The Ecology of Man: An Ecosystem Approach

The Ecology of Man:
An Ecosystem Approach

Robert Leo Smith
West Virginia University

Harper & Row, Publishers
New York, Evanston, San Francisco, London

THE ECOLOGY OF MAN: AN ECOSYSTEM APPROACH

To Bob, Tom, Pauline, and Maureen

Contents

Preface   **xi**

Part I. THE ECOSYSTEM AND MAN

1. *Concept of the Ecosystem* by Robert Leo Smith   **3**

   Commentary   **23**
2. *Odyssey* by Aldo Leopold   **24**

   Commentary   **27**
3. *The Strategy of Ecosystem Development* by Eugene P. Odum   **28**

   Commentary   **39**
4. *The Ecosystem View of Human Society* by Frank Fraser Darling and Raymond F. Dasmann   **40**

Part II. MAN AND THE FOOD CHAIN

   Introduction   **48**

   Commentary   **52**
5. *!Kung Bushman Subsistence: An Input-Output Analysis* by Richard B. Lee   **54**

   Commentary   **71**
6. *New Light on Plant Domestication and the Origins of Agriculture: A Review* by David R. Harris   **73**

   Commentary   **88**
7. *Domestication Features in Animals as Functions of Human Society* by H. Epstein   **91**

   Commentary   **102**
8. *Development of Modern Agriculture* by Wayne D. Rasmussen   **104**

   Commentary   **112**
9. *The Green Revolution: Cornucopia or Pandora's Box?* by Clifton R. Wharton, Jr.   **114**

   Commentary   **121**
10. *The Head Has a Stomach* by Gerald C. Anderson   **122**

Part III. MAN AND HIS HABITAT

   Introduction   **128**
11. *The Processes of Environmental Change by Man* by Paul B. Sears   **129**

   Commentary   **139**
12. *The Natural History of Urbanization* by Lewis Mumford   **140**

   Commentary   **153**
13. *Ecumenopolis, World-City of Tomorrow* by Constantinos A. Doxiadis   **154**

   Commentary **163**
14. *Our Treatment of the Environment in Ideal and Actuality* by Yi-Fu Tuan **167**

Part IV. MAN'S POPULATION

   Introduction **174**

   Commentary **180**
15. *The Origin of Man* by C. Loring Brace **181**

16. *Growth of the World's Population* by Robert Leo Smith **185**

   Commentary **189**
17. *Population Density and the Style of Social Life* by Nathan Keyfitz **190**

   Commentary **198**
18. *Overpopulated America* by Wayne H. Davis **199**

   Commentary **203**
19. *Cultural and Natural Checks on Population Growth* by D. H. Stott **206**

   Commentary **221**
20. *Evolutionary Response to Human Infectious Diseases* by George J. Armelagos
   and John R. Dewey **222**

   Commentary **228**
21. *On War and Peace in Animals and Man* by N. Tinbergen **230**

Part V. ENDANGERED ENVIRONMENTS

   Introduction **244**

   Commentary **246**
22. *Hormonal and Enzymatic Activity of DDT* by Joel Bitman **248**

   Commentary **255**
23. *Effects of Land Use on Water Resources* by W. E. Bullard **258**

24. *Thermal Pollution—A New Problem in Aquatic Ecosystems* by Robert Leo Smith **270**

   Commentary **279**
25. *Classification and Extent of Air Pollution Problems* by Leslie A. Chambers **284**

   Commentary **295**
26. *A Review of the Nature and Extent of Damage Caused by Oil Pollution at Sea* by
   Alfred L. Hawkes **296**

   Commentary **304**
27. *Radiation and the Patterns of Nature* by George M. Woodwell **306**

   Commentary **320**
28. *The Land: Its Future-Endangering Pollutants* by David E. Elrick **321**

Part VI. THE PROSPECT BEFORE US

   Introduction **332**

   Commentary **333**
29. *The World's Water Resources, Present and Future* by G. P. Kalinin and
   V. D. Bykov **335**

   Commentary **347**
30. *Mineral Resources: Challenge or Threat?* by Walter R. Hibbard, Jr. **349**

Commentary 358

31. *Photosynthesis and Fish Production in the Sea* by John H. Ryther 360

Commentary 368

32. *The World Outlook for Conventional Agriculture* by Lester R. Brown 369

Commentary 380

33. *The Tragedy of the Commons* by Garrett Hardin 382

34. *The Tragedy of the Commons Revisited* by Beryl L. Crowe 391

Commentary 399

35. *Growth Versus the Quality of Life* by J. Alan Wagar 400

Commentary 409

36. *The Ecosystem as a Criterion for Public Land Policy* by Lynton K. Caldwell 410

Epilogue 422

Contributors 423

Selected References 424

Index 431

Preface

Late 1969 and 1970 witnessed an expanding, almost explosive, interest in the environment. Since then the environment has become an object of concern for the man in the street. Sociologists, politicians, and economists have made the environment their sphere of interest and even expertise. The environmental crisis has inspired a rash of books and collections of readings on man and the environment, leaving ecologists almost breathless. Carefully surveying this mass of print, one becomes aware of two facts. One is that the terms *ecology* and *environment* are confused and misused. The other is that although the books survey the current environmental situation with varying degrees of success, most of them fail to view mankind's problems within the context of modern ecology, even though the word *ecology* is used with a happy abandon.

The objective of this book is to provide through a series of readings, introductions, and commentaries an insight into the ecology of man and the environmental problems facing the world within the conceptual framework of the ecosystem. The book began as an outline of topics developed around the theme of the ecosystem. After the topical outline was developed, papers were selected from a variety of sources. The final choice was based on a number of criteria, including readability, subject matter, scope, applicability to the ecosystem theme, and international or global approach. In some instances the papers available were either too technical or too narrow in their coverage, or did not fit the theme of the book. In these instances I wrote the selections myself. After final choices were made, introductions and commentaries were written to clarify, interpret, supplement, or expand the material in the selection.

The book is divided into six parts. In Part I energy pathways, mineral cycling, and ecosystem development are discussed, and man's place in the ecosystem is explored. This opening part sets the themes of the book, that the world is self-contained except for the input of solar energy, and that the functioning of the planet earth can be understood only in the terms of the ecosystem.

Part II deals with man and the food chain, his utilization of energy and materials. It begins with early man, who lived as a hunter-gatherer existing as a link in natural food webs. Then follows a series of articles and commentaries which explore how man modified energy flow and nutrient cycles by domesticating plants and animals and developing agriculture. This section also points out the cultural, social, economic, and nutritional aspects of man's food needs, which have changed considerably since man first walked on the face of the earth. If this part seems to be overdone it is deliberate, because I find among urban people a lack of appreciation both for the processes and problems involved in the growing and distribution of food and for the role agriculture plays in the life of the world.

Part III examines man and his habitat and his attitudes toward his environment. Man has exerted a tremendous ecological impact on the world ecosystems by modifying his own environment. This part explores how he modified the world environment from early times to the present, from primitive conditions to highly artificial urbanized society, and it speculates on the implications for the future.

Part IV looks at the population growth of man, how that population growth affects mankind, what controls have influenced animal numbers in the growth of animal population, and how the same mechanisms might affect human populations.

The impact of this population growth and accompanying technology on man's environment and world ecosystems is the subject of Part V. Its theme is the relationship of environmental degradation to the structure and function of ecosystems. Pesticides, eutrophication, thermal pollution, air pollution, oil pollution, relationships between water resources and land, ionizing radiation, and land pollution are considered.

Part VI is concerned with the future of the planet earth. What are the prospects that the earth will remain viable and functioning? This part takes a closer look at the capability of the earth to support a growing population. It examines the outlook of world resources in relation to population and economic growth and continued environmental degradation, points out why solutions have to be found here on earth and not in outer space, and suggests that a new approach in the management of the earth needs to be developed based on the concept of the ecosystem.

The book ends much as it began, with a view of the earth as a self-contained spaceship, but with a closer look at its passengers and crew, the situation in which all of us are in, and the decisions we have to make.

This book is not intended to be a study of the whole ecology of man. Such an undertaking would require volumes and would be beyond the capability of any one person. The ecology of man would have to include an examination of his social, cultural, and economic systems, behavior, nutrition, health and disease, movements and migrations, racial problems, and international problems. What I have aimed for in this book is simply an overview of human ecology. To achieve this I did not limit myself to selections from ecological literature alone. I also secured selections from such sources as cultural anthropology, geography, economics, political science, and agriculture. The book is intended as a supplement in any course dealing with man and the environment. If such a course happens to be in biology, the selections and commentary should give broader insights into the problems from a cultural or social point of view. If the course is in anthropology or social science, the book will provide some biological background. In fact, the book could stand alone as a text in ecology or environmental courses that are taught with a strong emphasis on current ecological problems and their economic, social, and cultural implications. In matters dealing with the earth, ecology, economics, and sociology can hardly be separated from one another.

Books are not produced by an author or an editor alone. They involve the help and assistance of others. Without the excellent cooperation of both contributors and publishers who graciously allowed me to include their material, this book would not have been possible. Rejections were rare, and unfortunately I could not include all the papers for which permissions had been obtained. The laborious details of securing permissions, handling correspondence, and typing the comments and introductions were efficiently handled by Charlotte Lemley. R. Wayne Oler of Harper & Row initially encouraged me to assemble this collection, and the book was guided to completion by Caroline Lanford. Thanks also go to Karen Judd, who made a number of excellent suggestions while editing copy and corrected flaws in writing. I would also like to thank Robert Leo Smith, Jr., for drawing several of the figures. Finally I want to acknowledge the patience and forbearance of my family, who live constantly in the shadow of some book.

ROBERT LEO SMITH

I/ The Ecosystem and Man

NASA

Introduction

THROUGH HIS RECORDED history man has rarely considered himself part of the natural world. It was there to be subdued, to be exploited, even to be enjoyed, but man himself stood aside, viewing it as a spectator from a distance. Even ecologists studied natural ecosystems as if they were apart from and wholly uninfluenced by man. Man was an intruder.

Yet we are a part of those natural systems; only because of them do we exist. Every decision we make in economic, social, and political life in some way affects those systems. When we build a dam, construct a road, develop a city, plow the ground, cut a forest, build an industry, pour our wastes into our water, air, and land, we influence or upset the life-supporting natural systems on earth.

Vital as they are, we have chosen to ignore them. Our environmental crisis, our population problems have not appeared overnight. They have been a long time in the making. But agriculture chose to ignore the increasing signs of ecological dangers ahead, as did industry, and government, and the people. Science, comfortable with its atoms and molecules and physical measurements, ignored the environment. Answers to the problems of life were to be found in biochemistry, and the rapidly developing environmental problems could be solved by technology. Those who looked at the environment were at best second-rate scientists and at worst alarmists.

But in the decade of the 1960s we had a rude awakening. Air had become so polluted that it was a major health hazard; waters were so contaminated that they were nearly unfit for either industrial use or human consumption. Waste, some 4.5 pounds per person per day in the United States, has created health and disposal problems all across the country. Pesticides used to promote public health and to increase food production contaminated the environment as well. Residues of pesticides resulted in the contamination of the 1968 catch of Coho salmon in Lake Michigan and the 1969 mackerel catch of California. In 1970, levels of mercurial compounds in many of the lakes and streams in various parts of the world were so high that fish were considered inedible. When industry faced serious financial losses, when sport fishermen could no longer cast their lines with the thought of a fish sizzling in a frying pan for a campside breakfast in the early dawn, when tourist industry found its summer trade cut in half, when people found water so polluted that they could no longer enjoy swimming at their favorite beaches, then some began to awaken to the fact that man indeed did depend upon and was a part of some larger system. Man got an even better appreciation of this fact when he saw home from outer space. Countries and political boundaries suddenly merged and became lost in a totality, the planet earth. And some have come to a jolting realization of what we have done to the earth and how we have indeed jeopardized its future. Man is a part of nature after all.

Although the word is out, the bulk of mankind has been rather unresponsive. Profit seeking and increasing the Gross National Product still take precedence over environmental conservation. Years ago, when the pressures on the environment were not as pressing as they are now, the problem was more simply solvable. Today solutions to the problem have become increasingly complex. The more industrialized society becomes, the larger its population, the more complex its governmental organization, then the more complex grows the pattern of organizing and governing men. This in itself makes the very process of problem solving a major task. The more people concerned and the more organizations involved, the less efficiently can the problem be attacked.

Somewhere there has to be a start. As George Woodwell[1] writes: "Ultimately there must come a recognition that the environmental crisis is a confrontation between man and nature; between human systems whose influence is now global, and the natural ecosystems that have built and maintain the biosphere as a place suitable for life." For everyone the beginning must come with some appreciation of man's place in the scheme of things, of his place in the global ecosystem.

---

[1] George Woodwell, "Science and the Gross National Pollution," in editors of *Ramparts* magazine, *Eco-Catastrophe*, San Francisco, Calif., Canfield Press (a department of Harper & Row), 1970, pp. 67–72.

2

Concept of the Ecosystem

by Robert Leo Smith

The planet earth hangs like a bright, bluish ball in the black void of space. Its surface is kaleidoscopic—white, blue, green, and shades of red constantly changing as the earth turns and the clouds move around its surface. It is alone, self-contained, and dependent on the outer reaches of space only for the energy of sunlight reflected from its surface. It is the sunlight flooding it that supports life on the planet, not so far away from the sun to be a cold body, not so close that the heat would be intolerable for life, yet protected from intense ultraviolet radiation by an atmosphere unlike that possessed by any of its sister planets.

Move in closer and the blues and the reds sharpen into broad outlines of deserts, mountains, flatlands, and seas. Still closer the patterns of the earth transform into expanses of grasslands, forests, and croplands, into rivers and lakes, estuaries, and oceans. Each is physically and biologically different. Each is occupied by different organisms well adapted to the environment in which they are found. Yet in spite of the differences, oceans and lakes, forests, grasslands and deserts—all function the same. Energy fixed by plants flows through them. Nutrients are deposited in the tissues of plants and animals, cycled from one feeding group to another, released by decomposition to soil and water and recycled again. Rarely are the desert or the forest, the stream, the lake, or the sea independent of one another. The energy and nutrients in one may find their way to another so that ultimately all parts of the earth are interrelated, comprising the total system that keeps the spaceship functioning. Each—the forest, the grassland, the lake, the sea, the total planet—is an *ecosystem*.

The word ecosystem comes from two words, *ecology* and *system*. Ecology, a word currently used with wild abandon and little under-

standing, comes from the Greek word *oikos*, meaning household, the same root word as that of economics. As Marston Bates (1) points out, ecology can be considered the study of the "economy of nature."

System, according to Webster, is an "aggregation of or assemblage of objects joined in regular interaction or interdependence; an orderly working totality." The definition implies homeostasis and feedback. "Every system," writes Ramon Margalef (2),

> is a set of different elements or compartments or units, any one of which can exist in many different states, such that the selection of the state is influenced by the states of the other components of the unit. Elements linked by reciprocal influences constitute a feedback loop. The loop may be negative or stabilizing, like the one formed by a heating unit and a thermostat or the mechanism regulating sugar level in the blood. Or the loop may be positive, or disruptive, like the spread of an annihilating epidemic.

The word ecosystem was coined by A. G. Tansley (3) back in 1935 in an article that appeared in the journal *Ecology*.

> The more fundamental conception is ... the whole *system* (in the sense of physics) including not only the organism-complex, but also the whole complex of physical factors forming what we call the environment.... We cannot separate them [the organisms] from their special environment with which they form one physical system. ... It is the systems so formed which ... [are] the basic units of nature on the face of the earth. ... These *ecosystems*, as we may call them, are of the most various kinds and sizes.

Thus, the "eco" part of the word implies

THIS SELECTION was written especially for this volume.

environment, the "system" an "interacting, interdependent complex" (4).

Ecology, then, to quote Margalef (2) again is "the study of systems at a level in which individuals or whole organisms may be considered elements of interaction, either among themselves, or with a loosely organized environmental matrix. Systems at this level are named ecosystems and ecology is the biology of ecosystems."

Look again at the natural ecosystem, a pond or a forest. It consists of a physical environment—in the case of the pond, water and the bottom mud and drainage system; in the case of the forest, the atmosphere and the climate, the soil, and hydrological influences. The environment is inhabited by a number of different plants and animals, each of which in turn modifies the climatic, the hydrological, and the nutritional aspects of the environment. Each group of species is made up of individuals, collectively a population, that are held together by some form of social and biological interaction. Populations and individuals within populations do not exist alone but form some kind of an association, not haphazard but orderly and well organized, utilizing and transferring energy and materials. These interacting plants, animals, and environment make up the ecosystem.

FLOW OF ENERGY

Within a structural framework of the environment and vegetation, consumer organisms, and decomposers, ecosystems function by maintaining a flow of energy and a cycling of materials.

Energy flow begins with its fixation by plants. The source of energy for ecosystems, local and global, is solar radiation that floods the earth. Solar energy reaches the atmosphere as visible radiation of light with wavelengths between 400 and 760 millimicrons; as ultraviolet and infrared radiation, X-rays, and charged and high energy particles. Charged particles are trapped in the Van Allen belt; X-rays and high energy particles are blocked out by the atmosphere; most of the ultraviolet radiation that could be damaging to life is absorbed by the ozone layer. The infrared or thermal end of the spectrum is reduced by absorption in water vapor and carbon dioxide. Light waves are thinned by scattering. The

scattering and reflection of light by small particles that retard and disperse shorter wavelengths while allowing heat rays and reds and yellows to pass through give blue light to the sky. Nearer the horizon, where there is a thicker layer of dust-laden atmosphere, the larger particles disperse and scatter the longer wavelengths producing the red, pink, orange, yellow, and white so characteristic of sunsets.

The amount of energy received on a surface outside the earth's atmosphere at the mean distance from the earth to the sun is 2.0 calories per square centimeter (cm^2) per minute, of which approximately 1.0 cal/cm^2/min reaches the earth's surface. Of this, about one-half is light; most of the remainder is infrared, the source of environmental heat, and a relatively small portion is ultraviolet.

The quantity of solar radiation reaching the earth at any one place varies considerably with daily and seasonal fluctuations. On cloudy days, for example, the infrared end of the spectrum is terminated, absorbed by water vapor. Less radiation reaches the northern hemisphere in winter than in summer. Topography and elevation influence radiation. South slopes, for example, receive more solar radiation and warmth than north-facing slopes, and high elevations with their thinner atmosphere receive more intense radiation than areas at lower elevations.

For the fixation of energy, light waves are the critical solar radiation, although thermal radiation is important in the heat budgets of plants, evaporation of water, soil moisture, and biochemical events within the plants. Of the light that strikes plants, only about 1 or 2 percent is utilized by green plants.

This light energy is fixed by the process of photosynthesis, a complicated process. When light strikes a chlorophyll molecule, it is absorbed and its energy is transferred to an electron of the chlorophyll molecule, now raised to a higher energy state. Once raised to this higher energy state, the electron is passed along through a series of chain reactions. This results in the synthesis of adenosine triphosphate, ATP, from adenosine diphosphate, ADP, by forcing a third phosphate group onto ADP. At the end of this synthesis the electron, drained of its excess energy, is passed to a compound called triphosphopyridine nucleotide, TPN. Acquiring this electron gives TPN a strong affinity for hydrogen ions, available from the ionized form of water ($H^+ + OH^-$). The energized TPN apparently pulls two hydrogen ions from the water molecule, splitting the water and forming $TPNH_2$, and retains the electron. The remaining OH ions form water, release some molecular oxygen, and supply the electron to replace the one lost by the chlorophyll molecule. This electron is then passed along a series of acceptor molecules until it arrives at the chlorophyll molecule. Further reactions involve the synthesis of carbohydrate from CO_2 in another series of reactions that incorporates the energy as well as the hydrogen and CO_2 into carbohydrates.

The rate at which energy is fixed by plants in photosynthesis is known as *gross production*. Plants use a considerable portion of the energy they fix for their own respiration. Gross production minus this respiration rate is *net production*, appearing as plant tissue or *biomass*. Biomass or organic matter present on a given area at a given time is the standing crop; it usually increases as the growing season progresses. Biomass is usually expressed as grams of organic matter per square meter, calories per square meter, or some other appropriate measure per unit area. Thus, biomass differs from production, which is the rate at which organic matter is created by photosynthesis. It is expressed as calories per square meter per year or grams dry organic matter per square meter per year. This meaning of production differs from other uses of the word. In agriculture, production refers to the amount of grain and the number or weight of cattle per acre, which in turn refers to the part of the standing crop harvested for man's use, the *yield*. To the wildlife and fishery biologist, production means the number of new individuals added to a population within some unit of time. To the ecosystem ecologist, production has a much more restricted meaning.

Productivity of different ecosystems varies considerably depending upon nutrient availability, water, temperature, length of the growing season, animal utilization, and the like. Productivity of the above ground parts of a tundra ecosystem where the growing season is only two months long is 21 to 219 g/m²/yr (5). For a deciduous forest, productivity is something on the order of 1200 g/m²/yr (6), and a tropical forest with its long growing season may average 2000 g/m²/yr (7). Temperate grasslands run about 500 g/m²/yr (8), estuaries 2000 g (9), and the open seas 125 g/m²/yr (10). Agricultural land runs about 650 g/m²/yr (11), but hybrid corn and other intensely cultivated crops may exceed 1000 g/m²/yr (12). As one might expect, there is a considerable range in the productivity of various ecosystems.

Net production theoretically represents the energy available either directly or indirectly to the consumer organisms and is the base upon which the rest of life on earth depends. This energy stored by plants is passed along through the ecosystem in a series of steps of eating and being eaten, a food chain (Fig. 1). Feeding on plant tissues are a host of plant eaters, or herbivores. Herbivores feed directly on plant tissue, converting it into animal flesh. In aquatic ecosystems the most important grazing animals are the zooplankton that feed on the microscopic plants, the phytoplankton. In terrestrial ecosystems, the important grazing herbivores are insects, such as grasshoppers and leafhoppers; the ruminants, such as cattle, buffalo, and deer; and the rodents. Only herbivores are adapted to live on a diet high in cellulose. Modification in the structure of the teeth, complicated stomachs, long intestines, a well-developed caecum, and a symbiotic flora and fauna enable many of these animals to digest plant tissue.

Herbivores are able to transform only a portion of the plant matter they consume to animal tissue. A good deal of the ingested energy is lost as feces, urine, and gas, or unassimilated energy. Much of the energy that is assimilated is lost. Part is utilized as heat increment, heat required for fermentation and nutrient metabolism above that required for basal metabolism. Energy left over from this loss represents net energy, part of which is used for body maintenance and is lost as heat. The remaining energy goes into growth and reproduction and represents secondary production.

Assimilation efficiencies vary considerably among herbivores. Grasshoppers, for example, assimilate only about 30 percent of what they ingest and lose 70 percent as feces (13). Immature spittle bugs assimilate about 36 percent of plant sap ingested, adults 76 percent (14), mud crabs 17 percent (15). A large herbivore, the elephant assimilates about 40 percent of its food intake (16), a steer about 60 percent (17), and the meadow mouse

5

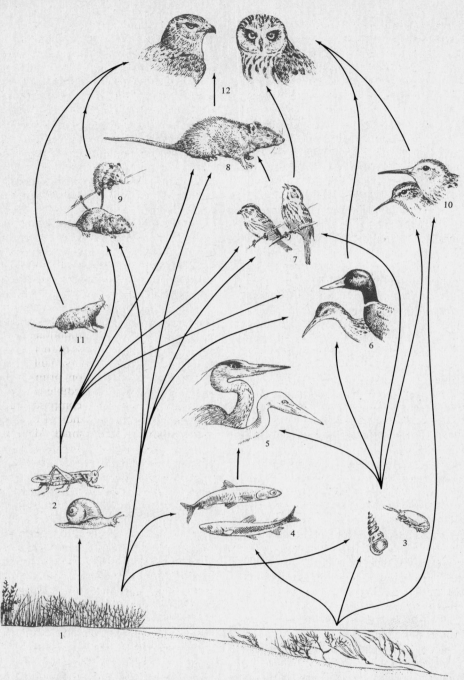

Figure 1. A midwinter food web in a *Salicornia* salt marsh (San Francisco Bay area). Producer organisms (1), terrestrial and salt marsh plants, are consumed by herbaceous invertebrates, represented by the grasshopper and the snail (2). The marine plants are consumed by herbivorous marine and intertidal invertebrates (3). Fish, represented by smelt and anchovy (4) feed on vegetative matter from both terrestrial and marine environments. The fish in turn are eaten by first-level carnivores represented by the great blue heron and the common egret (5). Continuing through the food webs, we have the following omnivores: clapper rails and mallard duck (6); savanna and song sparrows (7); Norway rat (8); California vole and salt marsh harvest mouse (9); least and western sandpipers (10). The vagrant shrew (11) is a first-level carnivore, while the top carnivores (second level) are the marsh hawk and the short-eared owl (12). (From R. L. Smith, *Ecology and Field Biology*, Harper & Row, New York, 1966.)

6

about 90 percent (18). Conversion of energy to animal tissue is low in herbivores, about 10 percent. A steer grazing on short grass plains utilizes about one-fourth of the primary production. Of the energy content of the forage consumed, 43 percent is lost as feces and urine; 48 percent is lost as heat, and about 9 percent goes to animal tissue (19).

The net secondary production of the herbivores is the energy base for the first-level carnivores. Again most of the energy ingested is lost as heat, feces, urine, and body maintenance, and only a small proportion goes into new animal tissue or production. According to available information, efficiency of conversion to secondary production among carnivores is on the order of 15 percent, probably due in part to the closer correspondence of the food to the carnivores' own chemical composition. Plant protein need not be converted to animal protein.

A first-level carnivore in turn may be a food source for a second-level carnivore and the second-level carnivore food for the third. But at each transfer, a large part of the energy transferred is lost as usable energy through dissipation as heat. The loss of energy at each transfer is so great that it limits the number of feeding steps involved. Animals out at the end of a food chain have a small energy base on which to support themselves.

Many animals, including man, occupy more than one position on a food chain. They may feed on both plant and animal sources of energy. Seed-eating song birds, such as sparrows, feed on both seeds and insects. Foxes eat wild fruits, which seasonally make up the bulk of their diet. Man consumes both vegetables and animal proteins. Such animals are omnivores, fulfilling the functions of both herbivores and carnivores.

Food chains in nature are difficult to study, but one of the best examples is the study of the old field food chain by Frank Golley (18). It involved bluegrass, meadow mouse, and weasel. The mouse was almost exclusively herbivorous and the weasel lived largely on mice. The vegetation converted about 1 percent of the solar energy into net production or plant tissue. The mice consumed about 2 percent of the plant food available to them and the weasels about 31 percent of the mice. Of the energy assimilated, the plants lost about 15 percent through respiration, the mice 68 percent, and the weasels 93

percent. The weasels used so much of their assimilated energy in maintenance that a carnivore preying exclusively on the weasel could not exist.

It is rather obvious that all of the net production of green plants is not consumed by the herbivores, nor are all the herbivores totally utilized by the carnivores. In fact, two-thirds to three-fourths of the energy stored by photosynthesis in a grassland ecosystem is returned to the soil as dead plant material, and less than one-fourth is consumed by herbivores (19). Of this about one-half is returned to the soil as feces. In the forest ecosystem only about 7 percent of the annual crop of leaves is consumed by herbivores, exclusive of the energy consumed by sap feeders (20). Grasshoppers consume just 2 percent of the net production available to them (13), and mice about 7 percent (18).

No predator, however skillful, completely exterminates its prey. The weasel in the old field ecosystem consumed 30 percent of the energy present (18). A mountain lion population in Idaho utilized less than 4 percent of the deer and elk population available to it (21). All of this unused production, primary and secondary, as well as the inedible and undigested portions, goes to the decomposers or the detritus food chain. Two kinds of organisms consume detritus: the small detritus-feeding animals, such as soil mites, earthworms, and millipedes in the soil, and mollusks, crabs, and worms in the aquatic ecosystem; and bacteria and fungi of decay. Their feeding relationships are so interwoven that it is impossible to separate their effects on the breakdown of organic matter. Some feed only on plant materials; others feed only on animal tissues. Each transfers energy into food chains that can reach up again into the grazing food chains. Mites feed on vegetation; mites are food for predacious mites that in turn are eaten by other soil invertebrates, such as spiders. These become food for shrews and birds. Earthworms feed in part on dead plant material, partially digest it, and make the organic matter available to still other decomposers, while in turn the earthworm becomes part of a food chain involving robins and other birds. The end result of the detritus is the ultimate breakdown and dissipation of all energy.

Within any ecosystem there are two major food chains, the grazing food chain and the detritus food chain (Fig. 2). Because of the high standing crop and relatively low harvest of

7

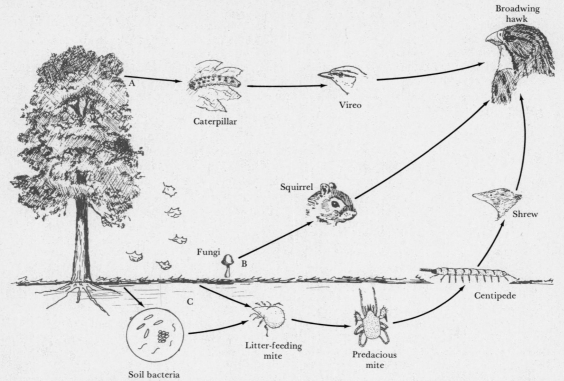

Figure 2. Examples of grazing and detritus food chains in the forest. The bulk of the primary production in the forest moves through the detritus food chain. (A) An example of a grazing food chain. Leaves are consumed by forest insects, represented by a caterpillar, which in turn is consumed by insectivorous birds; and they become food for birds of prey. (B) A detritus food chain in the organic matter in the form of fallen leaves supports a fungal population. The fruiting body of the fungi is eaten by such mammals as the squirrel which in turn is eaten by the hawk. (C) Organic matter on the forest floor is also utilized by decomposer bacteria and by detritus-feeding invertebrates such as mites. These mites become an energy base for predacious mites and centipedes. Larger forest-floor invertebrates are preyed upon by small mammals and they become food for larger predators. Detritus food chains often join the grazing chains at the higher consumer levels. These simple chains barely hint at the complexity of food webs in ecosystems.

primary production, the most important food chain in the terrestrial ecosystem is the detritus one. In most aquatic ecosystems with their low biomass, rapid turnover of organisms, and high rate of harvest, the grazing food chain is the dominant one.

An ecosystem consists of numerous food chains. Because no organism lives wholly upon another, the resources are shared especially at the beginning of the chain. Thus, food chains become interwoven into food webs, the complexity of which varies within and between ecosystems. If all the organisms that obtain their food in the same number of steps (that is, all of those that feed wholly or in part on plants, wholly or in part on herbivores, and so on) are superimposed, the structure can be collapsed into a series of single points, representing the trophic or feeding levels of the ecosystem. If

one then sums all of the biomass contained in each feeding level and all of the energy flowing in them, one can construct pyramids of biomass and energy for the ecosystem (Fig. 3). In general, the biomass of the producers must be greater than the biomass of the herbivores they support, and the biomass of the herbivores must be greater than that of the carnivores.

But this doesn't hold for all ecosystems. Terrestrial and some aquatic ecosystems have large standing crops in relation to energy flow, since primary production in them is characterized by an accumulation of organic matter, long life cycles of organisms, and a low rate of harvesting. In such aquatic ecosystems as lakes and open seas, primary production is concentrated in microscopic algae, characterized by short life cycles and rapid multiplication

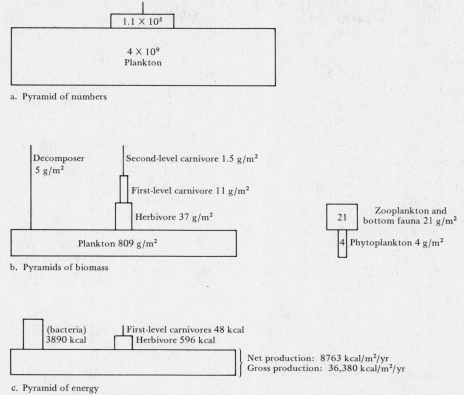

a. Pyramid of numbers

b. Pyramids of biomass

c. Pyramid of energy

Figure 3. Ecological pyramids. (a) Pyramids of numbers (marine ecosystem); (b) pyramids of biomass (freshwater spring and marine ecosystems); (c) pyramid of energy (cold spring). (From R. L. Smith, *Ecology and Field Biology*, Harper & Row, New York, 1966.)

of organisms, little accumulation of organic matter, and heavy grazing by herbivorous zooplankton. At any one point in time, the standing crop is very low. As a result pyramids of biomass for these aquatic ecosystems are top-heavy; the base is much smaller than the structure it supports. When measured in terms of energy flow, the pyramid of energy is applicable and comparable for all ecosystems. There is a stepwise reduction in rate of energy flow with succeeding trophic levels. The producer's base is much greater than the structure it supports.

This concept of energy flow in ecological systems is one of the cornerstones of ecology. The model was first developed by R. L. Lindeman (22) and is based on the assumptions that (1) laws of thermodynamics[1] hold for plants and animals; (2) plants and animals can be arranged into feeding groups or trophic levels; (3) at least three trophic levels—plants, herbivores, and carnivores—exist; and (4) the system is in equilibrium. From this model arise a number of other assumptions already discussed: Each succeeding trophic level has less energy flow than the preceding; assimilation efficiency, the ability of organisms to remove energy from ingested material, increases at higher trophic levels; however, respiration increases in proportion to assimilation; and although more energy is assimilated, more is lost. Thus, net productivity in relation to assimilation decreases high up in the trophic levels. The ratio of assimilation between one trophic level and another is about 10 percent.

---

[1]Briefly, the first law of thermodynamics states that energy is neither created nor destroyed, but is transformed from one state to another and the sum total can be accounted for. The second law states that during each energy transfer from one state to another, some of it is transformed into an unusable form, heat.

To understand the structure and function of energy flow through ecosystems, one has to know something of energy flow through populations within the ecosystem and relate this information to the flow of energy from one trophic level to another. Herein lies the weakness of the model. Energy budgets of several ecosystems to date are based in part on assumptions rather than known values of energy flow. Too little is known of energy flow through any population to allow any clear picture of energy flow through an ecosystem. Knowledge of energy flow through any given population often is unreliable. To be used, one has to assume that energy flow through a population is constant or, if fluctuating, at least predictable. But it probably is not, since energy flow through populations is variable depending upon ecological conditions. For example, the growth and thus energy storage by salmonid fishes is related to the size of food (23). When particle size is small, fish expend more energy obtaining food, and smaller proportion is used in growth. Variations in temperature affect the rate of food assimilation, and variations in salinity and nitrogenous wastes in the water affect both energy turnover and efficiency of utilization. Within any ecosystem, animal populations may have a pronounced influence on the rate of energy fixation by plants. Overgrazed range and overbrowsed forest may reduce the amount of primary production in grassland and forest ecosystems. Prey species, overexploited either by man or by predators, can affect the amount of secondary production. The nutrient composition of soil or plants can limit energy fixation and storage in both primary and secondary production. Lack of boron in the soil, for example, can severely depress growth of alfalfa and low nutrient status of soil, and thus plants can affect the production of animals. Thus, we lack enough trophic-efficiency studies either to give any clear picture of the structure of ecosystems or to strongly support the validity of the Lindeman model. Because they involve populations rather than trophic levels, the studies to date neither support nor refute the model of energy flow through ecosystems. But the concept of energy flow through ecosystems is valuable to provide a guideline for future study and a basis on which to attempt to understand some of the relationships and interactions of modern man and his environment.

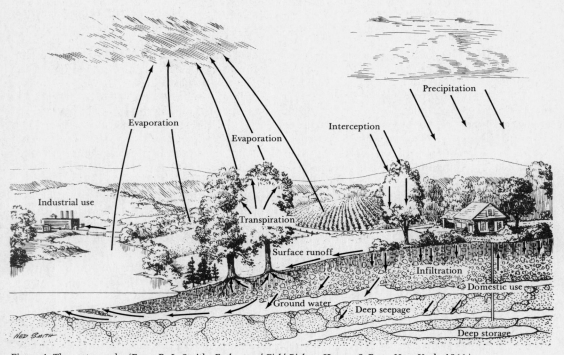

Figure 4. The water cycle. (From R. L. Smith, *Ecology and Field Biology*, Harper & Row, New York, 1966.)

NUTRIENT CYCLES

There are a number of nutrient cycles that keep materials moving through the global eco-systems. Basically they can be classified as gaseous and sedimentary; both are closely tied to and function within the water or hydro-logical cycle (Fig. 4).

An example of a gaseous cycle is nitrogen (Fig. 5), an element that makes up four-fifths of the earth's atmosphere and is a structural component of all proteins. The major source of nitrogen for the living world is the atmosphere, but plants cannot utilize nitrogen directly from the air as they can carbon dioxide and oxygen. Most of the nitrogen available to any ecosystem must come by the way of nitrogen-fixing bacteria found on the roots of legumes, alders, and a few other plants, or nitrogen-fixing blue-green algae found in both aquatic environments and

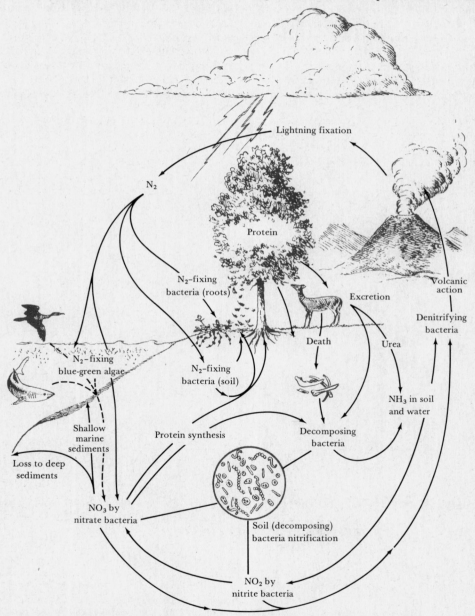

Figure 5. The nitrogen cycle. (From R. L. Smith, *Ecology and Field Biology*, Harper & Row, New York, 1966.)

the soil. Or nitrogen can come from such excretions of living organisms as ammonia, urea, uric acid, and other nitrogenous compounds and from the breakdown of dead plant and animal tissues by decomposers. The bacteria and other organisms of decay release ammonia from protein and other nitrogenous compounds. Nitrifying bacteria such as *Nitrosomas* convert ammonia to nitrites, and other bacteria such as *Nitrobacter* convert nitrites to soluble and usable nitrates. Denitrifying bacteria such as *Pseudomonas* break down nitrates and release molecular or free nitrogen back to the atmosphere.

Within an ecosystem, such as a forest, quantities of nitrogen are involved in short-term recycling from soil to plant to animal and back to soil again (Fig. 6). The same atom may be recycled within the same plant or the same ecosystem many times. Part of the nitrogen, as well as other elements, is stored in leaves to be returned with litter fall; part may be stored in wood tissue for a longer period of time. Nitrate in the soil below is easily leached and unless taken up by plants may be rapidly lost from the ecosystem through ground water circulation to streams, lakes, and seas. Excessive amounts of nitrogen carried by ground water to aquatic ecosystems are responsible for some major pollution problems.

Other materials are obtained through the mineral or sedimentary sources which at some point in time began with the breakdown of rocky material. The minerals are dissolved in

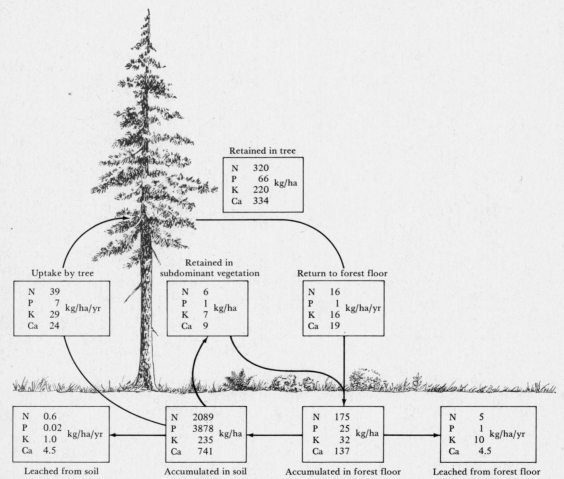

Retained in tree

N	320	
P	66	kg/ha
K	220	
Ca	334	

Uptake by tree

N	39	
P	7	kg/ha/yr
K	29	
Ca	24	

Retained in subdominant vegetation

N	6	
P	1	kg/ha
K	7	
Ca	9	

Return to forest floor

N	16	
P	1	kg/ha/yr
K	16	
Ca	19	

Leached from soil

N	0.6	
P	0.02	kg/ha/yr
K	1.0	
Ca	4.5	

Accumulated in soil

N	2089	
P	3878	kg/ha
K	235	
Ca	741	

Accumulated in forest floor

N	175	
P	25	kg/ha
K	32	
Ca	137	

Leached from forest floor

N	5	
P	1	kg/ha/yr
K	10	
Ca	4.5	

Figure 6. Distribution and short-term cycling of nitrogen, phosphorus, potassium, and calcium in a second-growth Douglas fir forest. (Based on data from D. W. Cole, S. P. Gessel, and S. F. Dice, in *Symposium on Primary Productivity and Mineral Cycling in Natural Ecosystems*, University of Maine Press, Orono, 1967.)

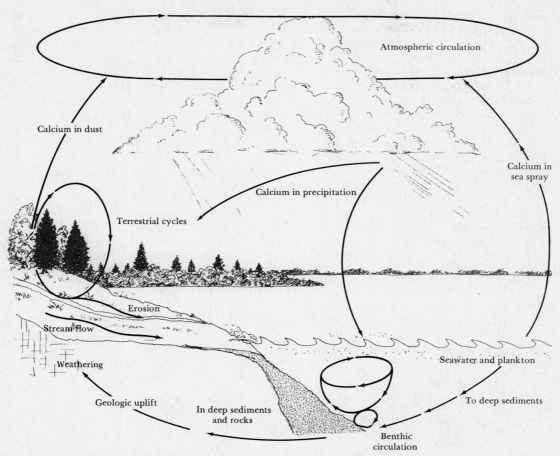

Figure 7. A generalized diagram of the calcium cycle showing the relationship between the rock and salt solution phases. Note how closely the sedimentary cycle is tied to the water cycle.

water and taken in by plants. Animals in turn get their nutrients from the plants or animals they consume; after death the material stored in their bodies goes back into the great cycle.

The calcium cycle is a good example (Fig. 7). It begins in the soil, where calcium is pulled from the ground by trees and other plants and deposited in leaves, trunks, stems, and roots. Rain dripping through the vegetation leaches some of the calcium from the leaves and carries it back to the soil, where it is quickly recycled through the plants again. Insects, rabbits, deer, and other plant eaters get their share of calcium from the plants. A bird gets its share of calcium when it consumes insects and deposits part of the element in the shells of eggs that it lays in the spring. When the young birds hatch, the bird removes the eggshells from the nest and the calcium contained in them goes back to the

soil. A squirrel feeds on a deer's antler that was shed in winter and the calcium goes into the building of bones. The time comes when the squirrel, the deer, the bird, and the insect die and the calcium contained in their bodies goes back into the soil and is recycled. In the fall the leaves containing a share of calcium drop to the ground and the minerals are eventually released by the organisms of decay.

Only a portion of the calcium and nutrients pulled from the soil by plants is returned each year. In a forest ecosystem, for example, a substantial amount is stored in woody tissue that eventually is released when the trees fall to the ground to decay or when they are destroyed by fire. A portion of the materials may be lost. Some is carried from the forest by animals that feed there and die elsewhere. A portion is lost by leaching of rainwater through the soil and more by surface run-off. But in a well-ordered forest, the spongy mass of litter holds most of the surface water and the bulk of the materials in place to be recycled through the trees and other members of the forest community. A great deal of the water that entered the undisturbed ecosystem is used by the trees and lost through evaporation and transpiration, leaving the minerals in place. A balance sheet of a forest ecosystem shows that gains from minerals dissolved in rainfall, from incoming dust, from animals and materials drawn from deep reservoirs of the soil equal losses. Thus, in the balanced ecosystem, gains equal losses, a condition that results because in natural ecosystems most wastes are recycled and not carried away.

The calcium and other minerals that are carried away find their way through ground water circulation and stream flow to lakes and seas, where they are recycled through phytoplankton, zooplankton, fish, and lake and ocean water. A portion is returned to land by sea spray to the atmosphere and back to land; part becomes incorporated in bottom sediments and rocks, where it is removed from circulation until it is released by weathering or other action.

In summary, the mineral cycle is bound closely to the energy flow, and both are carried largely by means of the water cycle. Energy flow is one way, with final dissipation of energy coming in decay, its renewal from light energy of the sun. Minerals or materials, on the other hand, are constantly being recycled through the ecosystem from soil and atmosphere and water to plants to animals to decomposers and back

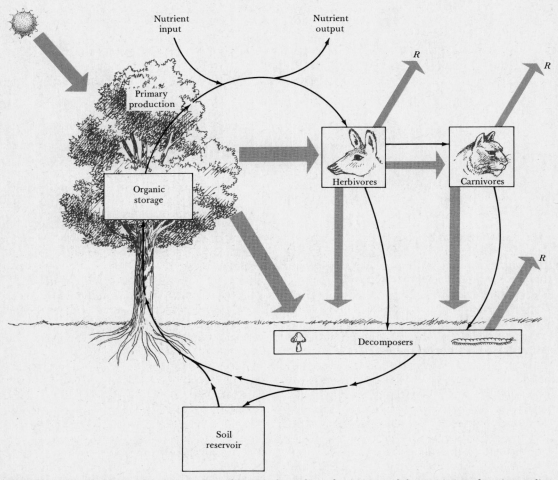

Figure 8. A model showing the one-way flow of energy, the cycling of nutrients, and the association of nutrient cycling with energy flow.

again (Fig. 8). Some materials enter the ecosystem through water, dust, precipitation, and the like, and a quantity is lost in a similar manner or through acts of man. Some are temporarily stored in organic storage, the tissues of plants and animals, until released by decay and made available; others are stored and withdrawn for longer periods of time in soil and rock minerals. Because of inputs and outputs, no ecosystem is entirely closed. And because of the close relationship between mineral cycling and atmospheric and water circulation, all ecosystems are interrelated into one large global ecosystem. Thus it is that radioactive elements from the atomic atmospheric explosions in the Pacific find their way into plants of arctic tundra, or DDT sprayed on the croplands of mid-America finds its way into Antarctic penguins (24).

STRUCTURE OF ECOSYSTEMS

The flow of energy and the cycling of materials is a functional aspect of the ecosystem. The ecosystem also has structure. A well-developed forest ecosystem, for example, has several layers of vegetation (Fig. 9), each of which provides a habitat for animal life in the forest. From top to bottom there is the canopy, the understory, the shrub, the herb or ground layer, and the forest floor.

The canopy, which is the major site of food production, has a major influence on the rest of the forest. If it is fairly open, considerable sunlight will reach the lower layers and the shrub and the understory tree strata will be well developed. If the canopy is closed, the shrub and the understory trees and even the herbaceous layers will be poorly developed.

The understory consists of tall shrubs such as the witch hazel, understory trees such as the dogwood and hornbeam, and younger trees; some are the same as those in the crown, others are of different species. Species that are unable to tolerate the shade and competition will die; others will eventually reach the canopy after some of the older trees die or are harvested.

The shrub layer differs with the type of forest. In oak forests on south-facing slopes, blueberries are most characteristic; in the

Figure 9. A diagram of forest succession from annual weeds to mature forest. Note the increasing stratification as one stage advances to another.

15

cove forests grow buffalonut, hydrangea, and rhododendron. In the northern hardwoods forest, witch hobble, maple-leaf viburnum, and striped maple are common.

The nature of the herb layer depends upon the soil moisture conditions, slope position, density of the overstory, and aspect of the slope, all of which vary from place to place through the forest.

The final layer, the forest floor, has already been mentioned as the site where the important process of decomposition of the forest litter takes place and where the nutrients are released to the nutrient cycle again.

The variety of life in the forest is directly related to the number and development of the layers of the forest. If certain layers are absent, then the animals they normally shelter and support are also missing. Thus, a well-developed forest supports a rich diversity of life that often goes unappreciated.

Other ecosystems have a similar if not as highly stratified structure. Grasslands have the herbaceous layer, the ground or mulch layer, and the root layer, the latter being more pronounced in grasslands than in any other ecosystem. Aquatic ecosystems such as lakes and oceans have strata determined by light penetration, temperature profile, and oxygen profile. In summer well-stratified lakes have a layer of freely circulating surface water, the epilimnion; a second layer, the metalimnion (thermocline), characterized by a very steep and rapid decline in temperature; below this the hypolimnion, a deep cold layer of dense water about 4°C often low in oxygen; and a layer of bottom mud (Fig. 10(a)). Each in season is occupied by its own forms of life. When the surface water cools in autumn, the difference in density between the layers decreases and the waters circulate throughout the lake. A similar mixing takes place in the spring when the lake water warms up. These seasonal overturns are important in recycling nutrients and in mixing the bottom water with the top. In addition, two other structural layers in lakes are recognized based on light penetration: the upper zone, roughly corresponding to the epilimnion, dominated by plant plankton, and the site of photosynthesis, and a lower layer in which decomposition is most active; this layer corresponds roughly to the hypolimnion and the bottom mud.

Thus, terrestrial and aquatic ecosystems are structurally similar. Each possesses an auto-trophic layer concentrated where the light is most available, which fixes the energy of the sun and manufactures food from organic substances. In the forest this layer is concentrated in the canopy; in the grassland the herbaceous layer; and in the lake and sea the upper waters. Each also possesses a heterotrophic layer that utilizes the food stored by autotrophs, transfers energy, and circulates matter by means of herbivory, predation in the broadest sense, and decomposition. Heterotrophic activity is most intense where organic matter accumulates. In terrestrial ecosystems this is in the upper layer of the soil, litter or mulch; and in aquatic ecosystems it is in the bottom sediments.

DIVERSITY AND STABILITY

Inherent in the concept of the ecosystem is the idea of stability and homeostasis. A stable system is one that responds to changes from a steady state by developing forces to restore it to its original condition. To effect this stability some homeostatic or feedback mechanism is necessary. In natural ecosystems this stability may mean that the system can survive many changes but still preserve some recognizably similar structure. Or stability may imply persistence; the system remains much the way it was.

Within an ecosystem, stability is related to the regulation of populations. Populations of plants and animals tend to maintain their numbers at some level. A population may fluctuate rather widely at times, but, if averaged over a long period of time, its numbers rise and fall about some point, a long-term constant mean.

A regulatory mechanism may be contained within the population, related to density (density dependent); or the population's fluctuation may be environmentally induced (density independent); or it may be an interaction of both.

Density dependent regulation implies some homeostatic mechanism at work within the population. As the population increases and approaches the point where the energy base or such environmental requirements as nesting sites and shelter will support few more, population growth slows and may actually decline. When the population declines considerably below a level which the habitat can support, the birth rate increases, the death rate declines,

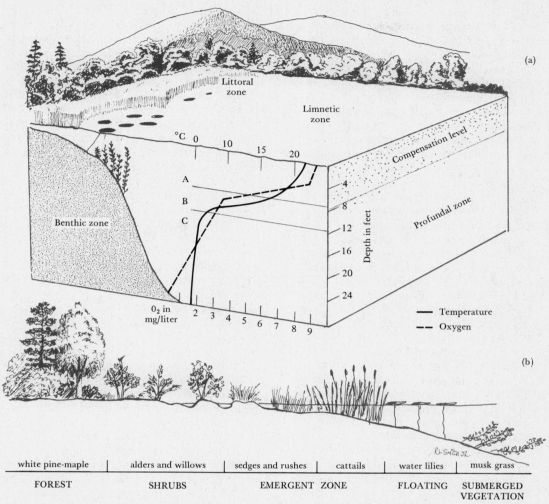

Figure 10. (a) A diagram of a lake in midsummer showing the major zones: the littoral or shallow-water zone and the limnetic or open-water zone to the depth of light penetration—the compensation level or maximum depth at which photosynthesis takes place. Also indicated is the stratification of oxygen and temperature in midsummer. Note the pronounced stratification. *A* is the epilimnion or layer of upper warm water; *B* is the metalimnion or layer in which temperature declines rapidly; *C* is the hypolimnion or deep, cold layer. (b) A diagram of succession around a pond. Successional stages embrace the littoral zone containing the submerged, floating, and emergent vegetation. The littoral zone in time is replaced by shrub and then forest growth. (Adapted from R. L. Smith, *Ecology and Field Biology*, Harper & Row, New York, 1966.)

and the population builds up again. Such a homeostatic process produces in part the long-term fluctuations in animal populations. When the population level of some mammals, such as the snowshoe hare, increases greatly, the reproductive rate declines and the death rate increases. Fewer young are born, few juveniles survive to adulthood, and adult mortality increases. As population rapidly declines and reaches a low point, adult survival and juvenile survival improve, and reproductive rates may double that of the decline (25). As population

levels reach a high again, another decline sets in. Increasing numbers in other populations may be checked by emigration of part of the population, as occurs among muskrats (26). Most emigrants find themselves in poorer habitat where they may succumb to disease, predation, or exposure. Well-situated residents maintain living area by territorial defense limiting the number that can occupy a given area. Such populations remain more or less stationary. Stress and failure of hormonal systems may reduce some populations (27), as well as decline in genetic quality (28). Population growth in plants may be inhibited by the excretion of growth inhibiting chemicals. Decline in algal blooms results from the inability of algae to tolerate their own extracellular products. Volatile terpenes produced by such shrubs as sagebrush inhibit growth of grass around them (29). Populations of both plants and animals may be limited by predation (grazing on plants being considered a form of predation), and predators may be limited by food shortages or disease.

Although not regulatory in the sense that they are homeostatic, density independent influences, particularly weather and climate, can have pronounced effects on population size. Like density dependent mechanisms, weather and climate act on population by influencing the birth rate and the death rate, but the effect is the same whether the population is large or small. For example, the population patterns of spruce budworms seem to be influenced by the mean of the daily maximum temperatures in June and the first fifteen days in July (30). A series of years with a high mean temperature is usually followed by an outbreak of the pest. Cold winters with deep snows and ice storms can cause widespread deaths in bobwhite quail (31), ring-necked pheasants (32), and white-tailed deer (33).

Or it may be a combination of both density dependent and density independent forces, as with ring-necked pheasants. Annual variations in the production of young are related as much to prenesting temperatures in the spring as to the breeding density. The former influences the viability of the eggs; the latter inversely affects reproduction and the spring-to-fall survival of the young. That is, the greater the density of hens, the lower the production of young (34). Whatever the reasons, many of them still conjectural and unproven, populations within natural ecosystems rarely reach a level at which they completely destroy their food supply or energy base.

At the community level, stability in ecosystems relates to ecosystem development. There is, according to current ecosystem theory, a tendency for the ecosystem to develop in the direction of a steady state, a stable ecosystem. This directional change is called *succession*, an orderly progression of developmental ecosystems in which the early stages are characterized by an excess of organic production, short food chains, and simplified food webs, to a highly stable situation with highly evolved structure, complex food webs, and portioning of energy among many units within the system.

Succession is a common phenomenon that can be observed during any trip through a countryside. A good example is the detailed study of old field succession in the Piedmont of North Carolina (35). When corn fields are abandoned in the fall, annual crabgrass becomes dominant. But seeds of horseweed are ripe and ready for germination in late summer. They sprout in the disturbed soil, and by early winter they have produced rosettes. The following spring, horseweed quickly claims the field. During the summer the field is invaded by another plant, the white aster. The combination of competition from the aster as well as the inhibiting effects of decaying horseweed roots on the horseweed itself allows the aster to achieve dominance. By the third summer, broomsedge, a perennial bunchgrass, invades the field. Abundant organic matter and the ability to exploit the soil moisture more efficiently eventually permit the broomsedge to dominate the field. About this time pine seedlings invade the broomsedge, and within five to ten years the pines have arrived at a low shrub stage and begin to shade out the broomsedge. The pine develops a duff layer on the forest floor where the shade is too dense to permit adequate growth of seedlings. Competition between the seedlings and the shallow-rooted parent pines, too, is intense, and the seedlings die from a lack of both light and moisture. In time, the understory of the pines is invaded by oaks and sweet gums that have long tap roots and can exploit a moisture supply, unavailable to the shallow rooted pines. Shade tolerant, the hardwoods grow up through the pines, and, as the pines die out (if they are not cut), the hardwood deciduous forest takes over. Further development of the hardwood forest continues as shade-tolerant trees and shrubs—dogwood, redbud, sourwood, hydrangea, and others—fill in the understory. The forest has arrived at the mature or tolerant stage in which only the dominant species of the crown are able to reproduce themselves in their own shade (see Fig. 9).

As the plants change, so do the animals: Early stages are characterized by such animals as arthropods, crickets, grasshoppers, spiders, and seed-eating birds, especially the mourning dove. Broomsedge brings in meadowlarks and meadow mice; the low pines, rabbits; and mature pines, pine warblers and sparrows. As pines decline and hardwood forest claims the area, downy woodpeckers, flycatchers, Kentucky and hooded warblers, ruffed grouse, and squirrels appear.

Parallel successional trends take place in such freshwater ecosystems as ponds and lakes, the rapidity of which is determined by the depth and deposition of silt from inflowing water and density of aquatic vegetation (Fig. 10(b)). Succession starts with open water and its planktonic communities until enough bottom silt accumulates to support submerged vegetation such as chara or muskgrass and pondweeds. As organic matter and sediments accumulate and water becomes more shallow, floating plants appear about the edge. These in turn are followed by emergents such as sedges and cattails. As emergents fill in the shore line, the floating plants reach further out toward the middle, eventually followed by the emergents. In time, such shrubs as alders and willows come in, followed by such trees as silver maple, red maple, and elm. In time, as the site becomes drier, these are replaced by the stable oak forest.

Studies of successional communities, especially in microcosms or laboratory cultures of algae and natural aquatic ecosystems, have led R. A. Margalef (36), H. T. Odum and R. C. Pinkerton (37), G. D. Cooke (38), and others to develop a model of succession (Fig. 11). According to the model, early stages of succession are characterized by low species diversity and low biomass. The ratio between gross production and biomass is high and production is greater than respiration ($P > R$). Energy is channeled through relatively few pathways to many individuals of a few species, and production per unit is high. Because of this, the ecosystem is very sensitive to disturbance, and a heavy interference with a major pathway of energy flow can disrupt it. Plants or autotrophs are more susceptible to exploitation by heterotrophs, such as outbreak of a plant pest or disease, and much the same holds true for the dependent consumers. Disturbance at one trophic level is quickly felt at other levels. In mature ecosystems, there is a greater accumulation of biomass, and although production may be high, the ratio between gross production and biomass is low and production equals respiration ($P = R$). In stable ecosystems according to the model, there is an increase in biomass, stratification, complexity, and diversity in flora and fauna. Energy is channeled down many diverse pathways and shared by many units. Thus, disturbance to one component of the food chain would not have a serious disturbing effect on the total ecosystem. The mature system, in effect, has a high degree of stability.

Diversity can become a measure of ecosystem maturity and stability. According to the model, diversity increases with maturity. By this measure, the tundra and croplands would be young, and immature or unstable ecosystems and the tropical forest would be the most mature and stable. Another point is that as diversity increases, dominance decreases. As more and more species make up an ecosystem and the energy is more finely shared, there are fewer true dominant species, ones that contain the most biomass or biologically control the environment.

Finally, diversity is related to stability. The more diverse the species composition, the more stable the ecosystem. Thus, most efficient ecosystems are ones in which biomass accumulates in large numbers of individuals of very few species. In species-rich ecosystems, biomass accumulates in few individuals of many species. Thus, the price for stability is decreased production, but the price for increased production is instability, which, with its extremely low species diversity, can create some problems in man's monocultural croplands.

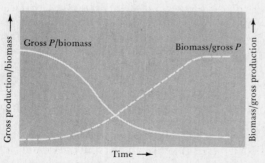

Figure 11. A graph showing the change in ratios between gross community photosynthesis and biomass, or production efficiency, and between biomass and gross community photosynthesis, or maintenancy efficiency, as succession proceeds. Note the high production efficiency of the early stages. In the later stages biomass has accumulated and gross production in relation to biomass is low. (Adapted from G. D. Cooke, 1967, BioScience 17(10):719.)

Although this concept of ecosystem development and stability has been widely accepted by ecologists, it has some shortcomings. Largely developed from experimental and field work in aquatic systems, it has not been tested adequately in terrestrial ecosystems and may not be wholly applicable. In the annual grasslands of California, for example, dominance declined as the diversity of grassland species increased as predicted by the model and biomass in the community was no longer concentrated in the top species (39). Likewise, as diversity increased, production declined. But stability of grasslands was unrelated either to production, diversity, or dominance.

In a study of the prairie, savannah, and oak woods ecosystems in Minnesota, J. D. Ovington, D. Heitkamp, and D. B. Lawrence (12) found that organic matter production increased with diversity. The oak woods was nine times as productive as the prairie, and the savannah five times as productive.

Another problem in terrestrial ecosystems is the question of stability itself. A mature oak-hickory or Appalachian cove hardwoods forest may approach stability, but there is no evidence that production equals respiration. Even in so-called old climax forests, new wood is still being added annually so that P still is actually greater than R. Some data on mineral cycling (7) indicate that in some mature ecosystems nutrients retained by plant biomass do not equal the difference between plant uptake and plant return, as should be the case.

The idea of succession is most applicable in biologically controlled ecosystems. Many major ecosystems, however, are controlled by physical conditions such as high temperature and low rainfall in the desert, or strong currents in streams and estuaries that restrict the kinds and numbers of organisms living there. For example, in a study of a cold spring, L. J. Tilly (40) found that the spring community supported largely by detritus was immature or young, yet was a stable ecosystem. It was maintained in that condition by a restricted space, a heavy flow of water, and a low but constant temperature. In such physically controlled environments, succession may never occur.

Although the trophic dynamic concept of energy flow and the model of succession and ecosystem development have their weaknesses, they are useful. They are highly applicable and valuable in appraising man's place in and effect on the world's ecosystems. Knowledge and understanding of energy flow and mineral cycling in ecosystems are important, for they relate directly to our well-being. We humans, like other heterotrophic organisms, depend upon the autotrophic energy base for the sustenance of life; but we also depend upon primary production and its derivatives for wood products and power. Since we require animal protein for part of our nutritional needs, we must understand energy transfers and efficiencies of production at the herbivore level. Increasing animal production means channeling as much primary production as possible into profitable forms of animal tissue. Agriculturalists know that young growing animals (like immature ecosystems) are much more efficient at converting primary production to animal flesh than older animals. Considerable advances have been made in developing early-maturing, fast-growing animals that can convert plant foods rapidly to animal tissue. In turn, we need more knowledge on energy fixation by green plants, especially the various grass species alone and in combination, and their short- and long-term responses to grazing.

A similar understanding of energy flow is important to the production of wood. Because useful forest lands are declining in the face of increasing populations and increasing demands for recreational use, we need more information about the utilization and wastage of energy in the forest ecosystem in the production of wood. How to increase production through fertilization and thinning to concentrate energy storage in fewer, faster-growing trees are some of the practical problems whose answers lie partly in the study of energetics of ecosystems. Knowledge of ecosystem functioning also can ensure rational exploitation of natural ecosystems; and data on the amount and pattern of energy flow before and after man's interference in natural ecosystems can permit us to guard against permanent damage.

In modifying ecosystems for our own use we simplify them. We shorten food chains by channeling all primary production either to ourselves or through specialized herbivores on which we alone are the predators. We attempt to prevent as much as possible from going through the decomposer food chain and to concentrate energy production on a few selected species of plants and animals. We are, according to ecosystem theory, creating instability in favor of production and low species diversity. The model of ecosystem development suggests that catastrophic problems of pest and disease might be prevented by adding diversity to our croplands. Since some natural ecosystems indicate that stability can be achieved even with low diversity, then perhaps a combination of crops in the same field may be an answer. Corn is being planted directly into pretreated sod fields reducing the amount of erosion and expenditure of energy on cultivation and permitting the harvesting of both fodder and grass by grazing animals.

Few of us ever consider ourselves part of a vast ecosystem. Yet each day we are utilizing both primary and secondary production and step directly into a food chain. Our wastes, our garbage, the addition of pesticides and chemicals to air and water and soil put us directly, for ill or for good, into the mineral cycle. Our pollution problems, our food problems, our population problems are all ecological ones. If we are to survive, we must gain far better knowledge of how ecosystems function and apply those principles to the systems, cultivated or natural, that we exploit and upon which we depend. The proper functioning of the spaceship earth demands it if we are to continue on our journey around the sun.

BIBLIOGRAPHY

1. Bates, Marston. 1960. *The Forest and the Sea.* New York, Random House.
2. Margalef, Ramon. 1968. *Perspectives in Ecological Theory.* Chicago, Ill., University of Chicago Press.
3. Tansley, A. G. 1935. The use and abuse of vegetational concepts and terms. Ecology 16: 284–307.
4. VanDyne, G. M. 1966. Ecosystems, systems ecology, and systems ecologists. Oak Ridge National Laboratory Report ORNL 3957. 31 pp.
5. Bliss, L. C. 1962. Net primary production of tundra ecosystems. In H. Leith (ed.). *Die Stoffproduktion der Pflanzendecke.* Stuttgart, Gustav Fisher Verlag.
6. Whittaker, R. H. 1970. *Communities and Ecosystems.* New York, Macmillan.
7. Rodin, L. E., and N. I. Bazilevich. 1968. *Production and Mineral Cycling in Terrestrial Vegetation.* Transl. by G. E. Fogg. Edinburgh, Oliver and Boyd.
8. Moir, W. H. 1969. Energy fixation and the role of primary producers in energy flux of grassland ecosystems. In R. L. Dix and R. G. Beidleman (eds.). *The Grassland Ecosystem: A Preliminary Synthesis.* Sci. Ser. No. 2, Range Sci. Dept., Colorado State University, Fort Collins.
9. Odum, H. T. 1967. Biological circuits and the Marine systems of Texas. In T. A. Olson and F. J. Burgess (eds.). *Pollution and Marine Ecology.* New York, Wiley (Interscience). pp. 99–157.
10. Ryther, J. H. 1963. Geographic variations in productivity. In M. N. Hill (ed.). *The Sea.* London, Interscience. Vol. 2. pp. 347–380.
11. Westlake, D. F. 1963. Comparisons of plant productivity. Biological Reviews 38: 385–425.
12. Ovington, J. D., D. Heitkamp, and D. B. Lawrence. 1963. Plant biomass and productivity of prairie, savanna, oakwood, and maize field ecosystems in central Minnesota. Ecology 44: 52–63.
13. Smalley, A. E. 1960. Energy flow of salt marsh grasshopper population. Ecology 41: 672–677.
14. Wiegert, R. G. 1964. Population energetics of meadow spittle bugs (*Philaenus spormarius* L.) as affected by migration and habitat. Ecological Monographs 34: 217–241.
15. Teal, J. M. 1962. Energy flow in the salt marsh ecosystems of Georgia. Ecology 43: 614–624.
16. Petrides, G. A., and W. G. Swank. 1965. Estimating the productivity and energy relations of an African elephant population. Proceedings IX International Grassland Congress. San Paulo, Brazil. pp. 831–842.
17. Pieper, R. D. 1969. The role of consumers in a grassland ecosystem. In R. L. Dix and R. G. Beidleman (eds.). *The Grassland Ecosystem: Preliminary Synthesis.* Sci. Ser. No. 2, Range Sci. Dept., Colorado State University, Fort Collins, pp. 316–329.
18. Golley, F. B. 1960. Energy dynamics of a food chain of an old field community. Ecol. Monographs 30: 187–206.
19. Hyder, D. N. 1969. The impact of domestic animals on the function and structure of grassland ecosystems. In R. L. Dix and R. G. Beidleman (eds.). *The Grassland Ecosystem: A Preliminary Synthesis.* Sci. Ser. No. 2. Range Sci. Dept., Colorado State University, Fort Collins, pp. 243–260.
20. Bray, J. R. 1964. Primary consumption in three forest canopies. Ecology 45: 165–167.
21. Hornocker, Maurice G. 1970. An analysis of mountain lion predation upon mule deer and elk in the Idaho primitive area. Wildlife Monographs No. 21. Wildlife Society. Washington, D. C.
22. Lindeman, R. L. 1942. The trophic-dynamic aspect of ecology. Ecology 23: 399–418.
23. Paloheimo, J. E., and L. M. Dickie. 1966. Food and growth of fishes III. Relations among food, body size, and growth efficiency. Journal Fishery Research Board of Canada 23: 1209–1248.
24. George, J. L., and D. E. H. Frear. 1969. Pesticides in the Antarctic. *Pesticides in the Environment and Their Effect on Wildlife.* Journal Applied Ecology 3(Suppl.): 155–167.

21

25. Meslow, E. C., and L. B. Keith. 1968. Demographic parameters of a snowshoe hare population. Journal of Wildlife Management 32(4): 812–834.
26. Errington, P. L. 1963. *Muskrat Populations*. Ames, Iowa, Iowa State University Press.
27. Christian, J. J., and D. E. Davis. 1964. Endocrines, behavior and population. Science 146: 1550–1560.
28. Wellington, W. G. 1964. Qualitative changes in populations in unstable environments. The Canadian Entomologist 96(1–2): 436–451.
29. Muller, C. H., W. H. Muller, and B. L. Haines. 1964. Volatile growth inhibitors produced by aromatic shrubs. Science 143: 471–473.
30. Morris, R. F. (ed.). 1963. The dynamics of epidemic spruce budworm populations. Mem. Entomological Society of Canada 31: 1–332.
31. Kozicky, E. L., and G. O. Hendrickson. 1952. Fluctuation in bobwhite populations, Decatur County, Iowa. Iowa State University Journal Science 26: 483–489.
32. Wagner, F. H., C. D. Besadny, and C. Kabat. 1965. Population ecology and management of Wisconsin pheasants. Wisconsin Conservation Dept. Tech. Wildlife Bull. No. 34.
33. Dahlberg, B. L., and R. C. Guettinger. 1956. The white-tailed deer in Wisconsin. Wisconsin Conservation Dept. Tech. Wildlife Bull. No. 14.
34. Wagner, F. H., and A. W. Stokes. 1968. Indices to overwinter survival and productivity with implications for population regulation in pheasants. Journal of Wildlife Management 32: 32–36.
35. Keever, Catherine. 1950. Causes of succession on old fields of the Piedmont, North Carolina. Ecological Monographs 20: 229–250.
36. Margalef, R. A. 1963. On certain unifying principles in ecology. American Naturalist 97: 357–374.
37. Odum, H. T., and R. C. Pinkerton. 1955. Times speed regulator: the optimum efficiency for maximum power input in physical and biological systems. American Scientist 43: 331–343.
38. Cooke, G. D. 1967. The pattern of autotrophic succession in laboratory microcosms. BioScience 17: 717–721.
39. McNaughton, S. J. 1968. Structure and function in California grassland. Ecology 49(5): 962–972.
40. Tilly, L. J. 1968. The structure and dynamics of Cone Spring. Ecological Monographs 38: 169–197.

Selection 2

Odyssey

Commentary

What did you have for dinner last night? Beef in some form, perhaps, and potatoes, corn, and lettuce. Where did it come from, the energy and the nutrients? Or haven't you ever given it a thought?

The potatoes, the beans, and the lettuce represent carbohydrates stored in the fields of Maine and on flat valley farms of California. The minerals contained in them came partly from reserves in soils that once supported forest and annual grassland and partly from commercial fertilizers, nutrients taken from some distant reserves stored up over the ages. Commercial nitrogen was in the form of ammonia, manufactured from bituminous coal, and processed into coke with ammonia a by-product. The phosphorus came from phosphate rock laid down in ancient seas and now mined in Idaho, Utah, and Florida. The potassium came from potash in Carlsbad, New Mexico. All this was transported to processing plants and then distributed to potato farmers in Maine and vegetable farmers in California.

The beef came from a steer that grazed on the open range of the high plains of Colorado and was fattened in a midwest feed lot on corn that pulled many of its nutrients from centuries of growth of prairie grasses. Too often the nutrients contained in the wastes trampled in the feed lots are washed by the rains to water courses and hurried off to the sea or deposited in the bottom mud of some flood control reservoir.

The table scraps from the meal were deposited in the garbage, carted away on collection day, and dumped offshore in the ocean or buried in a sanitary land fill. The undigested remains were flushed down a drain, carried off to a sewage disposal plant, or perhaps even dumped raw into rivers. In either event the nutrients were washed far downstream and deposited who knows where.

If there is one thing characteristic of man and the ecosystem, it is this removal of nutrients from one place and their transport to another. Atoms of calcium and phosphorus from the wheat fields of the midwest go to India, and those from tropical pineapple fields of Hawaii end up in offshore waters of New York harbor. Every item of food purchased in a supermarket and eaten at our dinner tables represents a quantity of mineral matter pumped out of some nutrient cycle and never recycled in that ecosystem again. The full effects of this impoverishment are prevented only by costly input of chemical fertilizers.

Food is not the only drain and transport from the ecosystem. Is the table made of wood? Are the walls of the den or office panelled? What about the morning paper you read? All these are wood products from forest trees. All represent nutrients stored in the biomass of a Rocky Mountain Douglas fir, Canadian spruce, and Appalachian oak. If left uncut to die naturally, the nutrients would have recycled through forest growth again. Instead they have been totally removed and even preserved from recycling by their special use.

The amount of nutrients removed by crops, grazing, and timber harvest is considerable. An acre of corn producing a very modest yield of 80 bushels of grain and 5200 pounds of fodder removes about 23 pounds of calcium and about 19 pounds of magnesium. An acre of wheat yielding 40 bushels of grain and 4000 pounds of straw removes about 8 pounds each of calcium and magnesium. A ton of alfalfa removes 31 pounds of calcium and 8 pounds of magnesium.[1] None of these figures includes the additional loss of nutrients from soil erosion. Removal of grazing animals can also be nutrient depleting. A yearling steer taken from the range after a six-month grazing season will remove 1.68 pounds of nitrogen, 0.62 pound of calcium, 0.44 pound of phosphorus, 0.02 pound of magnesium, and 0.11 pound of potassium.[2] Although the nitrogen losses are the greatest, the long-term consequences of grazing on the phosphorus, potassium, and other mineral reserves on natural grasslands may be more severe because of unreplaced losses from soil reserves.

Timber harvesting removes considerable quantities of nutrients. According to J. D. Ovington, the harvest of 55-year-old stand of Scotch pine removed per hectare 318 pounds of potassium, 732 pounds of calcium,

---

[1] K. Lawton and L. T. Hurtz, "Soil Reaction and Liming," in *Soil*, USDA Yearbook of Agriculture, Washington, D.C., 1957, pp. 184–193.
[2] R. D. Pieper, "The Role of Consumers in Grassland Ecosystems," in R. L. Dix and R. G. Beidleman, *The Grassland Ecosystem*, *Sci. Ser. No. 2*, Range Sci. Dept., Colorado State University, Fort Collins, 1969, pp. 316–329.

154 pounds of magnesium, 46 pounds of phosphorus, and 549 pounds of nitrogen.[3] Most serious was the loss of calcium and magnesium, for a relatively large portion is stored in tree trunks.

In addition to the loss from the removal of timber, further losses result from changes in the water cycle. Since the water is no longer being withdrawn from the soil by the trees during the growing season, more water is able to percolate through the soil, dissolving the nutrients and carrying them in solution. With the death of trees, the amount of roots and root surface is reduced. This in turn means that smaller portions of the nutrient in the soil water will be removed by the roots from the leaching water.

Loss of vegetation and the subsequent increased surface temperatures may speed up the action of decomposers and organisms. This enables them to convert the organic matter rapidly into mineral matter, which is then dissolved in the soil water. The amount of calcium ions, magnesium ions, sodium ions, potassium ions, and nitrogen ions lost by subsurface run-off in an experimental cutover forest in the Hubbard Brook Experimental Forest were 9, 8, 3, 20, and 100 times greater, respectively, than the amount lost from undisturbed forests.[4] As vegetation recovers, losses decline as recycling is restored. But temporary losses may be considerable.

The mass transport of food, fiber, and wood away from the ecosystems in which they were produced to distant points on the globe has radically changed nutrient cycles in world ecosystems. Impoverishment in one ecosystem leads to overenrichment and pollution in others. The nutrients have, as Aldo Leopold states, become itinerants.

"Odyssey" deals with mineral cycles. Although short, it says all that needs to be said. Scientific studies may quantify the cycle, posting the magnitudes of gains and losses of each nutrient. Technical publications may tell the same story in erudite and often unintelligible words and charts. But they will add nothing more than Leopold has already said. The atoms of nutrients, in this case calcium, have become itinerant, mostly because of the action of man. X remained a long time on the prairie before it finally arrived at the sea. Y never made it, ending instead in the bottom mud of some flood control dam, removed before its time.

Black and white buffalo are here to stay, as well as the red barns and the feed lots. We could not sustain ourselves otherwise. But only a fraction of the atoms need to be itinerants and none have to be trapped in oily sludge. Cattle need not be intruders on the plains or on the hillsides of an eastern dairy farm. They are components of modified but necessary ecosystems now, just as wheat, corn, alfalfa, and soybeans are. The solution comes in managing the ecosystems for stability to hold the itinerant atoms in their endless cycle.

---

[3] J. D. Ovington, "Some Aspects of Energy Flow in a Plantation of *Pinus sylvestris* L.," *Ann. Botany*, London N.S. **25**, 1961, pp. 12—20.

[4] F. H. Bormann, G. E. Likens, D. W. Fisher, and R. S. Pierce, "Nutrient Loss Accelerated by Clear-Cutting of a Forest Ecosystem." *Science* **159**, 1968, pp. 882—884.

Selection 2

Odyssey

by Aldo Leopold

X had marked time in the limestone ledge since the Paleozoic seas covered the land. Time, to an atom locked in a rock, does not pass.

The break came when a bur oak root nosed down a crack and began prying and sucking. In the flash of a century the rock decayed, and X was pulled out and up into the world of living things. He helped build a catkin, which became an acorn, which fattened a deer, which fed an Indian, all in a single year.

From his berth in the Indian's bones, X joined again in chase and flight, feast and famine, hope and fear. He felt these things as changes in the little chemical pushes and pulls which tug timelessly at every atom. When the Indian took his leave of the prairie, X moldered briefly underground, only to embark on a second trip through the bloodstream of the land.

This time it was a rootlet of bluestem which sucked him up and lodged him in a leaf, which rode the green billows of the prairie June, sharing the common task of hoarding sunlight. To this leaf also fell an uncommon task: flicking shadows across a plover's eggs. The ecstatic plover, hovering overhead, poured praises on something perfect; perhaps the eggs, perhaps the shadows, or perhaps the haze of pink phlox which lay on the prairie.

When the departing plovers set wing for the Argentine, all the bluestems waved farewell with tall new tassels. When the first geese came out of the north and all the bluestems glowed wine-red, a forehanded deermouse cut the leaf in which X lay and buried it in an underground nest, as if to hide a bit of Indian summer from the thieving frosts. But a fox detained the mouse, molds and fungi took the nest apart, and X lay in the soil again, foot-loose and fancy-free.

Next he entered a tuft of side-oats grama, a buffalo, a buffalo chip, and again the soil. Next a spiderwort, a rabbit, and an owl. Thence a tuft of sporobolus.

All routines come to an end. This one ended with a prairie fire, which reduced the prairie plants to smoke, gas, and ashes. Phosphorus and potash atoms stayed in the ash, but the nitrogen atoms were gone with the wind. A spectator might, at this point, have predicted an early end of the biotic drama, for with fires exhausting the nitrogen, the soil might well have lost its plants and blown away.

But the prairie had two strings to its bow. Fires thinned its grasses, but they thickened its stand of leguminous herbs: prairie clover, bush clover, wild bean, vetch, lead-plant, trefoil, and baptisia, each carrying its own bacteria housed in nodules on its rootlets. Each nodule pumped nitrogen out of the air into the plant, and then ultimately into the soil. Thus the prairie savings bank took in more nitrogen from its legumes than it paid out to its fires. That the prairie is rich is known to the humblest deermouse; why the prairie is rich is a question seldom asked in all the still lapse of ages.

Between each of his excursions through the biota, X lay in the soil, and was carried by the rains, inch by inch, downhill. Living plants retarded the wash by impounding atoms, dead ones, by locking them to their decayed tissues.

Animals ate the plants and carried them briefly uphill or downhill, depending on whether they died or defecated higher or lower than they fed. No animal was aware that the altitude of his death was more important than his manner of dying. Thus a fox caught a gopher in a meadow, carrying X uphill to his bed on the brow of a ledge, where an eagle laid him low. The dying fox sensed the end of his chapter in foxdom, but not the new beginning in the odyssey of an atom.

An Indian eventually inherited the eagle's plumes, and with them propitiated the Fates, whom he assumed had a special interest in Indians. It did not occur to him that they might be busy casting dice against gravity; that mice and men, soils and songs might be merely ways to retard the march of atoms to the sea.

One year, while X lay in a cottonwood by the river, he was eaten by a beaver, an animal which always feeds higher than he dies. The beaver starved when his pond dried up during a bitter frost. X rode the carcass down the spring freshet, losing more altitude each hour than heretofore in a century. He ended up in the silt of a backwater bayou, where he fed a crayfish, a coon, and then an Indian, who laid him down to his last sleep in a mound on the riverbank. One spring an oxbow caved the bank, and after one short week of freshet, X lay again in his ancient prison, the sea.

An atom at large in the biota is too free to know freedom; an atom back in the sea has forgotten it. For every atom lost to the sea, the prairie pulls another out of the decaying rocks. The only certain truth is that its creatures must suck hard, live fast, and die often, lest its losses exceed its gains.

It is the nature of roots to nose into cracks. When Y was thus released from the parent ledge, a new animal had arrived and begun redding up the prairie to fit his own notions of law and order. An oxteam turned the prairie sod, and Y began a succession of dizzy annual trips through a new grass called wheat.

The old prairie lived by the diversity of its plants and animals, all of which were useful because the sum total of their coöperations and competitions achieved continuity. But the wheat farmer was a builder of categories; to him only wheat and oxen were useful. He saw the useless pigeons settle in clouds upon his wheat, and shortly cleared the skies of them.

He saw the chinch bugs take over the stealing job, and fumed because here was a useless thing too small to kill. He failed to see the downward wash of over-wheated loam, laid bare in spring against the pelting rains. When soil-wash and chinch bugs finally put an end to wheat farming, Y and his like had already traveled far down the watershed.

When the empire of wheat collapsed, the settler took a leaf from the old prairie book: he impounded his fertility in livestock, he augmented it with nitrogen-pumping alfalfa, and he tapped the lower layers of the loam with deep-rooted corn. With these he built the empire of red barns.

But he used his alfalfa, and every other new weapon against wash, not only to hold his old plowings, but also to exploit new ones which, in turn, needed holding.

So, despite alfalfa, the black loam grew gradually thinner. Erosion engineers built dams and terraces to hold it. Army engineers built levees and wing-dams to flush it from the rivers. The rivers would not flush, but raised their beds instead, thus choking navigation. So the engineers built pools like gigantic beaver ponds, and Y landed in one of these, his trip from rock to river completed in one short century.

On first reaching the pool, Y made several trips through water-plants, fish, and waterfowl. But engineers build sewers as well as dams, and down them comes the loot of all the far hills and the sea. The atoms which once grew pasque-flowers to greet the returning plovers now lie inert, confused, imprisoned in oil sludge.

Roots still nose among the rocks. Rains still pelt the fields. Deermice still hide their souvenirs of Indian summer. Old men who helped destroy the pigeons still recount the glory of the fluttering hosts. Black and white buffalo pass in and out of red barns, offering free rides to itinerant atoms.

Selection 3

Strategy of Ecosystem Development

Commentary

If atoms have become itinerants in our modern world, it is because we have simplified ecosystems. We have destroyed high diversity for maximum productivity, and in doing so we have created problems for ourselves. The tendency in natural ecosystems, as Dr. Odum points out, is toward diversity and stability, but we have never made this ecological principle a part of our planning and thinking. Ecological principles apply to more than just natural systems. They also apply to man and his modern society. In his early history, man modified ecosystems, but he was still closely tied to them. Modern man cannot escape his past heritage. We may be far removed from soil, living in the heart of industrial and business complexes, shielded from environment by air conditioning, heating, lighting, and modern transportation. Yet in the air we breathe, the food we eat, the materials we consume, the wastes we discard, we are still a part of the ecosystem, still bound to its laws.

Young ecosystems, those in developmental stages, are the most productive for man. They represent production, growth, quantity. In their own economic growth, industry, cities, states, and nations strive for the same qualities. Just as a cropland or growing forest is characterized by a high ratio between gross production and biomass, so does a growing or young economy show a high ratio between Gross National Product and population growth. Both are terribly hard on nutrient budgets, financial or mineral, as is illustrated by the expanding cost of supporting governmental and business institutions as population growth and production keep soaring.

But the world still acts as if it were in the pioneering stage of succession. Emphasis is on production and growth, when in reality most of the world has passed far beyond this stage. Even the so-called underdeveloped countries can be considered overdeveloped.[1] They have passed their earlier stages of growth, have passed their maturity, and are now in a period, retrogressive succession, brought about by decadence and an impoverishment of the system. Respiration is greater than production. Like an overgrazed pasture or an overgrazed woods, the mature systems have been destroyed and the ecosystem has regressed to a stage from which it may never recover.

As populations grow and demands on resources and land increase, we have tended more and more toward youthful stages of development, both ecologically and socially. The world is becoming standardized. Cities, once distinctive, now have a monotony to them. At one time a worker did a variety of jobs. Now he is confined to the same dull task on an assembly line. Cities and regions come to rely on one type of industry, such as the coal industry of Appalachia. When there is a disturbance in the economy, the simplified ecosystem of man reacts violently to the disturbance. To feed an overpopulated world we have abandoned diversified agriculture. Thirty years ago many American farmers grew a variety of crops, from milk to fruits and vegetables, and supplied most of their own food. But that kind of agriculture cannot support a high population and it is unprofitable. So we traded diversified family farms for industrial-type farms specializing in wheat or corn and soybeans. Or such farms raise only beef or broilers or laying hens. Such systems are vulnerable to outbreaks of disease and pest, prevented only by constant vigilance and use of poisons that in turn contaminate our own environment.

What we need to do, suggests Raymond Dasmann in his book *A Different Kind of Country*,[2] is to plan against progress. Plan against uniformity of cities, against population increase, against an increased GNP; plan for the preservation of the irreplaceables, plan against unlimited growth of cities, plan for new ones and the rebirth of smaller towns, plan against use of prime agricultural land for urban development. He writes,

> The way out for us must lie in a deliberate effort to maintain and build diversity, so that in each section of this land there will be a different kind of country, with its different wilderness and wild land, its characteristic farmlands and rural landscapes, its varied cities that contain room for varied peoples. We have the power, the technology and the wealth with which to do this. We need only the will.

After explaining in considerable detail the strategy of ecosystem development, Odum sees the answer to

[1]G. Borgstrom, *The Hungry Planet*, New York, Macmillan, 1965.
[2]R. Dasmann, *A Different Kind of Country*, New York, Macmillan, 1968.

our problem in terms of increased diversity. We have to rethink the whole approach. In a pioneering or early successional stage, the emphasis is on high birth rates, high profits, and exploitation of resources. But as the population reaches a high level, its growth must slow, and the emphasis must be on those characteristics of later successional stage ecosystems: stability, quality and low rate of growth, recycling of nutrients. Somewhere we have to strike a balance between a productive environment and a protected environment.

Selection 3

The Strategy of Ecosystem Development

by Eugene P. Odum

The principles of ecological succession bear importantly on the relationships between man and nature. The framework of successional theory needs to be examined as a basis for resolving man's present environmental crisis. Most ideas pertaining to the development of ecological systems are based on descriptive data obtained by observing changes in biotic communities over long periods, or on highly theoretical assumptions; very few of the generally accepted hypotheses have been tested experimentally. Some of the confusion, vagueness, and lack of experimental work in this area stems from the tendency of ecologists to regard "succession" as a single straightforward idea; in actual fact, it entails an interacting complex of processes, some of which counteract one another.

As viewed here, ecological succession involves the development of ecosystems; it has many parallels in the developmental biology of organisms, and also in the development of human society. The ecosystem, or ecological system, is considered to be a unit of biological organization made up of all of the organisms in a given area (that is, "community") interacting with the physical environment so that a flow of energy leads to characteristic trophic structure and material cycles within the system.

DEFINITION OF SUCCESSION

Ecological succession may be defined in terms of the following three parameters (1). (i) It is an orderly process of community development that is reasonably directional and, therefore, predictable. (ii) It results from modification of the physical environment by the community; that is, succession is community-controlled even though the physical environment determines the pattern, the rate of change, and often sets limits as to how far development can go. (iii) It culminates in a stabilized ecosystem in which maximum biomass (or high information content) and symbiotic function between organisms are maintained per unit of available energy flow. In a word, the "strategy" of succession as a short-term process is basically the same as the "strategy" of long-term evolutionary development of the biosphere—namely, increased control of, or homeostasis with, the physical environment in the sense of achieving maximum protection from its perturbations. The strategy of "maximum protection" (that is, trying to achieve maximum support of complex biomass structure) often conflicts with man's goal of "maximum production" (trying to obtain the highest possible yield). Recognition of the ecological basis for this conflict is, I believe, a first step in establishing rational land-use policies.

The earlier descriptive studies of succession on sand dunes, grasslands, forests, marine shores, or other sites, and more recent functional considerations, have led to the basic theory contained in the definition given above. H. T. Odum and Pinkerton (2), building on Lotka's (3) "law of maximum energy in biological systems," were the first to point out that succession involves a fundamental shift in energy

---

THIS SELECTION is from *Science*, Vol. 164, pp. 262–270, April 1969. Copyright 1969 by the American Association for the Advancement of Science. Condensed and modified with kind permission of the author.

28

flows as increasing energy is relegated to maintenance. Margalef *(4)* has recently documented this bioenergetic basis for succession and has extended the concept.

Changes that occur in major structural and functional characteristics of a developing ecosystem are listed in Table 1. Twenty-three attributes of ecological systems are grouped, for convenience of discussion, under six headings. Trends are emphasized by contrasting the situation in early and late development. The degree of absolute change, the rate of change, and the time required to reach a steady state may vary not only with different climatic and physiographic situations but also with different ecosystem attributes in the same physical environment. Where good data are available, rate-of-change curves are usually convex, with changes occurring most rapidly at the beginning, but bimodal or cyclic patterns may also occur.

BIOENERGETICS OF ECOSYSTEM DEVELOPMENT

In the early stages of ecological succession, or in "young nature," so to speak, the rate of primary production or total (gross) photosynthesis (P) exceeds the rate of community respiration (R), so that the P/R ratio is greater than 1. In the special case of organic pollution, the P/R ratio is typically less than 1. In both cases, however, the theory is that P/R approaches 1 as succession occurs. In other words, energy fixed tends to be balanced by the energy cost of mainten-

Table 1. A TABULAR MODEL OF ECOLOGICAL SUCCESSION: TRENDS TO BE EXPECTED IN THE DEVELOPMENT OF ECOSYSTEMS

ECOSYSTEM ATTRIBUTES	DEVELOPMENTAL STAGES	MATURE STAGES
COMMUNITY ENERGETICS		
1. Gross production/community respiration (P/R ratio)	Greater or less than 1	Approaches 1
2. Gross production/standing crop biomass (P/B ratio)	High	Low
3. Biomass supported/unit energy flow (B/E ratio)	Low	High
4. Net community production (yield)	High	Low
5. Food chains	Linear, predominantly grazing	Weblike, predominantly detritus
COMMUNITY STRUCTURE		
6. Total organic matter	Small	Large
7. Inorganic nutrients	Extrabiotic	Intrabiotic
8. Species diversity—variety component	Low	High
9. Species diversity—equitability component	Low	High
10. Biochemical diversity	Low	High
11. Stratification and spatial heterogeneity (pattern diversity)	Poorly organized	Well-organized
LIFE HISTORY		
12. Niche specialization	Broad	Narrow
13. Size of organism	Small	Large
14. Life cycles	Short, simple	Long, complex
NUTRIENT CYCLING		
15. Mineral cycles	Open	Closed
16. Nutrient exchange rate, between organisms and environment	Rapid	Slow
17. Role of detritus in nutrient regeneration	Unimportant	Important
SELECTION PRESSURE		
18. Production	Quantity	Quality
OVERALL HOMEOSTASIS		
19. Internal symbiosis	Undeveloped	Developed
20. Nutrient conservation	Poor	Good
21. Stability (resistance to external perturbations)	Poor	Good
22. Entropy	High	Low
23. Information	Low	High

ance (that is, total community respiration) in the mature or "climax" ecosystem. The P/R ratio, therefore, should be an excellent functional index of the relative maturity of the system.

So long as P exceeds R, organic matter and biomass (B) will accumulate in the system (Table 1, item 6), with the result that ratio P/B will tend to decrease or, conversely, the B/P, B/R, or B/E ratios (where $E = P + R$) will increase (Table 1, items 2 and 3). Theoretically, then, the amount of standing-crop biomass supported by the available energy flow (E) increases to a maximum in the mature or climax stages (Table 1, item 3). As a consequence, the net community production, or yield, in an annual cycle is large in young nature and small or zero in mature nature (Table 1, item 4).

COMPARISON OF SUCCESSION IN A LABORATORY MICROCOSM AND A FOREST

One can readily observe bioenergetic changes by initiating succession in experimental laboratory microecosystems. Aquatic microecosystems, derived from various types of outdoor systems, such as ponds, have been cultured by Beyers (5), and certain of these mixed cultures are easily replicated and maintain themselves in the climax state indefinitely on defined media in a flask with only light input (6). If samples from the climax system are inoculated into fresh media, succession occurs, the mature system developing in less than 100 days. In Fig. 1 the general pattern of a 100-day autotrophic succession in a microcosm based on data of Cooke (7) is compared with a hypothetical model of a 100-year forest succession as presented by Kira and Shidei (8).

During the first 40 to 60 days in a typical microcosm experiment, daytime net production (P) exceeds nighttime respiration (R), so that biomass (B) accumulates in the system (9). After an early "bloom" at about 30 days, both rates decline, and they become approximately equal at 60 to 80 days. The B/P ratio, in terms of grams of carbon supported per gram of daily carbon production, increases from less than 20 to more than 100 as the steady state is reached. Not only are autotrophic and heterotrophic metabolism balanced in the climax, but a large organic structure is supported by small daily production and respiratory rates.

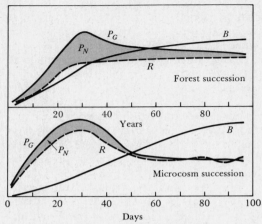

Figure 1. Comparison of the energetics of succession in a forest and a laboratory microcosm. P_G, gross production; P_N, net production; R, total community respiration; B, total biomass.

While direct projection from the small laboratory microecosystem to open nature may not be entirely valid, there is evidence that the same basic trends that are seen in the laboratory are characteristic of succession on land and in large bodies of water. Seasonal successions also often follow the same pattern, an early seasonal bloom characterized by rapid growth of a few dominant species being followed by the development later in the season of high B/P ratios, increased diversity, and a relatively steady, if temporary, state in terms of P and R (4). Open systems may not experience a decline, at maturity, in total or gross productivity, as the space-limited microcosms do, but the general pattern of bioenergetic change in the latter seems to mimic nature quite well.

These trends are not, as might at first seem to be the case, contrary to the classical limnological teaching which describes lakes as progressing in time from the less productive (oligotrophic) to the more productive (eutrophic) state. Table 1, as already emphasized, refers to changes which are brought about by biological processes *within* the ecosystem in question. Eutrophication, whether natural or cultural, results when nutrients are imported into the lake from *outside* the lake—that is, from the watershed. This is equivalent to adding nutrients to the laboratory microecosystem or fertilizing a field; the system is pushed back, in successional terms, to a younger or "bloom" state. Recent studies on lake sediments (10), as well as theoretical considerations (*11*), have indicated that lakes can and do progress to a more oligotrophic condition when the nutrient input from the watershed slows or ceases. Thus, there is hope that the troublesome cultural eutrophication of our waters can be reversed if the inflow of nutrients from the watershed can be greatly reduced.

FOOD CHAINS AND FOOD WEBS

As the ecosystem develops, subtle changes in the network pattern of food chains may be expected. The manner in which organisms are linked together through food tends to be relatively simple and linear in the very early stages of succession, as a consequence of low diversity. Furthermore, heterotrophic utilization of net production occurs predominantly by way of grazing food chains—that is, plant-herbivore-carnivore sequences. In contrast, food chains become complex webs in mature stages, with the bulk of biological energy flow following detritus pathways (Table 1, item 5). In a mature forest, for example, less than 10 percent of annual net production is consumed (that is, grazed) in the living state (*12*); most is utilized as dead matter (detritus) through delayed and complex pathways involving as yet little understood animal-microorganism interactions. The time involved in an uninterrupted succession allows for increasingly intimate associations and reciprocal adaptations between plants and animals, which lead to the development of many mechanisms that reduce grazing—such as the development of indigestible supporting tissues (cellulose, lignin, and so on), feedback control between plants and herbivores (*13*), and increasing predatory pressure on herbivores (*14*). Such mechanisms enable the biological community to maintain the large and complex organic structure that mitigates perturbations of the physical environment. Severe stress or rapid changes brought about by outside forces can, of course, rob the system of these protective mechanisms and allow irruptive, cancerous growths of certain species to occur, as man too often finds to his sorrow. An example of a stress-induced pest irruption occurred at Brookhaven National Laboratory, where oaks became vulnerable to aphids when translocation of sugars and amino acids was impaired by continuing gamma irradiation (*15*).

DIVERSITY AND SUCCESSION

Perhaps the most controversial of the successional trends pertains to the complex and much discussed subject of diversity (*16*). It is important to distinguish between different kinds of diversity indices, since they may not follow parallel trends in the same gradient or developmental series. Four components of diversity are listed in Table 1, items 8 through 11.

The variety of species, expressed as a species-number ratio or a species-area ratio, tends to increase during the early stages of community development. A second component of species diversity is what has been called equitability, or evenness (*17*), in the apportionment of individuals among the species. For example, two systems each containing 10 species and 100 individuals have the same diversity in terms of species-number ratio but could have widely different equitabilities depending on the apportionment of the 100 individuals among the 10 species—for example, 91-1-1-1-1-1-1-1-1-1 at one extreme or 10 individuals per species at the other.

While an increase in the variety of species together with reduced dominance by any one species or small group of species (that is, increased evenness) can be accepted as a general probability during succession (*18*), there are other community changes that may work against these trends. An increase in the size of organisms, an increase in the length and complexity of life histories, and an increase in interspecific competition that may result in competitive exclusion of species (Table 1, items 12—14) are trends that may reduce the number of species that can live in a given area. In the bloom stage of succession organisms tend to be small and to have simple life histories and rapid rates of reproduction. Changes in size appear to be a consequence of, or an adaptation to, a shift in nutrients from inorganic to organic (Table 1, item 7). In a mineral nutrient-rich environment, small size is of selective advantage, especially to autotrophs, because of the greater surface-to-volume ratio. As the ecosystem develops, however, inorganic nutrients tend to become more and more tied up in the biomass, so that the selective advantage shifts to larger organisms.

Thus, whether or not species diversity continues to increase during succession will depend on whether the increase in potential

31

niches resulting from increased biomass, stratification (Table 1, item 9), and other consequences of biological organization exceeds the countereffects of increasing size and competition. No one has yet been able to catalogue all the species in any sizable area, much less follow total species diversity in a successional series. Data are so far available only for segments of the community (trees, birds, and so on). Margalef (4) postulates that diversity will tend to peak during the early or middle stages of succession and then decline in the climax. In a study of bird populations along a successional gradient we found a bimodal pattern (19); the number of species increased during the early stages of old-field succession, declined during the early forest stages, and then increased again in the mature forest.

Species variety, equitability, and stratification are only three aspects of diversity which change during succession. Perhaps an even more important trend is an increase in the diversity of organic compounds, not only of those within the biomass but also of those excreted and secreted into the media (air, soil, water) as by-products of the increasing community metabolism. An increase in such "biochemical diversity" (Table 1, item 10) is illustrated by the increase in the variety of plant pigments along a successional gradient in aquatic situations, as described by Margalef (4, 20). Biochemical diversity within populations, or within systems as a whole, has not yet been systematically studied to the degree the subject of species diversity has been. Consequently, few generalizations can be made, except that it seems safe to say that, as succession progresses, organic extrametabolites probably serve increasingly important functions as regulators which stabilize the growth and composition of the ecosystem. Such metabolites may, in fact, be extremely important in preventing populations from overshooting the equilibrial density, thus in reducing oscillations as the system develops stability.

NUTRIENT CYCLING

An important trend in successional development is the closing or "tightening" of the biogeochemical cycling of major nutrients, such as nitrogen, phosphorus, and calcium (Table 1, items 15—17). Mature systems, as compared to developing ones, have a greater capacity to entrap and hold nutrients for cycling within the system. For example, Bormann and Likens (21) have estimated that only 8 kilograms per hectare out of a total pool of exchangeable calcium of 365 kilograms per hectare is lost per year in stream outflow from a North Temperate watershed covered with a mature forest. Of this, about 3 kilograms per hectare is replaced by rainfall, leaving only 5 kilograms to be obtained from weathering of the underlying rocks in order for the system to maintain mineral balance. Reducing the volume of the vegetation, or otherwise setting the succession back to a younger state, results in increased water yield by way of stream outflow (22), but this greater outflow is accompanied by greater losses of nutrients, which may also produce downstream eutrophication. Unless there is a compensating increase in the rate of weathering, the exchangeable pool of nutrients suffers gradual depletion (not to mention possible effects on soil structure resulting from erosion). High fertility in "young systems" which have open nutrient cycles cannot be maintained without compensating inputs of new nutrients; examples of such practice are the continuous-flow culture of algae, or intensive agriculture where large amounts of fertilizer are imported into the system each year.

Because rates of leaching increase in a latitudinal gradient from the poles to the equator, the role of the biotic community in nutrient retention is especially important in the high-rainfall areas of the subtropical and tropical latitudes, including not only land areas but also estuaries. Theoretically, as one goes equatorward, a larger percentage of the available nutrient pool is tied up in the biomass and a correspondingly lower percentage is in the soil or sediment. This theory, however, needs testing, since data to show such a geographical trend are incomplete. It is perhaps significant that conventional North Temperate row-type agriculture, which represents a very youthful type of ecosystem, is successful in the humid tropics only if carried out in a system of "shifting agriculture" in which the crops alternate with periods of natural vegetative redevelopment. Tree culture and the semiaquatic culture of rice provide much better nutrient retention and consequently have a longer life expectancy on a given site in these warmer latitudes.

OVERALL HOMEOSTASIS

This brief review of ecosystem development emphasizes the complex nature of processes that interact. While one may well question whether all the trends described are characteristic of all types of ecosystems, there can be little doubt that the net result of community actions is symbiosis, nutrient conservation. stability, a decrease in entropy, and an increase in information (Table 1, items 19—23). The overall strategy is directed toward achieving as large and diverse an organic structure as is possible within the limits set by the available energy input and the prevailing physical conditions of existence (soil, water, climate, and so on).

RELEVANCE OF ECOSYSTEM DEVELOPMENT THEORY TO HUMAN ECOLOGY

Figure 1 depicts a basic conflict between the strategies of man and of nature. The "bloom-type" relationships, as exhibited by the 30-day microcosm or the 30-year forest, illustrate man's present idea of how nature should be directed. For example, the goal of agriculture or intensive forestry, as now generally practiced, is to achieve high rates of production of readily harvestable products with little standing crop left to accumulate on the landscape—in other words, a high P/B efficiency. Nature's strategy, on the other hand, as seen in the outcome of the successional process, is directed toward the reverse efficiency—a high B/P ratio, as is depicted by the relationship at the right in Fig. 1. Man has generally been preoccupied with obtaining as much "production" from the landscape as possible, by developing and maintaining early successional types of ecosystems, usually monocultures. But, of course, man does not live by food and fiber alone; he also needs a balanced CO_2—O_2 atmosphere, the climatic buffer provided by oceans and masses of vegetation, and clean (that is, unproductive) water for cultural and industrial uses. Many essential life-cycle resources, not to mention recreational and esthetic needs, are best provided man by the less "productive" landscapes. In other words, the landscape is not just a supply depot but is also the *oikos*—the home—in which we must live. Until recently mankind has more or less taken for granted the gas-exchange, water-purification, nutrient-cycling, and other protective functions of self-maintaining ecosystems, chiefly because neither his numbers nor his environmental manipulations have been great enough to affect regional and global balances. Now it is painfully evident that such balances are being affected, often detrimentally. The "one problem, one solution approach" is no longer adequate and must be replaced by some form of ecosystem analysis that considers man as a part of, not apart from, the environment.

The most pleasant and certainly the safest landscape to live in is one containing a variety of crops, forests, lakes, streams, roadsides, marshes, seashores, and "waste places"—in other words, a mixture of communities of different ecological ages. As individuals we more or less instinctively surround our houses with protective, nonedible cover (trees, shrubs, grass) at the same time that we strive to coax extra bushels from our cornfield. We all consider the cornfield a "good thing," of course, but most of us would not want to live there, and it would certainly be suicidal to cover the whole land area of the biosphere with cornfields, since the boom and bust oscillation in such a situation would be severe.

The basic problem facing organized society today boils down to determining in some objective manner when we are getting "too much of a good thing." This is a completely new challenge to mankind because, up until now, he has had to be concerned largely with too little rather than too much. Thus, concrete is a "good thing," but not if half the world is covered with it. Insecticides are "good things," but not when used, as they now are, in an indiscriminate and wholesale manner. Likewise, water impoundments have proved to be very useful man-made additions to the landscape, but obviously we don't want the whole country inundated! Vast man-made lakes solve some problems, at least temporarily, but yield comparative little food or fiber, and, because of high evaporative losses, they may not even be the best device for storing water; it might better be stored in the watershed, or underground in aquafers. Also, the cost of building large dams is a drain on already overtaxed revenues. Although as individuals we readily recognize that we can have too many dams or other large-scale environmental changes, governments are so fragmented and lacking in systems-analysis capabilities that there is no effective mechanism whereby negative feedback signals can be received and acted on before there has been a serious overshoot.

33

Thus, today there are governmental agencies, spurred on by popular and political enthusiasm for dams, that are putting on the drawing boards plans for damming every river and stream in North America! Society needs, and must find as quickly as possible, a way to deal with the landscape as a whole, so that manipulative skills (that is, technology) will not run too far ahead of our understanding of the impact of change.

The general relevance of ecosystem development theory to landscape planning can, perhaps, be emphasized by the "mini-model" of Table 2, which contrasts the characteristics of young and mature-type ecosystems in more general terms than those provided by Table 1. It is mathematically impossible to obtain a maximum for more than one thing at a time, so one cannot have both extremes at the same time and place. Since all six characteristics listed in Table 2 are desirable in the aggregate, two possible solutions to the dilemma immediately suggest themselves. We can compromise so as to provide moderate quality and moderate yield on all the landscape, or we can deliberately plan to compartmentalize the landscape so as to simultaneously maintain highly productive and predominantly protective types as separate units subject to different management strategies (strategies ranging, for example, from intensive cropping on the one hand to wilderness management on the other). If ecosystem development theory is valid and applicable to planning, then the so-called multiple-use strategy, about which we hear so much, will work only through one or both of these approaches, because, in most cases, the projected multiple uses conflict with one another. It is appropriate, then, to examine some examples of the compromise and the compartmental strategies.

PULSE STABILITY

A more or less regular but acute physical perturbation imposed from without can maintain an ecosystem at some intermediate point in the developmental sequence, resulting in, so to speak, a compromise between youth and maturity. What I would term "fluctuating water level ecosystems" are good examples. Estuaries, and intertidal zones in general, are maintained in an early, relatively fertile stage by the tides, which provide the energy for rapid nutrient

Table 2. CONTRASTING CHARACTERISTICS OF YOUNG AND MATURE-TYPE ECOSYSTEMS

YOUNG	MATURE
Production	Protection
Growth	Stability
Quantity	Quality

cycling. Likewise, freshwater marshes, such as the Florida Everglades, are held at an early successional stage by the seasonal fluctuations in water levels. The dry-season drawdown speeds up aerobic decomposition of accumulated organic matter, releasing nutrients that, on reflooding, support a wet-season bloom in productivity. The life histories of many organisms are intimately coupled to this periodicity. The wood stork, for example, breeds when the water levels are falling and the small fish on which it feeds become concentrated and easy to catch in the drying pools. If the water level remains high during the usual dry season or fails to rise in the wet season, the stork will not nest (23). Stabilizing water levels in the Everglades by means of dikes, locks, and impoundments, as is now advocated by some, would, in my opinion, destroy rather than preserve the Everglades as we now know them just as surely as complete drainage would. Without periodic drawdowns and fires, the shallow basins would fill up with organic matter and succession would proceed from the present pond-and-prairie condition toward a scrub or swamp forest.

It is strange that man does not readily recognize the importance of recurrent changes in water level in a natural situation such as the Everglades when similar pulses are the basis for some of his most enduring food culture systems (24). Alternate filling and draining of ponds has been a standard procedure in fish culture for centuries in Europe and the Orient. The flooding, draining, and soil-aeration procedure in rice culture is another example. The rice paddy is thus the cultivated analogue of the natural marsh or the intertidal ecosystem.

Fire is another physical factor whose periodicity has been of vital importance to man and nature over the centuries. Whole biotas, such as those of the African grasslands and the California chaparral, have become adapted to periodic fires producing what ecologists often call "fire climaxes" (25). Man uses fire deliberately to maintain such climaxes or to set back succession to some desired point. In the southeastern coastal plain, for example, light fires of moderate frequency can maintain a pine forest against the encroachment of older successional stages which, at the present time at least, are considered economically less desirable. The fire-controlled forest yields less wood than a tree farm does (that is, young trees, all of about the same age, planted in rows and harvested on a short rotation schedule), but it provides a greater protective cover for the landscape, wood of higher quality, and a home for game birds (quail, wild turkey, and so on) which could not survive in a tree farm. The fire climax, then, is an example of a compromise between production simplicity and protection diversity.

PROSPECTS FOR A DETRITUS AGRICULTURE

As indicated above, heterotrophic utilization of primary production in mature ecosystems involves largely a delayed consumption of detritus. There is no reason why man cannot make greater use of detritus and thus obtain food or other products from the more protective type of ecosystem. Again, this would represent a compromise, since the short-term yield could not be as great as the yield obtained by direct exploitation of the grazing food chain. A detritus agriculture, however, would have some compensating advantages. Present agricultural strategy is based on selection for rapid growth and edibility in food plants, which, of course, make them vulnerable to attack by insects and disease. Consequently, the more we select for succulence and growth, the more effort we must invest in the chemical control of pests; this effort, in turn, increases the likelihood of our poisoning useful organisms, not to mention ourselves. Why not also practice the reverse strategy—that is, select plants which are essentially unpalatable, or which produce their own systemic insecticides while they are growing, and then convert the net production into edible products by microbial and chemical enrichment in food factories? We could then devote our biochemical genius to the enrichment process instead of fouling up our living space with chemical poisons! The production of silage by fermentation of low-grade fodder is an example of such a procedure already in widespread use. The cultivation of detritus-eating fishes in the Orient is another example.

By tapping the detritus food chain man can also obtain an appreciable harvest from many natural systems without greatly modifying them or destroying their protective and esthetic value. Oyster culture in estuaries is a good example. In Japan, raft and long-line culture of oysters has proved to be a very practical way to harvest the natural microbial products of estuaries and shallow bays. Furukawa (*26*) reports that the yield of cultured oysters in the Hiroshima Prefecture has increased tenfold since 1950, and that the yield of oysters (some 240,000 tons of meat) from this one district alone in 1965 was ten times the yield of natural oysters from the entire country. Such oyster culture is feasible along the entire Atlantic and Gulf coasts of the United States. A large investment in the culture of oysters and other seafoods would also provide the best possible deterrent against pollution, since the first threat of damage to the pollution-sensitive oyster industry would be immediately translated into political action!

THE COMPARTMENT MODEL

Successful though they often are, compromise systems are not suitable nor desirable for the whole landscape. More emphasis needs to be placed on compartmentalization, so that growth-type, steady-state, and intermediate-type ecosystems can be linked with urban and industrial areas for mutual benefit. Knowing the transfer coefficients that define the flow of energy and the movement of materials and organisms (including man) between compartments, it should be possible to determine, through analog-computer manipulation, rational limits for the size and capacity of each compartment. We might start, for example, with a simplified model, shown in Fig. 2, consisting of four compartments of equal area, partitioned according to the basic biotic-function criterion —that is, according to whether the area is (i) productive, (ii) protective, (iii) a compromise between (i) and (ii), or (iv) urban-industrial. By continually refining the transfer coefficients on the basis of real world situations, and by increasing and decreasing the size and capacity of each compartment through computer simulation, it would be possible to determine objectively the limits that must eventually be imposed on each compartment in order to maintain regional and global balances in the

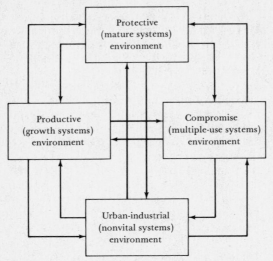

Figure 2. Compartment model of the basic kinds of environment required by man, partitioned according to ecosystem development and life-cycle resource criteria.

exchange of vital energy and of materials. A systems-analysis procedure provides at least one approach to the solution of the basic dilemma posed by the question "How do we determine when we are getting too much of a good thing?" Also it provides a means of evaluating the energy drains imposed on ecosystems by pollution, radiation, harvest, and other stresses (27).

Implementing any kind of compartmentalization plan, of course, would require procedures for zoning the landscape and restricting the use of some land and water areas. While the principle of zoning in cities is universally accepted, the procedures now followed do not work very well because zoning restrictions are too easily overturned by short-term economic and population pressures. Zoning the landscape would require a whole new order of thinking. Greater use of legal measures providing for tax relief, restrictions on use, scenic easements, and public ownership will be required if appreciable land and water areas are to be held in the "protective" categories. Several states (for example, New Jersey and California), where pollution and population pressure are beginning to hurt, have made a start in this direction by enacting "open space" legislation designed to get as much unoccupied land as possible into a "protective" status so that future uses can be planned on a rational and scientific basis. The United States as a whole is fortunate in that large areas

of the country are in national forests, parks, wildlife refuges, and so on. The fact that such areas, as well as the bordering oceans, are not quickly exploitable gives us time for the accelerated ecological study and programming needed to determine what proportions of different types of landscape provide a safe balance between man and nature. The open oceans, for example, should forever be allowed to remain protective rather than productive territory, if Alfred Redfields's (28) assumptions are correct. Redfield views the oceans, the major part of the hydrosphere, as the biosphere's governor, which slows down and controls the rate of decomposition and nutrient regeneration, thereby creating and maintaining the highly aerobic terrestrial environment to which the higher forms of life, such as man, are adapted. Eutrophication of the ocean in a last-ditch effort to feed the populations of the land could well have an adverse effect on the oxygen reservoir in the atmosphere.

Until we can determine more precisely how far we may safely go in expanding intensive agriculture and urban sprawl at the expense of the protective landscape, it will be good insurance to hold inviolate as much of the latter as possible. Thus, the preservation of natural areas is not a peripheral luxury for society but a capital investment from which we expect to draw interest. Also, it may well be that restrictions in the use of land and water are our only practical means of avoiding overpopulation or too great an exploitation of resources, or both. Interestingly enough, restriction of land use is the analog of a natural behavioral control mechanism known as "territoriality" by which many species of animals avoid crowding and social stress (29).

Since the legal and economic problems pertaining to zoning and compartmentalization are likely to be thorny, I urge law schools to establish departments, or institutes, of "landscape law" and to start training "landscape lawyers" who will be capable not only of clarifying existing procedures but also of drawing up new enabling legislation for consideration by state and national governing bodies. At present, society is concerned—and rightly so— with human rights, but environmental rights are equally vital. The "one man one vote" idea is important, but so also is a "one man one hectare" proposition.

Education, as always, must play a role in

increasing man's awareness of his dependence on the natural environment. Perhaps we need to start teaching the principles of ecosystem in the third grade. A grammar school primer on man and his environment could logically consist of four chapters, one for each of the four essential kinds of environment, shown diagrammatically in Fig. 2.

Of the many books and articles that are being written these days about man's environmental crisis, I would like to cite two that go beyond "crying out in alarm" to suggestions for bringing about a reorientation of the goals of society. Garrett Hardin, in a recent article in *Science* (*30*), points out that, since the optimum population density is less than the maximum, there is no strictly technical solution to the problem of pollution caused by overpopulation; a solution, he suggests, can only be achieved through moral and legal means of "mutual coercion, mutually agreed upon by the majority of people." Earl F. Murphy, in a book entitled *Governing Nature* (*31*), emphasizes that the regulatory approach alone is not enough to protect life-cycle resources, such as air and water, that cannot be allowed to deteriorate. He discusses permit systems, effluent charges, receptor levies, assessment, and cost-internalizing procedures as economic incentives for achieving Hardin's "mutually agreed upon coercion."

It goes without saying that the tabular model for ecosystem development which I have presented here has many parallels in the development of human society itself. In the pioneer society, as in the pioneer ecosystem, high birth rates, rapid growth, high economic profits, and exploitation of accessible and unused resources are advantageous, but, as the saturation level is approached, these drives must be shifted to considerations of symbiosis (that is, "civil rights," "law and order," "education," and "culture"), birth control, and the recycling of resources. A balance between youth and maturity in the socioenvironmental system is, therefore, the really basic goal that must be achieved if man as a species is to successfully pass through the present rapid-growth stage, to which he is clearly well adapted, to the ultimate equilibrium-density stage, of which he as yet shows little understanding and to which he now shows little tendency to adapt.

REFERENCES AND NOTES

1. E. P. Odum, *Ecology* (Holt, Rinehart & Winston, New York, 1963), chap. 6.
2. H. T. Odum and R. C. Pinkerton, *Amer. Scientist* **43**, 331 (1955).
3. A. J. Lotka, *Elements of Physical Biology* (Williams and Wilkins, Baltimore, 1925).
4. R. Margalef, *Advan. Frontiers Plant Sci.* **2**, 137 (1963); *Amer. Naturalist* **97**, 357 (1963).
5. R. J. Beyers, *Ecol. Monographs* **33**, 281 (1963).
6. The systems so far used to test ecological principles have been derived from sewage and farm ponds and are cultured in half-strength No. 36 Taub and Dollar medium [*Limnol. Oceanog.* **9**, 61 (1964)]. They are closed to organic input or output but are open to the atmosphere through the cotton plug in the neck of the flask. Typically, liter-sized microecosystems contain two or three species of nonflagellated algae and one to three species each of flagellated protozoans, ciliated protozoans, rotifers, nematodes, and ostracods; a system derived from a sewage pond contained at least three species of fungi and 13 bacterial isolates [R. Gordon, thesis, University of Georgia (1967)]. These cultures are thus a kind of minimum ecosystem containing those small species originally found in the ancestral pond that are able to function together as a self-contained unit under the restricted conditions of the laboratory flask and the controlled environment of a growth chamber [temperature, 65° to 75°F (18° to 24°C); photoperiod, 12 hours; illumination, 100 to 1000 foot-candles].
7. G. D. Cooke, *BioScience* **17**, 717 (1967).
8. T. Kira and T. Shidei, *Japan. J. Ecol.* **17**, 70 (1967).
9. The metabolism of the microcosms was monitored by measuring diurnal pH changes, and the biomass (in terms of total organic matter and total carbon) was determined by periodic harvesting of replicate systems.
10. F. J. H. Mackereth, *Proc. Roy. Soc. London Ser. B* **161**, 295 (1965); U. M. Cowgill and G. E. Hutchinson, *Proc. Intern. Limnol. Ass.* **15**, 644 (1964); A. D. Harrison, *Trans. Roy. Soc. S. Africa* **36**, 213 (1962).
11. R. Margalef, *Proc. Intern. Limnol. Ass.* **15**, 169 (1964).
12. J. R. Bray, *Oikos* **12**, 70 (1961).
13. D. Pimentel, *Amer. Naturalist* **95**, 65 (1961).
14. R. T. Paine, *ibid.* **100**, 65 (1966).
15. G. M. Woodwell, *Brookhaven Nat. Lab. Pub. 924(T-381)* (1965), pp. 1–15.

16. For selected general discussions of patterns of species diversity, see E. H. Simpson, *Nature* **163**, 688 (1949); C. B. Williams, *J. Animal Ecol.* **22**, 14 (1953); G. E. Hutchinson, *Amer. Naturalist* **93**, 145 (1959); R. Margalef, *Gen. Systems* **3**, 36 (1958); R. MacArthur and J. MacArthur, *Ecology* **42**, 594 (1961); N. G. Hairston, *ibid.* **40**, 404 (1959); B. C. Patten, *J. Marine Res. (Sears Found. Marine Res.)* **20**, 57 (1960); E. G. Leigh. *Proc. Nat. Acad. Sci. U.S.* **55**, 777 (1965); E. R. Pianka, *Amer. Naturalist* **100**, 33 (1966); E. C. Peilou, *J. Theoret. Biol.* **10**, 370 (1966).

17. M. Lloyd and R. J. Ghelardi, *J. Animal Ecol.* **33**, 217 (1964); E. C. Pielou, *J. Theoret. Biol.* **13**, 131 (1966).

18. In our studies of natural succession following grain culture, both the species-to-numbers and the equitability indices increased for all trophic levels but especially for predators and parasites. Only 44 percent of the species in the natural ecosystem were phytophagous, as compared to 77 percent in the grain field.

19. D. W. Johnston and E. P. Odum, *Ecology* **37**, 50 (1956).

20. R. Margalef, *Oceanog. Marine Biol. Annu. Rev.* **5**, 257 (1967).

21. F. H. Bormann and G. E. Likens, *Science* **155**, 424 (1967).

22. Increased water yield following reduction of vegetative cover has been frequently demonstrated in experimental watersheds throughout the world [see A. R. Hibbert, in *International Symposium on Forest Hydrology* (Pergamon Press, New York, 1967), pp. 527–543]. Data on the long-term hydrologic budget (rainfall input relative to stream outflow) are available at many of these sites, but mineral budgets have yet to be systematically studied. Again, this is a prime objective in the "ecosystem analysis" phase of the International Biological Program.

23. See M. P. Kahl, *Ecol. Monographs* **34**, 97 (1964).

24. The late Aldo Leopold remarked long ago [*Symposium on Hydrobiology* (Univ. of Wisconsin Press, Madison, 1941), p. 17] that man does not perceive organic behavior in systems unless he has built them himself. Let us hope it will not be necessary to rebuild the entire biosphere before we recognize the worth of natural systems!

25. See C. F. Cooper, *Sci. Amer.* **204**, 150 (April 1961).

26. See "Proceedings Oyster Culture Workshop, Marine Fisheries Division, Georgia Game and Fish Commission, Brunswick" (1968), pp. 49–61.

27. See H. T. Odum, in *Symposium on Primary Productivity and Mineral Cycling in Natural Ecosystems*, H. E. Young, Ed. (Univ. of Maine Press, Orono, 1967), p. 81;———, in *Pollution and Marine Ecology* (Wiley, New York, 1967), p. 99; K. E. F. Watt, *Ecology and Resource Management* (McGraw-Hill, New York, 1968).

28. A. C. Redfield, *Amer. Scientist* **46**, 205 (1958).

29. R. Ardrey, *The Territorial Imperative* (Atheneum, New York, 1967).

30. G. Hardin, *Science* **162**, 1243 (1968).

31. E. F. Murphy, *Governing Nature* (Quadrangle Books, Chicago, 1967).

Selection 4

Ecosystem View of Human Society

Commentary

Dr. Odum has suggested how certain ecological principles can be applied in a practical way to our environmental problems. Frank Fraser Darling and Raymond Dasmann, both eminent ecologists, go one step further and look at human society from an ecosystem point of view.

In the natural world each organism (including primitive man) performs a certain role in the overall scheme of things. The mink by preying upon the muskrat not only eliminates the weak but also helps dispose of the surplus population and thereby retains the flow of energy in the grazing food chain away from the decomposers. The crab consumes dead material or detritus in the pond. The robin feeds on the earthworm and the deer consumes herbaceous plants and woody browse. Each has a role in the transfer of energy and cycling of materials in the ecosystem. Among some organisms, such as the ant, the termite, and the bee, each animal in addition to the general functional role of the species in the ecosystem also performs a specific task in the maintenance of its own society. This division of labor reaches its most sophisticated level in human society. From an ecosystem point of view the occupational tasks that each individual performs is a niche, a functional role in the flow of energy. The achievement of the task in the natural ecosystem results in the cycling of materials; in the human ecosystem it is the cycling of money. The case may be somewhat overdrawn but the similarity should be obvious.

Human society can be observed in terms of a strategy of ecosystem development also. Underdeveloped countries, whether they are on the way up or, as suggested earlier, in a stage of retrogressive succession, represent simplified ecosystems occupied by ecological pioneers, the generalists. The generalists occupy very broad positions. They are able to perform a spectrum of activities of fairly simple tasks. As society becomes more complex and technology more important, there is less and less room for the generalist. The niche of the generalist has been taken over by and divided among specialists who are, in ecological terms, better competitors. The same is true for countries. Technical societies, in the short run at least, are better competitors than the less developed ones. The generalist countries remain economically poor and undeveloped.

In many ways this approach raises a number of conflicting questions and incongruities. To arrive at a more diverse stage of development, a society requires more resources. Is advanced technology, then, with its enormous drain on natural resources really a stage of immaturity, and the underdeveloped countries the mature stages? Ecologists have long considered succession in lakes to proceed from nutrient-poor, oligotrophic lakes to a more diverse, nutrient-rich eutrophic stage. However, the ecologist Ramon Margalef[1] has suggested that in lakes the reverse may be true. The oligotrophic lakes may be mature stages, the eutrophic lakes with their rich nutrient supply and diversity of life the immature system.

Generalists do not rely heavily on technology. If a technological or a specialized society is confronted with or destroyed by a major disaster such as nuclear war, would not the generalists out-compete the specialists? The technological society would revert back to the pioneering stages of the generalists.

The selection by Darling and Dasmann raises all sorts of controversial questions.

---

[1]R. Margalef, *Perspectives in Ecological Theory*, Chicago, Ill., University of Chicago Press, 1968.

Selection 4

The Ecosystem View of Human Society

by Frank Fraser Darling and Raymond F. Dasmann

THE ECOSYSTEM

Most ecologists who study an individual, a population, or a community, do so in the knowledge that the organisms under study exist as part of an ecosystem.

. . .

Any biotic community exists only as a part of its total environment. One cannot separate a forest from the air that surrounds it or the water and minerals in the forest soil since there is a constant interchange among these components. The forest changes the composition of the air, the air changes the physical and chemical composition of the forest. An organism apart from its physical environment is an abstraction. In nature, no such creature exists. A community therefore is a part of a physical and biological system including air, soil, water and all of the physical and chemical properties of these media. These form the reality of the ecosystem.

. . .

Energy stored by ecosystem powers most of our human activity today, since it is used by man not only in the form of food for himself and his domestic animals, but also in the form of fossil fuels which power most of his industrial activities. Only the relatively small percentage of energy in the human economy represented by hydroelectric power, solar power and nuclear power is derived from non-organic sources.

. . .

... Man has been a part of ecosystems throughout his time on earth, functioning originally as one of many consumer organisms. During human evolution, however, man has moved from being a simple component of an ecosystem to becoming a dominant force in the system. Today, with his new technology and his massive urban concentrations, he has assumed a new role on the planet, tying all ecosystems together in a higher level of organization comprising the entire biosphere itself. To understand this new global organization it is worthwhile to consider comparisons between human societies and biotic communities and the roles which they play within the broader natural systems of which both form a part.

THE ECOLOGICAL NICHE IN NATURE AND SOCIETY

The individual animal or plant survives in nature only to the extent that it can find and occupy successfully a place in the environment known as an 'ecological niche'. The niche is an individual's or species' place in a biotic community. It is defined both in terms of the surrounding environment, the habitat, and the role played by the organism within it. Niches may be either generalized in nature or specialized. Think of a pine tree, a very obvious entity in a biotic community and the component that leads to the identification of a type of community and ecosystem, the pine forest. The pine occupies a generalized niche. Its roots are in the soil, living commensally with mycorrhyzal fungi; its root tips are slowly dissolving the rock faces to which they come in contact; such roots hairs as die are bored by orybatid mites and the capillaries thus formed conduct air and water into the soil. The soil itself accrues from animal, plant, geological and climatic interdependencies and over time is subject to change. All

THIS SECTION is from *Impact of Science on Society*, Vol. XIX, No. 2, pp. 109–121, 1969. Reprinted by permission © Unesco.

this before the emergence of the tree we know so well.

Indeed, to go back to the humble mycorrhyzal fungi, it is very difficult to get a pine forest growing without them. We notice in Scotland after long deforestation, that regeneration is very slow; just a few pioneer pine trees seem to grow, then there is a relatively sudden spurt of regeneration and the forest is growing again. Are not those pioneer pine trees the ones that can get going with a minimum of mycorrhyzal help and then, when they are established, the pine seedlings that are not pioneers can come in and thrive?

The trunk of a pine tree has its own flora of lichens and fauna of tiny animals. When we see the tree-creeper hopping this way and that up the bark, it is no random movement but a pattern of behaviour found nutritionally rewarding by a species which has adapted to finding tiny animals in the interstices of bark. A flock of several species of titmice may also be going over the bark in search of similar food— overlapping in demand upon the resources of the environment, you might say. And yet if a birdwatcher observes closely enough—and several have—the over-all demands of each species are different. Each has its own niche.

When we reach the twigs and foliage we are in a different world again, and yet it is still intimately the tree's world. An osprey may nest in the pine tree, crossbills will open the cones with their seemingly deformed but truly functional mandibles to extract the seed. Other birds will use the tree for cover or shade, the black grouse and capercaillie will eat the shoots, and squirrels will consume the cones in different fashion from the crossbill. The pine marten will be seen in the trees hunting the squirrels and young wood pigeons.

Worlds of light and dark, of heat and cold, of plenitude and scarcity, all these are part of the ecosystem in which the pine tree is anchored. Together the trees of the forest are protecting the soil cover of each individual tree and the litter of pine needles helps the plants of the field layer which are themselves ameliorating the soil of the forest, restraining its acidity and lightening its texture, along with the worms, beetles, and field mice burrowing and aerating the surface layer. Shrubs such as rowan (*Sorbus*) and willow (*Salix*) have their own silent faunas and as little consociations further ameliorate the soil.

The generalized niche of the pine tree, defined in terms of sunlight, open space, air, water, and some broken-down rock and soil, is occupied by the pioneer pine trees. These in turn provide a niche for the more specialized mycorrhyzal fungi, and the two interact in a symbiosis that benefits both species. As the pine forest grows, more and more niches become available for those organisms that are specialized: the mites in the pine roots, the bark borers, tree creepers, titmice and crossbills.

All we have said of the world of the pine tree, a member in many strata of its own ecosystem, of the wholeness of its home place, could be said pretty well of a human being in his home place. His environment is his world, though he does not consciously take part in all the activities in his ecosystem.

Think of the interactions of rich and poor, of municipal government and of private organizations, of church, of art in its various forms, and of the many interests of people which bring about associations and consociations. They are all extremely complex, and to say 'I keep myself' or that 'I am not my brother's keeper' is to deny the facts of natural history. The unseen mite in the dead rootlets is not insignificant in the ecosystem of the forest, nor is the humblest of men in his own community.

The mathematician and student of evolution, G. F. Gause, postulated what is now an oft-quoted axiom, that two species with identical ecology—occupying exactly the same niche— cannot persist together in the same habitat. One or the other fails. Successful species are those that have by natural selection differentiated their niche in the ecosystem from that of other species. The science of natural history has constantly refined our knowledge of what plants and animals do and what differing demands they make on the environment—or in other words, how differently they exploit it.

To return to human society, the authors of this paper occupy a highly specialized niche, that of ecologists, within the highly complex technological society that has developed over the past century. A century ago there was no niche for ecologists in what was then a much more simple human community, but there was limited space for a more generalized individual, the biologist. Five hundred years earlier even the biologist as such had no specific place, but the society provided some small room for those able to exploit the role of natural philosopher or

41

scientist. Success and advancement in human society, as in nature, comes with the discovery and exploitation of new niches, but these are created by the presence and work of those who occupy more generalized places in the environment.

Each niche-exploiting species, whether a human specialist or some root-boring mite unknown to science, is seeking a place and the means to live; even in the human example it is moved at best only secondarily by altruistic motives for the good of the community. Nevertheless, integration of niche functions works naturally and unconsciously towards a more efficient and stable community, whether a human civilization or an ecosystem in nature. Shakespeare had the idea early when he wrote in *Romeo and Juliet*:

For nought so vile upon the earth doth live,
But to the earth some special good doth give.

The analogy between the natural world and the politico-economic world breaks down philosophically in one important aspect: evolution of living organisms in nature is not forethought and though there arises a momentum which gives quite unconscious direction in evolution there is no predetermination. Such is the infinite variety of the gene pool that individuals and populations vary and adapt to the environment or, because of their genetic constitution and behavioral expression, are able to exploit some new facet of it. Chance and natural selection are as well set today as when Darwin stated his thesis in 1858, though the ways they operate are, of course, much better understood.

We know of primitive human societies that have survived to the present time. However, like the pioneering stages of the pine forest ecosystem they offer niches mostly to those who are generalized and opportunistic. The authors have lived among such and marvelled at the way in which every man can do fairly well what every other man in the community can do and does it. If there is any sharp division of labour it is between what men do and what women do, but there again, the women all do the same thing as each other. To some degree the rigid customs and taboos that arise around the proper work of males and females represent an artificial creation of separate niches to allow each sex to fulfil more adequately its biological role. Such societies, however, offer little space for specialists. To survive, all must exploit the same environmental opportunities for the good of all.

Archaeological investigation has shown us how rapidly a degree of civilization was attained after men achieved a capability for food storage as a result of cultivation of cereal grains. This allowed them to live in larger groups than heretofore and a measure of certainty about food gave leisure.

One of the most striking phenomena in the course of what might be called the flocculation of scattered mankind into villages and towns was the division of labour—the exploitation of new niches created by the presence of surplus food, of leisure and of higher human densities. There were wood workers, stone workers and metal workers, and these differentiated into shipwrights, millwrights, wheelwrights, stonemasons, armourers, goldsmiths, and a hundred other crafts into which specialization brought skill and virtuosity unknown before. Such workers bound themselves to guilds, demanding loyalties which amounted almost to taboos and which served to firm up and define the boundaries between the separate niches. Priests became literate, and learning passed from the rigour of oral tradition to a freer accumulated culture of the mind.

The townsman has always thought himself rather superior to the simpler inhabitant of small, more or less communalistic societies, though some of us may think this a severely limiting conceit. Nevertheless, the village boy looks to the town for a career and correctly states, 'There are more opportunities there'. The capital city seems to offer more opportunities still and usually does: in Rome, London, Paris, and New York you can find immensely skilled practitioners in almost anything.

These great cities acquire a considerable stability beyond the political boundaries of their existence. Rome is no longer the city of the Roman Empire, but remains the capital city of a mighty church and a united Italy. Paris has withstood tremendous shocks and remained Paris, and London has gone steadily forward from being the capital of a Belgic tribe to become a provincial Roman capital, a Saxon capital, and a Norman one, gradually extending its influence to be the heart of a great empire. That empire has gone, but London remains a growing entity, pulsing with new life and adapting to new situations in the politico-economic environment.

The tendency to draw analogies with natural ecosystems is difficult to resist. In nature complexity brings stability. The most complex ecosystems, those of the humid tropics, provide the most niches, support the greatest variety of species, and have maintained themselves in close to their present form over millions of years. Our complex urban centres, in the human time-scale, show similar enduring qualities.

THE URBAN SYSTEM

In the new technoligical world, most people are urban dwellers. The modern metropolitan city is the most complex environment that man has created. It has many features in common with a complex ecosystem, however it transcends all local ecosystems. A city such as London has producer organisms in plenty: in the woodlands of Hyde Park, the gardens of St. John's Wood, to the plankton in the Thames. It has various levels of consumer organisms in the insects, birds and small mammals that feed upon plants or upon each other. However, the dominant mammal of the area does not feed to any noticeable extent upon either the plants or wild mammals that live in the city. Instead he lives independent of local food chains and uses the natural ecosystems of the city only as part of his living and playing space and not for their productive capacity.

If we consider the food relationships of man in the city and go on to consider his relationship to water, the disposition of his wastes, or even his seasonal travels, we find that the urban system to which he belongs does not stop at any describable geographic boundary. The food consumed in London by the final organisms in the various food chains, the people of London, represents the productivity of the lateritic soils of the African tropics, the fisheries of the North Sea and the Atlantic, the sugar plantations of the Indies, the tea-growing hillsides of Ceylon and India, the corn fields, leys, and truck gardens of all of England, the orchards of South Africa. The water used in London is not that which falls upon the city but that which has moved down by surface flow or aquifer from the distant hills. The wastes produced by London do not circulate back to the soils that produced the food, but move through treatment plants down the river to enter new food chains in the

estuaries and the sea. Even the human population that one might examine on a winter day in Piccadilly will be found on other days in California, France, Nigeria and Hong Kong.

Man's urban communities thus do not fit the usual definition of ecosystem because they have no definable boundaries. The system to which London belongs extends its physical and biological network over the entire face of the earth. It is, in fact, the global ecosystem or biosphere. No lesser entity can contain it. The functioning of any major metropolis is dependent upon the continued healthy functioning, not just of local ecosystems, but of the entire biosphere. This relationship, unfortunately, is one that is commonly overlooked. Only in times of war or catastrophe when networks of energy flow, chemical flow, or the movements of human populations are impeded, do we realize the global nature of our urban systems and our dependence upon the biological productivity and the natural resources of the entire earth.

The relationship between modern technological society and the entire biosphere in which it exists is a new phenomenon. Earlier, pre-industrial cities were a part of local regional combinations of ecosystems rather than a global combination. Today, however, everything that happens in the world biosphere has its effects upon the large urban centres, and the urban centres affect the far corners of the earth.

Unfortunately, this has ecological implications we have yet to face. Cities, and the nations of which they form the core, are attempting to occupy the same global niche within the biosphere and to exploit the same resources in the same way. If they are not to suffer the fate of species that attempt to occupy the same niche in a wild community, they must more clearly define their ecological roles, either in geographical or functional specializations. In the crises that have confronted the pound, the dollar and the franc, in the global tensions of today and the earlier horrors of two world wars we see consequences of failure to confront ecological realities.

BREAKDOWNS IN THE URBAN SYSTEM

The urban centres of today's world represent not only the highest achievement of human cultural evolution but also its greatest problem. This results in part from a failure to design such urban centres to fit ecological realities.

43

GENERALISTS VERSUS NICHE-OCCUPIERS

The advances of modern technological society have far outstripped the capacity of most of the world's people to keep up. They remain as ecological pioneers—generalists—in a world dominated by complex climax communities and have as little hope for survival as pine seeds shed in the shade of a mature forest. Unlike pine seeds, however, they will not succumb quietly. The influx of people trained only to survive in the simple ways of primitive agricultural communities into the world's major cities is a major ecological problem of today's world. The cities provide limited space for generalized humans with primitive skills, although they offer unlimited opportunities for those who can fill a specialized niche. In our concentration upon quantity of production and upon technological efficiency we have lost sight of the more primitive and fundamental knowledge that human societies exist for the benefit of people.

So we get automation and the population explosion in the same suffering world. Automation is beautiful, literally beautiful. Prevention of human suffering and of premature death is also surely desirable, compassionate and beautiful. Do not both have a profound significance for the utopian world to which our imaginations reach? But the practical Chinese decline to buy mammoth earth-moving machinery because they have so many people who, with little baskets, can move the earth. In India, pregnant women working on the roads with their little baskets shift a few pounds of earth at a time. Compassion wells up within one, but if the great machines were there what would the people do? Something is out of phase. Where most people are ecological generalists, space must be found for generalized occupations, or the people must be trained to occupy the specialized niches. Ecological reality becomes apparent in Harlem, the *barrios* of Lima and the *favelas* of Rio, and above all in the ports of Asia, such as Calcutta.

OVERCROWDING

Over-population is one of the greatest problems of the modern world, but we have yet to face up to all of its implications. Ecologists studying wild animals have great difficulty in finding out how many animals there are in a given area.

For man we have detailed information. We know that the range of densities under which humans live is enormous: from less than one to the square mile in some wild areas to thousands per square mile in our cities. We do not know very much about the significance of these density figures in relation to human health, both physical and mental, and to human welfare in the broad sense of the word.

Part of the reason for confusion is that high density and overcrowding commonly go together, whereas low density is often accompanied by an absence of cultural amenities. Let us get our definitions clear: 'density' refers to the number of people per unit area; 'overcrowding' refers to the arrangement of these people with relation to living space and environmental requirements—it is a localized, shifting excess in density. There can be overcrowding if there are not enough housing units, a poor system for distributing food or other essentials, an inadequate system for moving people about, and so on. It can be found in a small town in a low density region, but it is more common in large cities.

Many people have been impressed by the studies that have been made of the effects of overcrowding on populations of small mammals. Normal behavior seems to break down.

John Calhoun has described a situation in his rat colonies that he describes as a 'behavioural sink' in which one finds all varieties of abnormal behavior that could be described in human terms as murder, rape, robbery, perversion, an 'identity crisis' and so on. The situation forces comparison with what is observed on college campuses and slums in our urban centres. Konrad Lorenz has reported that rats get along well under conditions of high density so long as they are all known to one another and bear the appropriate smell belonging to friends and relations. Introduce a strange rat, a rat of different color so to speak, and violence erupts.

We know of a few studies that relate human behavior and welfare to density and overcrowding. The anthropologist, Edward Hall, has approached the problem. His work suggests deep-rooted cultural differences in people in their responses to various kinds of space relationships and consequently to high densities. It does not support the thesis of those apologists for high technology who say we need not worry about population because we can mass all of the world's people into monstrous super-cities and leave most of the world free for other productive purposes.

There is a tacit assumption among many apostles of urban renewal, new towns, and new cities, that they know the kind of habitat that is good for people, know how to build it, and are well able to answer all urban problems. However, we fail to investigate the question of racial, cultural, subcultural and individual differences among the genetically and culturally diverse peoples of the earth. The high-rise apartment building surrounded by open space, the detached suburban house, or the cluster development of the new town are supposed to hold all answers to human housing requirements. But people are difficult, individualistic, and contrary in nature, and would sometimes rather burn down a city or overturn a government than fit themselves into somebody else's formula.

THE PINE FOREST'S WASTES . . .

The functioning of a pine forest, or any other natural ecosystem, depends upon the breakdown of waste products and the turnover of chemical materials so that they re-enter the food chains. There is no waste in a natural ecosystem: the organic wastes of any one species are the raw material of others, returning the nutrients into the circulation when they are reduced finally to the inorganic salts which plants can take up. Plants cannot feed on organic matter, yet the accumulation of those wastes as humus represents the basis for their well-being. The humus is the factory for the conversion of wastes into useable form. Also, quite apart from nutrients processed, the humus provides physical qualities: it serves as a penetrable medium for roots, a water-retaining medium, and a storehouse of materials.

Each constituent organism below the ground surface is important: in an English woodland the loss of the pill millepede (*Glomeris marginata*) from the forest floor removes the one organism capable of processing the detritus of the grass *Brachypodium*. One might say that loss of species from an ecosystem is tantamount to the ecosystem's thereafter producing true wastes which are not processed; that means that the ecosystem becomes truly impoverished.

. . . AND THE CITY'S

In our urban systems we have generally failed to cope with the problem of wastes in an adequate manner. Pollution of the environment and over-population represent the twin major threats to human survival.

Man, in his state of euphoria over his technical cleverness, has been able to exploit natural resources at such a rate that he has felt—in his biological ignorance—that he could afford not to bother about the frugal use of materials or the disposal of the indestructible materials he is creating. Very little was indestructible in earlier phases of man's history—even galvanized iron sheeting rotted sometime. However, asbestos sheeting, one of our inert wastes, seems to have a life which is equal to that of the planet! And now we are deeply exercised as to what we are going to do with radio-active wastes. Old mine shafts are apparently promising, but dumping in the abysses of the ocean is found to be no solution at all. Some progress has been made in biologically activating the surface of shale heaps so that a woodland ecosystem can eventually establish itself on them. There is so much more to do.

Air, water and land are polluted more or less in different places, but to some degree all over the globe. Ducktown, Tennessee, was made a desert by sulphur dioxide fumes from a smelter. Smog is estimated to cost $124 million a year in California alone, where citrus orchards, vineyards and forests of ponderosa pine are affected. Speed in motor cars, made possible by leaded petrol, is contributing to a dangerous level of aerial pollution in some places, and the eutrophication of lakes through the deposition of sewage and drainage residues of fertilizers is common knowledge. Penguins and seals in the Antarctic carry DDT in their fat. So do you.

Because it yields more profits to broiler chicken rearers, intensive pig farmers and calf rearers, antibiotics are fed to the animals, substances which authority should withhold except to the medical profession. Chloramphenicol is the only effective biotic against typhoid fever and possibly against salmonellosis, yet it was being sold as a prophylactic to those so-called farmers of animals kept under conditions which many people consider unethical. Obviously, the development of any microbial resistance to these relatively rare antibiotics would be serious for their more humane medical use,

45

especially so since the discovery of the transfer of resistance from one species of bacteria to another.

NEEDED: THE ECOLOGICAL APPROACH

Has the efficiency applied to profitable extraction and exploitation of natural resources been applied equally to preventing pollution? We can definitely say not. The politico-economic world has not thought in terms of ecosystems and subtle interdependencies, either in nature or civilizations. It is no good blaming that world for what is past when the ecological approach as a whole is so recent and as yet even immature. The present scale of ecological research is quite inadequate and is still too individualistic to be an effective counter to the lack of balance in civilization's present state.

It is interesting to find that in the United States, where so much has gone wrong and yet where the ecological approach is perhaps strongest (we do not think this is an irrelevant inverse correlation), ten universities and the Smithsonian Institution, acting as a consortium, are proposing the creation of a national institute of ecology, following the pattern of the National Center for Atmospheric Research.

Such an institute could make a particular contribution to the solution of world problems of air and water pollution and of pesticide action and residues. Unfortunately some other sciences do not seem to have the same sense of urgency as ecology.

Systems analysis of entire ecosystems with the help of computers for data processing could give us answers quickly and prevent ecologists shuffling in their chairs from honest doubt.

Some ends seem so obviously desirable, such as freedom from hunger, that pursuit of them is direct without thought of what else is involved. This has been one of the troubles of the past quarter of a century since the so-called developed world accepted the task of giving help to the nations at a much earlier stage of technological development. Serious problems have arisen from such essentially altruistic action. Irrigation has meant a great spread of that debilitating liver-fluke disease, schistosomiasis, which afflicts hundreds of millions of people in Asia, Africa, and Latin America; unplanned watershed development has lowered water quality and quantity in the valleys; many square miles of African soils have been reduced almost to concrete by bush clearing and plowing; and the unplanned use of pesticides in the tropics has created a host of problems.

The agriculturist sees food production as an end in itself; there are times when medicine seems to neglect any consideration of the consequences of saving life; the engineer is fired with enthusiasm for technological possibilities. In such a group of do-gooders, the ecologist is apt to be looked upon as lacking in humaneness and as a back-to-nature fanatic. Each of us, of course, must examine his own motivations, but our own feeling is that the ecological approach is a compassionate concern for posterity and for the planet which we occupy.

Of course, there are not enough ecologists to go around, but we do not point that out simply because we are trying to get more scientists, as such, trained in this field. For what we equally need is more teachers in schools and more folk in many other fields with an ecological training. We need, in fact, a much wider general awareness. The ecological point of view and method of approach can be developed in most fields of thought. Medicine is fast absorbing it, we think. Toynbee has it in his historical and contemporary studies, and good poets are folk who can see from many angles.

When one is taught to drive a car, it is essential to take in the whole field of vision, not to focus on one point or object in the field. Furthermore, one must be a judge of behaviour: what is a dog on the pavement going to do in the next three seconds, and how slow are that old person's responses going to be? The good driver does not think consciously about all this as movements one, two, three: he has them established as second nature. That, we think, is how we should be able to approach our own problems, whether national or planetary ones—thinking in terms of time and space, causes and consequences.

. . .

That doyen of ecologists, Paul Sears, said in 1966: 'One could be an ecologist regardless of what he called himself . . . the true test is the breadth of his perspective—whether he knows what he is up to in terms of the great pattern of life and environment'.

II/Man and the Food Chain

Grant Heilman

Introduction

"THERE ARE TWO spiritual dangers of not owning a farm," wrote Aldo Leopold. "One is the danger of supposing that breakfast comes from the grocery, and the other that heat comes from the furnace. To avoid the first danger, one should plant a garden, preferably where there is no grocer to confuse the issue."

Relatively few in the United States plant gardens anymore, and most have succumbed to the first spiritual danger. To the mass of our people, breakfast does come neatly boxed from the grocery store and nowhere else.

Prior to World War II, the United States was largely rural. Small towns still ruled the city, and great proportions of our people living in the country, towns, and even on the edges of the city had a garden. Or if they lived in a city, they were at the most one generation removed from the soil and still knew something of the smells of newly plowed earth, ripening corn, and milk freshly drawn from the cow. Now less than 30 percent of our people live in the rural area, a majority are several generations removed from the soil, and it is probably safe to assume that a majority of city dwellers have never been on a farm. Indeed, I know some people who do not know that milk comes from a dairy cow, even if they could recognize one, or that steaks come from beef cattle. Yet the life of the city depends upon the primary and secondary production raised and harvested by only 5 percent of the population.

The amount of food consumed by the average American is three-quarters of a ton a year,[1] nearly three tons a year for a family of four. Only about 10 percent of this food is imported; most is produced in our own country. Such an achievement could be made only in a temperate zone with a wide range of climates and a variety of land types that are adaptable to growing many different crops. The principal milk-producing areas are in the climates adapted for lush pastures and hayland, the Northeastern and Great Lakes states. Broiler raising is concentrated in Maine, New Jersey, and Maryland, where western grain is easily shipped and where production is close to the centers of population. Southern delta states grow cotton, rice, and some soybeans. There are citrus groves in Florida and California. The corn belt extends from central Ohio to the Nebraska border. A region with rich soil, good climate, and adequate rainfall, it provides nearly one-fourth of our food supply—corn, beef, pork, soybeans, and some wheat. To the west of this belt are the Great Plains, the wheat belts, and the open range. The mountain states specialize in beef cattle and sheep, and their irrigated valleys produce sugar beets, potatoes, fruits, and vegetables. The Pacific coast states produce not only cattle but also fruits and vegetables.

Our food comes from farms that range in size from a hundred acres or less to thousands of acres. They may be part-time farms or family farms in which more than half the work is done by the farmer and his family. Such family farms make up 95 percent of all our farms and furnish 65 percent of all our food products.[2] Large commercial farms have factory-type systems of operation. To provide a minimum level of living, a family farm, if farming is the only source of income, must sell products worth at least $10,000. This nets only $4500. Not all farms produce this much. About 43 percent of our farms have sales amounting to less than $2500. These have to be classified as part-time and retirement farms; many are subsistence farms. On the average, farmers with such low sales receive more than five times as much income from off-farm work. One-fourth of the farms sell between $2500 and $10,000 worth of products and account for 12 percent of all sales. They too need supplemental income. The rest of our farms have gross sales of over $10,000 and provide 85 percent of our farm products. One percent of our farms have operations grossing at least $100,000 a year and account for 25 percent of all sales, 65 percent of our vegetables, 45 percent of our fruits and nuts, and 35 percent of our poultry.

---

[1] G. T. Barton, "Our Food Abundance," in *Protecting Our Food*, USDA Yearbook of Agriculture, Washington, D.C., 1966, pp. 16—24.

[2] D. D. Durost, "Where Food Originates: The Farmer and His Farm," in *Food for All of Us*, USDA Yearbook of Agriculture, Washington, D.C., 1969, pp. 8—14.

Even the best farms are plagued with problems that no city-bred person can appreciate. For example, 70 cents out of every dollar goes to production costs. Prices fluctuate from year to year, fluctuations that are rarely reflected in the prices consumers pay for food. At the same time farmers are faced with rising costs of machinery that wear out from hard usage. There are weather risks involved; a whole year's income can be wiped out by drought or frost.

Because of the tremendous investment needed in farming today and the necessity of farmers to expand their operations to make them profitable, fewer and fewer people—only one in every twenty Americans—are staying on the farm. Once a way of life, farming has now become business even on the larger family farms. Since 1950 the number of farms has declined to 3 million, one-half the former number. Yet the same acreage still remains in cultivation. The size of the average farm has increased from 225 to 360 acres. Since 1950, however, our population has increased 32 percent, our food supplies 41 percent. This has been achieved by mechanization (Fig. 1); improved management practices; better seeds, insecticides, and fertilizers; and more tractors, trucks, and harvesting machines (Fig. 2).

Figure 1. A decline in the number of farms, a decrease in the acreage of land devoted to agriculture, and a 37 percent increase in food production have been the result of the mechanization and industrialization of agriculture. This combine is harvesting wheat on a 2300-acre wheat farm in Washington. (Photo courtesy of U.S. Department of Agriculture.)

Figure 2. Modern harvesting equipment enables vegetable producers to pick and package the crop in the field. Here lettuce is being harvested, packaged, and boxed in a continuous operation. As the lettuce is picked it is put on conveyers that carry it inside the packing van. (Photo courtesy of U.S. Department of Agriculture.)

49

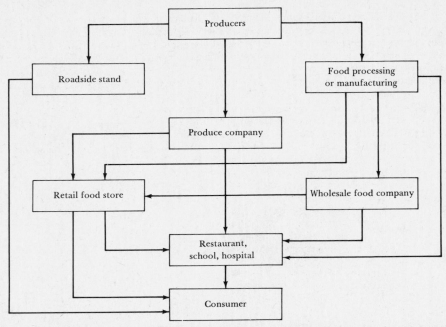

Figure 3. The principal supply routes that bring food from producers to consumers. (Adapted from *Protecting Our Food*, USDA Yearbook of Agriculture, Washington, D.C. 1966.)

Figure 4. The food distribution system in the United States ends in the supermarket, the largest of which may carry as many as 20,000 food and other items. (Photo courtesy of U.S. Department of Agriculture.)

The production of food means little if it cannot be distributed to the consumers. Among natural eco-systems, the organisms don't worry about distribution systems. The animal goes to the source of food (many aquatic organisms allow the currents to carry the food to them). Primitive man sought out sources of food and even followed his food supply. In subsistence agriculture, as was practiced in our pioneer days and is still practiced in most underdeveloped nations, food is consumed at the place where it was raised. But large urban societies require that food be transported to them. Unless a distribution system is available, high food production is of no consequence.

Nowhere in the world is there a more elaborate food distribution system than in the United States.[3] The marketing system must assemble products from farms across the country, sort them for uniformity, and combine them into units suitable for handling and shipping. To reach the American dinner table, food travels through a host of middlemen (each, incidentally, adding to the price of food paid by the consumer)—packers, processors, warehouse operators, wholesalers, and finally the retailer (Fig. 3). To preserve wholesomeness, quality, and freshness, the process must be continuous. Transportation must be rapid and there must be available storage space where at the end of the growing season fresh products, such as apples, can be stored and processed food stockpiled. Only in this way can regular flow of food be ensured throughout the year. To keep the food moving from farm to consumer requires the services of millions of employees in all phases of production. From farmers to retailers, the food industry in the United States is the largest in the numbers of persons employed.

The food distribution system puts at the disposal of the American consumers a wide variety of food prepared and packaged in hundreds of different ways to meet all their different tastes (Fig. 4). Yet we, the consumers, take for granted the food industry and our place in the food chain. As we go through the checkout line at the supermarket, we never stop to consider that the corn flakes originally came from an Iowa cornfield, the steaks from a midwest feed lot, the lettuce from a California truck farm; we never consider the work involved in getting the food to the grocery shelves. It is this technology which makes the Western world the best fed. The same technology is now being applied to underdeveloped countries.

---

[3] J. D. Gerald, "Food on the Go: The Long Haul from Farm to Shopping Bag," in *Food for All of Us*, USDA Yearbook of Agriculture, Washington, D.C. 1969, pp. 20—23.

Selection 5

!Kung Bushman Subsistence

Commentary

"Cultural man has been on earth for some 2,000,000 years. For over 99 percent of this period he has lived as a hunter-gatherer."[1] Modern man has occupied the planet earth for about 60,000 years, yet it was only 10,000 years ago that he began to domesticate plants and animals. Eight thousand years later agriculturalists and pastoralists replaced the hunters over half the earth. Today only a few pockets of hunting man survive. In spite of the hunters' more recent demise, the hunting way of life has been the most successful and persistent adaptation of man. It has dominated human evolution—agricultural way of life has influenced less than 1 percent of human history—and it enabled man to colonize the earth.

Throughout his long history as a hunter and gatherer, man was intimate with the natural world. He was a part of natural ecosystems in which he existed, just as were the animals that shared the same resources. He acquired his food by muscular energy. He was wholly dependent upon the productivity of his habitat. Although he had no control over scarcity and abundance, he was able to exploit a wide range of plants and animals, which tended to stabilize his food supply. To obtain his food he had to move about the countryside from areas of scarcity to areas of abundance. Like the animals he lived with, he expanded his hunting territory when prey was scarce, and he was able to contract the size of home range when game was abundant.[2]

As with other natural populations, man, the hunter and gatherer, achieved a sort of equilibrium with the parasites and diseases.[3] Parasites and the human host set up a sort of symbiotic relationship, and chronic disease was relatively infrequent (see Selection 20), but mortality of the young and the aged was high. Starvation occurred infrequently; it was less a problem among the tropical hunter but rather was most prevalent in winter among the peoples of the arctic and subarctic areas. Because his dietary resources were diverse, man was metabolically better fed than the agriculturalists who often suffered dietary deficiencies because of their dependence on limited kinds of food. His diverse food supply also made the hunter less vulnerable to famine and starvation than the agriculturalist, whose cultivated crops often failed because of drought, insects, or some other calamity.[4,5]

Hunting man, like most terrestrial warm-blooded vertebrates, evolved behavioral patterns that resulted in their efficient spacial distribution. If the food resources were concentrated seasonally and regionally, such as acorns and salmon, and the diet was specialized, as with the Northwest Indians,[6] then the size of the group the diet supported was large, perhaps 100 or more. If the food resources consisted of a wide variety of forms, as with the Shoshonean Indians, who utilized some 100 plants and a wide variety of animals,[7] then the exploitative groups were small. The size of the groups changed seasonally with the abundance and dispersion of food. Gregarious tendencies were limited in part by the food resource, the carrying capacity of the region. The size of the population on a long-term basis was stabilized at the carrying capacity, which may be limited, as much by social behavior as by food. In the Pleistocene epoch mean densities rarely exceeded one man per square mile.[8] Among many territorial vertebrates, the excess members are forced into submarginal

---

[1] R. B. Lee and I. Devore, "Problems in the Study of Hunters and Gatherers," *Man, the Hunter,* Chicago, Aldine, 1968, pp. 3—12.

[2] A. I. Hallowell, "The Size of Algonkian Hunting Territories: A Function of Ecological Adjustment," *American Anthropologist* **51**, 1949, pp. 35—45.

[3] F. L. Dunn, "Epidemiological Factors: Health and Disease in Hunter-Gatherers," in R. B. Lee and I. Devore (eds.), *Man, the Hunter,* Chicago, Aldine, 1968, pp. 211—228.

[4] J. B. Birdsell, "Some Predictions for the Pleistocene Based on Equilibrium Systems Among Recent Hunter Gatherers," in R. B. Lee and I. Devore (eds.), *Man, the Hunter,* Chicago, Aldine, 1968, pp. 229—240.

[5] Discussion, "Population Control Factors: Infanticide, Disease, Nutrition, and Food Supply," in R. B. Lee and I. Devore (eds.), *Man, the Hunter,* Chicago, Aldine, 1968, pp. 243—245.

[6] Wayne Suttles, "Variation in Habitat and Culture on the Northwest Coast," reprinted in Y. Cohen (ed.), *Man in Adaptation,* Chicago, Aldine, 1968, pp. 93—106.

[7] J. H. Steward, "The Great Basin Shoshonean Indians. An Example of a Family Level of Sociocultural Integration," *Theory of Cultural Change. The Methodology of Multilinear Evolution,* Urbana, Ill., University of Illinois Press, 1955.

[8] Birdsell, *loc. cit.*

habitat or eliminated by predators or starvation, or they emigrate from the area. Hunting man, anthropologists suggest, controlled his population by geronticide (the abandonment of the aged, sick, and wounded) and, more importantly, by infanticide. Since a mother could not possibly carry and nurse more than one child at a time, children were spaced about three years apart by systematic infanticide, which might have involved as high as 50 percent of the births.[9] Still emigration must have played an important part in reducing local population to an acceptable level.

Hunting society is characterized by the absence of any occupational choice. Hunter-gatherers are generalists. Every man is a hunter, every woman a gatherer. This division of labor, based partly on physical and physiological differences, apparently worked well. As the men pursued large mammals, the women gathered seeds, roots, and berries and procured insects and small mammals. This division of labor permitted simultaneous exploitation of the area for two different types of resources.

Even so, there is and was among hunting cultures a good deal of co-minglings of occupations. Among the Hadza of Tanzania,[10] for example, the men do not rely on the women to supply them with vegetable food. The women and children eat roots and berries which they gather, and bring back only the leftovers; Often less than half these are given to the men. Men go hunting when hunger demands it. On their forays men eat berries and cook the small animals they kill. His hunger satisfied, the hunter may not pursue large game. Like the women, the men bring back to camp only the leftovers. Men and women are more or less independent of each other for food, as are individuals who rarely cooperate with each other in either hunting or gathering. In other cultures there is a strong sense of sharing food and cooperation in obtaining it.

At the other extreme is the culture of the sedentary Indians of the northwest coast of North America, who lived by fishing and developed for hunter-gatherers a sophisticated social system. Fishing and the ability to exploit the resources of an aquatic ecosystem was a late acquisition by man. It demanded skills and abilities beyond those of a simple hunter. Man had to overcome his natural fear of water, devise methods to capture fish, and learn how to build and handle boats. An abundance of fish as well as a hospitable, food-producing terrestrial environment around them gave the Northwest Indians a wealth of food which they learned how to preserve to carry them through the winter. They developed surpluses and accumulated some wealth. Resources available to various groups were different enough to act as an incentive for exchange. Trade developed between groups, which in turn led to more highly developed political institutions with some form of leadership necessary to control simple commerce, social stratification, art, and ceremony, all lacking in simpler hunting cultures.[11]

Contrary to popular opinion, man the hunter and gatherer did not live on the edge of catastrophe, nor did he spend the greater part of his time seeking food. Studies of the few remaining hunting cultures indicate that he worked less than we do, that his quests for food took up only a small portion of his time, and that leisure was abundant. He was relatively happy and lacked any real concern for tomorrow. His wants were restricted, and, because of his need to move, wealth was a burden. Some wonder why, with his abundance of leisure time, the hunting man failed to build a more complex culture with its craftsmen and artisans and stronger political organization. The reasons, of course, rest in his way of life. He committed himself to nothing and he made no obligations. He possessed little or no wealth and did not own land or other resources, nor with a few exceptions did he accumulate food resources, both of which would necessitate some form of corporation and some means of defining the rights over the resource. Lacking this there was no need for any formal political institutions. The small band made necessary by the nature and distribution of food supply and the mobility required precluded the establishment of any large permanent settlement or great concentration of people with a strong sociopolitical organization out of which technology arises.

What life was like for the hunter-gatherer in the past can be reconstructed only from studies of modern-day hunting societies. Many of these are more complex than in the dim past, and many have become modified because of contacts with modern culture. But some idea of the life of the hunter and especially the energetics and ecology of the population emerges from a fascinating study by Richard Lee of the !Kung Bushmen of the Kalahari.

[9]Discussion, *loc. cit.*

[10]James Woodburn, "An Introduction to Hadza Ecology," in R. B. Lee and I. Devore (eds.), *Man, the Hunter*, Chicago, Aldine, 1968, pp. 49—55.

[11]Yehudi Cohen, "Culture as Adaptation," *Man in Adaptation: The Cultural Present*, Chicago, Aldine, 1968, pp. 41—60.

Selection 5

!Kung Bushman Subsistence:
An Input-Output Analysis[1]

by Richard B. Lee

I. INTRODUCTION

This paper examines the ecological basis of a hunting and gathering economy through an input-output analysis of work and consumption. The first goal of this exercise is to outline the subsistence strategy that enables the !Kung Bushmen, with only the simplest of technologies, to live well in the harsh environment of the Kalahari Desert. The second goal is to show that the Bushmen exhibit an elementary form of economic life. And the third goal is to trace, from a primate baseline, the origin and evolution of human energy relations.

The methodology I have used is adapted from the transactional models of input-output economics (Leontief 1966) and ecological energetics (Gates 1962; Kleiber 1961). At the outset an essential distinction should be made between these two approaches. Ecologists take as their unit of study a species which has energy relations with other species within an eco-system. A population is maintained by the energy absorbed in the course of food-getting activities of its members. The focus here is on *interspecific* trophic exchanges (Rappaport 1967: 18—19). Economists, by contrast, focus on the exchange relations within a single species. A productive unit, such as an industry in the American economic system, is maintained by the inputs from other productive units, and in turn allocates its outputs to other like units or to the "final demand" sector of the economy

(Leontief 1966:14—20). Viewed ecologically, these transactions can be considered as a highly evolved form of *intraspecific* exchange.

At first glance, the connection between, for example, the relations between predator and prey in an African savannah and the relations between industrial units in the American economy seems too remote to be worth considering. Yet this connection becomes meaningful when viewed in evolutionary terms. First of all, a human population, like all animal populations, has to expend energy in work in order to incorporate energy through consumption. In this respect energetics would apply equally well to the study of man as to the study of other animals.

However, in one important respect, human energy relations are unique among the higher animals. Whereas each adult non-human vertebrate organism is a self-sufficient subsistence unit, a large percentage of a man's energy expenditure goes to feeding others, and a large percentage of an individual's consumption is of food produced by others. Thus for humans, the minimal self-sufficient subsistence unit includes at least a social group, such as a family or "band," and at most includes economies involving hundreds of millions of persons. This central fact of cooperative consumption has been termed "division of labor" and "economic interdependence," and the study of the transactions and allocations so generated forms

THIS SELECTION is reprinted from "Ecological Essays: Proceedings of the Conference of Cultural Ecology," National Museum of Canada, 1966, David Damas, ed. Museum of Canada Bulletin No. 230. Crown Copyrights Reserved 1969. Reproduced with the permission of the publisher.

[1]The Bushman field research (August 1963 to January 1965) was generously supported by a U.S. National Science Foundation grant entitled "Studies in the Evolution of Human Behavior." To Irven DeVore, the principal investigator for this project, I owe special thanks for his unfailing support and good advice. Earlier versions of this paper were presented at the Conference on Cultural Ecology, Ottawa, August 1966, and at the University Seminar on Ecological Systems and Cultural Evolution, Columbia University, January 1967. For constructive criticism I owe a debt of gratitude to: Sally Bates, Mario Bick, David Damas, Henry Harpending, Marvin Harris, June Helm, Nancy Howell Lee, G. P. Murdock, Robert Murphy, Robert Netting, Roy Rappaport, R. H. S. Smithers, Louis Sweet, A. P. Vayda, and E. Z. Vogt.

the foundation of economic science. In man alone, these intraspecific exchanges have become extraordinarily pervasive and complex, so much so, in fact, that we take them for granted! Yet it is precisely in this form of trophic exchange that animal adaptation and human adaptation first part company. And it is here that the study of energetics and economics converge.

In evolutionary terms the origin of what we call an economic system is a relatively recent phenomenon. It appears in the Pleistocene, probably less than two million years ago, when early man began to pool resources and thereby break down individual animal self-sufficiency. Women are usually thought to be the original "scarce good," or medium of exchange (White 1949:316; Lévi-Strauss 1949: 35—86). It is more likely, however, that food was the original medium of exchange and that such exchanges are the foundation of social life.

Many economic transformations have occurred since the basic form of human exchange originated in the Pleistocene. Plant and animal domestication, the development of the market and money, and the harnessing of fossil and nuclear fuels have all contributed to making human energy exchange relations more complex.[2] The evolution of economic organization has reached the point at which an individual's productive activity is usually at the nth removed from the ultimate source of the food he consumes. He sells his labor (input) to the market and receives his consumption (output) in the form of cash, or some other convertible standard of value (Bohannan and Dalton 1962:9).

However, economies have evolved at different rates in various parts of the world. In some contemporary societies a much more elementary form of economic life can still be observed. I use elementary in the sense of an economy which exhibits the basic human pattern of exchange, without further elaboration.

In input-output terms, an economy exhibits an elementary form when the relation between the production and consumption of food is immediate in space and time. Such an economy would have the following properties:

minimal surplus accumulation; minimal production of capital goods; an absence of agriculture and domestic animals; continuous food-getting activities by all able-bodied persons throughout the year; and self-sufficiency in foodstuffs and generalized reciprocity within local groups.

Although no contemporary society exhibits all these properties, the !Kung Bushmen of the Dobe area of Botswana are a close approximation. The !Kung have a simple, small-scale, self-contained economy of a type that may have been characteristic of early man. Extreme isolation and a marginal environment have been responsible for the persistence of this form to the present. The Dobe area is surrounded by waterless desert, and the Bushman population within it is largely self-sufficient in terms of subsistence. The economy lacks trading posts, trade in foodstuffs, wage labor, cash, conversions, and markets—the features which are commonly taken to indicate economic interdependence (Bohannan and Dalton 1962: 1—26). Because the !Kung are hunters and gatherers, without agriculture and domestic animals (except for the dog), and because they do not amass a surplus of foodstuffs, the relation between local food production and consumption is an immediate one. A diagnostic feature of their subsistence economy is: *food is almost always consumed within the boundaries of the local group and within forty-eight hours of its collection.* This immediacy of consumption makes the !Kung Bushman an apt case for input-output analysis, since the level of work effort in a given period is a direct reflection of the food requirements of the local group. Such an analysis would be more difficult in a complex economic situation in which the work effort during a given period is dictated by the need for surplus accumulation for ceremonial purposes (Wolf 1966:7), for the conversion of subsistence goods into prestige (DuBois 1936), or for delayed consumption at a later period (Richards 1939:35—37).

Sections II through VI of this paper present the descriptive material on Bushman ethnography, demography, and subsistence strategies. These serve as a necessary introduction to the input-

---

[2]The implications of these developments have been documented by Marx (1867), Childe (1951), Polanyi (1944, 1957), and White (1949, 1959).

output analysis itself, presented in Sections VII and VIII. A concluding section (IX) returns to the problem of defining the properties of an elementary form of economy, and attempts to place the discussion in a comparative and evolutionary perspective.

II. ETHNOGRAPHIC BACKGROUND

The Dobe area lies in the northwestern corner of the Republic of Botswana and in adjacent areas of Southwest Africa. During my field work (1963—65), some 336 !Kung Bushmen were resident in the area, along with 340 Bantu pastoralists, mainly of the Herero and Tswana tribes.

!Kung Bushmen are known to have lived in the Dobe area for at least 100 years. Late Stone Age materials of Wilton Horizon are found at several localities, indicating that some hunting peoples have lived there for many hundreds of years (Malan 1950). There is no evidence that the present-day !Kung are recent refugees from other areas (Lee 1965:38—68). The introduction of metal tools and weapons can be provisionally dated to the period 1880—90 when iron replaced bone as the primary material for arrowheads and spears.

The first European known to have penetrated the area was Hendrick van Zyl in 1879 (Silberbauer 1965:115). The Tswana cattle herders appeared soon after, and from the 1890s onwards the area was used as a regular summer grazing ground by these pastoralists. The first year-round settlements by non-Bushmen were not established until 1925 when two Herero families set up a cattle post at !angwa. Effective administrative presence is even more recent, dating from 1948, the year in which a resident Tswana Headman was appointed by the Paramount Chief of the Batswana Tribal Administration. Apart from brief annual patrols by the British Colonial government starting in 1934, almost nothing was known of the Dobe area until the 1950s.

In 1952, for example, Sillery wrote:

> Not far from the border of South West Africa, near latitude 20° south, is a group of caves which occur in the limestone there. These caves have been visited by few white people. The journey involves a long and arduous trek across sandy country through which no road passes and a competent guide is essential. . . . The country in the vicinity of these caves is probably the least known in the whole Protectorate and Bushmen and wild animals have it to themselves (1952:198).

The Marshall family of Cambridge, Massachusetts, were the first "Europeans" to spend more than a few weeks in this area. Their expeditions (1951—59) focussed on the adjacent Nyae Nyae !Kung in Southwest Africa and their reports form the most complete and detailed record for any Bushman group (Lorna Marshall 1957, 1959, 1960, 1961, 1962; John Marshall 1956; Thomas 1959).

In 1960, the South African government initiated a scheme to settle the !Kung Bushmen of the Nyae Nyae area. By 1964 over 700 Bushmen had moved into the government station at Tsumkwe S. W. A. and were being instructed in agricultural and stock-raising techniques. As a result of political pressures, the South Africans have not permitted the !Kung Bushmen of the formerly British Bechuanaland Protectorate to participate in this settlement scheme.

The situation in the mid-1960s finds the !Kung on the Botswana side of the border primarily dependent on hunting and gathering for their subsistence. The Bushmen have now obtained some blankets, clothing, and cooking utensils from their Bantu neighbors. There is an inexhaustible supply of metal for arrowheads which are hammered out from scraps of fencing wire from the cattle enclosures built by the Botswana Veterinary Department. However, the !Kung still lack firearms, livestock, and agriculture. About 7 per cent of the Bushwomen have married Bantu; and 20 per cent of the young men are working for Bantu as cattle herders. Serious disputes, usually involving Bush-Bantu labor relations, are adjudicated by the Tswana Headman. Capital offenders are sent to Maun, the tribal capital, for trial. European presence amounts to a brief patrol once every six to eight weeks. The important point is that the Bushmen continue to hunt and gather because there is no viable alternative available to them.

III. POPULATION DYNAMICS

In a census made in November 1964, the resident !Kung population stood at 336. Of the

336 residents, 248 were organized into fourteen independent camps, ranging in size from nine to twenty-nine members (see Table I). The size of each camp is a statistical abstraction because individuals and families were constantly shifting from camp to camp. Subsistence at the camps was based on hunting and gathering. The remaining eighty-eight residents were associated with Herero and Tswana cattle posts (Table IIa). These people did some work for the Bantu and ate some of their foods, including milk, cheese, and meat. Because part of their diet came from external sources, these Bantu-

associated Bushmen groups are not included in the input-output analysis. In addition to the residents, fifty-five !Kung alternated in and out of the Dobe area (Table IIb) and thirty-four others emigrated permanently from the area (Table IIc). Thus the grand total Bushmen enumerated in 1964 was 425.

In the census, the population is divided by sex, and by age into three divisions: young, 0–15 years; adult, 16–59 years; and old, 60 + years. Several important demographic features should be noted. Eight percent of the population in camps (21 of 248) was determined to be

Table I. DOBE AREA CENSUS BY LIVING UNITS: RESIDENT CAMPS

NUMBER PLACE AND NAME	MALES Y*	A	O	FEMALES Y	A	O	TOTAL T	EFFECT.**	DEP	% EFFECT.
1. Dobe—n≠eisi	0	4	1	1	4	1	11	8	3	72.7
2. Dobe—≠oma//gwe	5	7	2	6	5	1	26	12	14	46.2
3. !angwa—bo	1	6	0	3	5	1	16	11	5	68.8
4. Bate—!xoma	3	7	0	3	5	1	19	12	7	63.2
5. Bate—Liceku	1	5	0	1	4	0	11	9	2	81.8
6. !ubi—Kamburu	3	5	0	1	10	0	19	15	4	79.0
7. !gose—/ise	1	7	0	5	7	2	22	14	8	63.6
8. !gose—/i!ay	0	6	0	1	4	0	11	10	1	90.9
9. !gose—Konguroba	3	4	0	5	7	0	19	11	8	57.9
10. /ai/ai—//aun!a	1	2	1	3	4	1	12	6	6	50.0
11. /ai/ai—//aiha	1	1	1	3	2	1	9	3	6	33.3
12. /ai/ai—≠oma!xwa	4	9	1	3	10	2	29	19	10	65.5
13. /ai/ai—x!am	2	3	1	5	5	1	17	8	9	47.1
14. /ai/ai—≠omazho	4	6	2	6	8	1	27	14	13	51.9
Total in resident camps	29	72	9	46	80	12	248	152	96	61.3%

*Age Divisions: Y = young, 0–15 years
                A = adult, 16–59 years
                O = old, 60+ years
**Effectives = adults
Dependents = young and old

Table II. DOBE AREA CENSUS BY LIVING UNITS: OTHER GROUPS

	MALES Y	A	O	FEMALES Y	A	O	TOTALS T
IIa *Residents living with Bantu*							
21 living groups	11	27	2	9	38	1	88
IIb *Alternators*							
6 living groups	13	14	0	12	15	1	55
IIc *Emigrants*							
3 living groups	10	7	0	6	11	0	34
Total IIa, IIb, IIc	34	48	2	27	64	2	177
Grand total of population	63	120	11	73	144	14	425

over sixty years of age.[3] These data contradict the view that Bushman life expectancy is short. Silberbauer, for example, says of the G/wi of the Central Kalahari that "life expectancy among Reserve Bushmen is difficult to calculate, but I do not believe that many live beyond 45" (1965:17). Among the Dobe area !Kung, every camp had at least several members over forty-five years of age, and ten of the fourteen camps had members over sixty years old; the oldest person was estimated to be 82 ± 3 years. These old people, although nonproductive in terms of food, played an important role in the social and ritual activities of the camps.

Since persons under fifteen and over sixty years of age do not contribute significantly to the food supplies of the camps, it is possible to use the census data to calculate the percentage of effective food producers and the percentage of dependents. The effectives comprised 61.3 per cent (152 of 248) of the total population in camps, in other words, every three effectives supported themselves and two dependents in subsistence. What is surprising is the wide variation in the percentage of effectives from camp to camp. In camp No. 11 (Table I), for example, three effectives supported themselves and six dependents (33.3 per cent effective), whereas in camp No. 8, ten of the eleven members (90.9 per cent) were effective. These variations were more apparent than real, however, since groups were constantly shifting in composition and the net effect was to produce work groups in which the ratio of effectives to dependents approached the mean.

In addition, these data show an unusual sex ratio favoring females. In the total population, the sex ratio is eight-four males per hundred females. The ratio for each age group is:

Young 86 males/100 females
Adult 83 males/100 females
Old 80 males/100 females

These data indicate a higher mortality rate for males in all age groups; although it is possible that the sex ratio at birth is anomalous, producing an initial excess of female over male live births. Another possible explanation is the practice of male infanticide. However, the overall incidence of infanticide (as well as invalidicide and senilicide) is so low that it is unlikely that this practice alone would account for the skewed sex ratio in the immature age group.

IV. SEASONAL SUBSISTENCE PATTERNS

The northern Kalahari Desert is characterized by a hot summer with a five-month rainy season from November to March, a cool dry winter from April to August, and a hot dry spring in September and October. During the spring and summer the diurnal temperature range is from a low of 60°F to a high of 100°F, with shade temperatures of as high as 108°F recorded. In the winter the diurnal range is from a low of 30°F to a high of 78°F. The annual rainfall varies from six to ten inches. The loose sandy soils support a surprising abundance of vegetation, in spite of the fact that the porosity of the sand is such that rainfall is rapidly absorbed and surface runoff is minimal. Permanent waterholes exist only where the underlying limestone strata have been exposed.

Because of these soil factors, the distribution of water sources is by far the most important ecological determinant of Bushman subsistence. The availability of plant foods is of secondary importance and the numbers and distributions of game animals are only of minor importance. Since the Bushman camps, of necessity, are anchored to water sources they can exploit only those vegetable foods that lie within a reasonable walking distance of water. Food sources that lie beyond a reasonable walking distance are rarely exploited.

The life of the camps surrounding the eight permanent waterholes are shown as solid dots on Figure 1. During the seven dry months of the year, April through October, these wells were the only sources of standing water and all the Bushmen camps were located within a mile of a well. During the summer rains (November–March) seasonal pools of water developed elsewhere, and virtually all the Bushmen went out to live at them.

The necessity for drinking water strictly defined the areas that people could exploit for food. On Figure 1 three divisions are plotted: (1) The shaded circles cover all the areas that

---

[3]The age estimates are based on a relative age ranking of the population from youngest to oldest; an event calender was used to establish birth dates. The accuracy of estimation is ± 3 years.

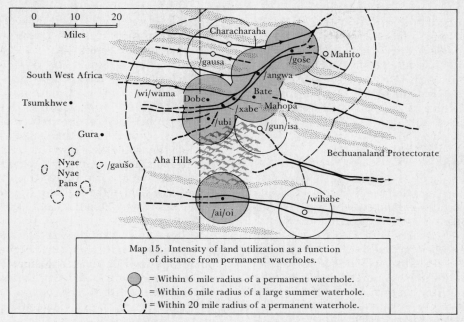

Map 15. Intensity of land utilization as a function of distance from permanent waterholes.

⬤ = Within 6 mile radius of a permanent waterhole.
◯ = Within 6 mile radius of a large summer waterhole.
⬭ = Within 20 mile radius of a permanent waterhole.

Figure 1. Intensity of land utilization as a function of distance from permanent waterholes.

lie within a day's walk, i.e., a six-mile radius of a permanent waterhole. This area of about 600 square miles supports all of the 248 Bushmen in camps for half the year. Thus the effective population density for the dry season is 42/100 square miles (2). The unshaded circles enclose an additional 400 square miles that lie within a six-mile radius of a large, seasonal summer waterhole. These areas support most of the resident population for the other half of the year (3). Finally, the dotted line encloses all the areas that lie within a twenty-mile radius of permanent water. None of the Bushmen were observed to camp or forage *outside* of this dotted line, and in fact the additional areas, so defined,

were rarely utilized by the Bushmen. Therefore about 1000 square miles was sufficient to support the entire population, plus visitors, at an effective density of 25 per 100 square miles, or four square miles per person.

Table III shows the actual numbers resident at each waterhole during the dry season of 1964. Two of the waterholes, !xabe and Mahopa, did not have an independent camp resident. The other six waterholes supported all of the 248 Bushmen in camps. The mean standing population per waterhole was forty-one and the range was from a low of sixteen at !angwa to a high of ninety-four at /ai/ai. These differences in standing population may reflect

Table III. THE NUMBERS AND DISTRIBUTION OF THE RESIDENT BUSHMEN AND BANTU BY WATERHOLE

NAME OF WATERHOLE*	NUMBER OF CAMPS	POPULATION OF CAMPS	OTHER BUSHMEN	TOTAL BUSHMEN	BANTU
Dobe	2	37	—	37	—
!angwa	1	16	23	39	84
Bate	2	30	12	42	21
!ubi	1	19	—	19	65
!gose	3	52	9	61	18
/ai/ai	5	94	13	107	67
!xabe	—	—	8	8	12
Mahopa	—	—	23	23	73
Totals	14	248	88	336	340

*For locations refer to Figure 1.

differences in the density of foodstuffs. It is probable that /ai/ai with ninety-four residents had more food closer to home than did !angwa, with only sixteen residents. Dobe with a standing population of thirty-seven was closest to the mean and was the subject of an intensive investigation of the relation of subsistence effort to food consumption.[4]

V. PATTERNS OF CONSUMPTION

The camp serves as a home base for its members. Each morning some people move out to collect plant food and/or hunt game, and each evening the workers return to the camp and pool the collected resources with each other and with the members who stayed behind. Food getting is not a cooperative activity. Collectors go out in twos and threes and each woman gathers plant foods on her own. Hunters usually work individually or in pairs and the success of the hunt is dependent largely on an individual's tracking ability and on the enthusiasm of his hunting dogs; there is no evidence of co-ordinated effort producing more meat than individual effort.

Cooperation is clearly in evidence, however, in the consumption of food. Not only do families pool the day's production, but the entire camp—residents and visitors alike—shares equally in the total quantity of food available. The evening meal of any one family is made up of portions of food from the supplies of each of the other families resident. Foodstuffs are distributed raw or are prepared by the collector and then distributed. There is a constant flow of nuts, berries, roots, and melons from one family fireplace to another until each person resident has received an equitable portion (cf. Marshall 1961). The following morning a different combination of foragers moves out of camp and, when they return late in the day, the distribution of foodstuffs is repeated. Except in the case of windfalls, such as the killing of a large ungulate, food rarely moves beyond the boundaries of a camp. People, however, move frequently from one camp to another. The boundary of the camp, therefore, can be considered to define the boundary of the co-consuming group; and the size of the consumption unit will depend on the number of personnel on hand in a given day.

The food resources of the Dobe area were both varied and abundant. I tabulated over 200 plant and 220 animal species known and named by the Bushmen (Lee 1965:98—121). Of these, eighty-five plant species and fifty-four animal species were classified by the Bushmen as edible. The basic food staple is the mongongo (mangetti) nut, *Ricinodendron rautanenii Schinz*; alone it accounted for one-half to two-thirds of the total vegetable diet by weight. This species was so abundant that millions of the nuts rotted on the ground each year for want of picking. The energy yield of the nut meat is remarkably high: 600 cals./100 gms. (see Section VIII below).

Of the fifty-four animals classified as edible, only ten species of mammals were regularly hunted for food. The ten species, listed in order of their importance in the diet, are: wart hog, kudu, diuker, steenbok, gemsbok, wildebeeste, spring hare, porcupine, ant bear, and common hare.

VI. FORAGING STRATEGY

The Bushmen were observed to be highly selective in their food habits. They stated strong likes and dislikes in foods and all of the eighty-five edible species of vegetable food were clearly ranked by the Bushmen on criteria of desirability: tastiness, nutritional value, abundance, and ease of collecting. As a rule people tended to eat only the most palatable and abundant foods available and to bypass the less desirable foods. Since the other major factor in subsistence was the distance between food and water, it is possible to summarize the basic principle of Bushman foraging strategy in a single statement: *At a given moment, the members of a camp prefer to collect and eat the desirable foods that are at the least distance from standing water.*

Given this principle, the optimum situation occurs when standing water and mongongo nuts are close together, and the worst situation occurs when water and nuts are far apart. The dynamics of the subsistence situation are made clear when we realize that the food that can be eaten in one week is a function of the food that has already been eaten in previous weeks.

The Bushmen typically occupy a camp for a period of weeks or months and eat their way out of it. For instance, at a camp in the nut

---

[4]The ecological and demographic determinants of group structure will be discussed in another paper.

forests (which form narrow belts along the crests of fixed dunes, see Figure 1), the members will exhaust the nuts within a one-mile radius during the first week of occupation, within a two-mile radius the second week, and within a three-mile radius the third week. As time goes on, the members of the group must travel farther and farther to reach the nuts, and the round-trip distance in miles is a measurement of the "cost" of obtaining this desirable food.

In Figure 2, the cost of obtaining mongongo nuts is plotted against distance. The cost curve for nuts rises slowly as the round-trip distance increases from two to twelve miles, climbs sharply from twelve to sixteen miles, then levels off for longer distances. The reason for the inflection in the cost curve is the difference between one-day trips and overnight trips. A round trip of up to twelve miles can be accomplished in a single day, but for trips to more distant points an overnight hike must be organized, involving the packing of drinking water and the carrying of heavy loads over long distances.

The alternative tactic to the longer trips is to stay at the home base, and to exploit foods of lesser desirability in terms of taste, ease of collecting, and abundance. At a given dry season camp one sees both alternative tactics in evidence. The older, less mobile members of the camp stay close to home and collect the less desirable foods, while the younger, more active members make the longer trips to the nut forests. As the water—nut distance increases, more and more attention is given to the lesser foods.

During the rainy season, a different and less costly strategy is employed. Since temporary pools of water form at a number of localities, when nuts are exhausted within a few miles of one pool the entire group moves camp to another where water and nuts are still abundant. Thus the "cost" of obtaining nuts during the rainy season never exceeds the level of a six-mile round trip. Towards the end of the rainy season, a temporary pool may dry up before the nuts in its immediate vicinity become exhausted. In this case the residents move camp to one of the large summer waterholes which usually persist until early autumn (April or May). When these latter pools dry up, then the entire population moves back to the areas around the eight permanent waterholes to spend the winter and spring dry season.

It is evident that the critical factor in the annual subsistence cycle is the distance between food and water. Basically, the Dobe area !Kung face three different sets of conditions through the year.

(I) FOOD ABUNDANT AND MANY WATER POINTS

During the rainy season (November—April) all the people live at the temporary pools in the midst of the nut forests. The water—food distance is short and the subsistence effort is minimal. This is also the season of plant growth when seasonal foods such as berries and leafy greens are available.

(II) FOOD ABUNDANT BUT ONLY EIGHT WATER POINTS

In the early half of the dry season (May—July), all the groups are based at the permanent waterholes. They eat out an increasing radius of desirable foods. As the water—food distance increases, the subsistence effort increases.

(III) FOOD SCARCE AND ONLY EIGHT WATER POINTS

By the end of the dry season (August—October) the water—food distance approaches an annual maximum. People must either walk long distances to reach the nuts, or be content to eat the less and less desirable foods, such as bitter melons, roots, Acacia gum, and the heart of the vegetable ivory palm. The diet is most eclectic at this time of year.

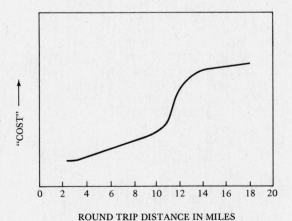

ROUND TRIP DISTANCE IN MILES

Figure 2. The cost curve for obtaining mongongo nuts.

With the onset of the first rains in late October or November, a new cycle of plant growth is initiated and seasonal pools again form in the hinterland. The subsistence effort decreases to the level of condition I.

VII. INPUT-OUTPUT: THE SUBSISTENCE EFFORT

As stated earlier, the purpose of Bushman work is to get food, and the amount of work expended is therefore a measure of the effort required to feed the group. In addition, the food gathered is equitably distributed among all members of the camp and rarely moves beyond camp boundaries. With these points in mind, we can apply the framework of input-output analysis to the Bushman data. The work input, or subsistence effort, is a compilation of all the days of work carried out by members of a group within a specified period of time. The subsistence effort could be stated in terms of the number of work days per week per hunter or gatherer. This, however, is a crude measure, since it does not define the size of the consumption unit. In addition one should know the number of dependents who are being supported by the work. The consumption unit, therefore, is defined by adding together the total number of effectives and the total number of dependents resident at a camp during a specified period.

I have found useful the following formula for measuring "S," the index of subsistence effort:

$$S = \frac{W}{C}$$

where W = the number of man-days of work and

where C = the number of man-days of consumption.

Example 1. Consider a hypothetical population of ten people subsisting for a thirty-day period. Since everyone eats every day, the value of "C" (man-days of consumption) is:

$$C = 10 \times 30$$
$$= 300$$

How many man-days of work will be necessary to provide 300 man-days of consumption? If every person worked every day of the thirty-day period, then:

$$W = 10 \times 30 \quad \text{and} \quad S = \frac{W}{C}$$
$$= 300 \qquad\qquad = \frac{300}{300}$$
$$= 1.00$$

Since every person works every day in order to eat every day, the value of "S" is unity.

Example 2. If everyone worked on alternate days, then:

$$S = \frac{10 \times 15}{300}$$
$$= .5$$

Example 3. If half the people worked every day and half the people were dependents, then:

$$S = \frac{5 \times 30}{300}$$
$$= .5$$

Example 1, in which everyone works every day, is not merely a hypothetical case. In fact, "S = 1.00" approximates the situation among the non-human primates (and most other vertebrates) in which every animal (save nursing infants) forages for its own food on every day of the year. For monkeys and apes (DeVore 1965) the value of "S" approaches unity and the actual value of "S" is simply a function of the percentage of nursing infants in the population.

A baboon troop, for example, leaves the sleeping area each morning and spends the day moving as a group through its range (Hall and DeVore 1965:70). Although the spatial cohesion of the group is maintained, each troop member acts as a self-sufficient subsistence unit, collecting and eating its own foods as it moves. There is no *exchange* of food between individuals, and this is truly a "hand-to-mouth" existence. The foregoing is not meant to imply that subsistence is precarious for baboons and other primates. On the contrary, the individual animal may spend only a few hours a day picking food, and this activity is interspersed with periods of social grooming, sexual and dominance behaviors, and sleeping. The point is that the work rhythm is such that every individual must do some subsistence work on *every single day of his adult life.*

The work rhythm of human groups is radically different. All human societies allocate some days to work and others to leisure, and in all human societies some people work harder than others. However, the condition "S = 1.00" can be regarded as the baseline from which man evolved. The sharing of food is part of a cluster of basic human institutions which also include the division of subsistence labor, the home base, the primary carrying device (for transporting foods to the home base for distribution), and the prolonged support of non-productive young and old people. These developments represent a quantum step in human affairs, for their presence means that not *all* of the people have to work *all* of the time.

The immediate implication of division of labor was that the value of "S," the index of subsistence effort, must have dropped radically during the early phases of hominid evolution. It is at this point that human economics parts company with animal energetics. The long-term implications of division of labor are manifold. Exchange opens up the possibility of more and more complex forms of surplus accumulation, either for the purpose of distribution to a wider social group or for the purpose of consumption by the producers themselves at a later date. Therefore one of the important dimensions along which economic evolution can be traced is the increasing separation between the production of food and its allocation to consumers.

Formally, the !Kung Bushmen economy corresponds to an early stage in this trend since the relation between production and consumption of food is immediate in space and time. Food produced by the local group is consumed within its boundaries, usually within forty-eight hours of production. The major concern, therefore, is to use the formula $S = \dfrac{W}{C}$ for the analysis of !Kung subsistence.

In any self-sufficient human group the magnitude of "S," the subsistence effort, is a function of the ease or difficulty of feeding the group. One would assume that hunter-gatherers such as the !Kung Bushmen, with a simple technology, living in a marginal desert environment, would have a difficult time getting food; therefore the index of subsistence effort should be relatively high.

For instance, in a group of ten people, if the six adults had to work $5\frac{1}{2}$ days per week to support themselves and four dependents, then the value of "S" would be ca. .5. A $5\frac{1}{2}$-day work week is not excessive by Western industrial standards. On the other hand, if the

work week were only three days long, then the value of "S" would fall to .26.

The calculation of the actual level of subsistence effort is, of course, an empirical question. Table IV tabulates the four-week work diary for the Dobe camp during the period July 6 to August 2, 1964. This period was chosen because it was neither the easiest nor the most difficult time of the year for subsistence, and it covered the period of transition from better to worse conditions.

Column 1 shows the number of adults at the camp on each day and column 2 the number of children. Column 3 tabulates the number of man-days of consumption (and incidentally documents the daily variations in group size). Column 4 counts the number of people who went out for food each day. Column 5 lists the meat output, in pounds of edible raw portion, for each day.

Table V is a summary, by week, of the work diary. Mean group size (column 1) varies from 25.6 to 35.6; the actual count of personnel on hand was rarely the same two days running. The work week (column 7) varies from 1.2 to 3.2 work days per adult. In other words, each productive individual supports herself or himself and dependents and still has $3\frac{1}{2}$ to $5\frac{1}{2}$ days available for other activities. The Index of Subsistence Effort (column 8) varies from .11 to .31. For instance, during Week I (July 6—12), thirty-seven man-days of work were expended to provide 179 man-days of consumption. The value S = .21 indicates twenty-one days of work per hundred man-days of consumption; or each day's work provided food for the worker and four other people. During Week IV (July 27—August 2), seventy-seven man-days of work provided 249 man-days of consumption for an "S" value of .31 (31 work days per 100 consumption days). The work input during Week IV is 50 per cent higher than in Week I. This rise reflects an increased difficulty in reaching food, although, in terms of actual time devoted to the food quest, the average rises from two days per week to three per week per individual producer.

In calculating the overall average value of "S" for this period, I have omitted Week II for the reason noted (Table IV, note 3); therefore the Index of Subsistence Effort for this camp of !Kung Bushmen is .23. Since the non-productive members comprised 35 per cent of the population, another way of expressing the

Table IV. DOBE WORK DIARY: A RECORD OF THE ACTIVITIES AT THE DOBE CAMP FOR THE 28-DAY PERIOD 6 JULY—2 AUGUST, 1964

WEEK	DATE	(1) ADULTS	(2) CHILDREN	(3) MAN-DAYS OF CONSUMPTION*	(4) MAN-DAYS OF WORK	(5) MEAT OUTPUT POUNDS
	July 6	18	9	27	9	—
	7	14	9	23	6	92
	8	15	9	24	2	—
I	9	15	9	24	3	12
	10	16	9	25	7	—
	11	18	11	29	3	—
	12	18	9	27	7	—
	13	20	11	31	5	—
	14	16	9	25	0	—
	15	16	9	25	1	—
II**	16	14	9	23	0	—
	17	19	12	31	11	80
	18	17	9	26	3	—
	19	23	14	37	2	—
	20	26	14	40	9	110
	21	24	11	35	3	24
	22	19	13	32	3	—
III	23	18	11	29	4	27
	24	23	13	36	10	16
	25	22	10	32	6	—
	26	24	12	36	7	—
	27	22	13	35	12	7
	28	27	13	40	12	80
	29	26	13	39	9	10
IV	30	24	11	35	16	12
	31	22	10	32	4	20
	Aug. 1	24	11	35	8	—
	2	22	11	33	16	—

*Each entry in column 3 equals the sum of the entries in columns 1 and 2 for the given date.
**Week II (July 13—19) shows an unusually *low* work output. The investigator contributed food on July 12 and 17, resulting in a decreased subsistence effort for the seven-day period. Week II therefore has not been included in final calculation of the S ratio (see Table V).

Index is to say that 65 per cent of the people worked 36 per cent of the time, and 35 per cent of the people did no work at all.[5]

Two of the ecological conditions noted above are represented in the work diary. The first week is condition II, in which food is abundant but only eight water points are available. People are making the daily round trips to the nut forests, giving an "S" value of .21. By the fourth week condition III has appeared; it is no longer possible to reach the nuts in one day, since a radius of over seven miles has been eaten

out. The round-trip distance to the nearest nuts is over fourteen miles and the "cost" curve of nuts has turned sharply upwards (see Figure 2). The higher value of "S" (.31) reflects the marked increase in overnight trips to reach the nut forests.

VIII. INPUT-OUTPUT: CALORIC LEVELS

Having considered the level of work effort required to feed the group, it is necessary to determine the quantity of energy yielded by this work effort. Since the actual time devoted to

[5]In calculating the Index, I have taken into account only the work actually devoted to getting food. The time spent on manufacturing the tool kit has not been included, nor has the time spent on processing food. However, in calculating the caloric requirements (Section VIII), I have included a value for the energy expended in such activities.

Table V. SUMMARY OF DOBE WORK DIARY

WEEK	(1) MEAN GROUP SIZE	(2) ADULT-DAYS	(3) CHILD-DAYS	(4) TOTAL MAN-DAYS CONSUMP-TION	(5) MAN-DAYS OF WORK	(6) MEAT LBS.	(7) WORK WEEK	(8) INDEX OF SUBSIS-TENCE EFFORT
I (July 6—12)	25.6 (23—29)	114	65	179	37	104	2.3	.21
II (July 13—19)	28.3 (23—37)	125	73	198	22	80	1.2	.11
III (July 20—26)	34.3 (29—40)	156	84	240	42	177	1.9	.18
IV (July 27—Aug. 2)	35.6 (32—40)	167	82	249	77	129	3.2	.31
4-wk. totals	30.9	562	304	866	178	490	2.2	.21
Adjusted* totals	31.8	437	231	668	156	410	2.5	.23

*See note** (Table IV)

KEY: Column 1: mean group size = $\frac{\text{total man-days of consumption}}{7}$

Column 7: work week = the number of work days per adult per week

Column 8: Index of Subsistence Effort = $\frac{\text{man-days of work}}{\text{man-days of consumption}}$

(e.g., in Week I, the value of "S" = .21, i.e., 21 days of work per 100 days of consumption or 1 work day produces food for 5 consumption days)

subsistence is modest, the question arises whether this low work effort produces a sub-standard diet.

The major constituents of the diet by weight during this period were:

1. mongongo nuts 33%
2. meat 37%
3. other vegetable foods 30%
   100%

During field work no direct caloric observations were made. It was difficult to measure a single individual's daily food intake, since this was eaten over a period of several hours in the late afternoon and evening and was made up of small portions from the supplies of different families. However, since foodstuffs are shared equitably throughout the camp, it was possible to measure gross per capita intake by estimating the total weight of food brought in and dividing it by the number of people on hand. A net per capita intake figure was calculated by deducting values for waste (inedible portions, bones, nutshells, etc.) and allowing for loss through cooking. An account follows of the methods and results.

1. The staple mongongo nut is particularly suitable for this kind of analysis; it is easy to count and weigh, and the percentage of edible constituents is precisely known. The nut consists of a hard outer shell and a soft inner shell (both inedible) and a core of edible nut meat. The whole nut weighs 5.0 gm. and the nut meat comprises 14 per cent of the total weight, or 0.7 gm. (Anon. 1917; author's field observations).

There are approximately 200 whole nuts per kilogram (91 nuts per lb.). Each kilogram of whole nuts yields 140 gm. of nut meats (64 gm. per lb.). I weighed the total back load of nuts brought in by a sample of women each day. A woman's daily collection of whole nuts weighed between 10 kg. (22 lbs.) and 15 kg. (33 lbs.), although back loads of as much as 20 kg. (44 lbs.) of whole nuts were recorded. Each back load contained on the average 2500 whole nuts, as well as smaller quantities of other foodstuffs. Since the edible portion of whole nuts is 14 per cent, each 12.5 kg. back load of nuts contained 1750 gm. of edible nut meats.

Records were also maintained for the number of nuts cracked and eaten by individuals and families on a single day. Women roast a quantity of nuts in the coals of the fire for a few minutes before cracking. The nuts are equally

Table VI. CALORIC AND PROTEIN LEVELS IN THE !KUNG BUSHMAN DIETARY, JULY—AUGUST, 1964

| CLASS OF FOOD | PERCENTAGE CONTRIBUTION TO DIET | PER CAPITA CONSUMPTION | | CALORIES PER PERSON PER DAY |
		WEIGHT IN GRAMS	PROTEIN IN GRAMS	
Meat	37%	230	34.5	690
Mongongo nuts	33%	210	56.7	1260
Other vegetable foods	30%	190	1.9	190
Total all sources	100%	630	93.1	2140

palatable when raw, but the brief roasting serves to drive off some of the moisture and makes the hard outer shell easier to crack. The nut is then cracked open, using a fist-sized limestone cobble as a hammerstone and a larger flat limestone block as an anvil. The shell is extremely hard, which accounts for the remarkable storage properties of the mongongo. Nuts are still perfectly edible after having lain on the ground for a year.

The cracking and shelling rate averages five or six nuts per minute and varies little from one woman to another. In one hour a woman cracks and shells 300—360 nuts, or one-eighth of a back load, and an hour's cracking yields 210—252 gm. of edible nut meats. On the basis of observations of cracking rates and time devoted to cracking, and on the basis of total weights of whole nuts brought into the camp, Bushmen were observed to eat about 300 nuts per person per day, yielding 210 gm. of nut meats. Thus one back load of whole nuts would feed a family of four for two days, with a little left over for the third day.

The constituents of the nut meat have been determined (Wehmer 1931, vol. 2:678)[6] and the nutritional yield can be calculated (Oser 1965: 1336).[7] The yield is 600 ($\pm$ 1 per cent) cal. per 100 gm. of edible portion and the protein yield 27 gm. per 100 gm. The caloric value of mongongo compares favorably with that of domesticated species of nuts such as almonds (600 cal. per 100 gm.), brazil nuts (653), cashews (563), and peanuts (583). In proteins, however, it exceeds the levels of these other nuts (27 per cent for mongongo vs. an average of 19 per cent for other species).

2. Complete records were kept for kills of game animals, and for the quantities of meat brought into the Dobe camp during the twenty-eight-day period of the work diary. Eighteen animals, totalling 206 kg. (454 lbs.) of edible meat, were killed and consumed by members of the camp.[8] In addition, 16 kg. (36 lbs.) of meat were brought into Dobe by visitors from other camps, for a total of 222 kg. (490 lbs.) of meat. Dividing this figure by the 866 man-days of consumption (see above) gives a daily allotment of 256 gm. (9.1 oz.) of uncooked meat per person. Even allowing for a 10 per cent shrinkage in cooking, the caloric yield of this allotment is estimated at 690 calories (based on a rate of 300 cal. per 100 gms., cooked). The protein content is estimated to be 15 per cent by weight, or 34.5 gms. per cooked portion.

3. The remaining vegetable portion of the diet consisted of small quantities of twenty species of roots, melons, gums, bulbs, and dried fruits. No caloric observations were made for these foods and their total caloric yield is estimated at 100 cal. per 100 gm. Protein yield is negligible, and is estimated at 1 per cent.

In Table VI the three main food sources (meat, mongongo nuts, other vegetable foods) are brought together in order to show the contribution each makes to the Bushman diet and to derive an estimate of daily per capita intake of calories and proteins. The results show a daily allotment of 2140 calories and 93.1 grams of proteins per person. Because of the high protein values for mongongo, the protein intake is unusually high even by American standards. It is also unexpected that a hunting people should get such a high proportion of their proteins from vegetable rather than from meat sources.

---

[6]Fats 59.4%, Protein 27.0%, Crude Fiber 5.9%, Water 4.7%, Ash 3.02%.
[7]Modified Atwater formulas used by the F.A.O. were employed, based on the following values:8.37 cal./gm. of fat, 3.4 cal./gm. of protein.
[8]Edible/waste ratios for various mammals were calculated by R. H. S. Smithers.

Does a per capita intake of 2140 calories meet the energy requirements of the group? The Bushmen are small in stature and weight. The average height and weight for adult males are 157 centimeters (5 ft. 2 in.) and 46 kilograms (101 lbs.) and for adult females 147 centimeters (4 ft. 10 in.) and 41 kilograms (91 lbs.) (Bronte-Stewart et al. 1960). Basal metabolic requirements for individuals of such heights and weights are calculated at 1400 cal. per day for males and 1100 cal. per day for females (Taylor and Pye 1966:45—48). Given an activity regime that varies from light—moderate to severe exercise (including an hour of nut-cracking per day and two ten-mile hikes per week), the caloric requirements can be estimated at 2250 calories for males and 1750 calories for females, per day of an average work week. These figures apply to adults thirty years of age and would necessarily be less for middle-aged and elderly persons. For children I have taken a median age of eight years for all individuals under age fifteen and estimate the daily requirements at 2000 calories (Taylor and Pye 1966:463).

To calculate the daily caloric requirement for the study group as a whole, it is necessary to take an average weighted according to the percentage of each age-sex class in the population. Since the population consists of 30 per cent adult males, 35 per cent adult females, and 35 per cent children under fifteen years (see Tables I and II), the mean daily energy requirement for a group of thirty-one persons is 61,300 calories, and for each group member, about 1975 calories.

The per capita yield of foodstuffs during the study period was estimated to be 2140 calories (Table VI) and therefore it is clear that food output exceeds energy requirements by about 165 calories per person per day. The conclusion can be drawn that the Bushmen do not lead a substandard existence on the edge of starvation as has been commonly supposed.[9]

A portion of these extra calories is absorbed by the food allocated to the maintenance of hunting dogs. The dog population of Dobe varied from five to eight animals. The dogs eat what is left over when people have eaten their fill, and it is worth noting that the physical condition of the animals seemed to show more seasonal variation than the conditions of the humans. It may be possible that, in input-output terms, Bushman dogs absorb most of the marginal variation in abundance of foodstuffs brought into the camp.[10]

The remainder of the extra calories may go into physiological accumulation of fat by the Bushmen during the good season, an accumulation which is then metabolized during the worst season of the year (September—October). Future research should include the weights and skin-fold measurements of individuals taken each month through the annual cycle. During the lean season of the year, the availability of the staple mongongo nut reaches an annual low, and the people have to walk farther and work harder in order to maintain an adequate diet. In other words, a higher energy input yields a relatively lower caloric output.

The significance of the differential activities of young and old people can now be appreciated. The more able, more mobile members of the group have higher energy requirements and they have the means to meet these by making the long hikes to the mongongo nut forests. The old people, with more modest energy requirements, remain close to home and gather a more eclectic diet of low-yield roots, bulbs, and edible gums. The group as a whole distributes the collective resources in such a way that the caloric needs of each age-sex class are met. In input-output terms this is a way of restating the classic dictum: *from each according to his means and to each according to his needs.* In principle the Bushman camp is a communistic society. In practice, sharing is never complete, but conflicting parties have the option of rearranging themselves spatially so that, when sharing breaks down, new groups can be constituted to ensure parity of production and consumption.

---

[9]The possibility that the Bushmen were enjoying an exceptionally good year can be discounted. The observations were made during the second year of a severe drought, which seriously dislocated the pastoral and farming economics of the Bantu, but apparently did not seriously affect the foraging economy of the Bushmen. If drought conditions demanded a three-day work week from the Bushmen, then one would have to postulate an even lower work input during years of average or higher rainfall.

[10]Pigs may play a similar role in the subsistence economy of Melanesians (Vayda et al. 1961; Rappaport 1967). Unlike the Melanesians, who eat their pigs, the Bushmen have never been known to eat their dogs.

The input-output approach to subsistence has shown that !Kung Bushmen in the Dobe area can derive an adequate living from only a modest expenditure of their time and effort. The analysis may help to correct the impression that their life is a constant struggle, maintained in the face of adversity, and ending in early death. As Sahlins (1968:85—89) has pointed out in a recent discussion, our view of the hunter has been conditioned by the traditional wisdom of the economics of scarcity. We have tended to equate poverty with the absence of material wealth. Sahlins suggests the alternative interpretation that hunters may be simply in business for their health, and that this modest end can be achieved even with the rudimentary technical means at their disposal. The result is that hunters may actually enjoy more leisure time per capita than do peoples engaged in other subsistence activities (see also Service 1966:13). In the Bushman case, food-getting is the primary productive activity, but the majority of the people's time (four to five days per week) is spent in other pursuits, such as resting in camp or visiting other camps.

Since the northern Kalahari Desert is by any account a marginal habitat for human occupation, it is likely that hunters in the past would have had an even more substantial subsistence base. Today the remaining hunters are confined to the least attractive environments of the world, but in Pleistocene times they would have had their pick of the richest areas, in terms of game, plant foods, and water supply.[11]

IX. ELEMENTARY FORMS AND THE LOGIC OF GENERALIZED RECIPROCITY

One of the most striking cross-cultural regularities yet discovered is the almost universal practice of voluntary food sharing among small-scale hunter-gatherers.[12] Sahlins has labelled this practice generalized reciprocity, and defines it as the giving of food, or other goods, without a definite expectation of return (1965:147). It is the kind of transaction that obtains in our own society between members of the nuclear family, and it falls at the solidary (sociable) extreme of Sahlins' continuum of reciprocities, ranging from generalized, through balanced, to negative reciprocity, the latter being the unsociable extreme (1965:147—49).

Viewed as a system of allocations, generalized reciprocity may be a necessary sociological outcome of the elementary form of economic life defined in Section I of this paper. The clue lies in the implications of this practice for the organization of subsistence. The obverse of sharing is, of course, hoarding, or witholding. The latter is reported to be a cardinal sin among hunter-gatherers (Service 1966:18; Sahlins 1965:200—1, 215—18). Yet hoarding is but a morally negative paraphrase of the respectable economic term "surplus accumulation." The act of setting aside a portion of one's production for consumption or distribution at a future date is the essence of bourgeois economics ("savings"), but it is regarded as stinginess or hardheartedness among the hunters. Since everyone in a hunter camp must be fed from the food supply on hand and since no one can be refused, the constancy of demand tends to keep food inventories at a minimum. It also tends to maintain "wealth" differences between people at an exceedingly low level. Constant turnover and low inventories are simply different facets of the earlier definition of an elementary form as an economy in which food production and consumption are immediate. In such an economy, the withholding of food by even one party would be incompatible with the model of generalized reciprocity. Only if all parties are equally wealthy—or, to be more accurate—equally poor, can the economic equilibrium be maintained.

What would happen if one individual in such an economy, against the expectations of his fellows, were to husband his resources and allocate his production to savings rather than to sharing? The short-term result of such a move would probably be ostracism for the individual; but if enough of his fellows were able to follow his example and did so, then the social fabric would be preserved and a new economic equilibrium would be established at a higher level of surplus accumulation. Wealth disparities would now become possible, and an

---

[11]The reconstruction of the prehistoric habitats of hunter-gatherers has been discussed in detail elsewhere (Lee 1963 and 1968).
[12]Some of the evidence has been brought together by Sahlins in his excellent review on reciprocity (1965:186—91, 200—1, 215—18). The practice of generalized reciprocity within local groups is found among: Mbuti Pygmies, Andaman Islanders, Australian Aborigines, Eskimos, Semang, and Great Basin Shoshone. For references consult Sahlins (op. cit.).

avenue for the conversion of subsistence goods into prestige would open up. Such a society would have embarked on the road to "economic development."

In human energy relations, no individual is self-sufficient. Human existence is made possible by the work effort of individuals, but social life is founded upon the principle of cooperative consumption of resources. It is fortunate for anthropologists that in some contemporary societies, the rudimentary forms of exchange may still be observed. In other societies higher orders of complexity can also be observed, enabling the analyst to trace the evolution of economic systems.

Starting from the primate baseline of a "hand-to-mouth" existence, one can discern several secular trends in human social evolution. One such trend leads to an increasing separation between the production of food and its final allocation in consumption. Another is in the direction of conversion of an increasing proportion of subsistence output into the production of durable goods. And a third trend is towards a greater and greater disparity in the distribution of wealth among individuals.

On all of these dimensions, the !Kung Bushmen exhibit an elementary form. Although the ideology of exchange is complex, the formal aspects of exchange are simple. Using input-output analysis may contribute, on a quantitative level, to our understanding of the origins and evolution of economics.

BIBLIOGRAPHY

Anonymous, 1917, "Manketti Nuts from South-West Africa." *Bulletin of the Imperial Institute*, 15: 35—38.

Bohannan, Paul, and George Dalton (eds.), 1962, *Markets in Africa*. Evanston: Northwestern University Press.

Bronte-Stewart, B., O. E. Budtz-Olsen, J. M. Hickley, and J. F. Brock, 1960, "The Health and Nutritional Status of the !Kung Bushmen of South West Africa." *South African Journal of Laboratory and Clinical Medicine*, 6: 187—216.

Childe, V. Gordon, 1951, *Social Evolution*. New York: Schuman.

DeVore, Irven (ed.), 1965, *Primate Behavior: Field Studies of Monkeys and Apes*. New York: Holt, Rinehart & Winston.

DuBois, Cora, 1936, "The Wealth Concept as an Integrative Factor in Tolowa-Tututni Culture," in R. H. Lowie (ed.), *Essays in Anthropology Presented to A. L. Kroeber*. Berkeley: University of California Press.

Gates, David Murray, 1962, *Energy Exchange in the Biosphere*. New York: Harper & Row.

Hall, K. R. L., and Irven DeVore, 1965, "Baboon Social Behavior," in I. DeVore (ed.), *Primate Behavior*. New York: Holt, Rinehart & Winston.

Kleiber, Max, 1961, *The Fire of Life: an Introduction to Animal Energetics*. New York: John Wiley.

Lee, Richard B., 1963, "Population Ecology of Man in the Early Upper Pleistocene of Southern Africa." *Proceedings of the Prehistoric Society*, 29: 235—57; 1965, *Subsistence Ecology of !Kung Bushmen*. Unpublished Ph.D. Dissertation, University of California, Berkeley; 1968, "What Hunters Do for a Living, or, How to Make Out on Scarce Resources," in R. B. Lee and I. DeVore (eds.), *Man the Hunter*. Chicago: Aldine.

Leontief, Wassily, 1966, *Input-Output Economics*. New York: Oxford University Press.

Lévi-Strauss, Claude, 1959, *Les Structures élémentaires de la parenté*. Paris. Presses Universitaires de France.

Malan, F., 1950, "A Wilton Site at Kaikai, Bechuanaland Protectorate." *South African Archaeological Bulletin*, 5:140—42.

Marshall, John, 1956, *The Hunters* (film). Film Study Center, Peabody Museum, Cambridge, Mass.

Marshall, Lorna, 1957, "The Kin Terminology System of the !Kung Bushmen." *Africa*, 27:1—25; 1959, "Marriage Among !Kung Bushmen." *Africa*, 29: 335—65; 1960, "!Kung Bushman Bands." *Africa*, 30: 325—55; 1961, "Sharing, Talking, and Giving: Relief of Social Tensions among !Kung Bushmen." *Africa*, 31: 231:49; 1962. "!Kung Bushman Religious Beliefs." *Africa*, 32: 221—52.

Marx, Karl, 1867, *Das Kapital*. New York: Random House (Modern Library Edition).

Oser, Bernard L. (ed.), 1965, *Hawk's Physiological Chemistry*, Fourteenth Edition. New York: McGraw-Hill.

Polanyi, Karl, 1944, *The Great Transformation*. New York: Rinehart; 1957, "The Economy as an Instituted Process," in K. Polanyi, C. W. Arensberg, and H. W. Pearson (eds.), *Trade and Market in the Early Empires*. Glencoe, Ill.: The Free Press.

Rappaport, Roy A., 1967, "Ritual Regulation of Environmental Relations Among a New Guinea People." *Ethnology*, 6: 17—30.

Richards, Audrey I., 1939, *Land, Labour and Diet in Northern Rhodesia*. London: Oxford University Press.

Sahlins, Marshall D., 1965, "On the Sociology of Primitive Exchange," in *The Relevance of Models for Social Anthropology*. A. S. A. Monographs 1. London: Tavistock; New York: Praeger; 1968, "Notes on the Original Affluent Society," comment in R. B. Lee and I. DeVore (eds.), *Man the Hunter*. Chicago: Aldine.

Service, Elman R., 1966, *The Hunters*. Englewood Cliffs, N.J.: Prentice-Hall.

Silberbauer, George B., 1965, *Report to the Government of Bechuanaland on the Bushman Survey*. Gabarones:Bechuanaland Government.

Sillery, Anthony, 1952, *The Bechuanaland Protectorate*. London: Oxford University Press.

Taylor, Clara M., and Orrea F. Pye, 1966, *Foundations of Nutrition*, Sixth Edition. New York: Macmillan.

Thomas, Elizabeth Marshall, 1959, *The Harmless People*. New York: Knopf.

Vayda, Andrew P., Anthony Leeds, and David P. Smith, 1961, "The Place of Pigs in Melanesian Subsistence," in V. E. Garfield (ed.), *Proceedings of the 1961 Annual Spring Meeting of the American Ethnological Society*. Seattle: University of Washington Press.

Wehmer, Carl, 1931, *Die Pflanzenstoffe*, 2 vols. Second Edition. Jena: Fischer.

White, Leslie A., 1949, *The Science of Culture*. New York: Farrar, Straus; 1959, *The Evolution of Culture*. New York: McGraw-Hill.

Wolf, Eric, 1966, *Peasants*. Englewood Cliffs, N. J.: Prentice-Hall.

Selection 6

Plant Domestication and Origins of Agriculture

Commentary

Preagricultural hunting man had already set the stage for agriculture. He had multiplied and the energy base of natural ecosystems was unable to support a high population of humans who depended solely on that source of food. Hunting man had learned the use of iron, and how to cook, and he made pottery. He had stones for grinding seeds into flour. In some regions he had developed a more complex social organization, including some trading.

For thousands of years hunter-gatherers in southwestern Asia lived by intensively collecting the seeds of wild wheat, barley, wild rye grass, wild flax, and large-seeded legumes such as vetch and chick peas. They also had access to dates in lowlands, acorns and almonds in the foothills, and grapes, apples, and pears in the mountains. They probably followed the ripening of plants as the seasons progressed up slope to the higher altitudes. Lowland hunters might have traded handfuls of seeds as well as asphalt used to fasten arrowheads to the shaft to mountain hunters for obsidian, the raw material for arrowheads.[1] Hunting man undoubtedly was aware that seeds thrown away subsequently sprouted. The transfer of wheat and barley seed from an environment to which they were indigenous to one to which they were exotic may have been the major step leading from food gathering to food raising. Planting such seeds in habitats to which they were not adapted exposed the plants to new selective pressures[2] as well as removing certain others. In addition, protection by man allowed new deviants and mutations to survive. When they benefited man, he kept them even though they were no longer suited to grow as wild plants.[3] For example, wild wheat tends to shatter, the seeds scattering at the slightest tug of the stem, and the tough husk holds the kernels stubbornly even after the seeds ripen. Both are adaptations for the dispersal and protection of seed. Consciously or unconsciously, man selected wheats whose grains would not shatter, whose heads would remain intact at harvest. Other random mutations, such as increased rows of grain, which would survive under his protection and prove advantageous would be planted by man. At any rate the cultivation and improvement of wild grains over areas where they previously had not grown gave rise to a number of different varieties, adapted to different elevations and different climatic conditions. In such a way did man the hunter become man the horticulturalist, the man with the hoe.

The shift from food gathering to food raising did not happen at any one place in the world or with only one group of men. It happened at different places in the New World as well as in the Old at approximately the same time. The Old World's major contributions were wheat, barley, and rye; the New World men contributed corn, potatoes, beans, squash, and tomatoes.

Corn was the only wild grass in the New World to be transformed into food grain. It began as a popcorn with a tiny cob about three-quarters of an inch long. On the lower part was a single spike that bore the ovules, the upper part was the pollen-bearing tassel, and the seeds were enclosed in a two-leafed husk.[4,5] Utilized for several thousands of years the plant apparently was first cultivated in the valley of Tehuacan, Mexico. With seeds transferred from one group of primitive agriculturalists to another and with the plant hybridizing freely with such other wild relatives as teosinte and tripsacum, a number of varieties developed. Through time the size of the cob and the rows and size of grain increased until an early variety of modern corn appeared about 1000 B.C.

This development of simple agriculture did not come about as a major revolution although it is often spoken of as such (the Neolithic Revolution). It developed in stages. Man did not trade a nomadic hunting way of life overnight for a sedentary horticultural existence dependent upon cultivated crops. In the first stage, man the

[1]K. V. Flannery, "The Ecology of Early Food Production in Mesopotamia," *Science* **147**, 1965, pp. 1247–1256.
[2]Selection pressures are those components of the environment such as competition, climate, disease, and day length which act on the whole genetic system. Some individuals of a species would be genetically more adaptable to a given situation than others. As a result their survival and ability to leave offspring would be greater than the poorer or maladapted individuals. The former would be "selected for" the given environment situation, the latter "selected against."
[3]Hans Helbaek, "Domestication of Food Plants in the Old World," *Science* **130**, 1959, pp. 365–375.
[4]Paul C. Mangelsdorf, "Ancestor of Corn," *Science* **128**, 1958, 1313–1320.
[5]R. S. MacNeish, "The Origins of New World Civilization," *Scientific American* **211**(5), 1964, pp. 29–37.

hunter probably grew some wild grains about his semipermanent settlement from which he left to hunt and to gather wild food and to which he returned to harvest his small crops. Cultivated food probably contributed little more than 10 percent to his diet.

Later as he became more proficient in growing the plants, man established permanent settlements and depended upon cultigens for perhaps a third of his diet. The women occupationally became the cultivators. The men still remained hunters or perhaps cared for domestic animals. Permanent settlements permitted a more complex development of social structure,[6] but the density of population still remained low.

Eventually man reached another plateau in which domesticates, plant and animal, made up two-thirds of his diet. This population density increased and more complex political systems developed with a village headman or chief who exercised some authority over life in the settlement. Eventually man reached the stage when domesticated plants and animals made up 85 percent or more of the food supply. Villages became larger and more compact, and political organization became more varied and complex. Now depending upon the foods he produced for a livelihood, desiring a variety of items no longer obtainable as they were at one time under a hunting culture, and knowing that certain villages or regions produced articles or items of food that could not be produced in his own settlement, horticultural man had a motivation to produce a surplus of his own goods for trade. This production of surplus under the stimulus of economic needs and political compulsion was a major force in the cultural development of man.

Early agriculture was hoe agriculture or horticulture. It fell short of being full-fledged agriculture, for it did not involve the turning of the soil and it still depended upon man's own muscular energy for power.

At the heart of horticulture is swidden agriculture, also known as slash and burn, or shifting agriculture. Swidden agriculture cannot be generalized beyond the statement that it involves the clearing of land by cutting and burning the vegetation to open the soil for planting. It varies widely from region to region, country to country, and culture to culture. It may involve year-long cropping of the land, seasonal cropping, fertilization, or no fertilization. Under ideal conditions the land is allowed to revert to and remain in wild vegetation for some time before it is cultivated again. The Indians of eastern North America and the southwest and the English colonists of Virginia practiced it. It is the major agricultural technique used by the people of Central and South America, of Asia, Africa, and other parts of the world.

A good example of swidden agriculture as it is practiced today is in tropical regions. First a plot of land up to perhaps three acres is cleared in the jungle. The clearing begins with the removal of underbrush and ends with the cutting of most of the larger trees. The trunks and branches are piled to dry and burn, the ashes acting as fertilizer. Having cleared the land, the farmers used a digging stick or hoe to plant the seeds or cuttings directly in the soil. No attempt is made to plow. Several crops are planted at once, creating a diversity absent in modern agricultural fields. In fact, the Hanunoo of the Philippines plant as many as fifty different kinds of plants in their plots. The fields are weeded by hand, by hoe, or by machete. As various crops ripen, they are harvested. In some systems the same crop may be replanted, resulting in a continuous, year-long production. Within two to three years the original plot is abandoned and a new clearing is opened to start the cycle over again.[7]

The reason for abandonment is open to considerable controversy. Some agriculturalists and anthropologists feel that the leaching of the nutrients by heavy rainfall as well as their removal from the soil by heavy crops so impoverishes the field that the site is abandoned.[8] Others disagree, citing experimental evidence which indicates that these fields can be recropped up to ten years before yields begin to seriously decline. The reason for abandonment, they claim, is fast invasion of the plots by jungle vegetation, since weeding methods of swidden agriculturalists are ineffective. It is easier for them to clear a new plot than it is to weed an old one. Whatever the reasons, the plots are abandoned, the jungle returns, old nutrient cycles are reestablished, and soil fertility is restored. Within twenty-five years, the people will return, clear the plot, and farm it again.

Most agriculturalists consider swidden agriculture to be wasteful and inefficient, robbing the soil of nutrients and requiring a considerable area of land. For every acre under cultivation, some fifteen to twenty other acres must lie fallow, especially if a plot is reopened only once every twenty to twenty-five years. Yet ecologically this type of agriculture is highly adapted to the region.[9] The plot is in cultivation a short time only. It is not open enough to be exposed to heavy erosion, nor is it so depleted of nutrients that new vegetation cannot quickly reclaim it. And by allowing natural vegetation to reclaim the area, the fertility is restored. As a form of agriculture it has stood the test of time. It is a method ecologically adapted to the region.

---

[6]Frank Hole, "Investigating the Origins of Mesopotamian Civilization," *Science* **153**, 1966, pp. 605–611.

[7]H. C. Conklin, "An Ethnoecological Approach to Shifting Agriculture," *Trans. N.Y. Acad. Sci.* Ser. 2, No. 17, 1954, pp. 133–142.

[8]D. E. Dumond, "Swidden Agriculture and the Rise of Maya Civilization," *Southwestern Journal of Anthropology* **17**, 1961, pp. 301–316.

[9]W. M. S. Russell, "The Slash and Burn Technique," *Natural History* **72**(3), March 1968, pp. 58–65.

A major drawback of swidden agriculture is the large amount of land required to operate it. Since only a fraction of the land area is under cultivation at any one time, and since a long period of time is necessary for the fields to lie fallow, the human population that such an agriculture can support is necessarily low. If a population increases at a significant rate, more forest land has to be cleared and a shorter time allowed between cycles of cultivation fallowing. Under extreme conditions the forest completely disappears and the land now continuously cropped becomes so depleted of nutrients and changed in structure by the eroding and leaching effects of the tropical climate that it is incapable of supporting a viable agriculture.[10] This is the fate of many areas today in the tropical regions. If high populations are to be supported in tropical regions, considerable research must be done on methods of developing intensive agriculture in the tropics. Simply transplanting agricultural practices of temperate regions to tropical regions is doomed to failure.

Swidden agriculture started with plant domestication. Although plant domesticates are now grown widely throughout the world where climate and soils permit, early domesticated plants and the agriculture they supported were determined by the wild plants and ecological conditions of the region. Agriculture had not one but many beginnings; its characteristics and the plants involved vary uniquely from region to region. A paper describing the rise of agriculture in any of one of these regions may have had a place in this collection. But I chose Dr. Harris' paper because it presents a broad and balanced view of plant domestication and agricultural development around the world. It will give the reader an appreciation of the development of agriculture in regions of the world other than southwest Asia and central America. Because it is a review paper, it is lacking in detail; but the extensive footnotes encourage the reader to seek out the details for himself.

---

[10]P. W. Richards, *The Life of the Jungle*, New York, McGraw-Hill, 1970.

Selection 7

New Light on Plant Domestication and the Origins of Agriculture: A Review

by David R. Harris

The problem of how, where, and when agriculture originated offers an intellectual challenge to all scholars concerned with the evolution of culture and the history of man's realtionship to the land. Few geographers or anthropologists can have failed to have their curiosity aroused at some time regarding the circumstances in which man took this decisive step. But progress in our understanding of the problem is hindered by the baffling diversity of the evidence that bears upon it. Even to geographers, accustomed to browsing in the undergrowth of neighboring subjects and sampling the fugitive literature of journalism, the range of evidence is daunting. It is doubtful whether any single individual can now assess with equal competence the findings of all relevant fields of inquiry, from genetics and the taxonomy of particular plant and animal species to archeology, linguistics, and even comparative mythology. Highly specialized investigations into the minutiae of the problem are essential, but expertness in one science sometimes leads to myopia in other directions; it is often easier to examine the trees than to attempt to comprehend the wood.

For this reason, and to bring together some of the more recondite aspects of the subject, it is worth reviewing from time to time advances in our knowledge of agricultural origins. The

---

THIS SELECTION is reprinted by permission from the *Geographical Review*, Vol. 57, 1967, pp. 90—107, copyrighted by The American Geographical Society of New York.

recent appearance in nongeographical publications of many significant comtributions calls for such an assessment. This discussion, however, is not intended to be all-inclusive. Attention is confined to certain aspects of the problem that are of current interest, and no attempt is made to review new evidence on the domestication of individual plants and animals.

PLANT DOMESTICATION

No general interpretation of how agriculture arose in both the Old World and the New has been put forward since Carl Sauer published his well-known hypothesis in 1952,[1] but notable advances have been made in our factual and theoretical knowledge of plant domestication. In a comprehensive factual summary Zukovskij[2] has gathered together available data on the uses, native habitats, wild ancestors, chromosome numbers, and history of cultivation of some 140 genera of cultivated plants. His account is more detailed and dependable than other compendia of economic plants—for example, that by Uphof[3]—and it makes clear the extraordinary diversity of man's cultigens. The impressive number of these that are "not known in the wild state" emphasizes the drastic nature of the morphological changes that domestication has so often brought about in the transition from wild ancestor to cultivated crop.

The processes of plant domestication and the problem of how agriculture originated are discussed by Darlington[4] in a new edition of his book on chromosome botany, in which the treatment of cultivated plants has been put "on an equal footing with that of wild plants." As a result, the book is of value to all students of agricultural origins. The section on cultivated plants itself serves as an introduction to the subject; for it ranges from the nineteenth-century pioneers—De Candolle, Darwin, and Mendel—to archeological evidence of early agriculture and the processes by which domesticated plants arise through cultivation, migration, and modern plant breeding. A more elementary discussion of agricultural origins is provided in a recent introduction to economic botany by Baker,[5] in which the ancestry of our major crops is outlined and the controversial question of pre-Columbian plant transfers between the Old World and the New is briefly considered.

The processes of plant domestication are explored both more selectively and in more detail in a recent survey of crop-plant evolution edited by J. B. Hutchinson.[6] This work contains essays by specialists on maize, sorghum, wheat, barley, oats, rye, potatoes, forage grasses, and legumes, and in conclusion Hutchinson elicits some of the biological principles that have governed plant domestication. He stresses the extremely rapid differentiation of our major crop plants into geographical races, which is a consequence of man's vast extension of their range into new and diverse habitats; and he contrasts the evolutionary effects of the different breeding systems established in crop-plant populations. These range from plants that maintain free gene exchange throughout large, wind-pollinated populations and are therefore highly variable (for example, maize), to those that are partly cross-pollinated and are therefore rather less variable (for example, cotton, wheat, barley, oats), to those in which sexual reproduction has given way to clonal propagation, with almost complete loss of variability (for example, bananas). The point of view is that of an agricultural geneticist interested in plant domestication as a guide to further crop improvement rather than as an unsolved problem of cultural history.

The importance of taxonomy and genetics in

---

[1] Carl O. Sauer: Agricultural Origins and Dispersals, *Amer. Geogr. Soc. Bowman Memorial Lectures*, Ser. 2, New York, 1952.

[2] P. M. Zukovskij: Cultivated Plants and Their Wild Relatives (abridged translation by P. S. Hudson; Commonwealth Agricultural Bureaux, Farnham Royal, Bucks., 1962).

[3] J. C. Th. Uphof: Dictionary of Economic Plants (Weinheim, 1959).

[4] C. D. Darlington: Chromosome Botany and the Origins of Cultivated Plants (2nd edit.; New York and London, 1963). An invaluable summary of the known chromosome numbers of wild as well as of cultivated plants, together with information on their common names, uses, and geographical distributions, is provided in C. D. Darlington and A. P. Wylie: Chromosome Atlas of Flowering Plants (2nd edit.; London, 1955; New York, 1956). This is a revised and much enlarged edition of C. D. Darlington and E. K. Janaki Ammal: Chromosome Atlas of Cultivated Plants (London, 1945; New York, 1946).

[5] Herbert G. Baker: Plants and Civilization (Belmont, Calif., and London, 1964).

[6] Sir Joseph Hutchinson, edit.: Essays on Crop Plant Evolution (London, 1965).

the study of plant domestication is further demonstrated in three recent papers, by J. R. Harlan, N. W. Simmonds, and W. T. Stearn.[7] These three authors approach the problem from different points of view but find common ground in their emphasis on the vital importance of conserving "primitive" varieties of cultivated plants as an irreplaceable and necessary source of genetic diversity for future plant breeding.

In his discussion of the geographical origins of crop plants Harlan stresses the significance of hybridization with weeds in the evolution of varietal diversity. Many weeds are derivative from, rather than ancestral to, their associated crops, and consequently Vavilov's centers of maximum diversity are not necessarily centers of primary domestication. Simmonds analyzes lucidly the relation between crop-plant variability and plant-breeding techniques. He examines different aspects of crop adaptation and suggests possible solutions to the apparently irreconcilable demands facing the plant breeder, who has to produce cultivars ever more closely adapted to modern agricultural requirements without at the same time reducing the reservoir of genetic variability on which further crop improvement depends. Finally, in the 1964 Masters Memorial Lecture of the Royal Horticultural Society, Stearn reviews such diverse topics as the morphological peculiarities of cultivated plants, the history of investigations into the origins of wheat and barley, the location of Vavilov's centers of crop diversity, the dispersal of cultivated plants about the world (particularly their introduction into Europe[8]), and the necessity of preventing the extinction of economically inferior but genetically diverse cultivars still in cultivation in "underdeveloped" areas.

All these recent publications are the work of botanists. Whether they approach the subject from the point of view of the taxonomist, the geneticist, or the agriculturist, the focus of interest tends to be the evolutionary and practical significance of plant domestication rather than the particular geographical and historical circumstances in which it took place. Curiosity is directed toward the biological questions raised by the problem of *how* agriculture began. For evidence on the time and place of agricultural origins we must turn principally to the work of archeologists, supplemented by that of the few paleobotanists who devote themselves to the identification of the macroscopic and microscopic remains of cultivated plants. Comparative and synoptic studies by a small number of geographers and anthropologists are also contributing to the interpretation of the archeological evidence. In what follows some of the more significant recent findings of archeology are reviewed regionally in order to throw light on the questions of *where* and *when* agriculture originated.

EURASIA

Archeology has long pointed toward the largest of the Old World landmasses as the likely scene of man's first experiments with agriculture. So far, the ecologically varied hills and valleys of Southwest Asia have yielded the richest and earliest evidence of plant cultivation and animal husbandry.[9] Excavation of Neolithic

---

[7]J. R. Harlan: Geographic Origin of Plants Useful to Agriculture, *in* Germ Plasm Resources (edited by Ralph E. Hodgson), *Amer. Assn. for the Advancement of Sci. Publ. No. 66,* Washington, D. C., 1961, pp. 3—19; N. W. Simmonds: Variability in Crop Plants, Its Use and Conservation, *Cambridge Philos. Soc. Biol. Reviews,* Vol. 37, 1962, pp. 422—465; W. T. Stearn: The Origin and Later Development of Cultivated Plants, *Journ. Royal Horticultural Soc.,* Vol. 90, 1965, pp. 279—291 and 322—340.

[8]Of interest to students of plant introduction is Dr. Stearn's elaboration of the six main periods of introduction into European botanical gardens distinguished by Gregor Kraus: Geschichte der Pflanzeneinführungung in die europäischen botanischen Gärten (Leipzig, 1894). To Kraus's six periods (European, to 1560; Near Eastern, 1560—1620; Canadian and Virginian herbaceous plants, 1620—1686; Cape, 1687—1772; North American trees and shrubs, 1687—1772; Australian, 1772—1820) Stearn adds three more (Japanese and North American tropical glasshouse and hardy plants, 1820—1900; West Chinese, 1900—1930; hybrids, 1930 on).

[9]At most sites remains of cultivated plants and of domestic animals occur in association, but at present the earliest evidence of domestic animals—sheep at Zawi Chemi Shanidar in northeastern Iraq (see Dexter Perkins, Jr.: Prehistoric Fauna from Shanidar, Iraq, *Science,* Vol. 144, 1964, pp. 1565—1566)—precedes that of cultivated plants by nearly two millennia. However, the apparent absence of cultivated-plant remains at this site shoud not be interpreted as positive evidence that animal domestication took place before, and independently of, plant domestication. The presence of sickle blades, grindstones, and polished-stone celts (axes? hoe blades?) at Shanidar and other very early sites suggests, though it does not prove, that cultivation was practiced.

village sites there has, during the past fifteen years, pushed back the earliest proven date of agriculture by more than two millennia, to *ca.* 7000 B.C., and at the same time has greatly extended the geographical range of known sites.

Current excavations continue to demonstrate the importance of Southwest Asia as a primary hearth of plant and animal domestication. Most impressive of these are Mellaart's investigations of two sites in southwestern Turkey, Haçilar and Çatal Hüyük, which have revealed the existence of substantial farming communities in the sixth and seventh millennia before Christ. At that time the inhabitants were evidently cultivating barley (the naked, six-row variety of *Hordeum vulgare*), wheat (einkorn, *Triticum monococcum*; emmer, *T. dicoccum*; and even a primitive variety of hexaploid bread wheat, *T. aestivum*), peas (both the field pea, *Pisum arvense*, and the purple pea, *P. elatius*), lentils (*Ervum lens*, syn. *Lens esculenta*, *L. culinaris*), and bitter vetch (*Ervum ervilia*, syn. *Vicia ervilia*, *Ervilia sativa*), and were raising sheep, goats, and cattle.[10] To the east and south,

especially along the western flank of the Zagros Mountains and in the Jordan Rift Valley, are other clusters of early Neolithic sites.[11] Some of them, such as Jarmo, in northeastern Iraq,[12] have yielded conclusive proof of agriculture, but at others, such as Jericho, near the north end of the Dead Sea,[13] the evidence is circumstantial only. The traces of cultivated plants recovered from many of these sites, and the possible stages in their domestication, are discussed in a series of useful papers by Hans Helbaek;[14] the evidence for animal domestication is similarly reviewed by Charles A. Reed.[15]

A promising new development in the study of Southwest Asian agricultural origins is the increasing effort being devoted to reconstruction of the environmental conditions that prevailed at the time. As the earliest date of proven agriculture is extended by carbon 14 determinations progressively nearer the close of the last phase of continental glaciation, it becomes increasingly imperative to learn how, if at all, the climate of Southwest Asia at that time differed from the present. Major contributions to this problem have been made by Butzer,

---

[10]James Mellaart: Excavations at Hacilar: First, Second, Third, and Fourth Preliminary Reports, *Anatolian Studies*, Vols. 8, 9, 10, and 11, 1958—1961, pp. 127—156, 51—65, 83—104, and 39—75; *idem*, Excavations at Çatal Hüyük: First, Second, and Third Preliminary Reports, *ibid.*, Vols. 12, 13, and 14, 1962—1964, pp. 41—65, 43—103, and 39—119; see also Hans Helbaek: First Impressions of the Çatal Hüyük Plant Husbandry, *ibid.*, Vol. 14, 1964, pp. 121—123; Harold B. Burnham: Çatal Hüyük—The Textiles and Twined Fabrics, *ibid.*, Vol. 15, 1965, pp. 169—174; M. L. Ryder: Report on Textiles from Çatal Hüyük, *ibid.*, pp. 175—176. More general accounts of the two sites are given in Mellaart's articles "Hacilar: A Neolithic Village Site," *Scientific American*, Vol. 205, No. 2, 1961, pp. 86—97, and "A Neolithic City in Turkey," *ibid.*, Vol. 210, No. 4, 1964, pp. 94—104.

[11]Discussions of the more important of these sites can be found in the following: Diana Kirkbride: Five Seasons at the Pre-Pottery Neolithic Village of Beidha in Jordan, *Palestine Exploration Quart.*, January—June, 1966, pp. 8—72; Frank Hole, Kent Flannery, and James Neely: Early Agriculture and Animal Husbandry in Deh Luran, Iran, *Current Anthropology*, Vol. 6, 1965, pp. 105—106; Ralph S. Solecki: Prehistory in Shanidar Valley, Northern Iraq, *Science*, Vol. 139, 1963, pp. 179—193; Robert J. Braidwood and Bruce Howe: Southwestern Asia beyond the Lands of the Mediterranean Littoral, *in* Courses toward Urban Life (edited by Robert J. Braidwood and Gordon P. Willey), *Viking Fund Publs. in Anthropol.*, No. 32, Chicago, 1962, pp. 132—146; Robert J. Braidwood, Bruce Howe, and Charles A. Reed: The Iranian Prehistoric Project, *Science*, Vol. 133, 1961, pp. 2008—2010; R. J. Braidwood and Bruce Howe: Prehistoric Investigations in Iraqi Kurdistan (Univ. of Chicago, Oriental Inst., Studies in Ancient Oriental Civilization, No. 31; Chicago, 1960); Robert J. Braidwood; Near Eastern Prehistory, *Science*, Vol. 127, 1958, pp. 1419—1430.

[12]Braidwood and Howe, Prehistoric Investigations in Iraqi Kurdistan [see footnote 11 above]; Robert J. Braidwood: The Agricultural Revolution, *Scientific American*, Vol. 203, No. 3, 1960, pp. 130—148; *idem*, From Cave to Village, *ibid.*, Vol. 187, No. 4, 1952, pp. 62—66.

[13]Kathleen M. Kenyon: Jericho and the Origins of Agriculture, *Advancement of Sci.*, Vol. 17, 1960—1961, pp. 118—120; *idem*, Earliest Jericho, *Antiquity*, Vol. 33, 1959, pp. 5—9; Carl O. Sauer: Jericho and Composite Sickles, *ibid.*, Vol. 32, 1958, pp. 187—189; F. E. Zeuner: The Goats of Early Jericho, *Palestine Exploration Quart.*, April, 1955, pp. 70—86.

[14]Palaeo-Ethnobotany, *in* Science in Archaeology (edited by Don Brothwell and Eric Higgs; New York and London, 1963), pp. 177—185; Paleoethnobotany of the Near East and Europe, *in* Prehistoric Investigations in Iraqi Kurdistan [see footnote 11 above], pp. 99—118; Ecological Effects of Irrigation in Ancient Mesopotamia, *Iraq*, Vol. 22, 1960, pp. 186—196; Domestication of Food Plants in the Old World, *Science*, Vol. 130, 1959, pp. 365—372.

[15]Osteological Evidences for Prehistoric Domestication in Southwestern Asia, *Zeitschr. für Tierzüchtung und Züchtungsbiologie*, Vol. 76, 1961, pp. 31—38; A Review of the Archeological Evidence on Animal Domestication in the Prehistoric Near East, *in* Prehistoric Investigations in Iraqi Kurdistan [see footnote 11 above], pp. 119—145; Animal Domestication in the Prehistoric Near East, *Science*, Vol. 130, 1959, pp. 1629—1639.

whose recent book contains a perceptive discussion of the geographical circumstances in which Southwest Asian agriculture arose.[16] Butzer believes that although there may have been a minor cold phase during the eighth millennium before Christ, and possibly a somewhat moister period locally in Palestine and Egypt between 9000 and 7000 B.C., there is no evidence to suggest a climate markedly different from the present in the foothill zones where the earliest Neolithic sites are concentrated. This conclusion should help finally to discredit the deterministic theory that agriculture and sedentary life arose in the Near East in response to progressive desiccation, a supposition which was championed by Childe and uncritically adopted by Toynbee, and which still appears in the writings of professional archeologists.[17] The question of the changes that have taken place in vegetation, soils, and animal life in Southwest Asia since the end of the Pleistocene is also under active investigation. In particular, pollen analysis beginning to provide some information on the nature of the vegetation cover before it was severely degraded by man.[18] It is likely that in the immediate future historical ecology will offer one of the most fruitful approaches to the problem of agricultural origins.[19]

Although Southwest Asia has been the main focus of interest and activity in the search for Old World agricultural origins, other parts of Eurasia have yielded fresh evidence in recent years. Many details have been added to our knowledge of how and when agriculture spread northwest from the Southwest Asian hearth area into temperate Europe, though they do not alter the main outline of this relatively well known story of cultural diffusion. The most significant new evidence has come from excavations in northern Greece and the southern Balkans, the intermediate area between the archeologically better-known cultures of the Near East and Central Europe.[20] The earliest known Neolithic site in Europe is in this area, at Nea Nikomedeia on the Macedonian plain west of Salonika. It dates from *ca.* 6000 B.C. and has yielded remains of wheat, barley, and lentils, sheep, goats, cattle, and pigs.[21] The further spread of Neolithic cultures northwestward across Europe has long been understood in considerable detail, but carbon 14 dating and pollen analysis have now made it possible to trace the spread of agriculture with much greater precision. Two useful recent summaries of evidence from these sources have been made by Clark, who has mapped all the carbon 14 dates for earliest sites of agriculture in Europe and the Near East that were available in October, 1964,[22] and Godwin, who has surveyed the palynological evidence for the beginnings of agriculture in Northwest Europe.[23]

Our knowledge of agricultural origins eastward from the Southwest Asian hearth is much more scanty. A few investigations have recently been carried out in Afghanistan and Baluchistan, where it appears probable that a rudimen-

---

[16] Karl W. Butzer: Environment and Archeology (Chicago, 1964; London, 1965), pp. 416–437.

[17] See, for example, Grahame Clark: World Prehistory: An Outline (London, 1961), p. 64.

[18] Willem van Zeist and H. E. Wright, Jr.: Preliminary Pollen Studies at Lake Zeribar, Zagros Mountains, Southwestern Iran, *Science*, Vol. 140, 1963, pp. 65–67; Ralph S. Solecki and Arlette Leroi-Gourhan: Palaeoclimatology and Archaeology in the Near East, *in* Solar Variations, Climatic Change, and Related Geophysical Problems, *Annals New York Acad. of Sci.*, Vol. 95, Art. 1, 1961, pp. 729–739.

[19] The ecological setting of early agriculture in Southwest Asia is considered in an interesting paper by Kent V. Flannery: The Ecology of Early Food Production in Mesopotamia, *Science*, Vol. 147, 1965. pp. 1247–1256.

[20] See, for example, Richard Pittioni: Southern Middle Europe and Southeastern Europe, *in* Courses toward Urban Life [see footnote 11 above], pp. 211–226; and Georgi Georgiev: The Azmak Mound in Southern Bulgaria, *Antiquity*, Vol. 39, 1965, pp; 6–8. Pittioni, however, regards most of the cultural traits of the Neolithic in Southeast Europe as having originated independently without stimulus from the Near East.

[21] Robert J. Rodden: An Early Neolithic Village in Greece, *Scientific American*, Vol. 212, No. 4, 1965, pp. 82–92. Until analysis of the large samples of cattle and pig bones has been completed, it remains uncertain whether they represent domestic or wild animals. If the cattle prove to have been domesticated, as seems likely, this will be the earliest dated occurrence of domestic cattle yet known.

[22] J. G. D. Clark: Radiocarbon Dating and the Spread of Farming Economy, *Antiquity*, Vol. 39, 1965, pp. 45–48.

[23] H. Godwin: The Beginnings of Agriculture in North West Europe, *in* Essays on Crop Plant Evolution [see footnote 6 above], pp. 1–22. An ecological interpretation of the spread of agriculture across Europe is also presented in Butzer, *op. cit.* [see footnote 16 above], pp. 441–499.

tary form of agriculture was being practiced by 5000 B.C.[24] Farther east and south, beyond the Indus lowland with its well-known Harappan civilization of the third millennium before Christ, Neolithic sites have been identified and dated from Kashmir in the north of the subcontinent to Mysore in the south,[25] but excavations have so far revealed few details of the crops and animals raised by the earliest Indian farmers. However, at one site in central India, Navdatoli on the Narbada River, which dates from 2000 B.C., remains of wheat, peas, broad beans, lentils, *Lathyrus sativus* and rice, together with bones of cattle, sheep and/or goat, and pig, have been identified,[26] suggesting derivation of agricultural traditions from both Southwest and Southeast Asia. The distribution of early agricultural sites in central India also shows an interesting concentration along the major river valleys, from the Ganges in the north to the Kistna and the Tungabhadra in the south.[27]

Beyond India the archeological record of early agriculture becomes even more meager. Only in the Huang Ho basin of northern China is there substantial evidence of a well-developed Neolithic farming economy. Within the valleys of the middle Huang Ho, the Fen Shui, and the Wei Ho are several hundred sites that have yielded remains of rice, millet (*Setaria* and *Panicum* spp.), and possibly kaoliang (*Sorghum* sp.) and soybean (*Glycine soja*), and also of domestic dog, pig, chicken, and probably sheep and/or goat and cattle.[28] Neolithic sites are not restricted to the Huang Ho basin—indeed, some three thousand are said to have been found in China since 1950[29]—but relatively few have been thoroughly excavated, and none has been dated by carbon 14 analysis. Until a much wider sample of plant and animal remains has been re-

covered and identified from sites of known age, the question how and when agriculture originated in China must remain open.

Still less is known about the beginnings of agriculture in Southeast Asia. An impressive number of tropical crops, particularly vegetatively reproduced roots and fruits, derive from the region, but there is virtually no archeological evidence by which to measure the antiquity of their domestication. This is due in part to the rate of decomposition of organic materials in the humid tropics, which greatly reduces the chances of recovery of identifiable plant and animal remains; but it also reflects the lack of archeological fieldwork. Where thorough excavation is being undertaken, it is proving possible to recognize cultural levels of Neolithic type and to recover remains of bone and shell as well as of stone and pottery. Exceptionally dry sites may also yield plant fragments. The longest cultural sequence under excavation at present is preserved in the great Niah caves of northern Sarawak, Borneo. There Harrisson has exposed an unbroken succession of deposits dating from the Middle Paleolithic to early Iron Age times (about 50,000 years ago to A.D. 1300), in which a period of nearly four millennia (*ca.* 4000–250 B.C.) is tentatively assigned to the Neolithic.[30] As yet there is no proof of the presence of domestic plants or animals except for a small dog in the later Neolithic (*ca.* 2000 B.C.), but remains of mats, nets, and elaborate boats suggest early and sophisticated use of plant materials. If plant remains are successfully recovered it may be that this important excavation will in due course confirm Harrisson's belief, based on nonarcheological premises, that rice is a relatively recent introduction into Indonesia and that before it came into general cultiva-

---

[24]Louis Dupree: Prehistoric Archeological Surveys and Excavations in Afghanistan: 1959–1960 and 1961–1963, *Science*, Vol. 146, 1964, pp. 638–640; *idem*, Deh Morasi Ghundai: A Chalcolithic Site in South-Central Afghanistan, *Amer. Museum of Nat. Hist. Anthropol. Papers*, Vol. 50, 1963, pp. 57–135; W. A. Fairservis, Jr.: Archeological Studies in the Seistan Basin of Southwestern Afghanistan and Eastern Iran, *ibid.*, Vol. 48, 1961, pp. 1–128; *idem*, Archeological Surveys in the Zhob and Loralai Districts, West Pakistan, *ibid.*, Vol. 47, 1959, pp. 273–448; *idem*, Excavations in the Quetta Valley, West Pakistan, *ibid.*, Vol. 45, 1956, pp. 165–402.

[25]B. B. Lal: Indian Archaeology since Independence (Delhi, 1964); V. D. Krishnaswami: The Neolithic Pattern of India, *Proc. 46th Indian Science Congr., Delhi, 1959*, Delhi, 1959, pp. 124–149.

[26]Hasmukh D. Sankalia: India, *in* Courses toward Urban Life [see footnote 11 above], pp. 60–83; reference on p. 75.

[27]*Ibid.*, pp. 71–72.

[28]Kwang-chih Chang: The Archaeology of Ancient China (New Haven and London, 1963); *idem*, China, *in* Courses toward Urban Life [see footnote 11 above], pp. 177–192. See also Te-kun Cheng: Archaeology in China: Vol. 1, Prehistoric China (Cambridge, England, 1959).

[29]Hsia Nai: Archaeology in New China, *Antiquity*, Vol. 37, 1963, pp; 176–184; reference on p. 177.

[30]Tom Harrisson: 100,000 Years of Stone Age Culture in Borneo, *Journ. Royal Soc. of Arts*, Vol. 112, 1963–1964, pp. 174–191.

tion times (about 50,000 years ago to A.D. 1300), there was an earlier agricultural phase in which taro (*Colocasia esculenta*) and other tuberous cultigens were the staple crops.[31]

AFRICA

It is one of the paradoxes of prehistory that agriculture seems to have developed late and haltingly in the continent that has the longest record of human occupation. The antiquity of man the toolmaker in Africa is now believed to reach back nearly two million years,[32] but at present the earliest definite evidence of agriculture comes from only the fifth millennium before Christ and is confined to the northeast corner of the continent. There the Neolithic cultures of the Faiyum Depression and the lower Nile Valley provide proof that cereal cultivation (barley and emmer wheat) and animal husbandry (sheep and/or goats) were practiced at this time.[33] That this agricultural complex (which also included flax) was introduced from Southwest Asia is clear from the fact that the crops and animals are Southwest Asian domesticates and appear substantially later in the archeological record of Egypt than in that of Southwest Asia.

The subsequent diffusion of seed agriculture and animal husbandry westward along the North African littoral[34] and southward up the Nile Valley as far as Khartoum[35] in the fifth and fourth millennia before Christ is relatively well known, but it now appears that cultiva-

tion and/or stock raising may also have spread extensively in the Sahara at this time. Evidence from plant remains, fossil soils, and rock drawings suggests that the desert may have experienced a moister climate from *ca.* 5000 to 2350 B.C., the so-called Saharan subpluvial, during the latter part of which many favorable mountain and valley sites were occupied by agriculturists.[36] They may have been primarily or even exclusively cattle pastoralists, but cereal pollen recovered at Meniet in the Ahaggar massif[37] and the presence of occasional grindstones suggest the possibility of seed agriculture as well. In the southern Sahara these "Neolithic" cultures are particularly closely associated with former waterside sites, at several of which Negroid skeletal remains have been found; and it may be that during the second half of the subpluvial period cultural contact in this region resulted in the initial transmission of a knowledge of agriculture from the core area of the Nile Valley to Africa south of the Sahara.[38]

Understanding of agricultural origins in Subsaharan Africa is still highly imperfect, but in recent years a number of archeologists and botanists have begun to question entrenched assumptions about the recency of agriculture in the southern half of the continent. This fresh approach is in large measure due to the publication in 1959 of Murdock's "Africa: Its Peoples and Their Culture History,"[39] in which the hypothesis of an early center of plant domestication in West Africa is proposed. Murdock's

[31]Harrisson, *op. cit.* [see footnote 30 above], p. 189; Tom Harrisson: Inside Borneo, *Geogr. Journ.,* Vol. 130, 1964, pp. 329—336. Compare also Harrisson's views with Carl Sauer's argument for the antiquity of vegetatively reproduced crops of Southeast Asian origin (Sauer, *op. cit.* [see footnote 1 above], pp. 25—28).

[32]J. Desmond Clark: Changing Trends and Developing Values in African Prehistory, *in* Proceedings of the First Conference of the African Studies Association of the United Kingdom Held at Birmingham University in September, 1964, *African Affairs,* Special Issue, Spring, 1965, pp. 76—95; reference on p. 83.

[33]Anthony J. Arkell and P. J. Ucko: Review of Predynastic Development in the Nile Valley, *Current Anthropology,* Vol. 6, 1965, pp. 145—166; J. D. Clark: The Spread of Food Production in Sub-Saharan Africa, *Journ. of African History,* Vol. 3, 1962, pp. 211—228, reference on p. 213; Charles B. M. McBurney: The Stone Age of Northern Africa (London, 1960), pp. 230—247.

[34]McBurney, *op. cit.* [see footnote 33 above], pp. 247—257; Charles B. M. McBurney and R. W. Hey: Prehistory and Pleistocene Geology in Cyrenaican Libya (London, 1955), pp. 237—269.

[35]Arkell and Ucko, *op. cit.* [see footnote 33 above]; Anthony J. Arkell: Khartoum's Part in the Development of the Neolithic, *Kush,* Vol. 5, 1957, pp. 8—12; *idem,* Shaheinab (New York and London, 1953).

[36]Butzer, *op. cit.* [see footnote 16 above], pp. 449—455; Théodore Monod: The Late Tertiary and Pleistocene in the Sahara, *in* African Ecology and Human Evolution (edited by F. Clark Howell and François Bourlière), *Viking Fund Publs. in Anthropol.,* No. 36, Chicago, 1963, pp. 117—229, especially pp. 196—203; P. Quézel and C. Martinez: Le dernier interpluvial au Sahara central: Essai de chronologie palynologique et paléo-climatique, *Libyca: Anthropologie, Préhistoire, Ethnographie,* Vol. 6—7, 1958—1959, pp. 211—227.

[37]A. Pons and P. Quézel: Première étude palynologique de quelques paléosols sahariens, *Travaux Inst. de Recherches Sahariennes,* Vol. 16, 1957, pp. 15—40; reference on pp. 26—27 and 35.

[38]Clark, The Spread of Food Production in Sub-Saharan Africa [see footnote 33 above], pp. 213—214.

[39]George Peter Murdock: Africa: Its Peoples and Their Culture History (New York, Toronto, London, 1959), pp. 64—77.

advocacy of the idea that ancestors of the Mande-speaking Negro peoples independently invented agriculture about 5000 B.C. in the region of the Niger headwaters is based both on the distribution of cultivated plants believed to be native to Negro Africa and on linguistic grounds. Working independently of Murdock and of each other, two botanists, Roland Portères and Edgar Anderson, have also suggested that West Africa may have been a primary center of plant domestication.[40]

The linguistic argument with which Murdock buttresses his case, namely that "the particular people who first advanced from a hunting and gathering economy to an agricultural one ... [would] have expanded geographically at the expense of their more backward neighbors, with the result that the group of languages which they spoke should have spread over an unusually wide expanse of territory,"[41] could be applied with greater force to the expansion of more mobile peoples than primitive cultivators, and it carries little conviction.[42] But the botanical evidence deserves closer examination.

Murdock assigns some thirty cultivated plants to his "Sudanic complex" and assumes for them a West African origin. But, as Baker has pointed out,[43] few of them are definitely known to derive from West Africa, and several have been so little differentiated from the wild that they cannot be assumed to have any great antiquity as cultivated plants. Furthermore, West African agriculture lacks an associated weed flora rich in indigenous species, such as might be expected to have evolved if cultivation had been practiced locally for seven millennia.

Although the botanical evidence adduced by Murdock does not adequately support his hypothesis, he has directed attention to an obscure group of cultivated plants, some of which, if investigated in detail, would probably yield fundamental intelligence on the origins of African agriculture.[44] At present it appears that most of the true cultigens on Murdock's list for which an African origin is highly probable—cereals such as sorghum (*Sorghum vulgare*) and millet (*Pennisetum typhoideum*) and vegetable crops such as cowpea (*Vigna sinensis*) and earthpea (*Voandzeia subterranea*)—could as well derive from central or eastern tropical Africa as from West Africa. It is at least as likely that they were introduced, already domesticated, into West Africa from the east as that they originated there and were carried in the opposite direction. And the small number of cultigens that seem definitely to have originated in West Africa—such as the Guinea yams (*Dioscorea cayenensis* and *D. rotundata*), oil palm (*Elaeis guineensis*), fonio (*Digitaria exilis*), and the geocarpa groundnut (*Kerstingiella geocarpa*)—probably represent local additions to an intrusive agricultural complex rather than components of an ancient indigenous one.

Conclusive statements, however, about the age of agriculture in this part of the continent must await the accumulation of archeological evidence. At present little is known of Neolithic cultures in either the humid or the dry tropical regions of West Africa, and positive evidence of agriculture, in the form of plant remains, is lacking. If, as seems likely, some of the polished-stone artifacts associated with these cultures are hoe or digging-stick blades, rather than wood-working tools or the points of digging sticks used for collecting wild vegetable foods, it can be inferred that cultivation was being practiced in northern Nigeria (Nok culture) and other

---

[40]Roland Portères: Berceaux agricoles primaires sur le continent africain, *Journ. of African History*, Vol. 3, 1962, pp. 195—210; *idem*, Géographie alimentaire, berceaux agricoles et migration des plantes cultivées en Afrique intertropicale, *Compte Rendu des Séances Soc. de Biogéogr.*, No. 239, 1951, pp. 16—21; *idem*, Vieilles agricultures de l'Afrique intertropicale, *L'Agronomie Tropicale*, Vol. 5, 1950, pp. 489—507; Edgar Anderson: The Evolution of Domestication, *in* Evolution after Darwin (3 vols.; Chicago, 1960), Vol. 2, The Evolution of Man (edited by Sol Tax), pp. 67—84.

[41]Murdock, *op. cit.* [see footnote 39 above], pp. 66—67.

[42]For critical comments on Murdock's explanation of Mande expansion in West Africa see an extended review of his book by J. D. Fage: Anthropology, Botany, and the History of Africa, *Journ. of African History*, Vol. 2, 1961, pp. 299—309.

[43]H. G. Baker: Comments on the Thesis That There Was a Major Centre of Plant Domestication near the Headwaters of the River Niger, *Journ. of African History*, Vol. 3, 1962, pp. 229—233.

[44]See, for example, a discussion of sorghum and cowpea by W. R. Stanton: The Analysis of the Present Distribution of Varietal Variation in Maize, Sorghum, and Cowpea in Nigeria as an Aid to the Study of Tribal Movement, *Journ. of African History*, Vol. 3, 1962, pp. 251—262; and Edgar Anderson's comments on the possible significance of several little-known crops anciently cultivated in both Africa and India (*op. cit.* [see footnote 40 above], pp. 77—79).

parts of West Africa by at least 1000 B.C.[45] And if a knowledge of agriculture was transmitted across the Sahara during the presumed subpluvial period it is to be expected that cultivation began in West Africa during or before the third millennium before Christ.

The only other part of Subsaharan Africa in which, on present evidence, agriculture may be of considerable antiquity is the Ethiopian and East African highlands, together with the Sudanic zone between the Sahara and the Congo forests that links the highlands with West Africa. Neolithic cultures with agricultural affinities have been found in Ethiopia, Kenya, and northern Tanzania.[46] Although remains of cultivated plants have not been recovered, the presence of polished-stone "hoes," grindstones, and bowls, and, in some of the East African Rift Valley sites, evidence of permanent dwellings as well, strongly suggest a tradition of sedentary cultivation. The principal crops raised in Ethiopia were probably wheat and barley, initially introduced from Southwest Asia, presumably via Egypt; sorghum, finger millet (*Eleusine coracana*), and teff (*Eragrostis abyssinica*), all believed to be of African origin; and ensete (*Ensete edulis*, syn. *Musa ensete*), a vegetatively reproduced banana-like plant originally domesticated, and still extensively cultivated, in southern Ethiopia.[47] In East Africa finger millet, sorghum, and *Pennisetum* spp. are likely to have been the basis of early seed agriculture, and there is evidence that cattle and sheep were raised.[48] The age of these Neolithic cultures is not definitely known, but they were certainly established in Kenya by the second millennium before Christ.[49] Although the French botanist Portères believes that agriculture evolved in the Ethiopian and East African highlands independently of external influence,[50] his view is difficult to reconcile with the evidence for Southwest Asian domesticates such as wheat, barley, cattle, and sheep in the Neolithic cultures of the region. It is more plausible to assume that knowledge of agriculture was introduced into East Africa, probably from the upper Nile Valley via the Ethiopian highland, during or before the third millennium before Christ, and that a selection of better-adapted indigenous plants were later domesticated locally.

Neither botanical nor archeological evidence points to any other region of Subsaharan Africa as a focus of early agriculture. Indeed, most of the subcontinent remained unoccupied by cultivators and pastoralists until after the beginning of the Christian era. The practice of agriculture did, however, gradually spread from the primary foci in western and eastern Africa, and from the intervening Sudanic zone, southward into the Congo forests and the plateau country of southeastern Africa.

The extension of agriculture into parts of the tropical rain forest may have been dependent on the introduction of those Southeast Asian cultigens, such as banana or plantain, taro, and the greater and lesser yams (*Dioscorea alata* and *D. esculenta*), which were the staple crops among the forest cultivators at the time of European penetration. Much controversy surrounds the question of when and by what route(s) these crops were introduced. Murdock postulates[51] their relatively late carriage by maritime peoples to the coast of East Africa, whence they spread northwestward along the Sudanic zone to West Africa about the beginning of the Christian era, were adopted there, and made possible the subsequent advance of cultivators south and east into the Guinea and Congo rain forests. An alternative possibility, originally proposed by Sauer[52] and recently modified by McMaster,[53] is that the banana

[45]J. Desmond Clark: Africa South of the Sahara, *in* Courses toward Urban Life [see footnote 11 above], pp. 1—33, reference on pp. 19—21; *idem*, The Spread of Food Production in Sub-Saharan Africa [see footnote 33 above], pp. 214—216.

[46]Clark, Africa South of the Sahara [see footnote 45 above], pp. 17—19; Sonia M. Cole: The Prehistory of East Africa (rev. edit.; New York, 1963; London, 1964), pp. 282—293.

[47]Frederick J. Simoons: Some Questions on the Economic Prehistory of Ethiopia, *Journ. of African History*, Vol. 6, 1965, pp. 1—13.

[48]Clark, The Spread of Food Production in Sub-Saharan Africa [see footnote 33 above], p. 217; *idem*, Africa South of the Sahara [see footnote 45 above], p. 18.

[49]Clark, The Spread of Food Production in Sub-Saharan Africa [see footnote 33 above], p. 217.

[50]Portères, Berceaux agricoles primaires sur le continent africain [see footnote 40 above], pp. 205—208.

[51]Murdock, *op. cit.* [see footnote 39 above], pp. 207—211, 222—225, 233, 238, 245, 252, 261, and 272—274.

[52]*Op. cit.* [see footnote 1 above], pp. 34—36 and Pl. I.

[53]D. N. McMaster: Speculations on the Coming of the Banana to Uganda, *Journ. of Tropical Geogr.*, Vol. 16, 1962, pp. 57—69.

and other vegetatively reproduced crops, which were part of an ancient Southeast Asian agricultural tradition (the "Old Planting culture"), reached Africa at a very early date via the coastal fringe of southern Arabia. It is assumed that they spread, by way of the Ethiopian highland and the Sudanic zone, to the Guinea coastlands of West Africa, which became a subordinate center of vegetative domestication (Guinea yams, perhaps *Coleus* spp.), and that much later, under pressure from cattle-owning, ironworking seed cultivators of the Sudanic zone, the planting peoples of the Guinea coast carried their agriculture into parts of the Congo rain forests. It is also suggested that this movement to the south and east resulted in the introduction of the Southeast Asian crops into East Africa, from which they had long been excluded by the barriers of swamp and desert between the Ethiopian and East African highlands. This hypothesis is geographically and historically attractive, but in the absence of definite evidence on the age of planting cultures in Ethiopia and West Africa it remains highly speculative. A third explanation of the planting cultures of the Guinea and Congo forests is the supposition that they arose independently of external stimulus and that the Southeast Asian cultigens were introduced later and adopted by forest farmers who were already cultivating the indigenous yams and other, locally domesticated, tuberous crops.[54] However, the very limited number of humid tropical cultigens of proven African origin argues against this possibility.

The last major phase in the spread of African agriculture before the arrival of the Europeans may have been associated with expansion of the ancestral Bantu-speaking peoples from West and Central Africa into the plateau country of southeastern Africa. This expansion is thought to have been contemporaneous with, and facilitated by, the diffusion of metalworking techniques, knowledge of which probably reached the Sudanic zone both via the Nile Valley and across the Sahara from about 500 B.C.[55] Possession of iron weapons may have stimulated the Bantu movements into southern Africa[56] that seem to have taken place, mainly down the highland spine of eastern Africa, from the early centuries of the Christian era.[57] These migrations resulted in the introduction of cultivation and pastoralism to the hunting and gathering populations of southern Africa, some of whom adopted the new way of life and became fully or partly sedentary, while others remained nomadic and were gradually driven back into the least accessible corners of the subcontinent.

MIDDLE AND SOUTH AMERICA

In recent years the findings of archeology have caused an even more drastic revision of accepted views on the time and place of agricultural origins in the New World than of those on Eurasia or Africa. Although one or two farsighted Americanists had long argued that the origins of cultivation must reach far back in time, it has been only in the last decade that the great antiquity of American agriculture has been accepted as a demonstrable fact. During that time excavation in a series of Mexican caves have yielded remains of cultivated plants dated by radiocarbon as far back as the seventh millennium before Christ.[58] As a result of these remarkable discoveries the earliest proven date of plant domestication and cultivation in the New World is now seen to be approximately the same as in the Old World: in both the beginnings of agriculture go back at least to 7000 B.C.

The evidence that has compelled this notable extension of the accepted time scale for American agriculture derives mainly from the investigations by MacNeish of cave sites in northeastern and south-central Mexico. Starting in 1948, he excavated a series of stratified

---

[54]This possibility is discussed by Christopher Wrigley: Speculations on the Economic Prehistory of Africa, *Journ. of African History*, Vol. 1, 1960, pp. 189—203; reference on pp. 198—199.

[55]Clark, The Spread of Food Production in Sub-Saharan Africa [see footnote 33 above], pp. 220—221.

[56]Wrigley, *op. cit.* [see footnote 54 above], pp. 201—202.

[57]J. D. Clark: The Prehistoric Origins of African Culture, *Journ. of African History*, Vol. 5, 1964, pp. 161—183, reference on pp. 181—182; *idem*, Africa South of the Sahara [see footnote 45 above], pp. 24—26.

[58]R. S. MacNeish: The Origins of American Agriculture, *Antiquity*, Vol. 39, 1965, pp. 87—94; Paul C. Mangelsdorf, Richard S. MacNeish, and Walton C. Galinat: Domestication of Corn, *Science*, Vol. 143, 1964, pp. 538—545; Paul C. Mangelsdorf, Richard S. MacNeish, and Gordon R. Willey: Origins of Agriculture in Middle America, *in* Natural Environment and Early Cultures (edited by Robert C. West; Handbook of Middle American Indians, Vol. 1; Austin, Tex., 1964), pp. 427—445.

cave deposits, first in southern Tamaulipas,[59] and later in the Tehuacán valley of southern Puebla.[60] In both areas long cultural sequences were recovered, which contained well-preserved plant remains going back to 7000 B.C. The oldest remains of probably cultivated plants found in Tamaulipas come from the period 7000–5500 B.C. (Infiernillo phase) and include seeds of annual pepper (*Capsicum annuum*), pumpkin (*Cucurbita pepo*), and the bottle gourd (*Lagenaria siceraria*, syn. *L. vulgaris*). By 1500 B.C. many additions had apparently been made to the local stock of cultigens, such as maize (*Zea mays*), amaranth (*Amaranthus leucocarpus*), sunflower (*Helianthus annuus*), squash (*Cucurbita moschata*), common bean (*Phaseolus vulgaris*), and, at the end of the period, lima bean (*P. lunatus*).

The comparable but even longer cultural sequence recovered from the Tehuacán caves has yielded a similar range of cultivated-plant remains. As in Tamaulipas, the earliest probable cultigens come from the seventh and sixth millennia before Christ (El Riego phase, 7200–5200 B.C.). They include annual pepper, amaranth, avocado (*Persea americana*), squash (*Cucurbita mixta*), and cotton (*Gossypium hirsutum*).[61] In the subsequent period (Coxcatlán phase, 5200–3400 B.C.) maize, common bean, bottle gourd, squash (*Cucurbita moschata*), black sapote (*Diospyros ebenaster*), and white sapote (*Casimiroa edulis*) appear in the archeological record, and at still later times a further selection of crops do so—tepary bean (*Phaseolus acutifolius*) and jack bean (*Canavalia ensiformis*) by 2300 B.C.; pumpkin by 900 B.C.; runner bean (*Phaseolus coccineus*) by 200 B.C.; peanut (*Arachis hypogaea*), tomato (*Lycopersicon esculentum*), and guava (*Psidium guajava*) by A.D. 700; and finally, lima bean by 1540.

Almost all these cultigens are believed to be of Middle American origin,[62] and most of them occupy important places in the local aboriginal tradition of seed-planting agriculture. Sauer has suggested that this "maize-beans-squash complex" became differentiated early in Middle America from the root-planting tradition of northern South America.[63] The anciently indigenous status of Middle American seed agriculture now finds support in the archeological evidence, but the question of links with the root-planting complex of South America remains open. Late contact between southern Mexico and northern South America may be inferred from the appearance of the peanut (probably a Brazilian domesticate) in the upper levels at Tehuacán; but the discovery of plant remains has not yet furnished definite evidence of earlier links.

More intriguing is the presence of the bottle gourd in the lower levels of both the Tamaulipas and the Tehuacán caves. The origin of this ancient domesticate is unknown, but it is usually assigned to India or Africa. Its proven status as an ancient American cultigen raises such unsolved questions as whether it may have had a natural pantropical distribution and been domesticated independently in the Old and New Worlds, whether it could have been transmitted accidently to America by ocean currents after it had been domesticated in Asia or Africa, or whether it was introduced deliberately by man at a very early date. Detailed taxonomic, genetic, and ethnobotanical study of the varieties and uses of the bottle gourd in both hemispheres would make a fundamental contribution of resolution of the question whether pre-Columbian contact with the Old World influenced the beginning of agriculture in the Americas.

At present, conclusions about the time and place of agricultural origins in Middle America must rest largely on the evidence from Tamaulipas and Tehuacán. This evidence suggests

[59]Richard S. MacNeish: Preliminary Archaeological Investigations in the Sierra de Tamaulipas, Mexico, *Trans. Amer. Philos. Soc.*, Vol. 48, Part 6, 1958.

[60]Richard S. MacNeish: The Origins of New World Civilization, *Scientific American*, Vol. 211, No. 5, 1964, pp. 29–37; *idem*, Ancient Mesoamerican Civilization, *Science*, Vol. 143, 1964, pp. 531–537.

[61]C. Earle Smith, Jr., and Richard S. MacNeish: Antiquity of American Polyploid Cotton, *Science*, Vol. 143, 1964, pp. 675–676.

[62]Darlington, *op cit.* [see footnote 4 above], pp. 141–142; R. L. Dressler: The Pre-Columbian Cultivated Plants of Mexico, *Harvard Univ. Botan. Museum Leaflets*, Vol. 16, 1953, pp. 115–172; Carl O. Sauer: Cultivated Plants of South and Central America, *in* Handbook of South American Indians (edited by Julian H. Steward), *Bur. of Amer. Ethnology Bull. 143*, Vol. 6, Washington, 1950, pp. 487–543.

[63]Sauer, Agricultural Origins and Dispersals [see footnote 1 above], pp. 62–73; Carl O. Sauer: Age and Area of American Cultivated Plants, *Actas XXXIII Congreso Internacional de Americanistas, San José, 1958*, Vol. 1, San José, Costa Rica, 1959, pp. 215–229.

that in both areas the transition from hunting and gathering to cultivation took place only slowly and that it was not closely associated from the first with the development of village life, pottery, polished-stone artifacts, and other "Neolithic" cultural traits. The distinctive character of the early archeological record in Middle America runs counter to deterministic interpretations of the development of civilization in terms of preconceived socioeconomic stages. The concept of the "Neolithic revolution" as applied by Gordon Childe to Southwest Asia appears to have little direct relevance to the rise of civilization in Middle America.[64] Opportunity to test this conclusion further will arise as continuing archeological investigation reveals more early agricultural sites. It is also likely that historical ecology will contribute data of critical importance to our understanding of agricultural origins in Middle America. As yet attempts to reconstruct the climatic, edaphic, and biotic conditions of the time are less far advanced than for Southwest Asia or Africa, but a useful beginning has been made.[65]

Elsewhere in the New World the archeological record of early agriculture is scanty. Only in the dry lands of coastal Peru[66] and the southwestern United States[67] has substantial evidence of cultivation been unearthed, and in both areas the earliest remains of cultivated plants date from a much later period than those in Mexico. All plant remains recovered from sites in the Peruvian desert up to 1960 have been analyzed in a comprehensive monograph,[68] and more recent excavations confirm the importance of Peru as an early center of agricultural development.[69]

The oldest plant remains come from coastal sites in central Peru, particularly those near Ancón, Chilca, Paracas, and Nazca. They consist of seeds and fragments of bottle gourd, lima bean, and two species of squash (*Cucurbita moschata* and *C. ficifolia*) and date from the period *ca.* 4000–2500 B.C. They are associated with remains of shellfish, seabirds, sea lions, and fish, and with elaborate fishing equipment, an association which suggests that the earliest Peruvian cultivators derived much of their food from marine resources. The abundance of gourds in these sites is due to their use not only as household containers but also as fishing floats and helps to explain why this domesticate, which was not used for food, is found among the earliest cultivated plants. From about 2500 B.C. other cultigens appear in the archeological record of the Peruvian coast, notably cotton (*Gossypium barbadense*), which was used in the manufacture of fishing nets and cloth, and pepper (*Capsicum* sp.). At one site recently excavated (Punta Grande, just south of Ancón) there is evidence that tuberous crops thought to derive from the Andean highland and eastern South America, such as potato (*Solanum tuberosum*), achira (*Canna* sp.), and sweet potato (*Ipomoea batatas*), may also have been in cultivation by about 2500 B.C.[70] This suggests the possibility of the early diffusion of a root-planting agricultural tradition from the highlands to the coastal lowlands. Somewhat later, during the second and first millennia before Christ, the coastal farmers seem to have acquired more new crops, including maize (which makes its appearance in the record about the same time as pottery), common bean, avocado, peanut, and manioc (*Manihot esculenta*).

The presence in Peruvian coastal sites of many cultigens believed to be of Middle American origin raises the question how far the development of Peruvian agriculture was due to stimulus from Mexico. The much greater proven antiquity of Mexican agriculture allows

---

[64]MacNeish, The Origins of American Agriculture [see footnote 58 above], p. 93; Gordon R. Willey: Mesoamerica, *in* Courses toward Urban Life [see footnote 11 above], pp. 84–105, reference on pp. 100–101.

[65]See, for example, G. E. Hutchinson, Ruth Patrick, and Edward S. Deevey: Sediments of Lake Patzcuaro, Michoacan, Mexico, *Bull. Geol. Soc. of America*, Vol. 67, 1956, pp. 1491–1504; Paul B. Sears, Fred Foreman, and Kathryn H. Clisby: Palynology in Southern North America, *ibid.*, Vol. 66, 1955, pp. 471–530; and Paul B. Sears: Palynology in Southern North America: I, Archeological Horizons in the Basins of Mexico, *ibid.*, Vol. 63, 1952, pp. 241–254.

[66]Donald Collier: The Central Andes, *in* Courses toward Urban life [see footnote 11 above], pp. 165–176; Janius B. Bird: Preceramic Cultures in Chicama and Virú, *Memoirs Soc. for Amer. Archaeol.*, No. 4, 1948, pp. 21–28; *idem*, America's Oldest Farmers, *Natural History*, Vol. 57, 1948, pp. 296–303, 334–335.

[67]Emil W. Haury: The Greater American Southwest, *in* Courses toward Urban Life [see footnote 11 above], pp. 106–131.

[68]M. A. Towle: The Ethnobotany of Pre-Columbian Peru, *Viking Fund Publs. in Anthropol.*, No. 30, Chicago, 1961.

[69]Edward P. Lanning: Early Man in Peru, *Scientific American*, Vol. 213, No. 4, 1965, pp. 68–76; Frederic Engel: A Preceramic Settlement on the Central Coast of Peru: Asia, Unit 1, *Trans. Amer. Phil. Soc.*, Vol. 53, Part 3, 1963.

[70]Lanning, *op. cit.* [see footnote 69 above], p. 74.

abundant time for the slow southward diffusion of crops and cultivation techniques. The recognition in Peru of improved varieties of maize closely related to races present much earlier in Mexico implies contact by the second millennium before Christ; and confirmatory evidence of contact between Middle America and northwestern South America, possibly by a direct sea route, comes from comparison of pottery styles in the two areas.[71] The problem of whether agriculture in coastal Peru owes its origin to southward diffusion of the Middle American seed-planting tradition may be resolved by close comparative study of the relevant crops. Certainly the occurrence of similar plants—bottle gourd, *Capsicum* peppers, species of squash and cotton—in the oldest agricultural horizons of both areas strongly suggests common origin. On the other hand, the discovery in a coastal site of remains of Andean root crops dating from the third millennium before Christ raises the possibility of links with an ancient center of root-planting agriculture in northern South America. At present the existence of such a center, which has been proposed by Sauer, has not been demonstrated archeologically, but excavation of selected sites in the Andean highland may throw some light on the question.[72]

The only other part of South America in which archeological evidence of early agriculture has been found is the southern margin of the Caribbean, particularly in Venezuela. Unfortunately, this evidence is indirect and does not include remains of cultivated plants. However, the presence in many sites of utensils similar to those still used locally in the preparation of flour from root and seed crops provides circumstantial evidence for cultivation. It is reasonable to assume that grindstones (*metates* and *manos*) found in archeological context imply the cultivation of maize or some other seed crop, and that the presence of clay griddles (*budares*) implies manioc cultivation. Working

on this assumption, Rouse and Cruxent have suggested that in Venezuela there was early differentiation between an eastern area of manioc cultivation and a western one dominated by maize.[73] According to available radiocarbon dates this may have occurred by *ca.* 1000 B.C. Evidence for earlier phases of agricultural development in the lands bordering the southern Caribbean is still more indefinite. The finding of budares at lower levels than metates and manos at two sites, one in western Venezuela (Rancho Peludo) and the other in Colombia (Momíl), may indicate an old agricultural substratum of root planting, which gave way to seed planting when maize reached the area from Middle America.[74]

This root-planting tradition may have originated in the interior, perhaps among fishing folk of the Orinoco Valley, and later have spread into parts of the Amazon Basin as well as to the Caribbean coast. Rouse believes that the spread of manioc cultivation can be inferred not only from the presence of budares but also from the distribution of a distinctive type of painted pottery (Saladoid series), which suggests that the main migration route of vegetative planters from the Venezuelan interior to the northeast coast was by way of the lower Orinoco.[75] At the coast these planting peoples may have acquired navigational skill from a preexisting population of strand gatherers and fishermen whose shell middens have been found on Cubagua and Margarita Islands as well as on the mainland. But it was probably not until the beginning of the Christian era that they began to occupy the West Indies, moving first north through the Lesser Antilles and then spreading out westward into the Greater Antilles.[76] It is likely that by that time they had already adopted such elements of Middle American seed agriculture as maize, beans, and annual pepper, in addition to their traditional root crops, so that aboriginal West Indian agriculture—which Columbus observed

---

[71] Michael D. Coe: Archeological Linkages with North and South America at La Victoria, Gautemala, *Amer. Anthropologist*, Vol. 62, 1960, pp. 363–393.

[72] For example, the investigation of high-altitude cave sites in southeastern Peru that Professor J. G. Hawkes of Birmingham University, England, hopes to initiate shortly with the aim of determining the age and character of root-crop cultivation in this part of the Andean highland.

[73] Irving Rouse and J. M. Cruxent: Venezuelan Archaeology (New Haven and London, 1963), pp. 5–6 and 53–54.

[74] Rouse and Cruxent, *op. cit.* [see footnote 73 above], p. 54; Irving Rouse: The Intermediate Area, Amazonia, and the Caribbean Area, *in* Courses toward Urban Life [see footnote 11 above], pp. 34–59, reference on pp. 48–49.

[75] Rouse and Cruxent, *op cit.* [see footnote 73 above], pp. 111–125.

[76] Irving Rouse: Prehistory of the West Indies, *Science*, Vol. 144, 1964, pp. 499–513; reference on pp. 508–509.

among the Arawaks of the Greater Antilles—was probably dependent from the first on cultigens of both Middle and South American origin.[77]

PROSPECT

The last two decades have seen spectacular though uneven advances in our knowledge of agricultural origins. While geneticists have revealed by painstaking observation and experiment the ancestry of some of our major crops, archeologists have successfully probed the beginnings of agriculture in several regions of the world where aridity favors the preservation of organic remains. The discoveries are impressive, but it is important not to overestimate their significance. Considered in its world context our knowledge of agricultural origins remains meager, both botanically and geographically. The number of cultigens of whose ancestry we have definite knowledge constitutes only a small proportion of those domesticated by man, and all the areas in which evidence of early agriculture has been sought constitute only a small proportion of the lands where it was practiced. On the basis of such an inadequate sample of the evidence we cannot expect to arrive at final answers to the questions of how, where, and when agriculture originated. But at least a review of recent progress suggests a number of promising themes for future investigation.

The most pressing need is for taxonomic, genetic, and ethnobotanical studies to be extended from the major crops, on which attention has been focused so far, to some of the minor cultigens whose domestication may date from the earliest phases of cultivation before agricultural systems became specialized toward the production of one or more major crops. With the spread of commercial farming in modern times these minor cultigens have tended to go out of cultivation, so that their study in remaining areas of primitive agriculture has become a matter of urgency. That many of them are among man's oldest cultivated plants is suggested by the multiplicity of uses to which they are or have been put. Some of the most interesting and deserving of detailed study are those which occupy a traditional place in the agricultural systems of more than one continent, such as the bottle gourd (*Lagenaria siceraria*) in Africa, Asia, and the Americas, finger millet (*Eleusine coracana*) and Galla potatoes (*Coleus* spp.) in Africa and India, or the grain amaranths (*Amaranthus* spp.) in Asia and the Americas.[78]

Among the minor cultigens, those raised for uses other than food have been particularly neglected and invite investigation. They include ornamental, protective, medicinal, dye, and fiber plants and plants used as utensils, stimulants, and poisons. Most of them are of tropical origin, and many have ritual associations. Some at least may have come under man's care and been domesticated well before the cultivation of food crops was achieved. Perhaps they offer a crucial clue to an understanding of the transition from nonagricultural to agricultural ways of life.

There is also need for concerted investigation of agricultural origins in particular regions. The importance of Southwest Asia and Middle America as centers of early agriculture has been amply demonstrated, but the wealth of evidence from these areas has tended to obscure the potential significance of other parts of the world. Among the regions most likely to repay close botanical and archeological study are the Ethiopian and Andean highlands, West Africa, central China, and the peninsular lands of Southeast Asia.

It is to be hoped also that new techniques of investigation will be brought to bear on the problem. Perhaps the most promising are those which offer the possibility of reconstruction of the ecological conditions under which early agriculture arose. Recently the relevance of small-scale environmental analysis to the problem of agricultural origins in Southwest Asia[79] and Middle America[80] has been demonstrated.

---

[77]For a discussion of cultivated plants introduced into the West Indies by the Arawaks see David R. Harris: Plants, Animals, and Man in the Outer Leeward Islands, West Indies, *Univ. of California Publs. in Geogr.*, Vol. 18, 1965, pp. 73–75.

[78]For a pioneer taxonomic and historical study of a minor cereal crop see Jonathan D. Sauer: The Grain Amaranths: A Survey of Their History and Classification, *Annals Missouri Botan. Garden*, Vol. 37, 1950, pp. 561–632.

[79]Flannery, *op. cit.* [see footnote 19 above].

[80]Michael D. Coe and Kent V. Flannery: Microenvironments and Mesoamerican Prehistory, *Science*, Vol. 143, 1964, pp. 650–654.

This work is valuable because it focuses attention on the question how many and what type of microenvironments were available for early hunters, gatherers, and cultivators to exploit. But it is liable to serious error if, like the studies cited, it assumes that ecological conditions were substantially the same in the past as they are today. Before such an assumption can be justified, it is essential for us to learn all we can of the ecology of the past. Pollen analysis can make a major contribution to this task, as it can also to the question when and where cultivated plants first appear in the prehistoric record. Indeed, as a method of tracing the origins and spread of agriculture it has great potential value, though as yet it has been effectively applied only to Northwest Europe.[81]

From the welter of new facts bearing on the problem of agricultural origins one general conclusion may be drawn. The transition from nonagricultural to agricultural ways of life can no longer be envisaged as a single "revolutionary" step. It is now clear that plant domestication and the beginnings of cultivation were slow and complex processes involving varied and gradual adjustments between man and the land over long periods of time and in many different habitats. The earliest steps toward agriculture were apparently taken in the tropics, and it is quite possible that cultivation began for reasons other than food production. Systematic inquiry into the role of nonfood plants in the economies of gathering, hunting, and fishing peoples might lead to the conclusion that the origins of plant domestication lie in remote times well before the development of food-crop agriculture.

In the present ferment of fresh facts and theories old orthodoxies, which envisage man's cultural development as proceeding through ordered stages, are dissolving and the problem has taken on greater but more realistic complexity. It remains far from a solution, but already these new approaches promise fundamental gains in our understanding of how, where, and when agriculture began.

---

[81]Godwin, *op. cit.* [see footnote 23 above].

Selection 7

Human Society and Domestication of Animals

Commentary

Ever since man emerged, he has had a close relationship in one way or another with other animals. The early relationship between man and animals was that of predator and prey. Man hunted them for food, and because man was the enemy they fled from him. Thus, to man, animals were wild and unapproachable. Where animals are not hunted by man, they are relatively tame. This fact is well illustrated by bear, deer, beaver, and other animals in National Parks where they are unhunted and in close contact with man. It is also illustrated by the behavior of the ruffed grouse in the northern and southern parts of its range. Once easily approachable over all of its range and called fool hen because it could easily be killed with a stick, the ruffed grouse where hunted has become extremely wild. In those regions where it is unhunted and man is relatively scarce, it still remains a fool hen.

Because of hunting man's close dependence on wild animals for food and the skill he undoubtedly developed in hunting them, some anthropologists[1] have suggested that the widespread and sudden extinction of a number of large terrestrial mammals in the Pleistocene some 10,000 years ago was the result of over-kill by man. Others argue that the massive exterminations were caused by climatic changes which the animals could not survive.[2,3] Caught in a diminishing range, human hunting then simply speeded their disappearance.

Another and highly plausible theory is that man, the hunter, indirectly caused their disappearance without killing off all the animals.[4] Man was a predator and a latecomer, and he shared the habitat with other large predators, such as the saber-tooth tiger. Both man and tiger lived on the same prey and it is an ecological and evolutionary principle that complete competitors cannot coexist.[5] Man simply out-competed the saber-tooth tiger, which depended on the old, young, and ill large herbivores for its prey. Man as a predator has a different impact on the prey than animal predators. Large predators concentrate their hunting on the young, the old, and the ill. As a result, survival of the young and the old is low. Man is not as selective. As a predator, he tends to remove animals from all age classes. More young survive, fewer live to old age, the life span decreases, the population becomes younger and more productive. Thus, herbivore populations that were man's principal prey species, especially the buffalo, simply out-produced and out-competed those species not hunted by man: horses, cattle, perhaps even mammoths. A similar situation might have existed in Europe with the reindeer, which under predation by man could have crowded out the bison and mammoth. The mammoth, because of its late onset of reproduction, might not have survived predation by man, just as the slowly reproducing whales are on the verge of extinction from overexploitation.

In parts of the world, other developments in man's relationship to animals led to some extinctions or at best to serious reductions in number. As man increasingly became a cultivator of crops he destroyed natural vegetation, both forest and grassland, and replaced it with cultivated plants, eliminating habitat for wild game. Fencing to protect crops may have interfered with movements of animals. By persecution of animals injurious to his crops, man seriously reduced the numbers of others. As man's settlements and modification of the natural environment increased, the wild animals retreated.

Man did something else to alter the relationship. He learned how to domesticate some of the animals he hunted. What prompted man to domesticate animals is a question that probably will never be answered satisfactorily. Two such domesticated animals, the dog and the pig, may have been volunteers, as Dr. Epstein

---

[1]P. S. Martin, "Prehistoric Overkill," in P. S. Martin and H. E. Wright, Jr. (eds.), *Pleistocene Extinctions, A Search for a Cause*, New Haven, Conn., Yale University Press, 1967, pp. 75–120.
[2]J. E. Guilday, "Differential Extinction During Late-Pleistocene and Recent Times," in Martin and Wright, *op cit.*, pp. 121–140.
[3]K. Kowalski, "The Pleistocene Extinction of Mammals in Europe," Martin and Wright, *op cit.*, pp. 349–364.
[4]G. S. Krantz, "Human Activities and Megafaunal Extinctions," *American Sceintist* **58**, 1970, pp. 164–170.
[5]Garrett Hardin, "The Competitive Exclusion Principle," *Science* **131**, 1960, pp. 1292–1297.

suggests, in that they stayed close to human habitation, where they fed on scraps of offal and received some protection from the weather. Eventually man assumed leadership and dominance over them. This idea does not go unchallenged. Carl Sauer[6] can find no reason to believe that dogs, as camp followers of the hunter, joined and became hunting companions. Instead, he argues that the dog, "as a prized and respected creature, became an object of sacrifice and of ceremonial consumption by the participants. As familial and religious connotations became blurred, the dog became a food item, especially at feasts." The pig in turn became an important source of food, especially in southeastern Asia.

There is still some question which of the herding animals was domesticated first, sheep, goats, or cattle. Sheep and goats were restricted more to the mountains, but wild cattle ranged widely throughout Asia and Europe, from the Eurasian tundra to northern Africa and the Indian Ocean. Perhaps his sedentary settlements, a growing scarcity of wild animals nearby, and an available surplus of grain prompted horticultural man to do something to ensure a supply of animals near his village for food and clothing. So he ventured into the habitat of animals, caught them, and corralled them near his village.

To domesticate smaller herding animals such as sheep and goats might have been relatively easy, but to capture and maintain the wild urus would not be an easy task. Some anthropologists suggest that the motivation was religious. The people of southwestern Asia, especially Mesopotamia, worshipped a lunar goddess. Because of its crescent-shaped horns, the urus was used as a sacrificial animal.[7] To have a supply of sacrificial animals available, man maintained a supply in captive state. The use of the animal for food, hides, and other by-products would have been a by-product of religious use.

Under the protection of the corral a number of deviations from wild stock appeared, deviants that would never have survived under wild conditions. When they appealed to man they were kept. Out of this breeding in confinement appeared two types, *Bos taurus primigenius*, which retained the massive long horns, and *Bos taurus longifrons*, a more retractable variety, the first cattle to be economically exploited. The more easily handled *longifrons* was put to a harness to pull sleighs or wagons in religious processions and from this eventually to pull loads and the plow. From both the *primigenius* and *longifrons* strains emerged the domestic cattle of today. Although the range of urus was wide, evidence indicates that cattle were domesticated only once and that took place in southwest Asia. When barbaric tribes began to push their way into Europe, they brought their animals of many sizes, shapes, and colors with them, which they used for milk, meat, and power. As these people settled down in various parts of Europe, they developed almost as many different races or breeds of cattle as they established provinces.

From the domestication of herding animals came a new way of life for some men, that of pastoralism. *Pastoralism* is a form of agriculture in which men gain a livelihood from the care of large herds of domestic animals. They are kept either for subsistence, that is, for milk, meat, or blood; for such economic products as wool; or as instruments of production, an example of which is the horse, used by the North American Plains Indians to hunt buffalo. Basically, pastoralism represents a cultural adjustment to a semiarid grassland ecosystem that can support grazing animals but is poorly suited for cultivated crops.

Pastoralism involves a mutual independence between man and animal. The livestock provides food, fuel in the form of dried dung, clothing, housing, a means of transport, and an item for trade. In return the pastoralist or herdsman provides the animals protection, shelter from climate extremes (in some cases), postnatal care of young, and in some instances winter food. Both man and animals extract more than they return to grassland ecosystem. Livestock in too many instances overgraze grassland, inducing water and wind erosion, and destroy vegetation around waterholes and even the waterhole itself. Dung, which might return some fertility to the grassland, is collected and used as fuel.

There are two types of pastoralism, transhumance and nomadism. Transhumance, common in eastern Europe and even the western United States, involves the periodic seasonal movement of livestock from low elevation and permanent villages in the winter or dry season to highland pastures in the summer or wet season. Movements are between two fixed points. Usually the core of the village remains behind to cultivate some crops while the herders drive the animals to pasture. In many instances the animals are housed in winter and fed forage and grain.

Nomadic pastoralists are people with no fixed settlements, no permanent agriculture, no provision for winter stalling and feeding. They move between summer and winter pastures, but at no time do they settle down in one place. In spite of the implication usually attributed to the word, nomadism should not imply indiscriminate wandering. Routes between pastures and the pastureland are both rights and territories which are defended.[8]

---

[6]C. O. Sauer, *Agricultural Origins and Dispersals*, New York, American Geographical Society, 1952.
[7]E. Isaac, "On the Domestication of Cattle," *Science* **137**, 1962, pp. 195–204.
[8]Lawrence Krader, "Ecology of Central Asian Pastoralism," *Southwest Journal of Anthropology* **11**, 1955, pp. 301–326.

Modern domestic animals have been selectively bred for qualities most useful to man. Modern breeds of sheep have been selected to produce a high grade of wool as well as superior mutton. (Photo by David Creel.)

When man achieved the domestication of animals, he more completely severed his dependence upon natural ecosystems as an energy base. As early as 9000 B.C. the Neolithic people of Mesopotamia had shifted their dependence from wild to domestic animals. This shift altered man's attitude and relations toward natural environment. No longer requiring wild animals for food, and secure with an energy base supported by domestic plants and animals, yet retaining his biological inheritance as a hunter, man began to kill animals indiscriminately and wastefully, something the cultural hunter rarely did. Many of the larger mammals were killed to protect both crops and livestock. But massive slaughters were the result of purposeful overkill in the name of sport. The Pharaohs of Egypt and other early rulers in southwestern Asia had animals driven into compounds for easy kill. The coliseum games of the decadent Roman empire consumed thousands of elephants, cattle, bears, lions, and other animals and were a major cause of their eventual extinction in North Africa.

Accompanying this change in attitude toward wild animals was the continued encroachment of agriculture on the habitat of wild animals and the constant competition between domestic livestock and wild ungulates for forage. This intense competition still continues, especially on the African savannah, on the savannahs of Australia, and on the range of western United States.

In the course of the history of the domestication of animals, man has adapted and changed originally wild animals to suit his religious, economic, and recreational needs. He has recognized the utilitarian value of mutants and deviants that could never have survived under natural conditions. By exposing these animals to new and often artificially applied selective pressure and protecting them, man has been able to expand the usefulness of animals to him for such specialized products as milk and wool; draft animals for work and war; dogs for protection, hunting, food; or simply household pets. How domestication changed the life of the beast as well as influenced the character of man and his course of history is discussed in detail by Dr. Epstein.

Selection 7

Domestication Features in Animals as Functions of Human Society

by H. Epstein

The creation of domesticated animals and cultivated plants is the oldest and grandest example of experimental biological activity of man. It is an example of the transformation and adaptation of nature by labor to the satisfaction of the needs of human society. Cultivation and domestication were the first steps in the economic and scientific revolution of the New Stone Age that ended the impasse of savagery and ushered in the age of neolithic barbarism.[1]

Domestication changed the life of the beast, the character of the animal, and its anatomy and physiology. The domesticated animal in its turn profoundly affected the life of human society, the character of man, and his physical development.

The domestication of the wolf may have been as much due to the animal's voluntary attachment to the offal and warmth of human habitation (a phenomenon that has been observed among foxes in the Arctic[2]) as to the human desire for companionship and the endeavor of women bereaved of their infants to reduce physical stress. In primitive human societies the rate of infant mortality is extremely high, and the geographically widespread custom to suckle young animals must be attributed to this cause. De Rienzi[3] recorded that on Tahiti young women whose children had died used to suckle dog pups to obtain relief.

The domestication of the remaining domestic animals seems to have had economic reasons: the provision of a reserve of animals for sacrificial purposes in the environment of settled cultivators that became progressively depleted of game (cattle); the substitution of wild species (reindeer) for domestic stock that could not be propagated in a new and unsuitable environment; and the provision of additional food reserves (rabbit) or beasts of burden (dromedary).[4] In close symbiosis with his domesticated animals, man soon learned to develop for his own benefit certain features—domestication features—that do not occur, or are excluded from propagation, in the wild animal.

Color. The first changes in domestication affect the size and color of the stock. Already in the wild state, leucism and albinism sporadically occur among species normally of a dark coloration. Wolves, in which the prevailing color is zonar-grey, may develop a more or less marked grey of red tinge, while in some cases the fur is much paler than usual, even pure white, and in others nearly or quite black.[5] Among birds, wild boar, and wild deer, white specimens are not uncommon, while among deer kept in parks, albinism frequently spreads throughout the herd within a few generations.[6] In the wild state, albinistic individuals of otherwise dark species are commonly eliminated by the process of natural selection. In arctic and subarctic regions, the reverse has

THIS SELECTION is reprinted by permission of the author and of *Agricultural History*, Vol. 29, No. 4, 1955. © Agricultural History Society, Washington, D.C.
[1] V. Gordon Childe, *What Happened in History* (Harmondsworth: Penguin Books, 1950), p. 48.
[2] A. Pedersen, "Eine Entdeckungsreise nach Nordost-Groenland," *Wild und Hund*, XLVIII (Berlin, 1926); Karl Kronacher, *Allgemeine Tierzucht* (6 vols.; Berlin: P. Parey, 1921—27), I, 56—73.
[3] D. De Rienzi, 1836. *Océanie ou cinquième partie du monde.* Vol. II. Paris.
[4] C. Daryll Forde, *Habitat, Economy and Society: A Geographical Introduction to Ethnology* (New York: Dutton, 1934), p. 455.
[5] N. A. Iljin, "Wolf-Dog Genetics," *Journal of Genetics*, XLII (1941), 359—414.
[6] Max Hilzheimer, *Natürliche Rassengeschichte der Haussäugetiere* (Berlin: W. de Gruyter, 1926), p. 32.

taken place in several species.

In domesticated animals, artificial selection of color variations has been practiced since early times. White used to be especially valued, and selection of breeding stock was directed accordingly. The Hottentots of the Cape of Good Hope selected their cattle according to color in order to facilitate distinction between the stock of different owners that was pastured in common. Every stock owner kept and bred only animals of his selected color, exchanging those that differed for animals of the desired pattern. However, none of the Hottentots ever exchanged a white ox or cow, which they looked upon as an invaluable leader of the herd. This preference for white cattle the Hottentots seem to have brought with them on their migration from their earlier home in East Africa.[7] The ancient Egyptians worshipped Isis in the likeness of a white cow, and used to pray that the deity send them a white ox. The half-Hamites of East and East Central Africa slaughter a white bullock at the great ceremony of handing over the country from one age-grade to the other.[8] In Cadzow Forest, Lanarkshire, Scotland, two white bulls were slaughtered in the Druid temple every year, on the sixth day after the first full moon following March 6. Among the German tribes, as among the Persians, Scyths, and Venetes, white horses were particularly esteemed. When Xerxes arrived at the Struma river, his magi sacrificed white horses in honor of the river. The Slavs held a white horse sacred to the sun god Svatovit, and a black one to Triglav, the god of darkness and evil.[9]

Many primitive pastoralists regard certain color patterns as the most desirable from an economic or social point of view. The Arabs of Najd breed their hairy sheep in a single color pattern—black, with the head, tip of tail, and lower part of the legs white. The sheep of Hijaz, on the other hand, are white with fawn-colored ears, while the goat of Hijaz, which furnishes the material for the tents of the Bedouin, is black.[10] In Ruanda-Urundi, East Africa, wealthy tribal chiefs keep herds of cattle of a uniform coloration—red, white, or variegated.[11] This custom is traceable to Ethiopia, where it may have originated. The custom of selecting cattle with a view to certain color patterns has extended also into southern Africa in the train of the Bantu migrations. Chief Lewanika of the Barotse people of Northern Rhodesia maintained a herd of pure white cattle with black points. These were all slaughtered when Lewanika died in the year 1916.[12] The Zulu have among their cattle a type with white body, black muzzle, black inside to the ears, and a few black spots near the tail setting. At one time these animals were regarded as royal cattle and treated with great respect; in fact, it is thought that to some extent they were held sacred.

Selection of domestic stock according to color is practiced even among modern breeders. Originally the cattle of the Netherlands were commonly red or red-and-white. Black-and-white cattle were imported from Jutland after rinderpest had destroyed many Dutch herds. However, this color pattern became predominant in Holland and other countries where Friesian cattle were bred only after U.S.A. breeders imported about 10,000 head of Dutch cattle during the decade 1875—1885, the importers insisting on the black-and-white pattern.[13] Similarly, Aberdeen-Angus cattle were originally found in several shades of color. The black color of the modern standard came to the fore during the seventies and eighties of the nineteenth century, owing to the demand of American importers for dark-colored specimens.[14]

[7]H. Epstein, "Animal Husbandry of the Hottentots," *Onderstepoort Journal of Veterinary Science and Animal Industry*, IX (1937), 653.

[8]Charles Seligman, *Races of Africa* (London: *T. Butterworth*, 1930 [2nd ed., London and New York: Oxford University Press, 1957]), p. 165.

[9]Victor Hehn, *Kulturpflanzen und Haustiere in ihrem Üebergang aus Asien nach Griechenland und Italien sowie in day übrige Europa* (7th ed.; Berlin: Gebrüder Bornträger, 1902), 44. [Published in English as *The Wanderings of Plants and Animals from their First Home* (London: Swan Sonnenschein, 1888).]

[10]H. Epstein, "The Fat-Tailed Sheep of Arabia," *Zeitschrift für Tierzüchtung und Züchtungsbiologie*, LXIII (1954), 381—96; *idem*, "The Hejas Dwarf Goat," *Journal of Heredity*, XXXVII (1946), 345—52.

[11]H. Kroll, "Die Haustiere der Bantu," *Zeitschrift für Ethnologie*, LX (1928), 241.

[12]H. H. Curson and R. W. Thornton, "A Contribution to the Study of African Native Cattle," *Onderstepoort Journal of Veterinary Science and Animal Industry*, VII (1936), 661.

[13]Dirk L. Bakker, *Studien über die Geschichte den heutigen Zustand und die Zukunft des Rindes und seiner Zucht in den Niederlanden* (Maastricht: Druck Leiter-Nypels, 1909).

[14]James MacDonald and James Sinclair, *History of Aberdeen-Angus Cattle* (London: Vinton, 1910).

Although color plays an important role in the breeding of cattle, it has commonly but a fictitious economic value. Occasionally the importance attributed to color markings may even be to the detriment of the breed if valuable breeding stock is culled owing to some minor color deviation from the established standard. An exception forms the absence of pigment which causes constitutional weakness of the skin, especially detrimental in tropical and subtropical climates with intense solar radiation. For this reason, breeders in subtropical countries show a justified reluctance to import white Shorthorn cattle. For a similar reason, dairy farmers in South-West Africa used to show preference for Friesian bulls excluded from registration in European herd books because of a black scrotum.

In early times, sheep breeders paid little attention to the color of their flocks, which comprised white, tan, grey, black, and variegated specimens. The purple dyeing industry, first developed by the Phoenicians on a large scale, provided the impetus for the gradual elimination of colored sheep from improved flocks; for none but a black dye can be used on wool that is black, tan, or grey. As the murex fishery started the Phoenicians on their maritime career, purple dyeing spread throughout the Mediterranean region, and with the dyeing industry extended the demand for white wool.[15] With the modern industrialization of weaving and dyeing, the elimination of colored sheep has spread so rapidly that all improved wool-bearing breeds now carry white wool; and there are only a few left in which some difficulty is still experienced in preventing a light scattering of dark fibers in the fleece.

A further illustration of the extent to which color in several domestic animals represents a function of modern society is provided by the large financial interests involved in the breeding of numerous color fads in dogs, cats, rabbits, poultry, pigeons, and fish. Even in the horse, kept singularly free from capricious color fancies, the white Appaloosa breed speckled with black in the manner of a leopard has been evolved for the purpose of furnishing a showy circus horse.

Horns. Among primitive pastoralists, it is a frequent practice to bend the horns of cattle, sheep, and goats into various shapes, or to increase their number by splitting the buds. Certain Nilotic tribes such as the Dinka and Nuer deform the horns of the cattle artificially— a custom believed to be of ancient Egyptian origin. Among the Dinka, the usual deformity is with the one horn forwards, the other back. Among the Nuer, one horn is trained to grow upwards, the other brought in a curve forwards across the beast's forehead. Cattle with artificially or naturally deformed horns have a social and emotional value, and the interest in such animals extends far beyond the Nile region into Kenya.[16] In South Africa, artificial deformation of the horns used to be practiced by several Bantu peoples; while in Northern Rhodesia, horns that hang down and swing owing to the lack of cores, or that are otherwise distorted, still excite high admiration.[17]

In several parts of Africa, horn gigantism in cattle has a high social value. Originally this feature was developed by Hamitic mountain dwellers in the western desert of Egypt. With the introduction of humped zebu cattle into Africa, horn gigantism passed into several hybrid (sanga) breeds derived from the crossing of the original straight-backed cattle of the Hamites with humped zebus. Single horns may attain a length of over 80 inches, and a basal circumference of 33 inches.[18] The reasons for the selection of giant-horned cattle are social and ceremonial rather than economic. Among the Masai and many other pastoral tribes throughout the savanna belts of Africa, animals with very large horns are held in high esteem. The cattle of the Masai are very mixed in type; for as a result of numerous predatory raids on their neighbors, nearly every variety of cattle in East Africa has found its way into the Masai kraals. All of these are humped, and two main types may be distinguished: a rather small, lightly built sanga strain with very long and

[15]Lucien Febvre and Lionel Bataillon, *A Geographical Introduction to History* (New York: Knopf, 1925), p. 259 [First published as *La terre et l'évolution humaine: introduction géographique à l'histoire* (Paris: La Renaissance du Livre, 1922.)]
[16]Charles G. Seligman, "Egyptian Influence in Negro Africa," in S. R. K. Glanvill (ed.), *Studies Presented to F. L. Griffith* (London: Oxford University Press, 1932).
[17]Edwin W. Smith and A. M. Dale, *The Ila-Speaking Peoples of Northern Rhodesia* (London: Macmillan, 1920), I, 128.
[18]Richard Lydekker, *The Ox and Its Kindred* (London: Methuen, 1912).

splendidly curving lyre-shaped horns, and a thickset short-horned zebu strain which yields nearly twice as much milk; nevertheless the sanga strain is more highly valued. Comparative study of other social traits of the Masai has suggested that their cattle complex developed farther north among the Hamitic Galla of Ethiopia and has been carried south by the advances of the Nilo-Hamitic pastoralists, of whom the Masai are the largest and most powerful group.[19]

In Uganda, the short-horned zebu is hardier and possesses greater power of resistance to rinderpest, tuberculosis, and other diseases, as well as to such adverse conditions as poor grazing or fly infestation, than the long-horned sanga cattle. In spite of this economic advantage of the zebu, the long-horned sanga cattle are more highly valued. In Tanganyika Territory, short-horned zebus are encountered in addition to giant-horned Ankole cattle. Economically, the zebu is definitely the more useful animal: hardier, maturing earlier, milking better, working better, and furnishing a superior carcass. It maintains its condition when food is scarce and innutritious, and water available only every other day. But the owner of an Ankole beast thinks altogether differently. He will not exchange a long-horned Ankole cow of poor conformation and production for a better but shorter-horned zebu.[20]

However, in some instances economic reasons operate against social forces. Among the Kivu cattle of the Congo, there are occasionally encountered horns of so huge a size that the animals suffer serious incommodation. The Warundi and Wawira consider such horns beautiful, but the Wanyabongo do not hold them in favor because the cows of the giant-horned variety are poor milkers and the breed is hard to fatten.[21] In general, the breeders of the giant-horned cattle are fighting a losing battle; for natural selection outweighs their preference for giant-horned stock. In the course of a few centuries, the short-horned zebu, introduced into East Africa by Indian and Arab traders, has superseded the longhorn cattle in nearly all low-lying areas and restricted their habitat to well-watered mountain grassland.

Under modern range conditions, horns in beef breeds of cattle are not only superfluous but an obvious disadvantage. Polled cattle are quieter and easier to handle and fatten. In general, their hides and carcasses are also more valuable, as polled cattle do not hurt each other on pasture or during shipment. Ranchers in the United States have therefore developed hornless types of the most popular beef breeds, Shorthorn and Hereford. Such cattle have been imported into Australia and the Argentine; and it is reasonable to assume that in the more advanced ranching countries the polled types will gradually gain on the horned.

Dwarfism. During the early stages of domestication, environmental conditions are generally less favorable to the development of the tamed animals than is the normal life of the wild beast. The beginnings of domestication are therefore frequently accompanied by a reduction in the body size of the domesticated stock, owing to natural selection in relation to the adverse conditions. The vast majority of these primitive dwarf breeds are pituitary dwarfs characterized by a hereditary underdevelopment affecting all parts and organs of the body alike so that the entire skeleton is well proportioned.

The number of achondroplastic breeds of domesticated animals is far smaller, and the reason for their evolution differs from that of the pituitary dwarfs. Achondroplasia is characterized by a marked difference in bodily proportions. There is an average size trunk coupled with abnormally stunted extremities.[22] The earliest record of an achondroplastic animal, dated to about 1900 B.C., is represented by the painting of a bitch from Beni Hassan, Egypt, where this type seems to have been evolved, because of its grotesque appearance. Judging from the care the Egyptians bestowed on the import of human dwarfs from Negroland, dwarfism was highly valued. Prior to the conquest of Peru by the Spaniards, the Incas had also developed an achondroplastic breed of

---

[19]Forde, *Habitat, Economy and Society,* p. 303.
[20]Curson and Thornton, "A Contribution to the Study of African Native Cattle." p. 658.
[21]F. Carlier, "L'Elevage au Kivu," *Bulletin Agricole du Congo Belge,* vol. III (1912).
[22]Epstein, "The Hejas Dwarf Goat," 345—52.

dog that vanished with the Inca civilization.[23] Among the Huancas and several other tribes of Peru, these dogs were regarded as sacred and some were mummified. The modern dachshund, extreme representative of achondroplasia in dogs, has been evolved for badger hunting from short-legged hounds similar to those still occurring among spaniels and bassets. However, the original purpose has now almost completely given way to the breeding of the type for fashion, as in the case of the Dandie Dinmont and Skye terriers, the pug, Pekinese, and other dwarfs of less pronounced achondroplasia, as well as in the numerous pituitary dwarf breeds of dogs.

In equatorial Africa, several achondroplastic breeds of goats are encountered in the general breeding area of pituitary dwarf goats.[24] In Busoga and eastern Uganda, an achondroplastic goat is bred that is prized for its unusual appearance. The hair grows extremely long over the back and sides and on the top of the head; it falls over the eyes like the hair of a Skye terrier. The Bongo, a true Negro people of the eastern Sudan, and the Mittu, of the high Nilotic group of inter-Congo-Nile tribes, have two different goat breeds, one of which is dwarfed and characterized by the heavy body and short legs.[25] A similar small and plump breed, distinguished by the heavy belly reaching nearly to the ground, is encountered among the Hausa in the region from Zaria to Katsina and Sokoto. In the most pronounced form, achondroplasia is met with in the dwarf goats of the Cameroons, which are distinguished by the heavy compact body on very short thick legs.[26] All these breeds, which are highly valued by their owners, have been developed solely for their strange appearance, in an environment that favors dwarf goats of any type—pituitary, achondroplastic, or mixed.

Among cattle, only a single achondroplastic breed is known—a humped zebu with a long deep body on tiny crooked legs.[27] This breed, which is held sacred, is kept in several

Indian temples for the attraction of visitors.

The only achondroplastic breed of livestock developed for a purely economic, rather than an aesthetic purpose, was the Ancon sheep that traced its origin to a male achondroplastic lamb born in a small flock of normal sheep in Massachusetts, in 1791. The Ancon breed, no longer extant, was characterized by the long body and the short, crooked legs which prevented it from jumping fences—the reason for its propagation.[28]

Weight and Speed in Horses. An increase in size and weight of domesticated animals has been brought about solely as a consequence of changes in human social relations. In the horse, increase in size and weight has proceeded in two different directions: one has led to the evolution of the heavy breeds of draft horses, the other to the Thoroughbred and its derivatives.

Horses of large size were first evolved during Roman times in response to the demand of the legions for a strong cavalry horse such as is represented in the equestrian statue of Marc Aurel. The foremost breeding center of heavy horses was Spain, where the ancestral stock, as illustrated by numerous iron age sculptures and rock drawings, seems to have been heavier than in other parts of Europe, Asia, or northern Africa. From Spain the Romans introduced these horses into several of their colonies, including Britain. The Roman importations altered the stock of western Europe to such an extent that by the middle of the second century A.D., the original small twelve-hand ponies were no longer easily obtainable along the routes traversed by the Roman legions and their auxiliaries.[29]

During feudal times, the increasing weight in armor made the breeding of a still larger horse essential. Horsemen commenced to wear some form of defensive armor during the early centuries A.D., but especially during the close of the twelfth century, when the use of the

[23]Hilzheimer, *Natürliche Rassengeschichte der Haussäugetiere*, p. 63.
[24]H. Epstein, "The Dwarf Goats of Africa," *East African Agricultural Journal*, XVIII (1953), 123–32.
[25]Georg Schweinfurth, *Im Herzen von Afrika* (Leipzig: F. A. Brockhaus, 1918).
[26]Adolf Staffe, "Die Haustiere der Kosi," *Zeitschrift für Tierzüchtung und Züchtingsbiologie*, XL (1938), 252–85, 301–42.
[27]J. Ulrich Duerst, *Grundlagen der Rinderzucht* (Berlin: J. Springer, 1931), p. 238.
[28]Kronacher, *Allgemeine Tierzucht*, II, 71.
[29]J. Cossar Ewart, "On Skulls of Horses from the Roman Fort at Newstead near Melrose," *Transactions of the Royal Society of Edinburgh*, XLV (1907), 555–87.

crossbow and the experience of the Crusades initiated a great development of European armor. The hauberk gave way to armor of interwoven chain, while the latter in its turn, from the year 1300 onwards, was gradually superseded by plates of metal until, at the beginning of the fifteenth century, the knight was sheathed in a complete panoply of plate armor. This ever increasing weight of mail demanded horses of increased size and strength, and induced the development of the large breeds of horses in those countries where knighthood flourished most, that is, in Spain, France, and Flanders. By the sixteenth century, a charger was capable of carrying a rider weighing, with his own armor and that of his steed, about 425 pounds.[30]

The horses of Britain gained considerably in size when the Saxons and Danes imported larger breeds from the Continent, and especially when the Normans introduced that large and heavy breed of horses which had been steadily developed for twelve centuries in northwestern Europe.

The origin of the recent breeds of heavy draft horses in France, Belgium, and Britain goes back to the seventeenth century when, after the introduction of firearms, the heavy armor of the feudal knights fell into disuse, and the powerful charger, no longer required for war, was made into an animal of draft. A heavy draft horse became necessary for several purposes: industrialization, by creating large urban centers with increasing demand for agricultural products, induced farmers to plow up heavy lands, so far used only as pastures, for the production of feeding crops, wheat, and sugar beets. Work on such land required a heavy type of horse which is now gradually being replaced by the tractor. Further, in Britain, Belgium, and northern France, the industrial revolution called for a suitable draft animal for the short-distance transport of heavy loads in urban areas. It took several decades until this task was taken over by motorized transport. Similarly, the ever increasing weight of cannons called for a progressive increase in the weight of horses until, in the course of the First World War, mechanization of transport became general in the armies at the western front.

The evolution of the racing type in horses is traceable to the second millenium B.C., when the peoples of the northern grassland zone, after the development of the light two-wheeled war chariot from the heavy ox-cart, carried their campaigns of conquest into China, India, western Asia, Egypt, and southern and western Europe. Chariot races for a long time remained a characteristic feature of all horse breeding peoples settling beyond the fringes of the grassland zone.[31] But the true racing type was evolved only after the horse was freed from the chariot. The peoples of northeastern Asia were the first to bring riding to the highest and most one-sided perfection, so that even the anatomy of the horsemen became adapted to their mode of life on horseback. We learn from Chinese sources that the Huns taught their children to ride on the backs of sheep at the age when other infants learn to walk. The most far-reaching development of the racing type was accomplished by the Arabs, who experienced the value of a horse of great speed and endurance in their intertribal raids characteristic of Bedouin society, as well as in the campaigns of Mohammed and his successors.

The Thoroughbred race horse, which has had such a profound influence on nearly every breed of riding horses throughout the world, was founded on oriental blood. It is significant that the development of the English race horse at the beginning of the seventeenth century followed the revolutionary changes in the art of warfare brought about by the introduction of firearms.[32] Instead of the knight's heavy charger, a light cavalry horse bred for speed, staying power, and maneuverability, became an essential part of nearly all European armies. And it is only since the introduction of the machine gun that the importance of the remount has begun to fade. Parallel with this recent development, the breeding of Thoroughbred horses has become largely the prerogative of a leisured class of society, the basis of an industry built on racing and betting.

With the reduced demand for remounts, racing itself has undergone significant changes.

---

[30]William Ridgeway, *The Origin and Influence of the Thoroughbred Horse* (Cambridge: Cambridge University Press, 1905), p. 336.

[31]Joseph Wiesner, "Fahren und Reiten in Alteuropa und im Alten Orient," *Der Alte Orient*, vol. XXXVIII (1939).

[32]Matthew H. Hayes, *Points of the Horse* (5th ed.; London: Hurst and Blackett, 1930), pp. 359–60.

The importance of long distance races has declined in favor of short distances. The resulting neglect of the stayer families in Thoroughbred breeding, and the coming to the fore of the sprinters, has been accompanied by genetic changes in the racing stock, both anatomically and physiologically; anatomically mainly in the skeleton of the shoulder and croup; physiologically in the capacity of the organism to incur a high "oxygen debt."

Meat and Fat. Since the beginning of domestication, all animals, with the exception of the cat, have furnished human society with meat. Even the flesh of the common pariah dog is still valued by several African native peoples. But until relatively recent times, the especial development of a meat-producing type was only occasionally accomplished. The ancient Egyptians evolved a beef type from their longhorn cattle when the wealth, amassed during the dynastic period in the palaces of the rulers and the temples of the priesthood, encouraged the demand for beef of a superior quality. However, it was only in the course of the industrial revolution that the concentration of large populations in towns and cities and the increasing accumulation of wealth created an unprecedented and persistent demand for animal products, particularly meat. Remunerative prices encouraged breeders to develop suitable breeds of livestock; and it is no coincidence that the second half of the eighteenth century witnessed Robert Bakewell's pioneer work in improved methods of breeding for beef and mutton, and that nearly all the more important breeds of beef cattle, mutton sheep, porkers, and bacon swine were developed in Britain, then industrially the most advanced country.[33]

In 1710, at the Smithfield Market, center of British meat trade, beefs averaged 370 pounds, and sheep 28 pounds in weight; whereas in 1795 average weights were 800 and 80 pounds, respectively.[34] In the course of the nineteenth century, the weights of cattle and swine in western and central Europe were more than doubled. In Bavaria, during the period 1816—67, the weight of cattle increased by 40 per cent

and of swine by 71 per cent; during the following 50 years, the weight of cattle by another 170 per cent and of swine by 70 per cent.[35]

During the period of development of the modern breeds, the value of fat and tallow greatly exceeded the value of lean meat. For prior to the introduction of petroleum, tallow was the principal material for lighting. In accordance with paragraph 35 of the "Capitulae de villis" of Charles the Great, the fattening of oxen was directed solely to the production of tallow, which was rendered at the place of slaughter. During the two decades, 1826—45, the average prices of beef and tallow in Austria were 6.9 and 16.8 kreuzers per one pound, respectively. Kidney fat during the same period cost twice as much as beef, and a large proportion of fattened cattle and sheep were sold direct to candle and soap factories.[36] For this reason, Bakewell was not worried when a customer complained that his sheep were so fat a gentleman could not eat them.

As soon as petroleum, gas, and electricity took over the role of the candle, the relative value of fat and meat changed in favor of the latter, and breeding and fattening methods were altered accordingly. While in France, 150 years ago oxen used to be fattened at the age of 10 to 15 years, since young beasts were merely growing and putting on flesh during the fattening process instead of large masses of valuable fat, the present demand in nearly all industrialized countries is for beef from early maturing cattle not older than 30 months at the time of slaughter. A contributory factor to this development is the growing percentage of married women employed in modern commerce and industry. While in a family in which the husband was the sole breadwinner, it was of little account if beef derived from old beasts had to be cooked for the formerly normal time of five hours; nowadays, with many married women having to add their income to that of their husbands in order to make ends meet, the demand is for tender cuts of young animals suitable for quick steaks and roasts. In consequence, the breeding for baby beef and fat lamb to meet these requirements is changing the breeding policy and thereby the anatomical and physi-

---

[33]Laurence M. Winters, *Animal Breeding* (4th ed.; New York: Wiley, 1948), p. 18.
[34]Victor A. Rice, *Breeding and Improvement of Farm Animals* (3rd ed.; New York: McGraw-Hill, 1942), p. 21.
[35]Kronacher, *Allgemeine Tierzucht*, IV, 144—45.
[36]Duerst, *Grundlagen der Rinderzucht*, p. 516.

ological character of many breeds of livestock in several countries such as Britain, the United States, New Zealand, Australia, and the Argentine, to an increasing extent.

In semiarid regions, the breeding of sheep and cattle with a view to fat-production has taken a different direction. In western Asia, cattle and sheep with store reserves of fat in various parts of their bodies were evolved about 5,000 years ago. In cattle, accumulations of fat are deposited in the hump, which may be either cervico-thoracic or thoracic in situation.[37] Such humped cattle, known as zebu, have since spread over a large part of southern Asia and throughout Africa south of the Sahara. They excel other types of cattle in hardiness and resistance to drought. The original zebu type had a cervico-thoracic flesh hump, not given to complete adipose deterioration, although in times of plenty a certain amount of fat may be deposited in layers, at first subcutaneous, then between Musculus trapezius and Musculus rhomboideus, and finally beneath the latter. The endeavor of pastoralists to increase the quantity of fat in the hump has led by way of selection to an overdevelopment of the thoracic part of M. rhomboideus, capable of considerable adipose development. Thereby the situation of the hump passed from the cervico-thoracic to the thoracic, M. trapezius simultaneously undergoing certain secondary structural and functional changes.

In sheep, the accumulation of fat is concentrated either in the rump or the tail. Fat-rumped breeds may have very short tails or be completely devoid of caudal vertebrae, while in fat-tailed breeds, the tail displays a marked variability in size and conformation, in some breeds attaining so great a length as to sweep the ground. Fat-tailed breeds extend over a large part of southern Asia, a small area in southeastern Europe, and the whole of Africa, excluding Somaliland and the tropical forest belt. Fat-rumped sheep are bred in the Horn of Africa, southern Arabia, and Iran, extending from the Black Sea through Turkestan, Mongolia, and Manchuria to China, and including the greater part of Siberia.

The development of store reserves of energy in the tail or rump, on which the animal draws during periods of nutritional scarcity, is explainable through the agency of artificial selection. This implies that fat deposits on the tail and rump of sheep may sporadically occur among any breed but that it was only in steppe and desert regions and among peoples lacking other fat-producing animals that these features were considered of sufficient economic importance to induce breeders to select specimens with adipose deposits for breeding purposes. Among ordinary sheep, the occurrence of both fat-rumped and fat-tailed animals has been recorded. The Cotswold and Romney Marsh breeds exhibit a marked tendency to accumulate fat on the rump almost to the degree of producing a deformity.[38] In some Border-Leicester rams there is a considerable amount of fat at the root of the tail or on the buttocks.[39] Since there exists no economic necessity in Britain to produce a fat-rumped or fat-tailed breed of sheep, such animals are not selected for breeding purposes; on the contrary, they are culled, as the fat deposits in the rump and tail are considered undesirable. Fat-tailed and fat-rumped sheep were developed in steppe and desert regions where such animals proved more resistant during periods of drought than the bulk of the ordinary stock, and where the fat-producing swine was lacking for religious reasons or because the nature of swine is unsuited to the roaming life of nomads.

Milk. The first development of a dairy type in cattle took place during the period of the urban revolution in Sumer and Elam, where the fertility of the soil and the cooperative effort of a planned society enabled farmers to produce a surplus of foodstuffs. Villages expanded into cities, surrounded by gardens, fields, and pastures. Artisans, laborers, transport workers, and traders were withdrawn from direct food production. The temples of the priesthood, where the wealth was concentrated, provided breeding stock, farm equip-

---

[37]H. H. Curson and J. H. R. Bisschop, "Some Comments on the Hump of African Cattle," *Onderstepoort Journal of Veterinary Science and Animal Industry*, V (1935), 621–44.
[38]Richard Lydekker, *The Sheep and Its Cousins* (London: G. Allen, 1912), p. 118.
[39]J. Cossar Ewart, "Domesticated Sheep and Their Wild Ancestors: Wild Sheep of the Argali Type," *Transactions of the Highland and Agricultural Society of Scotland*, XXVI (1914), p. 90.

ment, boats, and tools.[40] The demand of urban society for a regular supply of milk and dairy products called for a type of cattle adapted for this purpose. From Mesopotamia, this new type spread in three main directions: (1) eastwards, north of the zebu belt, to the shores of the Pacific; (2) along the eastern and southern coast belt of the Mediterranean, down the west coast of Africa as far as Nigeria; and (3) along the northern littoral of the Mediterranean through Switzerland and the coastlands of the North Sea to the Channel Islands and Britain (Celtic shorthorn).

When the industrialization of western Europe created a market for milk and dairy products, several breeds of cattle were developed to meet these requirements. Outstanding among these are the cattle of the Netherlands, the Jerseys and Guernseys, and the Brown Swiss, all of them either entirely or predominantly of the shorthorn type originally evolved for the purpose of supplying milk and dairy products to the urban populations of ancient Mesopotamia.

No other domestic animal, with the exception of the goat, has been developed for the purpose of milk production to the same extent as have cattle. Even the goat is not milked so universally. And the milk of the buffalo, camel, horse, and reindeer is used only in a few restricted areas; no special dairy breeds have been evolved from them. In certain conditions, the sheep approaches the goat as a milk producer. After the Thirty Years' War, milking of sheep became a general practice in central Europe, owing to the lack of cattle, the tremendous loss of population, and the reduced demand for wool. At that time several dairy breeds of sheep were evolved, a remnant of which is still found in the marsh sheep of East Friesland. The dairy properties of sheep have been developed also in some other conditions. Before the Hottentots of South-West Africa came in contact with goat-breeding Bantu peoples, they had no goats and used to milk their fat-tailed sheep and teach their infants to suck the milk straight from the udders.[41] In Southern France, where the true Roquefort cheese commands a high price, sheep are kept for their milk as well as their wool. In the more remote parts of the Balkans, western Asia, and North Africa dairy breeds of sheep are retained in agriculturally and industrially backward regions. But with the growing impact of industrialization on economic and social conditions, dairy sheep breeding is losing its importance even in these countries.

Wool. In the first stage of their exploitation by man, most domestic animals are of no use until they are killed. The sheep was domesticated in order to make human society independent of the vagaries of the hunt for meat and skins. In both the wild and primitive domesticated sheep, the body is covered with a coat of short hair, extending into a mane in mature rams. But already in wild sheep the hair in its structure is definitely wool although it is coarse, stiff, and nearly straight. It possesses the essential character of wool in the finely intricate arrangement of its serrated and imbricated scaly surface that gives to wool the remarkable felting property upon which its peculiar utility depends. Under domestication, the hair has become longer, finer, and wavier, chiefly through selection of suitable breeding stock that appeared either spontaneously or upon the crossing of various strains of domesticated sheep. And as the woolly fleece could repeatedly be plucked or shorn from the live animal, the sheep entered a higher stage of exploitation by man—the stage of its usefulness for its wool while alive, and for mutton and skin after exhaustion of its usefulness as a source of wool. Only in countries with a warm climate where people have no need for wool, as in southern Asia and in Africa south of the Sahara, primitive breeds of woolless sheep have survived to this day.

In goats, the hair has not developed the peculiar quality of felting. For this reason mohair and cashmere, although valuable textile fibers on account of their luster, length, fineness, and strength, have but a restricted use: mohair in the manufacture of upholstery and lining materials, rugs, summer suits, draperies, and decorative trimmings, and cashmere in the manufacture of shawls. And, unlike wool, which has been bred into every improved breed

---

[40]Childe, *What Happened in History,* p. 95.
[41]Epstein, "Animal Husbandry of the Hottentots," p. 660.

of sheep, mohair and cashmere have remained the respective properties of only two breeds of goat, the Angora and Cashmere.

Improvement of wool in sheep has taken two main directions: the elimination of colored wool and breeding for white fleeces as a prerequisite of dyeing, and the improvement in the weight and quality of fleeces, more especially the elimination of kemp.

With the gradual shift of economic power from western Asia to Greece, and from Greece to Rome, the wool industry migrated to the western Mediterranean region. Breeding stock was imported from Asia Minor by way of Samos to Attica and Epirus. From Greece, fine-wooled sheep were brought to Sicily and lower Italy, and to the ancient Greek colony of Massilia at the mouth of the Rhone, whence they reached the Iberian peninsula. During the 450 years of their rule, the Romans imported large numbers of fine-wooled sheep into Spain in order to improve the local breeds. Gades and Cordoba became the marketing centers that furnished Rome with the finest woolen cloth. The setback to the Spanish wool industry, caused by the Visigoth invasion in 456, was of short duration as the newcomers soon settled down to an agricultural existence. When the Moors conquered Spain in 712, they found a flourishing agriculture and soon developed an extensive weaving industry which became famous throughout the medieval world. As soon as the Moors were driven out, the Catholic church and nobility got hold of the merino flocks which produced the best type of wool then known anywhere.

During the latter part of the eighteenth century there was an ever growing demand for wool of an extremely fine fiber suitable for the manufacture of soft fabrics such as broadcloth. To meet this demand, merino flocks of Spanish origin, established in Saxony, Silesia, Prussia, Austria, and Italy, were bred for the single purpose of producing such fine wool. The flocks of Saxony in particular became world famous for the most marvelous fleeces ever known— wool of gemlike luster, so beautifully fine and even and of such exquisite downiness of touch that all other wools seemed base by the side of it.[42]

Social development in England favored the growing of wool, since the great plague of 1348 had reduced the number of laborers to such an extent that landowners were obliged to turn their lands into pastures. Wool became the sheet anchor of English farming. During the reign of Edward III (1327–1377), Flemish weavers, dyers, and fullers, skilled in the then most advanced methods of cloth making, were induced to settle in England by a grant of special protection. They were joined by others of their countrymen who came to England as refugees in the reign of Elizabeth.[43] However, climatic conditions did not encourage English farmers to produce so fine a wool as that of the Spanish merino; and at the time when the merino craze swept over Europe, the enormous industrial expansion and growth of urban populations caused such a rapid advance in land values that it no longer paid the English farmer to keep sheep for their wool alone. After the Napoleonic wars, England's export wool trade was cut away at its roots and English wool could not even hold its own in the home markets. By 1824, it had become unsalable in the face of competition by cheap Silesian and other German wools, and duties were unable to protect the local industry. The merino, therefore, could not gain a foothold in Britain and it is no coincidence that Robert Bakewell made a mutton breed of the Leicester sheep, with complete disregard for its wool, and that all the breeds of sheep subsequently evolved in Britain were of the mutton type. Wool could be grown more cheaply and profitably on the wide pastures of the colonies.

While this development started in Britain, then industrially the most advanced country, it did not end there. With the rise of industrialization, a similar development took place in central and western Europe. In Germany, within the nineteenth century the value of mutton increased five times in relation to the value of wool and the type of sheep bred in western Europe changed accordingly.

Even in Australia, New Zealand, and the Argentine, where the bulk of the wool was formerly produced by pure merinos, the rise in the importance of mutton, since the introduction of refrigerating plants in cargo vessels, has

[42]Robert H. Burns and E. L. Moody, "The Trek of the Golden Fleece," *Journal of Heredity*, XXVI (1935), 433–43.
[43]Walter C. Coffey, *Productive Sheep Husbandry* (3rd ed.; rev. by William G. Kammlade, Chicago, Philadelphia, etc.: Lippincott, 1937), pp. 6–7.

resulted in a large amount of cross-breeding and coarsening of the wool. The days have passed when in the more remote districts of Australia the value of a shorn sheep was approximately one shilling, that is, one fifth of the value of its annual yield of wool.[44] With the invention of combs that will comb comparatively short wool, long fine wool has become relatively less valuable than formerly. Manufacturers can now combine quality, length, and strength more cheaply and speedily than the wool grower can through breeding. Hence, sheep farmers no longer attempt to get into the fleece the maximum of fineness, length, and weight; and a different type of sheep producing a stronger wool and superior mutton, has gradually replaced the fine-wooled merino type all over the world.

---

[44]Friedrich Aereboe, *Allgemeine landwirtschaftliche Betriebslehre* (6th ed.; Berlin: P. Parey, 1923), p. 379.

Selection 8

Development
of Modern Agriculture

Commentary

Horticulture evolved into agriculture, most authorities agree in the Fertile Crescent—the border area of Iran and Iraq—and Mesopotamia. The change at first was one of degree, a transition from mixed crop fields of a swidden-type system to specialized crops, from the hoe to the plow, from simple gardening to technology and its subsequent development of complex social and political organization. In fact, it is difficult to separate the development of agriculture from the cultural development of man, from changes in political organization and stratification of social classes, and from the evolution of the modern state.

There are important differences between horticulture and agriculture. Horticulture depends upon natural husbandry. Ecologically, it is more closely tied to the functioning of natural ecosystems. Although the native vegetation is destroyed, the material is burned and the mineral matter at least is returned to the soil. The vegetation, even though domesticated and cultivated, is diversified and grows in layers or strata. A number of different crops are grown together from roots to grains and fruits. Even in simpler horticulture this is true. The Indian tribes of eastern North America grew corn, beans, and squash in the same plot, the three forming a sort of symbiotic relationship. The corn was dominant, grew tall, and claimed most of the sunlight. But the corn supported the beanstalks in their climb to sunlight, and the beans, being a legume, returned nitrogen to the soil. The lower stratum in the field was claimed by squash and pumpkins, whose vines covered the ground. The result was a protective cover of vegetation whose strata made full use of sunlight and moisture, an adequate substitute for the natural cover that once existed there. The crops in the tropics especially are continually being harvested and replanted and for a disturbed plot the nutrient cycle was nearly closed. When the plots are abandoned, the land reverts by natural succession back to natural vegetation. Under ideal conditions, the land is renewed and the nutrient cycles are restored to some degree of stability by ecological succession.

Agriculture, on the other hand, is characterized by a complete destruction of natural vegetation. The seed bed is carefully prepared and the seeds are drilled in the open soil. The growth of weeds is controlled and there is no stratification or layering. Only one crop is planted to a field; diversity is exchanged for mono-culture. Crops are further cultivated, keeping the soil disturbed and subject to erosion. The harvest is a one-time operation at the end of the growing season. Cover is removed from the soil and the field lies fallow until the next planting season. Nutrient cycles are open and nutrient outputs by leaching and erosion are great. Balance is maintained only by heavy inputs of fertilizer and manure. The output is greatest in grain agriculture. In northern Europe and in dairy and beef regions of the United States, animal husbandry is the most conservative in outputs. With a heavy emphasis on corn-grain-legume rotations or straight grassland farming, the ground cover is better protected from erosion, and manure provides top dressing for the fields.

In return for a dependable food supply, man exchanged mobility and dietary variety. He traded his role of a generalist in the production of food for that of a specialist. In so doing he made two critical changes from a horticultural existence, changes that affected the course of human history. One was the need for an extrapersonal source of power. The horticulturalist depends on his own muscular energy for the work involved in the production of food, a source of energy which is under his own control. The agriculturalist depends upon the draft animal (or mechanized power), or upon complex technology, such as elaborate irrigation works that involve skillful engineering, or upon terracing that requires careful construction and upkeep, or perhaps upon any combination of the three. To provide the power and the technology requires a much more sophisticated political organization than that needed by the horticulturalist's society. To furnish the necessary power, there arose a need for a system to supply draft animals, under which they could be borrowed, rented, or exchanged. A monopolistic control of draft animals arose which in turn eventually stimulated the development of a system of social stratification, as exemplified by the normal system of the middle ages. Where irrigation or terracing was necessary, the engineering involved and the sources of labor required were available only under some system or centralized control.

Sedentary agricultural man no longer had access to certain resources that he still desired. To obtain them he had to bargain and trade what surplus goods he had with neighboring peoples who had what he wanted and who needed what he could trade. Economic needs stimulated trade between and even specialization within villages. The conduct of trade required some political organization that could control production and redistribution. In early times it may have been an authoritative chief, a temple, a marketplace. In time, trade and redistribution of products and food required a more sophisticated political system.

A growing agricultural technology meant that fewer people were required to grow food. This freed a number of people from the land and stimulated the development of craftsmen, who were needed to support the technology, and bureaucrats, who were needed to run the political systems of emerging villages and cities. The craftsmen furnished the farmers with the goods they needed; the farmers in turn supplied both the craftsmen and the bureaucrats with food. Surpluses produced under economic incentives and political coercion were used by bureaucracy to support its own existence and to develop trade. This in turn encouraged regional specialization in production of foods that people could buy and sell to each other or even use to gain political advantages. At the same time it also increased stratification of social classes.

Along with rising technology in agriculture came land ownership. The hunting man and even horticultural man knew nothing of land ownership. All the land belonged to the tribe or the village. With the rise of agriculture, land ownership assumed considerable importance, especially when a certain amount of capital had to be invested for production. In time land ownership fell into the hands not of the farmer but of ruling classes. In England this reached its acme in the 1700s, when the aristocracy incorporated the bulk of the commons (common pasture used collectively by the peasants) into their own estates and drove small freeholders off the land and onto the relief rolls. Social relationships became further stratified with land ownership. At the top were the landowners or rulers, then the craftsmen who depended on both the rulers and the farmers, and finally the farmers or peasants. Each developed his own value systems, but the greatest division existed between the rural and the urban classes, particularly the rulers and landowners and the peasants.

Not only was this difference pronounced at the social level, it was also pronounced in the attitudes of each toward the land. The large landholders (or absentee landlords) and rulers looked upon land as an economic resource, a way to make money. The peasant and the small landholder both had a passion toward the land that became the mark of "peasantry—an attachment," as E. E. Evans writes,

> deepened by the devotion of daily work and seasonal festival and by the traditional use of home-grown foods, and of local materials for tools, crafts, clothing, and housing.... The peasant, in continuous touch with the whole cycle of production, can sense the wholeness of life and derive therefrom satisfaction and self-confidence.[1]

This quality was lacking in other classes.

Agriculture grew out of primitive technology, such as the invention of the plow, and perhaps the pressures of an increasing number of mouths to feed, although Carl Sauer[2] suggests that domestication and planting started from leisure and surplus. Before 3000 B.C. man learned how to make a rude plow, harness animals to wheeled vehicles, drain and reclaim swamps, irrigate dry land, and grow crops and fruits. Out of this knowledge grew cities and new technology that in turn was applied to agriculture. Technology begot advanced agriculture, advanced agriculture begot more technology.

Breakthroughs in science added to agricultural productivity. The discoveries of von Leibig that the addition of such nutrients as nitrogen, phosphorus, and potassium could renew the fertility of the soil led to the use of fertilizers to increase crop production without increasing acreage of land under cultivation. The discoveries of genetics, made possible by the work of Mendel, enabled plant breeders to tailor plants and animals to regional needs. Plants were made more tolerant to cold, more resistant to drought and disease, higher yielding, more responsive to fertilizers. Cows were bred for high milk production, chickens for maximum egg production, and meat animals for high gains and rapid maturity. The invention of the internal combustion engine enabled farmers to replace draft animals with tractors and thereby substituted the by-product of photosynthesis—petroleum—for corn, oats, and hay. This released vast acreages once needed to feed draft animals for food production and other purposes.

The replacement of draft animals by tractors was a technological change that took place most rapidly after World War II and led to another revolutionary development of agriculture in the United States—industrialization. Prior to and during World War II the United States was still a land of family farms. Loss of manpower on the farm during World War II and the failure of men to return to the land after the war forced increased mechanization. Mechanization involved a heavy outlay of capital that most family farms could not raise. The

[1]E. E. Evans, "The Ecology of Peasant Life in Western Europe," *Man's Role in Changing the Face of the Earth*, Chicago, Ill., University of Chicago Press, 1956, pp. 217–239.

[2]Carl. O. Sauer, "The Agency of Man on Earth," *Man's Role in Changing the Face of the Earth*, Chicago, Ill., University of Chicago Press, 1956, pp. 49–69.

return per unit of food produced was so low that only by expansion and specialization could the farmer make a living from the land. Small farms either were abandoned if marginal or absorbed into larger farms by owners or corporations who could afford them and obtain a return from the heavy investment. Food subsidies, whose original purpose was to aid the family farm, served instead the interests of commercialized farming. Thus, technology was eliminating the smaller farmer whose attachment for the land was similar to that of the older peasant and forcing him to the city. In too many instances he is being replaced with a commercialized, highly mechanized farmer whose interest in the land, like that of the lord of the manor, is wholly economic. Land becomes a commodity, something to be mined or exploited.

At least two aspects of technological agriculture tend to depress the effects of increased production. First, few people are needed on the land; more and more are sent unemployed to growing urban areas that draw their subsistence from the land. Second, too much technology may destroy agriculture. Modern commercial agriculture rests on a delicate base of chemical fertilizers, insecticides, too little return of organic matter back to the soil, and heavy machinery that can destroy the structure of the soil. Arthur Toynbee[3] advanced the theory that progress in the art of agriculture brought on a general decline in Greece and Rome. Their change from mixed crops to specialized agriculture for export was followed by an outburst of energy and growth. This greatly increased the productivity of the land and the profit of the capitalist but it reduced the land to social sterility. As Margaret Mead[4] points out, food divided from its primary function of feeding people and treated simply as a commercial commodity loses this primary significance. Land is mined instead of being replenished and conserved. "The social consequence," writes Toynbee, "was the depopulation of the countryside and the creation of a parasitic urban proletariat in the cities." The agricultural system persisted until it collapsed spontaneously in consequence of the breakdown of the money economy on which it depended.

---

[3]A. J. Toynbee, *Study of History*. New York, Oxford University Press, 1939.
[4]Margaret Mead, "The Changing Significance of Food," *American Scientist* **58**, 176—181.

Selection 8

Development of Modern Agriculture

by Wayne D. Rasmussen

When agriculture appeared in written history in the time of the Egyptians, Greeks, and Romans, it was already a highly developed art, backed by years of progress based on observation and trial and error. Some early Chinese historians assigned the beginning of agriculture in China to a specific year, 2737 B.C., when a continuous record of political life was started. Farming undoubtedly had been practiced before that particular year, but giving a new ruler credit for teaching farming to the people indicates the value they placed on it.

Agriculture enabled a man to produce more than enough food for himself and his family. Some labor thus could be released for the development of other aspects of civilization, such as industry, the arts and sciences, government, and writing.

Ancient civilizations, from the invention of writing to the beginning of the Christian Era, saw the adoption of systems of land use aimed at preserving or restoring soil fertility. The first farmers had practiced natural husbandry; that is, simply sowing and reaping. They moved on to new land when yields declined.

Sometimes the increase in population that usually followed the establishment of a settled village economy made it difficult to move to new land. In several parts of the world farmers then turned to fallow. Every year, according

---

THIS SELECTION is extracted from "Valley to Valley, Country to Country," in 1964 Yearbook of Agriculture *Farmer's World*, pp. 1—11. U.S. Department of Agriculture, Washington, D.C.

to some plan which became fixed, part of the land was given special treatment. No seed would be planted on it. The weeds and grass would be plowed under at least once during the growing season so as to rid it of some weeds and parasites, add vegetable matter, and conserve moisture. The fallow system was used in ancient Greece and Rome, in China from perhaps as early as 2000 B.C., and in Germany and northern Europe through medieval times.

But farmers of ancient times did not rely solely on fallowing to improve the soil. Ashes, animal manure, and composts were used in the Middle East, Greece, and Rome. The Greeks and Romans added lime in various forms.

The Roman farmers could draw upon farm manuals by Cato the Censor, writing about 200 B.C., or his successors, including Varro and Columella, for advice on ways to grow olives and grapes and press the fruits for oil and juice. Bread, oil, wine, figs, and grapes were staples in the ancient Mediterranean diet.

Improvements spread slowly.

The methods the ancients used survived with modifications in many parts of the world for centuries.

Fallowing, for example, was the basis for England's well-known two- and three-field systems of medieval times. The medieval English manor, with its villagers and lord, was divided into garden, arable, meadow, pasture, and waste land. The arable land was divided into two or three large fields, which in turn were divided into strips of an acre or less. Each villager would farm a number of scattered strips. Under the two-field system, half the land was left fallow. The other half was planted with winter and spring grain. In the three-field system, one field was fallow, one was planted in wheat or rye, and one was planted in some spring crop, such as barley, oats, peas, or beans. The three-field system permitted as much as 50 percent greater productivity than the two-field system.

Two other developments in northern Europe during medieval times also increased productivity: A heavy plow that could turn the soil was invented. The invention of the horse collar permitted the effective use of horsepower.

Fallowing sometimes gave way to rotations. Nitrogen-fixing legumes—peas, beans, vetches, alfalfa—would be grown on a field formerly fallow. The system arose through trial and error after it was noted that small grain planted on land formerly in legumes usually yielded more. It was practiced oftenest when towns and cities arose and farmers had a ready market for all they could produce. Legume rotation succeeded fallowing in limited areas of ancient Greece and Rome, in part of China shortly before the Christian Era, and in Germany and England in the 16th century.

As the medieval period passed in Europe, the beginning of the modern age was marked by a renewed interest of Europeans in other parts of the world, followed by exploration and by conquest. Some early explorers brought foreign plants and animals back to Europe.

. . .

The first European colonists in the New World, particularly in what is now the United States, found it difficult to adapt European methods to American conditions. They faced starvation and survived only because of supplies received from the mother countries and the food they bought or took from the Indians. The permanence of the Colonies was not assured until agriculture was securely established, and that came after they adopted the crops and tillage methods of the natives.

While the Indians of America contributed much to world agriculture, the Europeans who conquered and settled the New World introduced livestock, crops, and tools.

The axe and the plow, with the animals to pull the plows, were carried to America by all of the national groups entering the New World.

The Spaniards brought alfalfa, barley, flax, oats, sugarcane, wheat, and many others. They brought their grapes, oranges, peaches, pears, and other fruits and vegetables.

By 1606, the French had planted cabbage, flax, hemp, oats, rye, wheat, and other crops in Canada.

The English brought all the crops and livestock they had grown at home. Other nations introduced particular breeds and varieties of animals and plants.

The new settlers themselves made some improvements. For example, John Rolfe of Virginia obtained tobacco seed from South America in 1612 and raised a crop from it, which established American exports of tobacco to England.

The agricultural methods brought to the New World by the first European immigrants differed little from those of a thousand years earlier. Yet Europe, particularly England, was on the verge of a new era of developments that were to culminate in an agricultural revolution and were marked by the scientific rotation of crops and, in England, by the enclosure of many fields and scattered strips of land. Rotation and enclosure were a result of a growing market economy and the consequent emphasis on commercial farming.

Greater emphasis on commercial farming led to some consolidation of holdings in England under the open-field system. At the same time, some pastures and croplands were enclosed. The enclosure movement in the 16th century was undertaken mainly to furnish pasturelands for sheep—the demand for wool of the spinning and weaving industries was more effective than the demand for wheat.

The development of scientific rotations owed much to new methods and crops introduced from other European nations. Clover was introduced from Spain, turnip cultivation from Flanders, and new grasses from France. Although their value was recognized by the end of the 16th century, they were not widely grown until later.

Farm tools were crude at the beginning of the period. The large and cumbersome wooden plows usually were drawn by oxen. After the soil was broken, iron- or wooden-toothed harrows were pulled over the land. All crops were seeded by hand. Grain crops were cut with scythes or reaping hooks and threshed with flails. Hoes, mattocks, spades, and forks completed the list.

Often the ideas for machines were well known before they were adopted. Grain drills are an example. The Chinese had used a wheelbarrow drill as early as 2800 B.C. The first English patent was granted in 1623. A more practical drill was described by John Worlidge in 1669. Not until about 1700, however, when Jethro Tull made and publicized a seed drill, did these devices attract much attention. Tull also urged the adoption of the French horse hoe, or cultivator.

Many types of plows were used in Great Britain, but the first definite step toward making plows in factories came in 1730, when the Rotherham plow was introduced. It had a colter and share made of iron and may have been brought to England from Holland. It was called the Dutch plow in Scotland.

The introduction of root crops, clover, and grasses into a four-course crop rotation provided support for a larger number of livestock. The principle of selective breeding had been known for generations, but the creation of new breeds that gave general satisfaction was a long process. Improvement of the old native varieties by crossing with the newer breeds took longer.

The improvement of livestock was related to the enclosure of former open-field farms and the conversion of common and waste land into pasture. The movement began in the 16th century and was partly arrested by legislation; in the 18th century it received support from Parliament. The enclosure of pastures gave the livestock farmers control over breeding and permitted more rapid improvements in their herds.

All of these slow changes in English farming resulted in an agricultural revolution, which reached its peak in the first half of the 19th century. By then, greatly improved methods had been adopted, total output of farm products and output per man-hour had gone up, and livestock and crop husbandry seemed to be in balance with each other and the rest of the economy.

Over a period of 150 years, a number of agricultural leaders influenced British farmers and landowners to adopt improved practices. They were able to influence farming because industrialization, improved transportation, and other economic forces made the adoption of the improvements practical and profitable.

The most noted of the reformers were Jethro Tull (1674—1740), Charles Townshend (1674—1738), Robert Bakewell (1725—1795), Arthur Young (1741—1820), Sir John Sinclair (1745—1835), and Thomas Coke (1752—1842).

Tull invented a grain drill and advocated more intensive cultivation and the use of animal power. Townshend set an example of better farming through improvements in crop rotations and in emphasizing the field cultivation of turnips and clover. Bakewell devoted himself to developing better breeds of livestock. Young and Sinclair were influential writers, whose works were studied in many parts of the world. Coke developed a model agricultural estate, working particularly with wheat and sheep. Farm leaders and statesmen from many parts of the world visited his estate.

Other European countries contributed to the agricultural revolution, but advance was most rapid in England. The physiocrats, a school of economists who emphasized the importance and virtue of agriculture, influenced agricultural thought in France in the 18th century. They appeared to yearn for earlier days when agrarian interests were dominant but were indifferent to proved methods of progressive farming. For example, fallowing persisted in most of France, with little protest from the physiocrats, long after the value of the scientific rotation of crops had been demonstrated in England.

France contributed a new method of food preservation, canning. It permitted the year-round use of many otherwise perishable foods. In 1795, when France was at war, the Government offered a prize to the citizen who could devise a method of preserving food for transport on military and naval campaigns. The prize was awarded in 1810 to Nicolas Appert, a Parisian confectioner. He had filled bottles with various foods, sealed the bottles, and cooked them in boiling water.

The Napoleonic wars also gave impetus to the sugarbeet industry. Andreas Marggraf, a German chemist, in 1747 had crystallized sucrose from beets. One of his pupils, Franz Karl Achard, built the first sugarbeet factory in Silesia in 1802. With imports cut off because of war, Napoleon encouraged the building of a number of factories in France, where the industry persisted. Efforts were made to establish factories in the United States from 1830 on; the first successful American plant opened in California in 1879.

As the European nations expanded their colonies over the world, they influenced farming everywhere. The influence was greatest in the thinly populated regions, such as the New World and Australia, and least in densely populated regions like India.

When Napoleon led his armies into Egypt in 1798, he commented on the good quality of its agricultural produce and suggested that with French help the Nile Valley could become a Garden of Eden. He established a plant introduction garden in Egypt in 1800 and asked for French fruit trees. A group of French gardeners set out for Egypt the next year, but the British captured them at sea.

Many years later, in 1882, the British began a policy of agricultural reform and assistance in Egypt, building in part upon reforms introduced by the rulers of Egypt in the preceding decades. During the first decade of British rule, many irrigation works were completed and repaired, and the first Aswan dam was begun. The acreage brought under cultivation increased.

Europe's greatest impact on world agriculture followed the discovery, conquest, and settlement of the New World and, later, the development of reforms and improvements, which encouraged changes in farming.

For more than a century, however, Americans knew little of the changes in European agriculture. Gradually, scientific societies, such as the American Philosophical Society, founded in 1743, encouraged the investigation of European ideas and experiences and agricultural experimentation. Societies devoted entirely to agriculture were not organized until the United States had declared its independence. The first of record was established in New Jersey in 1781. The Philadelphia Society for Promoting Agriculture and the South Carolina Society for Promoting and Improving Agriculture were founded in 1785.

The early agricultural societies were groups of men of all professions who could afford to experiment and who would seek out the adapt to American conditions the progress made in other countries. None were farmers who depended solely on the produce of their farms for a living. Among them were George Washington and Thomas Jefferson. They corresponded with English agricultural reformers. Both were interested in soil conservation. Washington was first in this country to raise mules. Jefferson introduced upland rice and designed a hillside plow, a moldboard for a plow that would turn the soil, and other implements.

The changes in England during the 18th century included the development of improved breeds of livestock. The first importations of Bakewell's improved cattle were made by two gentlemen farmers of Maryland and Virginia in 1783. Large numbers of Merino sheep were imported from France and Spain a few years later. The first Hereford cattle were imported by another statesman, Henry Clay, in 1817. Nevertheless, most American livestock during the first half of the 19th century wandered about the open countryside.

Some leaders recognized the need to reach ordinary farmers. Elkanah Watson organized the Berkshire Agricultural Society at Pittsfield, Mass., in 1811. Its purpose was to hold an annual fair for the farmers of the community. The idea spread rapidly but declined when farmers did not realize their exaggerated hopes of benefits to be gained. Farm journals, first the *Agricultural Museum* in 1810 and then the *American Farmer* in 1819, also tried, but they received little support.

Production per man-hour in the United States increased only a little from 1800 to 1840 and somewhat more from 1840 to 1860.

But a technological foundation was being laid for a revolution in production. At the beginning of the period, the cotton gin, invented in 1793 by Eli Whitney, greatly changed agriculture in the South. The cheap, efficient separation of the seeds from the fiber encouraged planters to grow more cotton. The extensive commercial production of cotton dominated farming and led to the expansion of the plantation system. The South grew the one crop and neglected more diversified agriculture, while it depended on England and the North for markets and for supplies of other farm products and manufactured articles. At the same time, cotton cultivation brought about the rapid settlement of the region and returned large sums to the planters.

A cast-iron plow with interchangeable parts, patented in 1819 by Jethro Wood, was a major contribution. It would not scour in the heavy soils of the prairies, however; the soil clung to the moldboard instead of sliding by and turning over. Two Illinois blacksmiths, John Lane in 1833 and John Deere in 1837, solved the problem by using a smooth steel and polished wrought iron for the shares and moldboards of their plows.

The mechanical reaper was probably the most significant single invention introduced into American farming between 1800 and the Civil War. It replaced much human power at the crucial point in grain production when the work must be completed quickly to save a crop from ruin. The reapers patented by Obed Hussey in 1833 and Cyrus H. McCormick in 1834 marked the transition from the hand to the machine age of farming.

Many other farm machines were invented between 1830 and 1860, and the bases for other farm improvements were laid. Edmund Ruffin, sometimes called America's first soil scientist, had urged the chemical analysis of

soil and the use of marl as early as 1821. His work preceded that of Justus von Liebig, the great German chemist who published *Chemistry in Its Applications to Agriculture and Physiology* in 1840. Liebig's theories brought science to agriculture in Europe, and his influence was felt in America.

Commercial fertilizer was used in the United States, beginning with Peruvian guano in the 1840's. Mixed chemical fertilizer first appeared on the market in 1849. Modern irrigation agriculture began in the United States in 1847, when Mormon pioneers opened a ditch in Utah.

The United States Congress in 1862 passed four laws, all signed by President Abraham Lincoln, which were to help transform American agriculture. The Homestead Act encouraged western settlement. The Morill Land-Grant College Act encouraged agricultural education. The act establishing the Department of Agriculture provided a means for assisting farmers to adopt better methods. The act chartering the Union Pacific Railroad assisted in opening western land.

Agriculture from 1850 to 1870 was a decisive element in our economic development. The coming together of various lines of technology, the emphasis on agricultural revolution. The profitability of farming was due primarily to the greatly increased overseas demands for American farm products and the demand for products to support the armies in the Civil War.

The Nation's farms produced enough food and fiber to satisfy the needs of our growing population and to dominate our exports. Agricultural exports in 1865 were 82.6 percent in value of our total exports. This percentage declined slowly but did not fall below 50 percent until 1911. Both value and volume increased year to year, but less rapidly than other exports.

The United States was not alone in increasing its total volume of agricultural exports after 1865.

Argentina, Australia, Canada, and New Zealand became competitive with the United States in shipping grain and livestock products to Europe, although commercial agriculture began about a generation later than in America. The use of refrigeration in steamships, beginning in the 1870's, offered better opportunity to get livestock products to markets.

Refrigerated ships gave Argentina its opportunity to market fresh beef in England. Modern agriculture began in Argentina in 1856, with the arrival of 208 Swiss families. A considerable flow of European immigration fol-fowed. The immigrants established and developed the great cereal belt, and later the sugar, vineyard, cotton, and fruit belts. Herd improvement, beginning about 1860, aided sheep and cattle raising, which the Spanish settlers had established.

The manorial system, established in Canada by the first French colonists, was not abolished there until 1854. Agriculture thereafter developed more rapidly in Quebec, particularly after dairying became profitable. The Civil War in the United States hastened the transition from wheat growing to mixed farming in Ontario. At about the same time, wheat growing began in the Red River Valley and then spread slowly over the prairie provinces. The creation of a variety of wheat known as Marquis, by Sir Charles E. Saunders, and its distribution to Canadian farmers beginning in 1908, was a triumph for Canadian scientific endeavor.

Wool dominated exports from Australia throughout the 19th century. It more than quadrupled in value from 1861 to 1890. During this period, millions of acres of pasture were fenced, which led to better breeding, conservation of the soil, and greater production per man-hour.

European farming was not established in New Zealand until after 1840. The outbreak of war with the native Maoris in 1859, which led to the sending of British troops to the islands, and the discovery of gold in 1861 meant a great rise in population and a larger market for food products. Over time, wheat and wool came to be the major enterprises. Both were produced for export. The introduction of refrigeration in 1882 opened new possibilities. Meat—beef, mutton, and lamb—was shipped to England immediately. Exports of butter were large after 1900. Farming became a collection of specialized industries during the 20th century.

At about the same time New Zealand was developing as an agricultural nation, another country far to the north was opening its doors to Western civilization. Japan in 1854 granted the United States minor trading concessions, a major departure from its previous isolationism.

At about the same time, the feudal system collapsed, and Japan began rapid economic growth.

Concerned with its northern frontiers, Japan determined to colonize Hokkaido, an island that seemed to offer opportunity for agricultural development. The Japanese turned to America for help because weather conditions on Hokkaido and in the Northeastern United States were similar, America led the world in the use of farm machinery, and the United States was isolated from any international controversy.

The Japanese Government hired Horace Capron, Commissioner of the newly established Department of Agriculture, to head a mission to Japan. He arrived in Japan in the fall of 1871 with his group and remained there 4 years. Despite difficulties, which at times seemed insurmountable, the mission got a new, modern agricultural development underway in Hokkaido and had much to do with paving the way for better farming in Japan.

The Capron mission was responsible for establishing the first railway in Japan and encouraging the development of waterpower. By the First World War, Japan was a modern industrial nation. An authority on the economic history of Japan has said: "... it was the expansion of Japan's basic economy—agriculture and small-scale industry built on traditional foundations—which accounted for most of the growth of national productivity and income during this period."

Russia, Japan's rival in the Far East during the second half of the 19th century, liberated its serfs in 1861 and gave them allotments of land, administered through a communal system.

This accelerated a process of rural transformation, even though Russia suffered a great famine in 1891–1892. The period saw the encouragement of cotton growing in Turkestan and a sizable movement of peasants from European Russia into Siberia. The Russian Government made an effort to cultivate varieties of cotton that were suited to the climate of Turkestan and produced the finest staple. It kept in close touch with the U.S. Department of Agriculture, asking for samples of American cottonseed, information regarding types of staple, and advice in general. It was also cooperative in offering the United States its experience with American cotton, as well as with wheat and other crops that were of interest to American growers.

These vignettes indicate that the years between 1850 and the First World War were years of agricultural change and development in many parts of the world. In other areas, particularly those with large populations held in colonial status, there was little or no advance.

We should bear in mind, however, that technological improvement in any aspect of farming may draw on experience from several sources.

Several European nations, for example, made substantial contributions during the 19th century to the development of dairying.

Major breeds of dairy cattle developed in Europe included the Ayrshire in southwestern Scotland, the Guernsey and Jersey in the Channel Islands, the Holstein-Friesian and the Dutch-Belted in the Netherlands, and the Brown Swiss in Switzerland.

The modern silo for storing green forage for winter use had its beginning in Germany about 1860 and was quickly adopted in France.

A Swede, Carl de Laval, in 1878 invented the centrifugal cream separator, the most important of numerous inventions that helped dairying. An American, Stephen M. Babcock, in 1890 devised a test for measuring the quantity of fat in milk. Milking machines were patented in several countries during this period and came into wide use after the First World War. Taken together, these developments provided the technological basis for modern dairy farming.

American agriculture was approaching a balance with the rest of the economy as the 20th century began. Most farmers produced for the market. The prices they received for their products in relation to prices they paid for other products seemed fair. Horse-drawn machinery had replaced much hand labor on farms. Steam engines were used for plowing and threshing in parts of the West. Inventors were at work improving tractors with internal combustion engines. Lime and chemical fertilizer were widely used in the South and East. Draining in some areas and irrigation in others made land more productive. The agricultural colleges and the Department of Agriculture had brought science to bear on farming, even though farmers were sometimes slow to adopt their recommendations. The establishment of the cooperative extension service in 1914 meant that a college-trained county agent carried the results of research to farmers.

The First World War caused major dislocations in European agriculture for nearly 6 years. The food and fiber exporting nations found demand for their products virtually unlimited.

Prices rose, and many individual farmers in commercial farming areas throughout the world expanded their operations. Demand continued for about 2 years after the end of the war in 1918. By the summer of 1920, European agriculture had made a remarkable recovery, and some European countries embarked upon a program of agricultural self-sufficiency. World prices of many farm products declined sharply as a result.

World agriculture, at least among the countries producing surpluses for export, suffered chronic depression during the twenties and early thirties. Some countries developed plans to aid their farmers by influencing foreign marketing. In a few instances, where one controlled a substantial part of the supply of a commodity, attempts were made to control exports and thus raise prices.

Several nations, during the depression years, began to make particular efforts to help their farmers by extending credit, supporting farm prices, or establishing production control schemes.

The worldwide agricultural depression saw the continued development of agricultural technology, even though most farmers had neither the capital nor the financial incentive to change their methods.

Agricultural experiment stations in all parts of the world continued to develop better yielding plants and animals and to find new means to combat diseases and insects. Industry improved the tractor and other machines.

The Second World War provided the price incentives for farmers to increase production in every way possible, mainly by the adoption of the latest advances in agricultural technology. There was no postwar deflation like that following the first war. Continued postwar demand for food in many parts of the world and price supports of one type or another for farm products kept prices up. The result was great technological advance in much of the world.

In the United States, the revolution included widespread progress in mechanization, with gasoline tractors displacing horses and mules.

The commercial production of cottonpickers after the war completed the mechanization of cotton production.

Greater use of lime and fertilizer, the widespread use of cover crops and other conservation practices and improved varieties, the adoption of hybrid corn, a better balanced feeding of livestock, the more effective control of insects and disease, and the use of chemicals for such purposes as weed-killers and defoliants were part of the technological revolution.

Artificial breeding, which drew on earlier experiences in the Soviet Union and Denmark, brought major changes to the dairy industry. Such chemicals as gibberellic acid, a plant growth regulator first discovered in Japan, were placed on the market.

Hybrid sorghums, chickens, and pigs, following the great success of hybrid corn brought our production to new heights.

The successful development of freezing food for retail sale, beginning before the First World War, and the commercial adoption of freeze-drying in the early sixties improved food marketing. Sales of partially processed and ready-to-eat convenience foods, many of them frozen, increased markedly after the war. Attractive packaging, control of quality, and improvements in supermarkets helped give Americans a constantly improving diet.

Similar advances might be cataloged for most of western Europe and Canada, Australia, New Zealand, Japan, and other countries. Yet the agricultural potentialities of many nations are still underdeveloped.

One of the great opportunites in agriculture today is to help them take part in this technological revolution through the greater development of their own natural and human resources and greater participation in world trade.

The Green Revolution

Commentary

Green Revolution is a familiar term. Specifically it refers to the expanding production of certain food grains in the undeveloped parts of the world, especially Asia. It is touted as an answer to the problem of feeding the expanding population and growing food needs in that part of the world. Historically, the response to increased food needs in Asia, Mexico, and other undeveloped areas of the world was to expand the amount of land under cultivation. But by the early 1960s the supply of new land was used up. The only way to achieve greater food production was to apply technology to increase the production per acre of cropland. This was done with certain crops, particularly corn in Mexico, wheat in Mexico and India, and rice in the Philippines and southeast Asia.

Although the use of the term seems to imply that this is the first green revolution, there have actually been a number of Green Revolutions in the history of agriculture. The first occurred when man learned to domesticate plants, a second when he invented the plow, another when he learned the art of irrigation. Other green revolutions happened when man began to exchange crops from one country to another. Soybeans, the principle source of vegetable oil in the United States, was imported from China. The potato introduced to Europe from America permitted a rapid increase in population in Europe. The introduction of the potato in Ireland resulted in an expanded food supply that supported a rapid population increase until the potato blight devastated the potato crop and caused massive starvation. The history of the potato in Ireland points out both the strength and weakness of any green revolution. One successful crop can support an expanding population, but the heavy dependence upon it—a system of monoculture and its high susceptibility to disease—can lead to catastrophe.

The origin of the Green Revolution as we know it today began in the United States back in the late 1860s, just after the Civil War. At the time of the outbreak of the war, 95 percent of the people of the United States supported the other 5 percent. We were an agrarian country with a low industrial base. The Civil War pointed out the weakness of a nonindustrialized nation in a time of war. If the United States was to have an industrial revolution, she had to first release a great proportion of her population from the production of food. This could be achieved only with an agricultural revolution.

The revolution was accomplished in two steps. The first was the establishment of Land Grant Colleges under the Morrill Act of 1862. The purpose was "to donate public lands to the several states and territories which may provide colleges for the benefit of agriculture and the mechanic arts." Each state accepting the benefits of the Morrill Act was obligated to establish

> at least one college where the leading object shall be, without excluding other scientific and classical studies, and including military tactics, to teach such branches of learning as are related to agriculture and the mechanic arts . . . in order to promote the liberal and practical education of the industrial classes in the several pursuits and professions in life.

A combination of applied research in plant and animal sciences and an extensive educational system to bring the practical results of that research to the farmer resulted in the development and use of new management methods, new plants such as hybrid corn, disease control, and fertilization that tremendously increased production per acre. The second step was the application of industrial technology to the farm: tractors and new machinery starting with the binder and arriving at today's combines that can cut, thresh, and bag the grain, and harvesting machines that pick, package, and box lettuce in the field. The results of this Green Revolution, however, were seventy-five years in the coming. As was pointed out in the remarks prefacing the previous selection, the revolution was not achieved until after 1940. Today in the 1970s only 5 percent of the people are needed to feed the nation and supply a considerable surplus for export as well.

If the underdeveloped countries of the world are to feed their expanding population and at the same time industrialize, they too need a green revolution. Like the United States in the 1860s, the academic institutions in underdeveloped countries are interested only in turning out doctors and lawyers. There is no particular interest in training experts in agriculture, which many people still consider to be an inferior occupation. (In fact this was and in a way still is true in the United States. As Paul Ehrlich remarked concerning weaknesses in ecological knowledge and agricultural experts, "In my generation we were trained to think that anything pertaining to agriculture or applied to technical study was dirty, not to be mentioned, and we had to go into esoteric research." Now esoteric researchers are discovering that they are woefully handicapped in approaching the critical ecological problems that require an applied approach.) The United States in particular and other western countries attempted to fill in this gap and help increase food production of underdeveloped countries by sending in agricultural experts, seeds, and livestock. But the experts, after causing considerable ecological damage to many areas (for example, the groundnut scheme in East Africa), discovered you can't transplant temperate zone agriculture to the tropics (something applied ecologists could have predicted and did). They also found out that our varieties of grain were ill adapted to tropical and subtropical regions. The only solution was to duplicate in the underdeveloped nations the same program so successful in the United States.

The place to start was the development of new strains of grain that would produce more heavily and respond to fertilizers. Varieties of rice and corn and wheat being grown in the underdeveloped countries were producing at their maximum. Genetically ill adapted to respond to fertilization, they often produced even less when fertilizers were applied. The rice in southeast Asia is tall and thin strawed. When fertilized it becomes top-heavy and falls over, and the developing grain rots on the ground. The first improvement work in tropical grains was started by the Rockefeller Foundation in Mexico, where researchers concentrated on wheat. That successful wheat breeding program is now being continued under the Rockefeller- and Ford-sponsored International Maize and Wheat Improvement Center at Chapingo. The success with wheat prompted the establishment in 1962 of the International Rice Institute, co-sponsored by the Ford and Rockefeller Foundations in the Philippines. From this Institute came IR-8 miracle rice, a short-strawed variety that responded quickly to fertilization and in places doubled the yield of rice. This rice, which will be replaced by even better varieties, made the Philippines self-sustaining and even permitted the country to export a surplus. Similar successes have been registered for Mexican-type wheats, widely planted in India, Pakistan, and Turkey with marked increases in yields.

The new varieties of cereal grains are changing agriculture in a number of underdeveloped countries.[1] They are increasing yields of grains. Since the new varieties are early maturing, several crops can be grown in one year. The new varieties of rice ripen in 120 to 125 days, compared with 150 to 180 days for older varieties. They are also insensitive to day length and can be planted any time of the year. If temperature, water supply, and planting conditions are favorable, three crops can be harvested in one year.[2] Where water supplies are not adequate for rice during the dry season, rice can be replaced with wheat, grain sorghums, or corn. In northern India and Pakistan, wheat and corn are double-cropped, the wheat being grown during the winter season and corn during the summer season. As a result of double- and triple-cropping, yields of eight tons of grain per calendar year have been obtained, compared with two tons of high-yielding Japanese rice. This green revolution appears to offer some relief to food problems in underdeveloped countries, giving them some breathing time to solve the burgeoning population problem that is at the heart of the food crisis.

Promising as the Green Revolution may seem, it will not solve the food problems of the world as yet. Its full benefits can be enjoyed only when the program is accepted by all underdeveloped countries, when they make some effort to make needed agricultural reforms, to provide farm-to-market roads, to eliminate import taxes on agricultural inputs such as fertilizers, and to cut drastically their population growth.

But the Green Revolution is not without its built-in or second-generation problems, which even the most enthusiastic supporters of the Revolution recognize. Some are ecological. For one, will the soil hold up under such intensive cropping, or will the resource simply be mined? We do not know the effects of short-term, high-yield cropping obtained by heavy chemical fertilization on soils. Only in recent times have agricultural fields been subject to such intensive farming. We cannot compare the effects of this type of farming with the less intensive type that has kept soils productive over hundreds if not thousands of years.

Intensified farming on limited acres requires strong measures to control both pests and diseases. The use of pesticides has already created worldwide ecological problems (see Selection 22). There is a question whether chlorinated hydrocarbons can continue to be used without disastrous results to both animals and men. The effect of the Green Revolution may rest with the development of ecologically safe pesticides.

There is a problem of growing water scarcity. To provide needed water storage, rivers have been dammed, creating more ecological problems. The fertility of the lands along the Nile depended on deposition of fertile silt. Now the silt is depositied in the dam. Replacement of simple age-old irrigation practices with large-scale projects and slow, warm water in miles of irrigation ditches has created ideal conditions for certain species of snails that serve as secondary hosts for schistosomiasis, or bilharziasis, a growing health

[1]C. P. Streeter, *A Partnership to Improve Food Production in India*, New York, Rockefeller Foundation, 1969.
[2]L. R. Brown, "The Agricultural Revolution in Asia," *Foreign Affairs*, July 1968, pp. 687–698.

problem.[3] No one as yet can predict or foresee the ecological consequences of bringing more and more and often marginal land under cultivation.

But ecological problems are not the only ones created by the Green Revolution, as Clifton Wharton points out. The Revolution is creating a number of social, economic, and political problems that can affect the course of human history. Wharton's paper illustrates the comments made earlier that agricultural development cannot be dissassociated with the cultural development of man, that the two are inseparable. Wharton focuses on the economic strains of the agricultural revolution, on the economy of underdeveloped countries, and on the impact of technology on illiterate society. Remember, the American farmer was highly literate and able to grasp the new technology quickly. Only his conservation stood in the way. Wharton also points out that it is the commercial farmer with the capital who is able to seize upon the new technology and make it profitable. Thus, as Margaret Mead[4] contends, the production of food becomes a product of profit and commerce, separating it from its primary role of feeding people. The paper by Wharton demands careful study. The questions he poses are extremely important to the future.

---

[3]H. vander Schalie, "Schistosomiasis control in Egypt and the Sudan," *Natural History* **78**(2), 1969, pp. 61—65.
[4]Margaret Mead, "The Changing Significance of Food," *American Scientist* **58**, 1970, pp. 176—181.

Selection 9

The Green Revolution:
Cornucopia or Pandora's Box?

by Clifton R. Wharton, Jr.

The application of science and technology to traditional agriculture has begun to produce dramatic results, above all in Asia. The rapid expansion of certain food grains in the developing world is being particularly widely heralded, and justly so, as the "Green Revolution." The discussion of the phenomenon tends to cluster around two views. On the one hand, some observers now believe that the race between food and population is over, that the new agricultural technology constitutes a cornucopia for the developing world, and that victory is in sight in the "War on Hunger." Others see this development as opening a Pandora's box; its very success will produce a number of new problems which are far more subtle and difficult than those faced during the development of the new technology. It is important to give careful attention and critical analysis to both interpretations in order to be optimistic about the promise of the Green Revolution where justified, and at the same time to prepare for the problems that are now emerging. The Green Revolution offers an unparalleled opportunity to break the chains of rural poverty in important parts of the world. Success will depend upon how well the opportunity is handled and upon how alert we are to the inherent consequences.

It is now generally known that major technological breakthroughs in food production are believed to have lifted the spectre of famine in the immediate future and to have postponed the prospect of Malthusian population disaster. Startling developments have been accomplished in wheat, rice and corn—major food staples in much of the developing world. The possibilities for doubling or even tripling production are based upon new high-yield varieties coupled with adequate supplies of

---

water, fertilizer, pesticides and modern equipment. Overnight, the image of agriculture in the developing countries has changed from that of an economic backwater to that of a major potential contributor to overall development. The new varieties are rapidly spreading both within countries and across national boundaries. A recent estimate of the International Agricultural Development Service of the U.S. Department of Agriculture reveals that in Asia alone the estimated acreage planted with these new high-yield varieties rose from 200 acres in 1964—65 to 20 million in 1967—68. Traditional food-importing nations like the Philippines and Pakistan are becoming self-sufficient and have the prospect of becoming net food exporters.

It will be no easy task to achieve the potential increased production offered by the new technology, particularly when it involves millions upon millions of diverse farms and farmers scattered over the countryside. If the increased production is in fact obtained, this will automatically produce a whole new set of second-generation problems which must be faced if development is to be sustained and accelerated. Therefore, two considerations need to be borne in mind. First, there is reason to believe that the further spread of new varieties will not be as fast as early successes might suggest. Second, the new problems arising out of the spread of the new technology, whatever its speed, need to be foreseen and acted upon now. The probable developments in each case have the greatest significance for economic growth and for the conduct of international relations.

II

The reasons for believing that the new technology will not in fact spread nearly as widely or as rapidly as supposed and predicted include, first, the fact that the availability of irrigated land imposes at least a short-run limit to the spread of the new high-yield varieties. Most of these require irrigation and careful water control throughout the growing cycle. In most Asian countries about one-fourth to one-half of the rice lands are irrigated; the remainder are dependent upon monsoons and seasonal rains. The speed with which additional land can be converted to the new technology depends on the rapidity with which new irriga-

tion facilities can be constructed; and here the high capital costs are likely to be a retarding factor.

Large-scale irrigation projects can seriously strain the investment capacity of developing nations. For example, the massive Mekong River development scheme, involving Laos, Cambodia, Viet Nam and Thailand, has been estimated to require a capital investment over the next 20 years of about $2 billion, roughly 35 percent of the annual national income of the four countries involved and exceeding the annual net new investment of all the countries of Southeast Asia combined. Further, significant additional costs are involved in converting existing irrigation systems to the requirements of modern agriculture. Many of the old gravity irrigation systems were not designed to provide the sophisticated water controls demanded by the new varieties. (For example, each plot must be controlled separately throughout the growing season.)

Second, there are doubts about the ability of existing markets to handle the increased product. Storage facilities and transport are inadequate and crop grading often deficient. Not only must the marketing system be expanded to handle a larger output; there also is an increased need for farm supplies and equipment. Fertilizers, pesticides and insecticides must be available in the right quantities, at the right times, and in the right places. Given the inadequacy of the agricultural infrastructure, the need to expand and modernize marketing systems is likely to reduce the pace of the Revolution.

Because many of the new varieties, especially rice, do not appeal to the tastes of most consumers, it is difficult to calculate the size of the market. Some argue that until newer varieties which are closer to popular tastes are developed, the market will be limited.

Third, the adoption of the new technology is likely to be much slower where the crop is a basic food staple, grown by a farmer for family consumption. Such farmers are understandably reluctant to experiment with the very survival of their families. Peasant producers are obviously far more numerous in the developing world than are commercial farmers and the task of converting them to a more modern technology is considerably more difficult. So far, spectacular results have been achieved primarily among the relatively large commercial farmers. Some semi-subsistence farmers have begun to grow the new varieties, but the rate at which they adopt them may be slower.

Fourth, farmers must learn new farming skills and expertise of a higher order than was needed in traditional methods of cultivation. The new agronomic requirements are quite different as regards planting dates and planting depths; fertilizer rates and timing; insecticide, pesticide and fungicide applications; watering and many others. Unless appropriate extension measures are taken to educate farmers with respect to these new farming complexities the higher yields will not be obtained.

Fifth, many of the new varieties are non-photosensitive and the shorter term will allow two or three crops per year instead of one. Multiple cropping is good, but there may be difficulties if the new harvest comes during the wet season without provision having been made for mechanical drying of the crop to replace the traditional sun drying. In addition, there may be resistance if the new harvest pattern conflicts with religious or traditional holidays which have grown up around the customary agricultural cycles.

Sixth, failure to make significant institutional reforms may well be a handicap. There is evidence in several Latin American countries that a failure to make needed changes in policies now detrimental to agriculture, or a reluctance to effectuate the institutional reforms required to give real economic incentives to small farmers and tenants, has been primarily responsible for the very slow spread of Mexico's success with new varieties of wheat and corn to its neighbors to the south.

From all this one may deduce that the "first" or "early" adopters of the new technology will be in regions which are already more advanced, literate, responsive and progressive and which have better soil, better water management, closer access to roads and markets—in sum, the wealthier, more modern farmers. For them, it is easier to adopt the new higher-yield varieties since the financial risk is less and they already have better managerial skills. When they do adopt them, the doubling and trebling of yields mean a corresponding increase in their incomes. One indication of this is the large number of new private farm-management consultant firms in the Philippines which are advising large landlords on the use of the new

seed varieties and making handsome profits out of their share of the increased output.

As a result of different rates in the diffusion of the new technology, the richer farmers will become richer. In fact, it may be possible that the more progressive farmers will capture food markets previously served by the smaller semi-subsistence producer. In India, only 20 percent of the total area planted to wheat in 1967—68 consisted of the new dwarf wheats, but they contributed 34 percent of the total production. Such a development could well lead to a net reduction in the income of the smaller, poorer and less venturesome farmers. This raises massive problems of welfare and equity. If only a small fraction of the rural population moves into the modern century while the bulk remains behind, or perhaps even goes backward, the situation will be highly explosive. For example, Tanjore district in Madras, India, has been one of the prize areas where the new high-yield varieties have been successfully promoted. Yet one day last December, 43 persons were killed in a clash there between the landlords and their landless workers, who felt that they were not receiving their proper share of the increased prosperity brought by the Green Revolution.

III

Other experts argue that the new technology's stimulus to production and income cannot be stemmed. It is true that the rapidity with which the new seed varieties have spread in country after country belies the customary view of an inert, unresponsive peasantry. In 1965, India began a program of high-yield varieties which set a goal of 32.5 million acres by 1970—71; last year's crop season saw 18 million acres already planted, which contributed to the most successful year in recent Indian agricultural history (some 100 million tons of food grains, 11 million over the previous record year of 1964—65). Self-sufficiency in food grains is predicted in three or four years. Other countries are experiencing similar situations where the demand for the new seeds is outstripping the available supplies and black markets are even developing in seeds and fertilizer.

Nevertheless, if we assume that the new varieties will continue to live up to expectations and spread rapidly and widely, the increased production will in turn lead to a new set of difficulties. First, large tracts planted in one of the new varieties may be susceptible to disease and infestation which could cause massive losses. Heretofore, reliance upon seed selected by individual farmers meant that neighboring farms growing the same crop usually planted two or more different varieties or strains. This heterogeneity provided a built-in protection against widespread plant diseases, since not all varieties are equally susceptible. But where a single variety is introduced, covering large contiguous areas, the dangers of pathologic susceptibility are multiplied. For example, the new wheat introduced from Mexico into the Indo-Gangetic belt in India and Pakistan has involved a small range of genotypes—and the same has been true in Iran, Turkey and certain Middle Eastern countries. Any change in the spectrum of races of wheat rust in any of these countries could threaten the wheat crop on a massive scale, since it would involve the entire area.

Two steps are necessary to avoid these dangers: first, a diversified breeding program which can continually produce new varieties; second, an able and well-organized plant protection service which can quickly identify dangerous outbreaks and initiate prompt steps to combat them. Both activities must rely primarily upon national organizations rather than the regional or international ones. Both demand a skilled, well-trained staff. Some nations have recognized these dangers and are taking steps to meet them, but others still have not been made sufficiently aware. Aid givers—public and private—who are responsible for promoting the new varieties bear an equal responsibility to promote indigenous research and plant protection services. The outbreak of any major disease which wipes out the harvest of thousands of farmers is far more likely to be blamed on the producers and spreaders of the miracle seed than on Fate. Agricultural development could be set back several decades.

Second, it is vitally important to expand the entire complex of services and industries required to achieve the higher production. Any government or foreign-aid agency which distributes the "miracle" seed but fails to provide the insecticide and fertilizer in the appropriate quantities when and where needed is courting political disaster; unless these inputs are available and used, some local, traditional varieties will outyield the new ones. A seed

industry, agricultural chemical plants, processing and storage firms, factories producing hand sprayers, dusters, water pumps and engines—these are just a few of the agriculturally related industries which must develop if the Revolution is to take hold.

The skills and the capital needed cannot be provided solely by the public sector. Private capital must also be utilized. In a few countries the spread of the new technologies has already forced an abrupt departure from the previous practice of having government agencies serve as the major or sole distributor of the required inputs. Private industry, especially American, has stepped in to provide a new, more dynamic pattern of distribution. In the Philippines, for example, ESSO has become a major distributor of fertilizer and agricultural chemicals. Frequently, such ventures have involved links with local firms. In India, the International Minerals and Chemicals Corporation, with the Standard Oil Company of California, built a fertilizer plant with a yearly capacity of 365,000 tons; the U.S. firms provide the management but control is held by an Indian firm. Storage silos, seed multiplication firms and even integrated farm-to-retail firms are just a few of the activities where private U.S. resources are being harnessed to serve the Green Revolution.

Equally important are the increased farm services which are required, particularly agricultural credit. For example, from studies conducted at the International Rice Research Institute, it is estimated that whereas the total cash costs of production for the average Filipino rice farmer using traditional methods and varieties is about $20 per hectare, the cost rises to $220 when the new, high-yielding IR-8 is grown. Although the yield may increase three-fold, leading to a net return four times greater than with traditional varieties, the farmer must have access to substantially greater credit to finance his operations. Especially for the poorer farmers with low cash reserves, who may want to adopt the new varieties, the village money-lender and merchant will not be adequate unless they in turn have access to additional funds. Indeed, the Green Revolution must be accompanied both by an increase in the amount of credit available and by the expansion and modernization of credit institutions and mechanisms. Tapping the capital markets in the modern urban sector must be encouraged, and ways must be found at the village level to mobilize local capital, especially the increased savings which are possible from higher farm incomes. The Green Revolution will generate increased cash which, if properly marshalled, can contribute to capital formation and agricultural progress.

Third, much more attention must be devoted to marketing the increased output. Where there has been semi-subsistence agriculture, the impact of the new technology upon the *marketed* product is even greater than on total production. If the crop is a food staple and if the peasant farm family traditionally consumes some 70 to 80 percent of its total product each year, a doubling of output does not lead to a doubling in the amount retained for family consumption. Some modest increase in consumption is likely, but the bulk of the increased production will enter the market. Thus a doubling in yields in a semi-subsistence agriculture usually leads to much more than a doubling of the amount sold.

The impact of this explosive increase upon the traditional marketing network and storage capacity can be calamitous. The case of India is illustrative. During the past crop year, India experienced a marvelous increase in food-grain production, but the marketing network and storage facilities were not prepared to cope with it. The result can be seen in the mountains of food-grain stored in schools and in the open air under conditions which are apt to reduce if not negate the gains. The food-deficit psychology which underlies the failure of planners and policy-makers to anticipate these results is not limited to the developing nations. Aid givers were equally surprised. Strangely, the lessons of the Indian experience do not yet seem to have affected the thinking and planning of other nations which are promoting the new technology.

Fourth, the slowness with which the food-deficit psychology dies also has an important consequence in terms of government pricing policies. The fact that agriculture, even semi-subsistence agriculture, does respond to price, is only gradually becoming accepted. But the shock which quantum jumps in food production may have on domestic prices has not been sufficiently appreciated. The downward pressure on prices, especially where transport is deficient and storage is inadequate, may in fact be so severe as to have a disincentive effect upon producers. Unless adequate attention is given to

developing a sound pricing policy to prevent excessive dampening of incentives, the spread of the new technology may in fact be cut short before any "takeoff" has occurred. Premature discouragement could produce a reversion leading to a slowing up in food production or even a rejection of the new technology.

It has been amply demonstrated throughout the world that peasant and subsistence farmers are responsive to favorable prices, provided the return is real and they receive the benefit. For example, from 1951—53 through 1961—63, the farmers of Thailand in response to favorable prices increased their exports of corn at an average annual compounded rate of 35.8 percent; casava, 25.0 percent; and kenaf, 43.8 percent. Filipino farmers responded to a governmental price-support program for tobacco by changing from native to Virginia tobacco and then booming production from 3 million kilos in 1954 to over 30 million kilos in 1962. The list of crops where peasant farmers have responded to favorable prices is large—rubber, oil palm, coffee, jute, wheat, barley, sorghum, millet, gram, cotton. Thus, if the full potential offered by the new technology is to be realized, every effort must be made to insure that there is in fact a significant return to the producer and that the rapid rise in output does not lead to a counter-productive slump in prices.

Fifth, the goals of increased food production are frequently couched in terms of some desirable, minimal standards of nutrition. Such nutritional goals are commendable, but they can be attained only by individuals who have the income with which to purchase the better diet. Effective demand for food depends upon both the income of the demanders and the price of the food. If the increased production leads to lower costs and prices, then consumers will be able to increase their food purchases and hopefully to raise their levels of nutrition. Equally important is the need to increase incomes so that the greater production entering the market can be purchased. The food problem in a developing world is both a problem of production and supply and a problem of demand and income. Unless the higher levels of effective demand materialize, the prospect will be market gluts, price depression and, in certain cases, shifts by the farmers away from the higher-yielding varieties. Hence, every effort must be made both to reduce the unit costs of the increased food output and to augment the incomes of consumers who purchase food; otherwise, the second bowl of rice will not be bought—despite the technical feasibility of producing it.

Sixth, one of the major avowed aims of most nations which are eagerly promoting the Green Revolution is to achieve self-sufficiency in food production. In Southeast Asia, for example, the Philippines already claims to have become self-sufficient. Malaysia predicts that she will be self-sufficient by 1971; Indonesia by 1973. Some believe that these target dates are overly optimistic. But if the rice-deficit nations of the region such as Malaysia, Indonesia and the Philippines eventually become self-sufficient by successfully adopting the new technology, what will happen to the rice-surplus nations like Burma and Thailand whose economies are heavily dependent upon rice export? To whom will they sell their rice? Self-sufficiency will not only be detrimental to the rice-exporting nations, but will reduce one of the few areas of economic interdependence in the region. Unless action is taken in advance to offset the predictable impact of the new technology, hopes of promoting regional economic integration will be substantially reduced. Whether or not one agrees with the goal of self-sufficiency for these nations, the policies have been adopted and will be pursued. Many developing nations spend some 30 percent of their foreign exchange on food imports and wish to eliminate this drain as well as the irritation of chronic deficits in domestic production. We should anticipate the predictable consequences of these policies—in this case major economic dislocations in trade—so that we can be equally ready with developmental efforts or foreign assistance to reduce the dimensions of the problem. Unless the exporting nations take immediate stock of their prospects and seek to diversify their agriculture, the impact of such trade distortions could have major consequences for their economies and pace of development.

Seventh, a critical question is whether these technological developments are a "once-and-for-all" phenomenon. How likely is it that new technological improvement will continue to be made? The application of science to agriculture over the last 300 years has resulted in a tenfold increase in yield per acre on the best farmed lands in the temperate zone. This expansion is what led to the production

controls introduced by the surplus nations, such as the United States, to keep demand and supply in reasonable balance. Today's Green Revolution is the result of a similar application of science to agriculture in the developing world. But it should be noted that the institutionalized application of science is largely concentrated at present in food crops. Before World War II, primary attention in agricultural research in the developing world was devoted to the major crops—rubber in Malaysia, sugar in the Philippines, coffee in Kenya, palm oil in Nigeria, coffee in Brazil, bananas in Honduras. Staple food crops were either ignored or received scant attention. Thus the successes of the recent application of science to peasant agriculture could be interpreted as an exploitation of a "technical gap" in food crops left by years of neglect. If current developments merely represent a "catching-up," then as soon as population overtakes current developments, we are back to "square one."

Much will depend upon whether or not the necessary manpower is trained in each country to provide a continuing human resource which can produce a constant stream of new technology. The manpower trained in the Rockefeller Foundation's Mexican program has always been a greater contribution, in my view, than the new varieties. Successful adoption should not deflect attention from the importance and role of continuous agricultural research. The development of indigenous competence to engage in agricultural research is critical and becomes even more critical as the new varieties are adopted. The target should be not *a* new technology but ever-new technology, and this requires skilled manpower.

These are only a few of the possible consequences of the successful spread of the new technology. There are several broader consequences and issues which can be raised only as questions in this brief presentation:

To what extent will the diffusion of the new technology accentuate the displacement of rural people and heighten the pace of migration to the cities? If higher yields per acre, multiple cropping plus mechanization, force surplus manpower out of agriculture, what are the prospects for increased employment in industry and services to absorb this manpower?

For the average developing nation the Green Revolution means that instead of devoting two-thirds to three-fourths of its agricultural resources to food production, these resources may now be shifted to other higher paying crops. The question then becomes, what crops and for what markets?

If agriculture becomes more modern, dynamic and wealthy, will the non-agricultural sector allow agriculture to retain a significant share of this increased income or merely follow the previous patterns of taxing agriculture for non-agricultural development?

What will be the political significance of these changes if successful adoption of the new technology leads to an economically invigorated and strengthened rural population—almost invariably a large majority in developing nations? Will rural-based political parties and movements emerge to alter the recent dominance of urban centers?

What will be the global effect of a food explosion in the tropical and sub-tropical world? Will such developments lead to an improved reallocation of productive specialization among the developed and developing world, or will nationalistic trade barriers continue to flout natural comparative advantages?

One final danger lies in assuming that there is no longer an urgent need for measures to reduce rates of population growth. Quite the contrary. While the new developments are a splendid gift of time to allow a holding operation, effective population measures continue to be essential. Whether one assumes a growth rate of 2.5 or 3 percent, the inexorable fact is that, give or take a few years, the population of the developing world will double in about 25 years.

The significance of the food-population problem is more than humanitarian and developmental; it also has critical implications for the conduct of international relations. Relations between nations are often profoundly affected by long-run forces over which men can exercise only limited control in the short run. The food-population race is an excellent example of such a set of forces. Predictions regarding both population and food, as well as their interaction over varying lengths of time, must be taken into account in the conduct of developmental assistance, not only by aid-giving nations and international organizations, but by the governments of developing nations themselves. Policies and programs designed to win the race between food and population may have unintended, though often predictable, consequences which may have a very broad impact.

IV

Charles Malik once said that "one of the principal causes of both international conflict and internal strife is unfounded expectations. These are based ultimately either on deception or on a belief in magic."[1] What we have in hand seems to many people to approach magic; let us hope that it does not become the source of deception.

To speak of the possible consequences and problems associated with the next phase of the Green Revolution should not be misinterpreted as a plea for the suppression of the Revolution because, like Pandora's box, it will lead to even greater problems than those it was designed to eliminate. On the contrary, I would strongly argue that the list of second-generation problems is a measure of what great opportunities exist for breaking the centuries-old chains of peasant poverty. They also demonstrate how closely interrelated are the various factors which impel or retard agricultural development. This complex interrelationship makes interdisciplinary research and coöperation vital if the current problems are to be solved and future ones anticipated. The most realistic prediction is that each country is likely to experience a different set of these problems and that there will be variations among countries between the two extremes of optimistic and pessimistic prognoses.

The quiet, passive peasant is already aware of the modern world—far more than we realize—and he is impatient to gain his share. The Green Revolution offers him the dramatic possibility of achieving his goal through peaceful means. It has burst with such suddenness that it has caught many unawares. Now is the time to place it in its long-range perspective and to engage in contingency planning so that we may respond flexibly and quickly as the Revolution proceeds. Perhaps in this way we can ensure that what we are providing becomes a cornucopia, not a Pandora's box.

---

[1]Charles H. Malik, "What Shall It Profit A Man?" *Columbia Journal of World Business*, Summer 1966;

The Head Has a Stomach

Commentary

In spite of the Green Revolution, the seeming abundance of food in parts of the world, increased world food production, and technological developments in agriculture, much of the world goes hungry. Although there has not been a major famine (except for the man-caused one in Biafra) since World War II, the bulk of the world's population, including a surprising number in affluent nations, are inadequately nourished, suffering from the ills that accompany malnutrition.

Man has certain nutritive requirements necessary for his well-being. He needs carbohydrates—sugars and starches—as an energy source for daily activity, metabolism, and body maintenance and growth, as well as for storage for future energy demands. Carbohydrate intake greater than immediate demands is stored as liver glycogen and fat.

Fats, needed in lesser quantity, serve as a condensed reserve of energy, are an important structural component of cell membranes, and are essential for various reactions in intermediary metabolic reactions.

Proteins, the structural elements of life and the principle constituent of organs and soft tissues, are needed in continuous and liberal supply for body growth and maintenance throughout life. They are especially important to growing young. The thousands of different proteins all consist of different arrangements of amino acids of which eight (nine in the young) are essential. The quality of proteins varies considerably, determined by the ratio of the eight essential amino acids in the food.

In addition there are vitamins, essential nutrients needed in small amounts. Without them growth, metabolism, general health and vigor, and reproduction may be impaired. Humans in common with other vertebrate animals require some seventeen essential minerals, part of them needed in very small amounts, the trace elements. Details of their function can be found in books on nutrition and biology.

Man's metabolic energy demands can be met by many different combinations of proteins, carbohydrates, and fats, because both proteins and fats are also sources of carbohydrates. The requirements for energy, measured in calories, vary with sex, age, weight, occupation, and other variables. The calories needed for basal or resting metabolism generally decrease with increasing age. Children one to twelve require 1300 to 2500 Kcal per day; boys thirteen to fifteen years of age need 3100 Kcal per day; girls, 2600. Working adults may require 50 percent more calories a day than needed in resting metabolism, and the energy demands of pregnant and lactating women are much greater than those who are not.

Of all the nutrients required by man, proteins are the scarcest and the most expensive. They come from both plants and animals, but the most useful are of animal origin. The conversion cost is high. Four pounds of protein must be fed into poultry for every pound of egg protein, the most perfect of all for man. One pound of beef protein requires the consumption of 14 to 16 pounds of protein by the steer. Protein in plants, which is the source of most animal protein, varies widely. To obtain the daily requirements of protein from rice, which provides 60 percent of the energy to one-half the world's population, an adult would need to eat two pounds daily. To obtain sufficient protein from corn one would have to consume daily 1.75 pounds of corn and 1.25 pounds of wheat. And even then the protein would not be of the right quality.

Other plants commonly consumed provide even less protein. Two that form an important part of the diet of many in the world, potatoes and cassava, are extremely low in protein. The potato contains only 2 percent, and to obtain a minimum daily requirement from that source one would have to eat eight pounds daily. Cassava made into tapioca contains even less. Twenty-five pounds of that product would have to be eaten daily to meet protein requirements.

Some plants, on the other hand, are rich in high-quality protein, especially the pulses—beans, peas, and related plants. One cup of soybean concentrate, 170 grams, will supply the daily requirements of protein, vitamins, and minerals. Dried beans and peas contain 22 to 26 percent protein, yet in underdeveloped nations the full possibilities of these protein-rich plants are not realized. Crop production is concentrated in those plants such as rice, potatoes, cassava, bananas, and other carbohydrate-rich plants that have a high yield per acre. The total reference standard for protein is 60 grams per person per day. Many people in Latin America, Africa, and East Asia receive less than 7 grams a day.

It can be argued rather effectively, I think, that man's nutritional problems began when he became an agriculturalist. As a growing population began to depend more on plants and less on animals, the diversity of diet began to decline. Nutritionally, man the hunter was probably better off. He had a small population that apparently was held within the bounds of his food supply, and he consumed a diversity of plant and animal foods that gave him his daily nutritional needs. Agricultural man, by necessity in too many parts of the world, has sacrificed protein to meet the need of cheapness and ease of carbohydrate production.

The debilitating effects of low protein diet are observable throughout the world, including affluent nations. In the following selection Dr. Gerald Anderson calls attention to the protein deficiencies that exist in the United States, and discusses in detail the effects of a diet deficient in protein when man is short-changed in the food chain.

Selection 10

The Head Has a Stomach

by Gerald C. Anderson

Without question the paramount demand of man on his environment is for food. In the 10,000 years or so since agriculture emerged, man has steadily increased his ability to manipulate his environment toward the fulfillment of this need. Unfortunately, and paradoxically as his ability to produce food has grown, so have the number of his fellows who are inadequately fed.

An estimated half to a third of earth's residents suffer the debilitating effects of improper nourishment. Restrictions in resources both natural and human can be properly offered and accepted as an explanation for this condition in certain environments. But what can be the reasons for twenty million improperly fed persons in the United States?

Approximately one-third of these Americans are improperly nourished as a matter of choice. They have the dollars to feed themselves properly, but not the sense. The remaining fourteen million or so are malnourished because they do not have the resources to obtain enough food, or the knowledge to effectively use a limited income for the purchase of foods, or the knowledge to effectively use those foodstuffs provided by society.

The generous concern of Americans for international victims of errors of nature or society is repeatedly demonstrated. Why is it

then that this same concern cannot be extended to the victims of our own social errors? Kotz (1) in his recent book, *The Politics of Hunger in America*, provides some very disturbing insights, not the least of which are the views represented by Senator Strom Thurmond of South Carolina: "There has been hunger since the time of Jesus Christ and there always will be."

This view is not uncommonly held! "It took a major struggle to obtain $100,000 to find out who goes to bed hungry in America." (2) At least as heroic an effort was needed to bring about the White House Conference on Food, Nutrition and Health in order that Congress and the President could be advised on the development of a national policy aimed at eliminating hunger and malnutrition due to poverty.

Fully 3000 people from every part of the United States and its territories participated in this Conference. It transmitted to the White House very clear recommendations, the implementation of which could do much toward eliminating malnutrition in the United States. But, it is quite likely that the carefully made recommendations of the Conference will gather dust despite a public promise of the President to the contrary!

Can we continue to condone for the sake of

THIS SELECTION was written especially for this volume.

our national and individual health conditions which even approach these?

> ... We saw children being fed communally—that is by neighbors who give scraps of food to children whose own parents have nothing to give them. Not only are these children receiving no food from the government, they are also getting no medical attention whatsoever. They are out of sight and ignored. They are living under such primitive conditions that we found it hard to believe we are examining American children of the twentieth century. (3)

Certainly resources in the United States are not limiting the development and implementation of a national program to eliminate hunger in its most inclusive sense. It seems only fitting and proper that freedom from hunger is inherent in one of the world's most historic documents, the Bill of Rights. Could it be then that our dedication to it is being transferred to other areas, as is suggested by our budgetary program, which provides only eleven cents of every tax dollar to build America, whereas seventy cents is spent on wars past, present, and future? (4) Other suggestions can be offered as to why significant progress is not being made toward the elimination of hunger, but none can provide an acceptable reason.

Are there reasons which we cannot bring ourselves to recognize, let alone accept? Garrett Hardin's essay *The Tragedy of the Commons* [see Selection 33] suggests that there is no technological answer to the problems of modern man growing out of overpopulation. If this be the case, then a renovation of our attitudes, toward hunger and feeding hungry people, must take place as a prelude to any effective national program. There is considerable evidence at hand suggesting that we are unwilling or, worse yet, unable to accomplish this necessary renovation of our mores.

Perhaps our reluctance to dedicate more of ourselves toward the elimination of hunger reflects the function of a biological wisdom! I know of no system which is devoid of mechanisms for the control of its numbers, and this includes man, claims to the contrary. Fredericksen (5) in his valuable essay, *Feedbacks in Economic and Demographic Transition*, presents models that illustrate how population balance can be achieved. It is not difficult to see how a benign tampering with a model could destroy

its balance. Similar results could be achieved by ignoring warning signals calling for needed social-economic adjustments. In any case, the result would be demographic dementia and rapid deterioration of the environment.

The essence of this concept can be summed in Stott's (6) observation.

> For human beings we thus reach the paradoxical conclusion that in times of the pressure of population on food resources, any process which tended to *lower* the mental capacity, physical dexterity or perceptual acuity of a certain number of individuals might mean the saving of the race.

The validity of the foregoing can be questioned, but in so doing, the context must identify the time element which should be reckoned in units ordinarily beyond those commonly comprehensible. For expediency and for reasons less than humane, there are those who ignore the element of time and use this concept to rationalize their comfort. Disciples of this position also choose to ignore that a salient factor—pressure on food resources—does not apply in the United States.

As the foregoing intimates, imposed hunger and malnutrition are and have been effectively used to ensure survival of a way of life through oppression and contained genocide. It is no less disturbing to consider that the effects of malnutrition and hunger as an ingredient of poverty create for us a scapegoat that we inherently recognize to be useful and even essential.

One cannot deny from any stand that malnutrition degrades human health and achievement. This has been commonly appreciated for decades in respect to physical well-being and performance. But only recently has the impact of malnutrition on central nervous system development and function become well established. As previously unanswerable questions yield to increasingly sophisticated techniques of science and sociology, the more insidious effects begin to emerge.

The effect of early experience upon subsequent adult behavior is well accepted. Until recently most of these effects were attributed to psycho-social experiences, but it is now well established that factors of a biochemical nature are also involved. Of these biochemical factors, nutrition is the best studied.

From the evidence now at hand experiences

of malnutrition early in life may influence behavior directly through biochemical conditioning, creation of biochemical lesions, or indirectly by curtailing reactions to a limited environment, which in itself imposes a depressing social burden. Inadequate housing, inferior schools, disruptive home life, erosive attitudes toward education and technical competence, and substandard levels of health are as common accouterments of poverty as is malnutrition. Accordingly, it is hardly possible to determine the specific effects of early malnutrition upon subsequent adult behavior. Nevertheless the data from animal experiments and a host of clinical studies on the human leaves no doubt about the significance of malnutrition and its effects upon human behavior.

Because of the intimate association between nutrition and income level in almost all societies, malnourished persons as well as children previously at nutritional risk tend to cluster heavily in the underprivileged segments of a population. Such segments differ from the remainder not only in increased exposure to nutritional stresses but also in many other variables. They tend to have poorer housing, lower levels of formal education, higher incidence of infectious disease, greater attachment to outmoded patterns of child care, and obsolete concepts on causes of health and disease, and in general they live in circumstances less conducive to technologic and educational competence. Moreover, the effects of these circumstances may continue from one generation to another and suggest a familial or hereditary process. (7)

Malnutrition in the child can produce the most obvious and disturbing physical evidence which can usually be erased by a relatively short period of rehabilitation. But not so evident to the observer, nor so amenable to correction are the effects of malnutrition on cellular development and function.

Cravioto, Scrimshaw, Stock and their colleagues (7,8) among others have clearly established that central nervous system development in the infant can be seriously impaired by malnutrition. Effects are most damaging and least reparable the earlier in life the nutritional, or more correctly, the biochemical insult is experienced. Sensitivity decreases with the central nervous system development. Thus, an insult during the first six months of life is more damaging and permanent in nature than one

mediated eighteen months later. It would appear that sensitivity declines rapidly after the third year and that abuses after the sixth year are largely reparable.

Perhaps appreciation for the vulnerability of the central nervous system to biochemical insults can be properly emphasized by these observations.

Evidence is cumulative and impressive that severe undernutrition during the first two years of life, when brain growth is most active, results in a permanent reduction in brain size and a restricted intellectual development. (8)

... Children in the study group had reduced weight, height, and cranial circumference and ... differences were most marked in those children who had been malnourished for more than four months. The same findings are reported for developmental quotient. These data clearly indicate that conditions existing in urban America (United States) between 1965 and 1970 are such that children are being exposed to socioeconomic environments which breed malnutrition and limit growth and development. A large number of infants in this country are at risk, and the development of these children is being retarded. (9)

Eichenwald (10) neatly summarizes the effects of malnutrition on human development into these categories.

1. Physical growth retarded
2. Biochemical maturation inhibited
3. Neural development retarded or damaged
4. Mentation delayed or severely retarded
5. Debilitating interaction involving infection, growth, and environment caused

The effects of malnutrition upon human performance is easily enough recognized. But it is not likely that the lethargic and apathetic posture of poverty is commonly equated with the debilitating effects of chronic malnutrition. Neither is it likely to be commonly recognized that malnutrition during the critical periods of child development is most significant in perpetuating poverty.

For many years the only strong data supporting the concept that malnutrition in early life could influence central nervous system development came from animal experiments. Supporting data obtained on the human are difficult to obtain. As a result considerable time elapsed before the evidence reached an unassailable mass and it became recognized that the child's central nervous system is very sensitive to the effects of malnutrition during the first two or three years of life. The effect on central nervous system development is a function of the severity of nutritional deprivation, the length of time deprivation was experienced, and when it occurred.

While evidence to support the foregoing is available, this is not the case in respect to the influence of malnutrition on *in utero* development. There is, of course, a considerable amount of evidence obtained with experimental animals, but translation of this to the human is viewed with reservation.

The normal birth weight and appearance of babies born to malnourished and impoverished mothers seemed to isolate the *in utero* period of human life from careful study. However, since World War I evidence has been accumulating, and it now appears that a mother's ability to shield a fetus from the effects of malnutrition is far less than had been believed to exist.

The higher than normal incidence of stillbirths in malnourished mothers is widely recognized. It is also recognized that the incidence of congenital anatomical abnormalities in infants below expected weight is high, and it is very likely that an unfavorable uterine environment with a retarding effect on growth is responsible.

That the effects of malnutrition transcend maternal shields is no longer denied, as is evident from the following statements by Chow and colleagues. (11)

> ... Incidence of still births approximately doubled. The high incidence of congenital anatomical abnormalities among infants who are much below the expected weight for their gestational age suggests that early developmental abnormality may precede, and result in, growth retardation. ... A nutritional deficit can be

detrimental to the fetus without necessarily affecting its weight. It is possible, therefore, that the growth of a fetus may be retarded by maternal malnourishment but that this is partially concealed by a delay in parturition.

Beyond this, there are growing and impressive data showing that the nutritional well-being of the female from conception onward may influence the development of her children.

No one can deny that malnutrition and hunger make man less than he can be. This is true for those who suffer directly from effects of a restriction in life's essentials. It is no less true for those who condone it for whatever reason. For those of us in this group, Amos Tutola's Nigerian folk story (12) offers a disturbing eventuality.

> Now we started our journey from the Deads' Town directly to my home town which I had left for many years. As we were going on this road, we met over a thousand deads who were just going to the Deads' Town and if they saw us coming towards them on that road, they would branch into the bush and come back to the road at our back. Whenever they saw us, they would be making bad noise which showed us that they hated us and also were very annoyed to see alives. These deads were not talking to one another at all, even they were not talking plain words except murmuring. They always seemed as if they were mourning, their eyes would be very wild and brown and every one of them wore white clothes without a single stain.
>
> We met about 400 dead babies on that road who were singing the song of mourning and marching to Deads' Town at about two o'clock in the mid-night and marching towards the town like soldiers, but these dead babies did not branch into the bush as the adult-deads were doing if they met us. All of them held sticks in their hands. But when we saw that these dead babies did not care to branch for us then we stopped at the side for them to pass peacefully, but instead of that, they started to beat us with the sticks in their hands. ...

Literature Cited

1. Kotz, Nick. 1969. *Let Them Eat Promises: The Politics of Hunger in America*. Englewood Cliffs, N.J. Prentice-Hall.
2. *Ibid.*
3. *Ibid.* Quote attributed to Dr. Robert Coles, Harvard University, in describing his experiences with the Field Foundation in Mississippi. Page 9.
4. Barnet, Richard J. 1969. *The Economy of Death*. New York. Atheneum.

5. Frederiksen, H. 1969. Feedbacks in economic and demographic transition. *Science* **166**: 837—847.

6. Stott, D. H. 1969. *Cultural and Natural Checks on Population Growth in Environment and Cultural Behavior*, A. P. Vayda (ed). Garden City, N.Y. Natural History Press. [See Selection 19.]

7. Cravioto, J., and E. R. DeLieardie. 1968. *Intersensory Development of School-Age Children in Malnutrition. Learning and Behavior*. N. S. Scrimshaw and J. E. Gordon (eds.). Cambridge, Mass. M.I.T. Press. Also see Cravioto, J. 1966. *Malnutrition and Behavioral Development in the Pre-School Child in Pre-School Child Nutrition; Primary Deterrent in Human Progress*. National Academy of Sciences. National Research Council, Washington, D.C.

8. Stock, M. B., and P. M. Smythe. 1963. Does undernutrition during infancy inhibit brain growth and subsequent intellectual development? *Arch. Dis. Child.* **38**: 546.

9. Chase, H. P., and H. P. Martin. 1970. Undernutrition and child development. *New England J. Med.* **282**: 933.

10. Eichenwald, H. F., and P. C. Fry. 1969. Nutrition and learning. *Science* **163**: 644.

11. Chow, B. F., R. O. Blackwell, and R. W. Sherwin. 1968. Nutrition and development. Borden Review of Nutritional Research No. 39.

12. Tutola, Amos. 1952. The Palm-Wine Drinkard and His Dead Palm-Wine Tapster in Deads' Town. London. Faber and Faber.

III/Man and His Habitat

Georg Gerster from Rapho Guillumette

Introduction

RUSSELL LORD, one of the finest writers on agriculture and the land, wrote in his book *The Care of the Earth*,[1]

> Man as an implement maker, first and only such on earth, has the power to transform the landscapes and to manage soil and water sources so that he has become, in effect, himself a major force of geological change. When the first man or men began to fashion sticks, stones, and bones, to serve a given purpose, the metamorphosis began.

This is an important point to remember, because in this age of ecology we tend to consider that all of the sweeping and often disastrous changes around us are recent developments. Actually many are accumulations of past changes wrought by man, the effects of which we are just beginning to feel.

Ever since he appeared in some numbers on earth, man has altered the vegetation. Carl Sauer[2] has suggested that much of the world's grasslands, which occupy climatic regions that could support forest, developed because of man's recurrent use of fire. This theory has been supported by other geographers and ecologists.[3,4] Man cleared the forest by both ax and fire to make room for agricultural fields, and in so doing he destroyed much of the world's temperate forest, developed new plant communities, influenced the spread of weedy plants, and affected the hydrological cycle. Excessive soil erosion resulting from the destruction of forests and overgrazing of the hills by goats helped to destroy the "grandeur of Greece" and "the glory of Rome." Buried beneath the wind-drifted sands of the ancient Fertile Crescent are the remnants of ancient irrigation works, and the ancient seaport of Ur, now 150 miles from sea, is buried beneath 35 feet of silt. The remains of the Mayan civilization are overgrown with jungle vegetation.[5] It apparently collapsed because of an overexploitation of the soil and left behind the unproductive soils of present-day Guatemala.

The closer we come to the twentieth century, the faster the changes become. Increasing numbers of people possessing modern technology have completely transformed much of the globe. Free-flowing rivers have been dammed, creating enormous lakes and flooding out millions of acres. Highways and cities cover the landscape. Mountains and hills have been pared away for mineral exploitation. Refuse and debris of modern civilization litter the planet. The appearance of the landscape today bears little resemblance in most parts to what it was like even 100 years ago. In some places we have humanized the landscapes; in other places we have ravished it. The story of the development of our own habitat in the past and in the present, and the outlook of the future, are explored in the next four selections.

---

[1]Russell Lord, *Care of the Earth—A History of Husbandry*, New York, Nelson, 1962.

[2]Carl Sauer, "The Agency of Man on Earth," in W. E. Thomas (ed.), *Man's Role in Changing the Face of the Earth*, Chicago, Ill., University of Chicago Press, 1956, pp. 49—69.

[3]O. C. Stewart, "Barriers to Understanding the Influence of Use of Fire by Aborigines on Vegetation," *Proceedings Second Annual Tall Timbers Fire Ecology Conference*, 1963, pp. 117—126.

[4]E. V. Komarek, Sr., "Fire Ecology—Grasslands and Man," *Proceedings Fourth Annual Tall Timber Fire Ecology Conference*, 1965, pp. 169—220.

[5]Tom Dale and V. G. Carter, *Topsoil and Civilization*. Norman, Okla., University of Oklahoma Press, 1955.

Selection 11

The Processes of Environmental Change by Man

by Paul B. Sears

MAN'S PLACE IN NATURE

To understand and measure the change which man has produced in his environment, it is first necessary to view his place in nature. His flexibility as an organism is often emphasized, sometimes being referred to as his "unspecialization." What is meant is his freedom from evolutionary characteristics that would sharply restrict his activities and choice of habitat. That he is highly evolved cannot be questioned. Often overlooked is the fact that he exists by virtue of an environment which is itself highly evolved and specialized, having become so in the course of more than two billion years of earth history.

The most obvious features of this specialized environment include the presence of an angiosperm flora—notably grasses and legumes—and a mammalian fauna dependent upon it. From these sources man is able to derive sustenance with an ease and efficiency that would have been inconceivable had he been surrounded only by organisms of the remote geological past. Less obvious is the presence of a complex population of microörganisms and invertebrates which, among other functions, takes care of the breakdown of organic wastes and their return to chemical forms that can be reused to sustain life. Of major importance also is the persistence of numerous species of gymnosperms that, along with many kinds of woody angiosperms, furnish facilities without which man would have been severely handicapped throughout his existence. Indeed, that existence appears to have hinged upon trees, for his arboreal ancestors were obliged to develop the free shoulder articulation, grasping hands, and stereoscopic vision which serve him so well.

Least obvious, at any rate to modern urbanized man, is the effect of our present highly complex fauna and flora, organized as they are into communities, upon the environment itself. Through reaction upon habitat these communities not only insure an orderly cycle of material and energy transformations but also regulate the moisture economy, cushion the earth's surface against violent physiographic change, and make possible the formation of soil. In short, man is dependent upon other organisms both for the immediate means of survival and for maintaining habitat conditions under which survival is possible.

Man is also dependent upon minerals, his consumption of the two used longest, water and stone, still ranking first by volume. His present economy rests chiefly upon the use of fossil fuels and metals, both irregularly distributed and present in finite amounts. The fossil fuels, once used, can be restored only by the slow organic and tectonic processes which formed them, while the use of metals results in the dissipation of the ore concentrations by which they have been made available to man. Their present convenient form, like the character of the organic world, is the result of prolonged earth history before the coming of man. Man is clearly the beneficiary of a very special environment which has been a great while in the making. This environment is more than an inert stockroom. It is an active system, a pattern, and a process as well. Its value can be threatened by disruption no less than by depletion.

Any species survives by virtue of its niche—the opportunity afforded it by environment. But in occupying its niche it also assumes a role in relation to its surroundings. For further survival it is necessary that the role at least not be a disruptive one. Thus one generally finds in nature that each component of a highly organized community serves a constructive, or at any rate a stabilizing, role. The habitat furnishes the niche, and, if any species breaks

---

up the habitat, the niche goes with it. The guest who helps with the chores may prolong his stay, but the inconsiderate one may wreck the house. Systems or processes which involve organic activity resemble purely physical systems in being expressions of thermodynamic law, tending to approach a condition of minimum stress and unbalance. But, since living systems are active and dynamic, they tend to approximate what is known as a steady state rather than a condition of repose. That is, to persist, they must be able to utilize radiant energy not merely to perform work but to maintain the working system in reasonably good order. This requires the presence of organisms adjusted to the habitat and to each other, so organized as to make fullest use of the influent radiation and to conserve for use and re-use the materials which the system requires. The degree to which a living community meets these conditions is therefore a test of its efficiency and stability. This gives us a criterion by which the effects of environmental change can be judged.

While these principles have been shown to apply to what is generally called the world of nature, that is, the world apart from man, there is considerable resistance to the idea that they apply to him in any serious way. Much of this resistance is emotional, having its roots in that part of Judeo-Christian tradition which separates man from nature to a greater extent than perhaps was common in oriental and Mediterranean thought. Some of it certainly comes from those who resent, for whatever reasons, any warning sign along the road to a perpetually expanding economy. And surprisingly, perhaps, some resistance comes from scientists and technologists, especially those unacquainted with the general field that used to be called natural history. In defense of this last group it must be said that they are as aware of still unexploited reserves as the ecologist is of the existence of limiting factors. And, in view of the fabulous results they have produced, they are perhaps less concerned with the law of diminishing returns than their colleagues whose business it is to study the interrelationship of life and environment. As responsible scientists, both groups have an obligation to collaborate and to weigh scrupulously any pronouncements, whether these be cautions or promises. Mankind is not well served either by hysteria or by false visions.

It will be shown subsequently that the changes induced by man, whether by sheer destruction or indirectly by accelerating natural processes, are probably more serious to him than the so-called "natural changes" for which he is not responsible.

MAN AS AN AGENT OF CHANGE

Unfortunately, the situation is clouded by a widespread confidence that this impact of man upon environment can continue indefinitely. We are told that the greatest resource is human resourcefulness and that ways and means will be found, through the applications of science and technology, to meet all emergencies as they arise. The economy and the social and political policy of the United States are based upon this assumption of more and more, bigger and better. The phrase "an expanding economy" is frequently heard without any qualifying explanation.

It is true that we are far from the end of the rope. North of Mexico, America has great reserves of space and other essentials. Direct utilization of solar energy is a reasonable probability and with it the tapping of now unavailable mineral resources in igneous rocks. There is no call to sell applied science short. On the other hand, there is no justification for writing off the judgment of biologists, demographers, geologists, and anthropologists, all of whom have special competence with respect to the context of human activity—the broad but finite pattern within which man must operate.

THE PROBLEM

There are many interesting approaches to the problem of man and his environment, and all, save perhaps the technological, seem to lead to the same conclusions. With this possible exception, these various approaches indicate that humanity should strive toward a condition of equilibrium with its environment. This is the verdict of ethics, aesthetics, and natural science. And, despite the prevalence of the idea of a continually expanding economy, it is probably the verdict of that branch of economic analysis known as accounting.

Accounting seeks to identify certain entities—assets, liabilities, income, expense—and to construct therefrom its equations. It must be particularly careful to identify those changes in capital structure known as depreciation and not to confuse them with income. Assuming, therefore, that the physical environment represents the basis of humanity's capital assets, the question becomes: Does our levy upon it represent sustaining income in excess of expenditure, or has it been obtained through deterioration of the capital base, that is, through depreciation?

BY WAY OF BACKGROUND

An extensive literature upon man and his environment has appeared during the last twenty years, generally emphasizing the extent and seriousness of depreciation of the capital structure. Useful examples include Osborn's *The Limits of the Earth* (1953) and Brown's *The Challenge of Man's Future* (1954), the former written from the viewpoint of a biologist, the latter from that of a geochemist. So far as I know, the evidence of neither has been countered directly—that is, by demonstrating that humanity has not made serious inroads upon natural resources. The nearest exceptions to this have taken the form of statements that vast mineral resources remain to be discovered, though at increasing cost, and that the production of food and fiber can be greatly increased by better methods. Both assertions are probably true.

Rather has the rejoinder been indirect. Thus Hanson, in *New Worlds Emerging* (1949), stresses the vast potential of the tropics and the ocean, while De Castro, writing *The Geography of Hunger* (1952), advances the thesis (a curious one to biologists) that ample diet will slow down the birth rate and so relieve population pressure. Fortunately, our task is one of appraisal, not of passing on the merits of prophecy.

First, however, some comments on commercial economies are in order. Early commerce was probably on the basis of mutual plenty—tin for glass, wine for fish, wheat for lumber. But with the growth of empire and other forms of power a trend developed which can still be observed between nations and even within them. The flow is from the sources of raw materials and cheap labor toward the centers of power—military, political, or economic. And because of this drainage there is often left too little energy, capacity, or capital at the source for the exploited to safeguard their own interests. The process tends to become purely extractive, to the detriment of land

capital. Interesting exceptions, not fully appreciated at both ends of the line, are certain of our extra-territorial agricultural corporations whose net effect upon the economy of the countries where they work is constructive (Sears, 1953*b*). Unfortunately, the beneficiaries of this system may say, "Es bueno, pero no es nuestro," and who can blame them? We all like the privilege of making our own mistakes.

In spite of the recurring abuses of power throughout history, commerce and industry were until the Reformation, in principle at least, subordinate to other cultural forces and restraints, notably religion. The extent to which they took the bit in their teeth after the industrial revolution is shown by the demand for an antitrust law at a time in our history when the most radical leaders were men who would now be considered sober conservatives. Today—again in principle—no one seriously questions the social responsibility of those engaged in commerce. Little would be gained if he did!

Curiously, however, the very structure of our modern economy, based as it is on mass production, intensifies the problem that here concerns us. Everything is geared to the speedy conversion of raw materials into consumers' goods at a rate governed only—when it is governed—by the capacity of the public to buy. Presumably the public does not buy unless it needs, but there is sound, if sardonic, reason to believe that this is not always true.

Compared to the efforts at conversion of raw materials, the effort to conserve them is still relatively slight. But the growth of industrial enterprise is having a wholesome effect in some quarters. So much capital is being tied up that the larger concerns are beginning to think about their own permanence, and this in turn involves thinking about the continuing future supply of raw materials. Banks and public utilities, both dependent upon general prosperity, are taking an active interest in soil and water conservation. Some of the larger lumber companies have adopted excellent sustained-yield plans. And national associations representing various economic interests are paying at least lip service, often a good deal more than that, to the restoration and preservation of resource capital. The occasional sounding of a sour note is no cause for alarm, since it serves to keep vigilant those who are deeply concerned with the problem.

131

ENVIRONMENTAL CHANGES
PRODUCED BY MAN

THE INCREASING INTENSITY IN LAND USE

The effect of man upon vegetation before the origin of agriculture and pastoral life is not known. The incidence of fires, even during the hunting stage of economy, must certainly have increased. Man is known to have hunted Pleistocene mammals, for example, the mammoth and the bison. The mammoth, horse, and camel evidently became extinct in the Americas after man's arrival there.

Human influence on vegetation registers in many pollen profiles through the abrupt appearance of certain weeds, notably composites, amaranths, and chenopods. These multiply when the natural cover is destroyed and show up in prehuman pollen profiles following volcanic activity or erosion due to tectonic change. The chenopods are still used for food; thus they may be regarded as precursors of agriculture. Of especial interest is the recent evidence of their appearance during the second interglacial in association with artifacts of pre-Acheulean age.

Agriculture requires the removal of native vegetation, while pastoral life is sustained by such vegetation. Iversen's recent experiments (1949) demonstrate strikingly the effectiveness of stone tools and fire in clearing the drier types of forest. The practice of felling and burning trees and planting cleared ground until the yields decline, then abandoning it and moving on, is known in Latin America as the *milpa* system. It is not particularly harmful until the increasing pressure of population extends the system to the hills and shortens the cycle needed for the vegetation and soil to recuperate. Erosion then follows.

Similarly, so long as a pastoral economy has sufficient space to permit nomadic life, the grasses and other herbs which sustain it can recuperate between periods of heavy use. Moreover, the pastoral cultures tend to be somewhat more aggressive than the legend of Abel and other "gentle shepherds" would suggest. One cannot doubt that primitive herders knew good pasture when they saw it and took vigorous measures to prevent undue trespassing. Even so, the growth of population brought steady pressure on the world's natural grasslands. Under such conditions the floral com-

position of these grasslands is modified, and less nutritious species come in as weeds. If the pressure continues, and particularly if it is extended to arid or hilly land, erosion by wind and water ensues. All these effects are intensified and extended to forest country when goats, valuable as they are to man otherwise, are present in great numbers. The goat is a thin-lipped, destructive grazer, as is the sheep; but, to a greater extent than sheep, it is a resourceful browser, damaging to woody vegetation.

With agriculture, urban life and the leisure arts and crafts became possible. Repeatedly in human history, this appears to have thrown the art of husbandry and the importance of good land use out of perspective. Except perhaps in China, the status of the man who worked the land was gradually demeaned as cities grew in size, power, and prestige. The effect of such change on the quality of rural techniques was probably bad, and the effect on the land itself, intensified by increasing food demands, was clearly so.

Two aspects of the growth of cities were particularly important. One was the expansion of irrigation works; the other, the harvesting of timber for fuel and structural purposes, thus clearing land not needed for, or suitable to, agriculture. Early irrigation in both hemispheres seems to have been well engineered, probably because the irrigators of arid lands had the stark choice of doing a proper job or being eliminated.

Where such irrigation depended upon wells, these afforded a positive check upon expansion, and an equilibrium of land use was reached which persisted in parts of the Near East for millenniums, only to be broken by the growing cone of depression of the water table incident to modern pumping for water used in oil refining.

Important irrigation works of great antiquity, notably in Mesopotamia, were based on the use of streams arising in forested uplands. Here, the clearance of forests, no doubt followed by heavy grazing, stimulated erosion. Vast amounts of silt were washed down, so that increasing labor had to be used for the clearance of the otherwise excellent system of irrigation ditches. While it is true that this interfluvial culture persisted long after the empires which it built—until its ditches were wrecked by Mongol invaders during the thirteenth century—the immense piles of silt alongside the ditches show that the system was well on the way toward being choked out before it was destroyed.

It is in the world of today, where industrialization and death control have produced an explosive growth of population, that land-use problems have become most acute and dramatic. Man has long competed with other forms of life for space. Increasingly he is his own competitor—a situation made worse by the diversity of his interests as they affect land use. Residence, business, industry, transport, waste disposal, water supply, agriculture, forestry, military needs, recreation—not to mention many intangibles—all have intensified their rival claims, frequently upon the same limited area. The effect has been confusing almost to the point of disaster, as can be seen in any metropolitan "urban fringe" area.

Allocation of space by planning and zoning, while not a new idea, has been outlined on a scientific basis by Geddes and his followers. It has been rather effectively developed in Great Britain by Stamp (1952) and others and in some parts of western Europe. But in Holland, where it is extremely advanced, it now faces the crisis of a saturated population. In the United States it faces grave political obstacles, made worse by the fact that we do still have a margin of safety and by the prevalence of our conviction that an economy can continue to expand without limits. This of course runs counter to the scientific experience that the factors in any process must ultimately work toward some kind of equilibrium. This principle, so widely applied in the purely physical sciences, seems to be as widely ignored—or disbelieved—when it comes to land use. A curious and dangerous phenomenon in a technological culture!

SOIL EROSION

It would be misleading to say that man is the cause of erosion or that erosion per se is a bad thing. As frequently pointed out, it is a normal part of the natural process of base-leveling and has been the source of some of the richest alluvial terraces and plains on earth. But under natural conditions, and except in very arid mountainous regions, the rate of erosion is controlled by the presence of vegetative cover in the form of stable communities. Under these conditions erosion proceeds so slowly as not to interfere greatly with the normal process of soil

formation, which, in turn, is a resultant of the interaction of living communities with the physical environment. It is when we remove this natural cover *without providing a substantial artificial equivalent* that the rate of erosion is accelerated to a dangerous degree.

Where this occurs, soil is removed from the uplands, and the rich alluvium of the lowlands is buried, first by upland soil, later by the sterile mineral materials which have underlain the upland soil. In either instance the productive capacity of former surfaces is greatly reduced even where, as in sheet erosion, the surface form is not much affected. But sheet erosion, if not checked, rapidly passes into gullying, which frequently renders the topography unsuitable for use.

FOREST REGIONS

Because forest regions are usually well supplied with water and, at first, with fuel and building material, they often become heavily populated. But it is a characteristic of forest soils that the most fertile organic layer of the surface is shallow, thinly overlying a mineral layer from which the plant nutrients have been largely leached. This kind of soil profile under pressure of use rapidly loses its productivity; the result is likely to be extensive abandonment. This explains much of what happened in New England, which was under extensive cultivation in the early nineteenth century, later largely changed to pasture, and is today two-thirds in forest of such inferior quality that it yields less than 10 percent of the total rural income.

The situation is less serious where, as in Ohio, the minerals in the deposits brought in by glaciation are rich in nutrients and fairly deep. Here it is possible, through the use of cover crops and improved pastures and wood lots, to stabilize the surface and tap the underlying minerals, thus restoring the fertility lost when the original topsoil was removed. In western Europe, where relief is low, rainfall gentle, and economic pressure has enforced good husbandry, damage from removal of the original vegetation is relatively slight. Except for hunting preserves, the original forests of western Europe were largely destroyed during the Middle Ages in order to obtain not only building material but also charcoal for fuel and for the manufacture of steel. This is surprising in view of the fact that in the seventeenth century some 360 tons of steel more than met the annual needs of England—at least from the seller's point of view. Today, the art of forestry has reached such levels that, from Denmark to Italy, one finds that good agricultural land can be used profitably for the production of wood. Moreover, the forests of France and the pasture lands of Britain fill admirably the role of natural vegetation as a stabilizer of the landscape.

GRASSLANDS

Changes in forest cover are more obvious and better known than those in the grassland regions. Thus Ohio, once about 90 per cent forested, now is about 15 per cent in such cover. Farther west the proportion of native tall-grass prairie that has been destroyed is probably even greater. This is especially serious because of the remarkable resilience with which the rich prairie flora can adjust to the recurrent crises of climate—a property not shared by the plant cover which agriculture has substituted.

Where precipitation does not exceed the evaporating power of the atmosphere measured in inches of water, grassland, scrub, or desert occur. The subhumid grasslands of the world have developed a deep and fertile topsoil, well supplied with mineral nutrients and remarkably suited to the production of high yields of cereal protein. Because the thickness of the humus horizon varies from 3 to 5 feet, erosion goes largely unnoticed, and the use of artificial fertilizers can be prostponed for decades. Yet there is evidence that in Iowa, for example, an average of perhaps one-third of the original A-horizon of the surface has been lost since settlement, while the depletion of mineral nutrients is now making necessary the use of chemical additives.

The semiarid grasslands sustain a growth of short grasses and other low-growing herbs which have served to bind the soil into a turf or sod. Here there is a marked excess of evaporative power over precipitation and a consequent upward movement of water, bringing nutrient minerals to the surface. The soil is inherently productive except for the lack of moisture. Under natural conditions good, though sparse, grazing was afforded by the native grasses, which not only held the surface in place but cured on the stalk, retaining their value as forage.

Outward pressure from the centers of population brought these lands under settlement, and techniques of dry farming were developed. The level land being well suited to mechanized farming, good yields of high-protein cereal at minimum cost were found to be possible. The concurrence of moist years with periods of high demand and good prices encouraged the extensive plowing-up of the original short-grass sod during World Wars I and II. But in both instances the moist years were followed by dry, and the autumn-planted wheat either failed to germinate or made such feeble growth that it could not stabilize the lighter types of soil against the strong dry winds of late winter and spring. Severe dust storms were produced by the resulting erosion. This phenomenon is all the more remarkable for having repeated itself in less than a quarter-century in a literate, highly technological culture that had made notable efforts to repair the effects of the first series of dust storms and was well informed of the consequences to be expected from repeating the mistakes which had led to them. However, the fault does not lie entirely with the more speculative and less responsible segments of the free-enterprise system. Influential spokesmen for scientific agriculture, more concerned with the latent fertility of arid soils than with the inevitable pattern of recurrent drought, did too little to discourage exploitation and in some cases encouraged it.

Some confusion is due to the clear evidence of periods of rapid erosion and gully formation in recent geological time but before the known advent of man. This is especially noticeable in our own Southwest and has led some scientists to minimize the effects of overgrazing as a cause of accelerated erosion today. Past erosion cycles were due to intervals of dry climate, and we have been in the beginning of such an interval since about 1700; so, runs the reasoning, why blame man for a natural phenomenon? The answer lies in comparing such overburdened ranges as those of the Navaho with others which have been subjected to reasonable use. It is possible to find hillsides on which a fence separates a field of gullies from one which is intact. That we are in a time of increased climatic hazard is certain. It would seem equally certain that a scientific culture therefore should exercise more rather than less caution in its pattern of land use.

The effect of destroying or damaging natural

communities is not confined to increased erosion. Water, with wind, is the chief erosive agent. Besides stabilizing the land surface, natural vegetation is a major regulator of the hydrologic cycle—indeed, it is chiefly in this way that the surface is stabilized.

THE PROBLEM OF WATER

If the water cycle be roughly described as (1) evaporation from the seas, (2) transport over the land, (3) rainfall or snowfall, and (4) flow back to the sea, it is chiefly during stage (4) that water is available for the sustenance of life on land. By prolonging this stage, terrestrial life gets the maximum benefit from moisture. Whatever shortens the time that water is in or on the land decreases its utility to land life, including our own.

Continuous vegetative cover retards the flow of water. It also renders the ground more permeable, thus maintaining the water table. In one instance it has been shown (Mather, 1953) that, while pasture and cultivated land soon become saturated, forest absorbs the equivalent of nearly 500 inches of rainfall. It seems reasonable to suppose that the same relationship holds as between native prairie and average farmland derived from it. A number of factors, not the least of which is compaction due to increasing use of heavy farm machinery, are responsible for this reduction in permeability.

A closely related phenomenon is the rapid increase of virtually water-proofed surface areas represented by cities and highways. Except in isolated cases, notably parts of Texas, where highway drainage is channeled into storage ponds, the water falling on roofs, sidewalks, and roads is speeded on its way. If used at all, it is reclaimed from rivers and requires purification. At the same time the per capita demand for water in urban centers continues to rise for both domestic and industrial purposes. Our cities are almost wholly dependent upon water which falls in non-urban territory. Thus we have the phenomenon of a technological culture whose demand for water is steadily rising at the same time that its processes accelerate the return of water to the sea.

But the problem of water involves quality as well as quantity. In this respect, also, a curious picture is presented. No highly developed organism in nature carries massive effluent wastes and influent necessities in the same system of transport. No organized living community in nature is without components that transform waste materials back into harmless and usable form. Yet our streams are utilized as sources for domestic and industrial water supply and concurrently as convenient sewers for domestic and industrial waste—beyond the capacity of their normal process to purify.

To urban wastes is often added the silt from eroded surfaces. The net effect is not only to impair the quality of the water but seriously to affect it as a habitat for aquatic life, both in the stream bed and in the estuary into which it discharges. This has damaged recreation and sport as well as commercial fishing and shell fishing. Pearl Harbor is no longer hospitable to the mollusks which gave it its original name.

Commerce is affected also. Computations of the dredging costs due to erosional silt in Cleveland Harbor and at the mouth of the Brandywine show that these costs are equivalent to a tax of several hundred dollars on each ship that enters the two ports each year. Such are the hidden costs of man-made change, patent to the ecologist, yet largely ignored by the industrial and financial leaders of a great technological civilization, in which the art of accounting, or business analysis, has been carried to a high degree of perfection.

Any discussion of water involves not only shortage and quality but also the question of flood. It is difficult to say to what extent floods have been increased by man's activity, for certain catastrophic types of rainfall would almost certainly produce floods in any event. But buildings and other installations within the flood plain of a great river should be in the same category of calculated risks as vineyards on the sides of an active volcano. Though they are seldom so regarded, nevertheless it is man who is responsible for flood damages, if not for the floods which cause them.

On the other hand, there are at least local floods that can be traced to human disturbance. This applies to northeastern New Jersey, a country of ridges and folds, where clearing, building, and paving of the ridge tops for extensive suburban developments have left rainfall with only one course—that of running downhill and swamping the homes below. Similarly, burning of chaparral or forest clearance of mountain slopes above our western cities has been responsible for flash floods and mudflows of a serious character. On general principles we would expect denuded and exploited headwater regions to intensify the destructive character and frequency of floods. While this is assumed as a basic element in national forest policy, far greater funds are expended upon efforts to control flood *after* water has reached the river channels than are devoted to securing proper land use on the tributary uplands to retain the water where it falls. This is an interesting aspect of a technological culture whose emphasis is on engineering rather than on biological controls.

The impoundment of water for various reasons is rapidly increasing, owing to the substitution of powerful earthmoving machinery for hand labor. In some instances, most notably the Tennessee Valley Authority, there has been an attempt to relate such impoundments to the entire economy of a region, making them serve multiple purposes. Thus flood control, recreation, power, and water transport have been combined with measures to improve public health and land use in the Tennessee Valley. In numerous instances the approach has been on a narrower basis.

Small farm ponds are being used to compensate for the growing scarcity of suitable ground water. Great public works in arid and semiarid regions have made possible the extension of irrigation, generation of power, and augmented urban water supplies. Such irrigation has not been uniformly successful, as witnessed by the inability of the beneficiaries to carry out contract payments on schedule. In some instances the high rate of evaporation has resulted in the accumulation of salts which interfere with plant growth. Problems arise from the necessity, in heavily industrial-residential areas, of excluding recreational activities from public water-supply watersheds in order to protect them from contamination, even though suitable recreation space is at a premium.

THE ATMOSPHERE

The atmosphere has become a medium of transport and the scene of experiments to modify the weather. On this latter problem scientific opinion is divided as to both feasibility and wisdom. Our failure thus far to adjust our economy in marginal climatic areas to what we know about their compulsive and recurrent hazards suggests that, even if we can modify climate, the operation at this stage is somewhat premature. Modern society is not yet organized to control the powers which science already has placed at its disposal.

Of perhaps more immediate concern is the growing volume of volatile and solid wastes which pollute the air of great urban centers across the United States. Hydrocarbons from refineries and automobiles, no less than byproducts of chemical works, are particularly serious. Vegetation, not only in the vicinity of smelters, but in places like Pasadena, has been affected, and there have been instances of known damage to human beings. Pittsburgh has been greatly improved, and commissions are at work elsewhere; but the problem of protecting the quality of two basic resources, formerly regarded as free economic goods—water and air—remains urgent.

MINERAL RESOURCES

The per capita consumption of minerals, unlike that of renewable resources, has continued to rise steadily with the level of living. Re-use is growing but not sufficiently to offset the depletion of concentrated reserves. Once taken into the economic process, these minerals tend to become dissipated or, in the case of energy sources, altered beyond recovery except through the slow biological and geological changes which made them.

The measurement of reserves is difficult technically, and exploration is increasingly expensive. Strategic and business considerations may hinder us from finding out where we stand. As an official in the copper industry put it, no figures on reserves are given out, as a matter partially of protection to the American public!

However, a few figures will suffice to emphasize the situation. Department of Commerce figures for March, 1954, show that petroleum consumption within the United States is substantially in excess of domestic production. Again, the United States, with less than one-tenth of world population, is today consuming more than half of the world's mineral production. The fact that much of the wealth so created is being dispensed among other friendly nations is some compensation but no guaranty that this condition is either desirable or secure. And, finally, more than half of the many kinds of minerals used in the American economy must be imported, not being commercially available within our borders.

CHANGE AND ETHICS—A SUMMARY

Change in the ecosystem of which man is a part is inevitable, since this system is a process, and he is inevitably affected by such changes. On the whole, those changes which are natural (i.e., not due to his interference) take place on a scale and at a rate which is not disastrous to him. While some of his activities may regulate and utilize these changes to his benefit, more of them serve to accelerate the rate and widen the scope of natural changes in ways that lower the potential of the environment to sustain him.

For such effects man is responsible, and where responsibility enters so do ethical problems.

Through science, man now has the means to be aware of change and its effects and the ways in which his cultural values and behavior should be modified to insure their own preservation. Whether we consider ethics to be enlightened self-interest, the greatest good for the greatest number, ultimate good rather than present benefit, or Schweitzer's reverence for life, man's obligation toward environment is equally clear.

REFERENCES

Ahlmann, H. W., 1953, *Glacier Variations and Climatic Fluctuations.* (Bowman Memorial Lectures, Series Three.) New York: American Geographical Society. 51 pp.

Anderson, E., 1952, *Plants, Man and Life.* Boston: Little, Brown & Co. 245 pp.

Anonymous, 1953, *Desert Research: Proceedings of the International Symposium Held in Jerusalem, May 7–14, 1952, Sponsored by the Research Council of Israel and the United Nations Educational, Scientific, and Cultural Organization.* Jerusalem: Research Council of Israel. 641 pp.; 1954, *Growing Food for a Growing World.* ("The Work of FAO, 1952–53.") Rome: United Nations Food and Agriculture Organization. 37 pp.; 1955, "Europe Issues Aired on Overpopulation." *Christian Science Monitor,* January 29, p. 2.

Aveleyra, L., and Maldonado-Koerdell, M., 1952, "Asociación de artefactos con mamut en el pleistoceno superior de la cuenca de México," *Revista mexicana de estudios antropológicos,* XIII, 3–30.

Ayres, E., and Scarlott, C. A., 1952, *Energy Sources: The Wealth of the World.* New York: McGraw-Hill Book Co. 344 pp.

Benchetrit, M., 1954, "L'Erosion anthropogène: Couverture végétale et conséquences du mode d'exploitation du sol," *L'Information géographique,* XVIII, No. 3, 100–108.

Bliven, B., 1953, *Preview for Tomorrow: The Unfinished Business of Science.* New York: Alfred A. Knopf. 347 pp.

Brown, H., 1954, *The Challenge of Man's Future.* New York: Viking Press, 290 pp.

Castro, Josué de, 1952, *The Geography of Hunger.* Boston: Little, Brown & Co. 337 pp.

Coleman, E. A., 1953, *Vegetation and Water-shed Management: An Appraisal of Vegetation Management in Relation to Water Supply, Food Control, and Soil Erosion.* New York: Ronald Press Co. 412 pp.

Crawford, M. D. C., 1938, *The Conquest of Culture.* New York: Greenberg. 250 pp.

Curry, L., 1952, "Climate and Economic Life: A New Approach, with Examples from the United States," *Geographical Review,* XLII, No. 3, 367–83.

Darwin, C. G., 1953, *The Next Million Years.* Garden City, N.Y.: Doubleday & Co. 210 pp.

Diolé, P., 1954, *4,000 Years under the Sea.* New York: Julian Messner, Inc. 237 pp.

Douglass, A. E., 1935, *Dating Pueblo Bonito and Other Ruins of the Southwest.* ("Pueblo Bonito Series," No. 1.) Washington, D.C.: National Geographic Society. 74 pp.

Ellis, C. B., *et al.*, 1954, *Fresh Water from the Ocean for Cities, Industry, and Irrigation.* New York: Ronald Press Co. 217 pp.

Fox, Sir C. S., 1952, *Water: A Study of Its Properties—Its Constitution, Its Circulation on the Earth, and Its Utilization by Man.* New York: Philosophical Library. 148 pp.

Fried, M. H., 1952, "Land Tenure, Geography and Ecology in the Contact of Cultures," *American Journal of Economics and Sociology,* XI, No. 4, 391–412.

Good, R., 1953, *The Geography of the Flowering Plants.* 2d ed. London: Longmans, Green & Co. 452 pp.

Gottman, J., *et al.*, 1952, *L'Aménagement de l'espace: Planification régionale et géographie.* Paris: A. Colin. 140 pp.

Gutkind, E. A., 1953, *The Expanding Environment: The End of Cities, the Rise of Communities.* London: Freedom Press. 70 pp.

Hadlow, L., 1953, *Climate, Vegetation and Man.* New York: Philosophical Library. 288 pp.

Hanson, E. P. 1949, *New Worlds Emerging.* New York: Duell, Sloan & Pearce. 385 pp.

Hatt, P. K. (ed.), 1952, *World Population and Future Resources: The Proceedings of the Second Centennial Academic Conference of Northwestern University, Evanston, Illinois, March, 1951.* New York: American Book Co. 262 pp.

Horberg, L. 1952, "Interrelations of Geomorphology, Glacial Geology, and Pleistocene Geology," *Journal of Geology,* LX, No. 2, 187–90.

Howell, F. C., 1952, "Pleistocene Glacial Ecology and the Evolution of 'Classic Neandertal' Man," *Southwestern Journal of Anthropology,* VIII, No. 4, 377–410.

Hymans, E., 1952, *Soil and Civilization.* London: Thames & Hudson. 312 pp.

Iversen, J., 1949, "The Influence of Prehistoric Man on Vegetation," *Danmarks Geologiske Undersøgelse,* III, No. 6, 5–25.

Jarrett, H. (ed.), 1953, *The Nation Looks at Its Resources.* (Report of the Mid-century Conference on Resources for the Future.) Washington, D.C. 418 pp.

Jensen, L. B., 1953, *Man's Foods: Nutrition and Environments in Food Gathering and Food Producing Times*. Champaign, Ill.: Garrard Press. 278 pp.

Judson, S., 1952, "Arroyos," *Scientific American*, CLXXXVII, No. 6, 71—76.

Kendall, H. M., and Glendinning, R. M., 1952, *Introduction to Physical Geography*. New York: Harcourt, Brace & Co. 508 pp.

Kraemer, J. H., 1952, *Wood Conservation Bibliography: A Selection of References in the Field of Production and Utilization of Lumber and Other Wood Products*. Washington, D.C.: U.S. Department of Commerce, Office of Industry and Commerce. 77 pp.

Krick, I. P., 1954, "Weather Modification and Its Value to Agriculture and Water Supply," *Journal of the Royal Society of Arts*, CII, No. 4924, 447—68.

La Barre, W., 1954, *The Human Animal*. Chicago: University of Chicago Press, 371 pp.

Leet, L. D., and Judson, S., 1954, *Physical Geology*. New York: Prentice-Hall, Inc. 466 pp.

Leopold, A. 1949, *A Sand County Almanac*. New York: Oxford University Press. 226 pp.

Leopold, L. B., and Maddock, T., Jr., 1954, *The Flood Control Controversy*. New York: Ronald Press Co. 278 pp.

Lowdermilk, W. C., 1953, *Conquest of the Land through Seven Thousand Years*. (Agriculture Information Bulletin No. 99.) Washington, D.C.: U.S. Soil Conservation Service. 30 pp.

Malin, J. C., 1953, "Soil, Animal, and Plant Relations of the Grassland, Historically Reconsidered," *Scientific Monthly*, LXXVI, No. 4, 207—20.

Mangelsdorf, P. C., 1952, *Plants and Human Affairs*. ("Niewland Lectures," Vol. V.) Notre Dame, Ind.: University of Notre Dame. 29 pp.

Marsh, G. P., 1885, *The Earth as Modified by Human Action*. New York: Charles Scribner's Sons. 629 pp.

Mather, J. R., 1953, "The Disposal of Industrial Effluent by Woods Irrigation," *Transactions of the American Geophysical Union*, XXXIV, 227—39.

Meggers, B. J., 1954, "Environmental Limitation on the Development of Culture," *American Anthropologist*, LVI, No. 6, 801—24.

Minikin, R. R., 1952, *Coast Erosion and Protection: Studies in Causes and Remedies*. London: Chapman & Hall. 240 pp.

Monkhouse, F. J., 1954, *The Principles of Physical Geography*. London: University of London Press, 452 pp.

Odum, E. P., 1954, *Fundamentals of Ecology*. Philadelphia: W. B. Saunders Co. 384 pp.

Ojala, E. M., 1952, *Agriculture and Economic Progress*. London: Oxford University Press. 220 pp.

Ordway, S. H., Jr., 1953, *Resources and the American Dream*. New York: Ronald Press Co. 55 pp.

Osborn, F., 1953, *The Limits of the Earth*. Boston: Little, Brown & Co. 238 pp.

Peterson, E., 1954, *Big Dam Foolishness*. New York: Devin-Adair Co. 224 pp.

Sauer, C. O., 1952, *Agricultural Origins and Dispersals*. (Bowman Memorial Lectures, Series Two.) New York: American Geographical Society. 110 pp.

Sears, P. B., 1935, *Deserts on the March*. Norman: Oklahoma University Press. 231 pp.; 1949, "Integration at the Community Level," *American Scientist*, XXXVII, 235—42; 1953a, "The Interdependence of Archeology and Ecology, with Examples from Middle America," *Transactions of the New York Academy of Sciences*, Series II, XV, 113—17; 1953b, "An Ecological View of Land Use in the Middle America," *CEIVA*, III, 157—65; 1954, "Human Ecology: A Problem in Synthesis," *Science*, CXX, 959—63; 1955, "Changing Man's Habitat: Physical and Biological Phenomena," pp. 31—46 in Thomas, W. L., Jr. (ed.), *Yearbook of Anthropology—1955*. New York: Wenner-Gren Foundation for Anthropological Research, Inc. 836 pp.

Shantz, H. L., 1954, "The Place of Grasslands in the Earth's Cover of Vegetation," *Ecology*, XXXV, No. 2, 143—51.

Shapley, H. (ed.), 1953, *Climatic Change*. Cambridge, Mass.: Harvard University Press. 318 pp.

Stamp, L. D., 1952, *Land for Tomorrow: The Underdeveloped World*. Bloomington: Indiana University Press. 230 pp.

Sutton, O. G., 1953, *Micrometeorology: A Study of Physical Processes in the Lowest Layers of the Earth's Atmosphere*. New York: McGraw-Hill Book Co. 333 pp.

Thompson, L. M., 1952, *Soils and Soil Fertility*. New York: McGraw-Hill Book Co. 339 pp.

Thornbury, W. D., 1954, *Principles of Geomorphology*. New York: John Wiley & Sons. 618 pp.

Thornthwaite, C. W., 1953, "Topoclimatology." Seabrook, N.J.: Johns Hopkins University, Laboratory of Climatology. 13 pp. (Mimeographed.)

Verulam, J. B. G.; Angus, J. H.; and Chaplin, S., 1952, "The Geography of Power: Its Sources and Transmission," *Geographical Journal*, CXVIII, Part 3, 251—66.

Veyret, P., 1951, *Géographie de l'élevage*. Paris: Gallimard. 254 pp.

Vial, A. E. L., 1952, *Alpine Glaciers*. London: Batchworth Press. 126 pp.

Weaver, J. E., 1954, *North American Prairie*, Lincoln, Neb.: Johnsen Publishing Co. 348 pp.

Woytinsky, W. S. and E. S., 1953, *World Population and Production: Trends and Outlook*. New York: Twentieth Century Fund. 1,268 pp.

Yerg, D. G., under direction of Gray, D. E., 1951, *Annotated Bibliography on Snow, Ice, and Permafrost*. Wilmette, Ill.: U.S. Library of Congress, Science Division. 226 pp.

Natural History of Urbanization

Commentary

"The Natural History of Urbanization" Mr. Mumford entitled his essay. It is an apt title, for although he does not explicitly say so in his essay, Mumford does imply and demonstrate that urbanization is an ecological process. Not many ecologists recognize this, but a number of geographers do.

Urbanization is also an evolutionary process, a developmental strategy much like natural ecological succession. Hunting man with a loose social structure became agrarian and established villages. As villages were specialized and became centers of crafts and trade, they developed into cities. Over 10,000 years as agrarian, man is now becoming urban. He is engaged in an ecological revolution the likes of which man has experienced only once before in all history, when he abandoned a hunting way of life for an agrarian one.

This revolution will have its effects on both the natural landscape and man. Increasing urbanization and industrialization will continue to obliterate the natural environment, its wildlife, its wilderness. The tragedy is that first-class land for agriculture is also first-class land for urban development and housing. The vegetable fields of New Jersey and California and the cornfields of Iowa can disappear forever into the amoebic city. Unless efforts are made to prevent it, cities will become more and more parasitic on the land, working ruin on both surrounding and distant lands. For example, just as ancient cities destroyed forests for fuel, so our needs for power are destroying (but do not need to) the mountains of Appalachia; and wastes instead of being recycled are poured into air, water, and land.

As cities grow, they not only draw resources from the countryside; they also deplete its populations as the masses move to the city to find employment, excitement, and variety in their life experiences. But man can't shake his close to a million years' association with natural environment. So many who fled to the city flee away from it, rebelling against crowding and the impersonal life. Desiring that face-to-face social contact so characteristic of primitive society and the village, they move to special twentieth-century semicountry institutions, the suburbs. This aggravates rather than improves the problem. Suburbs devour land. The private lots—of up to an acre, the suburbanites' little peasant plots—eat up land at an enormous rate. They overextend sewage systems, if indeed any exist at all, and water systems. They demand more highways and air-polluting automobiles to get the suburbanites back to the city where the jobs still are. Highways and beltways proliferate, burying more and more of the countryside beneath the concrete and asphalt. The automobile becomes a way of life and the instrument for choking the life out of the central city. So the city extends outward to meet and eventually swallow up the suburbs. The result is large areas that are neither city nor countryside. As the 1970 census discovered, the United States is not urban but suburban.

The results are explainable. The urbanization process is developing so fast that the still agrarian man cannot adapt to it. Urbanization creates a synthetic environment. Edward Higbee states that, to help fit into this new synthetic environment, "each individual must undergo a formal process of adaptation to the man-made environment. This process of adaptation provides us with employable skills and behavioral codes; it guides our cultural growth so that it conforms to society's culture evolution."[1]

Involved in this evolutionary process must be a new adaptation of man for higher density living. The suburbs and the escape from his fellow creatures will no longer be possible. What is required, Higbee says, is an accelerated cultural revolution.

> We human beings are social animals with our own kind of herd instinct. We accept the familiar and reject the stranger. As our environment changes to accommodate higher densities and greater inter-action we must produce cultural changes so that we can relate to one another and to that synthetic environment we are creating. We must learn how to accept the stranger into our institutional net-

---

[1] Edward Higbee, "Consequences of Ecological Ignorance," *Proceedings Golden Anniversary Meeting*, New England Section, Society of American Foresters, 1970, pp. 26—29.

works, giving each person, known or unknown, the kind of elementary security which primitive peoples provided for one another as members of tribes in which there were no strangers.[2]

This means that the centuries-old relationship to the land is ending. Mumford chronicles it as he surveys the emergence of the city, the city's early relation to food production, and finally its complete alienation from the land. Cities began in a symbiotic relationship to the surrounding countryside; in spite of urban culture, man has to maintain that relationship, although he is personally divorced from the land.

---

[2]*Ibid.*, p. 26.

Selection 12

The Natural History of Urbanization

by Lewis Mumford

THE EMERGENCE OF THE CITY

The natural history of urbanization has not yet been written, for only a small part of the preliminary work has been done. The literature of the city itself, until a half-century ago, was barren to the point of nonexistence; and even now the ecologists of the city, dealing too largely with a late and limited aspect of urbanism, have hardly staked out the ground that is to be covered. Our present purpose, accordingly, is to make use of such studies as have so far been made in order to ask more pointed questions and so, incidentally, to indicate further fields of profitable study.

Whether one looks at the city morphologically or functionally, one cannot understand its development without taking in its relationship to earlier forms of cohabitation that go back to non-human species. One must remember not only the obvious homologies of the anthill and the beehive but also the nature of fixed seasonal habitations in protected sites, like the breeding grounds of many species of birds. Though permanent villages date only from Neolithic times, the habit of resorting to caves for the collective performance of magical ceremonies seems to date back to an earlier period; and whole communities, living in caves and hollowed-out walls of rock, have survived in widely scattered

areas down to the present. The outline of the city as both an outward form and an inward pattern of life might be found in such ancient assemblages. Whatever the aboriginal impetus, the tendency toward formal cohabitation and fixed residence gave rise, in Neolithic times, to the ancestral form of the city: the village, a collective utility brought forth by the new agricultural economy. Lacking the size and complexity of the city, the village nevertheless exhibits its essential features: the encircling mound or palisade, setting it off from the fields; permanent shelters; storage pits and bins, with refuse dumps and burial grounds recording silently past time and spent energy. At this early stage, at least, Mark Jefferson's observation (1931) holds true: urban and rural, city and country, are one thing, not two things.

Though the number of families per acre in a village is greater than the number per square mile under a pastoral economy, such settlements bring with them no serious disturbance in the natural environment; indeed, the relation may even be favorable for building up the soil and increasing its natural productivity. Archeological explorers in Alaska have been able to detect early settlements by noting the greenness of the vegetation around the otherwise submerged village sites, probably due to

---

THIS SELECTION is reprinted with permission of the author and publisher from W. E. Thomas (ed.), *Man's Role in Changing the Face of the Earth.* © The University of Chicago, 1956.

the enrichment of the soil from the nitrogenous human and animal waste accumulated near by. Early cities, as we find them in Mesopotamia and Egypt, maintain the symbiotic relation with agriculture that we find in the village. In countries like China, still governed by the principles of village economy, even contemporary cities with high population density, such as Keyes describes (1951), exhibit the same reciprocal relations: "The most concentrated highly developed agriculture is just outside the walls of cities." King estimated (1927) that each million city dwellers in China account for more than 13,000 pounds of nitrogen, 2,700 pounds of phosphorous, and almost 4,500 pounds of potassium in the daily night soil returned to the land. Brunhes' description (1920) of cities under "unproductive occupation of the soil" does not altogether hold for the earliest types or, as I shall show, for the latest types of city.

The emergence of the city from the village was made possible by the improvements in plant cultivation and stock-breeding that came with Neolithic culture; in particular, the cultivation of the hard grains that could be produced in abundance and kept over from year to year without spoiling. This new form of food not merely offered insurance against starvation in the lean years, as was recorded in the famous story of Joseph in Egypt, but likewise made it possible to breed and support a bigger population not committed to food-raising. From the standpoint of their basic nutrition, one may speak of wheat cities, rye cities, rice cities, and maize cities, to characterize their chief source of energy; and it should be remembered that no other source was so important until the coal seams of Saxony and England were opened. With the surplus of manpower available as Neolithic man escaped from a subsistence economy, it was possible to draw a larger number of people into other forms of work and service: administration, the mechanical arts, warfare, systematic thought, and religion. So the once-scattered population of Neolithic times, dwelling in hamlets of from ten to fifty houses (Childe, 1954), was concentrated into "cities," ruled and regimented on a different plan. These early cities bore many marks of their village origins, for they were still in essence agricultural towns: the main source of their food supply was in the land around them; and, until the means of transport had greatly improved and a system of centralized control

had developed, they could not grow beyond the limit of their local water supply and their local food sources.

This early association of urban growth with food production governed the relation of the city to its neighboring land far longer than many observers now realize. Though grains were transported long distances (even as special food accessories like salt had circulated in earlier times), cities like Rome, which drew mainly on the distant granaries of Africa and the Near East—to say nothing of the oyster beds of Colchester in England—were exceptions down to the nineteenth century. As late as fifty years ago large portions of the fruits and vegetables consumed in New York and Paris came from nearby market gardens, sometimes on soils greatly enriched, if not almost manufactured, with urban refuse, as Kropotkin pointed out in *Fields, Factories, and Workshops* (1899). This means that one of the chief determinants of large-scale urbanization has been nearness to fertile agricultural land; yet, paradoxically, the growth of most cities has been achieved by covering over and removing from cultivation the very land—often, indeed, the richest alluvial soils—whose existence at the beginning made their growth possible. The tendency of cities to grow along rivers or near accessible harbors was furthered not alone by the need for easy transportation but by the need to draw on aquatic sources of food to supplement those produced by the soil. This rich and varied diet may itself have contributed to the vital energy of city dwellers as contrasted with the more sluggish ways of hinterlanders and perhaps may also have partly offset the bad effect of close quarters in spreading communicable diseases. While modern means of transport have equalized these advantages, they have not yet hastened the migration of urban populations to upland sites on poorer soils, though often these present more salubrious climates and better living conditions.

The village and the small country town are historic constants. One of the outstanding facts about urbanization is that, while the urban population of the globe in 1930 numbered around 415,000,000 souls, or about a fifth of the total population, the remaining four-fifths still lived under conditions approximating that of the Neolithic economy (Sorre, 1952). In countries as densely peopled as India, as late as 1939, according to the *Statesman's Yearbook*, less than 10 per cent of the total population lived in cities. These "Neolithic" conditions include the utilization of organic sources of energy, vegetable and animal, the use of a local supply of drinking water, the continuous cultivation of land within walking distance of the village, the partial use of human dung along with that of animals for fertilizer, a low concentration of inorganic refuse, like glass and metals, and an absence of air pollution. In many parts of the world, village settlements, far from encroaching on arable land, occupy barren hill sites of little use for agriculture; the stony outcrop of an Italian hill town involves only a slightly more symmetrical arrangement of the original rock strata. The chief weakness of these settlements, particularly in parts of the world long cultivated, notably in Spain, Greece, or China, is due to the peasant's begrudging the land needed for forest cover; he thus tends, by overtillage, to promote erosion and to create a further imbalance among the bird, insect, and plant populations. But, just as the early village economy was indebted to the astronomical calendar produced in the temple cities for the timely planting of their crops, so the present development of ecological knowledge, which has led to increasing concern and care for the woodland preserves in highly urbanized countries, may in time counteract the otherwise destructive effects of earlier stages in urban settlement.

URBAN SYMBIOSIS AND DOMINANCE

With the first growth of urban populations in ancient Mesopotamia, the symbiotic relations that originally held between village and land were not greatly altered. "The city," as Childe (1942, p. 94) describes its earliest manifestations, "is girt with a brick wall and a fosse, within the shelter of which man found for the first time a world of his own, relatively secure from the immediate pressure of raw, external nature. It stands out in an artificial landscape of gardens, fields, and pastures, created out of reed swamp and desert by the collective activity of preceding generations in building dykes and digging canals." Though these cities represented "a new magnitude in human settlement," the populations of Lagash, Umma, and Khafaje are "reliably estimated to have been 19,000, 16,000, and 12,000 respectively during the third millennium." The Levitical cities described in the Bible, confirmed by modern excavations of Gezer, had a town area of about 22 acres, with pasture land, permanently reserved, amounting to about 300 acres (Osborn, 1946). More than four thousand years later, as late as the sixteenth century, the characteristic size of the city in western Europe ranged from 2,000 to 20,000 people; it was only in the seventeenth century that cities of more than 100,000 began to multiply. In both the Near East in ancient times and in western Europe in the Middle Ages, cities prudently retained some portion of the land within their walls for gardens and the harboring of animals for food in case of military siege. Even the vast domains of Babylon must not mislead us into looking upon it as comparable in density to modern London. A map drawn in 1895 by Arthur Schneider, and republished by Hassert (1907), shows that Babylon covered an area big enough to contain Rome, Tarentum, Syracuse, Athens, Ephesus, Thebes, Jerusalem, Carthage, Sparta, Alexandria, and Tyre, together with almost as much open space between these cities as they occupied in their own right. Even in Herodotus' time, Babylon had many of the aspects of an overgrown village.

The Neolithic economy appears to have been a co-operative one. The concentration upon plant cultivation in small neighborly communities, never with a sufficient surplus of food or power to promote too much arrogance in man's relation with other men or with nature, established a natural balance between fields and settlements. In Europe, as Élisée Reclus long ago noted, country towns and villages tended to spread evenly, as far as topography allowed, about the space of a day's walk apart. With the introduction of metallurgy, during the succeeding period of urbanization, came technological specialization, caste differentiation, and heightened temptations to aggression; and with this began a disregard for the welfare of the community as a whole and, in particular, a tendency to ignore the city's dependence upon its local resources. Excess of manpower abetted an excessive belief in the power of man—a belief deepened, no doubt, by the efficacy of the new edged weapons and armor in giving control to aggressive minorities who took the law into their own hands. With the development of long-distance trading, numerical calculation, and coinage, this urban civilization tended to throw off its original sense of limits and to regard all forms of wealth as purchasable by trade or procurable by a demonstration of military power. What could not be grown or produced in the local region could be, by theft or exchange, obtained elsewhere. In time this urban economy made the mistake of applying the pragmatic standards of the market place to the environment itself: the process began of building over the interior open spaces and building out over the surrounding land.

Until modern times the extension of a city's walls marked its growth as surely as does each additional ring of a tree. The wall had perhaps a formative role in the transformation of the village into the city; when made of heavy, permanent materials, surrounded by a moat, it gave the city a means of protection the little village could not afford. Not merely was it capable of military defense, but the city, through its surplus population, could muster enough manpower to hold against a large army of attackers. The earliest meaning of "town" is an inclosed or fortified place. The village that, because of its defensible site, offered protection against predators of all kinds would in times of peril attract families from more exposed areas and so, with a larger, mixed population, would turn into a city. Thus the temple citadel would add to its original population and, even after the danger had passed, would retain some of those who sought shelter and so become a city. In Greece, at least the city comes into existence, historically, as such a synoecism.

But the morphological difference between the village and the city is not simply the result of the latter's superior site or of the fact that its geographic situation enables it to draw on a wider area for resources, foods, and men and in turn to export their products to a larger market, though both are facts conducive to population growth and economic expansion. What distinguish city from village are mainly two facts. The first of these is the presence of an organized social core, around which the whole structure of the community coheres. If this nucleation may begin in the village stage, as remains of temples seem to indicate, there is a general shift of household occupations and rituals into specialized collective institutions, part of the intensified social division of labor brought in with civilization itself. But, from the standpoint of the city's relation to the earth, the important point to notice is that, in this social core or nucleus, the sharpest departures from the daily habits and the physical structure of the

village take place. Thus the temple, unlike the hut, will be built of permanent materials, with solid stone walls, often plated with precious stones or roofed with rare timber taken from a distant quarry or forest, all conceived on a colossal scale, while the majority of dwelling houses will still be built of clay and reed, or wattle and daub, on the old village pattern. While the temple area will be paved, the streets and alleys of the rest of the city will remain unpaved. As late as imperial Rome, pavement will be introduced first into the Forum, while most of the arteries remain uncovered, to become sloughs of mud in rainy weather. Here too, in the urban palace, as early as Akkad, such technological innovations as baths, toilets, and drains will appear—innovations that remain far beyond the reach of the urban populations-at-large until modern times.

Along with this bold aesthetic transformation of the outward environment, another tendency distinguishes the city from the village—a tendency to loosen the bonds that connect its inhabitants with nature and to transform, eliminate, or replace its earth-bound aspects, covering the natural site with an artificial environment that enhances the dominance of man and encourages an illusion of complete independence from nature. The first age of the "urban revolution," to use Childe's term, had little extrahuman power and few machines. Its technological heritage, once it had learned to smelt copper and iron, was in every sense a static one; and its major skills, weaving aside, were concentrated on fashioning utensils and utilities (pots, jars, vats, bins) and on building great collective works (dams, irrigation systems, buildings, roads, baths) and, finally, cities themselves. Having learned to employ fire of relatively high intensity to glaze and smelt ores, these early civilizations offset its danger by creating a fireproof environment. The importance of this fact, once papyrus and paper were in use, can hardly be overestimated. In this general transformation from the transient to the fixed, from fragile and temporary structures to durable buildings, proof against wind, weather, and fire, early man emancipated himself likewise from the fluctuations and irregularities of nature. Each of the utilities that characterized the new urban form—the wall, the durable shelter, the arcade, the paved way, the reservoir, the aqueduct, the sewer—lessened the impact of nature and increased the dominance of man. That fact was revealed in the very silhouette of the city, as the traveler beheld it from a distance. Standing out in the vegetation-clad landscape, the city became an inverted oasis of stone or clay. The paved road, a man-made desert that speeds traffic and makes it largely independent of the weather and the seasons; the irrigation ditch, a man-made river system that releases the farmer from irregularities of seasonal rainfall; the water main, an artificial brook that turns the parched environment of the city into an oasis; the pyramid, an artificial mountain that serves as symbolic reminder of man's desire for permanence and continuity— all these inventions record the displacement of natural conditions with a collective artifact of urban origin.

Physical security and social continuity were the two great contributions of the city. Under those conditions every kind of conflict and challenge became possible without disrupting the social order, and part of this new animus was directed into a struggle with the forces of nature. By serving as a secure base of operations, a seat of law and government, a repository of deeds and contracts, and a marshaling yard of manpower, the city was able to engage in long-distance activities. Operating through trade, taxation, mining, military assault, and road-building, which made it possible to organize and deploy thousands of men, the city proceeded to make large-scale transformations of the environment, impossible for groups of smaller size to achieve. Through its storage, canalization, and irrigation, the city, from its earliest emergence in the Near East, justified its existence, for it freed the community from the caprices and violences of nature—though no little part of that gift was nullified by the further effect of subjecting the community more abjectly to the caprices and violences of men.

URBAN DISPLACEMENT OF NATURE

Unfortunately, as the disintegration of one civilization after another reminds us, the displacement of nature in the city rested, in part, upon an illusion—or, indeed, a series of illusions—as to the nature of man and his institutions: the illusions of self-sufficiency and independence and of the possibility of physical continuity without conscious renewal. Under the protective mantle of the city, seemingly so permanent, these illusions encouraged habits of predation or parasitism that eventually undermined the whole social and economic structure, after having worked ruin in the surrounding landscape and even in far-distant regions. Many elements supplied by nature, necessary for both health and mental balance, were lacking in the city. Medicine, as practiced by the Hippocratic School in the great retreats, like that at Kos, concerned with airs, waters, and places, seems at an early age to have employed in therapy natural elements that were depleted or out of balance even in the relatively small Aegean cities of the fifth century B.C., though their ruling classes spent no small part of their leisure in the exercise of the body. Through the ages the standard prescription for most urban illnesses—and perhaps as effective as more specific remedies—is retreat to some little village by seacoast or mountain—that is, restoration to a pre-urban natural environment. In times of plague the retreat repeatedly has taken on the aspects of a rout. Though man has become the dominant species in every region where the city has taken hold, partly because of the knowledge and the system of public controls over both man and nature he exercises there, he has yet to safeguard that position by acknowledging his sustained and inescapable dependence upon all his biological partners. With the ecological implications of this fact, I shall deal later.

Probably no city in antiquity had a population of much more than a million inhabitants, not even Rome; and, except in China, there were no later Romes until the nineteenth century. But, long before a million population is reached, most cities come to a critical point in their development. That occurs when the city is no longer in symbiotic relationship with its surrounding land; when further growth overtaxes local resources, like water, and makes them precarious; when, in order to continue its growth, a city must reach beyond its immediate limits for water, for fuel, for building materials, and for raw materials used in manufacture; and, above all, when its internal birth rate becomes inadequate to provide enough manpower to replace, if not to augment, its population. This stage has been reached in different civilizations at different periods. Up to this point, when the city has come to the limits of sustenance in its own territory, growth takes place by colonization, as in a beehive. After

144

this point, growth takes place, in defiance of natural limitations, by a more intensive occupation of the land and by encroachment into the surrounding areas, with the subjugation by law or naked force of rival growing cities bidding for the same resources.

Most of the characteristics of this second form of urban growth can be observed in the history of Rome. Here the facts are better documented than they are for most ancient cities; and the effects upon the landscape have remained so visible that they suggested to George Perkins Marsh (1864, 1874) the principal lines of his investigation of *The Earth as Modified by Human Action*. Rome of the Seven Hills is an acropolis type of city, formed by a cluster of villages united for defense; and the plain of the Tiber was the original seat of their agriculture. The surplus population of this region conquered first the neighboring territories of the Etruscans and then those of more distant lands. By systematic expropriation, Rome brought wheat, olive oil, dried fish, and pottery back to the original site to sustain its growing population. To facilitate the movement of its legions and speed up the processes of administration, it carved roads through the landscape with triumphant disregard of the nature of the terrain. These roads and viaducts went hand in hand with similar works of engineering, the aqueducts and reservoirs necessary to bring water to Rome. By short-circuiting the flow of water from mountainside to sea, the city monopolized for its special uses a considerable amount of the runoff; and, to offset some of the effects of metropolitan overcrowding, it created a cult of the public bath that in turn imposed a heavy drain upon the fuel supplied by the nearby forest areas. The advance of technology, with central hot-air heating, characteristically hastened the process of deforestation, as was later to happen in the glass- and ironmaking and shipbuilding industries of northern Europe and to be repeated today in the heavy industrial demand for cellulose. Meanwhile, the sewers of Rome, connected to public toilets, polluted the Tiber without returning the precious mineral contents to the soil, though even in imperial Rome dung farmers still collected most of the night soil from the great tenements of the proletariat. At this stage the symbiotic relation turns into a parasitic one; the cycle of imbalance begins, and the mere massing of the demand in a single center results

in denudations and desiccations elsewhere. The more complete the urbanization, the more definite is the release from natural limitations; the more highly the city seems developed as an independent entity, the more fatal are the consequences for the territory it dominates. This series of changes characterizes the growth of cities in every civilization: the transformation of eopolis into megalopolis. If the process wrought damage to the earth even in the ancient world, when cities as big as Rome, Carthage, and Alexandria were the exception rather than the rule, we have good reason to examine carefully the probable consequences of the present wave of urbanization.

MODERN FORCES OF EXPANSION

Let me sum up the observations so far made with respect to the natural history of cities. In the first stage of urbanization the number and size of cities varied with the amount and productivity of the agricultural land available. Cities were confined mainly to the valleys and flood plains, like the Nile, the Fertile Crescent, the Indus, and the Hwang Ho. Increase of population in any one city was therefore limited. The second stage of urbanization began with the development of large-scale river and sea transport and the introduction of roads for chariots and carts. In this new economy the village and the country town maintained the environmental balance of the first stage; but, with the production of grain and oil in surpluses that permitted export, a specialization in agriculture set in and, along with this, a specialization in trade and industry, supplementing the religious and political specialization that dominated the first stage. Both these forms of specialization enabled the city to expand in population beyond the limits of its agricultural hinterland; and, in certain cases, notably in the Greek city of Megalopolis, the population in smaller centers was deliberately removed to a single big center— a conscious reproduction of a process that was taking place less deliberately in other cities. At this stage the city grew by draining away its resources and manpower from the countryside without returning any equivalent goods. Along with this went a destructive use of natural resources for industrial purposes, with increased concentration on mining and smelting.

The third stage of urbanization does not

145

make its appearance until the nineteenth century, and it is only now beginning to reach its full expansion, performance, and influence. If the first stage is one of urban balance and cooperation, and the second is one of partial urban dominance within a still mainly agricultural framework, behind both is an economy that was forced to address the largest part of its manpower toward cultivating the land and improving the whole landscape for human use. The actual amount of land dedicated to urban uses was limited, if only because the population was also limited. This entire situation has altered radically during the last three centuries by reason of a series of related changes. The first is that world population has been growing steadily since the seventeenth century, when the beginnings of reasonable statistical estimates, or at least tolerable guesses, can first be made. According to the Woytinskys (1953), the average rate of population increase appears to have gone up steadily: 2.7 per cent from 1650 to 1700; 3.2 per cent in the first half of the eighteenth century and 4.5 per cent in the second half; 5.3 per cent from 1800 to 1850; 6.5 per cent from 1850 to 1900; and 8.3 per cent from 1900 to 1950. As the Woytinskys themselves remark, these averages should not be taken too seriously; yet there is a high probability that an acceleration has taken place and hardly any doubt whatever that the world population has doubled during the last century, while the man-power needed to maintain agricultural productivity in mechanized countries has decreased.

By itself this expansion might mean no more than that the less populated parts of the earth would presently acquire densities comparable to those of India and China, with a great part of the increase forced to undertake intensive cultivation of the land. But this increase did not take place by itself; it was accompanied by a series of profound technological changes which transformed the classic "age of utilities" into the present "age of the machine" and a predominantly agricultural civilization into an urban one—or possibly a suburban one. These two factors, technical improvement and population growth, have been interacting since at least the sixteenth century, for it was the improvement in the sailing ship and the art of navigation that opened up the almost virginal territory of the New World. The resulting increase of food supply, in terms of added tillage,

was further augmented by New World crops like maize and the potato. Meanwhile, the increased production of energy foods—vegetable oils, animal fats, and sugar cane and sugar beet—not merely helped support a large population but in turn, through the supply of fat, turned soap from a courtly luxury to a household necessity; and this major contribution to hygiene—public and personal—probably did more to lower the death rate than any other single factor. From the beginning of the nineteenth century the surplus population made it possible for old cities to expand and new cities to be founded. As Webber long ago pointed out (1899), the rate was even faster in Germany in the second half of the nineteenth century than it was in the United States.

This wave of urbanization was not, as is sometimes thought, chiefly dependent upon the steam engine or upon improvements in local transportation. The fact is that the number of cities above the 100,000 mark had increased in the seventeenth century, well before the steam engine or the power loom had been invented. London passed the million mark in population by 1810, before it had a mechanical means of transportation or the beginning of an adequate water supply (in parts of London piped water was turned on only twice a week). But a marked change, nevertheless, took place in urban growth during the nineteenth century.

At this moment the four natural limits on the growth of cities were thrown off: the nutritional limit of an adequate food and water supply; the military limit of protective walls and fortifications; the traffic limit set by slow-moving agents of reliable transportation like the canalboat; and the power limit to regular production imposed by the limited number of water-power sites and the feebleness of the other prime movers—horse and wind power. In the new industrial city these limits ceased to hold. While up to this time growth was confined to commercial cities favorably situated at the merging point of two or more diverse regions with complementary resources and skills, urban development now went on in places that had easy access to the coal measures, the iron-ore beds, and the limestone quarries. Pottery towns, cotton towns, woolen towns, and steel towns, no longer held down in size, flourished wherever the tracks for steam locomotives could be laid and the steam engine established as a source of power. The only limitation on the spread and multiplication of towns under this regime was the disability of the steam locomotive to operate efficiently on grades of more than 2 per cent. Whereas the water power and wind power of the eotechnic period had tended to distribute industry in the coastal cities of high winds or along fast-running upland streams, coal power tended to group industry in the valleys near the mine pits or along the railroad lines that constituted a continuation of the mine and the mining environment (Mumford, 1934). Industry, like agriculture, competes for the heavy lowland soils. As for the railroad itself, it is one of the greatest devourers of land and transformers of landscape. The marshaling yards of its great urban terminals put large areas out of urban or agricultural use.

GROWTH OF THE CONURBATION

Up to the middle of the nineteenth century, water-power sites, the seats of earlier industrial improvements, continued to attract industries into mill villages; but, with the coming of the railroad, industries grouped together in cities in order to take advantage of the surplus labor that accumulated there. From this time on, whole districts, such as Elberfeld-Barmen, Lille-Roubaix, the Black Country, and the Delaware Valley, become urbanized, and the limits of city growth are reached only when one city, by its conversion of farmland into building lots, coalesces with another city engaged in the same process. Growth of this kind, automatic and unregulated, a result of the railroad and the factory, had never been possible before; but now the agents of mechanization not merely created their own environment but set a new pattern for the growth of already existing great cities. Looking at Bartholomew's population map of Britain early in the present century, Patrick Geddes discovered (1915) that urbanization had taken a new form: urban areas, hitherto distinct, both as political units and as topographic features, had in fact flowed together and formed dense population masses on a scale far greater than any of the big cities of the past, forming a new configuration as different as the city itself was from its rural prototypes. He called this new kind of urban grouping the "conurbation." This new urban tissue was less differentiated than the old. It presented an impoverished institutional life; it showed fewer signs of social nucleation; and it tended to increase in size, block by block, avenue by avenue, "development" by "development," without any individuality of form and, most remarkable of all, without any quantitative limits (West Midland Group, 1948).

This concentration of industry had marked effects upon the entire environment. The new source of power—coal; the new industrial processes, massed in the new steelworks and coke ovens; the new chemical plants for manufacturing chlorine, sulfuric acid, and hundreds of other potentially noxious compounds—all poured their waste products into the air and waters on a scale that made it impossible for the local environment to absorb them as it might have absorbed the effluvia of a village industry or the organic waste of a tannery or a slaughter-house. Streams hitherto well stocked with fish, salubrious for bathing, and even potable became poisonous sewers; while the fall of soot, chemical dust, silica, and steel particles choked vegetation in what open ground remained and left their deposits in human lungs. The effects of this pollution, and the possibility of more radical and irretrievable pollution to come through the use of atomic reactors, are dealt with in chapters that follow. Here the point to mark is that it was a natural penalty of overconcentration. The very ubiquity of the new type of city, coupled with its density, increases, for example, the threat of a lethal fog from chemicals normally in the air, such as wiped out over five thousand lives in a single week in London in 1952; a mass exodus by cars, at the low speed imposed by a heavy fog, would itself add to the deadly gases already in the air.

The extension of the industrial conurbation not merely brings with it the obliteration of the life-sustaining natural environment but actually creates, as substitute, a definitely antiorganic environment; and even where, in the interstices of this urban development, land remains unoccupied, it progressively ceases to be of use for either agriculture or recreation. The removal of the topsoil, or its effacement by buildings and slag piles, brings on no temporary denudation; it results in deserts that, even if every effort suggested by science were made, might take centuries to redeem for human occupancy, to say nothing of more organic forms of cultivation. Though the conurbation came into existence through the dense industrial occupation of a whole region rather than through the over-

147

growth of a single dominant city, the two types overlap. In England, Birmingham itself, though the center of congeries of smaller towns, has passed the million mark, to become the second city in Britain. By offering a big local market, the great conurbations, in addition to attracting the consumption trades and industries, have brought in petroleum refineries, chemical plants, and steelworks, which gravitate to the cheaper land on the edge of metropolitan areas. This tends to create industrial defilement at the point where Sir John Evelyn, in 1661 in his pamphlet *Fumifugium* (1933), proposed to create a protective green belt, filled with aromatic shrubs, to purify the already noisome air of London. This extension of the area of industrial pollution into the very land that the overgrown city needs for mass recreation—accessible to sunlight, to usable ocean, river front, and woodland—likewise lessens the advantage of the only form of temporary escape left: retreat to the suburb.

From the very nature of the city as a market, a workshop, and a place of civic assemblage, there is a direct relation between its growth and the growth of transportation systems, though, in the case of seaways and airways, the latter may be visible only in the increase of harbor facilities and storehouses. In general, one may say that, the heavier the urbanization, the heavier the transportation network, not merely within but without. From ancient Rome to recent times, the fifteen-foot roadway remained the outsize. But, with the eighteenth century, land transportation takes a new turn. In 1861, Wilhelm Heinrich Riehl noted it (1935) in the change from the rural highroads of the old town economy to the new *Landstrasse*, planned in more systematic fashion by the new bureaucracy—wider by three feet, more heavily paved, and often lined with trees, as in the beautiful highway lined with ancient lindens between Lübeck and Travemunde. With the coming of railroad transportation, the width of the new kind of permanent way again increased; the railroad made fresh demands for large areas of flat, low-lying land to serve as marshaling yards, adjacent to the city or even cutting a great wedge through it. The economy of the water-level route again turned to a non-agricultural use of precisely the land that was often the most fertile available and spoiled even its recreational value. With the introduction of the motorcar, even secondary roads demanded

pavement, and arterial roads both widened and multiplied, with the result that around great metropolises six-, seven-, and eight-lane highways with two-hundred-foot rights of way have become increasingly common. They are further complicated by great traffic circles or cloverleaf patterns of overpass and underpass to permit the continuous flow of traffic at intersections, however wasteful of land these junctions may be. In the case of parkways planned to follow the ridges, like the Taconic State Parkway in New York State, the land given over to the road may be of minor value either for agricultural or for civic use; but where the highway engineer ignores the contours, follows the valleys, and cuts through hills to maintain his level, the motorway may be an active agent both in eroding the soil and in disrupting the habitat. The yielding of water navigation to land transport has aggravated this damage; and every further congestion of population leads to still more highway-building of a permanent and costly kind to accommodate the mass week-end exit of motorists. Thus the city, by its incontinent and uncontrolled growth, not merely sterilizes the land it immediately needs but vastly increases the total area of sterilization far beyond its boundaries.

THE SUBURBAN OVERSPILL

At this point we are confronted with two special phenomena known only in embryonic form in other urban cultures: the production of a new kind of urban tissue, in the open pattern of the suburb, and the further development of a mass transportation by means of self-propelled, individual vehicles, trucks, and motorcars. The first change, the result of seeking an environment free from noise, dirt, and overcrowding of the city, actually antedated the means that made it possible on a mass scale. In London this suburban movement began as early as Elizabethan times as a reaction against the overbuilding and overcrowding that had then taken place in the center of the city; and at the end of the eighteenth century a similar exodus occurred among merchants who could afford a private coach to take them into the city. With increased facilities of transportation offered by the public coach and the railroad, this suburban movement became more common through the nineteenth century, as witness the growth of St. John's Wood, Richmond, and

Hampstead in London, of Chestnut Hill and Germantown in Philadelphia, and of the Hudson River suburbs in New York. But, up to 1920, it was mainly the upper-income groups that could afford the luxury of sunlight, fresh air, gardens, open spaces, and access to the open country. The new open-type plan, with houses set in gardens, at densities of from two houses to ten or twelve per acre, had long been characteristic of American country towns, most notably those of New England; indeed, this open pattern dominated west of the Alleghenies. But this standard now became universalized in the upper-class suburb, though its economic base lay outside the area the suburb occupied and from the beginning demanded a heavy sacrifice of man-hours in commuting to the distant metropolis. The low cost of suburban land and the possibility of economizing on local utilities like roads and sewers encouraged luxurious standards of space and gave those who could afford to escape a superior biological environment and perhaps, if Thorndyke is correct (1939), a superior social one. The initiative of a few farsighted industrialists, like Lever (Port Sunlight, 1887) and Cadbury (Bournville, 1895), proved that similar standards could be applied to building working-class quarters when land was sufficiently cheap.

Since 1920 the spread of private motor vehicles has completed the work of enlarging potential suburban territory, an expansion already well begun in the 1900's by interurban electric transit. The exodus to suburbia has taken in wave after wave of city dwellers, at lower and lower income levels, seeking to escape the congested and disordered environment of the big city. This removal from the city has not been accompanied by any equivalent decentralization of industry; rather it has served to sustain an antiquated pattern of concentration. The pattern of population distribution around great cities has been the product, not of social foresight for public ends, but mainly of private initiative for private profit, though it could not have taken place on its present scale in America without a vast public investment in highways, expressways, bridges, and tunnels. The result of this uncontrolled spread of the suburb has been to nullify the very purposes that brought the movement into existence.

But suburban agglomeration cannot be treated as a fact in itself; it carries with it, through

the demands of the motorcar, both for private transportation and for the movement of goods, an enormous increase in paved roads, which eat into the surviving agricultural and wilderness areas and permanently sterilize ever larger quantities of land. The filling-up of marshes, the coverage of rich soils with buildings, the felling of woodlands, the clogging of local brooks and streams, and the abandonment of local springs and wells were all secondary disturbances of the early type of metropolis, even when it reached a population of a million people. When Rome was surrounded by the Aurelian wall in A.D. 274, it covered, according to Carcopino (1940), a little more than 5 square miles. The present area of Greater London is about a hundred and thirty times as great as this, while it is roughly six hundred and fifty times as great as the area, namely, 677 acres, surrounded by its wall in the Middle Ages. The metropolitan area of New York is even more widespread; it covers something like 2,514 square miles; and already a good case could be made out for treating a wide coastal strip from Boston to Washington as one continuous conurbation, geographically speaking. This difference in magnitude between every earlier type of urban development and that characterizing our own age is critical. What is more, as population increases, the percentage of the population in cities increases, too, and the ratio of those going into metropolitan areas is even higher. Even in England, though the amount of land occupied by cities, "built-over land," is low (2.2 per cent) in proportion to the entire land area of the British Isles, this is more than half the area of "first-class" land available for agriculture and is a tenth of the "good land" available, according to Sir L. Dudley Stamp's classification (1952). Since requirements for manufacture and urban development are for accessible, graded land, these demands conflict with the needs of the farmer; they compete for the same good soils, and only goverment intervention in England, since 1932, has saved this misuse of valuable agricultural land.

Under modern technical conditions the open pattern of the residential suburb is not confined to domestic needs alone. The demand for large land areas characterizes modern factory organization, with its horizontally ordered assembly lines, housed in spreading one-story structures, and, above all, airports for long-distance flights, whose demand for landing lanes and approaches on the order of miles has increased with the size and speed of planes. In addition, the noise of planes, especially jets, sterilizes even larger areas of land for residential use as both hazardous to life and dangerous to health. There are many urban regions, like that tapped by the main-line railroads from Newark, New Jersey, to Wilmington, Delaware, where urban tissue has either displaced the land or so completely modified its rural uses as to give the whole area the character of a semi-urban desert. Add to this, in every conurbation, the ever larger quantity of land needed for collective reservoir systems, sewage works, and garbage-disposal plants as dispersed local facilities fall out of use.

As a result of population increase and urban centralization, one further demand for land, unfortunately a cumulative one, must be noted: the expansion of urban cemeteries in all cultures that maintain, as most "Christian" nations do, the Paleolithic habit of earth burial. This has resulted in the migration of the burying ground from the center to the outskirts of metropolitan areas, where vast cemeteries serve, indeed, as temporary suburban parks, until they become a wilderness of stone monuments. Unless the custom of periodically emptying out these cemeteries, as was done in London and Paris with the bones in old churchyards, takes hold, or until cremation replaces burial, the demand for open spaces for the dead threatens to crowd the quarters of the living on a scale impossible to conceive in earlier urban cultures.

URBAN-RURAL BALANCE

Whereas the area of the biggest cities, before the nineteenth century, could be measured in hundreds of acres, the areas of our new conurbations must now be measured in thousands of square miles. This is a new fact in the history of human settlement. Within a century the economy of the Western world has shifted from a rural base, harboring a few big cities and thousands of villages and small towns, to a metropolitan base whose urban spread not merely has engulfed and assimilated the small units, once isolated and self-contained, as the amoeba engulfs its particles of food, but is fast absorbing the rural hinterland and threatening to wipe out many natural elements favorable to life which in earlier stages balanced off against

depletions in the urban environment. From this, even more critical results follow. Already, New York and Philadelphia, which are fast coalescing into a single conurbation along the main-line railroads and the New Jersey Turnpike, find themselves competing for the same water supply, as Los Angeles competes with the whole state of Arizona. Thus, though modern technology has escaped from the limitations of a purely local supply of water, the massing of population makes demands that, even apart from excessive costs (which rise steadily as distance increases), put a definable limit to the possibilities of further urbanization. Water shortages may indeed limit the present distribution long before food shortages bring population growth to an end.

This situation calls for a new approach to the whole problem of urban settlement. Having thrown off natural controls and limitations, modern man must replace them with an at least equally effective man-made pattern. Though alternative proposals may be left to that portion of this volume dealing with the future, one new approach has fifty years of experience behind it and may properly be dealt with under the head of history. In the last decade of the nineteenth century two projects came forth relating to the need, already visible by then, to achieve a different balance among cities, industries, and natural regions from that which had been created by either the old rural economy, the free town economy, or the new metropolitan economy. The first of these suggestions was the work of the geographer Peter Kropotkin. His book *Fields, Factories, and Workshops* (1899) dealt with the alteration in the scale of technically efficient enterprise made possible by the invention of the electric motor. The other book, *Tomorrow*, published in 1898 by Howard, embodied a proposal to counteract the centralization of the great metropolis by reintroducing the method of colonization to take care of its further growth. Howard proposed to build relatively self-contained, balanced communities, supported by their local industry, with a permanent population, of limited number and density, on land surrounded by a swath of open country dedicated to agriculture, recreation, and rural occupation. Howard's proposal recognized the biological and social grounds, along with the psychological pressures, that underlay the current movement to suburbia. It recognized the social needs that were causing an exodus from rural regions or drab, one-industry towns into the big city. Without disparaging such real advantages as the concentrated activities and institutions of the city offered, Howard proposed to bring about a marriage between town and country. The new kind of city he called the "garden city," not so much because of its internal open spaces, which would approach a sound suburban standard, but more because it was set in a permanent rural environment.

Besides invoking the Aristotelian ideas of balance and limits, Howard's greatest contribution in conceiving this new garden city was provision for making the surrounding agricultural area an integral part of the city's form. His invention of a horizontal retaining wall, or green belt, immune to urban building, was a public device for limiting lateral growth and maintaining the urban-rural balance. In the course of twenty years two such balanced communities, Letchworth (1903) and Welwyn (1919), were experimentally founded by private enterprise in England. The soundness of the garden-city principle was recognized in the Barlow report (1940) on the decentralization of industry. Thanks to World War II, the idea of building such towns on a great scale, to drain off population from the overcrowded urban centers, took hold. This resulted in the New Towns Act of 1947, which provided for the creation of a series of new towns, fourteen in all, in Britain. This open pattern of town-building, with the towns themselves dispersed through the countryside and surrounded by permanent rural reserves, does a minimum damage to the basic ecological fabric. To the extent that their low residential density, of twelve to fourteen houses per acre, gives individual small gardens to almost every family, these towns not merely maintain a balanced micro-environment but actually grow garden produce whose value is higher than that produced when the land was used for extensive farming or grazing (Block, 1954).

On the basis of the garden-city principle, Stein (1951) and others have put forth the possibility of establishing a new type of city by integrating a group of communities into an organized design that would have the facilities of a metropolis without its congestion and loss of form. The basis for this kind of grouping was laid down in the survey of the state of New York made by the Commission of Housing and Regional Planning, of which Stein was chairman, and was published with Henry Wright in 1926. Wright, the planning adviser, here pointed out that the area of settlement was no longer the crowded terminal metropolitan areas of the railroad period but that electric power and motor transportation had opened up a wide belt on each side of the railroad trunk lines, equally favorable for industry, agriculture, and urban settlement. The most fertile soil and the most valuable geological deposits were almost entirely in the areas below the thousand-foot level; and, in planning for new urban settlement, the reservation of forest areas for water catchment and recreation, for lumber, and for electric power was important. Instead of treating the city as an intrusive element in a landscape that would finally be defaced or obliterated by the city's growth, this new approach suggested the necessity of creating a permanent rural-urban balance. In the regional city, as Stein conceived it, organization would take the place of mere agglomeration and, in doing so, would create a reciprocal relation between city and country that would not be overthrown by further population growth (Mumford, 1925, 1938; MacKaye, 1928; Stein, 1951).

With this statement of the problems raised for us today by the natural history of urbanization, our survey comes to an end. The blind forces of urbanization, flowing along the lines of least resistance, show no aptitude for creating an urban and industrial pattern that will be stable, self-sustaining, and self-renewing. On the contrary, as congestion thickens and expansion widens, both the urban and the rural landscape undergo defacement and degradation, while unprofitable investments in the remedies for congestion, such as more superhighways and more distant reservoirs of water, increase the economic burden and serve only to promote more of the blight and disorder they seek to palliate. But however difficult it is to reverse unsound procedures that offer a temporary answer and immediate—often excessive—financial rewards, we now have a prospect of concrete alternatives already in existence in England and partly established in a different fashion by the regional planning authority for the highly urbanized Ruhr Valley in Germany. With these examples before us, we have at least a hint of the future task of urbanization: the re-establishment, in a more complex unity, with a full use of the resources of modern science and techniques, of the ecological balance that originally prevailed between city and country in the primitive stages of urbanization. Neither the blotting-out of the landscape nor the disappearance of the city is the climax stage of urbanization. Rather, it is the farsighted and provident balancing of city populations and regional resources so as to maintain in a state of high development all the elements—social, economic, and agricultural—necessary for their common life.

REFERENCES

Barlow, Anthony M., 1940, *Royal Commission on Distribution of Industrial Population Report*. London: H.M. Stationery Office. 320 pp.

Block, Geoffrey D. M., 1954, *The Spread of Towns*. London: Conservative Political Centre. 57 pp.

Brunhes, Jean, 1920, *Human Geography, an Attempt at a Positive Classification: Principles and Examples*. 2d ed. Chicago: Rand McNally & Co. 648 pp.

Carcopino, Jerome, 1940, *Daily Life in Ancient Rome: The People and the City at the Height of the Empire*. New Haven, Conn.: Yale University Press. 342 pp.

Childe, V. Gordon, 1942, *What Happened in History*. Harmondsworth: Penguin Books. 288 pp.; 1954, "Early Forms of Society," pp. 38–57 in Singer, Charles; Holmyard, E. J.; and Hall, A. R. (eds.), *A History of Technology*. Oxford: Clarendon Press. 827 pp.

Evelyn, John, 1933, *Fumifugium: Or the Inconvenience of the Aer and Smoake of London Dissipated*. Reprint of 1661 pamphlet. London: Oxford University Press. 49 pp.

Geddes, Patrick, 1915, *Cities in Evolution: An Introduction to the Town Planning Movement and to the Study of Civics*. London: Williams & Norgate. 409 pp. (Rev. ed. by Jaqueline Tyrwhitt and Arthur Geddes. London: Williams & Norgate, 1949. 241 pp.)

Hassert, Kurt, 1907, *Die Städte: Geographisch Betrachtet*. Leipzig: B. G. Teubner. 137 pp.

Howard, Ebenezer, 1898, *To-morrow: A Peaceful Path to Real Reform*. London: Swann, Sonnenschein & Co. 176 pp.; 1902, *Garden Cities of To-morrow*. London: Swann, Sonnenschein & Co. 167 pp.; 1945, *Garden Cities of To-morrow*. With a Preface by F. J. Osborn and an Introduction by Lewis Mumford. London: Faber & Faber. 168 pp.

Jefferson, Mark, 1931, "Distribution of the World's City Folks: A Study in Comparative Civilization," *Geographical Review*, XXI, No. 3, 446–65.

Keyes, Fenton, 1951, "Urbanism and Population Distribution in China," *American Journal of Sociology*, LVI, No. 6, 519–27.

King, F. H., 1927, *Farmers of Forty Centuries*. New York: Harcourt, Brace & Co. 379 pp.

Kropotkin, Peter, 1899, *Fields, Factories, and Workshops*. New York: G. P. Putnam & Sons. 477 pp.

MacKaye, Benton, 1928, *The New Exploration: A Philosophy of Regional Planning*. New York: Harcourt, Brace & Co. 235 pp.

Marsh, George P., 1864, *Man and Nature*. London: Sampson, Low & Son. 577 pp.; 1874, *The Earth as Modified by Human Action: A New Edition of "Man and Nature."* New York: Scribner, Armstrong & Co. 656 pp.; 1885, *The Earth as Modified by Human Action: A Last Revision of "Man and Nature."* New York: Charles Scribner's Sons. 629 pp. (Note that in this last edition of *Man and Nature*, Marsh refers for the first time, in a long footnote [p. 473], under the heading "Inundations and Torrents," to the influence of large urban masses on climate, particularly heat and precipitation—an anticipation of present-day studies.) Last printing in 1907.

Mumford, Lewis, 1934, *Technics and Civilization*. New York: Harcourt, Brace & Co. 495 pp.; 1938, *The Culture of Cities*. New York: Harcourt, Brace & Co. 586 pp.

Mumford, Lewis (ed.), 1925, "Regional Planning Number," *Survey Graphic*, LIV, No. 3, 128–208.

Osborn, F. J., 1946, *Green-Belt Cities: The British Contribution*. London: Faber & Faber. 191 pp.

Riehl, Wilhelm Heinrich, 1935, *Die Naturgeschichte des Deutschen Volkes*. Reprint of 1861 edition. Leipzig: Alfred Kröner Verlag. 407 pp.

Schneider, Arthur, 1895, "Stadtumfänge in Altertum und Gegenwart," *Geographische Zeitschrift*, I, 676–79.

Sorre, Max, 1952, *Les Fondements de la géographie humaine*. 3 vols. Paris: Librairie Armand Colin.

Stamp, L. Dudley, 1948, *The Land of Britain: Its Use and Misuse*. London: Longman's Green. 570 pp.; 1952, *Land for Tomorrow*. New York: American Geographical Society; Bloomington, Ind.: Indiana University Press. 230 pp.

Stein, Clarence S., 1951, *Toward New Towns for America*. Chicago: Public Administration Service. 245 pp.

Stein, Clarence S., and Wright, Henry, 1926, *Report of the Commission of Housing and Regional Planning to Governor Alfred E. Smith, May 7, 1926*. (New York State Document.) Albany. 82 pp.

Thorndyke, Edward Lee, 1939, *Your City*. New York: Harcourt, Brace & Co. 204 pp.

Webber, Adna Ferrin, 1899, *The Growth of Cities in the Nineteenth Century: A Study in Statistics*. New York: Macmillan Co. 495 pp.

West Midland Group, 1948, *Conurbation: A Planning Survey of Birmingham and the Black Country*. London: Architectural Press. 288 pp.

Woytinsky, W. S. and E. C., 1953, *World Population and Production*. New York: Twentieth Century Fund. 1,268 pp.

Selection 13

Ecumenopolis

Commentary

Lewis Mumford offered some possible solutions to the growing crisis of the cities. He emphasized the achievement of some balance between city populations and regional resources, between urban and rural. He would seek to restore some ecological balance between city and country and half the forces of disorganized and unplanned urban sprawl.

In the next selection, Constantinos Doxiadis sees no stop to the spread of cities. Cities, he says, will continue to spread from the Megalopolis of today to the Ecumenopolis of tomorrow, a single global-wide city containing all the world's inhabitants. Perhaps Dr. Doxiadis is correct, for the trend is present through history. In 1850 no society could be called urbanized. The world was still agrarian. In 1900 only one country, Great Britain, was urbanized; by 1965 all industrial nations were urbanized—most of their people lived in cities. Like population growth, urbanization has increased rapidly in recent times. The rate of urbanization from 1950 to 1960 equaled the rate for a fifty-year period from 1900 to 1950. By 1990 one-half of the world's people will probably live in urban places of all sizes.

If the world city is coming about, the question is, Can man adapt to it? Edward Higbee states that "the speed of contemporary environmental change is too rapid for man's physiological evolution," and to adapt to urban world we must experience an accelerated cultural evolution which will enable us to "relate to one another and to that synthetic environment we are creating." Once urbanized, man is no longer dependent upon his locality, but rather upon the "globalized institutional network."[1] Man has been undergoing urban industrial evolution for only 200 out of his 10,000 years as an agrarian, yet we are moving so fast toward urbanization that we haven't had time to adapt, and we don't have 10,000 years in which to find the answers.

The apparent inevitable evolution of a world city has already begun: the tentacles of cities and suburbs reaching into natural areas, an expanding network of highways and utility lines, a large population living in cities, and the abandonment of the hinterlands. Worldwide transportation systems are becoming integrated with worldwide natural resources and manufacturing industries. Few countries manufacture all their needs anymore. Like the villages of old that specialized in manufacture and production of certain items of trade, the nations of the world are doing the same—electronics from Japan, clothes from Hong Kong, shoes from Italy and Spain. Eventually, Doxiadis concludes, the population of the earth will be living in small town-like units of 30,000 to 50,000 people.

To exist in an urban life, man is going to have to make some changes. According to Higbee,

> First of all, the ways we look at ourselves and our environment will have to change. The agrarian mind, with its idealization of physical work, rugged individualism, security in land ownership, preoccupation with scarcity, and its opposition to big government services (except when big government subsidizes farmers for not farming), will have to develop an urban outlook. It will have to recognize that in a world of science and technology mental work is more efficient than manual. The electron is cheaper and faster than human muscle. Security does not lie in the possession of land. Abundance of biological prerequisites for all is possible, and a commitment by big government to equitable, comprehensive services to all citizens in health, education, welfare and employment insurance is a biological must. The urban environment is capable, thanks to the mental labors of scientists and technologists, to replace the scarcities of unconscious nature with man-made abundances. That is the key ecological implication of urbanization—its unlimited potential for resource production and distribution.[2]

Lewis Mumford stopped at the present. Constantinos Doxiadis takes us into the future. Whether Ecumenoplis will come about or whether it is ecologically desirable for man or the planet are questions yet to be explored and answered. For the present the selection gives all of us something to ponder and discuss. We cannot ignore it.

---

[1]Edward Higbee, "Consequences of Ecological Ignorance," *Proceedings Golden Anniversary Meeting*, New England Section, Society of American Foresters, 1970, pp. 26–29.
[2]*Ibid.*, p. 28.

Selection 13

Ecumenopolis, World-City of Tomorrow

by Constantinos A. Doxiadis

WHY THE CRISES IN OUR CITIES

About thirty-five years ago, when one talked of cities, the only questions raised were, as a rule, questions of the aesthetics of buildings: whether a particular house or monument was beautiful or ugly. Later, when the world began to suffer severely from the poor state of communications, all one heard on every hand was about the crisis in urban communications, and more particularly about too many motor-cars. Later still, social problems arose in certain countries, and people began to view the urban crisis from that particular aspect. In some countries, the problems were specifically racial, as in the United States, where the situation is more delicate than elsewhere. And so the urban crisis then took on the appearance of a social crisis.

Sometimes, also, the urban crisis was poorly understood, because each person tended to regard it from his own particular point of view. Certain people, in fact, referred to it as a crisis in small-scale organic unity, that of the family; others saw it as resulting from the disappearance of small neighbourhoods and towns, and yet others as something inherent in large cities and big centres of population. Each one, in fact, saw only a single factor of the general crisis in space.

Actually, the crisis is nothing other than that of the entire system. This is an essential principle we must understand: it is the crisis of a system we commonly refer to as the city, but which it would be more accurate to call the human settlement.

The crisis is a general one. We shall understand this if we consider the city from a rational point of view. To do so, we must try to view it under three aspects.

THE FIVE ELEMENTS

First we must try to understand of what it is composed. Five elements enter into its composition (Fig. 1). The first of these is nature, the soil which gave it birth. By not taking this simple fact into account, our efforts have been doomed to failure. We have, in fact, polluted the atmosphere and the waters, destroyed beautiful country-sides, exhausted the natural resources, killed off the animals, insects and plants—in a word, annihilated the city's natural setting.

The second element is man, who is frequently left out of the calculations. All we need to do is look at a city from the air to realize that the most important place is allotted to motor-cars, and man occupies only the second place; that the city is covered with colossal buildings. We have so completely failed to recognize man's existence as to prevent our children from using the streets. In this way man is left exposed to various forms of psychosis and neurosis which are far more serious than the accidents which stain our streets with blood, for they are the diseases of a man who is no longer free to wander about and grows up, for the first time in history, with the feeling of being more at ease in the heart of nature than in the city.

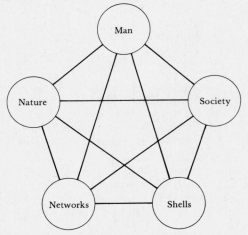

Figure 1. The five elements that compose the city.

THIS SELECTION is from *Impact of Science on Society*, Vol. XIX, No. 2, 1969. Reprinted by permission of ©Unesco.

Thirdly, society, painstakingly created by man, and producing, in turn, human settlements. We are incapable of creating a society. All we can create are enormous masses of people incapable of performing their normal functions. Men are more and more separated in space from each other; the necessary contacts between them are lacking. The women, left alone in the suburbs without a second car at their disposal become 'nervy', and the men who have to drive for several hours back and forth also become tense and nervous. It is curious to observe that when men are scattered over vast tracts of territory they lose contact with the small surface points of unity—the family, the neighbours. In this way we create a city with nothing human about it.

The fourth element is buildings in general, what the architectural trade refers to as 'shells'. Technically, there has certainly been progress. But does this progress serve man's true interests? This cannot be proved. On the other hand, we cannot help thinking that these great blocks isolate men and turn them into cave-dwellers. And the idea of wandering through car-choked streets admiring the beauty of some of the buildings as you go along is, strictly speaking, inconceivable.

The fifth and last element is the networks: highways, railways, water-supply systems, electricity and telecommunications. All these become more and more technically perfect every day. If they are underground systems, as in the case of water-supply, electricity and telephone, they cannot possibly inconvenience men from the technical or aesthetic point of view. If, on the other hand, they are on the surface, such as certain electrical and telephone systems, they can be disadvantageous, at any rate aesthetically. But it is in the road system that failure has been most marked. Motorways have the effect of breaking up a city's continuity and preventing it from functioning normally.

We therefore reach the conclusion that the failure of the system is due to the destruction of its elements and of the relationships between them. Because man cannot find joy in his home, because his habitation cannot offer him a better life, the entire city system suffers. Because the city expands rapidly, thanks to the motor-car and other centrifugal forces, it destroys the surrounding country-side and the entire system goes slowly from bad to worse.

THE FIVE POINTS OF VIEW

We can also regard this system in other ways, from the scientific point of view, for example; or we can regard it as an economic, social or political system or, again, as a technological, civilizing or aesthetic one. From whichever angle we look at it, we see that the city, the human settlement, the system, instead of getting better is only getting worse. Everything goes to show that the results obtained bear no relation to the progress being made nowadays in all the spheres of human activity.

The problem becomes even more complicated when, looking at these five elements from different angles and from the five basic points of view—economic, social, political, technological, and cultural—you arrive at a great number of combinations, which show just how many demands will have to be satisfied and how difficult it will be to meet them all. Figure 2 just shows a simple combination of these variables.

These problems become even more complex if we admit that what we understand by the word 'city' is only an extremely simplified term for a phenomenon of infinitely greater complexity. The significant feature of the way in which our life in space is organized is no longer the city *per se*, but rather a system of human settlements. In antiquity, at the time of the city-states, we could perhaps have claimed that the system was composed of a city and some villages. Such city-states varied neither in size nor in the relationships between them; these latter were few in number and often much more hostile than pacific.

In maintaining that the same is true today—

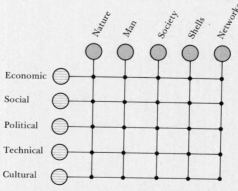

Figure 2. The five elements considered from five points of view.

which unfortunately is what we do—we make a profound mistake, for the city systems in which we live are not limited by cities' natural boundaries. No modern city could survive if its exits were to be closed. If its conduits were to be cut off, too, it would cease to exist, having neither water nor electricity. Moreover, even if it were allowed to maintain relations with the surrounding villages, the city, as we know it, would still be unable to live. Its system of communications is very extended; it imports goods from a great distance and exports likewise to remote countries, and as it functions at an intense rhythm it ends by absorbing the neighbouring villages. A village which has radio and television is no longer a village; it has been incorporated into the city network. It is ever receiving orders, and little by little begins to obey them.

Hence the following conclusion: we should not hold the concept of a dissociated 'city'—a concept which is, moreover, impossible to define—but envisage it as a system made up of many different units.

THE FIFTEEN SPACE-UNITS

If we closely and systematically analyse our living space, we shall discover that we live in fifteen different space units of increasingly greater dimensions (Fig. 3).

The first of these, and the smallest, is that of man himself—it is precisely the space occupied by the human body with all its limbs extended; the second is the room; the third, the dwelling; the fourth, the dwelling group; the fifth, the small neighbourhood. Leaping upward, we come to the eighth unit, the traditional town of 30,000 to 50,000 inhabitants; then to the tenth, comprising the metropolis

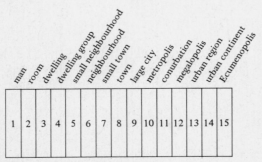

Figure 3. The fifteen space units.

with around two million inhabitants; the eleventh, the conurbation with several million inhabitants, and the twelfth, a new type of urban concentration going by the name of 'megalopolis', like the one stretching along the east coast of the United States or like those to be found in the region of the American and Canadian Great Lakes, or in the Netherlands, or along the banks of the Rhine, or yet again in the area stretching between Tokyo and Osaka which is known as Tokaido.

Finally, we come to the fourteenth and fifteenth units, the urban continent and Ecumenopolis, the universal city. These constitute a world system that we cannot, of course, actually see because it remains to be created, but which we should be able to visualize were we able to record the total movements of aircraft in the sky, those of trains and motor vehicles on the earth, and the torrents of news circulating by telephone, telegraph and television. These fifteen spatial units govern that total urban system which I call the city.

If we now consider this system with its fifteen units, and if we combine them with the five elements and five points of view so as to form a complex of forces exerting their influence on the city, we shall then realize that we are talking of billions and trillions of aspects and problems in an enormously complicated system.

We might naturally ask ourselves if this is the first time that the city has fallen sick. Obviously it is not. A city is, generally speaking, always sick. Sometimes it is the dwellings that are unsuitable for habitation and become slums; in other instances service installations are faulty or lacking, as in the past, when there were no town mains of any kind. In certain cases, it is the people themselves who are abnormal so that the community does not function properly. Diseases peculiar to cities, just as human diseases, have always existed. Sometimes remedies could be found for them, sometimes not. But all these diseases differed from our own in that they were restricted to a single element, a single aspect.

Nowadays, the disease of the city is also that of the whole system. It forms part of that system's very existence and increases as the system expands. We can say today that every city is, by definition, sick and that it is always moving towards a crisis, because no single one of its elements is immune from disease.

INTENSIFICATION OF THE CRISIS

If we have succeeded in understanding the exact nature of the crisis and the reasons for it, we shall also be able to realize easily enough that it can only get worse and worse as time goes on, if things are allowed to remain as they are. It is because we have been unable to grasp this state of affairs that we find ourselves incapable of dealing with it rationally and have no assurance that we will be able to avert the worst.

Since the cause of the crisis in the system is essentially the latter's size, obviously as the size grows, the problems arising out of it will grow in the same proportion. Assuming that the world population at the end of the century will be double the present population of 3,500 millions (and more likely it will be something more), that means it will have reached 7,000 million. In the generation immediately following, that is to say, by the year 2030, the population will probably have quadrupled, but even if this were not so, it is bound to be very much higher than 7,000 million. If this rate of increase continues, we shall have reached a figure of over 20,000 million by the end of the twenty-first century. Such a population increase will call for a corresponding increase in the units which compose the main elements of the city.

But population is only one aspect of the question. A city is not composed only of human elements; there are others besides, such as buildings and mains of various kinds, which complicate the problem. To be able to deal with questions of buildings and mains, we have to know something about the economy. We know, of course, that the economic potential of the population is expanding. We may therefore expect *per capita* income to rise steeply, to at least double the present one in the course of the generation. This means that the gross revenue of a medium-sized town will have quadrupled.

As a first approximation, as the population increases, the need for surface space increases proportionately. However, since incomes go up, people demand more space for their dwellings and service networks. They also have more cars at their disposal and they insist on more room for them, too. And with rising prosperity, the mileage covered by each car constantly increases, so that new motorways have to be built. We can, therefore, say that it is not just the city itself which needs more room, but also every individual in it. This explains how it is that in a good many urban centers, over the past forty years, the surface area has multiplied twice or even three times. We are led to face this additional problem: that the demand for urban space is bound to increase at a faster rate than the population and, in certain cases, will greatly outstrip the growth of the economy.

We now see that, where we have a population with an increased economic potential and therefore insisting on more living space, our whole system of human settlements is bound to become much more complex than the actual growth in population would seem to justify. Likewise, the whole body of problems increases at a faster rate than does either the world population or the urban population.

ESCAPIST SOLUTIONS

Most people are not yet aware of the major problems. But there are some who understand them because they think and they make calculations, even though these may not always be very accurate. Such people endeavour to find solutions. At present these are, in fact, but escapist solutions. I propose to enumerate the main ones in the order of their appearance.

In the first category we can place solutions based on various myths. These are, for example, the myth of optimism, which foresees the solution of all problems in emigration to other planets or in the abolishing of motor-cars; the myth founded upon imaginary concepts, such as the assertion that people are living today in high-density urban agglomerations, whereas the medium-sized town of today is in fact less densely populated than it was a generation ago; the myth that our problems would be solved by increasing the height of buildings, although, on the contrary, these enormous constructions create new problems without at all solving the human ones.

There is a whole series of other more realistic utopias, those which are based on some dream of reconstruction which is entirely divorced from logic. According to these, cities are no longer necessary.

There is still another form of utopia based on the application of the same abortive solutions to various problems which were tried at the end of the nineteenth century; these led to a host of

157

utopian groups which founded utopian communities. This is a typical escapist solution.

Then there are escapist-motivated solutions which take the form of ideal cities and technological utopias. These advocate the creation of parking lots on the flat roofs of dwellings, or the construction of buildings shaped like huge metal tanks capable of moving from place to place.

The most dangerous escapist solutions are those which advocate a return to small towns. Actually, many of us have been born and raised in such towns and we still see them in our mind's eye and dream of going back to them. This form of utopia takes on different aspects, such as the ideal little towns like those imagined by Skinner with his *Walden Two*, or like those described in Aldous Huxley's last book, *Island*, in which there is a small island where people live in little towns.

Still more dangerous is the theory recommending as the ideal solution the establishment of new satellite towns outside the large cities. Yet do we not now possess the evidence of experience, showing that the satellite towns established sixty years ago have for the past thirty years been urban sectors and that the same fate has befallen those established thirty years ago?

THE PATH OF THE FUTURE

We have now reached the point where we must decide on the future road to follow. The question is: are we now capable of examining systematically the various practicable alternatives for the future which are open to us? I believe we are.

First among the roads we can follow is that of research into basic causes, and the first among these to be studied must be the world population increase. Even if a decision on birth control could be adopted immediately, two generations would go by before we could convince the inhabitants of remote villages in India or South America to apply it. This means that in all probability we will reach the figure of 7,000 million and then 12,000 million before the population increase can be arrested.

Given this increase in world population, it is permissible to ask whether the urban population must necessarily rise too. Could we not arrange to keep this population in the countryside? That is something quite out of the question. Man's belief in the freedom of the individual

(which all peoples are coming to hold as firmly as their belief in human progress) makes it impossible for us to intervene directly in a man's decisions. We cannot say: 'Live in the villages, even if you are not needed for rural work to produce food, which can today be produced by a reduced number of people.'

The general increase in farm productivity will sustain the swelling of urban populations and the decrease of the rural population. The result will be that, in a world population of 7,000 million in the year 2000, 5,000 million will be city dwellers. Consequently, the urban population will not simply have doubled, as is sometimes naïvely thought, but will have quadrupled. And when the world population reaches 12,000 million, the lowest levelling-off point, 10,000 million people will be city-dwellers, six or seven times the present number.

Let us now consider the third road open to us. Given the fact of the increase in the urban population, might it not be possible to restrict the growth of our cities by directing the surplus population to new towns? We should give this solution serious thought. We could, indeed, build new towns to absorb that population if the necessary funds were available; for such towns call for a bigger capital investment per head for fewer services, especially during the first few years, the first decades, the first generations, until they reach the size of our present-day cities.

But why do we want the new towns to reach the size of today's cities? The answer is that only towns of a certain size can give men a greater number of options. Some people will say that even a town of modest size can have a theatre and a hospital, and, indeed, towns of 50,000, 80,000 or 250,000 inhabitants (this last being the fashionable figure just now) will be attractive to a certain proportion of the population.

The answer to this argument is simple. There was a time when a man was presumably content in a village of 700 inhabitants, which could support a primary school. What people forgot was that such a village could well have insisted on having a secondary school, a vocational school, and a university for its children.

Some will still argue that small towns like this can even meet the cost of maintaining a theatre. But where is the man who will be content with just one theatre, on the model of the small cities of ancient Greece, where the theatre was only obliged to open its doors during important festivals? Might he not well prefer a city with five, ten or twenty theatres, where he could choose between various productions? And why would he be content with a hospital with 200 beds if his disease calls for the attention of a number of specialists, which only university centres are able to provide? In fact, we cannot logically conceive of a city of fixed size which can satisfy our needs. The larger a city the more the needs it serves, which is why people are increasingly attracted to cities.

Should we enlarge our present cities or should we build new ones? The answer is that, theoretically, we could build new ones, provided we make them at least as large as the present ones. In view, however, of the fact that the exodus is from small cities to large ones and that, whatever the size of the new cities we wish to build, their actual construction is bound to take a considerable number of years—one, two or possibly three generations—the population flow will obviously be away from them. Consequently they will prove a failure, for we cannot possibly force these generations to accept dictated solutions to problems which involve their being told where they are to live.

So the answer to this difficult question is as follows: evolutionary and constructive forces will inevitably lead to the growth of cities of the present type in response to the need to satisfy all the requirements of the inhabitants. This does not mean that a certain number of cities of a new type will not be built, but the building of them will be difficult, and will only affect a small proportion of the population.

Thus we are led to the following conclusion: the most probable, logical and practical solution among the three we have been discussing is the progressive expansion of the present type of city as a result of the massive influx of an ever-increasing population.

TOWARDS ECUMENOPOLIS

Our present cities are developing into increasingly complex systems. Starting with the city which develops in concentric circles, we finally reach the one which is strung out along the main artery linking it up with the nearest town, port or coast. We thus pass naturally from the city we are familiar with to a system of cities linked together, forming an urban complex with great numbers of inhabitants.

This brings us at last to the following con-clusions: under the growing pressures of these various forces—economic, biological, demographic, etc.—we are gradually creating a bigger and bigger system of settlements, a system which, left to develop blindly, can only worsen daily and eventually bring us to catastrophe. This system will very quickly assume world proportions. From the megalopolis we shall pass to cities extending over continents, and thence to Ecumenopolis, or world-city. Its advent is inevitable. Any strict analysis reveals that there is nothing logical, rational or practical we can do to avoid it.

Ecumenopolis will be shaped by the forces engendered in cities of the present type as they attract huge populations in the future; by great systems for transportation, the inevitable magnet for industry and other activities; and by forces of an aesthetic nature, such as the attraction exerted by the seaboard on increasing numbers of people.

People will want to enjoy aesthetic pleasures at home; they will want to be able to build their houses overlooking an attractive valley, or along the coast with beaches opening before them, even though the crowded city centre is some distance away. At the same time, we must bear in mind the attraction of the vast plains, where water abounds, where the climate is mild.

All the above allows us gradually to form an idea of what the universal city will look like. As a result of research conducted by the Athens Centre of Ekistics we can already imagine to some degree how it will appear within a century or a century and a half (Fig. 4).

Ecumenopolis, this world-city that will englobe the whole of humanity, will be a frightening conurbation, but, as we made clear earlier, we have no evidences that enable us to conclude that a better sort of city can be created. Once we are convinced that this city is inevitable, we can only form one conclusion: if it is built on today's lines, according to present-day trends, it will be a city doomed to destruction, that which Lewis Mumford referred to some time ago as a necropolis—city of the dead.

There is still, of course, another road that could be followed: to avoid it altogether. But, as has been already pointed out, this is not a logical or practical solution. I would like to emphasize here that we have no reason to claim today that we know any more about the reasons why it would be a good thing to avoid

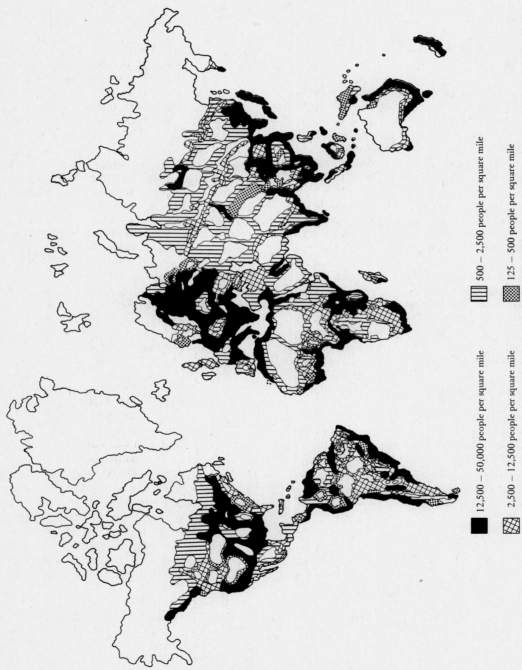

Figure 4. Ecumenopolis, 100—150 years from now.

establishing a universal city than did the citizens of ancient Athens, about 3,000 years ago, when Theseus decided to concentrate the rural population in one town, the tiny city of Athens, with only a few thousand inhabitants. How could they tell then whether or not they should avoid establishing this initial town in the plain of Athens? Doubtless similar arguments were used then in favor of the scheme and against it as are used today in the case of the universal city.

It is high time we accepted our responsibilities and started working toward something which must be done right. To do this, we must understand that the real challenge does not lie in whether or not to create the world-city; it lies in creating it correctly, taking into account the human factor, so that man who, at present, sees his values disintegrating around him, may be able to find them again.

THE OUTLINES OF ECUMENOPOLIS

In the preceding sections of this study, I have tried above all to clarify the problem so it can be fully understood, for understanding is an essential condition for success. If we fail today to deal with this problem, it will be because we have not understood it.

In Athens we are presently applying ourselves to the collection of data on human settlements. This systematized knowledge forms an organized discipline which is becoming a science, called 'ekistics'—the science of human settlements.

We must realize that ekistics cannot be restricted merely to understanding the problem; it must also lead to solutions for tomorrow. How is it that man in the past possessed the necessary strength, imagination and courage to build permanent settlements when he was still a hunter? How is it that he then went on to build villages, towns, industrial cities and metropolises? Why shouldn't we today have the necessary courage to conceive and build the world-city? To do it, we need, in addition to science, technology and art. Thus, we shall have to make ekistics a science, a technology and an art, all in one.

If we set to work in this way, we shall come to realize that we really can create. Ecumenopolis. It is of no special importance to us to know exactly what the size of the city will be. For it will not make much difference to us that,

going in certain directions, we would pass through hundreds of miles of urban centres. What will really matter is to know that, after a journey of ten or twenty minutes or of one to five hours, as the case may be, we can be certain of finding the country-side.

When we see the problem in this light, we shall understand that size and shape are of no special concern; what matters is a proper balance between elements. We shall then affirm this conclusion; that nature must be converted into a gigantic network with tentacles penetrating deeply into all parts of the universal city so as to reach every residential area—a system of woodlands transformed into parks, intersected by avenues and gardens, within easy reach of our homes.

The size of a city should not worry us if we know that we can control the atmosphere and keep it unpolluted. There are small towns where the atmosphere is contaminated by a great number of cars and large towns where the atmosphere is clean. What is important is to ensure that pollution from industrial plants and vehicular traffic is under control. Then we will be able to breathe better air in a large city than we could in a small town without proper pollution control.

Proceeding in this way enables us to understand, little by little, how the elements of nature will penetrate the city. A similar approach can establish the nature of the various networks. Transportation problems have nothing whatever to do with the size of a city. They are the result of lack of organization and because we have not yet learned that men and machines cannot exist on the same footing.

Urban transportation will function properly when it is placed beneath the surface, like arteries in the human body. As soon as we grasp this fact, we can take the first steps in the right direction—indeed, we have already done so. At one time, water was carried in surface conduits; the same was true—and still is in many places—of sewage drains; overhead electric and telephone wires are still a common sight.

The day will come when all such installations will be below the surface. Goods will be transported through underground tubes. Some of these already exist. In Canada, important networks of the kind are under construction for the transport of industrial products.

In the near future, no one will object to using underground roadways, just as no one

161

made objections when the subways began transporting people at speeds of 15—20 miles an hour in London, Paris and New York, considerably faster than they had been used to in their horse-drawn cabs. Before very long, we shall be travelling underneath our cities at speeds of 60—200 miles an hour, spending perhaps between 5 and 10 minutes below ground, instead of driving for hours on roads, constantly irritated by the stop and go of traffic lights.

These new transportation networks will be much more satisfactory and will make it possible to have cities spread over very much wider areas while being much better organized.

When this programme has been carried out, we will then attain the solution which is of prime importance to us: freeing the surface of the earth for man to enjoy and to use for the development of his artistic gifts. In a word, the earth's surface will be used in harmony with man's way of life. We harken back thus to the time, thousands of years ago, when man was both a researcher and a guinea-pig in the vast laboratory of life and did the experiments which enabled him to build throughout the world those beautiful cities which we still admire: ancient Athens, Florence, the old Paris and old London, as well as Williamsburg in the United States. An intrinsic worth attached to these cities because they had been built on a human scale, to man's own measurements.

A careful study of the cities of the past shows that they never exceeded more than about 1 mile in length or about 1.5 square miles in area, and included no more than 50,000 inhabitants, when they were at their most successful. Cities which were much bigger were, in fact, the capitals of large empires and were never able to retain their organization for very long. They often deteriorated into anarchy, as in the case of Rome and Byzantium. If they hoped to sustain an organized and integral life of their own, they had to be carefully planned from the start, like Peking and Changan (modern Sian), two ancient Chinese capitals.

Generally, then, any cities which exceeded the usual, the reasonable maxima were doomed to fail, were short-lived, and offer us no solution. Those that do offer a solution were the small cities of 30,000 to 50,000 inhabitants, covering an area of about 1.5 square miles. If we examine their structure rationally, we shall realize that we must return to something similar if we want to organize our life properly.

We thus reach what seems to be a paradox: on the one hand, the inevitable huge Ecumenopolis; on the other, the absolute need for man to live in small cities. But this only appears paradoxical. For following such reasonings to their logical conclusion, we arrive at a gigantic city of superhuman dimensions, made up of small units.

Thus, our thought processes have led us to the construction of huge cities composed of small towns, of vast urban complexes served by underground transportation systems, leaving the surface of the ground free, at man's disposal, and supplied with every human amenity. The conclusion we reach then is that Ecumenopolis, the world-city, will be made up of cells of 30,000 to 50,000 people.

In practice, we are already beginning to build such cities. Islamabad, the new capital of Pakistan, intended for 2.5 million inhabitants, has been laid out in this way. Before such cities are even finished, life there is already in full swing and anyone can go and study them in operation. It is very important to keep on studying them until they've been brought to perfection. Then by applying similar principles, it will be possible to transform some of the older cities.

Indeed, these principles have been applied to certain limited areas or even to certain cities which are planning the organization of the entire system on this sound basis. One example is Philadelphia (United States), which is now engaged in a gradual urban renewal project which will house 10,000 families on ground once covered with slums. There is also the immense urban region of Detroit, now in course of development and planned to accommodate by the year 2000 more than 10 million inhabitants enjoying maximum amenities.

So, after examining the nature of the crisis of the cities and the various escapist solutions, we have gradually synthesized a solution. This solution enables us to envisage the development of human settlements in a practical manner and to build in such a way as to offer men a much happier form of existence by combining the advantages of the small towns of old—which were certainly considerable from the point of view of a humane way of life—with those of the large cities which alone are capable of enlarging our freedoms and chances of development.

Our Treatment of the Environment

Commentary

The violence done to ecosystems and the massive changes made in the surface of the earth by man are blamed in part by a number of ecologists and geographers on the Western Judeo-Christian concept that man and nature are separate entities. Out of the idea expressed in Genesis, "Be fruitful, and multiply, and replenish the earth, and subdue; and have dominion over the fish of the sea, and over the fowl of the air, and over every living thing that moves upon the earth," comes the ideology that all nature has been put on earth for man's use and that land is an economic commodity rather than an ecological entity.

A lack of a land ethic as expressed by Aldo Leopold[1] which "reflects an existence of an ecological conscience" results in regarding land as a commodity on the marketplace, to be so managed or manipulated to bring in maximum profits. It is on this basis that forests have been destroyed, subdivisions created, coal stripmined, rivers dammed, water and air polluted. It is this dogma of land economics which has resulted in major modification on the face of the earth and created the ecological problems facing mankind today.

A great deal of the things that happen to land result from the fact that land in modern society is more than resource for the production of food and fiber. It is "our entire natural environment—all the forces or the opportunities that exist independently of man's activity."[2] Under such a theory little of our land is limited to the output of one commodity or service. What is a productive orange grove today may be more valuable economically as a housing subdivision, a turnpike interchange tomorrow.

The economic concepts behind decision in land use and thus the improvement or degradation of our environment are outlined by Walter E. Chryst and William C. Pendleton, Jr., in an article, "Land and the Growth of the Nation," in the 1958 Yearbook of Agriculture. Land use, they state, is based on the following general principle:

> Each acre should be devoted to the use in which its economic productivity is highest. Only by allocating land (or any other resource) according to productivity can we expect it to reach its highest efficiency in the satisfying of our wants.
>
> Another principle of land use . . . is that all land with any economic productivity should be used. The validity of this principle is clearer when we observe that a given output may be obtained from several different combinations of land, labor, and capital.

. . .

The implication of this principle is clear—to the extent that land can be used to free labor and capital for other types of production, land should be used. The failure to use land (when it is available) as a substitute for labor and capital results in a waste of human energy and the tools of production or in an output of the national economy that is less than the one that might be achieved if all resources were used.

The allocation of land and other resources is accomplished in an enterprise system such as ours largely in response to changes in relative prices—prices of the products and services the land can help produce, prices of the resources combined with the land, and the price of land itself.

When the price of beef goes up relative to the price of wheat, for example, some farmers who have a choice will shift into beef. When the wages of hired labor rise rapidly, the signal is given to farmers to mechanize. When paper companies can offer 30 dollars an acre for land that is worth no more than 20

---

[1]Aldo Leopold, "The Land Ethic," in *A Sand County Almanac*, New York, Oxford University Press, 1956.
[2]W. E. Chryst and W. C. Pendleton, Jr., 1958. "Land and the Growth of the Nation," in *Land*, USDA Yearbook of Agriculture, Washington, D.C., 1958.

dollars to farmers, a shift is indicated. Many other examples might be listed to underscore the principle: Relative prices and changes in relative prices are major factors in our decisions as to the use of land.

.   .   .

The framework of the decisions is a tenure system which is based on the principle of private property and through which the control of the various tracts of land and their earnings are identified with individuals.

Thus the responsibility for the decisions is tied to the consequences of the decisions.

If the person in control of land decides to use it to produce the items the consuming public prefers, his income is increased.

If he insists on not using the land or on using it to produce something the public does not want, he can expect little or no income from the land.

If a piece of land has a higher economic productivity in pasture than in wheat, he will be able to claim more of the total output of commodities and services if he devotes the land to pasture.

If the land has a higher economic productivity when it supports three-bedroom houses than when it is in corn or watermelons, the landowner's economic welfare will be improved if he permits the land to be used for building sites.

. . . It is clear that our economic system operates on the assumption that an individual who uses his land to get from it the maximum income uses it as efficiently as possible and that in this way his land makes the largest possible contribution to the output of the economy. Thus individuals, while acting in their own best interests, are assumed to act in the best interests of the public.

But the interests of the individual are not necessarily the interests of the public, and the mechanism of leaving decisions as to the use of land to the individual does not always result in the use the public wants.

The individual is concerned with how to use his own resources within the span of his lifetime and the lifetime of his immediate heirs. The public is concerned with the use of all resources over a longer period. These differences in expectations and orientation give rise to public intervention in decisions involving the use of land.

The need for public intervention will be observed when it is noted that each landowner uses his land within a much larger physical environment. The cost of cropping practices that increase the rate of runoff in the upper Mississippi Valley, for example, is not borne entirely by those who use those practices; it is borne partly by those downstream whose properties might be flooded by the practices. Similarly, the cost of producing wheat on land susceptible to wind erosion is borne partly by those who must live and work in areas affected by duststorms. The cost of chemical production may not be paid entirely by the producer who dumps his waste into a stream; it is paid partly by the downstream users of water who must install a more elaborate purification mechanism to eliminate the health hazard created by the presence of the waste.

Conversely, the least expensive way of eliminating a flood or erosion hazard on one farm may be to erect a dam on a farm higher up the slope. But the first farmer has no right to use the land of the other for this purpose, and the second has no incentive to provide this protection, as he does not participate in the benefits. Many similar examples might be cited, but it is evident that frequently, when there is an off-site benefit or cost for any land-use activity, there is need for public intervention if all of the land is to be used most effectively.

The foregoing examples pertain to the separation of benefits and costs of land-use practices in space.

.   .   .

A similar situation exists when the benefits and costs of a land-use practice are separated in time. The present landowner gets the benefit of a cropping system that leaves the land impaired in terms of its future ability to produce, but the cost must be borne by later generations, who either must have fewer agricultural products or must substitute labor and capital for the wasted land resource—labor and capital that could be used to produce something else. So, also, the use of timber, coil, oil, gas, or subsurface water can be excessive at one point in time if future needs are not taken properly into account.

The voice of the future is heard only feebly over the din of the market place, and the public has a responsibility to speak on behalf of future citizens.[3]

This short-term exploitative approach to the land is obviously incompatible with ecology. An ecological approach holds that economics does not determine all land use, that land use is more than just an economic problem. "Examine each question," writes Aldo Leopold, "in terms of what is ethically and esthetically right as well as what is economically expedient. A thing is right when it tends to preserve the integrity, stability, and beauty of the biotic community. It is wrong when it tends otherwise."[4]

The homocentric view of the world is regarded as wholly occidental, a culmination of modern technology and modern science that had its roots in the Middle Ages. It was a time wholly dominated by Christianity and the Christian view of the universe. Man was created in the image and likeness of God and all creatures were made by God to serve man's purpose. Man had no part in nature; rather he transcended it. This was in great contrast to the ancient paganism and Asian religions, especially Buddhism, which holds for a quiescent and adaptive approach toward nature.

The idea that the ecologically disastrous treatment of the environment is strictly Western or Judeo-Christian in origin has been voiced a number of times. Robert Redfield[5] in his book *The Primitive World and Its Transformation* notes that preliterate and ancient societies considered man and nature part of a single order. Man did not confront nature because "being already in nature, man cannot exactly confront it." In the development of Western thought, the world came to be viewed as one "in which God and man are both separated from nature, and in which the exploitation of material nature comes to be a prime attitude."

This idea is further elaborated by Alexander Spoehr in an essay "Cultural Differences in the Interpretation of Natural Resources." He points out that

> To the degree that the Western world is composed of almost complete urbanized individuals, it not merely regards habitat, and consequently natural resources, as an entity that is to be dominated and manipulated by man, but tends to relegate the whole matter to a handful of specialists and in effect to place nature outside its immediate sphere of concern.[6]

More recently the historian Lynn White, in a widely cited and reprinted paper, "The Historical Roots of Our Ecologic Crisis," expanded this thesis. He lays the blame on a medieval view of man and nature as it was colored by the Judeo-Christian viewpoints:

> No item in physical creation had any purpose save to serve man's purposes . . . . Christianity, in absolute contrast to ancient paganism and Asia's religions (except perhaps Zoroastrianism), not only established a dualism of man and nature, but also insisted that it is God's will that man exploit nature for his proper ends.[7]

He continues: "Our science and technology have grown out of Christian attitudes towards man's relation to nature which are almost universally held not only by Christians and neo-Christians but also by those who fondly regard themselves as post-Christians . . . . We are superior to nature, contemptuous, of it, willing to use it for our slightest whim."[8]

Looking at Western attitudes toward the wilderness, Roderick Nash in the first chapter of his book *Wilderness and the American Mind* explored the Western and Eastern attitudes of wilderness. He writes, "In early and medieval Christianity wilderness kept its significance as the earthly realm of the powers of evil that the Church had to overcome. Christians judged their work to be successful when they cleared away the wild forests and cut down the sacred groves where the pagans held their rites."[9] By contrast the Far East had a respect for a man-nature relationship that bordered on love. Wilderness was "venerated as the symbol and even very essence of diety." Taoists saw an infinite and benign force in nature and Shintoism was a form of nature worship.

In his book *Design with Nature*, Ian L. McHarg echoes the same ideas. Christianity absorbed unchanged from Judaism the idea of the

> exclusive divinity of man, his God-given dominion over all things and licensed him to subdue the

---

[3]*Ibid.*
[4]Leopold, *op. cit.*, p. 224.
[5]Robert Redfield, *The Primitive World and Its Transformation*, Ithaca, N.Y., Cornell University Press, 1953.
[6]A. Spoehr, "Cultural Differences in the Interpretation of Natural Resources," In W. E. Thomas (ed.), *Man's Role in Changing the Face of the Earth*, Chicago, Ill., University of Chicago Press, 1956, p. 100.
[7]Lynn White, "The Historical Roots of our Ecologic Crisis," *Science* **155**, 1967, p. 1205.
[8]*Ibid.*, p. 1206.
[9]Roderick Nash, *Wilderness and the American Mind*, New Haven, Conn., Yale University Press, 1967, pp. 17 and 20.

earth ... and that his literal belief permeates the western view of nature and man.... When this is understood, the conquest, the depredations and the despoliation are comprehensible, as is the imperfect value system.[10]

In contrast is the orient, which considers man and nature indivisible, man submerged in nature, although McHarg admits that the oriental harmony of man—nature has been achieved at the expense of the individuality of man.

I have presented these ideas to graduate seminars, and the students would not fully accept validity of the arguments. The North American Indian, some pointed out, had a reverence for nature, an ecological oneness with the land. Yet with economic incentives this did not stop them from helping to destroy both the fur resource and the buffalo; nor has it prevented the Navaho from overgrazing their range land with their sheep. I thought of the works of Walter Loudermilk[11] in which he describes how the Chinese, even though they knew the principles of soil conservation for centuries, allowed their soil to erode away and their forests to be destroyed. Only temple forests protected by Buddhists remain to show how the land was before it was exploited by man.

The weakness with the West—East arguments and the role of the Judeo-Christian concept in the mastery of nature is the total acceptance of the oriental philosophy without determining how well it was applied to the land. Now this has been done by Yi-Fu Tuan, an authority on Eastern culture and man's attitude toward nature. Tuan shatters the idea that the West's attitudes toward nature are solely its own. There isn't too much difference after all between the attitudes of the West and the East toward the land. It happens to be a universal attitude in man, the species, an idea emphasized by René Dubos, who wrote: "The Judeo-Christian civilization has been no worse and no better than others in relation to nature. Throughout history, men have disturbed the ecological equilibrium, almost universally out of ignorance and chiefly because they have been concerned more with immediate advantages than with long range goals."[12] R. T. Wright in an even more recent article critically examines the charges against Judeo-Christianity and concludes: "Christianity has become a scapegoat for human failure. It is not religious belief, but human greed and ignorance which have allowed our culture to come to the point of ecological crisis."[13]

We need not seek part of our solution in the mystic relation between man and nature in oriental philosophy, nor do we necessarily need to castigate the Judaism and Christianity. We simply need to evolve rather quickly, as Leopold has pleaded, a land ethic that considers the land as an ecological as well as an economic entity. Says René Dubos,

> The solution ... will not be found in a retreat from technological civilization, but rather in an enlightened transformation of it based on ecological understanding. We must learn to recognize the limitations and potentialities of the land and to manipulate it in such a manner that it remains a productive and desirable place for human life."[14]

[10]Ian L. McHarg, *Design with Nature*, Garden City, N.Y., Natural History Press, 1969, p. 26.

[11]W. Loudermilk, *"Conquest of the Land Through Seven Thousand Years,"* Agriculture Information Bulletin No. 99, Washington, D.C., U.S. Soil Conservation Service, 1953.

[12]René J. Dubos, "The Genius of the Place," The Tenth Horace M. Albright Conservation Lectureship, University of California, School of Forestry and Conservation, 1970, p. 4.

[13]Richard T. Wright, "Responsibility for the Ecological Crisis," *BioScience* **20** (15), 1970, p. 853.

[14]Dubos, *op. cit.*, p. 6.

Our Treatment of the Environment in Ideal and Actuality

by Yi-Fu Tuan

Ethnocentrism is characteristic of peoples all over the world. It is difficult for any viable culture to avoid seeing itself as the center of light shading into darkness. In Europe, to be sure, in the late seventeenth and early eighteenth centuries, this glorification of self was temporarily reversed. *Là-bas on était bien.* In the spirit of that age Europe was viewed as a portion of the earth afflicted with the blight of tyranny and superstition; beyond lay unspoiled Nature, unspoiled and rational peoples still appareled in celestial light (*1*). This romantic spirit has continued to affect the thinking of the West to the present day. Sensitive Westerners are wont to contrast their own aggressive, exploitative attitude to nature with the harmonious relationships of other times and other places. This view should be commended for generosity, but it lacks realism and fails to recognize inconsistency and paradox as characteristic of human existence.

In recent years two ideas that have bearing on our relationships to our environment are receiving greater recognition. One is that the balances of nature can be upset by people with the most primitive tools, the other that a wide gap may exist between a culture's ideals and their expression in the real world.

A current debate of interest in connection with the first point is the role of man in the extinction of Pleistocene mammals. Although the issue is far from resolution. I think we must admit that Paul Martin has made a good case for what he calls "prehistoric overkill" (*2*). We are readily persuaded that the disappearance of the bison was brought about by masterful and predatory white men, but find the thought that primitive hunters could cause the wholesale destruction of fauna somewhat unpalatable.

The second point is a commonplace of ex-perience in daily life; that a high-minded philosopher should actually live his philosophy is a matter for surprise, and we take it for granted that few of a politician's professed ideals are convertible into substance. But in the study of the ideas and ideals of cultures, especially non-Western cultures, there remains a tendency to assume that they have force and correspond to reality. It seems to go against the grain for a scientist to seek for polarities, dichotomies, and paradoxes; he would rather see unity and harmony. Contrarieties exist, however, in cultures as in individuals. A nonliterate, stable people such as the Zuñis of New Mexico do indeed make much of their aspiration to achieve harmonious order in the affairs of nature and of men, but their community is nonetheless wracked from time to time by bitter factionalism (*3*).

If small and stable societies do not often work as harmonious wholes, it is not surprising that large and complex civilizations like those of Europe and China should contain numerous dysfunctions. One of these is ecological imbalance. This is a theme I wish to take up—but indirectly; my primary concern is with the gaps that exist between an expressed attitude toward environment and actual practice. Such gaps may be taken as one of the signs of maladjustment in society.

To the question, what is the basic difference between European and Chinese attitudes to nature, many people might answer that whereas the European sees nature as subordinate to man the Chinese sees himself as part of nature. Although there is some truth in this generalization, it cannot be pressed too far. A culture's publicized ethos about its environment seldom covers more than a fraction of the total range of its attitudes and practices pertaining to that

THIS SELECTION is reprinted with permission of the author and publisher from *American Scientist*, Vol. 58, No. 3, 1970, pp. 244–249.

environment. In the play of forces that govern the world, esthetic and religious ideals rarely have a major role.

Christianity has often been blamed for Western man's presumption of power over nature. Professor Lynn White (4), for example, speaks of the Christian religion as the most anthropocentric the world has seen: it not only established a dualism between man and nature but insisted that it is God's will that man should exploit nature for proper ends. Christianity, White says, has destroyed antiquity's feeling for the sacredness of places and of natural things, and has made it possible for man to exploit his environment indifferent to the spirits that once guarded the trees, hills, and brooks. The Christian religion he further credits with Western man's prideful faith in perpetual progress, an idea that was unknown to Greco-Roman antiquity and to the Orient.

Opinions such as these reenforce the view that Christianity constituted a great divide. But the official triumph of Christ over the pagan deities brought no revolutionary change to the organization either of society or of nature. At the level of the actual impress of man on environment, both constructive and destructive, the pagan world had as much to show as Christianized Europe did, until the beginning of the modern period. Contrary to the commonly accepted opinion of twentieth-century scholars, classical antiquity knew progressivism. As Ludwig Edelstein has recently noted, the pre-Socratic philosopher Xenophanes believed in progress; and his faith could well have been buoyed up by the engineering achievements of this time (5). Lines in Sophocles' *Antigone* refer to the power of man to tear the soil with his plow. Plato in *Critias* described the negative side of that power—deforestation and soil erosion (6). By the early Hellenistic period, technical ingenuity was performing feats that justified Aristotle's boast: "Vanquished by nature, we become masters by technique" (7).

But the Romans did far more than the Greeks to impose their will on the natural environment. "Public roads," as Gibbons wrote in admiration, "ran in a direct line from one city to another, with very little respect for the obstacles either of nature or of private property. Mountains were perforated, and bold arches thrown over the broadest and most rapid streams" (8). An even more overriding example

of the triumph of the human will over the lineaments of nature is the Roman grid method of dividing up the land into *centuria quadrata*, each containing a hundred *heredia*. As John Bradford puts it (9), centuriation well displayed the arbitrary but methodical qualities in Roman government. With absolute self-assurance and great technical competence the Romans imposed the same formal pattern of land division on the well-watered alluvium of the Po Valley as on the near-desert of Tunisia. Even today the forceful imprint of centuriation can be traced across thousands of square miles on both sides of the central Mediterranean, and it can still stir the imagination by its scale and boldness.

Against this background of the vast transformations of nature in the pagan world, the inroads made in the early centuries of the Christian era appear relatively modest. Christianity teaches that man has dominion over nature—but for a long time this new dignity was more a tenet of faith than a fact of experience: for man's undisputed power over nature to become a realized fact Europe had to await the growth of human numbers, the achievement of greater administrative centralization, and the development and application of new technological skills. Farmsteads and arable fields multiplied at the expense of forests and marshes through the Middle Ages, but these lacked the permanence, the geometric order, and the prideful assertion of the human will that one can more readily read into the Roman road systems, aqueducts, and centuriated landholdings.

When we turn to China, we again find discrepancies between esthetic ideals and performance, as well as unforeseen conflicts and dysfunctions that are inevitable in a complex civilization. Western intellectuals who look at Chinese culture tend to be overgenerous, following the example of the eighteenth-century *philosophes* rather than the chauvinism of nineteenth-century European scholars.

Seduced by China's Taoist and Buddhist traditions, they like to compare the Oriental's quiescent and adaptive approach toward nature with the aggressive masculinity of Western man.

An adaptive attitude toward nature does indeed have ancient roots in China. Evidence of it occurs in diverse sources. Well known to the West is the concept of *feng-shui* or geomancy, aptly defined as "the art of adapting the residences of the living and the dead so as to co-operate and harmonize with the local currents of the cosmic breath" (*10*). A general effect of the belief in feng-shui has been to encourage a preference for natural curves—for winding paths and structures that seem to fit into the landscape rather than to dominate it—and at the same time to promote a distaste for straight lines and layouts.

Ancient Chinese literature contains scattered evidence that the need to regulate the use of resources was recognized. Even as early as the Eastern Chou period (8th–3rd century B.C.) the deforestation resulting from the expansion of agriculture and the building of cities seems to have led to an appreciation of the value of trees. In the *Chou Li*—a work which was probably compiled in the third century B.C. but may well include earlier material—two classes of conservation officials are mentioned: the inspectors of mountains and of forests. They were charged with protecting certain species, and with seeing to it that the common people cut trees at the proper season, except when emergencies required making coffins or strengthening dykes (*11*). Another ancient literary reference to conservation practice is Mencius' advice to King Huai of Liang that he would not lack for wood, if he allowed the people to cut trees only at the proper time (*12*).

Throughout Chinese history perspicacious officials have on various occasions warned against the dire consequences of deforestation. They deplored the indiscriminate cutting of trees in the mountains not only because of its harmful effect on stream flow and on the quality of soil in the lowland but also because they believed that forested mountain ridges slowed down the horse-riding barbarians. As one scholar of the Ming dynasty put it, "I saw the fact that what the country relies on as strategically important is the mountain, and what the mountain relies on as a screen to prevent advance are the trees" (*13*). The scholar-officials also recognized the esthetic value of forested mountains. The Wu-tai mountains in northern Shan-hsi, for example, were famous, but shorn of their trees can they retain their fame?

These references suggest that an old tradition of forest care existed in China. On the other hand it is clear that the concern arose in response to damages that had already occurred, even in antiquity. Animistic belief and Taoist nature philosophy lie at the back of an adaptive attitude to environment; alone these might have produced a sequestered utopia. But China, with her gardens and temple compounds, was also a vast bureaucracy, a civilization, and an empire. Opposed to the attitude of passivity was the "male" principle of dominance. One of the greatest culture heroes of China was the semi-legendary Yu, whose fame lay not in his precepts but in his acts—his feats of engineering.

An idea that lent support to the dominance side in Chinese culture was one which discerned a model of the cosmos in the earthly environment. It held that the regular motions of the stars could be expressed architecturally and ritually in space and time on earth. The walled city was given a rectilinear pattern, an orientation, and a grandeur that reflected the order and dimension of heaven (*14*). The earth's surface itself lacks paradigms of geometric order. Mountains and water are irregularly disposed. Experience of them has led to such unaggressive precepts as the need to observe and placate the spirits of the earth, the need for man to contemplate terrestrial harmony and adapt himself to it. By contrast observation of the stars has encouraged the aggressive side of Chinese culture, nurturing its predilections for order, hierarchy, and control.

Visitors to China in the nineteenth and early part of the twentieth centuries have often commented on the treelessness of the North, and the acute problems of soil erosion on the loess-covered plateaus. These areas were once well wooded. Deforestation on a vast scale took place as population increased and more and more land was taken over by farmers. But this alone does not account for the extent of the clearing. Other factors militated against prudence. One was the ancient custom, first recorded in the fourth century B.C., of burning trees in order to deprive dangerous animals of their hiding places (*15*). Even in contemporary China farmers are known to start fires for no evident purpose.

Asked why, they may say it is to clear land for cultivation—although the extent of burning far exceeds the needs for this purpose— or it is to leave fewer places in which bandits may hide, or to encourage the growth of small-sized sprouts in the burnt-over area and avoid the labor of splitting wood (*16*). The real reason for the burning is difficult to pin down.

Forests in North China were also depleted to make charcoal for industrial fuel. From the tenth century on, the expanding metallic industries swallowed up many hundreds of thousands of tons of charcoal each year, as did the manufacture of salt, alum, bricks, tiles, and liquor. By the Sung dynasty (960–1279 A.D.) the demand for wood and charcoal as both household and industrial fuels had exceeded the timber resources of the country; the result was the increasing substitution of coal for wood and charcoal (17).

An enormous amount of timber was needed for construction in the old Chinese cities, probably more than was required in European cities of comparable size. One reason for this is the dependence of traditional Chinese architecture on wood as the basic structural material. Great cities like Ch'ang-an, Lo-yang, and Hang-chou made severe demands on the resources of the surrounding country. The rapid expansion of Hang-chou in the thirteenth century to a metropolis of some one and a half million people led to the denuding of the neighboring hills. Despite the demand of the swelling urban population for food, some farmers found it more profitable to give up rice cultivation and grow trees (18). Rebuilding the wooden houses after fires put a further strain on timber resources; but of greater consequence was the deliberate devastation of whole cities in times of upheaval, when rebels or nomadic invaders toppled a dynasty. The succeeding phase of reconstruction was normally achieved in haste by armies of men who made ruthless inroads on the forest.

In a complex society benign institutions can introduce effects that were no part of their original purpose. The indirect results of any major action or event are largely unpredictable, and we tend to see the irony only in retrospect. For example, Buddhism in China is at least partly responsible for the preservation of trees around temple compounds, islands of green in an otherwise denuded landscape. On the other hand Buddhism introduced into China the idea of cremation of the dead; and from the tenth to the fourteenth centuries cremation was common enough in the southeastern coastal provinces to create a timber shortage there (19). Large parts of Mongolia have been overgrazed by sheep and goats. The most abused land appeared as sterile rings around the lamaseries, whose princely domains pastured large herds

though the monks were not supposed to consume meat. In Japan, the seventeenth-century official and conservationist Kumazawa Banzan was inclined to put most of the blame for the deforestation of his country on Buddhism; the Buddhists, he contended, were responsible for seven-tenths of the nation's timber consumption. One reason for this grossly disproportionate consumption was that instead of living in "grass hermitages" they built themselves huge halls and temples (20).

Another example of fine irony concerns that most civilized of the arts: writing. Soot was needed to make black ink, and soot came from burnt pine. As E. H. Schafer has put it, "Even before T'ang times, the ancient pines of the mountains of Shan-tung had been reduced to carbon, and now the busy brushes of the vast T'ang bureaucracy were rapidly bringing baldness to the T'a-hang Mountains between Shansi and Hopei" (21).

Although ancient pines may already have disappeared from Shan-tung by the T'ang dynasty, from the testimony of the Japanese monk Ennin we know that large parts of the peninsula were still well wooded in the ninth century (22). The landscapes described by Ennin provide sharp contrast to the dry, bare scenes that characterize so much of Shan-tung in modern times. Shan-tung has many holy places; the province includes the sacred mountain T'ai-shan and the ancient state of Lu, which was the birthplace of Confucius. The numerous shrines and temples have managed to preserve only tiny spots of green amid the brown. Around Chiao-chou Bay in eastern Shan-tung a conspicuous strip of forest lies behind the port of Ch'ing-tao. It is ironic that this patch of green should owe its existence not to native piety but to the conservation-minded Germans.

The unplanned and often careless use of land in China belongs, one hopes, to the past. The Communist government has made an immense effort to control erosion and to reforest. Besides such large projects as shelterbelts along the semiarid edges of the North, forest brigades of the individual communes have planted billions of trees around villages, in cities, along roads and river banks, and on the hillsides. A visitor from New Zealand reported in 1960 that as seen from the air the new growths spread "a mist of green" over the once bare hills of South China (23). For those who admire the old culture, it must again seem ironic that the "mist of green" is no reflection of the traditional virtues of Taoism and Buddhism; on the contrary, it rests on their explicit denial (*24*).

Problems of despoliation of the environment must be attacked along several fronts. Engineers offer technical solutions. Social scientists need to examine those societal dysfunctions that leave strains and scars on our habitats. One symptom of maladjustment lies in the conflicts between an ideal of nature or environment and our practice. Such conflicts are embarrassing to observe for they expose our intellectual failure to make the connection, and perhaps also our hypocrisy; moreover, they cannot always be resolved. Contradictions of a certain kind may be inherent in the human condition, and not even stable and simple cultures are exempt. Ideals and necessities are frequently opposed as, for example, on the most fundamental level, keeping one's cake and eating it are incompatible. Some consume beauty for gain; but all of us must consume it to live.

REFERENCES

1. Willey, B., 1962. *The eighteenth-century background* (Penguin Books), pp. 19—21.
2. Martin, P. S., 1963. *The last 10,000 years* (Tucson: Univ. of Arizona Press), pp. 64—65, 70; P. S. Martin and H. E. Wright, Jr., eds., *Pleistocene extinctions*, Proc. of the 7th Congress of the Internat. Assoc. for Quaternary Research, vol. 6, New Haven: Yale Univ. Press, 1967.
3. Vogt, E., and E. M. Albert, eds., 1966. *People of Rimrock: A study of value in five cultures* (Cambridge: Harvard Univ. Press), pp. 201—2.
4. White, L., 1967, The historical roots of our ecologic crisis, *Science* 155: 1205.
5. Edelstein, L., 1967. *The idea of progress in classical antiquity* (Baltimore, Md.: The Johns Hopkins Press), pp. 3, 11—13.
6. Sophocles, *Antigone*, trans. by Gilbert Murray, quoted in Arnold Toynbee, *Greek historical thought* (New York: New American Library, 1952), p. 128; Plato, *Critias*, ibid., pp. 146—47. On the theme of man-nature relationships in Western thought, see Clarence Glacken's monumental *Traces on the Rhodian shore*, Berkeley, Cal.: Univ. of California Press, 1967.
7. Aristotle, *Mechanics* 847, a 20.
8. Gibbons, E. *The decline and fall of the Roman Empire*, chap. 2.
9. Bradford, J., 1957. *Ancient landscapes* (London), p. 145.
10. Chatley, H., 1917. "Feng Shui," in *Encyclopaedia Sinica*, ed. by S. Couling (Shanghai), p. 175.
11. *Chou Li*, trans. by E. Biot as *Le Techeou-li* (Paris: 1851) 1: 371—74.
12. Mencius, Bk. 1, pt. 1, 3: 3.
13. Chen Teng, (1596). Gazetteer. Quoted by W. C. Lowdermilk and D. R. Wickes, *History of soil use in the Wu T'ai Shan area*, Monograph, Royal Asiatic Soc., North China Branch, 1938, p. 8.
14. Wright, A. F., 1965. Symbolism and function: reflections on Changan and other great cities, *J. Asian Studies* 24: 670.
15. Mencius, Bk. 3, pt. 1, 4: 7.
16. Steward, A. N., and Y. Cheo., 1935. Geographical and ecological notes on botanical exploration in Kwangsi province, China, *Nanking Journal* 5: 174.
17. Hartwell, R., 1962. A revolution in Chinese iron and coal industries during the Northern Sung, 960—1126 A.D., *J. Asian Studies* 21: 159.
18. Gernet, J., 1962, *Daily life in China on the eve of the Mongol invasion 1250—1276* (London: Allen & Unwin), p. 114.
19. Moule, A. C., 1957. *Quinsai* (Cambridge Univ. Press), p. 51.
20. McMullen, D., 1967. "Confucianism and forestry in seventeenth-century Japan." Unpublished paper, Toronto. I am grateful to Professor McMullen for allowing me to read this.
21. Schafer, E. H., 1962. The conservation of nature under the T'ang dynasty, *J. Econ. and Soc. Hist. of the Orient* 5: 299—300.
22. Reischauer, E. O., 1955. *Ennin's travels in T'ang China* (New York: Ronald Press), pp. 153—56.
23. Buchanan, K., 1960. The changing face of rural China, *Pacific Viewpoint* 1: 19.
24. Murphey, R., 1967, Man and nature in China, *Modern Asian Studies* 1, no. 4: 313—33.

IV/ Man's Population

Aoki from Monkmeyer

Introduction

THE PROBLEMS OF population are very much with us today, and it appears that they are going to remain with us very much in the future. This part deals with the various aspects of population: the beginnings of man, the growth of world population, the role of natural and cultural checks including disease, and a current subject of controversy, the aggressive tendencies of man.

An understanding of the worldwide problem of population and the attendant environmental crises requires an appreciation of how populations grow.

Population density and the rate of growth for an area depend upon the number of individuals entering the population and the number leaving or dying. The number of organisms depends upon births and immigration minus deaths and emigration. At local and national levels immigration and emigration are important, but since this is one world whether we recognize it as such or not, the effects of immigration and emigration are comparable to moving from one room to another. All individuals occupy the confining limits of the earth. From a world view it is only the birth and death rates that really count, so emigration and immigration will be ignored.

BIRTH RATES AND DEATH RATES

Birth rates in human population are usually expressed as births per 1000 population per year. This figure is obtained by dividing the number of births in a given year by the estimated population at the midpoint of the year and multiplying that result by 1000. This is the crude birth rate. A more precise way of expressing birth rate is the number of births per female of a specific age class or, even more precisely, the number of females left during a lifetime by newborn female, or the mean number of females born in each female age group. This is known as *net reproductive rate*. In humans this is usually modified as a fertility rate, the number of births per 1000 women fifteen to forty-four years of age. This compensates for differences in sex ratios and age structure.

Assuming there were no movement into or out of a population and no mortality, then birth rate alone would account for population changes. Under this condition population growth would simulate compound interest. If you refer to a mathematics handbook, you will learn that if interest is compounded annually, then

$$A = P(1 + r)^n$$

where A is the new amount at some given time
P is the original amount or principal
r is the rate of interest expressed as a decimal
n is the number of years

If the interest is compounded several times a year, then

$$A = P\left(1 + \frac{r}{q}\right)^{nq}$$

where q is the number of times interest is compounded during the year.

If interest is compounded continuously, then q approaches infinity. Letting r/q equal x, the expression can be written

$$A = P(1 + x)^{rn/x}$$

When q approaches infinity, x approaches 0, and from calculus it can be shown that

$$\lim_{x \to 0} (1 + x)^{1/x} = e$$

174

where e is the base of natural logarithms, which is approximately 2.7183. Thus, if the interest is compounded continuously, the expression reads

$$A = Pe^{rn}$$

In the symbols commonly used in population ecology, A, the amount at some time t, becomes N_t; P, the principal, becomes N_0, the initial population; r remains the growth rate or rate of increase; and t is the units of time. Then our compound interest formula will read

$$N_t = N_0 e^{rt}$$

the expression for logarithmic population growth, the accumulation of compound interest on the population. Changed to a logarithmic form,

$$\log_e N_t = \log_e N_0 + rt$$

If r is positive and the conditions remain the same, the exponential growth will increase faster and faster, like interest rapidly accumulating.

But this doesn't happen because death interferes, or because of a shortage of some aspect of the environment. Mortality, the second great influence on population size, is usually expressed as the number of deaths per year by the estimated population at the midpoint of the year multiplied by 1000. (Another way of looking at mortality and the one most useful in demography is probability of dying, the number dying during a given time interval divided by the initial population.)

Since births represent additions to the population and deaths subtractions from it, then birth minus death $(b - d)$ equals the rate of increase, or r in the formula above. When births exceed deaths, the population increases; when deaths exceed births, the population declines. This can be expressed by the simple formula $b - d = r$.

AGE STRUCTURE

The problem of population growth is not quite that simple. Buried in this formula is a variable, the age structure of the population. Since reproduction is restricted to certain age classes and mortality is most prominent in others, the ratio of the age groups bears on how quickly or slowly populations grow.

Populations can be divided into three ecological periods: pre-reproductive, reproductive, and post-reproductive. In humans these three periods also roughly correspond to the dependent young, the working ages, and the elderly dependents. These ratios can vary even though the densities remain the same.

Theoretically, all continuously breeding populations tend toward a stable age distribution; that is, the ratio of each age group in a population remains the same if the age-specific birth rates and age-specific survival rates are the same. The proportions of age classes in a closed population tend to become constant when mortality equals natality. If this stable situation is disrupted by any cause, such as a natural or man-caused catastrophe, disease, famine, or emigration, the age composition will tend to restore itself upon the return of normal conditions. Changes in age class distribution reflect changes in the production of young, their survival to maturity, and the period of life when most mortality occurs. Any influence which causes age ratios to shift because of changes in age-specific death rates affects the population birth rate. In populations in which life expectancy for the oldest age classes is reduced, a higher proportion falls into the reproductive class, automatically increasing the birth rate. Conversely, if life is extended, a great proportion of the population falls into the post-reproductive age, reducing the birth rate. Rapidly growing populations usually are characterized by declining death rates, especially in the very young age classes, which inflate the younger age group. Declining or stabilized populations are characterized by lower birth rates with fewer young to rise into the reproductive age classes and by a larger proportion in the older age classes.

Age structure is visualized best by means of age pyramids that relate the ratio in percent of one age group to another. The shape of the pyramid tells much about the present and the future of a particular population.

Figure 1(a)–(e) represents generalized age pyramids of human populations based on actual situations. Pyramid 1(a) with its broad base and narrow pinched top indicates an inflated younger-age group and a very small old-age group. Such a pyramid indicates a youthful population in which increasing numbers will enter the reproductive period. It foretells a rapid population growth. Pyramid 1(b) is a narrow one; the ratio between one age class to another is about the same. However, the dependency age groups are rather large in relation to the reproductive and working population. Such pyramids represent a situation of no significant population growth and even of an aging population. The narrow-based pyramid 1(c) illustrates a population with a large reproductive age group but declining young. This reflects a decreased birth rate, brought about by some form of birth control, and predicts a smaller reproductive age class later on. The rate of growth in

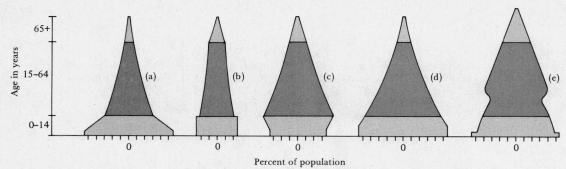

Figure 1. Diagrams of different types of age structure in populations. The diagrams are divided into three major parts: the prereproductive and young dependents, ages 0 to 14; the reproductive and economically active, ages 15 to 64; the postreproductive and elderly dependents, 65 years plus. (a) The broad base and the pinched top suggest a youthful population and foretell a rapid population growth. This is typical of Mauritius and certain South American and Asian countries. (b) The age structure suggests minimal population growth and even an aging population. This is characteristic of the United Kingdom and other western European nations. (c) The narrow base reflects a declining birth rate in spite of a high ratio of the reproductive age group. In time, if the trend continues, this structure will approach that of pyramid (e). (d) The age structure of a population in which death rates are declining. This profile will approach that of (a) as more young enter the reproductive age classes. (e) This age structure suggests a decline in the birth rate at an earlier time. The pyramid could change as the young enter the reproductive age period. This pyramid is characteristic of the United States.

such population is being checked. Pyramid 1(d) approaches that of 1(a). It represents a population in which the death rate is declining and the population is heading for rapid expansion. In contrast, pyramid 1(e) has a relatively large ratio of its population in the pre- and post-reproductive age periods and a marked indentation in the reproductive age period.

This suggests at least two situations. Either there was a period in the recent history of the population when the birth rate had declined markedly, as illustrated in pyramid 1(c), or the population experienced a heavy emigration of members of the younger reproductive age classes when they entered the working age period. Or it could be a combination of both. Whatever the reason, it suggests a declining population. (See also Fig. 2.)

GROWTH OF POPULATIONS

When a population first colonizes an unoccupied habitat, as often happened in the early history of man and even in the colonization of the New World, the environmental conditions in which it finds itself are for all practical purposes constant and the resources excessive. Under these conditions, the population increases geometrically in proportion to its numbers, as described by the formula previously given:

$$N_t = N_0 e^{rt}$$

The rate at first is influenced by hereditary or life history features, such as age at the beginning of reproduction, number of young produced, survival of young, and length of reproductive period. Regardless of the initial age of the colonizers, the number of animals or humans in the pre-reproductive category would increase because of births, while those in the older categories for the time being would be stationary. As the young mature, more would enter into the reproductive stage, and more young would be produced. Eventually after several generations, a population would grow at a fairly steady rate. If the number of animals are plotted against time, the points will fall into an exponential growth curve defined by the formula above. If the logs of the numbers of animals are plotted against time, the points fall into a straight line (Fig. 3).

But the environment is not unlimited, as man is rapidly discovering, nor does the age structure remain stable. As a population increases, detrimental effects of increased density, as was discussed in Selection 1 and will be in Selection 19 and its commentary, begin to inhibit the growth until it reaches some asymptotic level or the carrying capacity, the maximum number that can be supported in a given habitat.

This inhibition and slowing down of the growth rate can be described mathematically by taking the previous equation $N_t = N_0 e^{rt}$ and inserting into it some variables to describe the effects of density:

$$N = \frac{K}{1 + e^{a-rt}} \qquad a = r/K$$

where K represents the upper limit or carrying capacity.

176

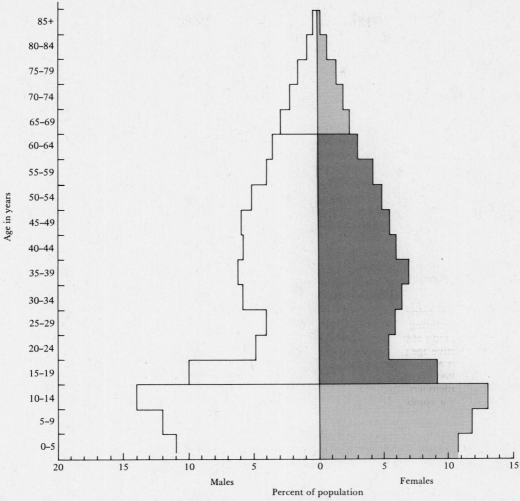

Figure 2. Age pyramid of a region in Appalachia which reflects the heavy emigration of the younger elements of the reproductive age group. This emigration results in a high ratio of dependent young and old to the economically active. It also reflects a declining population in the region.

This same equation is often written

$$\frac{dN}{dt} = rN \frac{K - N}{K}$$

In words, this equation says that the rate of increase of a population is equal to the potential increase of the population times the proportion of the carrying capacity of the habitat that is still unexploited (Fig. 4).

This idea of equilibrium which involves density dependence is not universally accepted. Indeed there is a great deal of debate concerning the effects of density-dependent and density-independent mechanisms in population regulation. Part of the arguments results from the observations that populations rarely exhibit any real equilibrium. They show constant fluctuation between some upper and lower limits, and where the asymptote falls depends on how one defines the carrying capacity.

Raymond Dasmann in his book *Wildlife Biology*[1] explores the concept of carrying capacity and suggests four different but overlapping types. One level is represented by *K* in the formula, the limit determined by the ability

---

[1]R. F. Dasmann, *Wildlife Biology*, New York, Wiley, 1964.

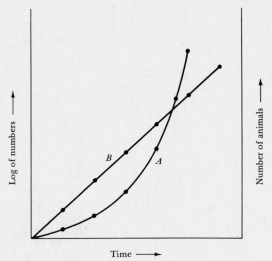

Figure 3. Exponential population growth plotted (A) arithmetically and (B) logarithmically.

of the environment to provide food to support the population at bare survival level. There is not enough food for optimum body growth nor vigor nor good health. The population flirts with disaster. A small change in the weather or failure of food supply can be catastrophic. Basically, this is the level at which populations of under-developed countries are existing.

Another concept is optimum density, which implies that the population has adequate food, water, and shelter to meet its needs. Individuals approach the maximum in body size and growth and in health and vigor. Rarely do populations remain at this level. Wild animals controlled by hunting or predation may hold at optimum level, as may a population controlled by territoriality or some form of birth control. Such levels may

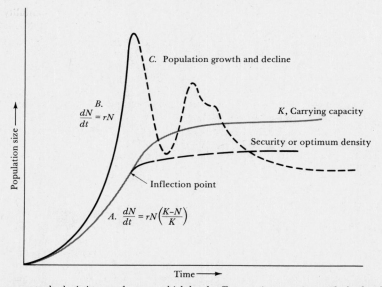

Figure 4. Curve A represents the logistic growth curve which levels off at carrying capacity, K. The broken line below starting at the inflection point represents what might be considered security or optimum density (see text). Curve B to the broken line is an exponential growth curve. C together with B represent a hypothetical situation based on data from several white-tailed deer populations in which a small population introduced into a vacant habitat expanded exponentially, then "crashed" to a point below K, the carrying capacity, recovered, and exhibited a renewed exponential expansion. The population was then reduced and held stationary at a level near or below optimum density by controlled hunting.

have been maintained by hunting-gathering cultures. By stretching the concept a bit, one could say that the United States, Canada, Western Europe, and the islands of Australia and New Zealand are at this level, although considering the pollution problems one might question this. Foodwise, these countries are fairly well off, and mortality from shortages does not occur although, due to social and economic reasons and inadequate welfare programs, a marginal part of the population does go hungry (see Selection 10). Optimum level represents the inflection on the growth curve.

Security density is a third type. It is based on Paul Errington's concept of the threshold of security, discussed briefly in the commentary to Selection 19. If the population density is above a certain size, there is instability in the population. Excess animals may be driven out or they may become very vulnerable to predation. Security density sometimes can correspond either to tolerance density, as in the case of territorial animals, or to optimum density. This concept of carrying capacity is not very applicable to human population, except perhaps in some primitive hunting societies or newly colonizing groups.

A fourth type is tolerance density. This is saturation density: the level at which intraspecific tolerance among animals of the same species or the lack of it permits no further increase. The degree of crowding tolerated usually sets the upper limit of population density. It is most marked in territorial species in which units of space are parceled out and defended by members of the population. Among territorial species, tolerance density may be the same level as optimum density. A similar type of density may occur among nonterritorial species that exhibit social hierarchy. The subordinate animals may be driven out or prevented from feeding or reaching shelter. Under such conditions, tolerance density might be nearly at the same level as subsistence density.

For man, the ideal is the optimum level, which probably would vary according to the desires, needs, and life styles of the population. The same might be said for tolerance density. What is a crowded condition for one individual or group may be desirable for another. But there are indications that man is rapidly reaching both a tolerance density and a subsistence density.

For most of his history man has reacted as if under the influence of tolerance density. If the population density became too great and a portion was forced out of the area, the excess population could move to empty lands or new habitats. In time even early man the hunter spread around the globe living at a low but probably optimum density. Hunting man increased the carrying capacity by becoming an agriculturalist and tapping a new energy source. Instead of living in small cooperative groups he began to live in clusters of varying densities. Even these had their limits imposed by food and other resources of the surrounding areas. The barbaric invasion of Europe by the Visigoths, Huns, and Mongols may have been the result of population pressures. When Europe, especially England, found herself becoming overpopulated, she could turn toward the New World, as well as toward the open lands of South Africa and Australia, even though this expansion meant the subjugation and in places extermination of indigenous peoples.

For all of his life on earth, man has lived in a frontier society with a frontier mentality. His success has been measured in terms of increasing population and increasing Gross National Product. No nation, state, or city likes to hear that its population is declining or its revenue from taxes and sales is dropping. So we behave as if there are always more space and more resources off somewhere in a new frontier. But there are no new frontiers of space and resources on the earth. As we have discovered but do not yet fully realize, we are living on a finite globe. We can hardly increase our habitat any further, for all but very marginal land has been occupied. The carrying capacity can be increased only by improving the habitat, by increasing food production, by utilizing new sources of raw materials, or by conquering the many environmental problems created by high populations in a technological age. But when carrying capacity of a habitat is increased, a population has a way of filling it up. The problems supposedly solved by such measures return even larger. Human population reacts the same way. As the capacity of the earth is increased, so does the population increase, and the problems worsen. Since there is a finite limit to which even the carrying capacity can be enlarged, the only alternative left is to check the growth of populations, to maintain numbers at a level that the earth can support.

Origin of Man

Commentary

There is no better place to start the considerations of the world population problem than at the very beginning with the origin of man. He began, all evidence seems to indicate, in tropical Africa. He apparently emerged from the lineage of apes as two separate forms. One was *Paranthropus*, barrel-chested, big-boned, massive-jawed, and small-brained. Living in the lushly vegetated regions of southern and east Africa he was largely a vegetarian, a grubber of roots and collector of fruits. The other was *Australopithecus*, short and slender, with a slightly forward-thrusting jaw and well-developed canines and incisors. A hunter and scavenger as well as a digger of roots, he ranged over a number of habitats and was an early maker of tools from animal bones. His habits as a hunter undoubtedly sharpened his intelligence, and evidence seems to indicate that since *Paranthropus* and *Australopithecus* both occupied the same areas, the latter out-competed the former and *Paranthropus* disappeared early from the African scene.

In time *Australopithecus*, too, faded away and in his place was *Homo erectus*, with long straight legs, flattened nose, sloping forehead, massive brow ridge, and a brain larger than that of *Australopithecus* and smaller than that of modern man. *Homo erectus* moved out of Africa. His fossils have been found around the world, in northern and central Africa, in eastern Europe, and in central China. He was a vegetarian turned meat eater, and he used fire. How he discovered it no one knows. Perhaps he obtained an occasional firebrand from naturally caused fires; or perhaps he made it accidentally by a spark made while chipping flint tools. *Homo erectus* was a toolmaker, progressing from a very primitive chopping tool to making a crude but efficient hand ax that advanced him to an excellent hunter, capable of killing large animals.

Like *Australopithecus* before him, *Homo erectus*, too, disappeared, apparently replaced by a not too well-known intermediate type, and eventually about 110,000 years ago by *Homo sapiens*, hunter, toolmaker, controller of fire, cave dweller, and home builder. One type of *Homo sapiens* was the much maligned but actually intelligent Neanderthal man who lived in Europe during the Glacial Age. He was a fire maker, and he used it to warm his cave and cook his food. He made a variety of cutting tools and weapon points. He showed a stirring of social and religious feelings, and by the way he buried his dead, it is probable that he believed in a life after death.

Neanderthal man disappeared abruptly, replaced by the physically more refined Cro-Magnon, a modern man who, having developed a distinctive culture, probably migrated from Asia to Europe and usurped the territory of Neanderthal man. Cro-Magnon man was further advanced than Neanderthal. He used the same tools, but he produced a more varied and elegant culture. He believed in magic and was an amazingly good artist who left cave paintings, small sculptures, and engravings on stone. He invented the eyed needle, made clothes from skins, and gave thoughtful treatment of the dead.

In the selection that follows, Dr. Brace traces the evolution of man to modernity and relates this evolution to the explosive spread of the species around the planet. For one and three-quarter million years in one form or another man has occupied the earth. For at least 10,000 years he has dominated it, but in turn he has literally been shaped by his own impact on the earth. He has the ability to forge his own destiny on the planet; whether he exercises that ability is a question only the future can answer. Perhaps like *Homo erectus* and Neanderthal man, modern-day *Homo sapiens* may disappear from the earth, an end brought on by his own ecological ineptitude and arrogance.

The Origin of Man

by C. Loring Brace

More than a century ago when Darwin published *On the Origin of Species*, it was authoritatively assumed by those who had not read the book that he was chiefly concerned with the origin of man. He actually mentioned the word *man* only once in the epoch-making work, and then in a cryptic sentence on the last page. But such is the strength of popular assumption that the title has been consistently misquoted. The popular press still refers to his book as *The Origin of the Species*, and *the* species is assumed to be man. This example typifies man's timeless fascination with himself, as well as his propensity for repeating misinformation about himself—a universal quality that may have been best summed up by the acerbic Ambrose Bierce early in the twentieth century when he defined man as "an animal so lost in rapturous contemplation of what he thinks he is as to overlook what he indubitably ought to be."

But what, then, is man? What was he in the past, and what has allowed him to survive to the present? If these questions are answered, we can then contemplate, perhaps with alarm, the basis for what is to come.

Central to any definition of man, and the key to his evolutionary success, is a phenomenon not immediately visible when specimens of the creature are scrutinized. This phenomenon is what the anthropologist calls culture. It includes not only the high points of art, music, and literature, but also all those things that result from the cumulative efforts of other people and previous generations. Tools, the traditions regulating their use, vital information, and language itself—all are included in the concept culture. Man is not just an animal that possesses culture, but an animal that cannot survive without it. Men could not exist if each had to discover anew the control of fire,

the manufacture of clothing and shelter, the sources of edible sustenance, and the guidelines for workable interpersonal relationships, to say nothing of the mechanics, electronics, chemistry, and physics on which human life depends today. These elements of culture are a cumulative continuation of simpler counterparts in the past.

In the beginning our ancestors, like other animals, must have been faced with the problem of surviving without the aid of culture. So much of culture is perishable or intangible that there is no way to determine when culture as a cumulative phenomenon began. Nonperishable cultural elements have an antiquity of about two million years in Africa. The cultural tradition of which they are a part continues without break, expanding to occupy the tropical and temperate parts of the Old World around 800,000 years ago, and ultimately developing into all the cultures in the world today.

From this we postulate an African origin for all mankind. The existence of crude stone tools in Africa a million and a half to two million years ago allows us to suppose the existence of culture at that time. Our guess suggests that the possessor of this culture could not have survived without it; therefore, he deserves the designation *man*—however primitive and crude he might have been.

We further postulate that culture existed a long time before the initial appearance of recognizable stone tools. This is speculation, but not idle speculation, because we could not otherwise account for the transformation of ape to man. Although small in quantity, supporting evidence exists in the form of skeletal material. Fossilized remains, including skulls, jaws, teeth, and a few other skeletal pieces have been found in association with the oldest known stone tools

THIS SELECTION is reprinted from *Natural History Magazine*, Vol. 79, No. 1, January 1970, pp. 46—49.

both in Olduvai Gorge in East Africa and in the Transvaal of South Africa. Since the discovery of these fossils in 1924, argument has continued over their status—ape? man? human ancestor? extinct side line? Brain size was within the range of that for the large modern anthropoid apes, but these early hominids walked erect on two feet as does modern man. Molar teeth were of gorilloid size, but the canines did not project beyond the level of the other teeth.

Despite continuing arguments over whether the balance of traits was on the human or simian side, it is apparent that the survival of these early hominids depended on a distinctly non-apelike adaptation. Bipedal locomotion did not enable hominids to escape predators by rapid flight. Neither could these hominids seriously threaten to bite a potential predator. Contrast this with such modern ground-dwelling primates as baboons and gorillas where the enlarged canine teeth of the males represent formidable defense weapons. We can guess that these early hominids depended for survival on something not visible in their anatomy, and our guess is that they used hand-held tools.

Possibly they defended themselves with the crude hunks of worked stone found at the sites where their skeletal remains have been discovered, but more likely they relied on pointed sticks. To use a rock as a defensive weapon requires close contact with the attacking creature, while the defender probably preferred to face his tormentor from the far end of a pointed stick. Not only is the pointed stick a simple and effective weapon—devisable with a minimum of manufacturing effort—but it can also double as a digging tool. Edible roots and bulbs are a substantial part of the diet of baboons that live today in the savanna, an environment typical of the areas inhabited by the earliest hominids. The addition of a simple digging stick of the kind used by the surviving hunting and gathering human groups—and probably by the early hominids—could easily double the baboons' food supply.

The huge, worn molars of the early hominids indicate that they relied on gritty, uncooked vegetables for subsistence. Unlike any other primates, their canine teeth are functionally indistinguishable from their small incisors. Assuming that the remote hominid ancestor had enlarged canine teeth like all other primates, then the creatures associated with the stone tools in East and South Africa two million years ago belonged to a line in which the selective pressures needed to maintain large canines had been suspended for a long time. Cultural means of defense must have existed long before the earliest stone tools.

Within the last three years jaws and teeth have been found in southwestern Ethiopia that are so like the Olduvai and Transvaal finds that they must be related. Their antiquity, however, extends back nearly four million years, and no stone tools are associated with them. The canine teeth in the fragmentary remains are not enlarged, leaving us to infer that defensive weapons must have been used some four million years ago—two million years before the earliest stone tools existed.

Reliance on hand-held weapons for defense (and perhaps also for food getting) did not automatically convert apes into men, but it altered the forces of selection so that evolution in the human direction was a consequence. For one thing, occupation with tool wielding reduced the locomotor role of hands. Legs and feet, as a result of natural selection, assumed the entire burden of locomotion. Tools usurped the defensive role of canine teeth, and, with an accumulation of mutations, these teeth were reduced. The vast majority of mutations interfere with the development of the structures that depend on their control, but usually these "deleterious mutations" are eliminated by selection. When selection is reduced or suspended—as when tools reduced the defensive role of teeth—the reductive mutations simply accumulate in the ongoing gene pool of the population. The structure controlled by the genes—the canine teeth, for example—eventually fails to achieve the full development once characteristic of the remote ancestral population.

Early in hominid development, when defensive weapons were not well developed, those charged with the task of defense, the males, must have been substantially more rugged than those less concerned with defensive activities, the females. Among terrestrial primates where a culture with weapons plays no defensive role, males tend to be much larger and stronger than females. Baboons, gorillas, and other ground-dwelling primates are good examples. Fossil fragments hint that this must have been the case for the earliest hominids as well. The difference in robustness of specimens from the early levels of Olduvai Gorge, the Transvaal, and now from Omo in southwest

Ethiopia has led some scholars to suggest that two different species of hominid—one small and slender, the other large and robust—shared the same habitat. However, now that we can demonstrate a time span of nearly three million years for the early hominids, it makes better ecological and evolutionary sense to explain the differences in size as sexual dimorphism—male-female difference—in a single species of early hominid.

The taxonomy of these earliest hominids continues to be debated. Genera such as *Australopithecus, Paranthropus, Zinjanthropus, Homo,* and others have been suggested, and even more species tentatively recognized. Whatever the taxonomic designation, these early hominids, except for their reliance on learned behavior and on hand-held tools for defense and food getting, lived more like apes than humans.

The evidence from Olduvai Gorge in East Africa shows that crude stone tools were added to the limited cultural repertoire toward the end of this long early hominid phase—a period I prefer to call the australopithecine stage. These tools belong to the incipient part of a tradition of butchering large animals in the Middle Pleistocene. At the end of the Lower Pleistocene, however, they occur mainly with the fossilized remains of immature animals. We can guess that this records the beginning of the adaptive shift that was largely responsible for the development of *Homo sapiens,* a shift related to the development of hunting as a major subsistence activity.

In the Middle Pleistocene, somewhat less than a million years ago, man emerges as a major predator. This adaptation is unique among the primates, and it is not surprising that many of the physical, behavioral, and physiological characteristics that distinguish man from his closest animal relatives are related to this adaptation. While we cannot make direct behavioral or physiological tests on fossils, we can make inferences based on their anatomy, on their apparent ecological adaptation, and on conditions observable in their modern descendants.

Anthropoligists generally agree that the men of the Middle Pleistocene are properly classified as *Homo erectus.* The first specimen to be discovered was classified in the genus *Pithecanthropus* at the end of the nineteenth century. While we no longer accept this generic designation,

pithecanthropine remains a convenient, non-technical term for Middle Pleistocene hominids.

Brain size was twice that of the preceding australopithecines and two-thirds that of the average modern man. With the absence of a specialized predatory physique, natural selection probably encouraged the evolution of intelligence. While brain size had increased, the size of the molar teeth had reduced, although they were still quite large by modern standards. This reduction may have been related to the shift from a rough vegetable-diet to one with a large proportion of meat. Meat, needing only to be reduced to swallowable pieces, requires far less mastication than starches, which begin the process of conversion to simple sugars by mixing with salivary enzymes through extensive chewing.

Evidence, although fragmentary, also suggests that bipedal locomotion in its modern form was perfected at this time, the Middle Pleistocene. While man's mode of locomotion may not be speedy, it requires an expenditure of relatively little energy. To this day, primitive hunters employ the technique of trotting persistently on the trail of an herbivore until it is brought to bay, often many days later.

Several correlates of this hunting life are suggested. Man, reflecting his primate heritage, is relatively night-blind and must, therefore, confine his hunting activities to the daytime. A tropical mammal (and physiologically man is still a tropical mammal) pursuing strenuous activities in broad daylight is faced with the problem of dissipating metabolically generated heat. The hairless human skin, richly endowed with sweat glands, is unique among terrestrial mammals of much less than elephantine size, and I suggest that this developed under the selective pressures of regular big game hunting early in the pithecanthropine stage.

The elimination of the hairy coat by natural selection left the skin exposed to the potentially damaging effect of the ultraviolet component of tropical sunlight. The obvious response was the development of the protective pigment melanin. Consequently the Middle Pleistocene ancestors of all modern men were probably what in America today is called black.

The conversion of this being into what is technically known as *Homo sapiens* requires only the further expansion of the brain from the pithecanthropine average of 1,000 cubic centimeters (actually well within the range of modern variation) to the average today of 1,400 cc. Fragmentary fossil evidence suggests that this transition had taken place by the beginning of the Upper Pleistocene, about 120,000 years ago. Men at that time—referred to as Neanderthals—still had an archaic appearance. In general these early representatives of *Homo sapiens* were more muscular and robust than their modern descendants—particularly the males. Jaws and teeth were large, especially the front teeth, which, from their wear patterns, evidently served as all-purpose tools.

Since the first appearance of *Homo sapiens* in his Neanderthal form, human evolution has been characterized by a series of reductions. Whenever human ingenuity made life easier, there was a relaxation of the forces of selection, and these reductions followed. More effective hunting techniques lessened the burden on the hunter's physique, and an eventual reduction in muscularity was the result. Manipulating tools lessened the stress on the anterior teeth, and the consequent reduction of these and their supporting bony architecture converted the Neanderthal face into modern form. In parts of the world where manipulative technology is a late phenomenon, such as aboriginal Australia, faces and teeth have remained large. Where clothing was developed for survival in northern climes, the significance of protective skin pigment was lessened, and the consequent

reduction produced the phenomenon that is euphemistically called white.

The only thing that has not been reduced is the number of human beings. We cannot even guess at the population density of the australopithecines. Throughout the Middle Pleistocene, the archeological record suggests a fairly constant population for the hunting pithecanthropines. Evidently the population increased dramatically with the Neanderthal form of *Homo sapiens*. The diversification of food resources and the increase in cultural complexity that accompanied the first appearance of modern *Homo sapiens* just under 35,000 years ago also signaled another sharp jump in population. This set the stage for the tremendous population growth made possible by the development of agriculture after the end of the Pleistocene 10,000 years ago.

Thus did *Homo sapiens* emerge—a manifestation of ecological imbalance, literally shaped by the consequences of his own impact upon the world. His fate, too, will be shaped by his future impact on the world—the result of his numbers and his actions. Malthus sounded the alarm nearly two centuries ago, but few listened to his warning. One who did was Ambrose Bierce, who added to his definition of man that "his chief occupation is extermination of other animals and his own species, which, however, multiplies with such insistent rapidity as to infest the whole habitable earth. . . ."

Growth of the World's Population

by Robert Leo Smith

The growth of the world's population has been so widely written about and debated over in all sorts of media from the popular press to scientific journals and on radio and television that there is no need to elaborate on the subject. But to put the discussions that follow in proper context, the growth of the world's population needs to be reviewed briefly.

How many people have inhabited the earth and how rapidly the populations grew is a matter of educated guesswork except for very recent times. Aside from local censuses there was no regular count of world population prior to 1800, and at best the censuses taken after that time have been incomplete for the world as a whole. However, there have been some rough estimates of past world populations based on knowledge of food needs, archaeological records, anthropological studies, and the like.

Man the hunter, requiring somewhere between 1000–2000 kilocalories of energy a day, would need at least one square mile to support one person. One million years ago in the lower Paleolithic, when man was probably confined to the African continent, he numbered somewhere around 125,000 (1). By the middle Paleolithic, 300,000 years ago, man had become a toolmaker and was acquiring a culture that enabled him to better exploit his environment. In addition he had expanded his range into Europe and Asia. By then man probably numbered 1 million. During the upper Paleolithic, 25,000 years ago, man, still occupying the same general range, increased his numbers to well over 3 million. By the Mesolithic, when man had emigrated to North and South America and Australia and had colonized most of the world, he probably numbered a little over 5 million. Man at this time had probably reached the carrying capacity of the earth for a hunting and gathering way of life.

Then man developed agriculture. By exploiting new resources and by making more efficient use of others, man in effect increased the carrying capacity of his habitat. Populations in the developing agricultural areas increased steadily, rising from perhaps 86 million 6000 years ago to 133 million 200 years ago. This comes to about three persons per square mile. As man began to crowd into farming villages and rapidly growing urban areas, problems developed. The concentration of humans made the spread of disease more rapid, and a close association with herding animals introduced such new diseases as anthrax, tuberculosis, and brucellosis. Breaking of new ground for agriculture and expansion into new areas exposed man to other diseases with which he had had no previous contact. As urban areas increased in size, providing sufficient food and eliminating human wastes became increasingly difficult. Polluted waters were a source of cholera, and the black rats, thriving in the unsanitary conditions of early cities, spread The Black Death. Life expectancy was fairly short, about 30 to 40 years. Lack of an ability to control disease, poor sanitation and hygiene, lack of transportation and a way to distribute food caused fluctuations in population size. The Black Death decimated populations of Europe in the Middle Ages, and outbreaks of typhus, smallpox, typhoid, and yellow fever spread through local populations. Man, especially the very young, also suffered from nutritional deficiencies, as well as from intestinal parasites. Local shortages of food often led to famines. Thus, for hundreds of years human populations, like natural populations of animals, fluctuated widely with local increases and declines common around the globe.

Then came the industrial revolution in Europe about 300 years ago, followed by a medical revolution—the discovery of the nature, spread, and prevention of disease. New resources and new sources of energy were available to the Europeans. Transportation was improved, agricultural knowledge was

---

THIS SELECTION was written especially for this volume.

increased, and techniques for food preservation developed. Population growth accelerated. In Norway, Denmark, and Sweden, for example, countries for which there are acceptable data, the death rate declined erratically until 1790, then dropped steadily and more rapidly. Between 1755 and 1775, 6.1 out of every 10 children reached the age of ten. Between 1901 and 1910, 8.5 children out of 10 reached the same age (2). Similar demographic situations existed in other European nations. From 1750 to 1850 the annual growth rate of European countries was 0.5 percent annually. Within 100 years the population doubled.

But Europe had an out in the New World, in Australia and New Zealand, in South Africa. This expanded land resource provided areas for increased food production, room for excessive population of European nations which numbered 27 per square mile, and economic enrichment. There was a heavy emigration especially of the young to new lands, and the European population declined. Between 1846 and 1932, 27 million people left Europe.

Emigration was not the only cause of population decline. The European nations were becoming both industrial and urban. People saw new economic opportunities and had new aspirations. They found that in cities children were strictly consumers, not producers, expensive to raise and educate. If they and their children were to succeed under urban conditions, they needed education, special skills, and freedom to move to places of new opportunity. Large families inhibited all of these. Even in rural areas of Europe large families were at an economic disadvantage. Mechanization reduced the number of laborers needed on the farm and required heavier capitalization. Parents, living out their three-score years and ten, remained on the land for a longer time, postponing the time when a son could take over the farming operation. As farms were subdivided among children, the point in time came when further subdivisions were no longer possible economically. There was no place for a large number of young in rural areas, most of whom had to leave for the city. Thus, all Europeans, urban and rural, began to restrict the size of the family by postponing marriages and by birth control measures. By 1930 the birth rate of European populations dropped to a low 15 per 1000. If such a trend had continued, the population would not have reproduced itself. This was the beginning of the demographic transition from high birth rates and low death rates to low birth rates and low death rates. Current population growth rates for some European countries are Denmark 0.9 percent, Norway and Sweden 0.8 percent, United Kingdom 0.6, Belgium 0.1, and Netherlands and France 1.0 percent (3).

While the Old World population growth was declining, the populations of the New World were expanding rapidly, brought on by a rapid influx of relatively young people into new country, a high birth rate encouraged by a situation in which opportunities were plentiful, and seemingly unlimited land resources. The population of the United States increased from 5.3 million in 1800 to 23 million in 1850. From 1850 to 1900 it increased to 76 million, in 1930 to 122.7 million, and in 1970 to 210 million. In the early part of the twentieth century the birth rate was exceptionally high, 30 per 1000. Since that time the birth rate in the United States has declined in a manner similar to that experienced by the European industrialized nations. It declined steadily to 18.4 per 1000 in the depression years of the 1940s, rose again after World War II, and has now fallen to a low of 16.8 per 1000. The current growth rate in the United States is around 1.0 percent.

Japan, the only heavily industrialized nation in Asia, has recently exhibited the same decline in birth rates. After World War I, Japan experienced a rapid decline in her death rate followed by a high rate of increase and a heavy emigration of her population to other lands, especially Asia, Australia, and the Americas. This increase was followed by a very rapid drop in the birth rate, especially after World War II. This was accomplished by voluntary family planning, late marriages, birth control measures, sterilization, and abortions. Japan is now experiencing the same demographic transition characteristic of the Western world. The growth rate of Japan has dropped to about 1.0 percent annually, the same as that of North America. This rate of growth still gives both a rather fast doubling time of 63 years (4).

Contrasting with the industrialized nations is the story of the underdeveloped countries. Although little is known of her population growth until the past several decades, Asia apparently has always experienced a high rate of growth brought on by the great number involved even if mortality was high. Between 1650 and 1750 the Asian population increased from 50 to 75 percent, although there were local reductions caused by famines. The dramatic increase did not come until after World War II, when the world entered a period of death control in the underdeveloped nations. The intervention of public health measures cut death rates by 50 percent and sent rates of population growth soaring. The spraying of malarial areas with DDT after World War II and other measures resulted in the population increase of 33 percent from 6.8 million to 9.1 million in less than a decade. A death rate of 22 per 1000 in 1945 was reduced to 10 per 1000 in 1954 to 8 per 1000 in 1969. Similar decreases took place in other highly populated underdeveloped countries. From 1940 to 1950 the death rate in those nations declined 24 percent on the average. This differs significantly from the decline in deaths that took place in the Western world. In the underdeveloped nations the decline in deaths required a remarkably shorter period of time than it did in the industrialized nations. The sugar-growing island of Mauritius in the Indian Ocean in an eight-year period after World War II increased her life expectancy from 33 years to 51 years, an accomplishment that Sweden needed 130 years to achieve (5). Taiwan in 20 years increased her life expectancy from 43 to 63 years; the United States required 80 years to achieve that goal.

The sharp drop in the death rate in the underdeveloped nations has not been followed by a similar decline in the birth rate. In Latin America, Asia, and Africa, the birth rate is still 40—45 per 1000, as it probably was 500—1000 years ago (2). These countries are experiencing an industrialized decline in death without the accompanying industrialization while still maintaining an agrarian birth rate.

The reasons are largely the attitudes of agrarian societies. In them children are considered blessings and a mark of male virility. Large families mean a labor force for the farm, an economic bonus, and old-age insurance. Since agriculture in the underdeveloped countries was largely subsistence, rural society had sufficient food. But overcrowding and lack of opportunity in the rural areas have forced massed emigration to urban areas, where immigrants have discovered that

opportunity does not exist either. They end up on governmental relief rolls and public charity yet still maintain their agrarian birth rates.

The result is an explosive population growth through the underdeveloped parts of the world. Costa Rica, for example, is increasing 3.8 percent per year and will double her population in 18 years (4). Mexico has a growth rate of 3.4 percent and a doubling time of 21 years; Brazil is growing 2.8 percent annually and will double her numbers in 25 years. For Latin America as a whole the growth rate is 2.9 percent and doubling every 24 years. A similar situation is in Africa. Kenya and Zambia have growth rates of 2.4 percent and a doubling time of 23 years, Nigeria 2.5 percent and 25 years, and the United Arab Republic 2.9 percent and 24 years. India is typical of southeast Asian countries. That nation has a 2.5 percent rate of increase and is doubling her population every 28 years.

Thus as much as some would like to believe, the population growth of the underdeveloped countries is not behaving like the growth of the industrialized Western world and Japan. It is happening without an expanding industrial or agricultural base on which to support a growing population. When Europe experienced her highest population growth, she was 38.5 percent industrialized and 27.9 percent of her labor force was engaged in manufacturing (5). Underdeveloped countries, now experiencing their highest population growth, find themselves 30 percent urbanized and with only 15 percent of their labor force in manufacturing. Further, these countries do not have the rich reserves of natural resources on which to draw, nor do their excess populations have new lands to which they can emigrate. This incredible rise in the number of people in the underdeveloped nations means that the economic resources of those countries must be used simply to maintain the people instead of being invested in education, labor skills, technology and administration, and planning. The world grows constantly more underdeveloped and impoverished.

Because the growth of populations varies from country to country, the population crisis is best viewed from a world viewpoint. Between the years 1650 and 1750 the world population grew at a rate of 0.3 percent per year to 728 million. From 1750 to 1850 the annual rate of growth rose to an estimated 0.5

percent and the world population stood at 1 billion. During the 100 years between 1850 and 1950 the world population increased even more dramatically. The death rate declined. Advances in agriculture and transportation, which lowered the prospects of crop failure and improved distribution systems, reduced incidences of local famine. Medical advances conquered a number of fatal diseases, reduced infant mortality, and increased longevity. As a result the world population grew at the rate of 0.8 percent a year. The numbers swelled to 2.5 billion. The populations of Asia, Europe, and Africa doubled; population increased five times in Latin America and six times in North America. The rate of growth for the world increased from 0.9 percent for the period 1940 to 1950, a doubling time of 77 years, to 1.8 percent and a doubling time of 37 years for the period 1950 to 1969. The world population jumped from 2.3 billion in 1940 to 2.5 billion in 1950 to 3.5 billion in 1969. If the present rate of growth of 1.9 percent annually continues, the world population will have doubled again by the year 2006. The United Nations medium estimate places the population of the year 2000 at 6.129 billion (6).

The greatest increase in populations, as the growth rates show, will be in those countries which can least support a larger population. Although projecting population increases is rather risky, particularly over a long period of time, some estimates have been made on population projections for the future. There is no question that it is on the way up. The estimated increase in population of Asia from 1950 to 2000 will equal the entire population of the world in 1958, and in 2000 the population of Latin America may be four times her own population of 1950.

Projections of the United States population made in 1967 estimated the population in the year 2000 to be between 283 million and 361 million. However, the 1970 census revised this downward. The projected population for the year 2000 is based on four possible birth rates. If the rate is that of the early 1950s, 3.1 children per woman of childbearing age in the population, then the population will be 321 million in A.D. 2000. If the birth rate is 2.78 per woman, the rate of the 1940s, then the population will be 301 million. For a rate of 2.45, which is the current one, then the population will be 281 million. If the birth rate is simply a replacement of 2.11, then the population will stand at 266 million. Current projections then place the population of the United States by the year 2000 at somewhere between 266 and 320 million. The errors in the 1967 projection resulted from the use of actual birth rates between 1960 and 1963, which seriously overestimated the number of babies born. The highest population projection—that of 361 million—is based on the number of children women are saying they will have, which suggests that a great deal of the concern about overpopulation still has not had an effect on the citizens of the United States. Zero population growth has yet to be sold to the United States citizenry, and it is making absolutely no headway in most of the world. There is a real danger that the lower estimates may result in a relaxation of concern about overpopulation in the United States. The age group 20–29 is the most fertile among American women and accounts for some 60 percent of births, which will increase from 15.5 million in 1970 to 20 million in 1980 and may cause a considerable rise in birth rate.

The question we have to ask is: "Is the world overpopulated?" Has it reached an asymptote that represents the bare subsistence level? For most of the underdeveloped countries it has. And although the developed countries do not appear to be overpopulated, they are, for they are living on resources outside their boundaries at the expense of the under-developed countries. If world resources were to be apportioned to all peoples, there would hardly be enough to go around.

BIBLIOGRAPHY

1. Deevey, E. S. 1960. The human population. Scientific American 209 (3) (Sept.).
2. Dorn, H. F. 1962. World population growth: an international dilemma. Science 135: 283–290.
3. Population Reference Bureau 1969. Data Sheet.
4. Ehrlich, P. R., and Anne H. Ehrlich. 1970. *Population, Resources, Environment. Issues in Human Ecology.* San Francisco, Freeman.
5. Davis, Kingsley. 1963. Population. Scientific American 209 (3) (Sept.).
6. United Nations. 1966. World population prospects as assessed in 1963. Population Studies, No. 41.

Population Density and Social Life

Commentary

In the first part of the following selection, Nathan Keyfitz reviews and summarizes part of what has been said in preceding material concerning the growth of agriculture and the development of cities. But he carries the discussions further to examine the reason for the expansion of cities in the developed and under-developed parts of the world. Industrialization was the power behind the growth of cities in developed nations. It drew people from rural areas because of employment opportunities; the new residents added wealth to the growing urban area. But in the underdeveloped countries the cities are growing not because of industrialization but because the hungry people move into seaport cities to be closer to the source of food, imported from other parts of the world. The new residents contribute nothing to the economy, but only add to its density.

As was pointed out in the previous section, man, evolutionarily speaking, is not a creature of the urban environment. He requires some time to evolve into his new role, and those best adapted to it now are ones who are second- or third-generation city dwellers. They have developed some of the changes necessary to cope with the environmental conditions encountered in high density populations, like the hens in a modern chicken house (the occupants of which, by the way, can be bred to exist under such conditions).

Keyfitz further expands the idea of the niche, introduced in Part I, as it relates to man. The modern Western city is livable because of niche segregation in occupations and interests. The life styles and interests of urbanized individuals differ from those of small town inhabitants. The impact of high density living on urban man shapes his awareness and efficiency in his own niche even down to social contacts and dulls his responses to other stimuli surrounding him. At professional and crafts levels urban man goes out of his way to cultivate ignorance of fields outside of his own (which can develop into major problems when major issues requiring specialized knowledge suddenly are claimed by those who have minimal knowledge and pass themselves off as authorities). One way urbanites attempt to escape the chicken house existence is to head for the country (see Part III), an escape obvious to those who travel the highways leading out of the cities on Friday evenings and into the cities on Sunday evenings. If such escapism continues, then in time the population expansion will arrive at a point where distribution is uniform and there will be no escape from the sight of one another.

As density increases and Ecumenopolis becomes a reality, it will be possible to exist in harmony only under intense regulations, just as the occupants of the chicken house are under intense regulation even to the point of having food brought to them individually, thereby eliminating any friction at the feed hoppers. To maintain high numbers of chickens in a limited space, the poultry man has to regiment the living arrangements. Urban man of the future will probably have to do the same, resulting in considerably less freedom of action.

Two different situations of density now exist in the world. In one we have increasing densities in the cities of industrialized affluent countries, with greater access to resources, accumulating wealth, and increasing densities still buffered by occupational niches. In the other we have increasing densities in cities that are growing without access to resources or industrialization, filling up with rural peasants removed from their way of life with no niche segregations to buffer them from the stress of density living. Keyfitz contrasts these two agglomerations, both urban, both growing, one rich, one poor, a situation that has important implications for the future.

Population Density and the Style of Social Life

by Nathan Keyfitz

To see how population density can occur at a rudimentary level of culture and what its effects may be, think of hunting groups with given apparatus, say spears or bows and arrows. Following Clifford Geertz (1963) and Julian Steward (1955) we observe that if the animals which they hunt move in herds, as do caribou, then large groups of hunters can pursue them. When they find a herd and attack successfully, there will be food for all. This herding of the animal prey is reflected in the gathering together of men, and communities can be large. If on the other hand the prey consists of small animals spread through a forest and caught one at a time, then men will have to spread out correspondingly; the large community cannot come into existence; human life will be lived out in isolated families. This latter condition, says Steward, applies to the Bushman and Eskimo, who have little in common but the dispersion of their game. Larger groups appeared among the Athabaskans and Algonkians of Canada and probably the prehorse plains' bison hunters.

This primary fact of dispersion or concentration will determine other circumstances. Isolated families cannot evolve the division of labor that is possible in bigger communities. In larger groups, specialization is likely to arise as some individuals become more adept at making spears, others at sighting herds, others at the tasks of surrounding the prey. Specialization will mean a variety of occupations, and, insofar as men are made by their work, a variety of men. Some of the occupations will have more prestige than others, perhaps because they require rarer skills. Even at this primitive level, where money may not exist in any form, the notion of a market for talent and a corresponding prestige hierarchy has a possible bearing.

Prestige is a source of power. Ambitious individuals can use occupational prestige to gain further power, especially if they have organizational ability. This suggests an interaction of economic and political phases, never entirely separated in real life. My only point here is that both the economy and the polity are more elaborated in large communities than in small, and hence more to be looked for in tribes living off herds of big game than in those living on dispersed small animals. The sociability of the animal, so to speak, permits a higher degree of sociability in the men; density causes density. To go one step more, and exaggerate somewhat, the animals have created the economic and political structures in the human group.

Human history and ecology did not stop at the hunting culture. The great change in society was the invention of agriculture, which even in the form of neolithic shifting cultivation permits much higher density than does hunting. Is the discovery of planting and tilling the cause of greater human density? Or was the causation the other way, the density coming first and forcing men to utilize their environment more intensively. Fortunately we do not need to stop here to investigate this question of metahistory. The important fact is that agriculturalists can produce a surplus, which hunters can rarely manage. Robert M. Adams (1965) has described the agricultural base of the early cities. The farmer can grow enough for himself and his family and have, let us say, 5% left over. Once this technological achievement occurs, then 5% of the population can live in cities. It becomes worthwhile for a ruler to dominate the farmer, to collect the food as booty or taxes, and use it to support an army and a court. The patriarch becomes a prince.

Some of the troubles, as well as the glories,

THIS SELECTION is reprinted by permission of the author and the American Institute of Biological Sciences from *BioScience*, Vol. 16, No. 12, pp. 868–873, 1966.

of civilization are implicit in the first cities, however small they may have been by modern standards. The total number of people which could congregate was limited, because strong political organization was needed to dominate a countryside, and an organization that tried to spread too far would be diluted and lose its control; the ancient empires often did outreach themselves in this way and fell apart. Physically, the area of control could not be too extended, since the transport of grain by ox-cart, the means used in the land empires of Asia, has natural limits set by the fact that the ox has to be fueled from the cargo. Among premachine cities, Rome did attain a population of nearly a million, but this was by virtue of extraordinarily competent, and harsh, organization of the lands around the Mediterranean, and by the use of sea transport for the movement of North African and Balkan grain.

Long before ecology or sociology became formal studies, a North African writer and politician called Ibn Khaldhun described with the utmost clarity how the population that could be concentrated in the capital city of an empire increased when the skill of the ruler and the discipline of his army and tax collectors enabled him to dominate a larger area of countryside, and how the population of the same city diminished when the rule was weaker so that the outlying provinces could successfully revolt from the exactions of the capital.

I have referred, then, to several levels of density—the dispersed hunters, the larger hunting group, the agriculturalists, the preindustrial city of landlords and princes organizing the countryside and living off the proceeds.

The city which constituted the capital of a despotic empire or of one of its provinces is not the only historical type. In Europe cities grew up specifically released from feudal ties, exempted from the domination of princes or landholders, their sustenance obtained by trade, religious, or entertainment functions, their independence assured by a sworn brotherhood of armed merchants. Not having to oppress a peasantry in order to secure their food, they could be loose in their internal arrangements; a medieval proverb says that "City air makes men free." The typical modern western city lives by a great extension of these same nonpolitical functions, and especially by manufacturing with mechanical power. Far from having to squeeze its food from the countryside, the city has be-

come an autonomous economic force. Today, the countryside wants city goods more than the city wants food. The concentrated population of cities, which in the preindustrial empires was parasitic, has now become incredibly productive. Exploitation, if that is the right word, goes the other way from that of Ibn Khaldhun's account; rural legislators tax the cities to maintain support prices for grains, butter and other foods. Today's pattern, at least in the United States, England, and other western countries, is that men are more productive in dense settlements than in sparse ones.

The increase of cities, especially the increase of very large cities, is to be seen on all continents. Not only in the rich countries as foci of industry and trade, but in the poorest, to which industry has hardly come, the cities are expanding. In fact, during the 1950's the urban populations of developed countries increased by 25%, while those of underdeveloped countries increased by 55%. The increase of poor, dense populations was twice as rapid as that of rich ones, Bourgeois-Pichat (1966) tells us.

How could that 55% increase occur, if what I have said about the preindustrial city being dependent on the limited surplus of a countryside is true? The surplus food of the Asian peasantry did not increase by 55% in the 1950's; it hardly increased at all. How can Djakarta be five times as populous as it was before World War II, and three times as populous as ancient Rome at the highest point of its imperial power? Djakarta has not much more industry than Rome had. Its weak civil or military domination of an island territory, in some degree democratic, cannot compare in extractive power with the iron rule of Rome. The answer, of course, is that it draws food from foreign territories, including the United States; some of it paid for with the export of raw materials; some of it borrowed; some as gifts.

Unable or unwilling to exploit its own peasantry, the large contemporary nonindustrial city more and more bases itself ecologically on the fields of the American west, together with the ships and harbors which link those fields with its massive populations. Population in the Asian countryside itself is growing beyond food supplies; far from having a surplus to ship to the city, the peasant is himself hungry.

Once the local countryside can no longer produce enough food for its own inhabitants so that these must be supported by foreign food, they tend naturally to gather into such seaport cities as Djakarta, Calcutta, and Rio de Janeiro, as close as possible to the spot where the boats will discharge their cargoes of American, or occasionally Burmese or Cambodian, grain. If people are to be fed from abroad it is cheaper to have them at the seaports than dispersed through the countryside. At the present time the United States is shipping about 800,000 tons of grain per month to India alone. At the Asian standard of about one pound per person per day, this is enough for 40,000,000 people to live on; that number happens to be about equal to all the citizens of India living in the seacoast cities. If population continues to increase in the countryside and food does not, one can expect further flight to those cities.

One could say much about what density and size will do to the condition of dependence of those cities. We know that their inhabitants tend to perform services rather than make goods. The services have the function of distributing the claim to the food shipments, the dominant ideal being to give employment rather than to get work done. Some studies have indicated that the new migrants to the cities retain links with the countryside. Others show that the simple and traditional patterns of association in the countryside are transferred to the city, which thereby seems like a number of contiguous villages, lacking only their fields and their crops. These dense cities of rural culture are a new phenomenon in the world.

For some quite different concomitants of density, shown in their most accentuated form, we must go to those world cities of the 19th century which were ecological consequences of the railroad and steamship—New York, London, Paris, Berlin. In the 20th-century West a process of dispersal has occurred; cities produced by the automobile are less dense than those produced by the railroad and street car. We are getting strip cities, of which the best known is Megalopolis, the name Jean Gottman (1961) gave to Boston-New York-Washington.

The industrial city of the 19th century as well as the strip city of the late 20th century intensifies competition on many levels. We must not only find a livelihood, we must find a life, each of us for himself, in the crowded city. This search for a tolerable physical and moral existence preoccupies every city dweller, and it has drastic consequences for urban society as a whole. Just as Darwin saw the animal or plant adapting to a niche in which it is partly sheltered from competition, so the sociologist Durkheim (1960) sees the city man restlessly searching for, and adapting to, a niche constituted by a specialized occupation and specialized personality. During the strike of airplane mechanics I was part of an undifferentiated mass seeking tickets at an airline counter. If one had to face daily the direct competition of millions of people, the struggle would so weigh on each of us that existence would be impossible for our spirits as well as our bodies. One's niche may be teacher, stock broker, or truck driver; it requires skills that others lack, or involves work that others do not want to do. It gives each a place with a certain minimum of predictable security. We are under constant inducement to better our position, and we seek to do so by further specialization.

Now the electronics engineer in Chicago, say, has to concern himself, at most, with the competition of other electronics engineers. But he does not even have to cope with them, at least in the short run. There are a hundred specialties within the field of electronics, and within each of these recognized specialties an individual practitioner, through his own tastes and capacities, can make himself unique. People in a particular plant come to depend on him. If the city is, on the one side, a jungle of potentially infinite and destroying competition, on the other, it shows a nearly infinite capacity of its members to differentiate themselves, to become useful to one another, to become needed.

The differentiated citizen can afford to be tolerant of those he meets, even to like them. This could not be true if competition were more direct, with individuals as personally ambitious as we know them to be in western countries. The struggle for upward mobility, characterizing all developed societies, can only through the process of specialization avoid the harshness of personal character that the blast of full competition would create.

The differentiation is only possible within an economic space that is honeycombed with organizations that are themselves competing, at a supra-individual level, and have their own lives, usually longer than those of individual men. The plants and firms live among a host of other organizations which serve varied interests—trade unions, professional societies, sporting clubs.

192

Corresponding to the infinite shades and gradations of personalities and types of work, spread through a complex social space, an unprecedented sensitivity to symbol systems comes into existence in the city. The contemporary mathematician, or biologist, or sociologist, along with such other products of city culture as the banker, the store manager, or the traffic analyst, each has his own characteristic set of symbols and has to cope with unprecedented variety, subtlety, and sheer mass of material. Typically 8 or 10 years of intense training, for most of us only possible between the ages of about 15 and 25, are the necessary means to develop the sensitivity, the awareness of issues, the minimum basic storehouse of facts in a given field. You only put up with me, if you do, because you suppose that I have an extensive and powerful storehouse of facts in my own field, which is the mathematics of population. This reciprocal imputation of subtle, mysterious, and extensive knowledge is what permits mutual respect in the more specialized residents of the city. We do not know just what it is that the other man knows, but we assume he knows something and is capable of doing his own job with reasonable competence, whether it is embryology or pants cutting.

Such a basis of respect is characteristically metropolitan. In a society of smaller volume such as a village, each gets to know all about the few score or the few hundred people with whom he will have contact in the course of a lifetime. He knows them as whole people, is concerned with literally everything about them.

Each of us as city people has contact in a day with as many individuals as the villager meets in the course of a lifetime; this includes store clerks, bus conductors, taxi drivers, students, colleagues, theater ushers, not to mention those we pass as we walk or drive along the street. It would destroy us if we had to react to every one of them as people. We want to know about each of them only enough to cover his particular relationship with us. We care only that the bus conductor is an authorized employee of the company and will take our fare and drop us at the corner of Madison and 42nd Street. Whether he is happily married with four children or a debauched bachelor, whether he is Presbyterian or Catholic, we never inquire. His uniform tells us everything about him that

we need to know. It is mere personal whim on our part if we even look at his face.

The well adapted citizen of the high income metropolis has learned to protect himself against its potentially infinitely varied stimulation. In some measure he becomes blasé; whatever happens he has seen something more exciting. He becomes absent-minded and dulls his recollection of gross stimuli and even his perception of them in order to accentuate his capacity to react to the subtler issues and symbols of his own business, professional, technical, or scholarly life. He goes out of his way to cultivate ignorance of fields outside his own. Whereas constant full exposure to what the city offers and demands would weary and frustrate him, by protecting himself sufficiently against stimuli he need show only a slight antipathy or even be perfectly good-natured. This is the nature of urban contacts, suggestively portrayed by Georg Simmel (1964). Note that this characterization applies only to those members of the city who have adapted to city life over two or three generations, and as a result are suitably educated, and are productive enough to command the facilities of the city. They do not apply to the recent migrant to Chicago from the rural south, or to Calcutta from inland Bengal.

The ultimate refuge against the pressures of the metropolis is flight. A quiet place in the country becomes the ideal of all and, in one form or another, the seasonal recuperation of most. But with the acceleration of the population growth, and especially with the improvement of transport through the private automobile, that quiet place in the country, the most precious of resources, is bound to become scarcer. We not only are a larger population, and able to get out of the city more easily, but a larger fraction of us has the means to travel. We are 197 million people in the 3.6 million square miles of the United States. Deducting the areas of the cities, superhighways, lakes, deserts (both natural and those made by man, for instance by mining operations), we could still each have 4 acres of countryside—which means just enough to get out of the sight of one another. But not very long ago the United States was growing at 1.5 percent per year, a pace which would double our numbers each 45 years. It would halve the 4 acres in 45 years, quarter it in 90 years. I mention these figures only to show that within the lifetime of children now born,

193

at an increase of 1.5 percent per year, dispersion would become impossible; no amount of redeployment would enable us to get out of sight of one another.

Simultaneous with the increase in numbers, the advance of technology makes each of us more mobile, and requires more space—especially highways—to be set aside merely for facilitating our movement. Aside from this, if effective density is counted in units of potential contact rather than in people per square mile, we increase our effective density merely in improving transportation. Man is unlike other creatures in drastically remaking his means of locomotion. United States' automobile and truck registrations were 86 million in 1964, and will pass the 100 million mark by the end of the 1960's. Nearly 10 million new vehicles are being put on the road each year, offset by only two-thirds that number of scrappings; this fact alone would tend to crowd us even if we were the same number of people. Year by year we are both more in numbers *and* are moving faster, always within a fixed people-container, the terrestrial area of the United States. The result is rising pressure and temperature, apparently under the operation of laws analogous to those governing the behavior of gases.

I do not know how we shall respond. Will we build up higher capacity for discretion and reserve? Will we develop the sort of etiquette of noninterference with our neighbors—silence, dignity, and good humor—that helps make life tolerable on a long submarine voyage? I knew a charming family in Paris during the housing shortage who had two and a half rooms, counting the bathroom, for five people. They managed the situation well, and despite proximity each was able to have his private thoughts without interference. The life required a degree of self-discipline that not all of us could furnish. Events on the city streets this hot summer do not suggest that our civilization is moving toward those standards of reserve, discretion, and respect for the rights of others that would make greater density acceptable.

In fact, the response of society to higher density is usually the very opposite of reserve and respect for the privacy of individuals; it is rather interference and planning. The frontier had no traffic lights or parking regulations. People did not have to regulate their activities by the activities of others. If the clocks and watches of frontier families were randomly in error, little inconvenience would have resulted; but if those of a modern city were wrong, say by 2 hours, all its activities would be brought to a halt. Everything we do interlocks with what others do. The frontier needed no zoning bylaws or building standards. The necessity for all these forms of planning has come with density. Richard Meier (1962) describes an arrangement of the city of Madras in South India, one of the growing harbor cities I have spoken of, such that 100 million people could live in it, but life would have to be planned in the most excruciating detail. People would not even be allowed to own bicycles, simply because parking individually owned bicycles would tie up the streets. Movement would be restricted, and all that was necessary would be provided by mass transportation.

The density continuum from the frontier to Meier's imaginary Madras is also a planning continuum; density and planning seem to be positively correlated.

Less clear is the degree in which freedom in the West has declined with planning, and hence with density. George Orwell's *1984* is inconceivable without high population density, supplemented by closed circuit television and other devices to eliminate privacy. It exhibits in extreme form an historical process by which the State has been extending its power at the expense of the Church, the Family, and the Local Community, a process extending over 150 years.

Though the trend to State power has accompanied the increase of density, I do not know whether, up to now, density, even combined with the march of technology, and combined with State control, has diminished the individual's effective freedom on balance. After all, the individual benefits from the State and from the increasing wealth that has gone along with density and with planning, including clocks and traffic lights. In the United States the gain to freedom through rising average wealth may offset the attack on freedom through State measures. In the USSR increasing wealth seems to be bringing about a loosening of totalitarian structures.

A convincing account of the relation between sparseness and abundance on the one side and national character on the other is presented by David Potter (1954). The wealth of the economy, first on the frontier and then in the cities, encouraged mobility and individual success as an ideal. The real wealth of the country—and this arose from spaciousness in the largely agricultural epoch when national character was being formed—was great enough that a mobile, optimistic, ambitious, and generous attitude would have scope for success and would often succeed. One man who succeeded with these traits encouraged the growth of similar qualities in others. In the United States, sparsely settled during most of its history, when men were scarce and resources plentiful, labor was sought after by employers rather than the other way round. This gave the common man confidence in himself; self-confidence made him open-handed and he taught his children open-handedness.

Plenty also encouraged freedom—if there are enough goods for everyone, let each one take the part of the patrimony he wants or can earn. If there are enough seats on the train each passenger can choose the one he wants without supervision; a shortage of seats compels a system of reservations, which is to say planning. Abundance brings men to potential economic equality—at least in the sense that each can hope to find the resources that will make his labor fruitful. By virtue of the same fact, it inclines them to political equality. Density and poverty make for the opposite of democracy—as Wittfogel (1957) argues in his study of hydraulic civilization.

If density tends to shackle us, and wealth to free us, then the question of what will happen in the United States in the 21st century that is only 34 years away is still an open question. I do not know enough of the conditions of the present race between exhaustion of raw materials on the one hand and technology on the other to make a firm statement, but suppose technology wins and we become much denser but also much richer. For us the wealth worked counter to the density. But what about those dense societies which have little prospect of attaining the wealth of the United States and whose density, combined with their traditional agricultural techniques, already places them near the point of starvation?

I started this discussion with the preindustrial environment, and went on to those contemporary preindustrial cities clustered around the coasts of the underdeveloped world in which ports, built for the export of now obsolete colonial tropical products, are operating at capacity to unload cargoes of food. Here are larger cities than Ibn Khaldhun contemplated. If those city dwellers oppress any peasantry it is that of the United States. But it is not that of the United States either, since American productivity has increased faster in agriculture than in industry these last years. The labor cost of that food to the American farmer is at an all-time low, and in any case, the city-dweller is paying for PL480 shipments, for which the Prairie farmer gets spendable cash. I said that if poor peasant populations are to be fed by imported grain rather than by grain from their own countryside, then it is convenient for them to bring their mouths to the harbors where the grain is unloaded, rather than having the grain carried to them dispersed over the countryside, and that this is the basis for much contemporary urban growth.

How different the case would be if the United States had given fertilizer factories rather than wheat. Then more grain could sprout throughout the South Asian mainland, and there would be no reason for the peasants to accumulate in the city in numbers beyond the industrial jobs available.

I have spoken of the problem of privacy in the dense industrial city. The problem is accentuated in the cities of Asia, where millions of similar beings exist in closer contact, without the shelter provided to each through specialization and the division of labor. In the West we each come to have a special claim on the production of others through our own specialized production, especially through the voluminous contribution which each of us can make in our highly capitalized society. We have some degree of uniqueness of personality through all those devices by which we differentiate ourselves, some of them arising out of our work, but others quite separate: sports and hobbies, for instance, which the affluent society lavishly supports and equips. Education, also a result of our wealth, inducts us into elaborate, differentiated symbol systems and into that etiquette of restraint and reserve which mitigates the closeness of city living.

The citizen of the poor crowded city is in all these respects disadvantaged. He has neither specialized work, nor capital to make his work productive, nor hobbies to reinforce a personal identity, nor education to make him sensitive to complex symbol systems. Here is the hurt of density without its benefits.

The only defense for the poverty-stricken urbanite in the tropics is through the retention of some of his rural habits; he may manage a kind of village existence, with village ecological relations complete in all respects except that the village fields are absent. The village within the city of Calcutta or Madras may well have its own temple and traditional service occupations: sweepers, watchmen, priests, headmen. Some physical production by village methods goes on, and there are tanners, potters, and makers of bullock-carts—but very few farmers. Each compressed village in the city may have some residue of the administrative structure of the village its inhabitants have left, and village factionalism need not be forgotten on the move to the city. The village in the city may have a rate of growth more rapid than the old village, because its death rate may be low, its birth rate remains almost up to rural levels, and the city is swelled by new entrants from the countryside. It is hungry, as the rural village often was, but now its hunger is a matter of high political importance, affecting both national and international politics.

Our picture now is of two dense agglomerations of mankind facing one another, both urban, one rich and one poor. America takes its cities into the countryside—it becomes an urban society through and through. Asia remains rural, even to parts of the dense agglomerations at the seaports—it brings its rural culture into the cities. In a sense, the rich city has called the poor one into existence, first by DDT and medicine which lower the death rate of India from perhaps 35 per thousand to 20 per thousand, and then by the provision of food.

In a quite different sense, Europe had earlier contributed to Asian population. The industrial revolution of Europe and America demanded raw materials, and this demand was translated into a demand for people who would produce its goods. The needs of Europe for sugar, spices, and rubber brought into existence large populations, for example in Indonesia; Java grew from under 5 million in 1815 to 40 million by World War II. And when our technical advance, especially western synthetics, enabled us to make the things that formerly could only be produced by tropical sunshine and tropical labor, those populations were left high and dry. They are functionless in relation to the Western industrial machine which brought them into

existence, but they keep growing nonetheless.

Western governments and electorates sense the tragic state of affairs, and, at least vaguely, feel responsible for this aftermath of colonialism; therefore we provide food and other kinds of aid. But such are the dilemmas of doing good in this difficult world that each shipment of food draws more people to the seaports, and we arrive at nothing more constructive than a larger population than before dependent on shipments of food. If the need for food is a temporary emergency, philanthropy is highly recommended, but the condition of tropical agriculture and population seems to be chronic rather than acute.

And yet the aid cannot be stopped. As the populations of these port cities grow so does the problem of producing and shipping food to them. But so also do the economic, political, and moral problems of cutting off the aid. When famine was the work of God, whose acts man lacked the technical capacity to offset, such issues did not arise.

The only escape is through the economic development of the countries of Asia, Africa, and Latin America. With increase of income arises the sort of communication system through which people can receive and act on signals in regard to the size of their families. Americans since 1957 have come to understand that their families had been too large—signals reach them to this effect through the price system and through the difficulties of placing children in college and in a job. For underdeveloped people such a signalling system of prices and costs is not in existence, and messages that create a desirable feedback and permit automatic control do not carry.

On the other hand, the growth of population for many reasons itself inhibits the development process which could solve the population problem. That is why some students of the matter think that the control of population should be tackled directly. Each point by which the birth rate falls makes the process of saving and investment and hence development that much easier.

I have spoken of two sorts of dense agglomerations of people looking at one another across the oceans. The one is wealthy, modern, productive, highly differentiated by occupation, handling complex symbol systems, dominating the environment. The other is poor, traditional, nonproductive except for services that are not badly wanted, less differentiated by occupation, illiterate or barely literate, highly dependent on the environment. Our rich American cities contain a minority which is taking refuge from rural poverty. Some Asian cities consist of a majority of such refugees.

I have refrained from reference to the individual human tragedy of the multiplying homeless sidewalk-dwellers of Calcutta and other cities of the tropics. No one can say that their plight is irremediable; evidently a number of countries are achieving development today, including Hong Kong, Taiwan, Mexico, Turkey. On the other hand, I see no grounds for the facile optimism that declares that development is inevitable for all. To turn the despairing kind of density into the affluent kind requires that three issues be squarely met: food supplies must be assured, industry established, population controlled. Only in some of the underdeveloped countries are these seen as key issues and seriously tackled.

Is the hardship of life in the crowded and poor city itself a stimulus to effective action? Do density and poverty make for greater sensitivity to the real problems, and greater judi-ciousness in their treatment? Not necessarily; especially not for the miserable newcomers, the first ill-adapted migrant generation to the city. In the slums of first settlement, whether in 19th century London and Paris or 20th century Chicago and Calcutta, city mobs can be readily aroused by their troubles to action and to violence, but they do not necessarily see the root of their frustrations and the way to overcome them. Penetrating analysis does not guide mob action. The crowd, mobilized by some incident, acts with a violence out of all proportion to the event that excited its anger. It streams through a city street, stops to throw bottles at the police who reply with tear gas, overturns automobiles, is finally dispersed by a National Guard armed with bayonets. Far from being a disappearing relic of the past, it is with us both in the temperate zone and in the tropics, in wealthy countries and in poor ones. Food riots occur in Bombay and civil rights riots in Chicago, New York and Cleveland. This ultimate manifestation of population density, which colors the social history of all continents, is a challenge to learn more about the causes of tension and frustration in city life.

REFERENCES

Adams, R. M. 1965. *Land Behind Baghdad.* University of Chicago Press, Chicago, Ill.

Bourgeois-Pichat, Jean. 1966. *Population Growth and Development.* International Conciliation, No. 556, January. Carnegie Endowment for International Peace.

Durkheim, Emile. 1960. *De la division du travail social.* 7th ed. Chap. III, La solidarité due à la division du travail ou organique, Presses Universitaires de France, Paris. pp. 79—102.

Geertz, Clifford. 1963. *Agricultural Involution: The Process of Ecologial Change in Indonesia.* University of California Press, Berkeley, Calif.

Gottman, Jean. 1961. *Megalopolis: The Urbanized Northeastern Seaboard of the United States.* Twentieth Century Fund, New York.

Hawley, Amos H. 1950, *Human Ecology: A Theory of Community Structure.* Ronald Press, New York.

Meier, R. L. 1962. Relations of technology to the design of very large cities. In *India's Urban Future* (Roy Turner Ed.). University of California Press, Berkeley, Calif. pp. 299—323.

Potter, David M. 1954. *People of Plenty: Economic Abundance and the American Character.* University of Chicago Press, Chicago, Ill.

Riesman, David. 1950. *The Lonely Crowd: A Study of the Changing American Character.* University of Chicago Press, Chicago, Ill.

Simmel, Georg. 1964. The Metropolis and Mental Life. In *The Sociology of Georg Simmel* (edited and translated by Kurt H. Wolff). Free Press of Glencoe, Collier-Macmillan, London. pp. 409—424.

Steward, J. 1955. *Theory of Culture Change.* University of Illinois Press, Urbana, Ill.

Wirth, Louis. 1964. Urbanism as a Way of Life. In *On Cities and Social Life.* University of Chicago Press, Chicago, Ill. pp. 60—83.

Wittfogel, Karl A. 1957. *Oriental Despotism: A Comparative Study of Total Power.* Yale University Press, New Haven, Conn.

Wolff, Kurt H. (Ed.) 1964. *The Sociology of Georg Simmel.* Collier-Macmillan, London.

Overpopulated America

Commentary

Mass production is the key to a successful poultry industry. Several thousand laying hens are housed in large, usually windowless laying houses, in which the temperature, humidity, and light are all carefully controlled. The hens are housed, three to a cage, carefully lined up in rows. Water is constantly available; feed, balanced to meet all dietary needs, is delivered to them on endless belts, and droppings are carried away in a similar manner. Denied a nest the birds lay eggs on the sloping floor of the cages. The eggs roll out onto another moving belt that carries them to the egg storage and packaging room. The chickens lack for nothing except space and freedom. They are protected against disease, enemies, heat, and cold.

I will be anthropomorphic enough to believe that even for a chicken there is a certain quality to life. Being penned up in an egg factory, no matter how amenable the climate, how dietarily correct the food, is not quality living for a chicken. I should imagine that a laying hen, housed in an old-fashioned chicken coop, fed a variety of food from mash to corn, with considerable room, and freedom of movement and access to the wide outdoors even though there were dangers of an occasional hawk, weasel, or dog, would enjoy quality living.

The world population is approaching the same situation. While I have no doubt that for a while at least, given a good food distribution system to reach all the world inhabitants, and dependent solely on plants as the source of food (which the factory chicken, by the way, is not), the world could be adequately fed but not at United States' standard. We can live at a high density packed into storied buildings with a highly artificial environment like the modern laying hen in a chicken farm.

When is the world overpopulated? When it lives at the subsistence density? at the tolerance density? or what? It all depends on what one is willing to accept as his norm. For many of us the world is already over-populated. When you have to fight your way bumper to bumper down a highway, force your way through a crowded street, move into a campground by 7 A.M. to get a tent site, or stumble over bodies and beach blankets to reach the water, then the world is overcrowded.

But all this has nothing to do with the density the world is able to feed, the subsistence density. Optimum density relates to quality of living. It relates to the impact that the population has on the environment. As Wayne Davis points out in the following selection, overpopulation does not relate to the number of people per se but to the demands they make on the environment. The crowded peoples of India, for example, are much less destructive to the land than we in the United States are with a much lower population.

So the optimum population is going to relate to the style of living (see Selection 17). The optimum population of an affluent industrialized country is considerably lower than that of a nonindustrialized nation whose population exists at the subsistence level. Quality living in an affluent country requires considerably more resources. The whole world population cannot live at the same level as the average citizen of the United States. The world for that style of living is already overpopulated. The difference is contrasted by some figures worked out by H. D. Hulett.[1] The average American consumes 3200 calories a day. Of this, one-third consists of meat, milk, eggs, and other animal products; two-thirds are plant products. If one also includes the amount of food grains fed to animals to produce the meat portion of the diet, daily requirements increase to about 11,000 calories.

But there is more to quality living than food. There is need for materials, such as wood and paper. If the world used wood products at the same annual rate as the United States, we could support only 1 billion people. The world could support only 600 million people if everyone used the same amount of energy, 700 million if all had the same steel requirements, 900 million with the same fertilizer requirements, 500 million with the same aluminum needs. To maintain our standard of living we act as parasites on the rest of the world.

In an original approach to optimum population, Dr. Eugene Odum[2] and his students worked out an optimum

---

[1] H. R. Hulett, "Optimum World Population," *BioScience* **20**(3), 1970, pp. 160–161.
[2] E. P. Odum, "Optimum Population and Environment: A Georgian Microcosm," *Current History* **58**, 1970, pp. 355–359, 365–366.

population for Georgia, a state that is close to the national mean in population density, growth rate, and distribution of human and animal population. They based their calculations on two principles: that the optimum is less than maximum and that affluence reduces the number of people that can be supported by a given resource base. Using for a norm of food requirements the diet recommended by the President's Council on Physical Fitness, they determined that 1.5 acres per person are required to produce that food, ten times that needed by an Asian on a rice diet. This emphasizes how much lower population density must be if the people want to enjoy bacon, eggs, and milk for breakfast and roasts for dinner. For present rate of use of fiber add another acre. Two acres are needed for greenways, recreation, watershed needs, and so on. For highways, airports, and waste treatment plants add another 0.5 acre. This comes to five acres per person. This amount of land applied only to those living in the temperate East. Considerably more land is required in sparse environments, such as the desert and the Arctic. Odum points out that Georgia would produce enough foodstuffs to feed 12 million people if the people were content to give up bacon and eggs and roast beef and live on a vegetable diet. If the affluent parts of the world were content to share their portion of the resource equally with the rest of the world, then the Western world's standard of living and especially that of the United States would have to drop drastically. As the density of our own country increases, we will place even greater demands on world resources. To maintain the same standard of living we either have to extract a greater portion of the world resources at the expense of underdeveloped nations or else reduce our own share of it. Since underdeveloped countries are slowly awakening to this proportionate sharing of resources the former cannot be continued indefinitely; the latter will probably come about. Which brings us to what Davis calls "Indian equivalents."

Selection 18

Overpopulated America

by Wayne H. Davis

I define as most seriously overpopulated that nation whose people by virtue of their numbers and activities are most rapidly decreasing the ability of the land to support human life. With our large population, our affluence and our technological monstrosities the United States wins first place by a substantial margin.

Let's compare the US to India, for example. We have 203 million people, whereas she has 540 million on much less land. But look at the impact of people on the land.

The average Indian eats his daily few cups of rice (or perhaps wheat, whose production on American farms contributed to our one percent per year drain in quality of our active farmland), draws his bucket of water from the communal well and sleeps in a mud hut. In his daily rounds to gather cow dung to burn to cook his rice and warm his feet, his footsteps, along with those of millions of his countrymen, help bring about a slow deterioration of the ability of the land to support people. His contribution to the destruction of the land is minimal.

An American, on the other hand, can be expected to destroy a piece of land on which he builds a home, garage and driveway. He will contribute his share to the 142 million tons of smoke and fumes, seven million junked cars, 20 million tons of paper, 48 billion cans, and 26 billion bottles the overburdened environment must absorb each year. To run his air conditioner we will strip-mine a Kentucky hillside, push the dirt and slate down into the stream, and burn coal in a power generator, whose smokestack contributes to a plume of smoke massive enough to cause cloud seeding and premature precipitation from Gulf winds which should be irrigating the wheat farms of Minnesota.

In his lifetime he will personally pollute three million gallons of water, and industry and agriculture will use ten times this much

---

THIS SELECTION is reprinted from *New Republic*, January 10, 1970, by permission of *The New Republic*, © 1970, Harrison-Blaine of New Jersey, Inc.

water in his behalf. To provide these needs the US Army Corps of Engineers will build dams and flood farmland. He will also use 21,000 gallons of leaded gasoline containing boron, drink 28,000 pounds of milk and eat 10,000 pounds of meat. The latter is produced and squandered in a life pattern unknown to Asians. A steer on a Western range eats plants containing minerals necessary for plant life. Some of these are incorporated into the body of the steer which is later shipped for slaughter. After being eaten by man these nutrients are flushed down the toilet into the ocean or buried in the cemetery, the surface of which is cluttered with boulders called tombstones and has been removed from productivity. The result is a continual drain on the productivity of range land. Add to this the erosion of overgrazed lands, and the effects of the falling water table as we mine Pleistocene deposits of groundwater to irrigate to produce food for more people, and we can see why our land is dying far more rapidly than did the great civilizations of the Middle East, which experienced the same cycle. The average Indian citizen, whose fecal material goes back to the land, has but a minute fraction of the destructive effect on the land that the affluent American does.

Thus I want to introduce a new term, which I suggest be used in future discussions of human population and ecology. We should speak of our numbers in "Indian equivalents". An Indian equivalent I define as the average number of Indian citizens required to have the same detrimental effect on the land's ability to support human life as would the average American. This value is difficult to determine, but let's take an extremely conservative working figure of 25. To see how conservative this is, imagine the addition of 1000 citizens to your town and 25,000 to an Indian village. Not only would the Americans destroy much more land for homes, highways and a shopping center, but they would contribute far more to environmental deterioration in hundreds of other ways as well. For example, their demand for steel for new autos might increase the daily pollution equivalent of 130,000 junk autos which *Life* tells us that US Steel Corp. dumps into Lake Michigan. Their demand for textiles would help the cotton industry destroy the life in the Black Warrior River in Alabama with endrin. And they would contribute to the massive industrial pollution of our oceans (we provide one third

to one half the world's share) which has caused the precipitous downward trend in our commercial fisheries landings during the past seven years.

The per capita gross national product of the United States is 38 times that of India. Most of our goods and services contribute to the decline in the ability of the environment to support life. Thus it is clear that a figure of 25 for an Indian equivalent is conservative. It has been suggested to me that a more realistic figure would be 500.

In Indian equivalents, therefore, the population of the United States is at least four billion. And the rate of growth is even more alarming. We are growing at one percent per year, a rate which would double our numbers in 70 years. India is growing at 2.5 percent. Using the Indian equivalent of 25, our population growth becomes 10 times as serious as that of India. According to the Reinows in their recent book *Moment in the Sun*, just one year's crop of American babies can be expected to use up 25 billion pounds of beef, 200 million pounds of steel and 9.1 billion gallons of gasoline during their collective lifetime. And the demands on water and land for our growing population are expected to be far greater than the supply available in the year 2000. We are destroying our land at a rate of over a million acres a year. We now have only 2.6 agricultural acres per person. By 1975 this will be cut to 2.2, the critical point for the maintenance of what we consider a decent diet, and by the year 2000 we might expect to have 1.2.

You might object that I am playing with statistics in using the Indian equivalent on the rate of growth. I am making the assumption that today's Indian child will live 35 years (the average Indian life span) at today's level of affluence. If he lives an American 70 years, our rate of population growth would be 20 times as serious as India's.

But the assumption of continued affluence at today's level is unfounded. If our numbers continue to rise, our standard of living will fall so sharply that by the year 2000 any surviving Americans might consider today's average Asian to be well off. Our children's destructive effects on their environment will decline as they sink ever lower into poverty.

The United States is in serious economic trouble now. Nothing could be more misleading than today's affluence, which rests precariously on a crumbling foundation. Our productivity, which had been increasing steadily at about 3.2 percent a year since World War II, has been falling during 1969. Our export over import balance has been shrinking steadily from $7.1 billion in 1964 to $0.15 billion in the first half of 1969. Our balance of payments deficit for the second quarter was $3.7 billion, the largest in history. We are now importing iron ore, steel, oil, beef, textiles, cameras, radios and hundreds of other things.

Our economy is based upon the Keynesian concept of a continued growth in population and productivity. It worked in an underpopulated nation with excess resources. It would continue to work only if the earth and its resources were expanding at an annual rate of 4 to 5 percent. Yet neither the number of cars, the economy, the human population, nor anything else can expand indefinitely at an exponential rate in a finite world. We must face this fact *now*. The crisis is here. When Walter Heller says that our economy will expand by 4 percent annually through the latter 1970s he is dreaming. He is in a theoretical world totally unaware of the realities of human ecology. If the economists do not wake up and devise a new system for us now somebody else will have to do it for them.

A civilization is comparable to a living organism. Its longevity is a function of its metabolism. The higher the metabolism (affluence), the shorter the life. Keynesian economics has allowed us an affluent but shortened life span. We have now run our course.

The tragedy facing the United States is even greater and more imminent than that descending upon the hungry nations. The Paddock brothers in their book, *Famine 1975!*, say that India "cannot be saved" no matter how much food we ship her. But India will be here after the United States is gone. Many millions will die in the most colossal famines India has ever known, but the land will survive and she will come back as she always has before. The United States, on the other hand, will be a desolate tangle of concrete and ticky-tacky, of strip-mined moonscape and silt-choked reservoirs. The land and water will be so contaminated with pesticides, herbicides, mercury fungicides, lead, boron, nickel, arsenic and hundreds of other toxic substances, which have been ap-

proaching critical levels of concentration in our environment as a result of our numbers and affluence, that it may be unable to sustain human life.

Thus as the curtain gets ready to fall on man's civilization let it come as no surprise that it shall first fall on the United States. And let no one make the mistake of thinking we can save ourselves by "cleaning up the environment." Banning DDT is the equivalent of the physician's treating syphilis by putting a bandaid over the first chancre to appear. In either case you can be sure that more serious and widespread trouble will soon appear unless the disease itself is treated. We cannot survive by planning to treat symptoms such as air pollution, water pollution, soil erosion, etc.

What can we do to slow the rate of destruction of the United States as a land capable of supporting human life? There are two approaches. First, we must reverse the population growth. We have far more people now than we can continue to support at anything near today's level of affluence. American women average slightly over three children each. According to the *Population Bulletin* if we reduced this number to 2.5 there would still be 330 million people in the nation at the end of the century. And even if we reduced this to 1.5 we would have 57 million more people in the year 2000 than we have now. With our present longevity patterns it would take more than 30 years for the population to peak even when reproducing at this rate, which would eventually give us a net decrease in numbers.

Do not make the mistake of thinking that technology will solve our population problem by producing a better contraceptive. Our problem now is that people want too many children. Surveys show the average number of children wanted by the American family is 3.3. There is little difference between the poor and the wealthy, black and white, Catholic and Protestant. Production of children at this rate during the next 30 years would be so catastrophic in effect on our resources and the viability of the nation as to be beyond my ability to contemplate. To prevent this trend we must not only make contraceptives and abortion readily available to everyone, but we must establish a system to put severe economic pressure on those who produce children and reward those who do not. This can be done within our system of taxes and welfare.

The other thing we must do is to pare down our Indian equivalents. Individuals in American society vary tremendously in Indian equivalents. If we plot Indian equivalents versus their reciprocal, the percentage of land surviving a generation, we obtain a linear regression. We can then place individuals and occupation types on this graph. At one end would be the starving blacks of Mississippi; they would approach unity in Indian equivalents, and would have the least destructive effect on the land. At the other end of the graph would be the politicians slicing pork for the barrel, the highway contractors, strip-mine operators, real estate developers, and public enemy number one—the US Army Corps of Engineers.

We must halt land destruction. We must abandon the view of land and minerals as private property to be exploited in any way economically feasible for private financial gain.

Land and minerals are resources upon which the very survival of the nation depends, and their use must be planned in the best interests of the people.

Rising expectations for the poor are a cruel joke foisted upon them by the Establishment. As our new economy of use-it-once-and-throw-it-away produces more and more products for the affluent, the share of our resources available for the poor declines. Blessed be the starving blacks of Mississippi with their outdoor privies, for they are ecologically sound, and they shall inherit a nation. Although I hope that we will help these unfortunate people attain a decent standard of living by diverting war efforts to fertility control and job training, our most urgent task to assure this nation's survival during the next decade is to stop the affluent destroyers.

Selection 19

Checks on Population Growth

Commentary

Considering the fact that natural populations of animals rarely seem to overpopulate their environment before some regulatory process steps in to reduce the population, one naturally asks the question, Is the population of man subject to similar regulatory mechanisms? Man the hunter probably was, but the agricultural revolution, the development of a complex culture, and the medical revolution eliminated many of the natural checks on population increase. A natural population receives, as it were, some signal from the environment that its population is reaching its environmental limits. Human populations seemingly receive no signal that populations are too dense. When population densities appeared to be reaching an upper limit of the environment, man by some fortuitous circumstance expanded his habitat by discovering and settling new land or increased the carrying capacity by improving agriculture or tapping some new resource. Today human population growth is unusual. It isn't exponential; it is as C. S. Holling[1] says, "superexponential," having all the attributes of a bacterial colony in the first stages of growth, at a time when density of the population is already very high. But we do seem to be reaching another limit of density. Although we proceed as if there were no signal of impending overpopulation, the signals are in the ghettos, in the poor, in the welfare rolls, in the drug addicts, and in numerous international crises.

D. H. Stott examines the role of cultural and natural checks on the growth of human population. In the first part he looks at some of the mechanisms that regulate the growth of animals populations; in the second part he discusses some of the same mechanisms that might be working in human populations (with little success). The first part needs some elaboration.

Stott early in the paper examines the role of predation as a regulatory mechanism and largely concurs with the theory of compensatory predation advanced by the late Paul Errington.[2] Briefly the theory goes like this. The maximum number of animals that can be carried through the most rigorous period of the year, usually the winter, depends upon the carrying capacity of the habitat. Any reproductive addition to the population in excess of this will be eliminated from the area in some manner. Many of these excess animals are easy victims of predators. If predators do not take them, then disease, starvation, or some other form of mortality will. If predation or other losses are exceptionally heavy and reduce the population far below the carrying capacity of the habitat, then the population responds with a heavier production of young. Predation, then, can be regarded as a function of density; it eliminates the subordinates, the weak, the young, and the infirm. Predation acts to eliminate the unfit.

Among some vertebrates this is true. Predators of ungulates succeed in taking largely the young and the old. Observations on hunting of moose by wolves[3] and of elk by mountain lions[4] tend to support this. Predatory pressures on an ungulate population can be great enough to reduce the population to a point at which it does not overgraze or overbrowse the range in stable environments. There is also some evidence that predation can hold local populations of a prey species down to a very low level.[5] But the exact role predation plays in the regulation of populations, if any, is still largely unknown.

Like so many other aspects of ecosystem functioning, predation is not subject to easy generalizations. What is the prey species—vertebrate or invertebrate? Who is the predator—bird, mammal, invertebrate? The life history, habits, habitat, population level, and movements of both predator and prey are important parameters in predation.

[1]C. S. Holling, "Stability in Ecological and Social Systems," in *Diversity and Stability in Ecological Systems*, Brookhaven Symposia in Biology, No. 22, 1969, pp. 128–141.
[2]P. L. Errington, *Muskrat Populations*, Ames, Iowa, Iowa State University Press, 1963.
[3]D. H. Pimlott, "Wolf Predation and Ungulate Populations," *Am. Zoologist* 7, 1967, pp. 267–278.
[4]M. G. Hornocker, "An Analysis of Mountain Lion Predation upon Mule Deer and Elk in the Idaho Primitive Area," Wildlife Monograph No. 21, Washington, D.C., The Wildlife Society, 1970.
[5]O. P. Pearson, "Carnivore—Mouse Predation: An Example of Its Intensity and Bioenergetics," *J. of Mammalogy* 45, 1964, pp. 177–188.

Among vertebrates the interaction between predator and prey can be a complicated one. The response of predator to the prey may be a functional one that relates to the reaction of the predator to density of a particular prey species.[6,7] Small mammalian and avian predators prey sparingly on a particular prey species if the density of that prey is low. If the density of a particular prey is moderate, there is a sharp rise in the intensity of predation. When the population of the prey species is high, the intensity of predation levels off, for if the prey species is increasing and the number of predators changes little, the predators can take only so many prey. The functional response of the predators depends upon food preferences, feeding behavior, hunting, and learning ability.

Predators can also respond to prey abundance numerically. One way is through breeding. The increased food supply may expand the energy base. Increased production and survival of young increase the population, although the upper limit to this increase will be limited by some other regulatory mechanism. Another type of numerical response would involve the movements of predators to areas of food abundance.

Stott also introduced the idea of cycles, and cites the work of Green and Evans[8] on the snowshoe hare. These two biologists studied the cyclic ups and downs of the snowshoe hare and concluded that the decline was caused in part by shock disease, a response to stress and high density. Since then there have been additional studies which relate the decline to reproductive failures and poor survival of adults and young without expressing any cause (see Selection 1).

Several theories not discussed by Stott have been advanced to explain the peaks and lows in the populations of both cyclic and irruptive species. Christian and Davis[9] suggest that a population decline can be associated with stress and changes in the adrenal-pituitary function. Physiological stress accompanying high densities is brought about by increased and exaggerated social intolerance and aggressiveness. Stress can progressively reduce reproduction or completely inhibit it at high densities. Stott suggests this for humans, also. In addition, stress leads to psychological disarrangement of adults, aberrent maternal behavior, and abnormal young. There is evidence that die-offs from overpopulation are not caused by disease or malnutrition but by adrenocorticular and other metabolic responses known to occur during increased density and social strife.[10]

The snowshoe hare, so named for its large, heavily furred hind feet which enable it to run easily across deep snow, is noted for its cyclic populations. (Photo courtesy of Pennsylvania Game Commission.)

---

[6]C. S. Holling, "The Components of Predation as Revealed by a Study of Small Mammal Predation of the European Pine Sawfly," *Canadian Entomologist* **91**(5), 1959, pp. 293–320.

[7]C. H. Buckner, "Avian and Mammalian Predators of Forest Insects," *Entomophaga* **12**, 1967, pp. 491–501.

[8]R. G. Green and C. A. Evans, "Studies on a Population Cycle of Snowshoe Hares on the Lake Alexander Area," *J. of Wildlife Management* **4**, 1940, pp. 220–238, 267–278, 347–358.

[9]J. J. Christian and D. E. Davis, "Endocrines, Behavior and Population," *Science* **146**, 1964, pp. 1550–1560.

[10]J. J. Christian, "Endocrine Adaptative Mechanisms and the Physiologic Regulation of Population Growth," in W. V. Mayer and R. G. van Gelder (eds.), *Physiological Mammology*, Vol. 1: *Mammalian Populations*, New York, Academic, 1963, pp. 189–353.

Another theory advanced by Chitty[11] and W. G. Wellington[12] involves genetic behavior. According to this theory, when animal populations increase in density, the quality of the population changes. During low and moderate population levels and during periods of environmental stability there is a high survival of individuals with variations in behavior, genetic constitution, physiological conditions, and the like. Large increases in population increase variability in the population, involving many inferior genotypes. As density becomes higher and as stress increases, brought about by climatic, food, behavioral, or other conditions, the inferior genotypes are eliminated and the population is reduced, often quite abruptly. Such reactions undoubtedly occurred in early human population, as both Stott and George Armelagos and John Dewey in Selection 20 suggest. But with the advent of the science of medicine, many physically inferior genotypes that might otherwise have been eliminated by natural selection have been retained in the population.

Recently a vegetation-herbivore-predator food cycle originally suggested by David Lack[13] and discussed by Stott has been revived in a different form by Arnold M. Schultz.[14] He relates the four-year cycle of the Arctic lemming to ecosystem function. According to the hypothesis the forage of the lemming is rich in calcium and phosphorus, but because of high production of forage much of these and other mineral elements are tied up in organic matter. Grazing by lemmings and their burrowing and tunneling reduce the organic insulation of the soil, and the soil thaws deeper. The next year the production of forage is low, there is poor cycling of nutrients, and the lemming population is now under stress from a low and nutrient-poor food supply. Nutrient depletion affects reproduction and lactation, and the lack of adequate protective cover exposes the population to excessive predation. A combination of the two factors causes a rapid decline of the population. The lower population permits the vegetation to recover and organic matter to accumulate, but the forage quality is still low. By the fourth year the plants have fully recovered, protective cover has returned, nutrient cycling is speeded up, and nutrients accumulate in the plants. The nutrient content of the forage is high enough to stimulate reproduction and support a large population again.

Another response of populations to high density is emigration. Most vertebrate populations and a number of invertebrate populations are characterized by a behavior and organization involving social hierarchy and territoriality or a combination of both. Evolutionarily, this is important because social competition eliminates the direct competition for environmental needs and subsequent food depletion. Among mammals and many birds, social behavior involves a series of dominance-subordination relationships between individuals within a given population. When stresses within a local population build up, low ranking individuals, usually the young, are forced out of optimum habitat by dominant individuals. These subordinate individuals carry with them a great deal of genetic variation, and out of the great number that leave, a few will establish themselves in marginal or alien habitats. It is not inconceivable that such immigration forced by the pressures of high density played a role in the early dispersal of man into suboptimal habitats, such as the desert and the Arctic, and in the development of the several races of man. Even in historical time immigrations were the result of social pressure, and the immigrants for the most part were subordinate individuals, the oppressed, the poor, the disadvantaged.

Dominance-subordination in the social hierarchy among some animals acts to limit the birth rate. An outstanding example is the social behavior of the wolf. Wolves live in small cooperative hunting groups or packs. The pack consists of a dominant male, a dominant female, subordinate males and females, peripheral males and females, and juveniles.[15] The alpha, or dominant, male is deferred to by all members of the pack; he is the focal point of solicitation and principal guard of the territory. The alpha female is dominant over all females and most of the males and controls the relationship of the rest of the females to the pack. The alpha male and female, and the subordinate males and females, form the nucleus of the pack; the peripheral males and females are kept out of it. Social relationships highly restrict fertile mating. The dominant female rather successfully prevents subordinate females from mating with other males. In addition, males exhibit preference for certain females. The dominant male, preferred by all the females, may himself actually prefer a peripheral female which the dominant female prevents from mating. Fertile mating usually occurs between the alpha male and the alpha female. This behavior places a severe restriction on mating habits and effectively

[11]Dennis Chitty, "Population Processes in the Vole and Their Relevance to General Theory," *Canadian J. of Zoology* **38**, 1960, pp. 99—113.

[12]W. G. Wellington, "Qualitative Changes in Populations in Unstable Environments," *Canadian Entomologist* **96**, 1964, pp. 436—451.

[13]David Lack, *The National Regulation of Animal Numbers*, Oxford, Clarendon Press, 1954.

[14]A. M. Schultz, "The Nutrient-Recovery Hypothesis for Arctic Microtine Cycles, II: Ecosystem Variables in Relation to Arctic Microtine Cycles," in D. J. Crisp (ed.), *Grazing in Terrestrial and Marine Ecosystems*, Oxford, Blackwell, 1964, pp. 57—68.

[15]J. H. Woolpy, "The Social Organization of Wolves," *Natural History* **77**(5), 1968, pp. 46—55.

limits the number of young. Perhaps there will be only one litter to a pack, the young being cooperatively raised by a number of the adults. Since optimum density of wolves in relation to an adequate supply of prey is about one wolf to ten square miles, the restrictive breeding limits population size. In areas where the wolf is heavily persecuted, however, the social restrictions break down. The birth rate is high, with nearly all mature females producing a litter each season.[16]

Social dominance can also be expressed as territoriality, a topic discussed in more detail in Selection 21. Territory implies defense of an area, usually by an individual against another of the same species and sex. In spite of some statements in popular writings and in some scientific writings (including this selection), territoriality is not found in all animals. Social behavior among animals ranges from simple hierarchy to strong expression of territoriality; and territorial animals themselves exhibit a wide expression of territoriality. Territoriality may even involve defense against members of other species, and it may serve a variety of functions, from providing an exclusive supply of food to a place to mate to an area in which to nest. Its function may differ considerably from species to species. However, territoriality does tend to distribute populations rather uniformly throughout the habitat. Each pair or group occupies a variable area of space which it tends to expand when population density is low and which each compresses when population density is high; but there is a limit to the compressibility of space. Territory then restricts the size of a population that can occupy a given area. The surplus represents unmated floating reserves, a reservoir for the replacement of losses within the territorial population.[17] Because of the great variability in the expression and functions of territory in animals, it is difficult and even dangerous to extrapolate the concept to man without considerable modification.

As Stott points out, stress and cultural attitudes affect human population more than any other mechanism, especially cultural. Man biologically is a mammal, but he has a nature different from the nonhuman species, no matter how valiantly some writers may try to prove otherwise. Animal populations are characterized by seasonal breeding, biologically controlled litter or brood sizes, and a wide variety of regulatory mechanisms. Man has lessened the biological aspects of reproduction and has imposed upon it cultural and social norms, taboos, myths, religious attitudes. The regulation of human densities is not through some natural regulatory mechanism but through cultural processes instead. That is considerably more difficult to achieve than possibly even population experts realize or are willing to admit, for it involves manipulation and painful restructuring of our social systems.

---

[16] R. A. Rausch, "Some Aspects of the Population Ecology of Wolves," *Am. Zoologist* **7**, 1967, pp. 253—265.
[17] Adam Watson and D. Jenkins, "Experiments on Population Control by Territorial Behavior in Red Grouse," *J. Animal Ecology* **37**, 1968, pp. 595—614.

Selection 19

Cultural and Natural Checks on Population Growth

by D. H. Stott

The study of the ways in which animal populations limit themselves to their means of subsistence has yielded many surprises, and explained many hitherto anomalous features of physical growth and behavior. The theme of the present contribution is to examine some of this work, and to ask whether certain unexplained, or poorly explained, features of human development and behaviour may be similarly understood. The writer has in mind in particular the regular appearance of reproductive casualties—infertility, stillbirth, infant death, malformation, mental deficiency, constitutional ill-health—which are commonly regarded as biological accidents or genetical vestiges of no value to the species. To these

---

THIS SELECTION has been condensed slightly and is reprinted by permission from Ashley Montagu (ed.), *Culture and the Evolution of Man*, New York, Oxford University Press, 1962, pp. 355—376.

must be added the behavioural maladjustments which, as the term implies, are viewed as failures to adapt to not very uncommon situations. Behavioural breakdown would have been many times more disastrous under primitive conditions; the capacity for maladjustment cannot thus be regarded even as a genetic survival. We must ask why, with the minutely fine instinctual equipment which regulates animal behaviour, human beings never evolved breakdown-immune patterns of conduct. The application of the criterion of survival-value to these human phenomena consequently leaves many facts unexplained.

For the individual, perinatal death, infertility, malformation, behaviour-disturbance, could obviously have no survival-value. But, as Simpson[1] points out, "selection favours successful reproduction of the population and not necessarily of any or of all particular individuals within it." It may seem implausible to suggest that the appearance of lethal disabilities could have survival-value even for the population as a whole, but if the limitation of fertility can be of advantage this might be the case. Similarly an increase in efficiency by natural selection may endanger the whole population if it reaches the point where the source of food is wiped out. A curb upon the presumed evolutionary trend towards greater hunting skill would therefore be of advantage. For human beings we thus reach the paradoxical conclusion that in times of the pressure of population on food resources any process which tended to *lower* the mental capacity, physical dexterity or perceptual acuity of a certain number of individuals might mean the saving of the race.

That the amount of food available sets the ultimate limit to the growth of all animal and human populations cannot be disputed. But this apparently self-evident proposition only holds good in a very rough way over a long period. The popular Malthusian notion that the number surviving from year to year is determined by the current supply of food, with the excess dying from starvation, is no longer supported by any student of natural populations. Even David Lack,[2] who among the authorities in this field lays the greatest emphasis upon food supply as the limiting factor, recognizes that the relationship is a complicated one. Food shortage severe enough to impair functional efficiency is critical, not because

more members of the species may die than need do in order to restore the ecological balance— a state of affairs that can and often is quickly made good by the excess reproductive capacity possessed by all species—but a general weakening threatens total annihilation from predators. Thus Chitty,[3] one of the best known students of animal populations, argued that "a species which frequently exhausted its food supply might be supplanted by one whose population densities were controlled at a safer level." This caused him to look for the alternatives to starvation as the regulating factors.

All the animal populations which have been the subject of observation have been found to suffer periodic declines in numbers which are not generally the result of starvation. These declines often continue in successive generations under conditions in which there could be no question of a shortage of food, and yet may result in the near-annihilation of a local population. The possibility that they may be due to epidemic diseases has been closely examined, but no greater incidence of such has been found in "dying" populations; and the pattern of the decline and recovery does not correspond to the progress and recession of an epidemic.

Lack[4] suggests that the fluctuations may reflect predator-prey cycles: overpopulation of the "consumers" reduces their food supply, whether it be animal or vegetable, to the point where recovery is slow. Consequently there is widespread starvation among them, until their numbers are so small that their source of food can recover. As will be noted in the discussion of the field-studies, this explanation does not fit the facts, since the "crashes" often occur when food is abundant, and the mass emigrations which sometimes mark their beginning almost invariably take place in the late summer and autumn, when food is plentiful, rather than in winter. There is in addition a theoretical reason why predator-prey cycles could not be the rule. Any major advantage gained by the "consumer" species over its prey implies that it has been able to make significant inroads into the numbers of healthy adults. If though only a more efficient minority of the predator-species are able to do this, their increased hunting capacity would spread by natural selection, and still further inroads, without limit, would be made into the

207

numbers of the prey, until they, and the predators themselves, were exterminated. It seems that predators only take a marginal toll in the form of the weakly and young animals (and the latter are naturally only at risk for a critical few weeks of their life). In his comprehensive collation of the evidence on predation Errington[5] quotes authorities on many wild animals to the effect that, on the whole, healthy adult populations suffer little from predators. In their home ranges at normal densities he observed that adult muskrats lived in noticeable security. The larger ungulates "suffer from subhuman predation chiefly when immature, aged, crippled, starved, sick, or isolated from their fellows." He advanced the theory of the *intercompensation* of factors limiting population: if predators and disease took little toll, self-limiting mechanisms came into operation to check the growth of numbers; if losses were great from external causes these mechanisms did not come into play. He concluded that "regardless of the countless individuals or the large percentages of populations who may annually be killed by predators, predation looks ineffective as a limiting factor to the extent that intraspecific self-limiting mechanisms basically determine the population-levels maintained by the prey." One might add that if predators only succeed in catching the vulnerable minority the balance would be smoothly maintained rather than cyclic, for a fairly constant proportion of the prey, other things being equal, would be eaten each year. (This argument does not hold in the case of a newly introduced predator, since time would be needed for a balance to occur by natural selection. There is also some anecdotal evidence that some ungulates, who rely for protection upon herding and flight, have at times been known in the absence of predators to eat up herbage to the point of starvation. In their case predators may be able to catch healthy adults, but since only one in a herd can be taken at a time, and the predators would be thinly spaced by territory, the toll might never exceed the replacement rate under normal conditions of abundance, and yet suffice to render other means of limiting numbers unnecessary.)

A record of typical population-cycle, that of the snowshoe hare, made by Green and Evans[6] is given in Table I. It is seen that the decline extended over five years, and then in 1938, when extinction seemed near, the trend was reversed. In their review of possible causes the

Table I

	EARLY SPRING POPULATION	YOUNG BORN DURING SUMMER	PERCENT OF YEARLINGS SURVIVING
1932		600	
1933	478 (peak)	1049	23
1934	374	818	29
1935	356	779	18
1936	246	541	12
1937	151	330	8
1938	32	66	91
1939	73	158	

authors of this, as of similar studies, discount the likelihood of an epidemic because the mortality did not abate after a first rapid spread. Nor could the losses have been due to emigration or an encroachment into adjoining regions: the snowshoe hares were seldom found more than one-eighth of a mile from the point where they were first trapped, even after a year or more.

The decline was chiefly a matter of the poor survival of the immature hares, as shown strikingly in the last column of the table.

It is indeed remarkable that the mortality among the yearlings should be so catastrophic in 1937, four years after the presumed overpopulation, and that this should occur during the summer months, whereas the greatest mortality of adult hares was, as would be expected, during the winter. Food shortage would thus seem to be ruled out as the immediate cause of this youthful mortality. That the young born during the summer of 1937 were still severely affected despite the fact that the parental population was little over half the peak density suggests that the noxious factors persisted through four generations.

During the peak, before the decline became general, occasional hares were found dead in the traps, the cause of which Green and Larson[7] diagnosed as "shock disease." As the decline became widespread during 1935 and 1936 this condition was observed over the entire area. The wider significance of this finding will be discussed later, but it may be noted at this stage that the parent-hares were found to be in a poor condition during the breeding season in which the generation of poor viability were produced.

In his study of a population cycle of ruffed

grouse in Ontario, Clarke[8] was similarly struck by the poor viability of the young, and by the fact that "even though the first year of dying off in an area has reduced numbers to a point where the birds may be regarded as scarce, the succeeding year may show a similar reduction of summer flocks."

From the study of a number of widely dissimilar species of animal one conclusion emerges with tolerable certainty: when population density reaches a certain point, even without actual shortage of food, changes take place which have the effect of reducing the population. These changes may even be in bodily form. Wilson[9] observed that when aphides become crowded on a plant the next generation grow wings to allow emigration. Uvarov[10] reported analogous physical changes in the locust. Preparatory to swarming and emigration locusts "moult" and change their exteriors from predominantly green to a brownish color, the two forms being originally thought to be different species. When studied in the laboratory this change was found to depend only on the density of population in a cage, and was notably independent of temperature, light or other obvious factors. The swarming is in no sense a migration, since it occurs irregularly in cycles of years. Nor, Uvarov points out, can they be driven by hunger, since they leave rich vegetation to enter the desert.

Among mammals the well known "suicidal" mass wanderings of the lemming offer a close parallel. Once again, as Elton[11] and others have shown, they occur in three to four year cycles, in periods of apparent high population in the home locality. Their emigration might be described as a behavioural aberration taking the form of always wandering downhill, which brings them to the sea, into which they then plunge, so that they are mostly drowned. The result is a periodic drastic thinning of the resident population, since none of the emigrants find their way back.

Lack draws attention to the genetic problem which these "suicidal" emigrations raise: if those who respond to this urge are eliminated while those in whom it is absent survive, why is it not rapidly eliminated by natural selection? If, however, the sacrificed individuals are the yearlings, their parents, who would as a whole be of the same genetic constitution, would have a certain advantage over other parent animals whose young caused dangerous overcrowding. In this way an inherited tendency to self-elimination, confined to the young, would be perpetuated by natural selection.

.   .   .

Errington's study[12] of . . . fluctuations in muskrat populations enables us to see, for this mammal at least, something of the detail of the interaction between crowding and the regulatory mechanisms. It would appear that at a certain degree of density the muskrats become intolerant of each other, as shown in greater dispersal, savage fighting among adults and attacks upon helpless young. . . . During the . . . upgrade, the muskrat population congregated within the choicer feeding grounds, at a density of about ten breeding pairs per acre, while leaving the unattractive areas uninhabited. But during the peak and decline the strife was so great that they distributed themselves at densities about one pair per acre through good and bad habitat alike.

The last of the field-studies to be considered, that of Chitty[13] in respect of voles upon a plantation in Montgomeryshire, contains an important suggestion as to the nature of the regulatory mechanism involved. He found that the offspring of the peak-generation either died prematurely or were infertile, as also was the case during the cyclic decline of the snowshoe hare. He concluded that, "in order to account for this decrease in viability and reproductive performance it is necessary to postulate a delayed effect of some previous condition. . . . We cannot at present be more precise about this supposed condition than to imagine some disturbance of the hormonal balance of the mother which in some way affected the foetus." He drew attention to the strife among the adults during the early part of the season in which the affected generation was born. That this caused congenital damage may be considered a bold hypothesis, but evidence is quoted below that the harassment and strife attendant upon overcrowding may produce psychosomatic illness in animals. Chitty arrived at his theory of prenatal damage only after reviewing and dismissing all other feasible causes, such as disease, food shortage, predation and migration.

In an experiment with wild rats Calhoun[14] showed that the regulatory mechanism consisted mainly of changes in social behavior. He bred a colony from a few individuals in a pen of 10,000 square feet, allowing them an abundance of food at all times. If over the 28 months of the experiment they had realized their breeding potential they would have numbered 50,000. If they had been content with the two square feet per rat allowed for caged rats in laboratories there could have been 5,000. In fact the population stabilized itself at less than 200. The social behaviour of the colony limited population growth in three ways. First, the rats split themselves up into local sub-colonies, between which were maintained buffer zones without burrows. Second, with crowding the normal dominance hierarchy broke down, leading to unstable groups. The effect of this was reduced frequency of conception and poor viability of the suckling young. Of the few which survived beyond weaning very few in turn had progeny of their own. Third, crowding caused increased attack upon the young, and those who received severe punishment were likely to succumb.

The behavioural breakdown of the rats living under conditions of social stress seems to have been manysided. Those which had suffered excessive punishment no longer made favorable use of their environment, that is, became "maladjusted," notably by losing their food-storage habits. The collapse of the social pattern also had a detrimental effect on fertility. Under conditions of crowding the dominant rats could no longer guard their own females from intruding males, for the latter pursued them and copulated frequently. Why the outcome was infertility may be gathered from the analogy of Bruce's[15,16] experiments with mice. From a chance observation that pregnancy sometimes unaccountably failed in the laboratory she was able to establish the cause as contact with a strange male. After mating with their familiar sire the females suffered a "blocking" of the pregnancy even if they only detected the odor of the intruder on nesting material. After some five days they came on heat again and could conceive, but a breakdown of social dominance and exposure to a succession of strange males would presumably inhibit pregnancy indefinitely.

A further effect of crowding in Calhoun's experimental colony was that "more and more individuals were stunted despite having plenty of food available. Such stunted rats seemed healthy ... they simply failed to grow very large and attained their mature weight very slowly." These stunted rats were also characterised by behaviour-disturbances. Again one

might infer prenatal damage, with a hint of the pregnancy/multiple-impairment syndrome hypothesized by the present writer in respect of human beings.[17]

The regulatory mechanisms which Calhoun observed in rats, and Bruce's "pregnancy-block" in mice, originated in the animals' becoming aware that something was "wrong" in their environment. No doubt to avoid the controversial term "psychological," Bruce described this type of influence as exteroceptive. Leaving terms aside, it can be said that a situation of a certain type, namely a relationship with other animals of their own species, was appraised as unfavourable, and that this act of appraisal initiated physiological processes which culminated in infertility. Barnett[18,19] has carried out experiments which showed that male rats in the unfavourable situation of being bullied become subject to adrenal cortical depletion, which may be followed by death, even though they suffer no actual wounding. It would appear that he induced in these bullied rats the condition of "shock-disease" which Green and Evans described in the snowshoe hare during the phase of population decline. With Larson, Green made a physiological study of a number of afflicted animals, and Christian[20] recognized their description of the disease as similar to Selye's stress adaptation syndrome: the animals had died of adreno-pituitary exhaustion.

Such a psychosomatic reaction to a situation appraised as unfavourable or disastrous does not, in itself, account for the continuance of the shock-state in subsequent generations, which did not experience the overcrowding. This could, however, result if the state of shock interferes with the reproductive processes, causing the next generation to suffer damage at the foetal stage. Two critical experiments demonstrate that the offspring can suffer prenatal damage as a result of the mother-animals' being subjected to exteroceptive or "psychological" shock. Thompson and Sontag[21] subjected pregnant rats to the constant ringing of an electric bell, to the extent that they broke down in convulsions. To eliminate the possibility that the after-effects upon the mothers retarded their young postnatally, the latter were changed around with the young of a control-group of unshocked rats. The offspring of the rats shocked in pregnancy were found to be significantly slower at maze-learning.

Thompson[22] carried out a further experiment to test the effects of anxiety pure and simple during pregnancy upon the offspring. Female rats were trained to expect an electric shock on hearing the sound of a buzzer, and to escape by opening a door. After being mated they were placed each day in the same compartment, without the electric shock being applied. But the escape-door was locked, so that they were reduced to a state of fear. Once again their offspring were randomly switched with those of control-rats. The young born to the rats which had been subjected to anxiety were much more sluggish, took twice as long to reach food when hungry, and nearly three times as long before they would venture forth from an open cage. In human terms we would say that they were suffering from a congenital impairment of motivation. Their timidity and "unforthcomingness" resembled a type of personality-defect which the present writer found to be associated with pregnancy-stress in the human mother. It is reasonable to suppose that such "substandard," unassertive young would be the bullied animals, which would succumb to attacks during the strife generated in phases of overcrowding. If so, the congenital damage they suffered might rank as a mechanism for the limiting of population.

The defence of territory is found in some form among almost all animals and must therefore have been a powerful factor in survival. Howard[23] put forward the most apparent reason why this should be so, that by defending a territory a nesting pair guarantees its family larder. Lack disputes this view, pointing out that the "territories" of some of the gregarious birds, such as the guillemot and heron, consist of a few feet or yards around their nests, which could not possibly serve as a source of food. He also draws attention to many anomalies: encroachment for feeding takes place regularly; during hard weather territoriality is suspended and birds congregate around any provision of food; and finally territories vary greatly in size for the same species (the largest held by the robins he studied being five times greater than the smallest.[24] These anomalies can better be explained if territorialism is seen as primarily a mechanism for the regulation of population-numbers. . . . The defending of territory may limit the population-density over the region as a whole from generation to generation. This is effected by preventing

more than a certain number of birds from breeding. That some fail to do so is shown by the rapidity with which a new mate is forthcoming when the former one dies. Lack has himself shown that in a covered aviary, where there was insufficient space for two territories, the non-dominant pair of robins failed to breed. The territories in miniature maintained by sociably breeding birds around their nests, and the destruction by rooks of "unpermitted" additions to their rookery, would have the analogous effect of limiting the number of birds who could forage over a day's flight or over the available fishing ground. The balance of evidence thus seems to favor the view of Huxley[25] that territorialism is "one of the more important of the factors determining the population of breeding pairs in a given area"; and of Carpenter[26] that it is "an important condition for optimal population density."

It has been seen that the postulated mechanisms for the limitation of population tend to centre around reproduction and the viability of the young, these being the stages at which they could operate most economically. This consideration brings us to another sphere of biology which is fraught with unsolved problems: the study and experimental production of congenital malformations. Traditionally these have been regarded as genetic in origin, but the most persistent attempts to fit their appearance into any of the known Mendelian patterns of inheritance have met with little success. Examples of standard types of malformation crop up in a strain of animal or human being without antecedents, and even where a certain familial tendency is observed the malformation, with a few exceptions, does not occur with the regularity that would be expected if it were entirely genetically-determined. The labelling of the isolated malformation as a "phenocopy" of the true genetic prototype, or the explanation of the sporadicity in terms of the varying "penetrance" of a gene, has brought little additional understanding of the causes of malformation. In the early years of the present century Stockard[27] observed that malformations could be produced in fishes by treating their eggs with a weak solution of alcohol and other noxious substances. It was not until 1935 that an analogous discovery was made in a mammal: Hale[28] demonstrated that pregnant sows deprived of vitamin A produced piglets with a tendency to severe malformation of or total lack of eyes, together with other malformations. These findings have been abundantly confirmed in respect of a number of species of animals. The degree of deprivation proved important. Summarizing his extensive work in this field Warkany[29] reported that, "a borderline deficiency is required to induce malformations; a slight improvement of the dietary situation may result in normal offspring, while a further deterioration may lead to embryonic death." Similarly Sobin[30] found that congenital heart disease could be induced in the offspring by revolving the pregnant rat 200 times in a drum; but if it was subjected to 800 revolutions no live offspring at all were produced. The effect of these phenomena under natural conditions would be to limit population-growth in times of shortage, and the greater the shortage the more severe would be the block to fertility. It is also significant that besides vitamin deprivation the administration of hormones such as cortisone and thyroxine tends to produce malformation. With the known effects of rage and fear on the endocrine system, strife and harassment resulting from shortage and overcrowding might thus be expected to reduce fertility.

A big advance in the study of malformation was made when it was realized that they were the result, not of either genetic or environmental influences as the case may be, but of an interaction of both. This was first hinted at by Malpas[31] in 1937: "The role of an unfavourable maternal environment is to facilitate the emergence of certain lethal genetic factors." Since then this concept of the *facilitation* of a genetic propensity to malformation has been experimentally confirmed by Landauer[32] and by Clarke Fraser and his co-workers[33]: the appearance of malformation under conditions of stress was found to depend on the genetic constitution of both mother and foetus. It would thus appear that there is *regular genetic provision* for the production of malformation, or poor viability, in the offspring in times of stress. This is consistent with the view that malformation must be accounted one of the mechanisms for adapting population-numbers to the resources of the environment, and as such to have survival value.

The existence of mechanisms for limiting population in man cannot be assumed because they are found in animals. On the other hand the fact that changes in viability and in fertility as well as aberrations of behaviour leading to reduction in numbers are widespread among animals indicates a strong probability that such will be found among the human species....

The most evident devices for limiting human population are cultural in character. In the case of infanticide it is a self-conscious one. Among the Polynesians for example not only was any weakly or malformed child disposed of as a matter of course, but it was by no means taken for granted that even a healthy child would be allowed to live; it was left for the father to decide as a matter of policy.[34] In many cultures the taboo upon sexual intercourse during lactation, and the long nursing period, would have the effect of spacing out births. The institution of marriage, and the customs and sexual morality that go with it, must have the effect of limiting the number of children. If a bride has to be bought, or only a suitor of substantial means is acceptable, young wives would tend to get paired with old men. In peasant communities marriage had to be postponed until the suitor got possession of a holding, and by the custom of gavelkind (gable-child) the youngest son was expected to remain unmarried to work his parents' holding until eventually, at a mature age, he inherited it himself.[35] In former times in England marriage was not socially sanctioned until the couple were able to get their own cottage, which usually meant waiting many years. Just what social institutions in each civilization have militated against population-increase would be a fruitful subject of study. Under the feudal system there was a residue of landless and homeless serfs or semi-slaves, inferior in status to the peasant, who slept around the log fire of the manorial hall, and who thus had no family life. In the ancient world the institution of slavery would similarly have made marriage and reproduction out of the question for a large section of the population, not to mention the effects of physical hardship and ill-treatment. In his historical novel, *Salammbô*, Gustav Flaubert[36] makes Hamilcar, prince of Carthage, express surprise at the small number of children among his slaves. He commanded that their quarters should be left open at night so that the sexes might mix freely. Since Flaubert was noted for the thoroughness and accuracy of his historical research, it is unlikely that he invented this episode.

The aborigines of Australia are of unique

scientific interest from the point of view of the limitation of numbers, since they were at the time of their discovery by Europeans the only extant example of a human population at the food-gathering stage covering a complete land mass, without anywhere to emigrate.... If, therefore, mechanisms for the limitation of human populations exist they should be found among them. That the density of the aboriginal population was closely related to the available food was cleverly demonstrated by Birdsell.[37] He found that the lower the rainfall, and hence the poorer the vegetation and the fewer the animals able to live on it, the larger was the area occupied by each tribe. This was all the more striking among tribes without any water or shore from which to get food.

Birdsell found a remarkable correspondence between rainfall and the practices of circumcision and subincision. These were the rule in the driest central areas. The eastern boundary of the region throughout which subincision was practised followed the eastern 8- and 10-inch rainfall line with a closeness which made a chance relationship out of the question. That for the practice of both circumcision and sub-incision ran further west, along the 5-inch rainfall line. Since these rites do not impair the fertility of the affected males, it must be asked what connection they can have with austere living conditions. The explanation which will be proffered involves reference to findings which will be described more fully below. These are that the commonest form of impairment of a disturbed pregnancy is to render the infant weakly and more liable to common infections. Under unhygienic conditions the chances of survival of such weakly children would be poor. Even in 20th century Britain, the writer observed that among mentally sub-normal children—who are very liable to infection in infancy—those coming from the lowest-standard of home had the best health-records, for the reason that the poorly children in such homes would have died in infancy. Similarly it is reasonable to suppose that under primitive conditions the infliction of wounding by the above rites, and similar operations upon the girls, would eliminate those of delicate health. In times of food shortage, with the consequent harassment, fatigue and anxiety, many more delicate children would be born, so that the numbers of the rising generation would be significantly reduced. Birdsell in fact found that

along the boundary marking the edge of the diffusion of these rites the tribes practising them were less numerous than those not doing so. Yet paradoxically the area in which the rites were practised had become progressively extended, which suggests that the numerically smaller tribes had gained an advantage in times of scarcity by avoiding starvation. Circumcision, subincision, and indeed the widely prevalent superficial mutilation inflicted during initiation ceremonies, may therefore be culturally effective means of adapting the size of primitive human populations to their food resources.

In the light of the work on animal populations, it would be surprising if there were no regulatory mechanisms in human beings operating at the physiological level. An observation by Smith[38] on the Ao Naga tribe of Assam may have wide implications. "The number of childless marriages is usually large, and very few women have large families. The Nagas take a pride in the strength and endurance of their women, saying they are inferior to the men by a narrow margin only. These qualities have no doubt been developed by the life of toil to which they have been accustomed from their earliest youth, but they have paid the price in a weakening of the reproductive power." Of all the hill tribes he writes, "The young women are generally stocky and plump; but this does not last long, because the hard life of carrying wood from the jungle, doing cultivation work, raising children and performing other hard tasks soon make old hags of them." Such a picture, with the women doing the hard work and the carrying, while the menfolk sit around and talk except for seasonable bursts of activity, is typical of primitive and many peasant agricultural communities. It may be that this unequal division of labour to the disadvantage of women is a cultural provision which has had survival-value by the limitation of fertility. In a study of pregnancy-factors among over 3000 women at the Watford Maternity Hospital near London, McDonald[39] found that "a statistically significant excess of mothers of children with major defects had been engaged in work they described as heavy—particularly laundry work"; work involving heavy pulling or lifting was reported in 20 per cent of the cases where the children were malformed, but in only 8 per cent where the children were normal.

If physiological mechanisms for limiting numbers in man exist, one would expect the reproductive rate to be sensitive to the quality of nutrition during pregnancy. Even in a middle-class population in Boston, women who had poor feeding habits during pregnancy were found much more likely to give birth to stillborn, malformed or otherwise defective children compared with mothers whose diet was good.[40] In Aberdeen, women belonging to the poorer sections of the community had twice as many premature babies, three times as many stillbirths and lost their infants in the first month four times as frequently, when compared with well-to-do women in a nursing home[41]. In Toronto it was found by a carefully controlled experiment that miscarriage, prematurity and stillbirth among ill-nourished women could be reduced to a small fraction of what it would otherwise have been by giving them a supplementary diet during pregnancy.[42,43]

As early as 1812 a doctor, Jacob Clesius, remarked that malformations were more frequent in times of war. Of the Thirty Years' War in Germany, Gustav Freytag wrote: "The effects which such a life, full of uncertainty and terror, exercised upon the minds of country people were very dire ... one observed the signs of terrible misery in numerous malformations." After the siege of Paris in 1870—71 the French doctor de Saulle reported a crop of malformations.[44] Systematic evidence of this phenomenon comes from studies in several centres in Germany of the incidence of malformation during the war and in particular during the post-war phase of acute hardship, housing shortage and despondency. The malformation rate in 55 German hospitals[45] showed a startling rise after the war—the average for 1946—50 being 6.5 per cent, but there was a smaller rise for the war years themselves (2.58 per cent compared with 1.43 per cent during the pre-war and pre-Hitler Weimar period). This began from the start of the war, when there was no question of food shortage. There would however have been many reasons for anxiety and fear among the civilian population; besides the bombing, husbands and sons would have been called up, reported killed, wounded or missing and so on. From the point of view of the role of anxiety in inducing malformations, it is also noteworthy that the rate reached a minor peak during 1933, in the

January of which year Hitler seized power and loosed his Storm Troopers upon the Jews and the politically opposed sections of the population; during the whole period of the Hitler terror up to the outbreak of the war (1933—39) the average rate was nearly double that obtaining during the last seven years of the democratic Weimar period. For Britain no general figures of incidence of malformation are published, but an indirect indication of the trend can be had from the death rate from malformation in the first month of life.[46] For both male and female infants it was fairly stable for the years 1932—39, but moved to a peak-level during 1940—43, the years of the heavy bombing and severest fighting, with the resulting news of casualties. Owing to full employment and the equalizing effect of an efficient rationing system, the general standard of nutrition, especially of pregnant and nursing mothers, was above the level of the pre-war years.[47] One can only conclude that the increase in malformations was due to the prevalence of fear and anxiety. A study of MacMahon, Record and McKeown in Birmingham[48] confirmed the existence of a distinct peak during the years 1940—43 for anencephaly and spina bifida, the malformations which seem to act as barometers of social stress. In Scotland, where there was very little bombing, there was no significant wartime peak but only the post-war downward trend presumably reflecting the general improvement in the standard of living and social security throughout Britain as a whole.

A remarkable inverse correlation has in fact been found between social amenities and the incidence of anencephaly.[49] It is highest in Glasgow (3.1 per 1000) where overcrowding is worst, and lower in regular succession in the other three chief cities of Scotland placed in order of amenities. In the widely spaced communities of the Highlands the rate was found to be only 1.29 per 1000. Edwards, also in Scotland,[50] showed that the anencephaly rate was about four times as high among unskilled town labourers as in the highest social class. Both in the United States[51] and in Britain[52] prematurity is significantly more frequent in the lower social classes, and Stewart has shown that the same also applies to death of the infant in the first month.[53]

There are some telltale findings concerning the greater risk attached to extramarital conception (illegitimacy and premarital conception). Stewart found prematurity to be over twice and death of the infant in the first month nearly three times as frequent among such children compared with those conceived after marriage. These findings may link up with some suggestive and unexplained features of the anencephaly studies referred to above. McKeown and Record report a consistently greater risk of this malformation in *first-born* children conceived during the summer months.[54] This could not have been due to a greater physiological risk in first-birth, otherwise the tendency would have been equally apparent in winter-conceived first-borns; nor could it have been due to seasonal infections, for second-born children conceived in the summer were not affected. But extramarital conception, owing to the greater opportunities for outdoor lovemaking, is probably more frequent during the summer months, and the resulting children would mostly be first-borns. It might be that the mental stress consequent upon becoming pregnant in the unmarried state can be one of the causes of this malformation.

This suggestion received confirmation in the above-mentioned study of anencephaly in Scotland by Edwards. Despite the general improvement in social conditions there was virtually no change in the rate between 1939 and 1956. But this global incidence disguised two opposing trends which cancelled each other out. During the peak period of the war, 1939—43, the figure for later births was consistently high, and indeed higher than for first-births. This would reflect wartime stresses. But that for first-births became markedly greater in 1944 and 1945, and except for two years when the rates were about equal, remained greater thereafter. This may well be the result of an increase in extramarital conception due to a measure of breakdown in traditional sexual morality. It is perhaps relevant that the Chief Medical Officer for England and Wales, in his Report for 1959,[55] infers an increased tendency to sexual promiscuity, especially among young people, from the steady rise in the number of new cases of gonorrhea in recent years.

It is, in short, apparent that sections of a population subjected to adverse social conditions tend to suffer more reproductive casualty. And there seems some evidence that, as in the case of some animal populations, the physiological process responsible is triggered off by exteroceptive stimuli which arouse anxiety or other emotion calculated to lead to adreno-pituitary exhaustion. That absolute infertility can be brought about by severe emotional stress was conclusively demonstrated by the well-known German anatomist, Stieve.[56,57] In the bodies of women who had been imprisoned during the Nazi terror and subsequently executed he found unmistakeable signs of degeneration in their reproductive organs which, he pointed out, must have been due exclusively to nervous shock, as they were in a well-nourished condition at the time of their death.

In his pioneer work on the effects upon the foetus of emotional disturbance in the mother Sontag observed that the children tended to suffer from gastrointestinal illnesses.[58,59] He suggested that these were in many instances of autonomic origin. In other words, the children may have already been born in the state of shock-disease found by Green and Larson in snowshoe hares during the phase of population decline. Striking also is the parallelism with Chitty's conclusion, that the poor viability in young voles during the population decline could best be accounted for by foetal damage.

The present writer made a study of 102 mentally subnormal children by case-study methods in order to make comprehensive soundings of causative factors.[17] The pregnancy was disturbed by either illness or emotional upsets in 66 per cent of the cases, compared with only 30 per cent among the mentally normal controls. Where there had been pregnancy-stress 76 per cent of the mentally retarded children were weakly and ailing or had serious illnesses other than epidemics during their first three years, as against only 29 per cent of those retarded children of whom no pregnancy-stress was reported. Among the 450 controls of normal mental ability a similarly close relationship between disturbed pregnancy and early illness was observed. Malformations in both groups followed the same pattern.

Of the pregnancy-stresses emotional upsets were more than twice as frequent as illnesses, and these showed a curious parallelism with the conditions attendant upon overcrowding in animal communities, namely strife, harassment and personal difficulties over having to share housing accommodation, shocks and anxiety-states. It is also significant that of the 24 maternal illnesses in pregnancy, 20 of which resulted in unhealthy children, all but three were stress-diseases, notably gastric ulcer, chronic heart disease, severe sickness and vomiting, and toxaemia.

It has been commonly observed that mentally retarded children tend to suffer from a multiplicity of handicaps; this was not only confirmed in the above study, but each handicap was related so closely to pregnancy-stress that the latter could be reckoned to be the common causative factor. This syndrome of pregnancy/multiple impairment, thus named, included impairment of temperament. Of this the most prevalent type was "unforthcomingness," seen in extreme unassertiveness, timidity and general lack of motivation.[60] It resembled the behaviour of the offspring of the rats which Thompson subjected to anxiety during pregnancy. There can be little doubt, also, that the other main type of impairment of temperament found in backward children, which one might term disorganized motivation (abnormal restlessness and inability to concentrate, and excitability), can also be congenital. In the important series of Baltimore studies conducted by Pasamanick, Lillienfeld and their co-workers behaviour-disturbance in the children, especially of the hyperactive, disorganized type, was found to be significantly related to certain stress-conditions of pregnancy (toxaemia and bleeding).[61] It goes without saying that these unforthcoming or disorganized children would have a very poor chance of survival under primitive conditions, and would be bullied and rejected in times of stress.

Even closer parallels can be seen between the behaviour-deterioration of animals during population-declines and that of human beings under stress. Before he was interested in the mechanics of the former, the writer, in his studies of the types of family-situation leading to maladjustment and delinquency, described the "irritable-depressive non-tolerance . . . in a severely overburdened or nervously exhausted mother (which) can assume the form temporarily of a heartless rejection of her child." During the phases of irritable-depressive character-change "the mother may express the greatest dislike of the child, or even commit some hostile act against it which earns her a prison sentence."[62] Such a reaction may be cognate with the attacks of the adult muskrats upon the young during the strife-phase of the population-cycle observed by Errington.

In the child who is the victim of parental rejection can be observed a typical and apparently instinctive behavioural-change, described as "an attitude of active hostility (which) it is hard to explain otherwise than as calculated to make its position in the family impossible." This was designated "a self-banishing reaction." Considering that at the food-gathering stage each family would need many square miles of territory per head, and that shortage and overpopulation would be likely to be general in a whole region, the chances of a rejected child being able to reattach itself to another family would be small indeed. The break-away from its own group would therefore be virtually suicidal in the same way as is that of the lemming. It is noteworthy that along with or alternative to this hostility-reaction the writer observed a "removal impulse," which had surprisingly recurrent features: a dislike of the home-locality, wanting to go to sea, join the army, or to get work on a farm or with a travelling fair, besides actually running away from home or committing such flagrant offences as will secure removal from home. In a study of approved-school boys the writer found that this unconscious urge for removal was the commonest motive underlying their delinquency.[63]

The most drastic way in which the reproductive capacity of a population can be reduced, short of sterility, is to limit the number of females born. In fact the incidence of anencephaly, which is a lethal malformation and the commonest of those which are sensitive to social environment, is three times as high among females. The slight preponderance of males born probably reflects the tendency for female embryos to be more subject to lethal anomalies; hence no doubt also the slight rise in the male-female sex-ratio during the war years, which has been explained by the myth that Providence supplies more males to replace those killed. The wartime rise in deaths of infants of under four weeks from malformation was more marked for female infants: the increase in the rate during the stress-years of 1940—42 compared with the eight pre-war years was 7.5 percent for boys and 14.3 percent for girls.

On other hand, non-lethal malformations and liability to disease in childhood are more common among boys. Among the 450 normal children studied by the writer, infantile ill-health was over twice as common among the boys, and it appeared that a greater degree of pregnancy-stress is needed to produce an unhealthy girl than an unhealthy boy. Boys are also more frequently mentally subnormal, and if their ten times greater proneness to delinquency is taken as an index thereof, they are much more liable to behavior-disturbance. (Contrary to popular impression and certain sociological theories, the great majority of delinquents are emotionally disturbed.[64])

In seeking an explanation of why males thus seem constitutionally to be the more vulnerable sex, it must be borne in mind that under primitive conditions the male was the chief predator. If a predatory species becomes too efficient it eats up its food resources and so exterminates itself. Consequently it would be of advantage to the species in times of too great numbers, when the prey would be over-hunted, for the predators to become less competent. The effects of pregnancy-stress on the male offspring is to make him more stupid, physically less robust, temperamentally less aggressive, and possibly more myopic and more gawky. There is indeed some evidence that deficiencies of diet in a poor community depress the level of intelligence. Harrell and Woodyard supplemented the diet of a group of pregnant and lactating women in Virginia (predominantly Negro); at the ages of 3 and 4 years their children had an average I.Q. five points higher than those whose mothers had only received dummy diet supplements.[65] Among a similar group of White women in Kentucky, the average I.Q. of whose children was 107.6, the vitamin supplement made no significant difference, presumably because the untreated diet was above the level which under primitive conditions would have indicated food-shortage. Evidence that eclampsia and pre-eclampsia, which are stress-conditions of pregnancy, may result in a certain impairment of intelligence in the children has been provided by Margaret Battle in her study of school children in Rocky Mountain City.[66] It may seem paradoxical that a lowering of intelligence in the next generation should be the biological response to stress, but this is consistent with the need to maintain ecological balance.

In yet another respect the handicaps following stress during pregnancy suggest a regulatory mechanism. Those children who suffer from early chronic ailments seem to grow out of them—hence no doubt the folklore that a

child's health will change for the better at 7 or 14 years. The writer has also observed that pathological unforthcomingness is often replaced at puberty in boys by normal assertiveness and confidence. Of these children who have overcome their initial handicaps one might say that under natural conditions their poor viability would have been only a provisional "death sentence": if the hardships which caused the impairment were replaced by communal well-being, so that a larger population could be tolerated, these children would be reprieved. The writer also found evidence that boys were more likely than girls to outgrow handicaps of intelligence.[67]

The tendency, to which Tanner has drawn attention,[68] for puberty to begin progressively earlier in recent generations would also seem to reflect a mechanism for the adaptation of numbers to food resources. Hammond, the leading British authority on farm animals, points out that high-plane nutrition brings earlier sexual maturity in poultry and cattle: "With seasonal breeding species like sheep, lambs reared on low-plane nutrition may completely miss the first breeding season and not come on heat for the first time until a year later."[69]

Once one gets the bit of a theory between the teeth there is no limit to the intriguing speculation in which one may indulge. The test is whether, having caused new questions to be asked, the theory can predict the answers to them better than other theories, and whether it can link into a meaningful whole what was previously thought of as separate, accounted for in a number of different ways, or just taken for granted. The case for the theory can be briefly summed up. Animal-populations would seem to be adapted to their food resources by a variety of built-in physiological and instinctive mechanisms rather than by starvation, and these come into play in response to signals of incipient overcrowding in advance of serious shortage of food. Among these signals are certain exteroceptive or "psychological" stimuli; that is to say, the perception by the animal of some factor in its environment—presumably unfavorable in the biological sense—triggers off a physiological or instinctive mechanism which has the effect of reducing fertility or the survival-rate of the young.

There was also some evidence that the same sorts of population-limiting mechanisms are found in animals and in man. In both, the severity of reproductive casualty is geared to the degree of stress upon the mother during and possibly prior to pregnancy. The most unfavourable conditions induce sterility or stillbirth; the somewhat less harsh result in a multiplicity of impairment in the young which reduces the chances of survival; more moderate hardships—sub-optimal diets, insufficient living space, strife and harassment—bring a reduction in competence, vigor or strength of motivation in the young. Perhaps the most striking and unexpected parallel is in the appearance of behavioural aberration, or perhaps more accurately, the substitution of the normal behaviour-pattern by a special pattern of stress-behaviour. In the adults this takes the form of increased irritability and intolerance of congeners, in particular of the young, who may—whether animal or human—be viciously attacked. In the young themselves the behavioural aberration is seen on the one hand in "unforthcomingness" and on the other in disorganized hyperactivity and an emigratory or "removal" urge.

The chief implication of the theory is that the predicted catastrophe of a world population increasing by geometrical progression to the point of starvation is unlikely to occur. It will be forestalled, if not by conscious human design, by the physiological mechanisms which have been evolved to obviate just such a calamity. Indeed we see that these mechanisms are already insidiously at work, and as in one region or another overpopulation and crowding cause increased hardship, so we may expect to find them more in evidence. Even among sections of the White populations of Britain and America reproductive efficiency is significantly reduced by sub-optimal living conditions.

This is not to minimize the fact that these mechanisms are themselves highly unpleasant. Nature prescribes happiness only when it has survival-value. If the survival of our species demands a certain amount of sterility, deaths of babies, unhealthy children, malformed and mentally deficient people, criminals and perverts, our feelings about these drastic measures are irrelevant. To man nevertheless is given an answer. We need not wait for the physiological killers and maimers to come upon us. Primitive man was able to evolve cultural means, even though harsh, for limiting populations. Apart from dropping the more barbarous, little real advance has been made on them by modern Western civilization. During the 18th and early 19th centuries in Britain the execution of child-delinquents, their transportation, or their being sent to sea with the poor viability which that entailed, must have been nearly as effective a means of elimination as the emigration of yearling animals. It should not, however, be beyond the capacity of man to develop cultural methods of regulating population-numbers which do not involve distress and unhappiness. The consideration of such is beyond the scope of this essay. All that can be said is that man has the choice of consciously maintaining population at a level, for each stage of economic development, at which welfare, health and ability will be at a maximum, or of allowing Nature to make the adjustment by genetic provisions which have been valuable in man's evolution but which are insensitive and amoral.

REFERENCES

1. Simpson, G. G. 1958 The study of evolution: methods and present status of the theory. Behavior and Evolution, ed. Simpson, G. G., and A. Roe, pp. 7—26. New Haven, Yale University Press.
2. Lack, D. 1955 The mortality factors affecting adult members. The Numbers of Man and Animals, ed. Craig, J. B., and N. W. Pirie, pp. 47—55. Edinburgh, Oliver and Boyd.
3. Chitty, D. H. 1952 Population dynamics in animals. J. Anim. Ecol. 21:340—41.
4. Lack, D. 1954 The natural regulation of animal numbers. Oxford, Clarenden Press.
5. Errington, P. L. 1946 Predation and vertebrate populations. Quart. Rev. Biol. 21:144—77, 221—45.
6. Green, R. G., and C. A. Evans 1940 Studies on a population cycle of snowshoe hares on Lake Alexander area. I, II, II. J. Wildlife Manag. 4:220—38, 267—78, 347—58.
7. Green, R. G., and C. L. Larson 1938 A description of shock disease in the snowshoe hare. Amer. J. Hyg. 28:190—212.
8. Clarke, C. H. D. 1936 Fluctuations in numbers of ruffed grouse. Univ. Toronto Studies. Biol. series No. 41. 1—118.
9. Wilson, F. 1938 Some experiments on the influence of environment upon the forms of aphis chloris Koch Trans. Roy. Ent. Soc. Lond. 87:165—80.

10. Uvarov, B. P.   1928   Locusts and grasshoppers. London. Imperial Bur. Entomology.
11. Elton, C.   1942   Voles, mice and lemmings: problems in population dynamics. Oxford.
12. Errington, P. L.   1954   On the hazards of over-emphasizing numerical fluctuations in studies of "cyclic" phenomena in muskrat populations. J. Wildlife Manag. 18:66—90.
13. Chitty, D.   1952   Mortality among voles (*microtus agrestis*) at Lake Vyrwy, Montgomeryshire, in 1936—39. Phil. Trans. Roy. Soc. London, B. 236:505—52.
14. Calhoun, J. B.   1952   The social aspects of population dynamics. J. Mammal. 33:139—59.
15. Bruce, H. M.   1960   A block to pregnancy in the mouse caused by proximity to strange males. J. Reprod. Fertil. 1:96—103.
16. ———   1960   Further observations on pregnancy block in mice caused by the proximity of strange males. J. Reprod. Fertil. 1:310—11.
17. Stott, D. H.   1957   Physical and mental handicaps following a disturbed pregnancy. Lancet, i, 1006—12.
18. Barnett, S. A.   1958   Physiological effects of "social stress" in wild rats. The adrenal cortex. J. Psychosom. Res. 3:1—11.
19. Barnett, S. A., J. C. Eaton, and H. M. McCallum   1960   Physiological effects of "social stress" in wild rats. 2. Liver glycogen and blood glucose. J. Psychosom. Res. 4:251—60.
20. Christian, J. J.   1950   The adreno-pituitary system and population cycles in mammals. J. Mammal. 31:247—59.
21. Thompson, W. R. Jnr., and L. W. Sontag   1956   Behavioral effects in the offspring of rats subjected to audiogenic seizure during the gestational period. J. Comp. Physiol. 49:454—6.
22. Thompson, W. R.   1957   Influence of prenatal maternal anxiety on emotionality in young rats. Science 125:698—9.
23. Howard, H. E.   1920   Territory in bird life. London, John Murray.
24. Lack, D.   1953   The life of the robin. Pelican books.
25. Huxley, J. S.   1933   A natural experiment on the territorial instinct. British Birds, 27:270—77.
26. Carpenter, C. R.   1958   Territoriality: a review of concepts and problems. Behavior and Evolution, ed. Simpson, G. G., and A. Roe, pp. 224—50. New Haven, Yale Univeristy Press.
27. Stockard, C. R.   1910   The influence of alcohol and other anaesthetics on embryonic development. Amer. J. Anat. 10:369—92.
28. Hale, F.   1935   Relation of vitamin A to anophthalmos in pigs. Amer. J. Ophthal. 18:1087—93.
29. Warkany, J.   1947   Etiology of congenital malformations. Advanc. Pediat. 2:1—63.
30. Sobin, S.   1954   Experimental creation of cardiac defects. Congenital Heart Disease. 14th M and R report of the Pediatric Research Conference, Ohio.
31. Malpas, P.   1937   The incidence of human malformations and the significance of changes in the maternal environment in their causation. J. Obstet. Gynaec. Brit. Emp. 44:434—54.
32. Landauer, W., and C. I. Bliss   1946   Insulin-induced rumplessness of chickens. J. Exp. Zool. 102:1—22.
33. Fraser, F. C., H. Kalter, B. E. Walker, and T. D. Fainstat   1954   Experimental production of cleft palate with cortisone, and other hormones. J. Cell. Comp. Physiol. 43 suppl.:237—59.
34. Danielsson, B.   1956   Love in the south seas. London, Allen & Unwin.
35. Rees, A. D.   1950   Life in a Welsh countryside. Cardiff, Univ. Wales Press.
36. Flaubert, G.   1874   Salammbô. Paris, éd. définitive.
37. Birdsell, J. B.   1953   Some environmental and cultural factors influencing the structuring of Australian aboriginal populations. Amer. Naturalist, 87:169—207.
38. Smith, W. C.   1925   The Ao Naga Tribe of Assam. London, Macmillan.
39. McDonald, A. D.   1958   Maternal health and congenital defect. New Engl. J. Med. 258:767—73.
40. Burke, B. S., V. A. Beal, S. B Kirkwood, and H. C. Stuart   1943   Nutrition studies during pregnancy. Amer. J. Obstet. Gynec. 46:38—52.
41. Baird, D.   1945   The influence of social and economic factors on stillbirths and neonatal deaths. J. Obstet. Gynec. Brit. Emp. 52:217—34, 339—66.
42. Ebbs, J. H., and W. J. Moyle   1942   The importance of nutrition in the prenatal clinic. J. Amer. Dietetic Assoc. 18:12—15.
43. Ebbs, J. H., W. A. Scott, F. F. Tisdall, W. J. Moyle, and M. Bell   1942   Nutrition in pregnancy. Canad. Med. Assoc. J. 46:1—6.
44. Gesenius, H.   1951   Missgeburten im Wechsel der Jahrhunderte. Berliner Med. Zeitschrift 2:359—62.
45. Eichmann, E., Gesenius, H.   1952   Die Missgeburtenzunahme in Berline und Umgebung in den Nachkriegsjahren. Arch. Gynäk. 181:168—84.
46. Registrar-General's reports for England and Wales (1932—57).
47. Garry, R. C., and H. O. Wood   1946   Dietary requirements in human pregnancy and lactation. A review of recent work. Nutr. Abstr. Revs. 15:591—621.
48. MacMahon, B., R. G. Record, and T. McKeown   1951   Secular changes in the incidence of malformations of the central nervous system. Brit. J. Soc. Med. 5:254.
49. Anderson, W. J. R., D. Baird, and A. M. Thompson   1958   Epidemiology of stillbirths and infant deaths due to congenital malformation. Lancet, i, 1304—6.
50. Edwards, J. H.   1958   Congenital malformations of the central nervous system in Scotland. Brit. J. Prev. Soc. Med. 12:115—30.
51. Pasamanick, B., and H. Knobloch   1957   Some early precursors of racial behavioural differences. J. Nat. Med. Assoc. 49:372.
52. Drillien, C. M., and F. Richmond   1956   Prematurity in Edinburgh. Arch. Dis. Child. 31:390.
53. Stewart, A. M.   1955   A note on the obstetric effects of work during pregnancy. Brit. J. Prev. Soc. Med. 9:159—61.
54. McKeown, T., and R. G. Record   1951   Seasonal incidence of congenital malformation of the central nervous system. Lancet, i, 192—96.
55. Chief Medical Officer for England and Wales, report 1959. London, H. M. Stationary Office.

56. Stieve, H.   1942   Der Einfluss von Angst und psychischer Erregung auf Bau und Funktion der weiblichen Geschlechts-organe. Zbl. f. Gynäk. 66:1698—1708.

57. ———   1943   Schreckblutungen aus der Gebärmutterschleimhaut. Zbl. f. Gynäk. 67:866—77.

58. Sontag, L. W.   1941   Significance of fetal environmental differences. Amer. J. Obstet. Gynec. 42:996—1003.

59. ———   1944   Differences in modifiability of fetal behavior and physiology. Psychosomat. Med. 6:151—54.

60. Stott, D. H.   1959   Evidence for pre-natal impairment of temperament in mentally retarded children. Vita Humana, 2:125—48.

61. Pasamanick, B., M. E. Rogers, and A. M. Lillienfeld   1956   Pregnancy experience and the development of behavior disorder in children. Amer. J. Psychiat. 112:613.

62. Stott, D. H.   1956   Unsettled children and their families. London, Univ. London Press; New York, Philosoph. Lib.

63. ———   1950   Delinquency and human nature. Dunfermline, Carnegie U.K. Trust.

64. ———   1960   Delinquency, maladjustment and unfavourable ecology. Brit. J. Psychol. 51:157—70.

65. Harrell, R. F., E. Woodyard, and A. I. Gates   1955   The effect of mothers' diets on the intelligence of offspring. New York Bureau of Publ., Teachers' Coll. Columbia Univ.

66. Battle, M.   1949   Effect of birth on mentality. Amer. J. Obstet. Gynec. 58:110—16.

67. Stott, D. H.   1960   Observations on retest discrepancy in mentally subnormal children. Brit. J. Educ. Psychol. 30:211—19.

68. Tanner, J. M.   1955   Growth at adolescence. Oxford, Blackwell.

69. Hammond, H.   1955   The effects of nutrition on fertility in animal and human populations. The Numbers of Man and Animals, ed. Cragg, J. B., and N. W. Pirie, Edinburgh, Oliver and Boyd, pp. 113—20.

Evolutionary Response
to Infectious Disease

Commentary

Stott in his essay hinted at but did not discuss pathogenic diseases as a control on the populations of man. The diseases with which he was concerned were degenerative, largely physiological, a response to genetic weaknesses and stressful situations. Other diseases outside the limits of Stott's essay did affect mankind and ravage human populations.

Don R. Arthurs in his book *Man and His Environment*[1] classified diseases as eco-alimental, ecopathogenic, ecometabolic, and ecophysical.

The first, eco-alimental, is largely nutritional, involving malnutrition, hunger, and famine at one extreme, and overeating at the other, which results in fat deposition and heart trouble. The latter was of little importance to early man, but in some affluent nations it is becoming increasingly important. Death from starvation and malnutrition is commonplace in many parts of the world. Great famines have swept parts of the earth in the past and, as in Biafra, they are with us today. The prospects are that they will be more frequent in the future.

Ecophysical disease includes automobile casualities, war injuries, murder victims, and the like.

Ecometabolic disease, which involves the intrusion of foreign matter or nonliving material into the metabolic system, is becoming increasingly important to human welfare. I was tempted to say it is not density dependent, but in many ways it is. Dust in coal mines, dust in air, noxious and poisonous gases, industrial pollutants in water supplies, stresses that produce heart diseases, all are the products of increased human densities. Ecometabolic diseases are becoming twentieth-century diseases brought about by industrialization, conglomerate living, automobiles, etc.

The paper by Armelagos and Dewey concerns ecopathogenic disease, one of the shadows that has hung over human population. Disease given a start in a dense population can wipe out an animal population. Rinderpest nearly wiped out the African buffalo; rabies has decimated fox populations. Man himself has not escaped—smallpox, often intentionally introduced, nearly exterminated some North American Indian tribes, and Eskimo populations declined rapidly when they came in contact with whites and contracted smallpox, measles, and other European diseases.

Disease has had a part in inhibiting the growth of world population in the past. The Black Death (bubonic plague), for example, repeatedly cut back populations in Medieval Europe. Between 1348 and 1350 The Black Death wiped out 25 percent of the inhabitants of Europe. And from 1348 to 1371 the same plague reduced England's population by nearly 50 percent. Malaria in the tropical regions, especially southeastern Asia prior to World War II, has been a depressant on population growth. Malaria control through DDT has decreased the death rate and contributed to the excessive population growth in that part of the world.

The role of pathogenic disease in the history of man changed with his cultural development. Diseases which were of little consequence when man lived in widely dispersed groups became highly contagious when man began to live in settled groups. As densities increased, the incidence of disease increased. But as with all animal species, man through selection began to acquire immunity and resistance to certain diseases common to the region. Then, as populations expanded, men moved to distant parts of the earth, and emigrants carried their diseases with them. Subsequently, they infected the indigenous peoples, who often rapidly succumbed to them. And in turn the emigrants contracted diseases for which they had little resistance. Syphilis, probably contracted from the Indians by Columbus' sailors, was introduced to Europe, where an epidemic swept the continent.

Today major diseases in many parts of the world are suppressed. Three to 4 percent of the budget of underdeveloped countries is spent on the conquest of disease, even before they have established a sufficient agricultural base to support the increased population. In affluent countries 6 percent of Gross National Product goes for medical services. Man protects himself by vaccines and antibiotics and by better food, housing, shelter,

---

[1] D. R. Arthurs, *"Man and His Environment,"* New York, American Elsevier, 1969.

and sanitation against some of the important diseases such as measles, diphtheria, and smallpox. But in protecting himself artifically he is interfering with the evolutionary response and creating a new pattern of disease. With rapid communication and mass transport of people around the globe, there exists the very real danger that new viruses or bacteria against which man has evolved no resistance could easily sweep the world.

Selection 20

Evolutionary Response to Human Infectious Diseases

by George J. Armelagos and John R. Dewey

The study of the evolution of man seldom takes into consideration the role of disease in this development. This is understandable since the evidence available is essentially inferential and consequently open to interpretation. These inferences are based on the actual paleontological record with additional information provided by the historical accounts of disease. We are also able to speculate on the occurrence of disease in prehistoric populations from the disease patterns in contemporary *Homo sapiens* and nonhominid populations. This study is an attempt to discuss infectious diseases in human evolution.

There are three variables which we must consider in the study of infectious diseases— the host, the pathogen, and the environment (Cockburn, 1963). The study of diseases in man, then, would involve the interrelationship of these variables. Although there have been changes in the host (in this case, man) and the pathogen, some of the most significant changes are those in the environment (Armelagos, 1967). It is important to note that the environment of man includes not only biotic, climatic, geologic, and geographic elements, but also all aspects of his culture (Bates, 1953). This presents somewhat of a dilemma, since man has used culture as his major mode of adaptation in an attempt to control the other aspects of his environment. The study of man's culture—his technology, social system, and even his idealogy

—must be considered if we are to understand the disease patterns of man.

The role of culture is so significant in understanding the disease process that May (1960) has constructed a model in which culture is dealt with as a separate factor, as are the environment (which includes the pathogen) and the host. May illustrates the role of culture with particular disease patterns in North Vietnam. North Vietnam has two relevant geomorphological features: fertile delta and the fertile hills. Although rice is grown in the hills, the major area of rice cultivation is in the delta. The rice growers in the delta build houses on the ground, with a stable on one side and a kitchen on the other. The hill people, on the other hand, build houses on stilts with living rooms about 8 to 10 ft above the ground. The animals are kept underneath the houses, while the cooking is done in the living room.

The vector for malaria, *Anopheles minimus*, occurs in the hills, but the flight ceiling of this vector is about 8 or 9 ft and, consequently, the *Anopheles* encounter only the animals under the house. If the vector were to stray to the living room, fumes from the cooking would tend to drive it away. The malaria vector does not occur in the delta.

Some people have been forced to move to the hills under pressure of overpopulation in the delta. Typically, movement of the delta people to the hills has not resulted in the acceptance of

---

THIS SELECTION, slightly condensed, is reprinted by permission of the American Institute of Biological Sciences from *BioScience*, Vol. 20, No. 5, pp. 271–275, 1970.

the culture of the hill people. The delta tribes still build their houses on the ground, with the animals kept in the stables on the side. Food is cooked outside and brought into the house to be eaten in the smoke-free living room. This results in the *Anopheles minimus* feeding on the humans, whom they prefer to the nonhuman animals. This transfer results in the transmission of malaria to the new inhabitants. According to May, the people of the delta have been discouraged from relocating, feeling that the evil spirits in the hills do not like them. The intimate relationship between disease and culture noted by May is not unique; others (Hackett, 1937; Livingstone, 1958; Lambrecht, 1964; Alland, 1967; and Hudson, 1965) have presented similar interactions.

. . .

The changes in cultural adaptation, with the resulting increases in population size, population density, and changes in the ecological balance, altered the disease pattern of man. Polgar (1964) suggests five stages in the disease history of mankind: hunting and gathering, settled villages, preindustrial cities, industrial cities, and the present. Our discussion of infectious disease in human evolution will utilize Polgar's description of these stages.

THE HUNTING AND GATHERING STAGE

For almost 2 million years man has subsisted on the animals he could hunt and on the edible plants he could gather. As one would expect, populations adapted to a hunting and gathering subsistence are small and are distributed over a wide area. In addition to their low density, these groups would have led a seminomadic existence. Small population size and low density would restrict the types of infectious disease which would have plagued them. Contagious diseases, for example, would not have had a large enough population base to have an impact on the evolution of these populations. Polgar suggests that the hunters and gatherers would have been afflicted with two types of disease—those which had adapted to the prehominids and persisted to infest them after speciation of the hominids, and those (zoonoses) which did not have human hosts but were accidentally transmitted to man. Such parasites as the head and body louse (*Pediculus*

humanus), pinworms, yaws, and malaria would fall into the first category. Cockburn (1967b) would add that most of the internal protozoa found in modern man and bacteria such as *Salmonella typhi* and staphylococci would have been present. It is interesting to note that Livingstone (1958) would argue against malarial infections in early man. The small population size and bipedalism indicating a savannah adaptation would preclude the presence of malaria.

The second type of disease is that which has adapted to another host and is transmitted to man accidentally by insect bite, wounds, or from consuming meat of the infected animal. Sleeping sickness, scrub typhus, relapsing fever, tetanus, trichinosis, tularemia, leptospirosis, and schistosomiasis are examples of diseases which, Polgar speculates, may have been transmitted accidentally to man.

The range of the hunters and gatherers is a limiting factor for the kinds of parasites which would have been present. During the earlier period of the hunting and gathering stage, the hominids were restricted to the tropical zone. With an expansion of hominids into the temperate zone (by the time of *Homo erectus*), new and different parasites would have been present. It is important to note that by this time some food was being cooked, a process which would kill some of the parasites present.

Missing from the list of diseases which would have involved man prior to the Neolithic are contagious community diseases such as measles, influenza, smallpox, and mumps (Polgar, 1964). Burnet (1962) goes further and suggests that few viruses would have infected early man. Cockburn (1967a) disagrees strongly, since there are a number of viral infections found in monkeys. Although it is possible that monkeys studied may have contracted the viruses in captivity, the differences in the form of these viruses, according to Cockburn, are enough to argue against this.

THE SETTLED VILLAGE STAGE

The semi-sedentary encampments of the Mesolithic and sedentary villages of the Neolithic resulted in the concentration of populations in relatively small areas. As one could expect, this would create new and different problems. In hunting and gathering societies, the disposal of human excrement presents no great problem since nomadic travel would preclude the accumulation of human waste (Heinz, 1961). It should be pointed out that in some cases, hunters and gatherers living in caves were forced to abandon them as the debris accumulated.

The sedentarism which is characteristic of the Mesolithic and Neolithic would provide new breeding places for many forms of life which harbor disease. In addition, domestication would have led to the herding of animals near the areas of habitation. Prior to this time, the dog was the only domesticated animal. *Salmonella* and *Ascaris* are carried by domesticated animals such as pigs, sheep, cattle, and fowl. C. A. Hoare (1957) has suggested that the trypanosomes were spread beyond the range of the normal host by domesticated animals. Polgar (1964) also suggests that the products of domesticated animals (milk, skin, hair) and the dust raised by the animals provide for the transmission of anthrax, Q Fever, brucellosis, and tuberculosis.

The expansion of agricultural societies into new environments created other problems. Audy (1961) has demonstrated that as new ground is broken for cultivation, scrub typhus increases. In this case, the agriculturalists exposed themselves to the bites of insects as they toiled in the fields. Livingstone (1958) has impressively illustrated the relationship between the spread of agriculture, malaria, and sickle cell anemia. As the West African agriculturalists expanded into the forest and destroyed the trees in the preparation of ground for cultivation, they encroached on the environment of the pongids. The pongids, which were the primary host of the *Plasmodium falciparum* carried by *Anopheles gambiae*, were exterminated or forced further into the forest. The mosquitoes quickly transferred to the hominids for their meals. Livingstone points out that agricultural activity, which provides new breeding areas for mosquitoes and provides a large population for the mosquitoes to feed, led to malaria becoming an endemic disease. Populations in this area have developed a genetic polymorphism—sickle cell trait—which gives those individual heterozygotes for the trait immunity to malaria. In other words, as the agriculturalists expanded, malaria would increase. In response to the increase in malaria, the frequency of the abnormal sickle cell hemoglobin would increase.

PREINDUSTRIAL CITIES

The expansion of the population which began in the Neolithic continued with the development of large urban centers in the preindustrial cities. The problem which faced the settled communities of the Neolithic are present but are significantly more difficult to control. The concentration of a large population in a small area creates problems in supplying food and water and removing human waste. Since many cities dispose of waste via their water supply, serious health hazards developed. Cholera, for example, was transmitted by polluted water. Even with our advanced technology, pollution is still a serious concern.

The increased frequency of contact between members of the population resulted in the transmission of disease by contact. Typhus was transmitted by lice which moved from person to person. Plague bacillus which was originally spread by rodents could, with the high population density, be transmitted by inhalation. During the preindustrial stage, viral diseases such as measles, mumps, chickenpox, and smallpox were also transmitted by contact.

Social change resulting from urbanization was responsible for alteration in the expression of some of the diseases. Prior to urbanization, syphilis was a nonvenereal disease, but with the changes in family structure, crowding, and sexual promiscuity, syphilis became a venereal disease (Hudson, 1965).

It was during this period that exploration resulted in the introduction of disease into new areas.

Population during this period approached a size for the maintenance of diseases in an endemic form. Cockburn (1967b) has suggested that a population of about one million is necessary for measles to be maintained as an endemic disease.

INDUSTRIAL CITIES

Increase in population size and density was again a consequence of the cultural advances of the industrial revolution. The social and environmental changes were important. Industrial wastes increased pollution of water and air. Unsanitary conditions in the slums were ideal focal points for the spread of infectious diseases, and imperialistic expansion transported disease into new areas.

Epidemics also created havoc in the industrial populations. Typhus, typhoid, smallpox, diphtheria, measles, malaria, and yellow fever epidemics are well documented for the late 18th and early 19th centuries (Polgar, 1964). Tuberculosis and respiratory diseases such as pneumonia and bronchitis were enhanced by the crowding and harsh working conditions.

Perhaps the saddest consequence of the industrial period was the spread of epidemic diseases to populations which had not developed an immunity to them. Although contact had occurred earlier, in the preindustrial period, the impact was greater during the industrial period.

PRESENT

The advances that have been made in recent times have been quite remarkable; our understanding of the relevant features of infectious diseases has allowed us to make significant strides in preventing and controlling some infectious diseases. Even with these advances, infectious diseases are still prevalent in many areas. Attempts to control disease are more difficult with rapid transportation. Infectious diseases may be transmitted in hours to populations which, 50 years ago, were 2 weeks distant.

THE EVOLUTIONARY RESPONSE

The study of infectious diseases and their impact on human development is the host and the parasite (Motulsky, 1960). The duration of a human generation is much longer than that of the parasites which feed on man. This would favor evolutionary changes in the parasites leading to less severe manifestations of the disease. This is understandable since a parasite which causes the death of the host can then die from lack of a host.

The responses in the host were also significant. Haldane (1949) suggests that infectious diseases have been the most important selective factor in human evolution. Since the factors (i.e., large, dense population) which led to epidemic infectious diseases arose rapidly following the Neolithic revolution, the genetic factors would not have been present to provide immunity against these infectious diseases. In other words, the genotypes that were selected during the hunting and gathering stage would have provided little protection against the infectious diseases, but the genetic heterogeneity of the population would have been adequate to protect some individuals from the diseases. Lederberg (1963) disagrees, since many of the diseases which have animal reservoirs would be important in an epidemic sense. Instead of rapid selection acting on a large population, Lederberg suggests that the persistent application of small differentials over a long period of time, as characteristic of "reservoir disease," could have developed factors of genetic immunity.

Motulsky (1963) states that there are three areas of concern in disease-susceptibility and resistance: (1) factors of immunity in the conventional antigen-antibody reaction; (2) generalized host factors; and (3) highly specific gene-determined factors which provide resistance.

Motulsky points out that there may be a genetic potential for antibody production, but it would be difficult to demonstrate in man. Lederberg (1959) has provided other data which would suggest a possible genetic variation in the response to antibody protection. Although not much is known about the inheritance of the nonspecific host factors in the response to infectious disease, they do appear to have a genetic basis. Efficiency of phagocytosis, levels of complements, antimicrobial factors in tissue, and serum inhibitors of microbial growth may have been important in providing immunity to diseases (Motulsky, 1963).

The highly specific genetic factors may have had a key role in the evolutionary response to infectious diseases. Although it would be impossible to demonstrate the genetic factors involved, populations appear to have developed a genetic immunity to disease. Motulsky (1960) states that when tuberculosis strikes a population which was not previously exposed to the disease, the mortality is high and the infection is acute. The individuals which are most susceptible to the disease would perish, while those with genetic characteristics which provide some resistance would survive. In subsequent episodes, the mortality is lower and infection is less severe. The differential susceptibility in different populations could result from a genetic difference. For example, American Indians and Eskimos developed a more acute tubercular infection. The evidence for genetic immunity is suggestive, however, since environmental differences in nutrition and sanitation may explain some of the population differences.

The evidence for highly specific genetic factors is more convincing in the metabolic polymorphisms which have evolved in response to disease (Motulsky, 1960). For example, the sickle cell trait, which provides resistance to malaria, has been discussed. Other polymorphisms have evolved in areas where malaria is endemic. The hemoglobinopathy thalassemia and glucose-6-phosphate dehydrogenase deficiency also appear to provide protection against malaria (Motulsky, 1963).

The evolution of genetic protection against infectious disease would have been essential for the survival of population, since epidemic diseases could destroy large segments of the population. In some instances, infectious diseases may act as a factor inhibiting population growth. In those populations in which epidemic diseases are still an important factor, increases in population are evidence. Cultural practices tend to maintain population size. As cultural groups are better able to prevent and control infectious diseases, the population increases at an alarming rate. In order to combat this increase in population, Polgar (1964) suggests that public health programs which are designed to control and prevent infectious diseases in countries with high fertility rates should include programs to limit population increase.

In addition to the problem of the exploding population, the control of infectious diseases has helped to increase life expectancy. The increase in longevity would have created new problems for the older segments of the population; increase in degenerative disease would have been a consequence. In a population in which the oldest individuals live to 60 years of age, degenerative diseases are relatively unimportant. Neel (1958) states that in the state of Michigan, of the deaths in 1953 from arteriosclerotic, hypertensive, or degenerative heart disease (which constituted 33.1% of all deaths), 7.4% occurred prior to age 50. By the 60th year, approximately 25% have died of degenerative heart disease. The remaining 75% of deaths due to degenerative heart disease occur after 60 years of age.

Recently, we were able to demonstrate that osteoporosis (loss of bone mass with age) occurs earlier and is more severe in prehistoric Nubian populations when compared to bone loss in a modern population. In the prehistoric Nubian population, the frequency of fractures due to severe bone loss was not evident. An examination of the mortality pattern would indicate why this should be the case. Approximately 40% of the population die before their 40th year. Only 15% live past 40 years and all are dead before age 60. In the United States, 91% live past their 40th year, 75% past their 60th, 29% past their 80th, and 6% past their 90th year. Since many individuals live past age 60 and osteoporosis continues, the decrease in bone mass becomes great enough to predispose the neck of the femur to pathological fracture. It should be pointed out that since these degenerative conditions occur in that segment of the population which is past reproductive age, selective responses to degenerative conditions could not occur.

With the possibility that we may be able to control infectious diseases in some populations, concern with degenerative conditions (Spiegelman, 1956) and population control should be two areas of future research.

ACKNOWLEDGMENT

Partial support was received from a grant (H. D. AM02771—01) from the National Institute of Child Health and Human Development, United States Public Health Service.

REFERENCES

Adams, R. M. 1964. The origin of agriculture. In: *Horizons in Anthropology*, S. Tax (ed.). The Johns Hopkins Press, Balimore, Md., p. 120—131.

Alland, A., Jr. 1967. War and disease: An anthropological perspective. *Natur. Hist.*, **76**: 58—61.

Armelagos, C. J. 1967. Man's changing environment. In: *Infectious Diseases: Their Evolution and Eradication*, A. Cockburn (ed.). Charles C Thomas, Springfield, Ill., p. 66—83.

Audy, J. R. 1961. The ecology of scrub typhus. In: *Studies in Disease Ecology*, J. M. May (ed.). Hafner Publishing Co., New York, p. 387—433.

Bates, M. 1953. Human ecology. In: *Anthropology Today*, A. L. Kroeber (ed.). University of Chicago Press, Chicago, Ill., p. 700—713.

Burnet, Sir F. M. 1962. *Natural History of Infectious Disease.* Cambridge University Press, England.

Cockburn, T. A. 1963. *The Evolution and Eradication of Diseases.* The Johns Hopkins Press, Balimore, Md.

———— 1967a. Infections of the order Primates. In: *Infectious Diseases: Their Evolution and Eradication,* T. A. Cockburn (ed.). Charles C Thomas, Springfield, Ill., p. 38—107.

———— 1967b. The evolution of human infectious diseases. In: *Infectious Diseases: Their Evolution and Eradication,* T. A. Cockburn (ed.). Charles C Thomas, Springfield, Ill., p. 84—107.

Davis, K. 1965. The urbanization of human populations. *Sci. Amer.,* **213**: 40—54.

Deevey, E. W., Jr. 1960. The human population. *Sci. Amer.,* **208**: 48, 194—198.

Griffin, J. B. 1960. Some connections between Siberia and America. *Science,* **131**: 801—812.

Hackett, L. W. 1937. *Malaria in Europe.* Oxford University Press, London.

Haldane, J. B. S. 1949. Disease and evolution. Supplement to *La Ricerca Scientifica,* **19**: 68—76.

Heinz, H. J. 1961. Factors governing the survival of bushmen worm parasites in the Kalahari. *S. Afr. J. Sci.,* **8**: 207—213.

Hoare, C. A. 1957. The spread of African trypanosomes beyond their natural range. *Z. Tropenmed. Parasitol.,* **8**: 1—6.

Howell, F. C. 1964. The hominization process. In: *Horizons of Anthropology,* S. Tax (ed.). Aldine Publishing Co., Chicago, Ill., p. 49—59.

Hudson, E. H. 1965. Treponematosis and man's social evolution. *Amer. Anthropol.,* **67**: 885—902.

Lambrecht, F. L. 1964. Aspects of evolution and ecology of tsetse flies and trypanosomiasis in prehistoric African environments. *J. Afr. Hist.,* **5**: 1—24.

Lederberg, J. 1959. Genes and antibodies. *Science,* **129**: 1649—1653.

———— 1963. Comments on A. Motulsky's *Genetic Systems in Disease Susceptibility in Mammals.* In: *Genetic Selection in Man,* W. J. Schull (ed.). University of Michigan Press, Ann Arbor, p. 112—260. (The comments are interspersed with motulhoup text.)

Livingstone, F. B. 1958. Anthropological implication of sickle cell gene distribution in West Africa. *Amer. Anthropol.,* **60**: 533—562.

Martin, P. S. 1967. Pleistocene overskill. In: *Pleistocene Extinctions: The Search for a Cause,* P. S. Martin and H. E. Wright (eds.). Yale University Press, New Haven & London, p. 75—120.

May, J. M. 1960. The ecology of human disease. *Ann. N. Y. Acad. Sci.,* **84**: 789—794.

Motulsky, A. G. 1960. Metabolic polymorphism and the role of infectious diseases. *Hum. Biol.,* **32**: 28—63.

———— 1963. Genetic systems involved in disease susceptibility in mammals. In: *Genetic Selection in Man,* W. J. Schull (ed.). University of Michigan Press, Ann. Arbor, p. 112—260.

Neel, J. V. 1958. The study of natural selection in primitive and civilized human populations. *Amer. Anthropol. Assoc. Mem.,* **86**: 43—72.

Polgar, S. 1964. Evolution and the ills of mankind. In: *Horizons of Anthropology,* S. Tax (ed.). Aldine Publishing Co., Chicago, Ill., p. 200—211.

Sears, P. B. 1956. The processes of environmental changes by man In: *Man's Role in Changing the Face of the Earth,* W. L. Thomas (ed.). University of Chicago Press, Chicago, Ill., p. 471—484.

Sjoberg, G. 1965. The origin and evolution of cities. *Sci. Amer.,* **213**: 55—63.

Spiegelman, M. 1956. Recent trends and determinants of mortality in highly developed countries. In: *Trends and Differentials in Mortality,* F. C. Boudreau and C. V. Kiser (eds.). Milbank Memorial Fund, New York, p. 51—60.

Stewart, O. C. 1956. Fire as the first great force employed by man. In: *Man's Role in Changing the Face of the Earth,* W. C. Thomas (ed.). University of Chicago Press, Chicago, Ill.

Woolley, L. 1965. *Beginnings of Civilization, History of Mankind.* Vol. 1, Part II. The New American Library. Mentor Books, New York & T oronto.

Selection 21

On War and Peace

Commentary

Back in my high school days when the threat of World War II was facing Europe, my civics class (a subject now called social studies) was discussing war. "Are there any advantages to war?" the teacher asked. It was rather obvious that she felt there were none. The silence in the classroom suggested that no one could think of any either. Then one boy raised his hand, stood up, and said, "I know one. War kills off the excess population." There were a few snickers in the class and a horrified look on the face of the teacher. But my classmate, of course, was right. War has killed off the excess population a number of times in history, from early recorded biblical times through the Crusades, the Thirty Years' War, which destroyed nearly one-third of the population of Germany and Bohemia, and the several World Wars and other conflicts, let alone many of the tribal war-fares. In the long run it has not been effective, but at points in history it has served as a temporary check on population growth.

War is an expression of aggressive behavior of the group; it is also an expression of territorial expansion by the group. If war is examined closely, one finds that in most instances it has been brought on by population expansion within a limited resource base and available land. This in part was the reason behind the militarism of Rome, who had to expand her resource base to support a growing population that could be maintained by resources near at hand. It sent the German armies moving through Europe and caused Japan's expansion into China and Korea. The Chinese hordes that now stand on the borders of relatively open lands of Siberia present a future threat to world peace. War then seems to reflect some ecological pressures on localized populations of man.

What is the relationship of aggressiveness and war to population density? Several books published in the past few years have concerned themselves with the aggressive tendencies of man and related problems: Robert Ardrey's *The Territorial Imperative*; Konrad Lorenz's *On Aggression*; and Desmond Morris' *The Naked Ape* and *The Human Zoo*. Several of these have prompted N. Tinbergen to write the selection which follows.

Ardrey's thesis in *The Territorial Imperative*[1] is that man is a territorial animal. He writes:

> We act as we do for the reasons of our evolutionary past, not our cultural present, and our behavior is as much a mark of our species as is the shape of a human thigh bone or the configuration of nerves in the corner of the human brain. If we defend the title to our land or the sovereignty of our country, we do it for reasons no different, no less innate, no less ineradicable, than do lower animals.

> Instinct exists and it makes use of learning the way a furnace sucks in air. One may consider the scientist as an example. Many a physicist or chemist, deficient not at all in the humanitarian virtues, has in our time placed at the disposal of the machinery of war the most sophisticated attainments of his discipline. All apparent conscience, all cultural instruction and religious teaching concerning the immorality of killing vanish before the higher command to defend his country. . . . He fills out from the particularity of his learning the generality of that open instinct, the territorial imperative.[2]

"The territorial imperative is blind as a cave fish", Ardrey writes, "as consuming as a furnace, and it commands beyond logic . . . strives for no goal more sublime than survival. . . . The principle cause of modern warfare arises from the failure of an intruding power correctly to estimate the defensive resources of a territorial defender."[3]

Perhaps, but it doesn't quite measure up to the behavior of a truly territorial animal. As Tinbergen points out in his article, territorial animals once settled in a territory attack intruders, and on his territory the owner is virtually invulnerable. Territorial animals do not seek to expand their territory once settled. In fact they may be forced to compress it up to a limit to make room for another. But in most cases an animal seeking a territory avoids established owners. Intruders are driven off by hostile behavior more ritualistic

---

[1] R. Ardrey, *"The Territorial Imperative,"* New York, Atheneum, 1966, p. 5.
[2] *Ibid.*, p. 25.
[3] *Ibid.*, p. 236.

than combative that rarely involves the demise of the intruder. A country's defense of its national boundaries is an overt act of territoriality. The invasion of a territory can hardly be called an example of territorial behavior. More wars are caused by invasions than by the defense which would never come about if aggression had not been committed in the first place.

The premise that man is a territorial animal has never been proven by scientific study in a manner that territoriality has been studied in other animals. Tinbergen makes much of this point. Our ideas of territoriality in man are subjective based on historical observation. The relative proof of man's territoriality could come from objective studies of more primitive societies of man, those still in the hunting or early swidden agricultural stages of cultural development. The anthropologist Anthony Vayda[4] suggests that warfare, rather than being an expression of pent-up aggression, as a number of anthropologists claim, or a means of attaining social cohesiveness, must have another reason for existing in man. As a means to attain solidarity of a social group, warfare is highly maladaptive, for it results, as animal aggressiveness rarely does, in the death of a portion of the population. Since this maladaptation does exist in warfare, the losses must have some survival value. Some advantages of warfare might be adjustment of male-female ratios in the population by the capture of women and children, spacing out of a relatively stable population, the prevention through death by war of a population increase so great that it would lead to overexploitation of the habitat.

Although Vayda has no empirical data, he does present a hypothesis about the functions of war among the slash and burn or swidden agriculturalist of New Guinea. Primitive wars, Vayda suggests, come about because "a diminishing per capita food supply and increasing intragroup competition for resources generate intense domestic frustration and in-group tensions."[5] When these tensions reach a certain level, release is sought in warfare with an enemy group. This warfare then results in "the reduction of the pressure of the people on the land, either because of heavy battle mortality or because of the victorious group's taking its defeated and dispersed enemy's territory. This reduced pressure on the land means the diminution of per capita food supply and the increase of intragroup competition over resources are arrested." Thus, war "regulates population size, population dispersion, intersocietal offenses, tension or aggressiveness, and inequalities in goods or resources."

Tinbergen considers man an animal exhibiting group territoriality. As a social hunting primate, man must have been organized on the principle of group territory. But Tinbergen is quick to point out what Ardrey completely misses—that not all of our territorial behavior is as characteristic of animal ancestors as Ardrey would have us believe. Man's territoriality has been enhanced by cultural evolution, which permits him to invade another territory with force. If man were more animal, this would not occur. But man is human, and it does occur.

Konrad Lorenz has somewhat the same attitude toward man's behavior as Ardrey. Or rather Ardrey based much of his arguments on the thoughts of Lorenz. According to Lorenz,[6] aggression is innate in man. If at one time he had any inhibition about killing, as lower animals possess, he lost it by rapid changes in human ecology and sociology. Militant enthusiasm he considers a specialized form of communal aggression in which inhibition against hunting and killing are removed by impersonal distance. The social unit with which the subject identifies itself must appear to be threatened from outside, which can cause the group or nation to engage in aggressive action to eliminate that threat. Militant enthusiasm in man, Lorenz declares, is a true autonomous instinct; it has its own appetitive behavior, its own releasing mechanisms, and it engenders a specific feeling of intense satisfaction. Its stimuli[7] are the subjects' social unit threatened from the outside, the presence of the hated enemy, an inspiring leader, and other individuals all inspired or agitated by the same emotions. The excitation grows in proportion, perhaps even in geometrical progression, with the increasing number of individuals. This is exactly what makes militant mass enthusiasm so dangerous. One does not need to mention any examples.

If man is aggressive to the point of being able to kill his fellow members, then, according to Lorenz, it is because of the obliteration by his intelligence of those instincts which prevent other animals from engaging in undue violence. A man's hope lies in finding some substitute objects toward which he can direct his aggressive instincts.

Desmond Morris argues that man is still a humble animal subject to all of the basic laws of animal behavior. Aggressiveness in man, he says, "is the evolution of a deep-seated urge to help our fellows that has been the main cause of all the major horrors of wars. It is this that has driven us on and given us our

---

[4]A. P. Vayda, "Expansion and Warfare Among Swidden Agriculturists," *American Anthropologist* **63**, 1961, pp. 346–358.

[5]A. P. Vayda, "Hypothesis About the Functions of War," *Natural History*, Special Supplement: *The Anthropology of Armed Conflict and Aggression*, Vol. 76, No. 10, December, pp. 48–50.

[6]K. Lorenz, *On Aggression*, New York, Harcourt Brace Jovanovich, 1966.

[7]*Ibid.*, p. 262.

lethal gangs, mobs, hordes, and armies."[8] All of our problems Morris relates back to our animal origins. In *The Naked Ape* he goes to considerable length to show how man behaves like other species. The examples are overdrawn. He interpolates too much for lower animals to man, ignoring the fact that man is a cultural animal as well as a biological one. Tinbergen takes issue with him. In his other book, *The Human Zoo*, Morris continues in the same vein. Cities are human zoos, a place where the modern human animal is no longer living in conditions natural for the species, a point that has been raised in a somewhat different context in Selection 12. Morris predicts that if population densities continue to increase at the present rate, uncontrollable aggressive behavior will be dramatically increased. The secret to man's survival, Morris claims, will be his ability to design civilizations which do not clash with or tend to suppress his basic animal demands.[9] In light of these viewpoints, Tinbergen proceeds with his carefully reasoned arguments against making too much of an animal out of man and adds his views on the aggressive behavior of man.

[8]Desmond Morris, *The Naked Ape*, New York, McGraw-Hill, 1967.
[9]Desmond Morris, *The Human Zoo*, New York, McGraw-Hill, 1969.

Selection 21

On War and Peace in Animals and Man

by N. Tinbergen

In 1935 Alexis Carrel published a best seller, *Man—The Unknown* (1). Today, more than 30 years later, we biologists have once more the duty to remind our fellowmen that in many respects we are still, to ourselves, unknown. It is true that we now understand a great deal of the way our bodies function. With this understanding came control: medicine.

The ignorance of ourselves which needs to be stressed today is ignorance about our behavior—lack of understanding of the causes and effects of the function of our brains. A scientific understanding of our behavior, leading to its control, may well be the most urgent task that faces mankind today. It is the effects of our behavior that begin to endanger the very survival of our species and, worse, of all life on earth. By our technological achievements we have attained a mastery of our environment that is without precedent in the history of life. But these achievements are rapidly getting out of hand. The consequences of our "rape of the earth" are now assuming critical proportions. With shortsighted recklessness we deplete the limited natural re-

sources, including even the oxygen and nitrogen of our atmosphere (2). And Rachel Carson's warning (3) is now being followed by those of scientists, who give us an even gloomier picture of the general pollution of air, soil, and water. This pollution is seriously threatening our health and our food supply. Refusal to curb our reproductive behavior has led to the population explosion. And, as if all this were not enough, we are waging war on each other—men are fighting and killing men on a massive scale. It is because the effects of these behavior patterns, and of attitudes that determine our behavior, have now acquired such truly lethal potentialities that I have chosen man's ignorance about his own behavior as the subject of this paper.

I am an ethologist, a zoologist studying animal behavior. What gives a student of animal behavior the temerity to speak about problems of human behavior? Of course the history of medicine provides the answer. We all know that medical research uses animals on a large scale. This makes sense because animals, particularly vertebrates, are, in spite of all differences, so similar to us; they are our blood relations, however distant.

But this use of zoological research for a better understanding of ourselves is, to most people, acceptable only when we have to do with those bodily functions that we look upon as parts of our physiological machinery—the functions, for instance, of our kidneys, our liver, our hormone-producing glands. The majority of people bridle as soon as it is even suggested that studies of animal behavior could be useful for an understanding, let alone for the control, of our own behavior. They do not want to have their own behavior subjected to scientific scrutiny; they certainly resent being compared with animals, and these rejecting attitudes are both deep-rooted and of complex origin.

But now we are witnessing a turn in this tide of human thought. On the one hand the resistances are weakening, and on the other, a positive awareness is growing of the potentialities of a biology of behavior. This has become quite clear from the great interest aroused by several recent books that are trying, by comparative studies of animals and man, to trace what we could call "the animal roots of human behavior." As examples I select Konrad Lorenz's book *On Aggression* (4) and *The Naked Ape* by Desmond Morris (5). Both books were best sellers from the start. We ethologists are naturally delighted by this sign of rapid growth of interest in our science (even though the growing pains are at times a little hard to endure). But at the same time we are apprehensive, or at least I am.

We are delighted because, from the enormous sales of these and other such books, it is evident that the mental block against self-scrutiny is weakening—that there are masses of people who, so to speak, want to be shaken up.

But I am apprehensive because these books, each admirable in its own way, are being misread. Very few readers give the authors the benefit of the doubt. Far too many either accept uncritically all that the authors say, or (equally uncritically) reject it all. I believe that this is because both Lorenz and Morris emphasize our knowledge rather than our ignorance (and, in addition, present as knowledge a set of statements which are after all no more than likely guesses). In themselves brilliant, these books could stiffen, at a new level, the attitude

of certainty, while what we need is a sense of doubt and wonder, and an urge to investigate, to inquire.

POTENTIAL USEFULNESS OF ETHOLOGICAL STUDIES

Now, in a way, I am going to be just as assertative as Lorenz and Morris, but what I am going to stress is how much we do not know. I shall argue that we shall have to make a major research effort. I am of course fully aware of the fact that much research is already being devoted to problems of human, and even of animal, behavior. I know, for instance, that anthropologists, psychologists, psychiatrists, and others are approaching these problems from many angles. But I shall try to show that the research effort has so far made insufficient use of the potential of ethology. Anthropologists, for instance, are beginning to look at animals, but they restrict their work almost entirely to our nearest relatives, the apes and monkeys. Psychologists do study a larger variety of animals, but even they select mainly higher species. They also ignore certain major problems that we biologists think have to be studied. Psychiatrists, at least many of them, show a disturbing tendency to apply the *results* rather than the *methods* of ethology to man.

None of these sciences, not even their combined efforts, are as yet parts of one coherent science of behavior. Since behavior is a life process, its study ought to be part of the mainstream of biological research. That is why we zoologists ought to "join the fray." As an ethologist, I am going to try to sketch how my science could assist its sister sciences in their attempts, already well on their way, to make a united, broad-fronted, truly biological attack on the problems of behavior.

I feel that I can cooperate best by discussing what it is in ethology that could be of use to the other behavioral sciences. What we ethologists do not want, what we consider definitely wrong, is uncritical application of our results to man. Instead, I myself at least feel that it is our method of approach, our rationale, that we can offer (6), and also a little simple common sense, and discipline.

The potential usefulness of ethology lies in the fact that, unlike other sciences of behavior, it applies the method or "approach" of biology to the phenomenon behavior. It has developed a set of concepts and terms that allow us to ask:

1. In what ways does this phenomenon (behavior) influence the survival, the success of the animal?
2. What makes behavior happen at any given moment? How does its "machinery" work?
3. How does the behavior machinery develop as the individual grows up?
4. How have the behavior systems of each species evolved until they became what they are now?

The first question, that of survival value, has to do with the effects of behavior; the other three are, each on a different time scale, concerned with its causes.

These four questions are, as many of my fellow biologists will recognize, the major questions that biology has been pursuing for a long time. What ethology is doing could be simply described by saying that, just as biology investigates the functioning of the organs responsible for digestion, respiration, circulation, and so forth, so ethology begins now to do the same with respect to behavior; it investigates the functioning of organs responsible for movement.

I have to make clear that in my opinion it is the comprehensive, integrated attack on all four problems that characterizes ethology. I shall try to show that to ignore the questions of survival value and evolution—as, for instance, most psychologists do—is not only shortsighted but makes it impossible to arrive at an understanding of behavioral problems. Here ethology can make, in fact is already making, positive contributions.

Having stated my case for animal ethology as an essential part of the science of behavior, I will now have to sketch how this could be done. For this I shall have to consider one concrete example, and I select aggression, the most directly lethal of our behaviors. And, for reasons that will become clear, I shall also make a short excursion into problems of education.

Let me first try to define what I mean by aggression. We all understand the term in a vague, general way, but it is, after all, no more than a catchword. In terms of actual behavior, aggression involves approaching an opponent,

and, when within reach, pushing him away, inflicting damage of some kind, or at least forcing stimuli upon him that subdue him. In this description the effect is already implicit: such behavior tends to remove the opponent, or at least to make him change his behavior in such a way that he no longer interferes with the attacker. The methods of attack differ from one species to another, and so do the weapons that are used, the structures that contribute to the effect.

Since I am concentrating on men fighting men, I shall confine myself to intraspecific fighting, and ignore, for instance, fighting between predators and prey. Intraspecific fighting is very common among animals. Many of them fight in two different contexts, which we can call "offensive" and "defensive." Defensive fighting is often shown as a last resort by an animal that, instead of attacking, has been fleeing from an attacker. If it is cornered, it may suddenly turn round upon its enemy and "fight with the courage of despair."

Of the four questions I mentioned before, I shall consider that of the survival value first. Here comparison faces us right at the start with a striking paradox. On the one hand, man is akin to many species of animals in that he fights his own species. But on the other hand he is, among the thousands of species that fight, the only one in which fighting is disruptive.

In animals, intraspecific fighting is usually of distinctive advantage. In addition, all species manage as a rule to settle their disputes without killing one another; in fact, even bloodshed is rare. Man is the only species that is a mass murderer, the only misfit in his own society.

Why should this be so? For an answer, we shall have to turn to the question of causation: What makes animals and man fight their own species? And why is our species "the odd man out"?

CAUSATION OF AGGRESSION

For a fruitful discussion of this question of causation I shall first have to discuss what exactly we mean when we ask it.

I have already indicated that when thinking of causation we have to distinguish between three subquestions, and that these three differ from one another in the stretch of time that is considered. We ask, first: Given an adult animal that fights now and then, what makes each outburst of fighting happen? The time scale in which we consider these recurrent events is usually one of seconds, or minutes. To use an analogy, this subquestion compares with asking what makes a car start or stop each time we use it.

But in asking this same general question of causation ("What makes an animal fight?") we may also be referring to a longer period of time; we may mean "How has the animal, as it grew up, developed this behavior?" This compares roughly with asking how a car has been constructed in the factory. The distinction between these two subquestions remains useful even though we know that many animals continue their development (much slowed down) even after they have attained adulthood. For instance, they may still continue to learn.

Finally, in biology, as in technology, we can extend this time scale even more, and ask: How have the animal species which we observe today—and which we know have evolved from ancestors that were different—how have they acquired their particular behavior systems during this evolution? Unfortunately, while we know the evolution of cars because they evolved so quickly and have been so fully recorded, the behavior of extinct animals cannot be observed, and has to be reconstructed by indirect methods.

I shall try to justify the claim I made earlier, and show how all these four questions—that of behavior's survival value and the three subquestions of causation—have to enter into the argument if we are to understand the biology of aggression.

Let us first consider the short-term causation; the mechanism of fighting. What makes us fight at any one moment? Lorenz argues in his book that, in animals and in man, there is an internal urge to attack. An individual does not simply wait to be provoked, but if actual attack has not been possible for some time, this urge to fight builds up until the individual actively seeks the opportunity to indulge in fighting. Aggression, Lorenz claims, can be spontaneous.

But this view has not gone unchallenged. For instance, R. A. Hinde has written a thorough criticism (7), based on recent work on aggression in animals, in which he writes that Lorenz's "arguments for the spontaneity of aggression do not bear examination" and that "the contrary view, expressed in nearly every textbook of comparative psychology . . ." is that

fighting "derives principally from the situation"; and even more explicitly: "There is no need to postulate causes that are purely internal to the aggressor" (7, p. 303). At first glance it would seem as if Lorenz and Hinde disagree profoundly. I have read and reread both authors, and it is to me perfectly clear that loose statements and misunderstandings on both sides have made it appear that there is disagreement where in fact there is something very near to a common opinion. It seems to me that the differences between the two authors lie mainly in the different ways they look at internal and external variables. This in turn seems due to differences of a semantic nature. Lorenz uses the unfortunate term "the spontaneity of aggression." Hinde takes this to mean that external stimuli are in Lorenz's view not necessary at all to make an animal fight. But here he misrepresents Lorenz, for nowhere does Lorenz claim that the internal urge ever makes an animal fight "in vacuo"; somebody or something is attacked. This misunderstanding makes Hinde feel that he has refuted Lorenz's views by saying that "fighting derives principally from the situation." But both authors are fully aware of the fact that fighting is started by a number of variables, of which some are internal and some external. What both authors know, and what cannot be doubted, is that fighting behavior is not like the simple slot machine that produces one platform ticket every time one threepenny bit is inserted. To mention one animal example: a male stickleback does not always show the full fighting behavior in response to an approaching standard opponent; its response varies from none at all to the optimal stimulus on some occasions, to full attack on even a crude dummy at other times. This means that its internal state varies, and in this particular case we know from the work of Hoar (8) that the level of the male sex hormone is an important variable.

Another source of misunderstanding seems to have to do with the stretch of time that the two authors are taking into account. Lorenz undoubtedly thinks of the causes of an outburst of fighting in terms of seconds, or hours —perhaps days. Hinde seems to think of events which may have happened further back in time; an event which is at any particular moment "internal" may well in its turn have been influenced previously by external agents. In our stickleback example, the level of male sex hormone is influenced by external agents such as the length of the daily exposure to light over a period of a month or so (9). Or, less far back in time, its readiness to attack may have been influenced by some experience gained, say, half an hour before the fight.

I admit that I have now been spending a great deal of time on what would seem to be a perfectly simple issue: the very first step in the analysis of the short-term causation, which is to distinguish at any given moment between variables within the animal and variables in the environment. It is of course important for our further understanding to unravel the complex interactions between these two worlds, and in particular the physiology of aggressive behavior. A great deal is being discovered about this, but for my present issue there is no use discussing it as long as even the first step in the analysis has not led to a clearly expressed and generally accepted conclusion. We must remember that we are at the moment concerned with the human problem: "What makes men attack each other?" And for this problem the answer to the first stage of our question is of prime importance: Is our readiness to start an attack constant or not? If it were—if our aggressive behavior were the outcome of an apparatus with the properties of the slot machine —all we would have to do would be to control the external situation: to stop providing threepenny bits. But since our readiness to start an attack is variable, further studies of both the external and the internal variables are vital to such issues as: Can we reduce fighting by lowering the population density, or by withholding provocative stimuli? Can we do so by changing the hormone balance or other physiological variables? Can we perhaps in addition control our development in such a way as to change the dependence on internal and external factors in adult man? However, before discussing development, I must first return to the fact that I have mentioned before, namely, that man is, among the thousands of other species that fight, the only mass murderer. How do animals in their intraspecific disputes avoid bloodshed?

THE IMPORTANCE OF "FEAR"

The clue to this problem is to recognize the simple fact that aggression in animals rarely occurs in pure form; it is only one of two com-

ponents of an adaptive system. This is most clearly seen in territorial behavior, although it is also true of most other types of hostile behavior. Members of territorial species divide, among themselves, the available living space and opportunities by each individual defending its home range against competitors. Now in this system of parceling our living space, avoidance plays as important a part as attack. Put very briefly, animals of territorial species, once they have settled on a territory, attack intruders, but an animal that is still searching for a suitable territory or finds itself outside its home range withdraws when it meets with an already established owner. In terms of function, once you have taken possession of a territory, it pays to drive off competitors; but when you are still looking for a territory (or meet your neighbor at your common boundary), your chances of success are improved by avoiding such established owners. The ruthless fighter who "knows no fear" does not get very far. For an understanding of what follows, this fact, that hostile clashes are controlled by what we could call the "attack-avoidance system," is essential.

When neighboring territory owners meet near their common boundary, both attack behavior and withdrawal behavior are elicited in both animals; each of the two is in a state of motivational conflict. We know a great deal about the variety of movements that appear when these two conflicting, incompatible behaviors are elicited. Many of these expressions of a motivational conflict have, in the course of evolution, acquired signal function; in colloquial language, they signal "Keep out!" We deduce this from the fact that opponents respond to them in an appropriate way: instead of proceeding to intrude, which would require the use of force, trespassers withdraw, and neighbors are contained by each other. This is how such animals have managed to have all the advantages of their hostile behavior without the disadvantages: they divide their living space in a bloodless way by using as distance-keeping devices these conflict movements ("threat") rather than actual fighting.

GROUP TERRITORIES

In order to see our wars in their correct biological perspective one more comparison with animals is useful. So far I have discussed animal species that defend individual or at best pair territories. But there are also animals which possess and defend territories belonging to a group, or a clan (*10*).

Now it is an essential aspect of group territorialism that the members of a group unite when in hostile confrontation with another group that approaches, or crosses into their feeding territory. The uniting and the aggression are equally important. It is essential to realize that group territorialism does not exclude hostile relations on lower levels when the group is on its own. For instance, within a group there is often a peck order. And within the group there may be individual or pair territories. But frictions due to these relationships fade away during a clash between groups. This temporary elimination is done by means of so-called appeasement and reassurance signals. They indicate "I am a friend," and so diminish the risk that, in the general flare-up of anger, any animal "takes it out" on a fellow member of the same group (*11*). Clans meet clans as units, and each individual in an intergroup clash, while united with its fellow-members, is (as in interindividual clashes) torn between attack and withdrawal, and postures and shouts rather than attacks.

We must now examine the hypothesis (which I consider the most likely one) that man still carries with him the animal heritage of group territoriality. This is a question concerning man's evolutionary origin, and here we are, by the very nature of the subject, forced to speculate. Because I am going to say something about the behavior of our ancestors of, say, 100,000 years ago, I have to discuss briefly a matter of methodology. It is known to all biologists (but unfortunately unknown to most psychologists) that comparison of present-day species can give us a deep insight, with a probability closely approaching certainty, into the evolutionary history of animal species. Even where fossil evidence is lacking, this comparative method alone can do this. It has to be stressed that this comparison is a highly sophisticated method, and not merely a matter of saying that species A is different from species B (*12*). The basic procedure is this. We interpret differences between really allied species as the result of adaptive divergent evolution from common stock, and we interpret similarities between nonallied species as adaptive convergencies to similar ways of life. By studying the adaptive functions of species characteristics we understand how natural selection can have produced both these divergencies and convergencies. To mention one striking example: even if we had no fossil evidence, we could, by this method alone, recognize whales for what they are——mammals that have returned to the water, and, in doing so, have developed some similarities to fish. This special type of comparison, which has been applied so successfully by students of the structure of animals, has now also been used, and with equal success, in several studies of animal behavior. Two approaches have been applied. One is to see in what respects species of very different origin have convergently adapted to a similar way of life. Von Haartman (*13*) has applied this to a study of birds of many types that nest in holes—an anti-predator safety device. All such hole-nesters center their territorial fighting on a suitable nest hole. Their courtship consists of luring a female to this hole (often with the use of bright color patterns). Their young gape when a general darkening signals the arrival of the parent. All but the most recently adapted species lay uniformly colored, white or light blue eggs that can easily be seen by the parent.

An example of adaptive divergence has been studied by Cullen (*14*). Among all the gulls, the kittiwake is unique in that it nests on very narrow ledges on sheer cliffs. Over 20 peculiarities of this species have been recognized by Mrs. Cullen as vital adaptations to this particular habitat.

These and several similar studies (*15*) demonstrate how comparison reveals, in each species, systems of interrelated, and very intricate adaptive features. In this work, speculation is now being followed by careful experimental checking. It would be tempting to elaborate on this, but I must return to our own unfortunate species.

Now, when we include the "Naked Ape" in our comparative studies, it becomes likely (as has been recently worked out in great detail by Morris) that man is a "social Ape who has turned carnivore" (*16*). On the one hand he is a social primate; on the other, he has developed similarities to wolves, lions and hyenas. In our present context one thing seems to stand out clearly, a conclusion that seems to me of paramount importance to all of us, and yet has not yet been fully accepted as such. As a social, hunting primate, man must originally have been organized on the principle of group territories.

Ethologists tend to believe that we still carry with us a number of behavioral characteristics of our animal ancestors, which cannot be eliminated by different ways of upbringing, and that our group territorialism is one of those ancestral characters. I shall discuss the problem of the modifiability of our behavior later, but it is useful to point out here that even if our behavior were much more modifiable than Lorenz maintains, our cultural evolution, which resulted in the parceling-out of our living space on lines of tribal, national, and now even "bloc" areas, would, if anything, have tended to enhance group territorialism.

GROUP TERRITORIALISM IN MAN?

I put so much emphasis on this issue of group territorialism because most writers who have tried to apply ethology to man have done this in the wrong way. They have made the mistake, to which I objected before, of uncritically extrapolating the results of animal studies to man. They try to explain man's behavior by using facts that are valid only of some of the animals we studied. And, as ethologists keep stressing, no two species behave alike. Therefore, instead of taking this easy way out, we ought to study man in his own right. And I repeat that the message of the ethologists is that the methods, rather than the results, of ethology should be used for such a study.

Now, the notion of territory was developed by zoologists (to be precise, by ornithologists, 17), and because individual and pair territories are found in so many more species than group territories (which are particularly rare among birds), most animal studies were concerned with such individual and pair territories. Now such low-level territories do occur in man, as does another form of hostile behavior, the peck order. But the problems created by such low-level frictions are not serious; they can, within a community, be kept in check by the apparatus of law and order; peace within national boundaries can be enforced. In order to understand what makes us go to war, we have to recognize that man behaves very much like a group-territorial species. We too unite in the face of an outside danger to the group; we "forget our differences." We too have threat gestures, for instance, angry facial expressions. And all of us use reassurance and appeasement signals, such as a friendly smile. And (unlike speech) these are universally understood; they are cross-cultural; they are species-specific. And, incidentally, even within a group sharing a common language, they are often more reliable guides to a man's intentions than speech, for speech (as we know now) rarely reflects our true motives, but our facial expressions often "give us away."

If I may digress for a moment: it is humiliating to us ethologists that many nonscientists, particularly novelists and actors, intuitively understand our sign language much better than we scientists ourselves do. Worse, there is a category of human beings who understand intuitively more about the causation of our aggressive behavior: the great demagogues. They have applied this knowledge in order to control our behavior in the most clever ways, and often for the most evil purposes. For instance, Hitler (who had modern mass communication at his disposal, which allowed him to inflame a whole nation) played on both fighting tendencies. The "defensive" fighting was whipped up by his passionate statements about "living space," "encirclement," Jewry, and Freemasonry as threatening powers which made the Germans feel "cornered." The "attack fighting" was similarly set ablaze by playing the myth of the Herrenvolk. We must make sure that mankind has learned its lesson and will never forget how disastrous the joint effects have been—if only one of the major nations were led now by a man like Hitler, life on earth would be wiped out.

I have argued my case for concentrating on studies of group territoriality rather than on other types of aggression. I must now return, in this context, to the problem of man the mass murderer. Why don't we settle even our international disputes by the relatively harmless, animal method of threat? Why have we become unhinged so that so often our attack erupts without being kept in check by fear? It is not that we have no fear, nor that we have no other inhibitions against killing. This problem has to be considered first of all in the general context of the consequences of man having embarked on a new type of evolution.

CULTURAL EVOLUTION

Man has the ability, unparalleled in scale in the animal kingdom, of passing on his experiences from one generation to the next. By this accumulative and exponentially growing process, which we call cultural evolution, he has been able to change his environment progressively out of all recognition. And this includes the social environment. This new type of evolution proceeds at an incomparably faster pace than genetic evolution. Genetically we have not evolved very strikingly since Cro-Magnon man, but culturally we have changed beyond recognition, and are changing at an ever-increasing rate. It is of course true that we are highly adjustable individually, and so could hope to keep pace with these changes. But I am not alone in believing that this behavioral adjustability, like all types of modifiability, has its limits. These limits are imposed upon us by our hereditary constitution, a constitution which can only change with the far slower speed of genetic evolution. There are good grounds for the conclusion that man's limited behavioral adjustability has been outpaced by the culturally determined changes in his social environment, and that this is why man is now a misfit in his own society.

We can now, at last, return to the problem of war, of uninhibited mass killing. It seems quite clear that our cultural evolution is at the root of the trouble. It is our cultural evolution that has caused the population explosion. In a nutshell, medical science, aiming at the reduction of suffering, has, in doing so, prolonged life for many individuals as well—prolonged it to well beyond the point at which they produce offspring. Unlike the situation in any wild species, recruitment to the human population consistently surpasses losses through mortality. Agricultural and technical know-how have enabled us to grow food and to exploit other natural resources to such an extent that we can still feed (though only just) the enormous numbers of human beings on our crowded planet. The result is that we now live at a far higher density than that in which genetic evolution has molded our species. This, together with long-distance communication, leads to far more frequent, in fact to continuous, inter-group contacts, and so to continuous external provocation of aggression. Yet this alone would not explain our increased tendency to kill each other; it would merely lead to continuous threat behavior.

The upsetting of the balance between aggression and fear (and this is what causes war)

is due to at least three other consequences of cultural evolution. It is an old cultural phenomenon that warriors are both brainwashed and bullied into all-out fighting. They are brainwashed into believing that fleeing—originally, as we have seen, an adaptive type of behavior—is despicable, "cowardly." This seems to me due to the fact that man, accepting that in moral issues death might be preferable to fleeing, has falsely applied the moral concept of "cowardice" to matters of mere practical importance—to the dividing of living space. The fact that our soldiers are also bullied into all-out fighting (by penalizing fleeing in battle) is too well known to deserve elaboration.

Another cultural excess is our ability to make and use killing tools, especially long-range weapons. These make killing easy, not only because a spear or a club inflicts, with the same effort, so much more damage than a fist, but also, and mainly, because the use of long-range weapons prevents the victim from reaching his attacker with his appeasement, reassurance, and distress signals. Very few aircrews who are willing, indeed eager, to drop their bombs "on target" would be willing to strangle, stab, or burn children (or, for that matter, adults) with their own hands; they would stop short of killing, in response to the appeasement and distress signals of their opponents.

These three factors alone would be sufficient to explain how we have become such unhinged killers. But I have to stress once more that all this, however convincing it may seem, must still be studied more thoroughly.

There is a frightening and ironical paradox in this conclusion: that the human brain, the finest life-preserving device created by evolution, has made our species so successful in mastering the outside world that it suddenly finds itself taken off guard. One could say that our cortex and our brainstem (our "reason" and our "instincts") are at loggerheads. Together they have created a new social environment in which, rather than ensuring our survival, they are about to do the opposite. The brain finds itself seriously threatened by an enemy of its own making. It is its own enemy. We simply have to understand this enemy.

THE DEVELOPMENT OF BEHAVIOR

I must now leave the question of the moment-to-moment control of fighting, and, looking further back in time, turn to the development of aggressive behavior in the growing individual. Again we will start from the human problem. This, in the present context, is whether it is within our power to control development in such a way that we reduce or eliminate fighting among adults. Can or cannot education in the widest sense produce non-aggressive men?

The first step in the consideration of this problem is again to distinguish between external and internal influences, but now we must apply this to the growth, the changing, of the behavioral machinery during the individual's development. Here again the way in which we phrase our questions and our conclusions is of the utmost importance.

In order to discuss this issue fruitfully, I have to start once more by considering it in a wider context, which is now that of the "nature-nurture" problem with respect to behavior in general. This has been discussed more fully by Lorenz in his book *Evolution and Modification of Behaviour* (18); for a discussion of the environmentalist point of view I refer to the various works of Schneirla (see 19).

Lorenz tends to classify behavior types into innate and acquired or learned behavior. Schneirla rejects this dichotomy into two classes of behavior. He stresses that the developmental process, of behavior as well as of other functions, should be considered, and also that this development forms a highly complicated series of interactions between the growing organism and its environment. I have gradually become convinced that the clue to this difference in approach is to be found in a difference in aims between the two authors. Lorenz claims that "we are justified in leaving, at least for the time being, to the care of the experimental embryologists all those questions which are concerned with the chains of physiological causation leading from the genome to the development of . . . neurosensory structures" (18, p. 43). In other words, he deliberately refrains from starting his analysis of development prior to the stage at which a fully coordinated behavior is performed for the first time. If one in this way restricts one's studies to the later stages of development, then a classification in "innate" and "learned" behavior, or behavior components, can be considered quite justified. And there was a time, some 30 years ago, when the almost grotesquely environmentalist bias

of psychology made it imperative for ethologists to stress the extent to which behavior patterns could appear in perfect or near-perfect form without the aid of anything that could be properly called learning. But I now agree (however belatedly) with Schneirla that we must extend our interest to earlier stages of development and embark on a full program of experimental embryology of behavior. When we do this, we discover that interactions with the environment can indeed occur at early stages. These interactions may concern small components of the total machinery of a fully functional behavior pattern, and many of them cannot possibly be called learning. But they are interactions with the environment, and must be taken into account if we follow in the footsteps of the experimental embryologists, and extend our field of interest to the entire sequence of events which lead from the blueprints contained in the zygote to the fully functioning, behaving animal. We simply have to do this if we want an answer to the question to what extent the development of behavior can be influenced from the outside.

When we follow this procedure the rigid distinction between "innate" or unmodifiable and "acquired" or modifiable behavior patterns becomes far less sharp. This is owing to the discovery, on the one hand, that "innate" patterns may contain elements that at an early stage developed in interaction with the environment, and, on the other hand, that learning is, from step to step, limited by internally imposed restrictions.

To illustrate the first point, I take the development of the sensory cells in the retina of the eye. Knoll has shown (20) that the rods in the eyes of tadpoles cannot function properly unless they have first been exposed to light. This means that, although any visually guided response of a tadpole may well, in its integrated form, be "innate" in Lorenz's sense, it is so only in the sense of "nonlearned," not in that of "having grown without interaction with the environment." Now it has been shown by Cullen (21) that male sticklebacks reared from the egg in complete isolation from other animals will, when adult, show full fighting behavior to other males and courtship behavior to females when faced with them for the first time in their lives. This is admittedly an important fact, demonstrating that the various recognized forms of learning do not enter into the programing of these integrated patterns. This is a demonstration of what Lorenz calls an "innate response." But it does not exclude the possibility that parts of the machinery so employed may, at an earlier stage, have been influenced by the environment, as in the case of the tadpoles.

Second, there are also behavior patterns which do appear in the inexperienced animal, but in an incomplete form, and which require additional development through learning. Thorpe has analyzed a clear example of this: when young male chaffinches reared alone begin to produce their song for the first time, they utter a very imperfect warble; this develops into the full song only if, at a certain sensitive stage, the young birds have heard the full song of an adult male (*22*).

By far the most interesting aspect of such intermediates between innate and acquired behavior is the fact that learning is not indiscriminate, but is guided by a certain selectiveness on the part of the animal. This fact has been dimly recognized long ago; the early ethologists have often pointed out that different, even closely related, species learn different things even when developing the same behavior patterns. This has been emphasized by Lorenz's use of the term "innate teaching mechanism." Other authors use the word "template" in the same context. The best example I know is once more taken from the development of song in certain birds. As I have mentioned, the males of some birds acquire their full song by changing their basic repertoire to resemble the song of adults, which they have to hear during a special sensitive period of some months before they sing themselves. It is in this sensitive period that they acquire, without as yet producing the song, the knowledge of "what the song ought to be like." In technical terms, the bird formed a *Sollwert* (*23*) (literally, "should-value," an ideal) for the feedback they receive when they hear their own first attempts. Experiments have shown (*24*) that such birds, when they start to sing, do three things: they listen to what they produce; they notice the difference between this feedback and the ideal song; and they correct their next performance.

This example, while demonstrating an internal teaching mechanism, shows, at the same time, that Lorenz made his concept too narrow when he coined the term "innate teaching

mechanism." The birds have developed a teaching mechanism, but while it is true that it is internal, it is not innate; the birds have acquired it by listening to their father's song.

These examples show that if behavior studies are to catch up with experimental embryology our aims, our concepts, and our terms must be continually revised.

Before returning to aggression, I should like to elaborate a little further on general aspects of behavior development, because this will enable me to show the value of animal studies in another context, that of education.

Comparative studies, of different animal species, of different behavior patterns, and of different stages of development, begin to suggest that wherever learning takes a hand in development, it is guided by such *Sollwerte* or templates for the proper feedback, the feedback that reinforces. And it becomes clear that these various *Sollwerte* are of a bewildering variety. In human education one aspect of this has been emphasized in particular, and even applied in the use of teaching machines: the requirement that the reward, in order to have maximum effect, must be immediate. Skinner has stressed this so much because in our own teaching we have imposed an unnatural delay between, say, taking in homework, and giving the pupil his reward in the form of a mark. But we can learn more from animal studies than the need for immediacy of reward. The type of reward is also of great importance, and this may vary from task to task, from stage to stage, from occasion to occasion; the awards may be of almost infinite variety.

Here I have to discuss briefly a behavior of which I have so far been unable to find the equivalent in the development of structure. This is exploratory behavior. By this we mean a kind of behavior in which the animal sets out to acquire as much information about an object or a situation as it can possibly get. The behavior is intricately adapted to this end, and it terminates when the information has been stored, when the animal has incorporated it in its learned knowledge. This exploration (subjectively we speak of "curiosity") is not confined to the acquisition of information about the external world alone; at least mammals explore their own movements a great deal, and in this way "master new skills." Again, in this exploratory behavior, *Sollwerte* of expected, "hoped-for" feedbacks play their part.

239

Without going into more detail, we can characterize the picture we begin to get of the development of behavior as a series, or rather a web, of events, starting with innate programming instructions contained in the zygote, which straightaway begin to interact with the environment; this interaction may be discontinuous, in that periods of predominantly internal development alternate with periods of interaction, or sensitive periods. The interaction is enhanced by active exploration; it is steered by selective *Sollwerte* of great variety; and stage by stage this process ramifies; level upon level of ever-increasing complexity is being incorporated into the programing.

Apply what we have heard for a moment to playing children (I do not, of course, distinguish sharply between "play" and "learning"). At a certain age a child begins to use, say, building blocks. It will at first manipulate them in various ways, one at a time. Each way of manipulating acts as exploratory behavior: the child learns what a block looks, feels, tastes like, and so forth, and also how to put it down so that it stands stably.

Each of these stages "peters out" when the child knows what it wanted to find out. But as the development proceeds, a new level of exploration is added: the child discovers that it can put one block on top of the other; it constructs. The new discovery leads to repetition and variation, for each child develops, at some stage, a desire and a set of *Sollwerte* for such effects of construction, and acts out to the full this new level of exploratory behavior. In addition, already at this stage the *Sollwerte* or ideal does not merely contain what the blocks do, but also what, for instance, the mother does; her approval, her shared enjoyment, is also of great importance. Just as an exploring animal, the child builds a kind of inverted pyramid of experience, built of layers, each set off by a new wave of exploration and each directed by new sets of *Sollwerte*, and so its development "snowballs." All these phases may well have more or less limited sensitive periods, which determine when the fullest effect can be obtained, and when the child is ready for the next step. More important still, if the opportunity for the next stage is offered either too early or too late, development may be damaged, including the development of motivational and emotional attitudes.

Of course gifted teachers of many generations have known all these things (*25*) or some of them, but the glimpses of insight have not been fully and scientifically systematized. In human education, this would of course involve experimentation. This need not worry us too much, because in our search for better educational procedures we are in effect experimenting on our children all the time. Also, children are fortunately incredibly resilient, and most grow up into pretty viable adults in spite of our fumbling educational efforts. Yet there is, of course, a limit to what we will allow ourselves, and this, I should like to emphasize, is where animal studies may well become even more important than they are already.

CAN EDUCATION END AGGRESSION?

Returning now to the development of animal and human aggression, I hope to have made at least several things clear: that behavior development is a very complex phenomenon indeed: that we have only begun to analyze it in animals; that with respect to man we are, if anything, behind in comparison with animal studies; and that I cannot do otherwise than repeat what I said in the beginning: we must make a major research effort. In this effort animal studies can help, but we are still very far from drawing very definite conclusions with regard to our question: To what extent shall we be able to render man less aggressive through manipulation of the environment, that is, by educational measures?

In such a situation personal opinions naturally vary a great deal. I do not hesitate to give as my personal opinion that Lorenz's book *On Aggression*, in spite of its assertativeness, in spite of factual mistakes, and in spite of the many possibilities of misunderstandings that are due to the lack of a common language among students of behavior—that this work must be taken more seriously as a positive contribution to our problem than many critics have done. Lorenz is, in my opinion, right in claiming that elimination, through education, of the internal urge to fight will turn out to be very difficult, if not impossible.

Everything I have said so far seems to me to allow for only one conclusion. Apart from doing our utmost to return to a reasonable population density, apart from stopping the progressive depletion and pollution of our habitat, we must pursue the biological study of animal behavior for clarifying problems of human behavior of such magnitude as that of our aggression, and of education.

But research takes a long time, and we must remember that there are experts who forecast worldwide famine 10 to 20 years from now; and that we have enough weapons to wipe out all human life on earth. Whatever the causation of our aggression, the simple fact is that for the time being we are saddled with it. This means that there is a crying need for a crash program, for finding ways and means for keeping our intergroup aggression in check. This is of course in practice infinitely more difficult than controlling our intranational frictions; we have as yet not got a truly international police force. But there is hope for avoiding all-out war because, for the first time in histroy, we are afraid of killing ourselves by the lethal radiation effects even of bombs that we could drop in the enemy's territory. Our politicians know this. And as long as there is this hope, there is every reason to try and learn what we can from animal studies. Here again they can be of help. We have already seen that animal opponents meeting in a hostile clash avoid bloodshed by using the expressions of their motivational conflicts as intimidating signals. Ethologists have studied such conflict movements in some detail (*26*), and have found that they are of a variety of types. The most instructive of these is the redirected attack; instead of attacking the provoking, yet dreaded, opponent, animals often attack something else, often even an inanimate object. We ourselves bang the table with our fists. Redirection includes something like sublimation, a term attaching a value judgment to the redirection. As a species with group territories, humans, like hyenas, unite when meeting a common enemy. We do already sublimate our group aggression. The Dutch feel united in their fight against the sea. Scientists do attack their problems together. The space program—surely a mainly military effort—is an up-to-date example. I would not like to claim, as Lorenz does, that redirected attack exhausts the aggressive urge. We know from soccer matches and from animal work how aggressive behavior has two simultaneous, but opposite effects: a waning effect, and one of self-inflammation, of mass hysteria, such as recently seen in Cairo. Of these two the inflammatory effect often wins. But if aggression

were used successfully as the motive force behind nonkilling and even useful activities, self-stimulation need not be a danger; in our short-term cure we are not aiming at the elimination of aggressiveness, but at "taking the sting out of it."

Of all sublimated activities, scientific research would seem to offer the best opportunities for deflecting and sublimating our aggression. And, once we recognize that it is the disrupted relation between our own behavior and our environment that forms our most deadly enemy, what could be better than uniting, at the front or behind the lines, in the scientific attack on our own behavioral problems?

I stress "behind the lines." The whole population should be made to feel that it participates in the struggle. This is why scientists will always have the duty to inform their fellowmen of what they are doing, of the relevance and the importance of their work. And this is not only a duty, it can give intense satisfaction.

I have come full circle. For both the long-term and the short-term remedies at least we scientists will have to sublimate our aggression into an all-out attack on the enemy within. For this the enemy must be recognized for what it is: our unknown selves, or, deeper down, our refusal to admit that man is, to himself, unknown.

I should like to conclude by saying a few words to my colleagues of the younger generation. Of course we all hope that, by muddling along until we have acquired better understanding, self-annihilation either by the "whimper of famine" or by the "bang of war" can be avoided. For this, we must on the one hand trust, on the other help (and urge) our politicians. But it is no use denying that the chances of designing the necessary preventive measures are small, let alone the chances of carrying them out. Even birth control still offers a major problem.

It is difficult for my generation to know how seriously you take the danger of mankind destroying his own species. But those who share the apprehension of my generation might perhaps, with us, derive strength from keeping alive the thought that has helped so many of us in the past when faced with the possibility of imminent death. Scientific research is one of the finest occupations of our mind. It is, with art and religion, one of the uniquely human ways of meeting nature, in fact, the most active way.

241

If we are to succumb, and even if this were to be ultimately due to our own stupidity, we could still, so to speak, redeem our species. We could at least go down with some dignity, by using our brain for one of its supreme tasks, by exploring to the end.

REFERENCES

1. A. Carrel, *L'Homme, cet Inconnu* (Librairie Plon, Paris, 1935).
2. AAAS Annual Meeting, 1967 [see *New Scientist* **37**, 5 (1968)].
3. R. Carson, *Silent Spring* (Houghton Mifflin, Boston, 1962).
4. K. Lorenz, *On Aggression* (Methuen, London, 1966).
5. D. Morris, *The Naked Ape* (Jonathan Cape, London, 1967).
6. N. Tinbergen, *Z. Tierpsychol.* **20**, 410 (1964).
7. R. A. Hinde, *New Society* **9**, 302 (1967).
8. W. S. Hoar, *Animal Behaviour* **10**, 247 (1962).
9. B. Baggerman, in *Sump. Soc. Exp. Biol.* **20**, 427 (1965).
10. H. Kruuk, *New Scientist* **30**, 849 (1966).
11. N. Tinbergen, *Z. Tierpsychol.* **16**, 651 (1959); *Zool. Mededelingen* **39**, 209 (1964).
12. —, *Behaviour* **15**, 1—70 (1959).
13. L. von Haartman. *Evolution* **11**, 339 (1957).
14. E. Cullen, *Ibis* **99**, 275 (1957).
15. J. H. Crook, *Symp. Zool. Soc. London* **14**, 181 (1965).
16. D. Freeman, *Inst. Biol. Symp.* **13**, 109 (1964); D. Morris, Ed., *Primate Ethology* (Weidenfeld and Nicolson, London, 1967).
17. H. E. Howard, *Territory in Bird Life* (Murray, London, 1920); R. A. Hinde *et al., Ibis* **98**, 340—530 (1956).
18. K. Lorenz, *Evolution and Modification of Behaviour* (Methuen, London, 1966).
19. T. C. Schneirla, *Quart. Rev. Biol.* **41**, 283 (1966).
20. M. D. Knoll, *Z. Vergleich. Physiol.* **38**, 219 (1956).
21. E. Cullen, *Final Rept. Contr.* AF 61 (*052*)-*29*, USAFRDC, 1—23 (1961).
22. W. H. Thorpe. *Bird-Song* (Cambridge Univ. Press, New York, 1961).
23. E. von Holst and H. Mittelstaedt, *Naturwissenschaften* **37**, 464 (1950).
24. M. Konishi, *Z. Tierpsychol.* **22**, 770 (1965); F. Nottebohm, *Proc. 14th Intern. Ornithol. Congr.* 265—280 (1967).
25. E. M. Standing, *Maria Montessori* (New American Library, New York, 1962).
26. N. Tinbergen, in *The Pathology and Treatment of Sexual Deviation*, I. Rosen, Ed. (Oxford Univ. Press, London, 1964), pp. 3—23; N. B. Jones, *Wildfowl Trust 11th Ann. Rept.*, 46—52 (1960); P. Sevenster, *Behaviour, Suppl. 9*, 1—170 (1961); F. Rowell, *Animal Behaviour* **9**, 38 (1961).

V/Endangered Environments

Aero Service Corporation / Division of Litton Industries

Introduction

FOR THE SOME $2\frac{1}{2}$ million years that man has inhabited the earth, he has, as previous selections described, extracted his livelihood from earth's lands and waters. During his early history, his impact on the earth was scarcely felt. He was in many ways simply a part of the ecosystem he inhabited, utilizing a small share of its energy input and utilizing and recycling its materials. As his numbers increased and his culture and technology changed, he found it impossible to exist within the framework of mature natural ecosystems. They provided neither sufficient food for a growing population nor sufficient resources. So man simplified ecosystems, destroying the natural ones and replacing them with more or less artificial, young, highly productive systems that provided him with the energy and nutrient resources he desired. Improved technology, new discoveries, and urbanization encouraged, if not forced, man to seek new sources of raw materials to improve or continue his way of life. He began to extract more and more from the environment and to produce more by-products and wastes.

So long as his numbers were relatively small in relation to the total environment available, his wastes and even his extractive processes produced little more than local effects. The water, the land, and the air seemed able to absorb the wastes and the abuse. The wastes man poured into the water were diluted and purified before the same waters had to be used by settlements further downstream. The burning of fossil fuels created local air pollution problems, but the gases and particulates became well dispersed over the countryside. As cities grew, more sewage emptied into waterways, more carbon and sulfur poured into the atmosphere, and conditions gradually worsened. To provide the needs of industry, ore and fuel had to be extracted from the earth, degrading the landscape. As technology created new products and processes, toxic chemicals and nondegradable solid wastes began to pollute both land and water. Plants, animals and even ecosystems were unable to adapt to the changes.

Unknown, unnoticed, or ignored by man, environmental problems began to accumulate. Local problems of pollution have become global problems in the latter half of the twentieth century. It was not just the air over Pittsburgh or New York, London or Tokyo, that was polluted, or the Thames or Hudson River. Also polluted were air over regions remote from cities and industry and waters of the high seas. The problem of global pollution, of total environmental degradation, seemed to appear overnight. It did not, of course; it is the accumulation of pollution problems that developed over the ages.

Now man is suddenly realizing that he has fouled his own nest, that he is destroying his own habitat, and that in so doing he is destroying myriads of living things. He has changed or destroyed ecological systems to his own detriment; he has decreased the productivity of many parts of the earth; he has caused the death and extinction of many forms of life; he has allowed toxic substances to accumulate in ecosystems to a point where they threaten his own life. And as Lewis Mumford writes, "Modern man . . . is bringing into existence an environment degraded by garbage dumps, auto cemeteries, slag heaps, nuclear piles, superhighways and mega-structural conglomerates—all destined to be architecturally homogenized into a planetary Megalopolis."[1]

Part V examines in some detail what man has done to his habitat. It looks at the problem of pesticides, water pollution, air pollution, land pollution, radiation dangers, and it examines what these have done to global ecosystems.

One type of pollution is not included: noise, variously defined as "unwanted sound" or "vibrational energy out of control." But noise must be considered, if only briefly, for it is destructive to man's well-being and to man's environment in ways we are only beginning to realize. The controversy over supersonic planes and their effect on the environment reflects this growing concern.

As a pollutant, noise is unique. It is not persistent; it is not cumulative, nor is it transported great distances. But like other pollutants, it is a product of technology. Noise, as a nuisance, is growing at an accelerating rate,

---

[1] Lewis Mumford, *The Myth of the Machine: The Pentagon of Power*, New York, Harcourt Brace Jovanovich, 1970.

especially in the United States, the noisiest nation in the world. Noise surrounds us in the home: the radio, the TV, the air conditioner, the dishwasher, the electric sweeper, the blender, the electric mixer. Outside the house there are lawn mowers, minibikes, cars and trucks on highways, aircraft overhead and airports. At work there are all sorts of occupational noises: copying machines, electric typewriters, factory equipment.

Noise damages our health and lowers the quality of life. It can cause temporary or permanent damage to the ears, provoke emotions, increase irritability, and cause loss of sleep. It prevents us from enjoying our surroundings, the songs of birds, a walk in the woods, a quiet evening on the lake.

But what of the effect of rising noise levels on the physical environment as such? This effect is almost totally unexplored. Of special environmental concern are supersonic planes. A supersonic plane would fly at a speed of about 1700 miles an hour. It would create a continuous sonic boom over a forty- to fifty-mile area below the plane's flight path during the interval of time it is flying above the speed of sound. Multiply that figure by the length of the flight and you get some idea of the magnitude of the area that would be covered by the sonic boom. Sonic booms have triggered rock slides, damaged buildings, and disturbed, startled, and annoyed nearly everyone within the flight path. What effect a continuous boom produced daily would have on human life, not to mention animal and plant life, or what effect it would have on the marine life over which it would occur, are unanswered questions. Apparently many nations do not wish to find out: they are banning the planes from flying over their land or landing in their countries.

Selection 22

Activity of DDT

Commentary

Although the term *pesticide* is usually equated with DDT and organochloride hydrocarbons, it has a much broader meaning. It covers all chemical compounds used by man to kill or control plants and animals, including herbicides used as weed killers and defoliants, fungicides, insecticides, rodenticides, and others.

All pesticides, and there are some 200 different kinds in use, have some certain characteristics. They are highly toxic and have been compounded and used by man to kill some form of living organism. To achieve this kill, man habitually uses them in quantities far in excess of that needed to kill the pest. Pesticides are generally brought into use when the population of some unwanted species is high. The action against the pest is not density related—the effectiveness of the kill is not influenced by the size of the population. Pesticides are nonspecific—they do not kill one species only. At best they kill species restricted to one taxon, or group; at worst they eliminate many different species as well as the pest. Thus, spraying a field for weevils can also destroy bees. Although pesticides may be directed against very few wild species, their effects are felt in a wide number of plants and animals against which the pesticides are not directed.

Agricultural and medical science and the chemical industry assume a direct relationship between pesticide and pest. Any other effects are regarded as side effects, which is a rather euphemistic way of admitting, but not really saying, that the true relationship is that of pesticides to the ecosystem in which the pest occurs.

The pesticide can react in two ways. It can kill the organism directly, especially the pest. But in the process it can also remove one species from the web of energy flow in the ecosystem and in so doing can eliminate the source of food for another higher link in the food chain. More importantly the nonspecificity of the pesticide often results in the elimination of predators, parasites, and competitors of the undesirable species, and the pest against which the control was directed might resurge in even greater numbers.[1,2]

However effective the pesticide may be, it rarely kills all the individuals of the population. Some may occupy microhabitats where the pesticide cannot penetrate. Or they may possess some behavior pattern that reduces their contact with the spray. Others carry within them a genetic constitution that makes them resistant to the effects of the spray. They were, in effect, preadapted to organochloride sprays. With less resistant members of the population removed, and with the resistant individuals now comprising the breeding population, a strain unaffected by the spray rapidly evolves. A new and more powerful spray is then called for to combat that species of pest.

The pesticide can build up in the organism and produce a change in the metabolic efficiency or alter the behavior of a species, the consequences of which may be greater than the death of individuals. The latter effects can result in evolution of a resistant strain, the former in the slow extinction of a species.

Organochloride pesticides are highly persistent and resistant to biological degradation. Relatively insoluble in water, they cling to plant tissues or accumulate in the soil or in the bottom mud of ponds, lakes, and streams. From there pesticides follow the mineral cycle. The pesticide is either ingested by the plant feeders from the plant, or in the case of fish and aquatic invertebrates may be absorbed directly from the water. The pesticide is further concentrated as it is passed from the herbivorous to the carnivorous level of the food chain. Each step ingests and concentrates a much heavier dose than the previous one. For example, in a food chain studied by Woodwell, Wurster, and Isaacson,[3] DDT was present in the algae Cladophera, which contained 0.80 ppm (parts per million). This was grazed upon by the fluke that contained 1.28 ppm of DDT. The fluke in turn were eaten by cormorants that accumulated 26.4 ppm in their tissues. Quantities as high as 99 ppm have been found in the breast muscles of healthy herring gulls[4] and 2800 ppm in the fatty tissue of bald eagles. Thus, chlorinated

---

[1]R. C. Muir, "The Effect of Sprays on the Fauna of Apple Trees," *J. Applied Ecology* **2**, 1965, pp. 31–41, 43–57.

[2]G. R. Conway, "Pests Follow the Chemicals in the Cocoa of Malaysia," *Natural History* **78**(2), 1969, pp. 46–51.

[3]G. M. Woodwell, C. F. Wurster, P. A. Isaacson, "DDT Residues in an East Coast Estuary: A Case of Biological Concentration of a Persistent Insecticide," *Science* **156**, 1967, pp. 821–823.

[4]G. M. Woodwell, "Toxic Substances and Ecological Cycles," *Sci. Amer.* **216**(3), 1967, pp. 24–31.

hydrocarbons, especially DDT, which metabolizes to DDE and DDD,[5] are concentrated in successive trophic levels with the carnivores containing the greatest amount.

The pesticides once ingested or absorbed through the integument enter the metabolic pathway. Part is eliminated and part is stored in body fat, material in which it is highly soluble. So long as the animal has no need for the fat reserves, the pesticide as far as is known has little effect on the body, but when the fat reserves are utilized, particularly during the migratory or reproductive periods, then the "side effects" show up. Migratory birds may die, growth rates may be inhibited, and reproduction may be impaired.

Some pesticides, especially DDT, seem to be attracted to the reproductive cells. DDT concentrates in the eggs and spermatozoa of oysters.[6] It does likewise in the eggs of fish, greatly increasing the mortality of young fish hatching from them.[7] The spectacular decline of predatory birds, especially the peregrine falcons,[8] ospreys,[9] bald eagles,[10] and pelicans[11] has been associated with the decreases in eggshell thickness and weight of the egg, seemingly caused by some interference of DDT with calcium metabolism in the birds.[12,13] Thin-shelled eggs increase the eating of eggs by parents and the breakage of eggs. Other effects appear to be the decreased size of the clutch and the increased mortality of the embryos.

This relationship between DDT, eggshell thickness, and the decline of certain birds has been based on field evidence rather than on laboratory data. It remained only a hypothesis until 1970, when Dr. Joel Bitman, of the U.S. Department of Agriculture Hormone Physiology Laboratory, published the results of his carefully controlled experiments on the effects of DDT on hormonal and enzymatic activity of the animal body, particularly birds. His results confirm the hypothesis that among birds certain levels of DDT do cause thin eggshells and a decreased number of eggs laid. Dr. Bitman's paper differs somewhat from others in this volume. I include it because it gives insight into how scientists can approach a problem to confirm a hypothesis, and because by its very results it indicates that many of the pollutants now pouring into our environment may have serious effects on metabolism that are still unrecognized.

DDT is indeed the culprit in the decline of our colorful birds of prey. Even if DDT and similar pesticides are totally banned now, they will continue to damage ecosystems for a long time to come. DDT is highly persistent and global in its distribution. N. W. Moore[14] estimates that perhaps 1 million tons of DDT are now concentrated and/or stored in the earth's surface. Some 50,000 tons are being used annually in the world for malaria and pest control. Man's body contains upwards of 12 ppm of DDT, apparently the maximum that can be stored, with the excess eliminated metabolically. Before DDT is completely degraded, which may take well over a decade assuming use is stopped now, many birds in the upper trophic levels will be extinct. What effect the concentration of DDT will have in man over a period of time is anyone's guess.

[5]C. M. Menzie, *Metabolism of Pesticides*, Spec. Sci. Rept. Wildlife No. 127, U.S. Bureau of Sport Fisheries and Wildlife, Washington, D.C., 1969.

[6]P. A. Butler, "The Problem of Pesticides in Estuaries," in *A Symposium on Estuarine Fisheries*, Spec. Publ. No. 3, *Transactions American Fisheries Society*. 1966.

[7]G. E. Burdick, E. J. Harris, H. J. Dean, T. M. Walker, J. Skea and D. Colby, "The Accumulation of DDT in Lake Trout and the Effect on Reproduction," *Transactions American Fisheries Society* **93**, 1964, pp. 127—136.

[8]D. A. Ratcliffe, "Population Trends of the Peregrine Falcon in Great Britain," in J. J. Hickey (ed.), *Peregrine Falcon Populations, Their Biology and Decline*, Madison, Wis., University of Wisconsin Press, 1969.

[9]P. L. Ames, "DDT Residues in the Eggs of the Osprey in the North-Eastern United States and Their Relation to Nesting Success," *J. Applied Ecology* **3**(Suppl.), 1966, pp. 87—97.

[10]Lucille F. Stickel and R. G. Heath, "Effects of Pesticides on Birds of Prey," in *The Effects of Pesticides on Fish and Wildlife*, USDI Fish and Wildlife Service Circular 226, 1965, pp. 3—17.

[11]J. O. Keith, L. A. Woods Jr. and E. G. Hunt, "Reproductive Failure in Brown Pelicans," *Transactions North American Wildlife Conference*, **35**, 1970, pp. 56—63.

[12]J. J. Hickey and D. W. Anderson, "Chlorinated Hydrocarbons and Eggshell Changes in Raptorial and Fish Eating Birds," *Science* **162**, 1968, pp. 271—273.

[13]L. J. Blus, "Measurements of Brown Pelican Eggshells from Florida to South Carolina," *BioScience* **20**, 1970, pp. 867—869.

[14]N. W. Moore, "A Synopsis of the Pesticide Problem," in J. B. Cragg (ed.), *Advances in Ecological Research*, vol. 4, New York, Academic Press, 1967, pp. 75—129.

Selection 22

Hormonal and Enzymatic Activity of DDT

by Joel Bitman

The strengths of DDT are also its weaknesses. In other words, the problems currently being encountered with DDT are inherent in its advantages.

First, it has a wide spectrum of action and is extremely potent. But this characteristic also poses a problem, since DDT also affects many living things besides insects.

Second, DDT is easy to manufacture and therefore is cheap—about 17 cents a pound. This factor has resulted in widespread and somewhat indiscriminate use.

A third advantage of DDT as an insecticide is its prolonged stability. Its environmental half-life is 15 to 20 years, and a major portion remains in the upper soil layers. This extreme persistence is also one of its hazards. It has been estimated that there is now 1 billion pounds of DDT in the biosphere.[1]

A fourth advantage of DDT is an apparently low mammalian toxicity. Few people or mammals are killed outright by DDT. Yet it is this characteristic that has, in a way, contributed indirectly to the dearth of knowledge about its sublethal effects over a long period of time on man, plants, and animals.

It was this fourth advantage/disadvantage and several associated factors that led the staff of USDA's Pioneering Research Laboratory in Hormone Physiology to initiate research on DDT. Earlier research had shown a marked similarity between the geometry of the DDT molecule and the synthetic estrogen, diethylstilbestrol. This finding in turn prompted investigations of the estrogenic activity of DDT in mammals and birds. But the studies have yielded conflicting results. Because the research

of the Hormone Physiology Laboratory has, for some years, involved the biochemical and physiological effects of estrogens, our staff was quite well prepared to determine in detail the estrogenic activity of DDT.

DDT AND THE MAMMALIAN UTERUS

Estrogenic activity can be followed by using the uterus as a target tissue for estrogen—the female hormone. The uterus responds by growing; it increases in weight, in water content, and in carbohydrate, RNA and DNA. By using an immature female rat at 22 days of age, long before any estrogen is produced by the rat, we have sensitive biological tissue with which we can measure estradiol or any estrogenic compound, such as o,p'-DDT.[2]

Previous studies have yielded both positive and negative evidence of estrogenicity. In 1952, Fisher et al. (8)[3] tested their working hypothesis of an estrogen by using DDT and its analogs, methoxychlor and 2,2-bis (p-hydroxyphenyl), 1,1,1-trichloroethane. DDT and methoxychlor were not able to produce estrus, but the di hydroxy compound did.

The conflicting results continued. In a three-generation test in rats, DDT produced no significant effects upon number of pregnancies, litter weight, or litter number. But during the suckling period, DDT had an adverse effect upon mortality of the young (18).

Results in mice were also inconsistent. Deichmann and Keplinger (6) found an adverse effect of DDT on several aspects of fertility and reproduction. Another group, however, found that technical DDT produced some trends

THIS SELECTION is reprinted with permission of the author and publisher from *Agricultural Science Review*, Vol. 7, No. 4, pp. 6–12. Published by the U.S. Department of Agriculture.

[1]This figure, proposed by ecologist G. M. Woodwell, is purely an estimate. Presumably it is based on manufacturers' production records during the past two decades and the measurement of DDT stability. Since 1949, the United States alone has produced more than 2 billion pounds of DDT.

[2]Abbreviations: p,p'-DDT, 1,1,1-trichloro-2,2, bis(p-chlorophenyl) ethane; o,p'-DDT, 1,1,1-trichloro-2-(o-chlorophenyl)-2-(p-chlorophenyl) ethane; p,p'-DDD, 1,1-dichloro-2,2-bis(p-chlorophenyl) ethane.

[3]Italic numbers in parenthesis refer to Literature Cited, p. 254.

which were not significantly different from controls (*19*).

A report at the 1968 Federation Meetings by Levin, Welch and Conney (*12*) provided results which offered a possible explanation of the existing differences in the published literature. They found that o,p'-DDT and technical DDT exhibited estrogenic activity in immature female rats while p,p'-DDT showed only weak activity. Since technical DDT contains about 80 percent p,p'-DDT and 15—20 percent o,p'-DDT, the activity of the technical product can be ascribed to the presence of the o,p'-isomer.

On this bases, investigations using pure p,p'-DDT might demonstrate no estrogenic effects while studies with technical DDT might yield other results. And since technical DDT, containing both isomers, is the commercial product which is universally used as the pesticide, an estrogenic action of the ortho-para isomer takes on great significance for mammals, fish, and birds.

The initial work at our laboratory began by comparing the time course of effects of DDT isomers (o,p'-DDT and p,p'-DDT) with 17β-estradiol on several biochemical constituents of the immature rat uterus. Glycogen, an extremely sensitive indicator of estrogen action (*1*), increased after o,p'-DDT administration in a manner very similar to 17β-estradiol (fig. 1), while p,p'-DDT exhibited only slight activity. The o,p'-DDT stimulated characteristic estrogenic responses in the uterus—increases in wet weight, water content, and RNA content 24 hours after administration being similar to those elicited by estradiol.

Using the glycogen response at 18 hours to establish a dose response curve for o,p'-DDT, we found that 6 mg of o,p'-DDT gave a maximal glycogen response and the minimal effective single dose of o,p'-DDT was 0.4 mg. When we examined the route of administration, we found that 6 mg of o,p'-DDT gave a maximal were as effective as subcutaneous injection in rats.

Our tests showed that MER-25[4] inhibits the estradiol glycogen response and is almost equally effective in reducing the o,p'-DDT response. The antibiotic actinomycin D has been widely used to inhibit protein synthesis and inhibits the RNA increase which estrogen induces in the uterus. In our tests, the RNA

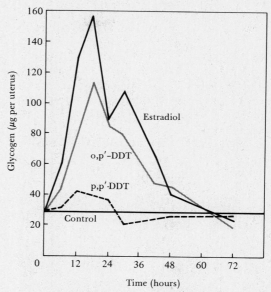

Figure 1. Glycogenic response of immature rat uterus to DDT isomers and 17β-estradiol. Four milligrams of o,p'-DDT or p,p'-DDT, or 0.4 mg of 17β-estradiol, was injected subcutaneously at 0 time. Each point consists of determinations of 4 to 14 uteri of 22- to 25-day-old rats; the control level was established by use of 70 rat uteri. Glycogen was determined by the anthrone procedure.

increase which o,p'-DDT induces was also blocked by treatment with actinomycin D.

These results were all obtained by administering a single dose of a rather large amount of o,p'-DDT. The amount of estradiol or diethylstilbestrol which will bring about the same type of estrogenic response is about 10^{-4} of this amount of o,p'-DDT. We were interested in determining what lower level of DDT contamination in the diet, on a continual feeding basis, would be necessary to produce a definite estrogenic effect. Although these experiments are not fully completed, rates of 1,000 ppm and 500 ppm of o,p'-DDT in the diet are estrogenic and cause the vagina of immature rats to open early. In another study, 50 μg of o,p'-DDT per day given to immature rats caused the vagina to open early while p,p'-DDT did not.

DDT AND THE AVIAN OVIDUCT

In 1950 Burlington and Lindeman (*5*) injected DDT into White Leghorn cockerel chicks from 8 days of age to 89 days. After 25 days, the comb and wattles were much smaller than controls.

---

[4]MER-25 is 1-(p-2-diethylaminoethoxyphenyl)-1-phenyl-2-p-methoxyphenyl ethanol.

249

When the birds were killed, the testes of the DDT-treated birds were only $\frac{1}{6}$ the size of the controls, suggesting that DDT exerted an estrogen-like action. In a later report, however, they found no significant differences in red cell numbers, hemoglobin, blood sugar, plasma proteins, plasma calcium, phosphorus, fibrinogen or prothrombin time in DDT and control birds.

DeWitt (7) at the Patuxent Wildlife Refuge showed some effects of 200 ppm of DDT upon reproduction in quail. In a later report, he found little effect at a 100-ppm level on egg production and fertility but found that chick survival was reduced. Pheasants appeared to be more sensitive to DDT.

Woodwell (20) and Wurster and Wingate (22) have determined DDT residues in a number of species of bird and have implicated contamination by insecticides as a probable major cause of the decline in reproduction in several species. In view of the estrogenicity of o,p'-DDT in the uterus of a mammalian species, it was of interest to determine whether sublethal concentrations of this isomer of DDT would have an effect upon the oviduct, the reproductive tract of avian species (2).

In experiments with chickens at our laboratory, a single dose of o,p'-DDT, even up to 400 mg, would not stimulate the oviduct in 24 hours. Chickens are able to handle a great quantity of o,p'-DDT if given subcutaneously or orally. But if given by intraperitoneal injection and given repeatedly, the oviduct will respond to the o,p' isomer. Three daily doses of 50 mg of o,p'-DDT doubled oviduct weight—from 65 to 122 mg—and more than doubled glycogen content. p,p'-DDT had no effect. Experiments with Japanese quail produced a very similar effect; o,p'-DDT doubled oviduct weight and tripled oviducal glycogen.

One possible hypothesis for an action of o,p'-DDT, in contrast to p,p', is that the o,p' isomer might accumulate to a greater extent and exert an estrogenic action because of this preferential uptake. We examined this possibility by determining the pesticide content of rat, chicken, and quail tissues after 4 days of pesticide treatment. In rats, o,p'-DDT was found to accumulate to a much lesser extent than p,p'-DDT, by a factor of 5 to 8.

In chickens and quail, the accumulation of o,p'-DDT was similar to the p,p' accumulation, indicating that no selective accumulation took place. It was concluded that the estrogenic activity of o,p'-DDT was associated with the o,p'-DDT molecule or a metabolite or impurity rather than any preferential uptake of the compound as compared to p,p'-DDT.

STRUCTURE ACTIVITY RELATIONSHIPS

Since the physio-chemical basis for estrogenic activity is still not known, we became interested in learning whether the estrogenic activity of the o,p'-isomer has important implications for the mechanism of estrogen action. The exact nature of the active estrogen structure arising from o,p'-DDT—if it is not o,p'-DDT itself—might provide important theoretical information about the spatial configuration of an active estrogen. Schueler (17) had proposed that a large, rigid molecule with the same spatial characteristics as diethylstilbestrol would be estrogenic. Although p,p'-DDT comes fairly close to the proper measurements, o,p'-DDT is much too short.

This problem was approached in a largely empirical way. By having a similar spatial or molecular configuration, DDT or an analog might occupy receptors in reproductive organs and tissues and thereby exert direct estrogen action. We used the 18-hour glycogen response in the immature rat and determined the presence or lack of estrogenic activity in a series of DDT analogs and in a series of structurally related compounds, which had halogen or other substituted atoms. The information gleaned for this study may provide a link to the nature of the chemical structure that induces estrogenic response.

About 50 compounds have already been tested. Nine of these compounds have been positive; all are diphenylmethane compounds and are not dibenzyl or stilbene structures. All were active at a 4-mg dose; several of them seemed to be active at much lower concentrations. This research will continue.

THE THIN-EGGSHELL THEORY

Much has been written about the effects of DDT on wild bird species. Declines in populations of some species have been linked to increased levels of DDT and other pesticides in the environment. The problem here, however, is whether the relationship is a causal one or a casual one, which statistically would be a nonsense correlation.

That some birds species have declined since the introduction of DDT is, of course, a documented fact—although it is known that similar declines have occurred among both avian and mammalian species long before the use of pesticides. Presently, decreases are occurring mainly in predatory birds that eat fish or small mammals: bald eagles, osprey, peregrine falcons, sparrow hawks, kestrels, herring gulls, and Bermuda petrel. The decline in these bird populations is assumed to be due to greater shell breakage, because of eggs with thinner shells.

The basis for the thin-eggshell theory originated primarily in two studies. In 1967 Ratcliffe (15) examined blown eggs of 3 British species—the peregrine falcon, sparrowhawk and the golden eagle—which had been collected from 1900 to 1966. He plotted time versus an index of eggshell thickness. He noted a decrease in eggshell weight, which he contended was correlated to exposure of the eggs to persistent organic chemicals. Ratcliffe based his conclusion solely on the fact that pesticides were becoming more prevalent in the environment.

In 1968 Hickey and Anderson (9) examined eggshell weight and thickness in 1,729 blown eggs that had been collected from 1880 to 1967. These eggs were in museums and private collections, and in 30 percent of the eggs they were able to insert a micrometer to measure shell thickness directly. They found a decrease of 19 percent in peregrine falcon shell weight in the 1947–52 period. Hickey and Anderson also collected eggs from 5 herring gull colonies in 5 different states and analyzed the eggs for DDE and measured the shell thickness. They found a high correlation between DDE content and thinner eggshells.

Thus, from these two studies, came the hypothesis that eggshell thickness is affected by certain chlorinated hydrocarbons.

Acting on the decision that such a hypothesis needed to be tested directly, we began a study in which o,p'-DDT and p,p'-DDT were incorporated into the diet of Japanese quail (3).

Birds were divided into 3 groups—controls, o,p'- and p,p'-DDT. Birds in the control group received *ad libitum* a chick starter diet of low calcium content, which provided a calcium stress during egg laying. The o,p'-DDT and p,p'-DDT groups received the same diet modi-

fied by the addition of 100 ppm of the pesticide.

Eggs were collected daily for a 45-day experimental period and the presence of broken eggs was recorded. During this period, 1,020 eggs were collected.

Egg production, egg weight, eggshell thickness, eggshell calcium, bone calcium, blood calcium, bird weight, and pesticide residues in the eggs, liver, and lipid—all were measured. We determined calcium by atomic absorption analysis after wet ashing of eggshells and bone. Pesticide residues were determined by gas chromatography. Eggshell thickness was measured at 3 places at the waist of each egg with a micrometer, after removing the shell membranes. The beta backscatter method of James and Retzer (10) was used to study the relationship between eggshell thickness and backscatter.

The o,p'- and p,p'-DDT diets produced a lag in egg production during the 1st half of the experiment (fig. 2). During the last half of the experiment there was little difference in num-

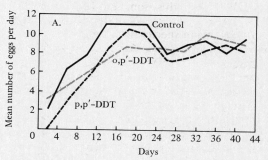

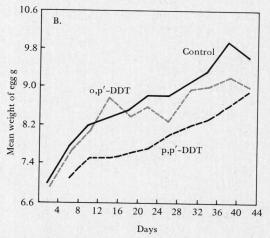

Figure 2. (A) Effect of DDT on egg production. (B) Effect of DDT on egg weight.

bers of eggs produced. This lag suggested a lag in ovulation in these groups and a delay in ovulation produced by p,p'-DDT has been reported by Jefferies in the Bengalese finch (11). Eggs produced by birds on the p,p'-DDT diet were significantly smaller than those produced on either the o,p' or control diet.

The p,p'-DDT diet produced a great number of broken eggs—15.6 percent as compared to 11.1 percent in the control group. Individual egg-laying records of the birds showed that most of the broken eggs were coming from a few birds. The quail responsible for producing most of the broken eggs were classified as susceptible, but the o,p'- and p,p'-groups had 5 and 6 birds producing broken eggs.

Eggs from the o,p'- and p,p'-groups were significantly lower in percent of shell calcium and had thinner shells than eggs in the control group. In these experiments broken eggs which fell through the screen floors to the pans below the cages were not recovered. It is very likely that these broken eggs would have had thinner shells and lower calcium contents. Accordingly, there is a bias in the data, and the decreases observed would probably have been greater if all eggs had been recovered and measured.

Individual egg-laying records also showed what was happening as successive eggs were laid in a clutch. Typically, quail and chickens lay an egg 1 day, another on the next day, another on the third day, another on the 4th day, and so on. Then there may be a break of a day or two and egg laying resumes. The group of eggs laid successively is called a clutch, and can consist of a 2-egg clutch, 3-egg clutch, 4-egg clutch, and so on. Egg-laying records showed a decrease in thickness and in percent shell calcium in the o,p'- and p,p,'-DDT groups as successive eggs were laid, and only a slight decrease in control eggs. At the end of a clutch, during the nonlaying interval, the bird restores the drain on the calcium balance and the first egg of the next clutch has a higher shell-calcium content and a thicker shell. Pooling of all data tends to mask this effect and calculation of group means reflects only part of the calcium decline.

Regression lines for the o,p'- and p,p'-DDT groups were significantly different from the control regression lines and exhibited 10 to 20 percent decreases in percent shell calcium as clutch size increased. Also, eggshell thickness decreased as clutch size increased.

Blood calcium concentrations were deter-mined on the birds at the end of the experiment. No significant differences in the three groups were noted.

Although o,p'- and p,p'-DDT were fed at the same rate, approximately 20 times more p,p' was accumulated than o,p'. The liver of the p,p'-group had 1,400 ppm compared to only 56 ppm of o,p' in the o,p'-group. These results suggest a much greater metabolism and excretion of o,p'-DDT than p,p'. In spite of the relatively low body or egg burden of o,p'-DDT compared to p,p'-DDT, the two compounds were equally effective in reducing eggshell thickness. This suggests that toxicological effects are more closely related to intake than to body or egg burden.

Relatively low amounts of p,p'-DDE were found in the bird tissues and eggs. Only about 10 percent of the total pesticide residue was p,p'-DDE. Several bird investigators have reported that p,p'-DDE usually makes up 80—90 percent of the total pesticide residues found in environmentally collected avian samples. The explanation for this difference probably lies in three factors: (1) our relatively short-term experiment; (2) immediate workup and (3) no prior conversion of DDT to DDE by the environment.

The experiment we conducted confirms in a direct way the previously reported correlative evidence of Ratcliffe and Hickey and Anderson that DDT induces a decrease in eggshell calcium. Although the dietary levels used in our experiments were high and seed-eating birds would probably never encounter DDT concentrations of this magnitude, there is evidence in the literature that carnivorous birds have been exposed to extremely high DDT concentrations. Riseborough (16) had reported total DDT accumulation levels of 5,000 and 2,600 ppm in the lipid of North American falcons— considerably above the 1,500 ppm in our study. These higher residue levels suggest that predatory birds in the field are exposed to body burdens of DDT which could readily exert the adverse effects upon calcium metabolism and eggshell thickness which we demonstrated in the laboratory.

MECHANISM OF DDT ACTION

The mechanism by which DDT exerts its effect upon eggshell calcium is one of the most interesting problems of the DDT picture. Several possible modes of action have been suggested.

1. Stimulation of liver enzymes which degrade steroids necessary for calcification resulting in an upset in hormonal balance.
2. Inhibition of medullary bone deposition —the primary source of calcium during eggshell formation.
3. Inhibition of the parathyroid gland .
4. Inhibition of the thyroid gland.
5. Inhibition of calcium absorption from the gut.
6. Inhibition of carbonic anhydrase activity in the avian shell-forming gland.
7. Abnormal stimulation of the nervous system resulting in premature extrusion of the egg.

Not much has been published about these possible modes of action, but apparently the liver microsomal enzyme theory is the favored one at present. Peakall (14) used pigeons treated with p,p'-DDT and found that the liver microsomes formed greater amounts of polar metabolites from estradiol, testosterone, and progesterone than microsomes from untreated birds. A direct link between this finding and the calcification process has not yet been reported.

One of the approaches our laboratory has been using to determine the effect of DDT upon the liver is to measure sleeping times. The rationale for this method is the fact that essentially only the liver metabolizes barbiturates. A given dose of barbiturate will put an animal to sleep for a certain length of time. Liver metabolism eventually removes the anesthetic from the system. If liver enzymes are stimulated, the dose of barbiturate will be metabolized in a shorter period of time and the animal will be asleep for a shorter period. Conversely, if the liver enzymes are inhibited, it would take a longer time to handle this dose of barbiturate and the animal would stay asleep longer.

Because organochlorine insecticides such as DDT stimulate liver enzymes in the rat, sleeping times of DDT-treated rats are shorter than those of controls. The o,p' and p,p' isomers of DDT, DDD, and DDE were fed to immature and mature rats to determine the time course of their effect upon sleeping time. p,p'-DDT reduced sleeping time to 50 percent of control after 2 days and to 5 percent of control at 7 days. There was little further reduction at 14 days. p,p'-DDT had less effect in mature rats, reducing

sleeping time to 75, 40, and 40 percent at 2, 7, and 14 days, respectively. Body lipid residues of o,p'-DDT were only about $\frac{1}{10}$ those of p,p'-DDT.

In contrast to the shortening of sleeping time observed in rats, the DDT isomers and metabolites prolonged sleeping time in Japanese quail (4). p,p'-DDT produced the greatest prolongation of sleeping time—to over 300 percent of controls. In quail lipid, p,p'-DDE and p,p'-DDT increased linearly with increasing time on the diet. Prolongation of sleeping time, however, was not maintained although p,p'-DDE and p,p'-DDT lipid residues increased, which suggested an adaptation to this stimulus. All o,p' compounds and p,p'-DDD were metabolized rapidly and exhibited very low accumulations in quail lipid.

The prolongation of sleeping time in the quail suggests that the liver microsomal enzymes which metabolize pentobarbital were inhibited by prior DDT treatment. The data that Peakall has reported in the pigeon indicate that the liver microsomal enzyme system which metabolizes steroids was stimulated. Although these systems usually go together, there is a dissociation of effects here.

FUTURE RESEARCH ON DDT

The persistence of the organochlorine compounds, especially DDT, in the environment insures their presence in biological systems for many decades even if future use is further limited by legal or scientific considerations. DDT, DDD and DDE presently account for over 50 percent of the total chemical residues present in human food. The nature of the biological effects which DDT and its metabolites produce in farm animals, birds, and man are thus problems of significant biological importance and merit continued study.

There have been a number of previous studies of the gross effects of large and near lethal amounts of DDT (13) and an extensive literature exists of a survey nature detailing the organochlorine content of animals, animal products and plant materials. It seems fair to state, however, that our information on the mechanism of action of DDT and on subtle low-level effects is still meager. This has now become a focal point of widespread concern. Since we must continue to live with these residues for some time to come, we would do well to learn as much as we can about them.

LITERATURE CITED

(1) Bitman, J., Cecil, H. C., Mench, M. L., and Wrenn, T. R., 1965, Kinetics of in vivo glycogen synthesis in the estrogen-stimulated rat uterus. Endocrinology 76, 63—69.

(2) Bitman, J., Cecil, H. C., Harris, S. J., and Fries, G. F., 1968, Estrogenic activity of o,p'-DDT in the mammalian uterus and avian oviduct. Science 162, 371—372.

(3) ———, 1969, DDT indulges a decrease in eggshell calcium. Nature 224, 44—46.

(4) ———, 1969, Comparison of DDT effects on pentobarbital metabolism by rats and quail. 158th National Am. Chem. Soc. Meeting.

(5) Burlington, H., and Lindeman, V. F., 1950, Effect of DDT on testes and secondary sex characters of white leghorn cockerels. Proc. Soc. Exp. Biol. Med. 74, 48—51.

(6) Deichmann, W. B., and Keplinger, M. L., 1966, Effect of combinations of pesticides on reproduction of mice. Toxicol. Appl. Pharmacol. 8, 337—338.

(7) DeWitt, J. B., 1955, Effects of chlorinated hydrocarbon insecticides upon quail and pheasants. J. Agr. Food Chem. 3, 672—676.

(8) Fisher, A. L., Keasling, H. H., and Schueler, F. N., 1952, Estrogenic action of some DDT analogues. Proc. Soc. Exp. Biol. Med. 81, 439—441.

(9) Hickey, J. J., and Anderson, D. W., 1968, Chlorinated hydrocarbons and eggshell changes in raptorial and fish-eating birds. Science 162, 271—273.

(10) James, P. E., and Retzer, H. J., 1967, Measuring egg shell strength by beta backscatter technique. Poultry Sci. 46, 1200—1203.

(11) Jefferies, D. J., 1967, The delay in ovulation produced by p,p'-DDT and its possible significance in the field. Ibis 109, 266—272.

(12) Levin, W., Welch, R. M., and Conney, A. H., 1968, Estrogenic action of DDT and its analogs. Fed. Proc. 27, 649.

(13) Muller, P., 1959, The insecticide dichlorodiphenyltrichloroethane and its significance. Vol. 2. Birkhauser, Basel.

(14) Peakall, D. B., 1967, Pesticide-induced enzyme breakdown of steroids in birds. Nature 216, 505—506.

(15) Ratcliffe, D. A., 1967, Decrease in eggshell weight in certain birds of prey. Nature 215, 208—210.

(16) Riseborough, R. W., Reiche, P., Peakall, D. B., Herman, S. G., and Kirven, M. N., 1968, Polychlorinated biphenyls in the global ecosystem. Nature 220, 1098.

(17) Schueler, F. W., 1946, Sex hormonal action and chemical constitution. Science 103, 221—223.

(18) Treon, F. J., Boyd, J., Berryman, F., Gosney, J., Hartman, L., Brown, D., and Coomer, J., 1954, Final report. Kettering Laboratory, Univ. of Cincinnati, College of Medicine.

(19) Ware, G. W., and Good, E. E., 1967, Effects of insecticides on reproduction in the laboratory mouse. Toxicol. Appl. Pharmacol. 10, 54—61.

(20) Woodwell, G. M., 1967, Toxic substances and ecological cycles. Sci. Amer. 216, 24—36.

(21) Woodwell, G. M., Wurster, C. F., Jr., and Isaacson, P. A., 1967, DDT residues in an east coast estuary: a case of biological concentration of a persistent insecticide. Science 156, 821—823.

(22) Wurster, C. F., Jr., and Wingate, D. B., 1968, DDT residues and declining reproduction in the Bermuda petrel. Science 159, 979—981.

Effects of Land Use
on Water Resources

Commentary

As the title of the following selection suggests, a very close relationship exists between land and water, between terrestrial and aquatic ecosystems. Primarily through the water cycle one feeds upon the other. The water that falls on the land runs from the surface or percolates through the soil and deeper layers of the earth to enter springs, streams, lakes, estuaries, and oceans. The water carries with it silt and nutrients in solution, all of which enrich aquatic ecosystems. Of late, man has been adding considerably more to the material interchange than occurs under natural conditions. Agriculture, road construction, and building have added incalculable tons of silt, which have clogged rivers and streams and filled lakes, dams, and estuaries. Man has added a heavy load of nutrients, especially nitrogen, phosphorus, and organic matter from sewage and industrial effluents. He has poured in thousands of different chemicals and wastes, including pesticides, which natural ecosystems are ill-adapted to handle.

One of the outcomes has been excessive nutrient enrichment of our waterways. Because of it a term once only in the vocabulary of ecologists, *eutrophication*, is becoming commonplace. *Eutrophic* means well nourished, and *eutrophication* refers to the natural or artificial addition of nutrients to lakes, streams, and estuaries and to the effects of the added nutrients.

In classical limnology natural eutrophication is considered an aging process. Inflowing waters carry silt, which builds up bottom sediments and fills in the basins of lakes and estuaries. Nutrients carried in from surrounding watersheds stimulate the growth of phytoplankton. The increased production of phytoplankton increases total biological productivity and gradually causes major changes in the lake. Phytoplankton, one-celled algae, become concentrated in the upper layer of water or epilimnion, giving the water a murky green cast. This turbidity reduces light penetration and restricts biological productivity to the surface waters. Zooplankton feed on phytoplankton and bits of organic matter and they in turn become food for fish. Algae as well as inflowing organic debris and the remains of rooted plants, drift to the bottom, where bacteria convert the dead matter into inorganic substances. The activity of these decomposers depletes the oxygen supply of the bottom sediments and the benthic waters to the point that the region is unable to support aerobic forms of life. The numbers and biomass of organisms are high although the diversity of species is often low.

This circumstance is in contrast to oligotrophy, or poor nourishment. Oligotrophic lakes are relatively impoverished in nutrients, especially nitrogen and phosphorus, and the nutrients normally added by inflow are quickly taken up by the phytoplankton. The density of algal growth is low, and light easily penetrates to considerable depth. The water is clear and appears blue to blue-green in the sunlight. The oxygen profile is nearly the same at all depths, and the bottom fauna are well developed. Although the number of organisms may be low, the diversity of species is high. Fish life is dominated by members of the salmon family.

When nutrients in moderate amounts are added to oligotrophic lakes, they are rapidly taken up and circulated. As increasing quantities are added, the lake or pond begins to change from oligotrophic to mildly eutrophic to eutrophic conditions. This has been happening to the clear oligotrophic lakes of the world at an increasing rate.

In fact, this "galloping" eutrophication has been changing even the naturally eutrophic lakes to a hypereutrophic condition. An excessive nutrient input results from a heavy influx of wastes: raw sewage, drainage from agricultural lands, river basin development, recreational use of water, industry, run-off from urban areas, burning of fossil fuels. This accelerated enrichment has been called *cultural eutrophication*.[1]

Cultural eutrophication has produced significant biological changes in many lakes and estuaries. The tremendous increase in nutrients stimulates a dense growth of planktonic algae, dominated by the blue-green forms, and rooted aquatics in shallow water. This upsets normal food chains. The herbivores, principally grazing zooplankton, are unable to consume the bulk of the algae as they would normally. Abnormal quantities

---

[1]A. D. Hasler, "Cultural Eutrophication Is Reversible," *BioScience* **19**, 1969, pp. 425–431.

of unconsumed algae as well as the rooted aquatics die and sink to the bottom. On the bottom the aerobic decomposers are unable to reduce the organic matter to inorganic matter and perish from the depletion of oxygen. They are replaced by anaerobic organisms that only incompletely decompose the organic matter. Partially decomposed bottom sediments accumulate on the bottom, and sulfate-reducing bacteria release hydrogen sulfide that can poison benthic waters. These chemical and environmental changes cause major shifts in the plant and animal life of the affected aquatic ecosystem.

Examples are some major shifts that resulted in part from cultural eutrophication in Lake Erie.[2,3] In 1930 before it was subject to enormous quantities of pollutants, the dominant bottom organism was the burrowing mayfly *Hexagenia*. In 1961 the mayfly in the western part of the lake was virtually extinct and was replaced by tubificid worms. Between 1911 and 1963 the phytoplankton production increased significantly. Spring and fall blooms increased in intensity and duration. Dominant phytoplankton in spring bloom in western Lake Erie shifted from *Asterionella* to an exotic species, *Melospira binderana*, not reported in the United States prior to 1961. Now the dominant species, it comprises in certain areas of the lake as much as 99 percent of the total phytoplankton. In 1940 the major commercial species of fish were the cisco or lake herring, whitefish, blue pike, walleye, and yellow perch. In the past twenty-five years, the catch, still averaging 50 million tons a year, consists of yellow perch, smelt, fresh-water drum, sheepshead, white bass, and carp. The lake herring population collapsed in 1925 and the blue pike and whitefish after 1950. Apparently environmental conditions became unsuitable for reproduction. The blue pike collapse, for example, was associated with oxygen depletion and extensive changes in the bottom sediments. Only after 1952 did smelt become important in the lake fishery.

A similar and even more disastrous example of biological change can be found in many lakes.[4] These changes affect the value of water for man. Murky green water and algal scums make lakes and ponds undesirable for recreational use. Phytoplankton and products of decomposition impart unsatisfactory flavor to the water and interfere with its proper treatment. The rotting mass of vegetation and the die-off of fish create objectionable odors.

Cultural eutrophication has been attributed largely to the increase of nitrates and phosphorus added to the water from many sources. Both are important, but of the two, phosphorus is considered the most important because it is an element naturally in short supply. Because the principle sources of phosphorus are human sewage (each human produces about 1.5 to 4 pounds per year), agricultural drainage (each cow produces about 1.5 pounds per year), and detergents, some consideration is being given to its removal from sewage plant effluents.[5] The phosphorus is readily precipitated by the addition of ferric chloride, slaked lime, or aluminum sulfate to the inflow or outflow of final settling tanks.

Recent research, however, has suggested that carbon dioxide rather than phosphorus may be the major cause of cultural eutrophication. In 1967 a paper by Willy Lange appeared in *Nature*.[6] He advanced the thesis, based on his own experimental work, that algae exist in mutualistic association with bacteria. Algae use the carbon dioxide and sunlight to produce organic matter and oxygen. Bacteria utilize the oxygen to break down the organic matter and produce carbon dioxide. In the presence of a large amount of organic matter, bacteria release large amounts of carbon dioxide available for algal growth. This theory was further supported by work done by a plant physiologist, Pat Kerr, working for the Federal Water Quality Administration. As a result, there are two polarized views concerning the major cause of cultural eutrophication.[7] Both sides agree that for growth, algae need carbon dioxide, which can be limiting, phosphorus, and nitrogen, and that a symbiotic relationship does exist between algae and bacteria. The carbon school argues that carbon dioxide controls growth; that only small amounts of phosphorus are needed for algae blooms; that phosphorus is recycled and rapidly made available during periodic die-offs of algae; that massive blooms occur even when dissolved phosphorus is low; that a severe reduction in phosphorus will not halt algal growth; and that carbon dioxide diffused from the atmosphere cannot provide the carbon necessary for heavy algal growth.

The phosphorus school, on the other hand, argues that no matter how much carbon dioxide is present,

[2]A. M. Beeton, "Eutrophication of the St. Lawrence Great Lakes," *Limnology and Oceanography* **10**, 1965, pp. 240–254.
[3]A. M. Beeton, "Changes in the Environment and Biota of the Great Lakes," in *Eutrophication Causes, Consequences, Correctives*, National Academy of Sciences, Washington, D. C., 1969, pp. 150–187.
[4]W. T. Edmondson, "Eutrophication in North America," in *Eutrophication Causes, Consequences, Correctives*, National Academy of Sciences, Washington, D.C., 1969, pp. 124–149.
[5]G. A. Rohlich, "Engineering Aspects of Nutrient Removal," in *Eutrophication, Causes, Consequences, Correctives*, National Academy of Sciences, Washington, D.C., 1969, pp. 371–382.
[6]W. Lange, "Effect of Carbohydrates on the Symbiotic Growth of Planktonic Blue-Green Algae with Bacteria," *Nature* **215**, pp. 1277–1278.
[7]D. H. M. Bower, "The Great Phosphorus Controversy," *Environmental Science and Technology* **4**(9), 1970, pp. 725–726.

phosphorus is still needed for growth; that phosphorus concentrations are low during algal blooms because most of the phosphorus is incorporated in the algae; that recycling is ineffficient and much of the phosphorus is lost in the bottom sediments; that while bacteria produce carbon dioxide, the bulk of carbon is supplied from disassociation of the bicarbonates in solution in the water; and that a reduction of phosphorus will curtail algal production.

In many ways both are probably right. But algae blooms require other nutrients, such as sodium and potassium, and such growth substances as vitamin B_{12}. Any environmental condition such as bottom muds and suspended particulate matter which favors bacterial growth would be vitamin rich. A large source of vitamins and other growth substances, too, could encourage algal growth. Whatever the biological causes of cultural eutrophication, man is responsible for the rapid eutrophication of natural waters.

Accelerated enrichment of water resulting from man's activities raises some questions concerning eutrophication. From a developmental point of view, limnologists consider eutrophic bodies of water as mature or aged and oligotrophic lakes as young ecosystems. Natural succession is assumed to proceed from an oligotrophic to eutrophic state accompanied by a filling in of the basin and subsequent conversion to land. Yet the characteristics of oligotrophic and eutrophic bodies of water do not conform to those characteristics of young and mature ecosystems (see Selection 3 and commentary). Eutrophic lakes possess a relatively low diversity of species, a high ratio of primary production to biomass, a circulation of nutrients, and a high rate of exploitation, all characteristic of immature ecosystems. Oligotrophic bodies of water have a high diversity of species and a low ratio of production to biomass. Nutrients and tightly circulated and quantities are tied up in biomass. These are all characteristics of mature ecosystems. In addition, culturally eutrophic lakes are kept in a continuous state of immaturity by heavy influx of nutrients.

The terms *eutrophic* and *oligotrophic* were introduced by the German biologist C. A. Weber in 1907, when he applied them to the evolution of peat bogs. In his studies he found that the upper layers of the peat bogs were nutrient poor and the deeper layers reflected a much richer supply of nutrients.[8] Thus, the development of bog from a lake proceeded from a eutrophic to an oligotrophic state.[9] Somewhere and somehow the terms as used in context of lake succession became reversed. Perhaps it might be advisable to separate the terms from ecosystem development.

Lakes and other bodies of water in many ways passively exploit terrestrial ecosystems. The characteristics of streams, lakes, and estuaries are heavily influenced by their drainage basins and the sediments they receive. Thus, as Hutchison[10] suggests, it might be more useful to stop thinking in terms of eutrophic and oligotrophic *water types* and instead to consider rivers, lakes, and estuaries and their watersheds as eutrophic or oligotrophic *systems*. A northern bog lake is oligotrophic because its watershed, the terrestrial ecosystems feeding it, are nutrient poor. A lake fed by drainage from urban and agricultural watershed is eutrophic because the watershed is eutrophic. The validity of such an approach is supported by the next selection, which emphasizes how inseparable an aquatic ecosystem is from the surrounding terrestrial ecosystems that feed it.

[8]L. Provasoli, "Algal Nutrition and Eutrophication," in *Eutrophication, Causes, Consequences, Correctives*, National Academy of Sciences, Washington, D.C., 1969, pp. 574—593.

[9]W. Rodhe, "Crystallization of Eutrophication Concepts in Northern Europe," in *Eutrophication, Causes, Consequences, Correctives*, National Academy of Sciences, Washington, D.C., 1969, pp. 50—64.

[10]G. E. Hutchison, "Eutrophication, Past and Present," in *Eutrophication, Causes, Consequences, Correctives*, National Academy of Sciences, Washington, D.C., 1969, pp. 17—26.

Selection 23

Effects of Land Use on Water Resources

by W. E. Bullard

I. INTRODUCTION

The land areas included in drainage basins or watersheds constitute a source of water supplies. Rain and snow are received on the watersheds and converted into runoff or absorbed into the soil to add to groundwater. The relative amounts of conversion or absorption, the losses by evaporation and transpiration, and the quality of the water produced as streamflow depend to a considerable extent on the condition of the land that receives the precipitation. This paper describes the effects of land use on land conditon and thus on water resources.

The principal effects are those concerned with amount of surface flow, with timing and magnitude of flow maxima and minima, and with the quality of the water produced. Of these three effects, that on water quality will be the major subject for discussion. This is not to say that the effects are separable and unrelated.

HOW THE WATERSHED OPERATES

Water reaches the surface of the land as falling drops of rain, as particles of ice in sleet and hail, or as flakes of snow. Snow floats down gently and forms a blanket that melts more or less slowly. Sleet and hail are infrequent enough to be relatively insignificant and may be ignored. Although rain falls as a liquid, it usually falls in drops of sufficient mass to strike the ground with considerable impact.

If the ground is covered with a canopy of vegetation, and beneath that a layer of leaf litter over the soil surface, the raindrops are dispersed and their force is broken. They trickle slowly through the litter to the soil surface and infiltrate into the soil. Any rainfall in excess of the soil infiltration rate will run off over the surface, but will be slowed mechan- ically by the surface litter and the stems of the cover vegetation.

Rain falling on bare ground beats the soil surface, breaking down the soil aggregates and causing the fine particles to rise to the surface where they create a seal. Infiltration is reduced greatly and surface runoff greatly increased. There is no litter or interlacing of plant stems to hinder the runoff, and it is rapid. Fast-moving runoff erodes and carries away soil particles. Rills and gullies form and concentrate the runoff still more rapidly. Streamflow rises abruptly to high levels carrying a heavy load of sediment, then dwindles away rapidly when the rain stops.

Water moving from vegetated areas moves slowly, causes little or no erosion, remains fairly clear and clean, and builds up much more slowly to lesser levels than the flashy flows from barren watersheds. The soil beneath the cover remains open and receptive to infiltration and temporarily stores water for slow release to streamflow later.

On a vegetated watershed there are often rather large water losses by transpiration. There are also losses from direct evaporation of water intercepted by leaves and stems or caught in the litter. This is the price paid for protection by the cover. The only loss from the barren watershed is from evaporation of whatever amount of water may be held against gravity in the topmost foot of the soil profile. Removal of cover definitely will increase water yield from a watershed, perhaps by 20 percent; but there are two significant differences in the water produced.

From the protected watershed the flow is regulated and the water most of the time is clear and clean. From the barren watershed the runoff, except in periods of low flow, is flashy and dirty. Any gain in quantity often is made at the sacrifice of quality, and the timing of

THIS SELECTION is reprinted with permission of the author and publisher from *Journal Water Pollution Control Federation*, Vol. 38, No. 4, pp. 645—659.

the gain is such that artificial storage space is needed to take advantage of it. Storage space in the soil is not utilized fully.

Barren watersheds are not natural; the trend in nature is toward cover. Rocks break down by mechanical weathering processes to form soil particles. Lichens and mosses work on these to speed up the soil-building process, adding some organic matter. As the soil develops a greater variety of plant life develops. Limited in rate and extent by the climate, there is a slow but regular succession toward forest. The succession may be interrupted occasionally by catastrophic occurrences such as landslides, avalanches, or fires set by lightning, but the greatest setbacks are caused by man.

II. EROSION AND SEDIMENTATION

LAND USE FACTORS IN SEDIMENTATION

Use of the land for agriculture has caused the greatest changes on the face of the landscape. Forest and grassland have been converted to cropland over nearly 25 percent of the area of the country. On more than half of the cropland, from one-fourth to three-fourths of the soil has been lost by erosion. On more than 10 percent of the cropland, erosion has been so severe that the land essentially has been destroyed for tillage. Grazing by domestic livestock has depleted the cover and led to severe erosion on great areas of uncultivated land. It is estimated that more than 3 bil tons (2.7 bil metric tons) of soil are washed annually from cultivated or barren fields and from overgrazed ranges, to be poured into streams, reservoirs, lakes, and tidewaters (1). This does not help water quality.

Erosion of land surfaces unprotected by vegetation causes siltation of streams, lakes, and estuaries and removes nutrients from the land. (Photo courtesy of Soil Conservation Service.)

More recently, the rapid expansion of the timber harvest has opened up mountain forest areas. These are the most productive watersheds, receiving the largest amounts of rain and snow, and furnishing regular flows of water of good quality. But forest development has involved considerable soil disturbance and in many areas the quality of the water produced has deteriorated. Scars on the landscape made by access roads and the areas disturbed by poorly planned timber harvest operations, as well as areas denuded by fire, contribute quantities of sediment to streams. This contribution, while often significant, is not as extensive as from cultivated land. Forest lands recover their vegetation after cutting or after fire in most cases and, in a few years, generally are in good condition from the water production standpoint.

Urbanization is changing the watersheds in the lower-lying areas. Many cities occupy areas of several square miles each. These areas are paved and roofed and produce almost 100-percent runoff from every storm. As cities grow, additional clearing for construction involves additional soil disturbance. Because of the rapid and almost complete runoff from every storm, any material eroded is flushed away immediately to become sediment. Notorious examples of this are in the Anacostia River and Rock Creek in Washington, D.C. The stream load from urban areas also carries considerable dust, ash, soot, and oil washed from rooftops, sidewalks, and pavements.

Cross-country construction—roads, highways, powerlines, and pipelines—changes the watersheds at all levels. The original plant cover is cleared away and replaced by packed gravel or concrete in the case of roads and highways, and by smaller growth that is thinned and kept down by constant maintenance in the case of powerlines and pipelines. Openings in the cover created by rights-of-way for these operations affect snowcatch and melt rate in the mountains, and the soil disturbance increases the sediment load in the streams that drain affected areas. Surfaced roads contribute high rates of runoff, their drainage systems often overload the natural drainageways, and extensive raw cut-and-fill slopes erode and contribute markedly to stream sediment loads. Construction and maintenance operations without particular regard for the streams move huge quantities of rock and earth and plant

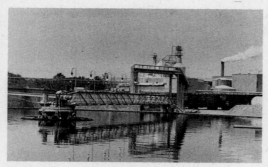

Sewage and waste treatment plants can reduce the amount of pollution entering rivers and lakes. This 190-ft diameter clarifier at a Maine paper mill removes fibers and other solids after which the water is subject to further treatment. (Photo courtesy of Georgia-Pacific.)

debris into channels where it is carried away at each high flow.

SPECIFIC EFFECTS

Changes made on the land through its use by man result primarily in erosion, sedimentation, turbidity, and modifications of streamflow regimes. So far as water is concerned, the products of erosion lower the quality of water, making it unfit for many uses and necessitating complex and expensive purification treatment. Sediments fill reservoirs and so destroy storage capacity. Sediments are deposited on flood plains and lower the productive capacity of rich bottom lands—this in addition to the lowering of productive capacity by loss of soil on the lands from which the sediments were derived originally. Fine sediments deposited on stream beds ruin the habitat for aquatic life. Turbidity destroys the aesthetic attractions of streams and lakes and cuts down recreational opportunities. Sediments and turbidity may make water treatment more difficult and more expensive.

The changes in streamflow regime usually are adverse. The increased volume of flow following denudation of the land comes largely at times when it is not wanted, when it causes damage instead of serving useful purposes. This necessitates additional storage space to hold the water for periods of need and channel protection works to keep high flows within bounds. There is less water in the streams in the dry periods, lowering the usefulness of the stream as an aquatic habitat as well as cutting down the volume of water for other beneficial use. Stream temperatures often are raised by

the removal of riparian vegetation in logging and road construction. This physical change may be beneficial sometimes, but usually is detrimental both to water quality and the aquatic habitat.

There are losses on the land itself. When most of the water received quickly runs off the surface of the land there is a deficiency of moisture in the soil. This in turn slows the growth of what cover vegetation is present and deters establishment of additional cover. Also, the erosion pavement of stones left behind does not make a good seed bed to encourage new plants. When the processes of deterioration reach a certain level they tend to be self-perpetuating. On mountain grazing lands, for example, this level is at about two-thirds of full plant cover density.

PROBLEM AREAS AND PRACTICES

To be specific in terms of problem areas would require identifying geographic locations. This can be done for certain areas in the Northwest, but perhaps it would be simpler to begin with problem situations and then cite certain locations as examples.

Three aspects of agricultural land use affect water quality: soil erosion, leaching or runoff of chemicals applied to the soil or to crops, and the disposal of agricultural wastes. It is the purpose of this section to consider the first of these problems, that of soil erosion and consequent sedimentation.

Anywhere that soil is disturbed, and cultivation disturbs it exceedingly, there is opportunity for erosion. The amount of erosion depends on the slope of the ground, the type of soil, the amount and intensity of rainfall, and the cultivation practices. In the Northwest the bulk of the rainfall comes in the winter season; if the soil is left bare over winter, it is apt to suffer considerable erosion. However, if there is a cover crop, erosion largely will be prevented.

Erosion rates from cultivated land in the Northwest are probably highest in the wheat belt where fine-grained soils on steep slopes are left open to erosion over winter. Some fields have lost more than 300 ton/acre (670 metric ton/ha) of soil in a single season. Average erosion losses on 2 mil acres (810,000 ha) over a 5-yr period are estimated at 10.5 ton/yr/acre (23.5 metric ton/yr/ha). At least 25 percent of this amount is estimated to have become sediment in the major streams draining the area. Sediment loads measured have ranged from 20,000 to a maximum of 82,000 g/l (2). Clean-tilled orchards in hilly country also suffer heavy erosion, and sometimes over-application of irrigation water causes considerable erosion in the summer season.

Studies by fisheries biologists have traced heavy sedimentation in streams in Montana to irrigation return flows; measured sediment loads ranged to more than 200 mg/l below the wastewater outlets, but to 25 g/l at most above the outlets. The upper reaches of the streams had good trout populations, but only a fiftieth as many in the warmer turbid waters below the outlets. Tests with live trout eggs showed 98 percent successful hatching in the clean upstream gravels and none in the silt-smothered downstream gravels (3). Whatever the source, the eroded soil takes away the productivity of the land and becomes sediment in the streams to the detriment of water quality and the aquatic habitat.

The problems created by forestry are similar to those from agriculture, but rarely are as significant. Erosion can and does occur on logged areas and on burns, but is not often severe or long-continuing because of fairly rapid regeneration of cover vegetation. However, burned slopes in areas of high-intensity rainfall may lose tremendous volumes of soil in a single storm and contribute markedly to flood damages. In Southern California erosion rates from fresh burns have been measured at several thousand cu yd/sq mile of contributing watershed (4). In several instances this has reduced storage capacity significantly in reservoirs where the sediments were trapped. The organic matter and ashes brought down with the soil particles add solutes to the water and lower its quality and usefulness.

Most of the erosion associated with logging comes from skidtrails and landings where the soil is churned and compacted to depths of 2 or 3 ft (0.6 or 0.9 m). Yarding logs across channels drags soil and litter into streams and provides vertical paths for erosion from the disturbed slopes above. Amount of erosion loss varies with the logging method, steepness of slope, and season of work. There is less damage to the soil in the dry season and less with uphill highlead cable yarding than with downhill tractor skidding.

Construction of roads and highways involves both considerable soil disturbance and exten-sive interference with drainage patterns and stream channels. Powerline and pipeline construction similarly involve soil disturbance, but to a lesser degree. Not only is the soil disturbed and laid bare to erosion on the slopes of road cuts and fills, but excess soil and rock material often are dumped in the nearest channel for disposal. Where construction is difficult, as in the rough topography of forested mountain areas, the amount of soil movement is tremendous. It commonly is estimated that at least four-fifths of the erosion and sedimentation caused by development of mountain forests is the result of access road construction (5). Eroded material from road construction has in many cases moved downstream in sufficiently large quantities to reduce significantly the storage capacity of reservoirs below. There are many examples of silting of stream bottoms with road-derived sediments that damage the aquatic habitat and ruin fish spawning grounds (6).

Road drainage led directly to streams carries material eroded from the ditches as well as oil and grease drippings washed from the road surface. Where roads encroach on channels, as they often do in narrow valleys, normal road maintenance work results in pushing material from slides and slumps directly into the channels. The encroachment itself narrows the channel and adversely affects streamflow and the aquatic habitat in additon to the sedimentation damage.

Impermeable surfaces of highways, airports, and urban and suburban developments change the hydrology of the streams in the watersheds where they are located. Some channels are blocked and their flow diverted to others. Slow-moving underground waters are intercepted in road cuts and carried away by different routes. Rapid runoff from even relatively small paved areas increases streamflow so that it exceeds the capacity of existing natural drainage channels. These changes result in channel down-cutting and sidecutting to adjust to the need for additional flow capacity. The erosion thus induced adds to stream turbidity and sediment loads and degrades water quality. The constant expansion of paved areas brings with it increasing problems in the disposal of water and in control of water quality. This expansion also means that more and more land is being taken out of crop and forest production and the pattern of expansion is often such as to interfere markedly with the use of the land left in production.

Mining is a widespread land use, and in some areas is a significant source of pollution. Mining operations include dredging, placer operations, gravel removal, strip mining, and augering, as well as hardrock mining and oil drilling. Mine access roads create problems similar to those from forest access roads. The most serious problems, however, derive from streamside mine tailing dumps, the drainage of toxic mineralized mine waters directly to streams, the destruction of stream channels by dredging and placer operations, and the disturbance of channels by gravel removal. All these have immediate and highly adverse effects on stream turbidity and sedimentation, the aquatic habitat, and water quality. Acid drainage from coal mines presents a pollution problem that affects ten states and two major river basins, the Ohio and the Susquehanna.

The only natural phenomenon contributing as much sediment as the erosion from disturbed and abused lands is the undercutting and scouring of streambanks at times of high flow. In the Willamette River in western Oregon it has been estimated (7) that slightly over half of the total sediment load measured in the river comes from the eating away of the streambanks through the main valley. The process may go on in all reaches of the stream, but appears to be at its worst in the lower flatter areas with a deep alluvial fill. The process is not entirely natural, for stream behavior is affected by upstream riparian and cross-channel works. The amount of runoff and the peaks reached are to some degree dependent on conditions of the land brought about by development and use.

Landslides may be locally significant in causing sedimentation. But while some may be triggered by an earthquake, or by ground saturation in an exceptionally wet season, many are set in motion or their effects increased by carelessness in land development. This is particularly true with regard to road construction.

RECOMMENDATIONS

Many of the adverse effects of land use on water quality can be avoided or minimized. If soil disturbance and denudation are kept to the minimum, erosion losses can be reduced greatly. In agriculture this involves such practices as contour cultivation on sloping lands,

maintenance of cover vegetation, efficient application of irrigation waters, and provision of protected drainageways. In the timber harvest it means adapting logging methods to the slope of the land and the condition of the soil, avoiding the use of heavy equipment along channels and channel banks, planning the operation to remove logs without dragging them across channels and to avoid repeated use of the same skidtrails, and postoperative treatment to control drainage and stabilize disturbed soil.

In road and highway construction it means avoidance wherever possible of areas of unstable soil and rock formations, bench and ridge rather than sidehill or streambank locations, keeping excess soil and rock out of stream channels and hauling the excess to locations safe from erosion, disposing of road drainage where it can filter into undisturbed soil rather than flow directly to stream channels, stabilization of exposed soil in cut and fills, laying culverts on channel gradients with a minimum of channel disturbance, providing both inlet and outfall protection against erosion at culvert ends, and preparation and maintenance of road surfaces to avoid rut formation and drainage concentrations.

Rehabilitation of lands damaged by misuse also is needed. Restoration of cover by ground preparation and seeding and planting on denuded range and forest lands; contour furrowing and trenching to retard runoff, prevent erosion, and afford rain and snowmelt water opportunity to soak into the soil; and a variety of gully control measures all may be necessary. Quick application of emergency measures on newly burned areas usually is desirable where there is a possible hazard of flood damage or degradation of water supplies.

A number of references give details for specific preventive control or rehabilitation measures (8) (9) (10) (11) (12) (13). What must be emphasized is avoidance and prevention of problem situations by thorough consideration of all the possible effects of any given land use and development, in terms of soil and water and public health, and advance planning to incorporate into land use practices and the development job whatever requirements appear necessary. Cost is sometimes a factor, but additional costs may be far outweighed by the tangible benefits gained; in many cases it costs no more to do the job properly to protect soil and water resources, and often returns direct benefits in terms of lower maintenance and rehabilitation needs on the particular development itself.

SUMMARY—SECTION II

Water falling as rain on disturbed soil and moving across it as rain and snowmelt runoff detaches soil particles and carries them away. This is erosion. Eroded particles flushed into stream channels cause turbidity and sedimentation, lower the quality of the water in the streams, and damage the aquatic habitat for fish. Land use and development involve varying degrees of soil disturbance and subsequent erosion. On croplands and range lands, on some forest lands, and on lands occupied by urban and related developments, the disturbances induced by man's activities have accelerated erosion much beyond natural rates. Of these activities, agriculture has had perhaps the greatest total effect, although road and highway construction have had and continue to have the most spectacular effects in the Northwest.

These effects need not be suffered. Many of them can be avoided or minimized. Soil-conserving cultivation practices, efficient use of irrigation, timber harvest methods adapted to the soil, careful road location and construction—all will reduce the erosion and sedimentation hazards. Lands which contribute significant amounts of sediment because of past abuse can be rehabilitated. Even natural sources of sediment often can be checked.

The basic need, to quote Cordone and Kelley (6), "is to develop a philosophy of land husbandry that will avoid the creation of untreated and running sores on the earth's surface, . . . a responsibility to future generations that matches the power gained through the development of heavy machinery."

III. TOXINS AND NUTRIENTS INTO THE ENVIRONMENT

PESTICIDES

The category "pesticides" includes a wide variety of toxic substances used for many purposes and applied to the land in a variety of ways. Four major groups named and classified by purpose are insecticides, fungicides, herbicides, and rodenticides. They include organic and inorganic metallic compounds; some formulations have been in use for a great many years. Some are lethal to the target life form on contact, others when inhaled, eaten, or otherwise absorbed by it.

The first and most widespread use of insecticides and fungicides was and is in agriculture. Many of the same compounds used in agriculture also are used on open range and on forest lands, often at the same application rates, to control grasshoppers, lygus bugs, pipe-tip moths, spruce budworms, and hemlock loopers, to name a few of the major targets.

Arsenical compounds provided the first insecticides, and still are used widely. Sodium arsenite was used as early as 1681. Paris green, a mixture of arsenic trioxide and copper acetate, has been used since 1870. It was applied by aerial dusting for mosquito control in 1923. The first aerial dusting in 1921, however, used lead arsenate. Calcium arsenate was used in 1923 for cotton dusting. The use of these metallic toxins involves certain difficulties—they are by no means target-specific, being toxic to nearly all life forms; and they accumulate in the environment with continued use since they are not converted readily to less toxic compounds. They can poison the soil of areas to which they are applied and they can poison the water draining from that soil.

One of the first fungicides, Bordeaux mixture, was discovered accidentally to be such. A mixture of lime and water and copper sulfate, it was first sprinkled on grapevines in the Medoc region of France to discourage theft of the ripe grapes by boys of the neighborhood. Vines so treated were observed to be free from mildew. The metallic element copper that is the base of this fungicide also is used as an algicide, having been applied in lakes as early as 1918; it has been used, too, as a bactericide in swimming pools.

Some use is made of the metallic toxins as plant killers. Arsenic salt solutions are used for injection to kill trees; unfortunately, they have been known to kill deer and porcupines at the same time. (Since porcupines have a taste for salt, wooden blocks soaked in arsenic salts and hung in porcupine den trees serve to reduce populations that threaten forest stands.) Sodium borate has been used as a spray to kill brush. Some mercury and zinc compounds are also in use; movement of these compounds to water, either accidentally or by leaching from treated lands, could impair seriously water quality and damage the aquatic habitat.

Both arsenicals and thallium compounds have been used as rodenticides. In ordinary situations they were used to coat seed baits which were placed in rodent burrows and runways. This usage posed no great threat to water or to the environment, although birds occasionally were poisoned by seeds that were left exposed, secondary poisoning of animals feeding on carcasses of target animals now and then resulted, and accidents involving children did occur. Better substances for rodenticides now are available, more target-specific and less hazardous to other life forms. Still, the exceedingly dangerous sodium fluoroacetate (1080) is in use as a rodenticide.

Natural substances, from plants or from minerals as they came from the earth, were, as might be expected, among the earliest insecticides. Pyrethrum dust originally was the powdered dried flowers of a certain chrysanthemum; pyrethrin, the active principle, is still an important insecticide. Sulfur was another "dusting" agent. Petroleum fractions early were found effective; a kerosene and soap emulsion was used against aphis and scale insects in 1877. Oil sprays still are used for weed control. Nicotine sulfate, a plant extract, has been used since 1690.

Compounds derived from minerals, particularly from petroleum, are very much in use directly or form the bases for synthesizing other compounds. Naphthalene has been used as an insecticide since 1900; its more recent derivatives are used for thinning orchard crops. Neither these nor the natural substances provide serious pollution hazards if carefully applied; most of them will break down fairly rapidly to harmless substances. It is the synthetic materials, principally those developed within the last 20 yr, that are the most hazardous. DDT first was used as an insecticide in 1939, and was the forerunner of a flood of synthetic organic insecticides (14). Many are highly toxic to all life forms, can be leached by water, and do not decompose readily and disappear from the environment.

These are of several types: halogenated hydrocarbons, organophosphates, carbamates, and thiocyanates being common ones. Some of the halogenated hydrocarbons and organophosphates appear to be quite durable in the natural environment, as evidenced by several studies and some recent fishkills, for example,

in the lower Mississippi River in the winter of 1963–1964, attributed to endrin and other pesticides. Even worse, they tend to accumulate in the food chain.

Equally significant with the types of compounds used are the amounts used, the frequency of application, the season of application, the method of application, and the extent of area treated. Despite all the precautions specified by law, prescribed by agricultural extension agents, and recommended by the manufacturers and vendors of pesticides, incidents and accidents happen. Tanks leak, trucks spill, barges overturn, streams are sprayed or dusted inadvertently, equipment is washed where waste water can drain to streams, or surplus material is dumped where it can contaminate streams or groundwater. Toxic "slugs" pass down the streams, destroy aquatic life, prevent the use of the poisoned water for many purposes, and provide a serious threat to human health.

Millions of acres of farm and range and forest lands are treated annually with millions of pounds of pesticides. In 1962, for example, more than 125 mil lb (57 mil kg) of halogenated hydrocarbons (principally DDT, aldrin, toxaphene, and BHC), 20 mil lb (9 mil kg) of organophosphates, and 14 mil lb (6.3 mil kg) of arsenates were used in the United States (15). These are much lower than the amounts cited for 1958 (16), when 280 mil lb (127 mil kg) of halogenated hydrocarbons were sold, though, in the main, this means only that newer formulations are replacing the older. Many of the most commonly used halogenated hydrocarbon and organophosphate insecticide compounds are toxic in the aquatic habitat at levels of less than 1 mg/1.

It has been predicted that present use of pesticides will increase tenfold within the next 20 yr. Obviously, tight control at every step in such intensive use is an absolute necessity to prevent excessive pesticide contamination of the human environment. Substitution of target-specific chemicals that decompose rapidly will help prevent serious hazards from developing. Substitution of methods, adoption of biologic controls, or changes in land use and management may provide even better answers to the threat of poisoning the environment.

The herbicides and algicides furnish good examples of threats to the aquatic environment. The 2,4-D family of chemicals used as weed killers are highly toxic to aquatic life, too much so to be favored for killing aquatic weeds. They also have been found toxic to animals fed on sprayed vegetation. For application in water there are petroleum solvent compounds available that are good plant-killers but which break down and disappear from the environment in a very short time. These latter formulations are widely used for keeping irrigation canals clear of weeds, with no damage to the crops irrigated, and with no damage to the streams receiving the return flows.

FERTILIZERS

The addition of various materials to soil to stimulate the growth of crops goes back to prehistoric time. Man early learned how to improve on nature. Animal manures and plant wastes (plant, in the botanical sense) have been applied for thousands of years to increase crop yields. Only within the last three centuries has science looked into the matter of soil and plant needs to prescribe the most efficient fertilizer formulations. Today, though we still use natural organic (manure, compost, sawdust) and inorganic (crushed limestone, gypsum, sulfur, rock phosphate) materials as fertilizers in great quantity, we also apply to the land vast amounts of manufactured chemical compounds of nitrogen, potassium, phosphorus, and sulfur. Most of these are quite soluble and easily leached away or exchanged in the soil chemistry system. Their movement out of the soil by runoff or by drainage may have a significant impact on water quality.

About 500 mil acres (202 mil ha) of cropland and pasture in the United States receive about 30 mil ton (27 mil metric ton) of fertilizers each year. Generally these nutrient materials are added in such a manner and at such a time that the growing plants make full use of them and little is lost by leaching and runoff. The farmer tries to get efficient use of the fertilizers to keep his costs down. If 300 lb/acre (336 kg/ha) are applied at a cost of $10, and 1 percent is leached away, the loss to the farmer is only 10¢/acre (25¢/ha). However, that 3 lb (1.4 kg) of fertilizer in an acre-ft of water (which we may take to represent runoff for an average growing season) amounts to about 1 mg/l. While this is very small, this amount of phosphate, for example, could trigger troublesome algal blooms resulting in considerably more than 10¢ worth of damage of water quality.

Recent studies around the world (17) indicate that fertilization of forests producing sawtimber and pulpwood is a paying proposition. Rates of application of superphosphate from 150 to 500 lb/acre (168 to 560 kg/ha), of nitrate up to 300 lb/acre (336 kg/ha), and of similar amounts of other macro- and micronutrients may be expected eventually over great areas of forest as well as cropland. Since the forest lands are the source of many of our domestic and industrial water supplies, any nutrient loss following fertilization becomes a matter of keen interest (18). There is as yet no serious or widespread hazard, and there is still time to work out management controls to prevent any from developing.

Even urban areas contribute nutrient loads from fertilizers to runoff. Because of the high proportion of impervious rooftop and pavement, runoff rates are very rapid in cities and suburbs. The city dweller tends to be less scientific about using fertilizers—being perhaps not as cost-conscious—and spreads them on lawn and garden with a lavish hand. The surplus is readily lost to runoff. While it would be difficult to separate the sources of the various nutrient substances in the enriched urban runoff, use of fertilizers is undoubtedly a significant contributor. What is said about fertilizer application is equally true about pesticides in urban use.

OTHER ADDITIVES

Urban areas make their major contributions, however, in materials associated with building, with streets, with industry, with people in great concentrations. The high runoff cited for urban areas will carry a wide spectrum of nutrients. Fallout from smoke; particles and solubles from roofs, from paint, and from cement in buildings; from oil, rubber, asphalt, dirt, and trash on streets; from de-icing compounds in the winter; and from carwashing in the summer all help degrade urban runoff and the streams that receive it (19). The loads carried are considerable, and the runoff needs treatment to remove them. Sometimes some of the runoff goes to the same treatment plant that handles domestic wastewater, but wastewater treatment plants rarely are designed to cope with this kind of load. Most urban-suburban runoff, therefore, receives no treatment and finds its way rapidly to streams.

Urban runoff unfortunately does not occur

in regular, readily manageable flows. It comes in surges, following thaw or storm periods. It often overtaxes local drainage capacity and storage for it rarely is provided. The dissolved and suspended solid loads move through the drainage system in slugs. As the result of a thaw in February or March a slug may consist largely of calcium chloride or sodium chloride de-icers spread on the streets and of soot trapped by snowfall; following a thunderstorm in July a slug may consist principally of oil, rubber, cement and asphalt particles, and solutes. Trickles flowing at times between surges and slug occurrences will carry the detergents from car washing and the nutrients and pesticides from irrigated lawns and gardens.

Where streets are not paved, dust-settling materials are applied often. These may be washed away by summer rains. Also associated with streets and highways in the rural environment are soil-binders used along rights-of-way, the creosoted timbers used in bridges and retaining walls along streams, and the chemicals from concrete in pavements. Accidental spills of many kinds of materials can happen anywhere, and may be quite frequent in the rural environment along the higher speed country routes; concentrated slugs of milk, molasses, gasoline, or other products in commerce can move rapidly from roadside ditch spills into waterways. Accidents in water transport are actually the most frequent, and may be the most directly damaging to water quality and aquatic habitat.

Farms can contribute a variety of direct as well as accidental and incidental additives to streams. The contributions may include drainage from silos, corrals, and compost; leaching of antibiotics and preservatives used on stock and poultry feed; and leaks from fuel storage. Some of these materials may be nutrient, some toxic, but all have an impact on water quality.

Materials are added even from the much less intensively managed "wild" forest and range lands. Chemicals used only infrequently and applied to only limited areas in aid of fire control have at times damaged water supplies. The hazard was considered sufficiently great that use of non-toxic bentonite slurry now is favored over borate slurry for bombing running fires. The fires themselves may have quite adverse chemical effects—alkali materials readily leach from the ashes. Without fire, the accumulation of leaves and twigs forms an organic mulch on the soil through which rain and snowmelt must percolate; tannins and humates are leached away to streamflow.

SUMMARY—SECTION III

The many sources of contaminants described present a variety of problems in prevention and control. For urban runoff, with its peculiar and widely varying types of pollution loading, collection, storage, and special treatment may be a simpler and easier solution than prevention. Accidental occurrences may prove much more amenable to control than traditional practices in construction and maintenance. It is not likely that there will be much change in the pollution loads contributed from farmsteads and from crop, range, and forest lands. Indeed, in areas of severe pollution by substances derived from intensive irrigated farming, treatment of return flows may be necessary to clean them up before putting them back into circulation.

Wherever we use water, for whatever purpose, insofar as possible and in every way possible, we must protect its quality to enable its full reuse. We do not have water to waste.

IV. WASTES

AGRICULTURAL

Crop residues and crop processing wastes occasionally constitute sources of stream-pollution contributing substances that increase the oxygen demand and stimulate algal blooms as well as adding other materials that are undesirable in the aquatic habitat. These are natural organic materials in varying stages of decomposition. They generally are similar to the natural litter and humus of the uncultivated wild lands, though they tend to be released in more concentrated form, and often in "slugs."

Irrigated agriculture involves the leaching and transport of materials dissolved from the soil, and the mixing of these materials with others already in the water. Heavy irrigation often is used specifically for flushing from the soil unwanted salts that inhibit crop growth. Return flows from such treatments carry large quantities of solutes that degrade water quality for subsequent uses. Insofar as the leachings are plant nutrients, they also may lead to algal blooms in the receiving streams.

Animal manures and dairy wastes are other sources of damaging contaminants to streams. They may provide viable disease organisms that attack people as well as putting unwanted degrading elements into the water. Nutrient contributions from such sources are very high. Dairy wash water carries a rich load of suspended and dissolved materials (20). Spreading the wastes, or diverting the drainage therefrom to infiltrate into the soil where the nutrients can be taken up by plants is one solution to the problem.

TIMBER HARVEST

The principal immediate waste from timber harvest is logging slash. In chemical makeup, this material is identical to natural forest litter, though logging leaves larger pieces and amounts than normal leaf and twig fall and the occasional broken tree. The slash presents no problem except where it accumulates in stream channels; then it may contribute tannins, oils, resins, and sugars to the water with deleterious effect. Accumulation of slash in channels can be avoided by leaving an uncut strip of trees to protect the stream, by logging uphill from streams, or by collecting and piling the slash away from streams.

Where slash is burned or where wild fire has run through the forest, there are sharp changes in the local soil chemistry that temporarily may affect water quality in streams draining the burned area. The soil is normally slightly acid under the influence of decomposing organic litter but, when the litter is burned, the soil— sometimes for a year or two—may become quite alkaline at the surface. Available phosphorus, exchangeable bases, and total soluble salts usually are increased (21). Nitrates, however, tend to be destroyed by burning (8). Denuded soil, under the impact of raindrops, puddles and seals and rapidly loses much of its surface infiltration capacity; runoff increases and carries with it the soluble material from the litter, ash, and burned soil. Thus, an abnormal surge of various salts may occur in the streams below.

One interesting but damaging effect of burning slash after logging occurred on a city water supply watershed. The slash (from resinous conifers) was bulldozed into piles, covered with paper, and not burned until there was a snowfall to prevent the fire from spreading. However, the snow was so heavy that it roofed over one burning pile near a stream and resulted more in wood distillation than combustion. Condensed tars and resins from the fumes under the snow cap trickled into the stream and caused a serious taste problem in the city water. Fortunately, such occurrences are rare and easily avoided by piling the slash well away from streams.

Sawdust from streamside and waterfront sawmills too often becomes a pollution source for close-at-hand bodies of water. Materials leached from waterlogged wood particles discolor the water in streams, lakes, and estuaries, and lead to growths of undesirable organisms. Decomposition of the wood increases oxygen demands and exhausts the supply of DO in the water. The settling particles blanket stream, lake, and bay bottoms and smother aquatic life.

A common method of storing logs before milling is to put them in water. Natural streams, ponds, or bays may be used, or artificial ponds may be built. The purpose is to keep the wood from drying and checking, to protect it against insect attack, and to facilitate log sorting and handling. Sometimes the logs are in the water many months; quantities of tannins and resins and sugars leach out. Bark, in particles and in slabs, scales off and accumulates in the water. It likewise contributes to discoloration, the nutrient load, and all the associated water quality problems.

MINING

Mining wastes that damage water quality and the aquatic habitat bear in solution toxic minerals derived from exposed rock formations and from various ore-processing operations. A widespread and well known example is that of the sulfuric acid, iron oxides, and hydroxides in the drainage associated with coal mining. Many thousands of miles of streams in 10 states from Pennsylvania to Missouri have been degraded both as sources of water supply and as aquatic habitat by this one kind of pollution (22). Some acid drainage also is associated with certain metal-mining operations in Arkansas, Colorado, and other states.

Another well known example is that of the oil field salt brines that pollute streams in Kansas, Oklahoma, Texas, Arkansas, and Louisiana (23). Saline waters have limited usefulness, and treatment costs are high. Even though the average salt load in a stream may not appear excessive, the salt content during low flow periods—perhaps more than half the time—may be above acceptable limits.

Other salts, including toxic metallic compounds, may be drained off with mine wastewaters or leached from mine dumps. The dissolved load sterilizes the aquatic habitat, as well as making the water of receiving streams unfit for other use. Considerable dilution is necessary to counteract the damaging effects. Where abandoned mines are left unsealed, the toxic drainage waters may continue for many years to affect the streams to which they flow.

Smelting of minerals has created air pollution that in turn has created water pollution. Smelter smoke—acid fumes and particles carrying toxic metallic salts—has killed vegetation and poisoned the soil within a several mile radius around some smelters. Southeast Tennessee's copper basin and the Kennett area of Northern California are notable examples. Water draining from the affected areas becomes degraded by the toxic materials it picks up and carries away. There was a case in British Columbia where a heavy snowfall trapped arsenic particles from smelter smoke; when the snow melted, it released to the nearby streams a slug of material sufficiently toxic to concern public health and wildlife agencies. Stack controls to filter out the harmful particles and reclaim lost metals have and will cut down the threat from this source.

URBAN

Stream degradation by urban runoff already has been mentioned. In this connection, however, two additional waste sources should be mentioned. One is the fallout from industrial smokes, which, like smelter fumes, may have serious impact on water quality. The other is drainage from garbage and refuse dumps. If their relation to land use activities seems far-fetched, it is necessary only to recognize that urban-suburban development is taking up more and more land. Smoke particle fallout is incidental to such development while refuse and garbage disposal represents a specific land use aspect of urbanization. Unfortunately it carries considerable pollution threat; drainage from garbage and refuse concentrations may supply both nutrients and toxic materials to receiving waters and damage the aquatic habitat as well as degrade water quality.

RECREATION

Pollution associated with recreation area wastes is similar to that from urban areas and, in fact, is often part of the urban problem. But, for the most part, recreation areas occupy a much less developed environment and bring special problems to it. Most of the time solutions have not accompanied the problems; there have not been many wastewater treatment plants installed at recreation areas, for example.

Heavily used recreation areas will have wash waters from spigots, kitchens, laundries, and bath houses; these will carry soaps and detergents and present a special disposal problem. Where there are only pit privies for human wastes, there may be a contamination hazard to groundwater and to nearby streams. Drainage from garbage and refuse pits may pose similar dangers. These are problems which develop because of concentrations of people and of their wastes.

Litter is a form of waste that endangers the environment even if from the aesthetic rather than the chemical or bacteriological standpoint. Collections of litter—papers, metal cans, glass bottles, and plastic containers of all kinds—may be found in most roadside ditches and in the vicinity of recreation areas. Breakdown of the metal and plastic, and of the remnants of materials once contained, often provides a threat to the environment, including water. Again, in the ditches and in the streams, litter can be a source of degradation to water quality and the aquatic habitat.

SUMMARY—SECTION IV

Wastes encompass the third and last class of pollutants derived from land use and development. Whether their release into the environment is intentional or not is beside the point. The volume released and the damage it causes have grown sufficiently to require strong controls. Some of the wastes are toxic, others enrich the streams with nutrients; neither type can be tolerated at present levels, nor need they be. Most agricultural wastes can be redirected and used as fertilizers. Wastes from timber harvest and processing, similarly, do more good when put back on the land as mulches, soil amendments, or fertilizers than when released to streams. Toxic wastes from mining, ore-processing, and other industry, from urban and recreation area sources, all can be controlled or prevented by one means or another. It is part of the land manager's job to see that this is done; to this end he needs advice and help from the water resources managers and the waste disposal experts.

REFERENCES

1. "Soils and Man." In "Yearbook of Agriculture." U.S. Dept of Agr., Washington, D.C. (1938).
2. "Report on Agriculture Program, Big Bend-Palouse Sub-Area, Columbia River Basin Area." U.S. Dept. of Agr., Washington, D.C. (1954).
3. Peters, J., "Agricultural Pollution and Trout." Report to Water Pollution Control Advisory Board, Washington, D.C. (1961).
4. "Flood Control Survey Report, San Gabriel River, California." U.S. Dept. of Agr., Washington, D.C.
5. Dunford, E. G., "Effect of Logging and Forest Roads on Stream Sedimentation." Pacific-Northwest Forest and Range Exp. Sta. (1960).
6. Cordone, A. J., and Kelley, D. W., "The Influences of Inorganic Sediment on the Aquatic Life of Streams," *California Fish and Game*, **47**, 189 (1961).
7. Anderson, H. W., "Suspended Sediment Discharge." *Trans. Amer. Geophys. Union*, **35**, 286 (1954).
8. "Watershed Control for Water Quality Management." Pollution Control Council, Pacific-Northwest Area (1961).
9. "2533—Land Treatment Measures Handbook," and "2534—Watershed Structural Measures Handbook." U.S. Forest Service, Washington, D.C. (1958 and 1959).
10. "Forest Watershed Management Symposium." Oregon State Univ., Corvallis, Ore. (1963).
11. "Design of Roadside Drainage Channels." Hydr. Design Ser. No. 4, Bur. of Pub. Roads, U.S. Dept. of Commerce, Washington, D.C. (1965).
12. "A Guide for Revegetating Bituminous Strip-Mine Spoils in Pennsylvania." Res. Comm. on Coal Mine Spoil Revegetation in Pa., Harrisburg, Pa. (1965).
13. Limstrom, G. A., "Forestation of Strip-Mined Land in the Central States." Handbook No. 166, U.S. Dept. of Agr., Washington, D.C. (1960).
14. "Handbook of Toxicology, Vol. III. Insecticides." Natl. Acad. of Sciences, Natl. Res. Council, Washington, D.C. (1959).
15. Taylor, F. B., "Current Status of the Pesticide and Insecticide Problem." Paper presented to New England Section, Amer. Water Works Assn. (1964).
16. Woodward, R. L., "Pesticides and Water Supplies." Paper presented to Canadian Section, Amer. Water Works Assn. (1960).
17. Swan, H. S. D., "Reviewing the Scientific Use of Fertilizers in Forestry." *Jour. Forestry*, **63**, 501 (1965).
18. Cole, D. W., and Gessel, S. P., "Movement of Elements through a Forest Soil, etc." In "Forest-Soil Relationships in North America." Oregon State Univ. Press, Corvallis, Ore. (1963).
19. Weibel, S. R., Anderson, R. J., and Woodward, R. L., "Urban Land Runoff as a Factor in Stream Pollution." [*Jour. Water Pollution Control Fed.*], **36**, 7, 914 (July 1964).
20. "Farm Wastes Studied." [*Jour. Water Pollution Control Fed.*], **36**, 12, 1566 (Dec. 1964).
21. Spurr, S. H., "Forest Ecology." Ronald Press Co., New York (1964).
22. "Acid Mine Drainage." U.S. House of Representatives Print No. 18, 87th Congress, 2nd Session, Washington, D.C. (1962).
23. "Arkansas-Red River Basins Water Quality Conservation." U.S. Pub. Health Service, Washington, D.C. (1964).

Thermal Pollution—A New Problem in Aquatic Ecosystems

by Robert Leo Smith

A new dimension is being added to the problems of water quality and the maintenance of aquatic ecosystems. It goes by a variety of names: thermal pollution, thermal loading, thermal enrichment. It has been with us in some form for years. Dams, including beaver dams, raise the temperature of streams and rivers. Irrigation practices and industrial and steam electrical plants have been returning heated waters to rivers and lakes. But only in recent years, with the tremendous increase in electrical power plants and their need for cooling water, has thermal pollution entered our vocabulary and become a problem of great concern. The term *thermal pollution* must be used with discrimination. Heat becomes a pollutant only in those situations in which it is inimical to the interests and needs of man, including the adverse effects it has on the aquatic ecosystem.

Posing the greatest problem to thermal pollution are steam electric stations. Producing electricity by steam generation, whether by coal or by nuclear power, is highly inefficient, somewhere between 37 to 39 percent efficient for coal, 31 percent for nuclear power. Much of the energy of the fuel that cannot be converted to electricity is lost as heat. Yet in spite of this loss, the steam turbine provides the highest efficiency of all heat machines in operation. The automobile engine is less than 10 percent efficient. The ideal way to get rid of this heat is to release it to the atmosphere. But the most economical way is to use water with its ability to store tremendous quantities of heat with a small rise in temperature as the coolant and allow the water to discharge the heat to the air. The most common method of employing water to remove heat is to circulate fresh water from a river or lake through the condensers and back to the river or lake again without precooling.

Where ample supplies of cooling water are not available, plants may use cooling reservoirs or storage dams, which need a steady flow of water. Fresh water is drawn from the dam, circulated through the condensers of the plant, and returned to the cooling lake, where the heat is lost by radiation and convection. A 1000-megawatt station would require a 2000-acre lake four feet deep at one end, fifty feet at the other. Cooling water is drawn from the bottom, circulated through the condensers, and pumped out 20° higher at the rate of 500,000 gallons a minute to the shallow end of the pond. Complete overturn of the water would require about fifteen days.

Or the plant may use cooling towers, of which the most common is the evaporative or wet cooling tower (Fig. 1). Instead of dis-

Figure 1(a). The Fort Martin Power Station near Morgantown, West Virginia. The concrete hyperbolic-shaped towers, two of the world's largest, cool the hot water coming from the plant's condenser by the inflow of great masses of air drawn up by the draft action of the towers. The tower in the foreground is in operation, the one in the background is in the construction stage. (Photo courtesy of Consolidation Coal.)

THIS SELECTION was written especially for this volume.

Figure 1(b). The Fort Martin plant with both towers in operation. Note the clouds of water vapor rising from the cooling towers. Also note the empty coal barge moving up river and another loaded one moving down river. The photo represents the heart of energy production, fossil fuels and thermal plants. (Photo by Shelby Young, courtesy of Dominion-Post.)

charging the heated effluent back to the river, the power plant sends the water into the lower part of a 300- to 500-foot tower with sloping sides. The heated water drops from large pipes atop a tressel-like fill section and cools as it drips down through a series of slats or baffles. Temperature and atmospheric differences created by the heated water cause the outside air to be sucked in over the baffles and up the chimney-like tower (Fig. 2). The water is collected in a basin at the foot of the tower and is recirculated back to the condenser. Some water, on the order of 2.8 to 4 percent of daily requirements, is lost as evaporation, an amount which on a local basis can be considerable. A 1000-megawatt plant can discharge 20,000 to 25,000 gallons of evaporated water a minute.

Another type of cooling tower is the non-evaporating closed-circulating dry tower. It utilizes air-cooled radiators through which a large volume of air is passed either by natural draft or, more frequently, by mechanical fans powered by the plant itself. The heat is transferred directly from cooling tubes to the air, and the water is recirculated for continuous use, as it is in an automobile radiator (Fig. 3). Such towers are very expensive, costing two to

three times as much as wet or evaporative cooling towers. The tower consumes significant quantities of electrical energy, but it can completely eliminate thermal pollution and cut down the water loss from accelerated evaporation. This benefit in itself in some area could balance the construction investment where water supplies are limited.

The amount of water used for industrial cooling has increased tremendously in the past decade, and most of the increase is directly attributable to increased demand and production for electricity (Fig. 4). In 1958 steam generating utilities required 90 billion gallons of water daily for cooling purposes. In 1965 the electric power industry used 128 billion gallons of water per day. By the year 2000, if no other methods of cooling are introduced and if nuclear power becomes the common source of power, the cooling water requirements will be 1250 billion gallons of water per day. If 30 percent of the power generated waste heat is discharged to seawater cooling systems, 875 billion gallons of cooling water per day will have to be supplied by inland freshwater sources. Since the average daily run-off in the United States is about 1200 billion gallons per day, the power industry

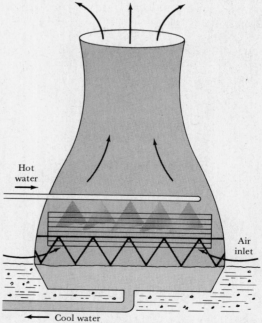

Figure 2. A cross-sectional diagram of the wet cooling tower. The heated water sprayed over wooden baffles is cooled by the inrushing air.

Hot water

Air inlet

← Cool water

271

would need nearly three-quarters of the total run-off for cooling purposes (1). This is a nationwide average. Locally, the problems could be much greater especially during the summer when the flow is naturally low. In some Delaware River watersheds, power plants by reuse utilize 150 percent of the freshwater flow during the low flow periods of summer. Power plants can increase water temperatures 10 to 30°F above ambient temperatures. If the ambient temperature of water is 70°F, the discharge water will be 80 to 100°F. In summer the discharges may reach 100 to 115°F. Except for local situations, thermal pollution is not yet a major problem, but with the increased demands for power and the extensive construction of a number of steam electric plants on the same waterways, thermal pollution stands as a major threat to the aquatic ecosystems.

Increased temperatures in natural waters place a stress on aquatic life. Through long periods of evolution, poikilothermal, or cold-blooded, aquatic organisms have become adapted to a particular range of temperatures. Each species has its optimum, which may vary with several stages in the life cycle. Within limits these organisms are able to adjust to higher or lower temperatures. If an organism lives at the higher end of the tolerable range, the animal acclimatizes itself sufficiently so that the lethal temperature will be somewhat

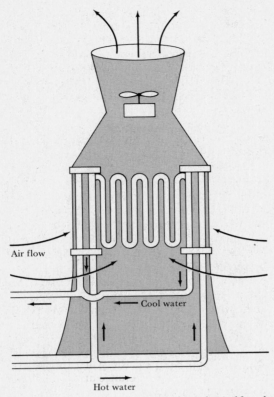

Figure 3. A cross-sectional diagram of a mechanical forced-draft dry cooling tower. The heated water from the condenser passes through a series of radiator-type systems and water is cooled by inflowing air.

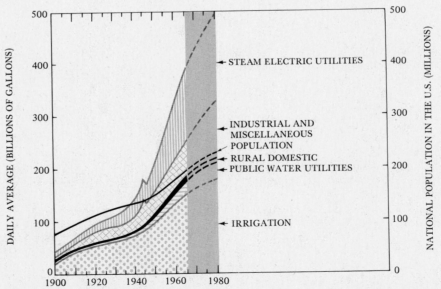

Figure 4. A comparison of the growth of consumptive uses of water compared with population growth.

higher than it would be if the animal were acclimatized at a lower temperature. Most aquatic organisms can acclimatize more quickly to rising temperatures than they can to dropping temperatures. But this ability to adjust is limited, and there is no absolute maximum upper or minimum lower limit to which an organism can be acclimatized without dying: it varies with the species (2).

Under natural conditions with a slow rise and fall in temperature, fish and other organisms gradually adjust to changing environmental temperatures. But if a new temperature regime is imposed quickly, such as when a slug of hot water is poured into rivers and lakes, the lack of sufficient time for acclimatization can produce thermal shock and death.

Thermal shock is an extreme result of thermal pollution. There are other effects, often more insidious, that result from heated effluents entering the waterway. One is the effect on metabolic processes. According to van't Hoff's law, the rate of chemical reaction doubles with every 18°F rise in temperature. Because the body temperatures of poikilothermal animals are influenced by environmental temperatures, a rise in environmental temperature increases the metabolic rate of fish and aquatic invertebrates, which in turn increases their oxygen demands. At the same time high temperatures decrease the oxygen content of the water when the organism needs it the most. The situation in fish is further aggravated by the reduced affinity of hemoglobin for oxygen. Increased oxygen demand, the decreased availability, and the reduced efficiency for obtaining it cause severe physiological stress, even death. In summer only a few degrees' rise in temperature may cause a 100 percent mortality among fish and invertebrates, especially those living in areas near the southern extremities of their ranges.

Many aquatic organisms have a range of temperature optima, one for several different stages in the life cycle. The Atlantic lobster (*Homarus americanus*), for example, can inhabit waters that range from 32 to 62°F, but it will breed only in waters warmer than 52°F. Largemouth bass (*Micropterus salmoides*) start nest building at 58°F and begin to spawn at 66°F, although the preferred living temperature is 80 to 82°F (3). Higher spring temperatures force the bass to move elsewhere to spawn. Among the Pacific salmon the best growth for fry is obtained between 60 to 65°F (4). Eggs develop best between 38 and 55°F, but they will survive temperatures ranging from 34 to 62°F.

The temperature tolerances vary with the species. Cold-water fish represented by such salmonids as the brook trout (*Salvelinus fontinalis*) and such invertebrates as the stonefly (*Plectoptera* spp.) are very sensitive to warm water. The brook trout rarely occurs in water whose temperatures exceed 68°F (5). Peak of activity as measured by oxygen consumption is reached at 66.2°F (6), and 77°F is the upper lethal limit for brook trout acclimatized for 77°F. The optimum temperature for a food source of the brook trout, the stonefly, is 50 to 60°F (7). Temperatures above 60°F are detrimental to these insect larvae. Warm-water species are much more tolerant of high temperatures. The preferred temperature of largemouth bass is 80 to 82°F and for bass acclimatized to 86°F the lethal temperature is 97.5°F. *Trichoptera*, or caddis fly, larvae occur in water up to 95°F (8), whereas the majority of the midge larvae (Tendipedidae) live in water 86 to 91°F (9).

The temperature of the water can be well within the range of tolerance and still have an adverse effect by limiting or eliminating the food supply. In the Patuxent River estuary of Chesapeake Bay the juvenile striped bass (*Roccus saxatilis*) feeds heavily on the opossum shrimp (*Neomysis americana*). This shrimp, a northern latitude species, is at the southern extremity of its range in the Chesapeake Bay. It is highly intolerant of high temperatures, failing to survive above 87.5°F (10). This temperature is occasionally reached and even exceeded in the waters of Chesapeake Bay.

Behavior of fish can be changed or modified by heated waters. Warmer water in winter may cause spawning out of season. Most aquatic organisms reproduce when a given temperature level is reached after a period of increasing or declining temperatures. The eastern brook trout and the brown trout (*Salmo trutta*), for example, spawn under conditions of declining temperatures, and rainbow trout (*Salmo gairdneri*) spawn under conditions of increasing temperatures. If the temperature change, normally a seasonally dependent environmental phenomenon, is altered by addition of heated water, then the fish may spawn out of season. Mayflies and other aquatic insects may hatch early and emerging from the water enter an environment too cold to permit the completion of their life cycle, mating and egg laying. Altered temperatures interfere with the migratory behavior of fish. Anadromous fishes, highly sensitive to temperature, have rigid time schedules for upstream and downstream migrations. High temperatures act as a barrier both to the spawning of adults and to the downstream migration of young. Heated water also interferes with the timing of migration or may actually inhibit movements altogether. The bluefish (*Pomatomus saltatrix*) is rarely found in water colder than 43 to 46°F. Normally the species leaves Long Island Sound in October when the water has cooled below the tolerable limits (11). But heated effluents encouraged the bluefish to remain in the Sound when they should have migrated. Remaining in the plume of heated water discharged from power plants, they are subject to changes in water discharges and in circulatory patterns, often with disastrous results. It happened in Long Island Sound in 1968. Small bluefish eleven inches long were suddenly taken by some change in circulation from balmy waters of 52°F to seasonal wintertime waters of 31°F. Other kills have been reported about the intake and outfall structures of power plants. In 1966 some 40,000 blue crabs were killed in the Patuxent River estuary. The crabs apparently became trapped in the discharge. Many species of plankton in estuaries exhibit daily movements from lower depth to upper and a return to the deep again. Little is known about what effect a layer of heated surface water might have on the movements or the fate of the organisms when they enter the heated waters.

Artificially warming natural waters can change the structure and functioning of aquatic ecosystems. Results of a number of studies suggest what impact heavy thermal pollution can have on aquatic environments. Most species of fish are eliminated from the zone of maximum heat in summer (12), and the diversity, numbers, and biomass of invertebrate fauna of the riffles are reduced substantially (13,14). At Cousins Island Cove in Maine where three different effluent discharges raised the temperature of the estuarine waters 42 to 77°F above the ambient temperature, the rockweeds *Fucus* and *Ascophyllum* and their associated invertebrate fauna were eliminated (15). Increased temperatures of the water affected competition. Elimination of rockweeds

enabled a suppressed species *Enteromorpha* to flourish and permitted populations of the blue mussel *Mytilus edulis* to establish large colonies and grow throughout the year. In the Patuxent River estuary, eelgrass, *Ruppia maritima*, a valuable duck food has declined and is being replaced by a more tolerant pondweed, *Potamogeton perfoliatis* (16). As temperatures rise, diatoms characteristic of cool water are replaced by green algae and finally at high temperatures by blue-green algae. In freshwater streams such cold-water species as trout, dace, and stoneflies are replaced by largemouth bass and carp, and even these fish disappear if water temperatures exceed 86°F. These observations suggest that heated water can change environmental conditions to a point where heat-tolerant species can out-compete the cold-water species, even though the temperatures of the water may be below the lethal levels for cool-water species.

Disease, parasitism, and predation may be influenced by changing temperature. Heated water may bring new predators into the area; it may influence the ability of the predators to capture prey, or of the prey to escape their predators. Experimental brook trout living in 63°F water were comparatively slow in capturing minnows, and at 70°F they were incapable of capturing them. Thus, increased temperatures favored the prey species and were detrimental to the trout, which literally starved to death in the midst of plenty. Warming of the Columbia River by nuclear power plants encouraged a once rare but deadly bacterial disease of fish, columnaris, to flourish. It has caused extensive mortality among salmon ascending the river.

Extension or contractions of natural range and the introduction and spread of exotic species are other possible effects of thermal pollution. In marine environments where certain cold-water species such as the American lobster and Ipswich clam reach their southernmost distribution and certain warm-water species are at the northernmost part of their range, heated effluents can tip the scales in favor of the warm-water species, enabling them to breed and expand their range, something they were unable to do at ambient temperatures. Northern species would be forced to retreat into cooler waters. On the other hand, in areas where the ranges of such species do not overlap, there may be a scarcity of replacement species. In such situations the niche remains vacant unless some species adapted to warmer water are deliberately introduced or accidentally carried there by currents or on the hulls of boats (17). Often such colonizers are species that are able to live on piling and other structures located near discharges of heated effluents. For example, *Vallisneria spiralis* has become naturalized in British coastal waters heated by thermal effluents, as well as the subtropical barnacle *Balanus amphitrite* var *denticulata* (18). In Maine the oyster, *Crassostrea virginica*, a relatively warm-water species, was introduced into some heated waters, where it spawned and exhibited accelerated out-of-season growth (15).

There is a relationship, too, between production and cycling of minerals, and the influx of heated effluents. This in turn can have a pronounced effect on food webs. A measure of primary production is carbon assimilation. In the York River estuary of Virginia, heated water increased primary production over what it would have been at ambient temperatures. When river water reached a temperature of 59 to 69°F, a rise of 10° increased carbon assimilation. Heating river water by 6°F when its water temperature was above 87°F depressed production (14). The higher the ambient water temperature, the greater production was depressed when heated effluents were added. Part of this depression of productivity may relate to the requirements of phytoplankton for certain growth substances, such as vitamin B_{12}. The requirement for this vitamin increases 300 times between a temperature rise from 96.8 to 98.2°F. Since this vitamin is naturally limiting, heated effluents may decrease production by increasing vitamin needs (19). A rise in water temperature at the same time speeds up the rate of decomposition of organic matter. This increase in bacterial action lowers oxygen supply especially in summer months. Great loads of nitrogen and phosphorus poured into cool water may produce a minimal immediate biological effect. A rise in temperature in the presence of these nutrients can trigger massive blooms of algae.

In addition to altering the environment, power plants can also have a physical effect on life in the water. A number of steam plants use salt, brackish, or hard water for cooling. These waters can be highly corrosive to metallic surfaces and can cause a loss of metallic ions, especially copper, to the water. Shellfish con-

centrate the copper in such quantities that make them unfit for human consumption. In fact, oysters in the Patuxent River estuary have turned a metallic blue-green from the concentration of copper in the tissues (16). Biological growths on the walls of condenser tubes and intake and outflow pipes reduce their capacity for heat exchange and lower electrical generating efficiency. To rid the tubes of these deposits power companies resort to a variety of biocides and cleaning agents, such as detergents, acids, and chlorines. The latter is especially important, because its ability to kill attached organisms extends to free-floating organisms in the waters receiving the discharges.

Water drawn into plants for cooling contain phytoplankton, zooplankton, shellfish larvae, and fish eggs and larvae. Many of these suffer 95 percent destruction (16) from thermal shock in the condenser. If the predatory action of the power plant exceeds the ability of the species affected to reproduce itself, the population declines. Such is the case of the sea nettle on the Patuxent River estuary. So great is the number of sea nettle killed as they pass through the condensers that the local population of the species has decreased. What has happened to the sea nettle can also happen to other species.

Although the discussion so far has concentrated on the detrimental effects of heated effluents, thermal loading, if not carried to an extreme, can have some beneficial effects for man. It can improve the quality of winter fishing, often making this sport available when the fishing season would normally be over. This beneficial effect may be negated by the mortality that can result when fish return to cooler water or when summer temperatures reach lethal levels. Heated effluents have been used successfully in culture of oysters in lagoons receiving the heated water directly from a power station. The heated water not only enables oysters to continue their growth through the winter when growth is normally slowed; it also permits oyster culture in cooler waters north of normal range. The use of heated effluents also can be extended to lobster culture, especially since the waters of its normal Maine habitat are gradually becoming too cold for spawning. Heated effluents can be used to speed up the decomposition of sewage and organic matter, although this results in lower oxygen levels, inimical to other aquatic life.

A modest rise in temperature within tolerable limits can increase the growth rate of fish and many aquatic invertebrates. The heated effluents also make possible the pond culture of such fish as Tilapia and milkfish. Use of artificially heated natural water has been used extensively in the U.S.S.R. for the commercial production of carp (*Cyprinus carpio*) in those parts of Russia where carp culture was restricted by low water temperatures. Studies are under way to utilize waste for food production. Inorganic wastes obtained from sewage treatment might be used as a source of nutrients for the growth of algae. These in turn would provide a food source for the quahog (*Venus mercenaria*) or perhaps for zooplankton which in turn would support a population of pond fish (20). The fish would provide both food for man and fish meal for livestock. Organic wastes from man shunted through sewage treatment plants would be utilized as a source of inorganic fertilizer again (21). A number of steps in the process would depend in part on heated water provided by power plants.

What is known about thermal pollution is small in relation to what needs to be known before greater quantities of heated effluents are poured into the world's aquatic ecosystems. How are heated effluents dispersed in the waters that receive them? Theoretically, heated water, because it has a lower density, remains on top of the cooler, denser receiving waters and moves rapidly down the waterway. But in some estuarine situations heated effluents may become sandwiched between the cooler, fresh surface layer and the cooler, heavier salt-water on the bottom. Thus, heated waters may actually occur at unpredicted depths, where it effects the benthic organisms as well as the fish and plankton. Before the effects of thermal pollution can be predicted, one needs to know the general pattern of water distribution in estuaries, the surface and bottom profiles of temperature and oxygen, and the rate of heat dissipation. Since temperature does not act alone, one requires some information about the interaction of temperature with dissolved oxygen, carbon dioxide, salinity, and various pollutants at different temperature levels. We have little understanding of the effect of thermal pollution on the growth of freshwater and marine algae and on the growth and survival of fish and aquatic invertebrates. We do not know what temperature conditions block estuarine fish from entering spawning areas or the effects of thermal pollution on spawning and survival of eggs and larvae. Possessing only the knowledge we now own, we can hardly predict what can happen to aquatic ecosystems receiving heated discharges.

To minimize the damage to aquatic habitats from heated effluents, the Federal Water Pollution Control Administration has made the following recommendations covering the release of heated waters into streams and lakes:

1. At any season of the year, heated water should not be added in quantities that will raise the temperature more than 5°F under conditions of minimum flow for that month. In larger streams, lakes, and reservoirs, peak water temperature should not exceed 86 to 90°F or prevail for more than 6 hours in any 24-hour period.
2. The maximum temperatures of streams or lakes should be restricted by known maximums tolerated by aquatic life inhabiting different environments. For example, temperatures of trout streams should not exceed 68°F. For warm water streams the temperature should not be raised more than 5°F above the monthly average of the maximum daily water temperature. In lakes the limitation should be a 3°F rise in the waters of epilimnion. In marine and estuarine situations the monthly means of daily maximum temperature should not be raised more than 4°F in winter, spring, or fall months. For summer months the limitations should be 1.5°F.
3. The rate of temperature change should not be more than 1°F per hour or more than 7 to 9°F in a 24-hour period except when due to natural phenomena.

Several states have established their own regulations. Pennsylvania has set the following:

1. The temperature of the waters shall not be increased artificially by amounts that shall be inimical or injurious to the public health or to animal or aquatic life or prevent the use of water for domestic, industrial, or recreational purposes.
2. The heat content of discharges shall be limited to an amount that could not raise the temperature of the entire stream at

the point of discharge above 93°F assuming complete mixing. The heat content of discharges may be increased or further limited where local conditions would be benefited thereby.

3. Where downstream circumstances warrant, the area in which the temperature may be artificially raised above 93°F will be prescribed.

4. A fishway will be required in streams receiving heated discharges where this is essential for the preservation of migratory pathways of game fish, or for the preservation of important aquatic life.

5. There shall be no new discharge to waters providing a suitable environment for trout if as a result the temperature of the receiving stream exceeds 58°F or stream temperature, whichever is higher.

6. Reduction of the heat content of discharges to estuarial waters will be required where necessary to protect the public interest. Estuarial waters are those containing ocean salts. Tidal waters not containing ocean salts are considered as freshwater streams.

And the state of Maryland has recommended the following for steam electric stations:

1. No thermal additions may be made to trout streams.

2. Temperature increases through condensers are not to exceed 5°F during those seasons when natural water temperatures are 60°F or higher.

3. Temperature increases through condensers are not to exceed 10°F during those seasons when natural water temperatures are 55°F or lower.

4. Discharge temperatures are not to exceed 65°F when natural water temperatures are between 55 and 60°F.

5. Discharge temperature is not to exceed 90°F at any time.

6. Thermal additions are not to affect more than 25 percent of the cross-sectional area of any stream, river, or part of the Chesapeake Bay.

7. No plant may pump more than 10 percent of the net flow of any surface water system through its condenser system.

8. There may be no toxic chemicals in effluent water from plant operations.

9. There must be adequate barriers to prevent large invertebrates and fish from entering intake and discharge structures, including canals.

Such recommendations, even if followed, are only stopgap measures. The problem can be met only after we have first acquired sufficient information about the behavior of heated effluents in lakes, rivers, and estuaries, about the effects of temperature on mortality, behavior, and physiology of aquatic organisms, to predict effects of thermal pollution on any site. Ways must also be sought for alternative methods of cooling, such as the use of dry towers or closed-circuit cooling systems. Careful consideration must be given to each and every site of proposed steam electric stations to determine its possible detrimental effects on environment and public welfare. Consideration must also be given to the possible constructive uses of waste heat. Unless the problems of thermal pollution are solved before they become unsolvable, irreparable and costly damage will be done to aquatic ecosystems and man's environment.

BIBLIOGRAPHY

1. Wright, J. H. 1970. Electric power generation and the environment. Westinghouse Engineer 30(3): 66—80.
2. Fry, F. E. J. 1947. Effects of environment on animal activity. Univ. Toronto Studies Biol. Ser. 55 (Ontario Fish. Res. Lab. Pub. 68). 63 pp.
3. Brett, J. R. 1960. Thermal requirements of fish—three decades of study, 1940—1970. In *Biological Problems in Water Pollution*, 2nd Seminar, 1959. Robert A. Taft, Sanitary Engineering Center Tech. Rept. W60—3. pp. 110—117.
4. ———. 1956. Some principles in the thermal requirements of fishes. Quart. Rev. Biology 31(2): 75—87.
5. Henderson, N. E. 1963. Influence of light and temperature on the reproductive cycle of the eastern brook trout, *Salvelinus fontinalis*. (Mitchell). J. Fish. Res. Bd. Canada 20(4): 859—897.
6. Fry, F. E. J. 1951. Some environmental relations of the speckled trout (*Salvelinus fontinalis*). Rept. Proc. N. E. Atlantic Fish Conf.
7. Gaufin, A. R. 1965. Environmental requirements of Plecoptera. In *Biological Problems in Water Pollution*, 3rd Seminar, August 1962. Public Health Service Publ. No. 999-WP-25. pp. 105—110.

8. Robach, S. S. 1965. Environmental problems in Trichoptera. In *Biological Problems in Water Pollution*, 3rd Seminar, August 1962. Public Health Service Publ. No. 999-WP-25. pp. 118—126.

9. Curry, L. L. 1965. A survey of the environmental requirements for the midge (*Diptera tendipedidae*). Hearings Before the Subcommittee on Air and Water Pollution of the Committee on Public Works. United States Senate. pp. 127—141.

10. Mihursky, J. A., and V. S. Kennedy. 1967. Water temperature criteria to protect aquatic life. Symposium on Water Quality Criteria to Protect Aquatic Life. Am. Fish. Soc. Spec. Pub. No. 4. pp. 20—32.

11. Jensen, A. C. 1970. Thermal pollution in the marine environment. The Conservationist 25(2): 8—13.

12. Trembley, F. J. 1965. Effects of cooling water from steam electric power plants on stream biota. In *Biological Problems in Water Pollution*, 3rd Seminar, August 1962. Public Health Service Publ. No. 999-WP-25. pp. 334—345.

13. Coutant, C. C. 1962. The effect of heated water effluents upon the macroinvertebrate riffle fauna of the Delaware River. Proc. Penna. Acad. Sci. 36: 58—71.

14. Warinner, J. E., and M. L. Brehmer. 1966. The effects of thermal effluents on marine organism. Air and Water Pollution Int. J. 10: 227—289.

15. Arndt, H. E. 1968. Effects of heated water on a littoral community in Maine. Hearings Before the Subcommittee on Air and Water Pollution of the Committee on Public Works. United States Senate. pp. 246—349.

16. Mihursky, J. A., and L. E. Cronin. 1968. Progress and problems in thermal pollution in Maryland. Thermal Pollution—1968. Hearings Before the Subcommittee on Air and Water Pollution of the Committee on Public Works. United States Senate. pp. 136—139.

17. Naylor, E. 1965. Biological effects of a heated effluent in docks at Swansea. S. Wales, Proc. Zool. Soc. Lond. 144: 253—268.

18. ———. 1965. Effects of heated effluents upon marine and estuarine organisms. In F. S. Russell (ed.). *Advances in Marine Biology*, New York. Academic Press, Vol. 3, pp. 68—103.

19. Glooschenko, Walter. 1968. Thermal Pollution—1968. Hearings Before the Subcommittee on Air and Water Pollution of the Committee on Public Works. United States Senate. p. 752.

20. Gaucher, T. A. 1968. Monoculture from Study of Means to Revitalize the Connecticut Fisheries Industry—reprinted. Thermal Pollution—1968. Hearings Before the Subcommittee on Air and Water Pollution of the Committee on Public Works. United States Senate. pp. 293—306.

21. Mihursky, J. A. 1967. On possible constructive uses of thermal additions to estuaries. BioScience, 17(10): 698—702.

Air Pollution Problems

Commentary

Of all the environmental degradations caused by man, none is of greater public concern than air pollution. It creates problems of visibility, nuisance odors, and dirt. It has created massive public health problems: bronchitis, asthma, emphysema, increased death rates among older people and those with chronic respiratory problems. Although the human species seems to be highly adaptable to air pollution, it is highly susceptible to it as well, given certain conditions.

Ecosystems are the same. Air pollution poses a threat to the functioning of ecosystems as well as a threat to health. Actually the two cannot be separated, for health problems are also ecological. Thus, no matter from what viewpoint air pollution is considered, it is an ecological problem.

Heat, gases, aerosols, and dust of some form or another have always been discharged into the atmosphere. Under normal loads these pollutants were dispersed and recycled by ecosystems. But like other pollutants, man's activity and technology have discharged into the atmosphere all forms of pollutants, including many new ones in amounts far exceeding the ability of ecosystems to recycle them.

Although air pollution is global, its most immediate effects are local. Air pollution is caused by an interaction of large amounts of pollutants poured into the air and physics of the atmosphere.

The atmosphere that envelops the earth is a gas and behaves according to the general law of gases. When the pressure of a mass of gas changes, the volume and temperature of that gas also change. The column of air above the earth has a measureable mass and exerts a pressure that decreases with increasing altitude. If a mass of air rises, it moves into a region of lower pressure, and its temperature decreases at the rate of $5\frac{1}{2}°F$ per 1000 feet. If this mass moves downward to lower elevations, the air is compressed and warmed at the same rate. When heat is neither gained nor lost by mixing with the surrounding air, it is an adiabatic process, and the rate of change in temperature in going from either a higher or a lower pressure is called a "dry adiabatic change." If a mass of air is cooled at the dry adiabatic rate, it will rise; and if it becomes immersed in warmer air, it will fall to its original level or to a level where the surrounding air has the same temperature. If the air mass lowers and is surrounded by cooler and denser air, it will rise to its original level. When this condition prevails the atmosphere is said to be stable. But if the mass of air moves up or down and continues to rise or fall, the atmosphere is unstable.

Instability of the atmosphere is created by differential heating of the earth and lower atmosphere. The earth by day is heated by short-wave solar radiation (Fig. 1(a)), which is absorbed in different amounts over the land, depending on vegetation, slope, soil, season, etc. Lower layers of the atmosphere, heated by the earth's surface below by radiation, conduction, and convection, rise in small volumes and colder air falls. This turnover of the atmosphere produces a turbulence that is increased by strong winds on the earth's surface and aloft. Under such conditions pollutants are carried aloft and are mixed and diffused both vertically and horizontally.

After the sun goes down, the heating of the earth stops and the earth begins to lose heat (Fig. 1(b)). This loss of heat causes both the earth and the lower atmosphere to become cooler. This nighttime radiational cooling is most pronounced on calm clear nights. The layer of surface air is cooled while the air aloft remains near daytime temperatures. This forms a surface inversion in which the temperature of the air increases rather than decreases with altitude, as it normally does. In mountainous or hilly country, cold dense air flows down slopes and gathers in the valleys. The cold air then is trapped beneath a layer of warm air (Fig. 2). Such inversions trap impurities and other pollutants. Smoke from industry and other heated pollutants rise until the temperature matches the surrounding air. Then the pollutants flatten out and spread horizontally. As pollutants continue to accumulate, they may fill the entire area with smog. Such inversions are most intense if the atmosphere is stable. Inversions break up when surface air is heated during the day to create vertical convections up through the inversion layer, or when a new air mass moves in.

Similar but more widespread inversions occur when a high pressure cell stagnates over a region. In a high pressure area the air flow is clockwise and spreads outward. The air flowing away from the high must be replaced, and the only source for replacement air is from aloft. Thus surface high pressure areas are regions of sinking air movement from aloft, called subsidence. When high level winds slow down, cold air

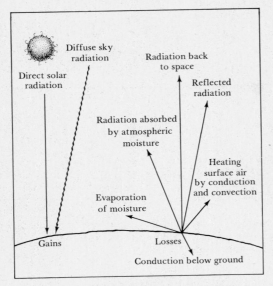

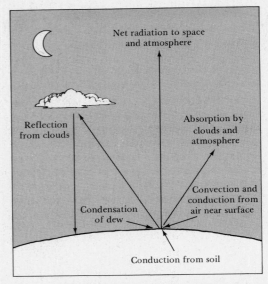

(a) DAYTIME SURFACE HEAT EXCHANGE

(b) NIGHTTIME SURFACE HEAT EXCHANGE

Figure 1. (a) Solar radiation that reaches the earth's surface in the daytime is dissipated in several ways, but heat gains exceed heat losses. (b) At night there is a net cooling of the earth's surface, although some heat is returned by various processes. (Adapted from *Fire Weather*, USDA Agricultural Handbook 360, Washington, D.C., 1970.)

at high levels in the atmosphere tends to sink. As this air moves from the high altitude and low atmospheric pressure to lower altitude and higher atmospheric pressure, it heats up at the dry adiabatic rate. The sinking air becomes compressed as it moves downward, and as it warms it becomes drier. As a result a layer of warm air develops at a higher level in the atmosphere (Fig. 3). Rarely reaching the ground, it hangs several hundred to several thousand feet above the earth, forming a subsidence inversion. Such inversions tend to prolong the period of stagnation and increase the intensity of pollution. Subsidence inversions are often accompanied by

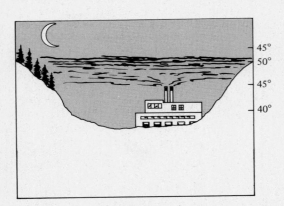

Figure 2. Smoke released into an inversion layer will rise only until the temperature equals that of the surrounding air. Then the smoke flattens out and spreads horizontally. The zone of warm nighttime temperatures near the top of the inversion is known as the thermal belt.

lower level radiation inversions that bring about our highest concentrations of pollution of the type that spread over the East and West coasts, Tokyo, and other areas of the globe in the fall of 1970.

Along the West coast and occasionally along the East coast, the warm seasons often produce a coastal or marine inversion. In this case, cool, moist air from the ocean spreads over low-lying land. This layer of cool air, which may vary in depth from a few hundred to several hundred thousand feet, is topped by warmer, dryer air, which also traps pollutants in the lower layers.

Aside from the health problems created, the ecological effects of air pollution are pronounced. Pollution can influence local weather. Particulate effluents seed clouds, a natural process. Pollen, sea spray, bacteria, volcanic and other natural dusts, all are important in seeding clouds and influencing precipitation. But man

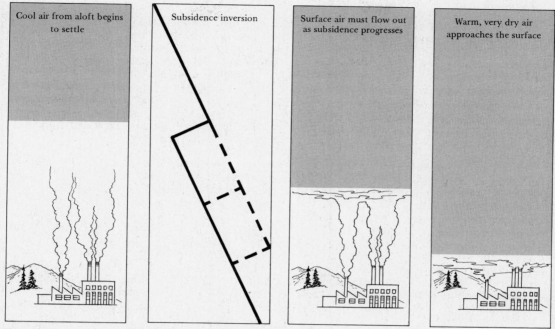

Figure 3. The descent of a subsidence inversion may be followed by successive temperature measurements as shown by the dashed lines. As more humid air flows outward, the drier air aloft is allowed to sink and warm adiabatically. (Adapted from *Fire Weather*, USDA Agricultural Handbook 360, Washington, D.C., 1970.)

has greatly increased the amount of particulate matter in the atmosphere, especially through ashes, soot, and dust from disturbing the surface of the earth. These particulates vary widely in size. Large particulates fall out, quickly producing the nuisance dirt and dust so characteristic of industrial and mining areas. Other particulate matter remains for some time in the atmosphere, reducing ultraviolet penetration and providing condensation nuclei.

The latter are of considerable local interest. Particulate matter smaller than 10 microns act as nuclei for the condensation of water vapor and the freezing of atmospheric water. Many particulate pollutants are hydroscopic, possessing the marked ability to attract water and to speed up the condensation of water vapor. Close to the earth condensation on this particulate matter produces damp haze, mist, and fog. Higher up in the atmosphere it produces cloud droplets. At temperatures below 32°F some types of pollutants, such as metallurgical fumes, certain organic compounds, and lead iodine, effectively act as surfaces on which ice crystals form.[1] Lead iodine is a leading one, for it is produced in large quantities by a combination of iodine vapor in the atmosphere with submicron-sized lead particles from auto exhausts. The man-made pollutants increase the frequencies of fog, haze, and rainfall over urban and industrial areas. Cities in the United States experience 5 to 10 percent more cloud cover, 5 to 10 percent more precipitation, and 100 percent more winter fog than rural areas.[2] An evidence of weather modification by pollution is the increase in precipitation and stormy weather about La Porte, Indiana, downwind from the heavily polluted areas of Chicago, Illinois, and Gary, Indiana, and close to moisture-laiden air over Lake Michigan.[3] Since 1925 there has been a 31 percent increase in precipitation, a 38 percent increase in thunderstorms, and a 240 percent increase in the occurrence of hail.

Man-derived particulate matter comes not only from the city but from rural areas over the earth as well. Smoke from slash-and-burn agriculture in southeast Asia, South America, and Africa produces great areas of

[1] V. J. Schaefer, "The Inadvertent Modification of the Atmosphere by Air Pollution," in S. F. Singer (ed.), *Global Effects of Environmental Pollution*, New York, Springer-Verlag, 1970, pp. 158—174.

[2] H. E. Landsberg, "City Air—Better or Worse?" in *Symposium—Air over Cities*, Robert A. Taft. Sanitary Engineering Center Tech. Rept. A62-5, Cincinnati, Ohio, 1962, pp. 31—36.

[3] S. A. Changnon, "La Porte Weather Anomaly, Fact or Fiction?" *Bull. Amer. Met. Soc.* **49**, 4—11.

blue haze.[4] Summer dust storms in India and dust from the winter monsoons in China both have some effect on local as well as global climatic conditions.

Whatever the source, turbidity of the atmosphere has increased in recent times. Some estimates place the increase at 30 percent in the past decade;[4] other estimates place it at 10 to 15 percent.[5] Part is due to the activities of man. Who or what has contributed the largest share in the past decade is open for debate. Some meteorologists estimate that man-derived dust load in the atmosphere is comparable to the average stratospheric dust load from volcanic activity; but the global variation in dust pollution due to man's activities is one full magnitude lower than that of the injection of dust by volcanoes. The effect of atmospheric dust is to increase the reflection of solar radiation back to space and to reduce the amount of radiation reaching the earth.

Aggravating the situation are the contrails of jet aircraft. Flying at high altitudes, jets leave condensation trails that persist and spread to form high altitude cirrus clouds that could modify solar radiation balances over well-traveled areas.[4]

Another major global pollutant of the atmosphere is carbon dioxide. The amount of CO_2 in the atmosphere has increased 10 percent over the past 100 years and roughly 20 percent over the past 30 or 40 years.[5] Most of this increase is due to the increased burning of fossil fuels, the reserves of products of photosynthesis that have not been oxidized. If large quantities of fossil fuels are not burned, a sort of balance exists between the amount of CO_2 produced by respiration and the amount consumed in photosynthesis. As a world average, roughly 11×10^{16} g of CO_2 annually is consumed in photosynthesis.[6] This amount nearly matched the amount of CO_2 released by oxidation, of which some 10^{13} g/yr is deposited as new fossil carbon. Through the combustion of fossil fuels man is releasing some 1.5×10^{16} g/yr of CO_2, three orders of magnitude greater than that returned to fossil state. We are depleting the resource 1000 times faster than it is being replaced. Although early estimates suggested that most of the CO_2 produced by the burning of fossil fuels remains in the atmosphere, recent measurements indicate that a considerable portion is shared with the oceans. The rate of increase of atmospheric CO_2 from 1958 to 1963 is 0.5×10^{16} g annually, about $\frac{1}{3}$ the rate of release of CO_2 from burning of fossil fuels.

Considering that the level of CO_2 in the atmosphere in the nineteenth century was 290 parts per million, CO_2 in the atmosphere increased by 5 percent by 1944 and 10 percent by 1960. It is projected to increase to 15 percent by 1980, 20 percent by 1990 and 27 percent by 2000, for a doubling time of twenty-three years.

The effect of this increase is to raise the global temperature. Carbon dioxide is a strong absorber of longwave infrared radiation and acts something like the glass in greenhouses, to raise the temperature of the earth. The earth has been experiencing a warming trend of about 1.8°F since 1900. One-third of the world-wide warming trend between 1880 to 1940 has been ascribed to an increase in atmospheric CO_2. All things remaining equal, the present rate of CO_2 accumulation in the atmosphere will cause the global temperature to rise 0.2°F by 1980, 0.5°F by 1990 and 0.8°F by 2000.

But, paradoxically, the temperature of the earth has decreased 0.5°F since 1940. This fact is thought to be due to an interaction between the warming properties of CO_2 and the cooling effect of atmospheric dust, both man-derived and natural, particularly volcanic dust.

Certain implications appear. In the past, warming influences of man-derived CO_2 exceeded the cooling effect of man-induced particulates in the atmosphere. The doubling time of the accumulation of CO_2 in the atmosphere is twenty-three years, and the doubling time of man-derived particulate matter is fifteen to twenty years. If these rates remain the same in the future, the cooling effect will catch up with the warming effect and eventually surpass it, sometime after A.D. 2000. Thus, an additional warming of perhaps 1.8°F over that period will be followed by a temperature decline. All of this is speculation, for no one can foresee other forces that are involved in climatic change. There may be an increase or lessening of the particulate load in the atmosphere; volcanic activity may increase or decrease; and man may reduce his load of dust pollutants in the air or increase cloud cover because of the increased traffic of jet planes, especially supersonic transports.

Some concern has been raised about the possible depletion of oxygen, the other half of the oxygen—carbon dioxide cycle. Supposedly this would come about through the increased burning of fossil fuels and a decreased biomass of photosynthetic plants brought about by deliberate destruction and by pollution. The earth is envel

---

[4]R. A. Bryson and W. M. Wendland. "Climatic Effects of Atmospheric Pollution," in S. F. Singer (ed.), *Global Effects of Environmental Pollution,* New York, Springer-Verlag, 1970, pp. 130—138.

[5]J. M. Mitchell, "A Preliminary Evaluation of Atmospheric Pollution as a Cause of the Global Temperature Fluctuation of the Last Century," in S. F. Singer (ed.), *Global Effects of Environmental Pollution,* New York, Springer-Verlag, 1970, pp. 139—155.

[6]F. S. Johnson, "The Oxygen and Carbon Dioxide Balance in the Earth's Atmosphere," S. F. Singer (ed.), *Global Effects of Environmental Pollution,* New York, Springer-Verlag, 1970, pp. 4—11.

oped in a cloak of oxygen, approximately 60,000 moles per square meter.[7] To this photosynthesis adds 8 moles per square meter annually. Most of the oxygen released to the atmosphere by photosynthesis is consumed by animals and bacteria. The bulk of the remainder is utilized by the oxidation of geological materials. Only a very small fraction, about one part in 10,000, escapes oxidation and remains in the atmosphere. Thus the amount of oxygen in the atmosphere remains rather stable and resistant to short-time changes of 100 to 1000 years. If we were to completely burn our fossil fuel reserves, we would still use up less than 3 percent of our oxygen reserves.[7] And if photosynthesis should cease and all organic matter were decomposed, we would still have a large reserve of molecular oxygen on which to draw. The point is before oxygen is depleted by any cause man will have died from starvation because of the loss of photosynthesis, or from pollution. The major problem is not oxygen depletion but an accumulation of harmful gases and dusts in the world's atmosphere.

What harmful gases can do is indicated by the response of plants to pollution. Already air pollution is altering ecosystems and interfering with the production of food. Plants, the basic component of ecosystems, are vulnerable to much lower levels of air pollution than man or animals and to a greater variety of pollutants. Sulfur dioxide, PAN (peroxyacetylnitrates), fluorine, and ozone (an active form of oxygen) are among some of the pollutants to which plants are most highly sensitive. Plants may be sensitive to all, or sensitive to some and resistant to others. Each pollutant produces certain symptoms in each sensitive plant that are distinguishable from the effects of other pollutants. Thus, plants serve as detectors of air pollution useful to such agencies as the U.S. Forest Service and the Public Health Service.[8] Injuries to plants are convincing indicators of harmful air pollution. And the response of plants to pollutants influences primary production and ecosystem structure.

Among the forest trees, pines are highly vulnerable. White pine is very sensitive to sulfur dioxide and ozone. Spotted and yellowed needles, dead tips, and stunted growth are some characteristics of pollution damage to white pine. In a number of localities air pollution is killing plantations of Christmas trees as well as eliminating pines from the forest.

In the San Bernadino Mountains of Southern California smog from Los Angeles is killing ponderosa pine. Ozone, a by-product of pollutants from automobile exhausts, and other oxidants cause a rapid loss of chlorophyll. The loss of chlorophyll reduces the ability of pines to carry on photosynthesis, often to a level too low for plant growth and maintenance. Stunted growth, loss of needles, reduced moisture in the sapwood and phloem so weaken the pines that they are very susceptible to the attack of bark beetles, which subsequently kill the trees.[9] Because of air pollution, well-stocked stands of ponderosa pine are being converted to poorly stocked stands of Douglas fir, incense cedar, and sugar pine, which are more resistant to air pollution.

Air pollutants interfere with food production. Ozone is particularly harmful to such important food plants as tomatoes, beans, spinach, potatoes, and tobacco. Ozone injury, appearing as dark stipples or light flecks on the upper surface of the leaf, damages the palisade layer of cells just under the upper epidermis of the leaf. Sensitive to sulfur dioxide are alfalfa, barley, cotton, wheat, and beans. Plants resistant to sulfur dioxide are potatoes, corn, onions, and celery. The sensitivity of plants often prevents the growing of important agricultural crops for hundreds of miles around large cities.

Some plants resistant to certain pollutants build up the material in their tissues. Alfalfa, tobacoo, cotton, and tomatoes, for example, are resistant to fluorine, yet the plants may accumulate hundreds to several thousands parts per million without injury. When these plants are consumed by animals, the fluorine is transferred to the next trophic level. Cattle feeding on fluorine-contaminated alfalfa may develop fluorosis and die. Death results from the interference of enzymatic processes by fluorine that brings about a rapid buildup of fluorocitrate.

Air pollution—its cause, its complex chemical interaction both in the atmosphere and within organisms, its impact on ecosystems, and its interference with food production—represents an enormous environmental problem. The nature and extent of air pollution is examined in some detail in the following selection by L. A. Chambers.

[7]W. S. Broecker. "Man's Oxygen Reserves," *Science* **168**, 1970, pp. 1537—1538.

[8]C. R. Berry and H. E. Heggestad, "1968 Air Pollution Detectives," in *Science for Better Living*, USDA Yearbook of Agriculture, Washington, D.C., 1968, pp. 142—146.

[9]F. W. Cobb, Jr., and R. W. Stark, "Decline and Mortality of Smog-Injured Ponderosa Pine," *J. Forestry* **68**, 1970, pp. 147—149.

Selection 25

Classification and Extent of Air Pollution Problems

by Leslie A. Chambers

HISTORICAL PERSPECTIVE

AIR POLLUTION PRIOR TO THE INDUSTRIAL REVOLUTION

The quality of the atmosphere, on which all terrestrial forms of life are dependent, has been recognized as an important variable in the environment only during the past few decades. It may be supposed that smoke and fumes from forest fires, volcanoes, and crude "domestic" heating and cooking arrangements were troublesome or lethal in discrete localities even before our human ancestors became organized in fixed communities, and that the odors of decaying animal and vegetable refuse, attested to by existing residues of prehistoric garbage dumps in and near Stone Age dwellings, were cause for protesting comment in such language as may have been available to the temporary residents.

However, it is unlikely that such circumstances can have been regarded as more than incidental to devastating natural cataclysms, or as cause for transfer to another dwelling site, until social evolution reached the husbandry level involving association of family units into more or less fixed communities. Only then could human activities in the aggregate have produced sufficient effluvia to affect an occupied neighborhood. To what extent they did so is entirely conjectural with respect to all of prehistory and can be guessed only by tenuous inference with respect to most of the ancient and medieval periods. The embodiment in folk knowledge of the middle ages, and in pre-scientific belief, of the concept of "miasmas," or poisonous airs, as etiological agents of certain diseases, may indicate a deduction from ages-old survival experience related to recognized sources of unwholesome air, but is more likely a mistaken association of "malarias" with the odors of swamps rather than with their mosquitoes.

Historically oriented writers on air pollution occasionally have cited classic references to blackened buildings and monuments as evidence that the smoke nuisance has a reality spanning thousands of years. But the grime of antiquity, while a reasonable expectation, does not suffice to indicate a contemporary recognition of its impact on ancient communities or their members. In fact, accumulated knowledge of domestic heating practices, and of the available primitive metallurgical and other limited industrial processes utilized during the first 13 or 14 centuries of the Christian era, leads to the inference that generalized air pollution could not have been an important problem in the villages and towns of the time; cities, in the sense of modern magnitudes, were nonexistent. The frequently cited references to deaths caused by toxic atmospheres, e.g., the suffocation of Pliny the Elder by volcanic fumes as recorded by Tacitus, seem not to be pertinent except in the sense of demonstrating that the human species was then, as now, physiologically responsive to anoxia or to excessive amounts of poisonous gases.

Throughout the earlier periods of history wood constituted the prime source of energy; dependence on it undoubtedly slowed the evolution and use of industrial processes, and eventually limited the per capita availability of heat as the depletion of nearby forests proceeded. The discovery of the energy potential of coal and its gradual replacement of wood

---

THIS SELECTION is reprinted with permission of the author and publisher from A. Stern, *Air Pollution*, 2nd ed; New York, Academic Press, Vol. 1, pp. 1—21. A short introductory section has been omitted to save space.

took place in Europe about the time of Marco Polo's return from his travels through the more technologically advanced civilizations of Asia. But in spite of its abundance in the West and its retrospectively apparent advantages, the European adaptation to its use, which culminated in the Industrial Revolution, proceeded slowly and against all the resistance normal to economic readjustments. Coal was an "unnatural" fuel; its sulfurous combustion products confirmed its suspected association with anticlerical forces at a time much too closely related to the ascendancy of strict orthodoxy; above all, as a matter of record, it caused neighborhood "action committees" to protest against its evident pollution of the atmosphere.

In England, Germany, and elsewhere on the continent various limitations and prohibitions relative to the use, importation, and transport of coal were proclaimed officially, and in isolated instances there is evidence that capital penalties were imposed. Nevertheless the overriding necessities for domestic heat and industrial power made these efforts useless generally and assured their disposal in the limbo of unenforceable law. Coal—the revolutionizer—made possible the Industrial Revolution. And then there was smog.

AIR POLLUTIONS AS RELATED TO COAL SMOKE AND GASES

From the beginning of the 14th century to the early part of the 20th, air pollution by coal smoke and gases has occupied the center of the stage almost exclusively, and in many industrialized areas of the world is still the dominant concern. That it is still a community problem, in spite of a repeatedly demonstrated technological capability for its control, would be surprising if public and official hesitance to pay the price were not so characteristic a factor in the historical evolution of all types of health protection programs. Positive action has seldom been anticipatory; instead it has occurred only after dramatic disasters or large-scale sensory insults have aroused public clamor based on fear. We build levees only after floods have devastated whole regions; we abate pollution of water supplies only after typhoid epidemics or similarly impressive episodes; and we take necessary action to control air pollutants only after their killing or irritating potentials have been realized on a large scale as in London in 1952, or in Los Angeles around 1945.

In no case is the very early recognition of a public health problem, and the failure to take any effective action until it threatened personal survival, better illustrated than in the case of air pollution produced by the unrestricted use of coal in Great Britain. During the reign of Edward I (1272—1307) there was recorded a protest by the nobility against the use of "sea" coal; and in the succeeding reign of Edward II (1307—1327) a man was put to the torture ostensibly for filling the air with a "pestilential odor" through the use of coal.

Under Richard III (1377—1399) and, later, under Henry V (1413—1422) England took steps to regulate and restrict the use of coal, apparently because of the smoke and odors produced by its combustion. The earlier action took the form of taxation, while Henry V established a commission to oversee the movement of coal into the City of London.

Other legislation, parliamentary studies, and literary comments appeared sporadically during the following 250 years. In 1661 a most remarkable pamphlet was published by royal command of Charles II. It consisted of an essay entitled "Fumifugium; or the Inconvenience of the Aer and Smoke of London Dissapated; together with Some Remedies Humbly Proposed," written by John Evelyn, one of the founding members of the Royal Society. It is unfortunate that the author's 17th century style has attracted more attention in the 20th century than has the content of his paper. Evelyn clearly recognized the sources, the effects, and the broad aspects of the control problem, to an extent not far surpassed at the present time except for detail and for chemical and physiological terminology. Thus it is clear, not only that the London of 1661 was plagued by coal smoke, but also that the problem and its content were recognized by at least one of the leading scientists of the period.

Some evidence exists that methods for abatement of the smoke nuisance were being sought immediately after the appearance of Evelyn's pamphlet. In 1686 a person named Justel presented before the Philosophical Society "An Account of an Engine that Consumes Smoke." The nature of this and other very early control devices is unimportant, since the rapid increase in smoke density through the next century and a half indicates that they were, like many more recent procedures, either ineffective or not widely used.

By the beginning of the 19th century the smoke nuisance in London and other English cities was of sufficient public concern to prompt the appointment (in 1819) of a Select Committee of the British Parliament to study and report upon smoke abatement. Immediately available sources do not include the substance of any resulting publication, but the effect of the study is suspected of having been similar to that of dozens of other committee recommendations made during the ensuing 133 years. The gradual development of the smoke problem was culminated in the action-arousing deaths, within a few days, of 4000 persons in London in December, 1952.

Records of lethal air pollution concentrations during the 19th century are not definitive; in fact, recognition of their occurrence seems to have resulted largely from retrospective examination of vital records and contemporary descriptive notes. 1873 an episode having the characteristics of the 1952 event occurred in London, and more or less severe repetitions have affected metropolitan life at irregular intervals up to the present time.

The term "smog" originated in Great Britain as a popular derivation of "smoke-fog" and appears to have been in common usage before World War I. Perhaps the term was suggested by H. A. Des Voeux's 1911 report to the Manchester Conference of the Smoke Abatement League of Great Britain on the "smoke-fog" deaths which occurred in Glasgow, Scotland in 1909. During two separate periods in the autumn of that year very substantial increases in death rate were attributed to smoke and fog and it was estimated that "1063 deaths were attributable to the noxious conditions."

With few isolated exceptions, the extreme atmospheric concentrations of pollutants produced by coal burning in Britain have not been duplicated elsewhere. Nevertheless, coal-based industrial economies on the continent of Europe and in the United States have caused discomfort, public reaction, and regulatory action. A generation before the dramatic incident which killed 20 and made several hundred ill in the industrial town of Donora, Pennsylvania in 1948, public action and protest groups had appeared in several American cities. In some, such as St. Louis, Cincinnati, and, more recently, in Pittsburgh, popular movements have resulted in substantial elimination of the smoke nuisance, by substitution of less smoky fuels and by enforced employment of combustion practices designed to eliminate smoke. It has thus been demonstrated that high smoke densities are preventable, although the cost may be great. London and other English cities are handicapped in their current smoke abatement effort by a lack of domestic low volatility coal supplies, almost complete dependence on imports for other fossil fuels, and a centuries-old pattern of household heating, the physical characteristics of which can be changed only gradually and at a very high price.

No rigorous identification of the constituents of coal smoke responsible for the respiratory illnesses with which it has been associated has been produced, although the effects have been generally attributed to sulfur dioxide and trioxide. Recently the probability of a role of tar, soot, and ash particles in the total irritative effect has been the inspiration for several investigations. But the information available to us on the relationship of coal smoke to human health has been insufficient to explain the death and discomfort it has caused.

Smoke and gases from the burning of coal have been the chief atmospheric pollutants in all parts of the industrialized world for more than 400 years. In spite of the recent rapid shift to petroleum and natural gas, coal smoke still is a major contributor to poor air quality in all but a few metropolitan areas.

POLLUTION BY SPECIFIC TOXICANTS
While pollutants resulting from use of the dominant energy sources—coal and petroleum products—generally arise from a large number of points within a community and therefore often cause a general deterioration of the air supply over large areas, more restricted regions closely adjacent to individual sources may be even more seriously affected. Many localized events have emphasized that critical concentrations of pollutants other than smoke, having proven toxic properties, can adversely affect air quality. A large number of substances used in manufacturing and commerce have been recognized officially by the American Conference of Governmental Industrial Hygienists as hazards to industrial workers, and maximal limits of acceptable concentration for eight-hour exposures have been established. While the MAC's (maximum acceptable concentrations) are not applicable where intermittent

exposure of an unselected population is the concern, they do indicate the classes and species of substances potentially hazardous.

Perhaps the most publicized recent example of serious air pollution by an identified toxicant was the episode at Poza Rica, near Mexico City, in which numbers of people were affected and a few died, from exposure to hydrogen sulfide. Metallic fumes and acid mists from metallurgical processing have occasionally rendered downwind regions wholly uninhabitable for plants as well as man. Fluorides escaping from aluminum processing and other industrial sources have been the cause of losses to cattle farmers. Malodorous pollutants from a wide variety of source types have produced responses ranging from public irritation to overt and wholesale illness.

But such unquestionable local reactions to specific pollutants are fortunately rather infrequent. Usually, dispersive processes reduce the concentrations of emitted toxic materials to levels below the probability of immediate or acute biological response. Under such circumstances the pollutants may provide a more or less continuous low dosage to occupants of an extended area, providing the possibility of slow concentration of substances such as lead, or a continuum of low grade physiological insults which may eventually overpower physiological defenses. The whole area of potential knowledge of the effects of low dosages of pollutants long continued is virtually unexplored; and the possibilities of synergism among two or more substances simultaneously breathed at subacute concentrations for extended periods of time have been suggested but scarcely examined, even theoretically.

EMERGENCE OF PETROLEUM PRODUCTS

It is possible that future historians may recognize a Second Industrial Revolution born in the years following the successful completion (1859) of Drake's first oil well in Pennsylvania. Subsequent release of a flood of fossilized energy in the form of petroleum and natural gas not only has transformed industrial and domestic heating practices, but has made possible wholesale changes in transportation, and has provided the raw materials for petrochemical products in almost infinite variety.

Combustion of oil and gas has diminished the nuisance and hazard of coal smoke to the extent that the use of these fuels has displaced coal. With more than one type of mineral energy source available, the magnitude of the change has varied markedly among geographical regions, in a manner closely related to propinquity of oil and gas fields, extension of pipeline networks and other transport facilities, relative local costs of delivered fuel, and other logistic factors. Within the United States, for example, large areas of the Southwest now consume negligible quantities of coal, while portions of the eastern seaboard, the Southeast, and the midwestern industrial complexes exhibit mixed patterns of coal, oil, and natural gas use.

Throughout the United States and in many other parts of the world the use of petroleum products, in the forms of gasoline and oil, has been tremendously accelerated, especially since World War II, by the almost exclusive employment of internal combustion engines in highway, railway, and marine transport. Thus, even in those regions unfavorably situated for the rapid adoption of oil and gas for heating and manufacturing, the combustion residues of petroleum products have become a factor in community air pollution.

As a matter of fact, the physical system underlying the obvious manifestations of smog in Los Angeles includes neither smoke nor fog. Early in the hastily organized effort to abate the air pollution which became irritatingly evident during the wartime industrialization of southern California, Professor A. J. Haagen-Smit demonstrated that the eye irritation, damage to green leaves, and light-scattering characteristic of smog could be produced by ultraviolet irradiation of a mixture of hydrocarbon vapors and nitrogen dioxide. This, as well as much subsequent work, has proved that the "new" kind of air pollution results from exposure to sunlight of mixtures of olefins and other reactive products of petroleum manufacture and use, mixed with oxides of nitrogen. The variety of intermediate and terminal products formed under different conditions of relative concentration, humidity, temperature, solar radiation intensity, and admixture with other reactive gases and particles is certainly very great. Among them are ozone, organic hydroperoxides, peroxyacyl nitrates or nitrates (PAN); several aldehydes and other irritants which have been positively identified, a wide variety of free radicals not experimentally demonstrated but necessary intermediates in the photochemical transitions from primary

287

reactants to more stable products, and a number of possibly troublesome substances whose occurrence is still hypothetical.

Most of the pollutants related to petroleum production, processing, and use have intrinsic toxic or irritative potentials of a rather low order. By contrast, their photochemical reaction products may affect biological systems at extremely low concentrations. Thus, the control of the primary reactants must be based on their identification and their regulation to atmospheric levels at which they are incapable of generating effective amounts of secondary products. Ozone, for example, is not known to be produced in significant quantity from direct sources within the Los Angeles area; yet it occurs frequently at levels greater than 0.25 ppm as the result of photoenergized reactions involving hydrocarbons at the level of 1 ppm or less and NO_2 in the same range of concentration. To prevent toxic accumulations of ozone, it is necessary to control sources of both hydrocarbon vapor and nitrogen oxides which, except for the intervention of reaction in the general atmosphere, would be harmless.

Current economic trends and knowledge of proven world petroleum resources indicate that air pollution due to hydrocarbons, petrochemical products, and engine exhausts will become increasingly evident in most metropolitan areas for many years to come. Eventually, of course, retarding pressures generated by depletion of supplies will become operative, but the present and at least one or two future generations will find it necessary to protect local air supplies against contamination by gasoline vapors and exhaust gases.

RELATIONSHIP TO ENERGY SOURCES

The material which a biological system utilizes as its source of energy determines the characteristics of its waste products. Similarly, the fuel used by a community governs the kinds, amounts, and properties of its refuse to a major degree. The aerial excreta of a city may be modified by local patterns of industry, solid waste disposal practices, or occasional counteracting "perfumes" such as paper mill mercaptans, but the products generated in energy transformations constitute the core of the community air pollution problem.

It is not necessary to discount the importance of localized nuisances in order to accept this primary thesis. Odors, toxic dusts and fumes, and corrosive acid mists are of great importance to the locality directly affected. But the primary threat to the air resources of modern cities may be firmly attributed to the kinds of stuff they use for fuel and to the ways in which they use it.

A major change in the nature of the air pollution problem could occur only with a major change in energy sources. It is interesting, but probably of little immediate import, to speculate on what may occur if nuclear power, or direct utilization of solar energy, become practicable and economically competitive. In the one case a totally different kind of air pollution will require careful control; radioactive by-products of nuclear fuels could be troublesome to an extent not foretold by any previous experience with products of fossil fuels. In the present state of nuclear power technology the magnitude and quality of the potential air pollution problem cannot be defined, but it can be hoped that power packages will be so constructed as to minimize emission of active wastes.

Since about the beginning of the 20th century world-wide atmospheric concentrations of carbon dioxide have been increasing steadily in a manner related to the increased global use of fossil fuels. Carbon dioxide is not often considered to be an air pollutant since it produces adverse physiological effects only at relatively high concentration, and because biological and geochemical processes are known to provide a sufficient natural disposal system. Its atmospheric increase apparently reflects an accelerating disparity between the CO_2 production rate and the rate of approach to equilibrium with marine and terrestrial sinks. Unchecked increase in the rate of combustion of carbon fuels apparently will increase general CO_2 levels eventually to meteorologically and physiologically significant levels. Perhaps it may, within a few generations, compete with radioactive wastes for the dubious distinction of being a world-wide air polluter.

Any substantial shift of energy dependence from fossil fuels to nuclear or solar power plants will tend to re-establish the planetary CO_2 equilibrium. It is especially exciting to consider the air conservation potential of solar energy, certain types of fuel cells, and related nonpolluting power sources now being explored. Should these prove capable of displacing current combustive transformations, the community air pollution problem would be reduced to more or less routine policing of localized sources.

PRIMARY CONCEPTS OF AIR POLLUTION

A variety of definitions of air pollution have been devised, each expressing more or less completely the individual philosophical, theoretical, practical, or protective motivation of its author. Any circumstance which adds to or subtracts from the usual constituents of air may alter its physical or chemical properties sufficiently to be detected by occupants of the medium. It is usual to consider as pollutants only those substances added in sufficient concentration to produce a measurable effect on man or other animals, vegetation, or material.

Pollutants may therefore include almost any natural or artificial composition of matter capable of being airborne. They may occur as solid particles, liquid droplets, or gases, or in various admixtures of these forms. Pollution of the air by a single chemical species appears to be a most unusual event; certainly, most community problems involve a very large number of kinds and sizes of substances.

In an effort to classify the pollutants thus far recognized, it is convenient to consider two general groups: those emitted directly from identifiable sources and those produced in the air by interaction among two or more primary pollutants, or by reaction with normal atmospheric constituents, with or without photoactivation. But any taxonomic system based on available sampling and analytical methods is almost certain to fall short of a complete description of the qualities of a polluted air supply. This is true because few, if any, of the polluting entities retain their exact identities after entering the atmosphere. Thermal and photochemical reactions, often catalytically facilitated by gases or solid and liquid surfaces, provide a dynamic, constantly changing character to the total system, and to its individual constituents. Eventually it may be possible to characterize a polluted air mass in space and time by a complex integration of reaction pathways and rates as governed by fluctuating free energy levels. But that capability is only a present dream.

PRIMARY EMISSONS.

Fortunately, it is usually possible to determine with reasonable assurance the kinds and amounts of primary pollutants emitted from each source in a community. Much information is available as to the chemical species and physical states of discharges from most types of artificial and natural generators. While the end effect of the emissions cannot be predicted with certainty from these data alone, they do define the primary reactants, and after other troublesome reaction chains have been identified, enable retroactive abatement with respect to the primary species contributing to the chains.

Primary emissions are often categorized, quite illogically because of our imperfect knowledge, under a mixture of headings defining chemical properties, physical phases, and magnitudes. For purposes of generalization a listing of the following type is probably as inclusive as any:

Fine solids (less than 100 μ in diameter)
Coarse particles (greater than 100 μ in diameter)
Sulfur compounds
Organic compounds
Nitrogen compounds
Oxygen compounds
Halogen compounds
Radioactive compounds

The finer aerosols include carbon particles, metallic dusts, silicates, fluorides, tars, resins, some pollens, fungi and bacteria, solid oxides, nitrates, sulfates, chlorides, aromatics, and a host of other species obviously overlapping all of the more specific categories. As particles, they scatter light in conformance with well-established physical laws relating wavelength and particle size. As suppliers of large specific surface they afford opportunity for catalysis of normally slow interactions among adsorbed pollutants. As charged entities they govern to a substantial degree the condensation and coalescence of other particles and gases. As chemical species per se some of them exhibit high orders of toxicity to plant and animal species, or are corrosive to metal structures and other materials. To the extent that they are radioactive they increase the normal radiation dosage and are suspected of being factors in abnormal genetic processes. And finally, as plain dust, deposited in accordance with the physical laws governing precipitation

289

and electrostatic attraction, they soil clothing, buildings, and bodies, and constitute a general nuisance.

The coarser particles, 100 μ and greater in diameter, present the same types of problems in greatly diminished degree. This is true because their mass assures rather prompt removal from the air by gravitational attraction, because physiological defensive mechanisms prevent their penetration into human or animal lungs, and because the same mass of substance in such large units affords substantially less opportunity for interaction with other components of the polluted air supply. On the other hand, their soiling effect may be more evident simply because after leaving a source they are readily deposited without opportunity for wide dispersal.

Interest in the sulfur compounds has been prolonged and intense because of their suspected role in the London disasters of 1952 and other years, and because of the extreme toxicity of hydrogen sulfide. Combustion of sulfur-containing fuels contributes large amounts of SO_2 and some SO_3, many industrial processes and waste disposal practices generate H_2S, and the nauseous odors of mercaptans are well-recognized associates of some paper-manufacturing and petrochemical processes. All of these affect plants and animals adversely at different, but generally low, concentrations. There is substantial evidence that the full air-polluting potential of SO_2 is realized only after it has reacted with other substances in the atmosphere.

Organic compounds released to typical community air supplies include a very large number of saturated and unsaturated aliphatic and aromatic hydrocarbons together with a variety of their oxygenated and halogenated derivatives. They are emitted principally as vapors, but the less volatile compounds may occur as liquid droplets or solid particles. Some have odors which are characteristic and often objectionable. A number, notably the polynuclear aromatics, have been associated with carcinogenesis. But the majority have relatively low potential for serious air pollution effect so long as they retain their specific identities. Outstanding exceptions may be found, e.g., formaldehyde, formic acid, acrolein, and some compounds containing phosphorus and fluorine.

The nitrogen compounds most abundantly generated and released are nitric oxide, nitrogen dioxide, and ammonia. The first two of these are produced in high temperature combustion and other industrial operations by the combination of normal atmospheric oxygen and nitrogen. While NO_2 is irritating to tissues at relatively low concentration, the major interest in both the oxides is related to their participation in atmospheric photochemical reactions.

Carbon dioxide and carbon monoxide arise in huge amounts from the complete and incomplete combustion of carbonaceous fuels. In Los Angeles County the daily production of CO is estimated to exceed 10,000 tons daily, with more than 80% of it resulting from incomplete utilization of the carbon content of gasoline in automobile engines. CO is not known to participate in secondary atmospheric reactions, but its ability to impair the oxygen-carrying capacity of hemoglobin gives it special status as a primary pollutant. Carbon dioxide in very high concentration affects the cardiac control mechanism, but the quantity required is too great to be of much concern. Mention has already been made of the possible long-range influence of the general rise in atmospheric CO_2 on world temperatures and related phenomena.

Certain inorganic halogen compounds, among them HF and HCl, are produced from metallurgical and other industrial processes. Both are corrosive and irritating per se, and the metallic fluorides have toxic properties which have precipitated some intricate and costly legal actions among operators of producing factories and neighboring residents whose crops and cattle have been severely damaged.

It is not within the scope of this discussion to elaborate on the very specialized nature, sources, or properties of radioactive pollutants. Except for fallout of nuclear weapon residues, these materials have not yet presented a major practical problem beyond the vicinities of Atomic Energy Commission operations. That they will do so with increasing use of nuclear power and industrial applications of isotope techniques is unquestioned.

SECONDARY POLLUTANTS

It was suggested earlier that the total polluted air mass over a populated area is chemically and physically unstable. As a whole, the system tends, like everything else in nature, to approach a state of minimal free energy. The rates, reaction routes, and intermediate steps involved in the process are influenced by many factors such as relative concentration of reactants, degree of photoactivation, variable meteorological dispersive forces, influences of local topography, and relative amounts of moisture.

In the simplest case two species may react thermally, as in the formation of a halide salt by combination of acid mists with metallic oxides. When water droplets are airborne, solution reactions may occur, as in the formation of acid mists by reaction of dissolved oxygen and SO_2.

The formation of sulfuric acid in droplets has been shown to be enormously accelerated by the presence in the droplets of certain metallic oxides such as those of Mn and Fe. This illustrates the well-established role of catalytic processes in affecting step rates in the over-all system.

Surface of liquid and solid particles contribute variously to the energy degradation processes. They may be able to adsorb gases from very dilute mixtures, thereby accelerating normal reactions by providing discrete sites of high reactant concentration. In the adsorbed form the retention of toxic gases in the respiratory system of man may be enhanced, and the apparent irritative effect of the gas may be greatly increased. This kind of phenomenon is well illustrated by Amdur's work relating NaCl aerosols with SO_2 and certain other irritating gases in their effect on pulmonary function. Some species of particles provide sites for surface catalysis of simple and complex reactions, and at least a few cases have been studied in which semiconducting metallic oxide surfaces are active in the catalysis of photoenergized events.

Photochemical reactions involved in air pollution have been studied enough in recent years to prove their major role in smog manifestations of the type experienced in Los Angeles. The primary photochemical event appears to be the dissociation of NO_2, providing NO and O radicals which are able to initiate sustained free radical reaction chains. The number and kinds of transient radicals and semistable compounds formed is then governed by the relative abundance and susceptibility of other chemical species in the system, and by environmental energy factors.

The secondary pollutants produced during events of this type are among the most troublesome that air pollution control agencies are required to abate. They include ozone, formaldehyde, organic hydroperoxides, PAN, and other very reactive compounds, as well as potentially damaging concentrations of short-lived free radicals, so long as photoactivation is maintained in the presence of a sufficient supply of primary and secondary reactants. It will be recognized that free radical mechanisms do not preclude the participation of O_2, H_2O or other normal atmospheric constituents in the formation of end products.

To unravel so complex and temporally variable a system will challenge air pollution research for a long time to come, and the precise prediction of the characteristics of the system one hour ahead may never be more reliable than a probability function. On the other hand, it is clear that the simple process of collecting and analyzing stable chemical species and physical entities as is now practiced cannot provide much knowledge of the continually changing assemblage of transient entities which are prime factors in the effects produced by air pollution.

RECOGNIZED ATMOSPHERIC PROCESSES

In addition to chemical recombinations, several other major factors regulate the impact of primary and secondary pollutants. Principal among these are processes of nucleation and condensation, sedimentation, and other air-cleansing phenomena which tend to remove substances from the atmosphere, and meteorological processes that may dilute the reactants or tend to concentrate them.

Condensation nuclei released from many sources both natural and artificial, under appropriate circumstances can induce the accumulation of vapors into aerosols. These in turn may coalesce with other particles to an extent great enough to permit their eventual deposition on exposed surfaces. As in the case of chemical reaction, such physical processes are rate-related to concentrations; it is questionable whether aggregation and sedimentation play a significant role in air purification except under unusual circumstances, or with respect to coarse particles.

The energy-degrading mechanisms discussed in the previous section may be regarded as natural purification processes, in the sense that their end products are less reactive and therefore usually less troublesome than the primary or intermediate pollutants. The mechanism is analogous in its effect to the biological oxidation of organic pollutants in sewage and water supplies; in each case the oxidized products are relatively ineffective physiologically. Thus, the development of a large excess of ozone during a Los Angeles "alert" usually signals an ensuing rapid decline in eye irritation, presumably because the primary organic reactant in the air mass is near exhaustion and the ozone itself assures final oxidation of the irritating intermediate compounds.

Much closer analogies between water pollution and air pollution problems are apparent when physical dispersive factors are considered. In each case the volume of medium available for dilution of contaminants, and the speed of mixing, are dominant in determining the capability of the stream or air mass of accommodating a given output without presenting localized or general affronts to users of the water or air.

Air supplies are affected, in this quantitative sense, by the degree of containment beneath inversions, the magnitude of horizontal and vertical wind movements, and by the degree of turbulence induced by convection and nonlinear flow. As is the case with all types of meteorological phenomena these factors are governed by both external, synoptic forces, and by localized topographic and thermal influences.

It is possible, given sufficient data to establish wind direction and velocities, local and regional thermal variations, and other pertinent factors, to develop equations expressing the most probable concentrations of pollutants likely to occur in relation to a source of known characteristics. Hypothetically, it is also possible to relate these influences to future air pollution events in, and adjacent to, a large community of different sources. Some suggestive elementary models have already been proposed. But as practical tools for the regulation of regional problems, meteorological analyses have not been used effectively except in relation to localized emissions and their effects in the immediate vicinity.

The existence of usual patterns of air movement over specific geographical areas has suggested to many the possibility of affecting favorably the quality of air supplies by some form of zoning or regulated placement of sources. Sites in deep valleys and elsewhere, subject to frequent inversion entrapment, can be recognized as unfavorable to maintenance of good air quality. However, it is unfortunately true that the acute air pollution episodes in affected localities occur when the meteorological pattern is not "usual." For this reason, a question may reasonably be raised as to the ultimate usefulness of regional zoning as a means of controlling air pollution. The whole matter of the relationship between meteorological probability and the relatively infrequent atypical pollutional occurrences associated with unusual air movement, or lack of it, is intensely interesting. But it is currently a mathematical exercise in topologic nonlinear differential equations, the number of solutions of which may well approach infinity.

Meteorological factors are the chief diluters and dispersers of pollution. Where and when they fail to perform these functions adequately, the sources of pollution must be controlled.

TYPES OF EFFECTS ASSOCIATED WITH AIR POLLUTION

In the following sections detailed attention is devoted to the kinds and magnitudes of effects known and suspected of being produced by air pollution. They may be grouped under five general headings:

VISIBILITY REDUCTION

Historically the earliest noted, and currently the most easily observed, effect of air pollution is the reduction in visibility produced by the scattering of light from the surfaces of airborne particles. The degree of light obstruction is a complex function of particle size, aerosol density, thickness of the affected air mass, and certain more subtle physical factors. Particulates responsible for the phenomenon may be either primary pollutants, e.g., coal smoke, or secondary, e.g., Los Angeles photochemical smog. At times London and cities in the eastern United States have been so seriously affected by pollutional reduction in visibility as to have experienced severe curtailment of transport and other municipal activities. It has frequently been pointed out that the attenuation of ultraviolet and other radiations reaching the surface through layers of aerosols may be associated with adverse physiological effects in men and vegetation.

MATERIAL DAMAGE

Direct damage to structural metals, surface coatings, fabrics, and other materials of commerce is a frequent and widespread effect of air pollution. The total annual loss from these and incidental increases in cleansing and protective activities in the United States is not accurately known but has been estimated at a level of several billions of dollars. The destruction is related to many types of pollutants but is chiefly attributable to acid mists, oxidants of various kinds, H_2S, and particulate products of combustion and industrial processing. Secondary pollutants contribute a substantial share. For example, O_3 is known to cause rapid and extensive damage to all kinds of rubber goods in Los Angeles and elsewhere in the United States.

AGRICULTURAL DAMAGE

A large number of food, forage, and ornamental crops have been shown to be damaged by air pollutants. The curtailed value results from various types of leaf damage, stunting of growth, decreased size and yield of fruits, and destruction of flowers. Some plant species are so sensitive to specific pollutants as to be useful in monitoring air supplies. Annual bluegrass, the pinto bean, spinach, and certain other forms are so employed in southern California.

Again, no satisfactory estimates of dollar loss due to air pollutants are available. California places agricultural damage at a current annual rate of about $6,000,000 but this figure seems to exclude losses incidental to the enforced total abandonment of certain commercial crops, such as spinach, in the Los Angeles area.

Substances thus far identified as responsible for the damage include ethylene, SO_2, acid mists, fluorides, O_3, and a number of organic oxidants. Research on the etiology, physiology, and biochemistry of air pollution pathologies in plants is proceeding at a pace which promises early contributions to knowledge of related phenomena in man.

PHYSIOLOGICAL EFFECTS ON MAN AND DOMESTIC ANIMALS

Donora, Poza Rica, London, and the Meuse Valley of Belgium have given dramatic proof that air pollution can kill; together with other evidence, they have implied less shocking but more extensive effects of air pollutants on the health of affected populations. Long-continued exposure to sublethal concentrations of many substances, and combinations thereof, are suspected of having physiological effects, but in most cases the quantitative aspects of the relationships remain undefined.

The high incidences of "chronic bronchitis" in British cities, of nasopharyngeal and optic irritation in Los Angeles, and the rapid rise in lung carcinoma among metropolitan populations appear to be closely associated with air pollution. Fluorosis in cattle exposed to fluoride-containing dusts has been proved to be related to emissions from certain industrial operations. More subtle physiological effects of air pollution are suggested by laboratory observations of suppression of ciliary action, alterations in pulmonary physiology, specific enzymatic inhibitions, and changes in blood chemistry.

PSYCHOLOGICAL EFFECTS

Since fear is a recognizable element in public reactions to air pollution, the psychological aspects of the phenomenon cannot be ignored. Psychosomatic illnesses are possibly related to inadequate understanding of a publicized threat. Little effort has been directed toward evaluation of such impacts in relation to general mental health of affected groups, or determination of their role in individual neuroses. Only in practical politics has any significant action been based on recognition of the psychological attitudes induced by periodic public exposure to an airborne threat.

AIR POLLUTION AS A PROBLEM OF THE FUTURE

In spite of its long history of development, community air pollution must be looked upon as a problem of the future. Only a few of the largest population concentrations of the present day are occasionally using their air supplies faster than natural processes can replenish them. Such overuse must be expected to occur with increasing frequency as populations increase, since per capita demands for air cannot be expected to decline.

So long as the air resource was almost infinitely large with respect to its daily withdrawal and use, its pollution caused discomfort and illness only in areas immediately adjacent to individual sources. As regional and world populations increase exponentially, a time must come when human occupation of the medium will threaten the quality of the total air resource. On a world scale, residues of nuclear weapon testing and huge outpourings of CO_2 from fossil fuel combustion are already demonstrating the extent to which human activity can affect the total gaseous milieu.

Air pollution shares with all other threats to public health and welfare the certainty of becoming more and more severe as long as the population increase remains unchecked. Unless some effective population control is permitted to intervene, the monetary cost of maintaining an acceptable air quality can be expected to rise in some exponential relationship to the numbers of people and associated activities requiring it. This will be true regardless of the speed with which fossilized energy sources are replaced by thermonuclear or solar power plants. Nevertheless, such substitutions can be expected to delay, perhaps for generations, the development of large-scale completely intolerable and economically uncontrollable situations.

The emergence of air pollution as a regional, or even global, phenomenon has already had some impacts on governmental and administrative procedures. Air masses recognize no political jurisdictions, and in their movements frequently do violence to democratically evolved concepts of local autonomy. As the geographic breadth of air resource problems increases there will be a need to develop administrative mechanisms capable of dealing with them as regional, national, or international entities. Since they involve aspects of transportation, refuse disposal, industrial zoning, and power utilization, it is difficult to believe that future jurisdictional adjustments, made to meet the regulatory need, will conform with traditional governmental concepts.

Water, food, and air must forever constitute the survival bases of human and other populations; we will pay for them whatever they cost in time, money, and effort, since without them we die. It is therefore shortsighted to consider the air resource as a competitively priced commodity; it is priceless. In 1962 it may be appropriate to consider which of several alternative air pollution control measures may be imposed without their affecting the public purse unduly; this is true because there are still not enough of us to pose more than a marginal threat to air quality. However, the quadrupled population anticipated by the year 2062, if realized, may force consideration of basic resources as fundamental limits to survival, rather than as dollar-valued items affecting the cost of comfort.

Selection 26

Oil Pollution at Sea

Commentary

The ocean, Thor Heyerdahl reported after completing his trip across the southern Atlantic on the papyrus raft Ra II, is polluted. For weeks along the route, Norman Baker, navigator on the Ra II, writes, "We saw no land, no ship, no light, no man, all we saw was his garbage and we saw that all the time." Among this garbage were floating globs of oil ". . . as far as I could see," Baker continues, "below as well as to the sides, the entire visible layer of the ocean was infested with hanging bits of hardened oil."[1] Although oil for a long time has been a pollutant of the seas, largely from natural leakages out of deposits on the ocean floor, only in recent times has oil become a major pollutant of oceans. Errors in handling oil cargos, accidents involving tankers and barges, and illegal washing of tanker bilges have all created problems which in the past attracted the attention of only wildlife and fishery biologists and conservationists. Not until Santa Barbara and Torrey Canyon became words synonymous with oil pollution did the people of at least the United States, England, France, and some other countries become alerted to the threats of oil pollution.

Oil pollution is increasing. The worldwide demand for oil means more transportation of oil by tankers and underwater pipelines. Continental shelves carry 20,000 miles of rusting pipeline capable of releasing an oil disaster. Growing numbers of large tankers increase chances of accidents such as that of the Torrey Canyon. Oil on the continental shelves of North and South America, Africa, Australia, and in the North Sea and the Persian Gulf will eventually be exploited. And drilling at sea, as the Santa Barbara and Gulf of Mexico oil spills have emphasized, is environmentally risky. Then there are the environmental problems raised by oil in Alaskan tundra.

Oil is a collection of hundreds of substances that react with the environment. When released in water it spreads in a thin film over the surface. The lighter fractions evaporate or are absorbed by particulate matter and sink to the bottom. Some become dissolved in seawater. Much is oxidized by bacteria, yeasts, and molds, which attack different fractions of crude oil.[2] Bacteria can digest straight-chain hydrocarbons. They have more problems with the branched-chain hydrocarbons, which persist for a long time as tarry chunks bobbing on the surface and lying on the bottom of the sea.

Much of the recent outcry against oil pollution is not because of the ecological damage it does, but because of its economic and esthetic damage.[3] Oil slicks on the water ruin the beaches and waters for recreation, damage property, and blight the seascape. Aside from loss of birds, the most obvious victims of oil pollution, ecological losses are not fully appreciated. Studies following oil spills[4] indicate that oil kills plant and animal life of the intertidal zones, especially that of the upper and middle littoral zones—barnacles, mussels, crabs, rockweeds, and their associated invertebrate fauna. It may take two to ten years for the area to fully recover. Sandy beaches become permeated with oil. The surface oil film brought ashore is deposited on the top and eventually is pressed into the sand by the waves. There it kills the inhabitants of sandy beaches; and it becomes mixed with subterranean currents and is carried back out to the lower depths of the sea.

The ecological effects of oil pollution on marine life have hardly been studied. Little is known about the toxicity of hydrocarbons in oil to marine life, about the effects of oil on bottom life, about the impact oil has on marine food chains, or about the subtle long-term effects of sunken, absorbed, or dispersed oil. A. L. Hawkes in the following selection, written well before the Santa Barbara oil spill or the Torrey Canyon wreck, delineates and explores the problem of oil pollution at sea.

---

[1] Norman Baker, "Science, Solitude and Slime," *Industrial Ecology* **1**, 1970, pp. 9—11.
[2] R. W. Holcomb, "Oil in the Ecosystem," *Science* **166**, 1969, pp. 204—206.
[3] H. Molotch, "Santa Barbara: Oil in the Velvet Playground," in editors of *Ramparts magazine, Eco-Catastrophe*, San Francisco, Canfield Press, (a department of Harper & Row), 1970.
[4] K. Rützler and W. Sterrer, "Oil Pollution," *BioScience* **20**, 1970, pp. 222—224.

A Review of the Nature and Extent of Damage Caused by Oil Pollution at Sea

by Alfred L. Hawkes

Oil pollution of the sea has been a recognized problem since 1754 when Jonas Hanway described oil leaking from wooden vessels at Holy Island in the Caspian Sea as covering the sea "for leagues together." Prior to the first World War the problem remained relatively small and only certain oil-producing areas were involved. With the advent of oil-burning ships, the automobile and airplane, asphalt roads and the thousands of other devices and processes which demand that oil be produced, transported, and disposed of, oil pollution of the sea has become an international problem which is reaching the proportions of a disaster in some of its aspects.

From the time oil is taken out of the ground until it is burned, broken down by bacterial action, or destroyed by some other process, it is a constant hazard to every living thing and every piece of property with which it comes in contact. Nowhere and at no time is oil more likely to get where it is not wanted than when it is being transported at sea, either as cargo on a tanker or as fuel on dry cargo or passenger vessels.

The U.S. Coast Guard's Proceedings of the Merchant Marine Council for April 1960 lists the principal sources of oil pollution of the oceans. Two of the commonest from shipping are spills during bunkering operations and discharges from bilge and ballast tanks. Nearly half of all the oil spills whose causes were determined by the U.S. Coast Guard from January 1, 1956, to September 22, 1959, originated while oil-burning ships were taking on fuel. Bilge pumping ranked third as a traceable cause of oil pollution.

There is little excuse for either of these sources to be a menace. Almost all spills occurring while loading fuel are attributable to carelessness or faulty equipment. Port facilities for receiving excess oily water are available in many U.S. harbors. Few ship handlers are ignorant of the law forbidding discharges of bilge and other oily waste water within territorial limits. Most violations of this law are completely avoidable. The same may be said of pollution due to ballast dumping and tank cleaning operations. Both are necessary but both can be done at times and places where they cause a minimum of concern.

Another common source of trouble from shipping is leaking hulls. This is more frequent on riveted vessels which are now being replaced by ships whose plates are welded. Hull leakage, however, accounted for 20 per cent of the traceable spills over the four-year period mentioned previously.

Casualities such as collisions, groundings, and fires cause the worst pollution problems since they frequently occur near shore and release thousands of barrels of oil at a time. A recent grounding in Narragansett Bay flooded the area around Newport, Rhode Island, with an estimated 10,000 to 50,000 barrels of so-called "bunker C" oil. The resulting mess had to be seen to be believed, and the Rhode Island governor was forced to declare a state of emergency to deal with the situation. Many of the worst oil strandings on Cape Cod occur as a result of wrecks in those particularly hazardous waters. In spite of modern technology and the equipment and facilities now available, these casualties still remain a principal source of pollution as well as loss of life at sea. Many of them admittedly serve also as monuments to careless seamanship. Gradual rusting out of tanks on sunken vessels makes

THIS SELECTION is printed from *Transactions of the North American Wildlife Conference*, 1961, pp. 343–355, by permission of the author and the Wildlife Management Institute.

them major sources of oil pollution for years after the date of sinking.

Deliberate release of oil at sea is permitted only in cases of extreme emergency and is seldom a serious source of pollution except in groundings and other casualties. It is interesting that the most objectionable types of oil from the pollution standpoint are crudes and fuel oils and that the British Ministry of Transportation, to avoid endangering human lives, recommends throwing almost *any* other oil than these overboard to quell waves when men are in the water.

Still a minor, but rapidly increasing, cause of oil pollution is the more than 8,000,000 small craft now plying our bays, rivers and lakes. The average weekend captain probably gives little or no thought to where and when he pumps the bilge or to the pint or so of oil that goes overboard with it. Thousands of him in one area at one time, however, may compound this into a problem of major proportions in the near future. Much of the oil involved from small craft is lighter than crude or fuel oil but correspondingly less care is used in handling it. Bodies of fresh water are likely to feel this before it becomes a severe threat on salt water.

All oil pollution of marine waters does not originate with shipping, although it is the principal cause. Shore installations are frequent trouble spots. Disasters such as fires, explosions, and floods often spread oil in harbors and rivers. Obsolete or worn equipment accounts for many spills. Spillage during transportation to or from docking areas and leaky storage equipment account for more oil on our waters. Effluents from a wide variety of shoreside industries contain significant amounts of oil along with other pollutants and can be among the most difficult of sources to locate. About one third of the recorded oil spills on Narragansett Bay over the past four years originated at shore installations of one type or another. While the oils used are light, spraying of salt marshes with insecticides in an oil vehicle adds another mite to the total. In some areas oil drilling operations and the associated brines, drilling muds and leaks are sources of marine oil pollution. In Cuba and on the United States West Coast and Gulf Coast natural oil seepage causes still other troubles.

The total effects of the enormous amounts of oil released on the marine waters of the world can never be accurately assessed. We can assume, however, that what happens in one area of the world is also going on in similar areas elsewhere and that similar results are sequential. The principal uses of salt water the world over may be listed more or less as follows:

Propagation and harvesting of fin fish;
Propagation and harvesting of shellfish;
Propagation and maintenance of other vertebrate and invertebrate marine life including waterfowl;
Swimming, boating, sport fishing, and other forms of recreation and esthetic enjoyment;
Navigation and commercial transportation;
Dilution and dispersion of wastes;
Domestic water supply—in the near future;
Industrial water supply—in the near future.

Contamination of salt water with oil diminishes the usefulness of that water for nearly every one of the above purposes in direct proportion to the amount of oil thrown out.

Certainly the prime hazard from oil spillage is the danger to human life. The greatest and most immediate threat is that of fire. Oil and oil soaked debris on the waters of any harbor or coastline or washed up on shore offer almost unequalled opportunities for major fire disasters. The potential is so obvious that it needs no further elaboration here.

Oil washed directly onto beaches by winds, tides and currents creates a variety of problems. It would seem, according to a recent report by the American Petroleum Institute, that seasonal currents may be more responsible for the location of the landings of these spills than either tides or winds, when the spills occur on the open sea. Beach strandings of oil are annoying to bathers and expensive to those whose livelihood comes in whole or part from sales and services to seashore users. In the small resort community of Narragansett, Rhode Island (population—3,444), the estimated loss to local businesses of one day's closing of their beaches in good weather runs between $10,000—$50,000.

Then there is the cost of cleaning up. At one state beach in Rhode Island the cost of cleaning the beach and adjacent buildings as a result of a severe oil spill last fall, will run into several thousand dollars and has yet to be completed. Cleaning oil from bathing beaches in many areas along the east coast of North America is a more or less continuous process all during the swimming season. In some instances it has been necessary to set up "detergent stations" at the entrances to public bathhouses and to compel bathers to clean the oil off themselves before entering. A report from Texas relative to the Gulf Coast indicates that "It is a common occurrence in recent years for beach enthusiasts to pick up waste oil and tars on their feet and subsequently leave oil deposits on expensive rugs and furnishings in their motel and hotel accommodations, causing considerable costs to owners of these accommodations for rehabilitation." That the extent of damages of this type is not made public by those affected is indicated in a communication from John W. Mann, Executive Secretary of the U.S. National Committee for Prevention of Pollution of the Seas by Oil. Mr. Mann stated that hotel and resort owners are often reluctant to call attention to beach pollution problems because they fear the adverse publicity will affect their patronage. The bather himself certainly has no desire to come in contact with oil or to swim where it is visible or can be smelled. The after-dark shore fishermen who has never reeled in a long cast only to discover that his entire line passed through floating oil has a memorable experience waiting for him.

The fouling of boats of all kinds is another result of oil pollution. The cost of repainting a boat, and this is frequently the only recourse, varies with the size and type of the craft. An oil spill which floats into an exclusive yacht club anchorage can be an expensive proposition. Certain oil companies in the Narragansett Bay area have from time to time undertaken to repaint boats so damaged when there was no question as to the source of the oil. This has given rise to a class of yachtsmen on that bay who now await the first reports of a traceable oil spill, immediately sail their boats into the middle of it, and then indignantly demand a free paint job from the oil company. Fraud is only one of the consequences of oil pollution. The problem of boat fouling takes on a more serious complexion when commercial fishing vessels are involved. Hauling oil-smeared lobster pots, crab pots, or seines into a small craft can create serious problems and the waste of time and money for cleaning may mean the difference between profit and loss for a small operator.

In entering the area concerning the effects of oil on various forms of animal life, we approach one of the most widespread and tragic results of oil pollution of the sea. The world's only major and relatively untapped source of food is the ocean, and the most productive portions of it, the surface and shallow waters, are those portions most acutely affected by oil pollution. If we could count on the dilution of every oil spill by the entire volume of water in all the oceans our problem would indeed be a small one for many years to come. This is not the case, however. It is safe to assume that due to the confluence of major world shipping lanes in the areas of continental coastlines and harbors and the development of refineries and industrial centers near marine oil transportation terminals, the major portion of oil pollution of the sea will continue to occur in these areas—the same areas from which the greatest potential harvest of marine life should come.

There is some difference of opinion as to the exact nature and variety of the effects of oil on different forms of marine life. In general, there are five principal ways in which oil may affect salt water animals. These are:

The tainting of the flesh of fin fish and shellfish thus rendering them inedible;
Poisoning of animal life by ingestion of oil or its soluble fractions;
Upsetting of food chians;
Mechanical fouling of animals;
Repellent effects.

The tainting of the flesh of marine animals which have come in contact with oil is largely self-evident. While the notion that oil and water do not mix is a common one, it is not entirely correct. Particles of clay or other fine sediment quickly absorb large amounts of the oil and it then sinks to the bottom where it may remain for long periods of time. Disturbing the bottom in any way can refloat much of it at a later date. Oils, particularly the residual products of modern refining methods, are frequently almost the same density as water, and under certain conditions, sink readily. In extremely cold weather oil may quickly sink only to reappear when warm weather returns. By these means oil reaches the bottoms of marine environments and tends to remain there in direct contact with bottom-dwelling organisms. Many forms of marine life are killed outright by such contact and the best evidence of this is the almost complete absence of living things from the bottoms of bays and harbors where oil spills occur regularly. Those animals which can survive direct contact take on highly objectionable tastes and odors.

This can be a serious economic problem in certain areas. The quahog or hardshelled clam (*Venus mercenaria*) is the foundation of an industry in Rhode Island which grosses over $2,000,000 annually for commercial diggers. Quahogs seem to be practically immune to oil pollution. The Rhode Island Department of Health states that there are quahogs flourishing in Narragansett Bay in the area of Providence where the Bay bottom is literally paved with oil. They also assure me that each and every one of these quahogs has a taste and odor which would make the strongest stomach turn. If oil settled undetected on the bottom in a portion of Narrangansett Bay where quahogs are normally harvested—and the Health Department attests that there are many such unreported spills—and these flavored shellfish reached the New York markets on about two different occasions, Rhode Island quahoging would be a thing of the past. Tainting of European mussel beds by oil has caused serious problems there in the past, and Walter Gresh, regional director, U.S. Fish and Wildlife Service, Atlanta, Georgia, states that, "Fishermen in the lower St. Mary's and Savannah Rivers in Gerogia, have reported that the fish caught in these reaches are unfit for human consumption. Pumping of bilges is thought to be responsible for the taste in the lower Savannah River."

Many marine animals are susceptible to certain fractions of oil which are soluble in water and are highly toxic. Dr. Paul Galtsoff, biologist for the U.S. Fish and Wildlife Service, established this in 1935 and again in 1949 working with oysters and other marine invertebrates. These toxic substances are released for long periods of time from oil in the water. While these substances are undoubtedly diluted below dangerous levels in small or infrequent spills, areas where oil tends to accumulate on the bottom may be slowly building up long-term problems. In spite of the common notion of tides washing nearly everything in bays and estuaries out to sea, it simply isn't always true. In most estuaries the total result of surface flow is eventually to the sea, but the total result of bottom flow is upstream. Oils deposited on the bottom of an estuary then are sending a constant stream of toxic materials into the estuary and if the bottom is disturbed frequently the oils themselves may gradually work farther and farther upstream. Since the rates of microbial decomposition and other factors destructive to oil will vary enormously from place to place even in the same body of water, the length of time this process of accumulation may go on is problematical. A report presented to this body in 1953 by Hunt and Ewing indicated that during annual dredging operations in the lower three miles of the Rouge River in Michigan more than 17,000 gallons of oils and greases are scooped out daily for a period of fifty days. This is presumably a one year accumulation. Some of our salt water environments have been badly polluted for many years.

An additional hazard to animals from these toxic fractions exists when other forms of pollution are present in addition to oil. An animal which might otherwise resist the effects of an oil spill may succumb instead if it has already been weakened by other pollutants. The converse can be equally true.

In experiments with *Nitzschia*, a diatom food of the oyster, Dr. Galtsoff found that these microscopic plants were seriously inhibited in their growth if oil remained for more than one week on the surface of the water in which they were living. Another effect of the presence of oil was to stimulate the growth of certain bacteria which in turn became so numerous that the *Nitzschia* died. Presumably, the effects of longlasting oil spills would be the same on many of the other minute organisms at the base of oceanic food chains.

Oil smeared on exposed intertidal flats quickly coats all life including commercially valuable softshelled clams (*Mya arenaria*) and razor clams (*Ensis directus*), and a variety of other more or less sessile dwellers of this zone on both muddy and rocky shorelines. The famous Dungeness crab of the West Coast is another casualty of this type of pollution. Even fur seals have been killed as a result of contact with oil.

A less direct effect of oil pollution on marine life is its repellent effect. Fish in particular are possibly affected this way when ther are migrating. Fish, such as flatfish of various kinds which breed in salt marshes, may well refuse to enter a good breeding marsh if sufficient quantities of oil or other pollutants are flowing out of the area. The same causes might well affect selection of migration routes and in turn affect commercial fishing grounds and methods.

The most obvious and spectacular loss of

animal life due to oil pollution of the sea, and one of the principal reasons this subject is being reviewed at this time, is the enormous annual toll taken of marine waterfowl as a result of contamination by floating oil. There is ample evidence from both Canada and England that serious reductions in the populations of certain species of oceanic birds have taken place as a result of oil dumped at sea. While it is admittedly extremely difficult to pin down the cause of these reductions directly to oil, every piece of circumstantial evidence points to this source. The most convincing evidence is that certain colonies of seabirds subject to continued oil pollution have declined over periods of time while other colonies composed of the same species and in nearby areas but not subject to pollution have not declined in the same periods.

Oil affects birds in several ways. The principal damage is simple mechanical fouling of the feathers. Fuel and crude oils are thick and sticky to the point of being impossible to remove without the aid of solvents. Once a bird has come into contact with the oil by landing in it, swimming into it from the surface or by coming up underneath it, he is almost invariably doomed. In cold weather a spot of oil the size of a coat button is sufficient to cause death, particularly if located over the vital organs. The oil mats the contour and down feathers into strings instead of the broad water-repellent and circulation-resistant surfaces normally sealing the insulating layer of air between feathers and body. Once this seal is opened icy water seeps in against the skin and body heat is lost faster than it can be renewed. The process of degeneration is speeded up if there is also oil on the wings since this inhibits movement and thus feeding. If the oil covering is extensive, the bird must swim for all it is worth just to stay afloat since the oil destroys natural buoyancy. This may be the main reason why so many oiled birds head for shore and are so reluctant to take to the water again once there. Certainly when oil spills affect birds any distance at sea, most of them will sink long before they reach land.

Even in warm weather, oiling is fatal to birds. Inability to fly or swim properly interferes with feeding. Preening in an effort to remove the oil transfers much of it to the beak and from there to the digestive tract. Following a recent severe spill in Narragansett Bay, a large number of ducks killed by the oil were examined internally and found to have the entire alimentary canal coated with a layer of oil. Those ducks which survived in captivity for a few days frequently showed oil in the droppings. There is evidence that oiled birds spend so much time preening that they neglect to feed properly and become much emaciated even when food is available. There is no reason for not assuming that all of these same conditions apply to other birds such as alcids caught in oil spills at sea. Even unoiled birds may feel the effects of oil they feed on plants or bottom organisms which have become contaminated. The oil itself is toxic and undoubtedly can be fatal if sufficient amounts are consumed.

Attempts to save individual birds by various washing and cleaning processes have not been noticeably successful. If the birds survive the cleaning process many of them seem to perk up for a day or two but then suddenly expire. An occasional individual will survive for an extended period of time and apparently recover completely. It is very likely that these are birds which had not had time to preen and consume oil. Also, some birds apparently survive handling better than others. Even if this approach to recovering oiled birds were successful, it is impractical because of the sheer weight of numbers and the time necessary—several hours—to do a through cleaning job on one bird.

Reports from many sources indicate that the kill of birds by oil has been getting progressively worse over the past few years. Mr. L. M. Tuck of the Canadian Wildlife Service in Newfoundland has estimated that one nesting colony of auks in his area has been decimated by nearly a quarter of a million birds within the last two years and that it cannot survive comparable losses for more than another two or three years. Mr. Lester Giles, director of the American Humane Education Society, has counted approximately 4,000 oiled birds on Nantucket Island in December and January of 1960 and 1961 and this is a time of year when currents are carrying oil away from this area. In Narragansett Bay approximately 4,000 ducks, nearly one fifth of the entire wintering flock, were killed by an oil spill in early February of this year. Mr. Oliver Beckley, supervisor of game management for the Connecticut Board of Fisheries and Game estimates a kill of 4,000 more ducks as the result of an oil spill in Long

Island Sound in mid-December, 1960. While not an oil spill at sea, as many as 10,000 ducks may have died as a result of oil on the Detroit River in April, 1960. Going back only a few years to 1955, a report from Germany indicates a kill of over one quarter of a million birds in the North Sea, mostly as the result of one spill. These figures represent typical reports from many sources. A long list of reported kills of this sort can easily be compiled but only begins to indicate the real extent of the problem, since, without any doubt, the major portion of bird kills go unnoticed at sea. The most spectacular slaughter results from disasters to ships. The slow steady kill of sea birds as a result of bilge pumping and tank washing may, however, in the long run account for more losses than ship disasters. In any event, if the smaller and more frequent, and preventable, spills were halted, the larger, and presumably unavoidable, disasters would be less devastating in their effects on populations of oceanic birds.

There are still other deleterious effects of oil on the sea. The facts that in 1936 the River and Harbor Act of 1899 was interpreted by the Appellate Court to include oil as a hazard to navigation and that this decision has been standing firm since that time is indication enough of the menace of oil to shipping itself. There is no longer much question in the minds of conservationists that the sea is soon to become a major source of domestic and industrial water supply. Even if we cannot bring down the cost of desalinization the demand will soon make present costs seem reasonable. The effects of marine oil pollution as it exists today on such a water supply will present a real problem for sanitary engineers. Finally, a rather paradoxical hazard exists, in that except for the fire dangers involved some of the methods involved in cleaning up or disposing of oil spills may be nearly as harmful as leaving the oil on the water. Carbonized sand used to sink floating oil is an "out of sight, out of mind" technique which simply puts oil on the bottom and in direct contact with many of the organisms we wish to protect. Contrary to earlier beliefs, carbonized sand will not sink oil indefinitely but releases it slowly for return to the surface. Sinking the oil does not decrease the toxicity of the soluble fractions and in fact gets them closer to the organisms most affected by them. At the recent Governor's Emergency Conference on Oil Pollution in Rhode Island

several commercial oil solvents were suggested as a means of getting rid of the oil in particularly critical areas. Marine biologists questioned this technique on the grounds that the solvents or emulsifiers or their effects on the oil might be equally or more harmful to marine life than the floating oil itself. Although representatives of several commercial manufacturers of these substances were present, no concrete evidence was offered to meet these objections.

The direct financial losses involved in oil pollution of the sea can probably never be accurately assessed on a dollar basis. Their magnitude can be implied, however, in a simple review of some of the factors involved. A few of the more important ones are as follows:

Loss of natural resources which could be harvested, held as reproductive stock, serve as links in oceanic food chains, or provide esthetic values;

Destruction of bottom areas to produce the above-mentioned natural resources;

Loss of revenue to resort areas;

Costs to local and state governments of cleaning up when spills cannot be traced;

Loss to those sources responsible for the pollution in fines, cleaning expenses, legal expenses, loss of valuable oil, and poor public relations;

Costs of investigation to determine sources and responsibility for pollution;

Costs of prosecution when pollution cases go to court.

One of the conclusions which can be drawn from this review is that in addition to the many problems created by it, there are three basic reasons for oil pollution of the sea. These are: economic expediency, carelessness and negligence, and inadequate regulation and enforcement. All of these causes can be reduced, if not eliminated, by concerted action on the part of all the interests involved in oil pollution. Oil handlers and producers must shoulder the major portion of the responsibility since they alone are responsible for the problem. There is much evidence that they are becoming aware of this responsibility and are taking steps to live up to it. The extent to which they can control the problem within their own ranks and by their own methods will determine the extent to which they will be controlled by regulations imposed upon them by outside, and not entirely sympathetic, interests. They will need all the help and cooperation they can get from conservationists but this does not imply any cessation or letting up of criticism or pressure to get the job done.

In placing the onus of elimination of oil pollution directly on the oil industry, let us not overlook two closely related problems with which the oil industry has little to do. First—many of the saline waters we are demanding be rid of oil pollution are so badly contaminated by other pollutants that they would be valueless even if 100% free of oil. Second—those most aware of and concerned about oil pollution have failed to present clear, well documented, and voluminous information relative to the real extent of this problem. There is no question that the problem exists and is of disastrous proportions in some areas but there is real need for sound information making this clear to all concerned. There-in lies one of the major contributions needed from the biologists and conservationists of the world.

SUMMARY

The principal source of oil pollution of the sea is shipping. Oil is spread from ships when taking on fuel, pumping bilges, and washing tanks. Much oil is also lost through leaking hulls. Ship casualties such as groundings cause the most damaging spills of oil. Oil drilling and natural seepage are two less significant causes of oil pollution of the sea.

Some of the potential hazards and consequences of oil pollution are fire, poisoning of animal life, upsetting of oceanic food chains, mechanical fouling of animals, pollution of beach and resort areas, fouling of boats, tainting of fin fish and shellfish, interference with navigation, damage from some removal techniques, degradation of oceanic waters as a source of industrial and domestic water supply, and repellent effects on marine fauna.

Financial losses as a consequence of marine oil pollution stem from loss of valuable natural resources, loss of revenue to resort areas, loss of time and revenue for cleaning operations on commercial fishing gear, loss to sources responsible for the pollution, costs to local and state governments for cleaning shorelines and property, costs of investigations, costs of prosecution. Intangible losses may be even greater than those mentioned.

REFERENCES

Angus, K. C., 1959, No Title—Address before International Conference on Oil Pollution of the Sea—Copenhagen, Denmark.

Anonymous, 1949, Oil and refuse pollution: Navigable waters of the United States: California—Corps of Engrs., U.S. Army, So. Pacific Div.; 1959a, Part 1—Determination of the quantity of oily substances on beaches and in nearshore waters. "Part 2—Characterization of Coastal Oil Pollution by Submarine Seeps"—State Water Pollution Control Board, Room 316, 1227 O Street, Sacramento 14, Calif.; 1959b, Official Report of the United States National Committee for the Prevention of Pollution of the Seas by Oil—Dept. of State, Washington, D.C.—Aug. 1959; 1960a, Proceedings of Governor's Emergency Conference on Oil Pollution of Narragansett Bay—Preliminary Conference and Main Conference—Sept. 8, 1960—R. I. Department of Agriculture and Conservation—Providence, R. I.; 1960b, Thousands of ducks die in Detroit River oil slick—Michigan Out-Of-Doors, Vol. 11, No. 4. Apr.; 1960c, Shore birds die in hundreds as oil pollutes beaches—Edgartown, Mass. Gazette, Dec. 30; 1960d, International Convention for the Prevention of Pollution of the Sea by Oil—Certified Copy—86th Congress—Senate Executive C.—Feb. 15; 1960e, International Convention for the Prevention of Pollution of the Sea by Oil Report submitted by Mr. Fulbright from the Committee on Foreign Relations—86th Congress, 2nd Session, Senate—Executive Report No. 6—June 2; 1961, Oil spillage imperils more ducks—New York Herald Tribune, New York—Jan. 12.

Boyer, George F., 1948, pollution—Informal report to: Chief, Canadian Wildlife Service, Ottawa, Canada—Mar. 18; 1950, Oiling of sea birds and other waterfowl—Informal report to: Chief, Canadian Wildlife Service, Ottawa, Canada—Apr. 29.

Chipman, Walter A. and Paul S. Galtsoff, 1949, Effects of oil mixed with carbonized sand on aquatic animals—Special Scientific Report: Fisheries No. 1, U.S. Dept. of the Interior, Fish and Wildlife Service.

Dennis, John V., 1959a, Oil pollution survey of the United States Atlantic Coast with special reference to Southeast Florida coast conditions. American Petroleum Institute, Division of Transportation, 1625 K St., N.W., Washington 6, D.C.; 1959b, Can oil pollution be defeated? Mass. Audubon Magazine—Vol. 44, No. 2, pp. 66-73, Mass. Audubon Society, Lincoln, Mass; 1960a, Oil pollution conditions of the Florida East Coast—American Petroleum Institute, Division of Transportation, 1625 K St., N.W., Washington 6, D.C.; 1960b, Oil pollution survey of the Great Lakes within United States territorial limits. American Petroleum Institute, Division of Transportation, 1625 K. St., N.W., Washington 6, D.C.; 1961. The relationship of ocean currents to oil pollution off the Southeastern Coast of New England. American Petroleum Institute, Division of Transportation, 1625 K. St., N.W., Washington 6, D.C.

Doudoroff, P. et al., 1951, Bio-assay methods for the evaluation of acute toxicity of industrial wastes to fish. U.S. Dept. of Health, Education and Welfare—Reproduced from, Sewage and Industrial Wastes, Vol. 23, No. 11, Nov.

Eldridge, E. F., 1953 Oil on our waters. Washington Pollution Control Commission—Information Series No. 2, Olympia, Wash.

Frome, Michael, 1959, What's happening to our shoreline? Parade, Feb. 15, 1959, Parade Publications, Inc., New York, New York.

Galtsoff, Paul S., Herbert Prytherich, Robert O. Smith, and Vera Koehring, 1935, Effects of crude oil pollution on oysters in Louisiana waters. Bull. No. 18. U.S. Dept. of Commerce—From Bulletin of the Bureau of Fisheries, Vol. XLVIII.

Galtsoff, Paul S., 1936, Oil pollution in coastal waters. Trans. No. Amer. Wildlife Conf., Feb. 3-7; 1959, Environmental requirements of oysters in relation to pollution. Trans. Second Seminar on Biological Problems in Water Pollution, April 20-24. U.S. Public Health Service, Robert A. Taft Sanitary Engineering Center, Cincinnati 26, Ohio.

Giles, Lester A., Jr., and John A. Livingston, 1960, Oil pollution of the seas. Trans. No. Amer. Wildlife and Natural Resources Conf.

Hadley, Alden H., 1930, A Sea Bird Tragedy. Bird Lore, 32(1):169. National Audubon Society—New York.

Horwood, Harold, 1959, Death has a rainbow hue. Canadian Audubon, 21(3):69—Audubon Society of Canada, Toronto.

Hunt, George S., and Howard E. Ewing, 1953, Industrial pollution and Michigan waterfowl—Transactions of the 18th North American Wildlife Conference, March 9, 10, 11, 1953.

Livingston, John A., 1958, The senseless slaughter of our seabirds—Maclean's Vol. 71, No. 16, 1958—Toronto, Canada; 1959, No title—Address to the International Conference on Oil Pollution of the Sea—Copenhagen, Denmark—Audubon Society of Canada, Toronto; 1960, Toll of seabirds by oil worst in history—Press release, Audubon Society of Canada, Toronto—February 19, 1960.

Lunz, G. Robert, Jr., 1950, The effect of bleed water and of water extracts of crude oil on the pumping rate of oysters—Research conducted for the Texas A. & M. Research Foundation, Biology Research Laboratory, College Station, Texas.

McGowan, Charles B., A man-made disaster in Rhode Island—Unpublished manuscript for Audubon Magazine, National Audubon Society, New York, New York.

Menzel, R. Winston and Sewell H. Hopkins, 1951, Report on experiments to test the effects of oil well brine or "bleed-water" on oysters at Lake Barre oil field. Vol. 1—Research Conducted for the Texas A. & M. Research Foundation, Biology Research Laboratory, College Station, Texas; 1952, Report on commercial-scale oyster planting experiments in Bayou Bas Bleu and in Bay Sainte Elaine oil field. Research Conducted for the Texas A. & M. Research Foundation, Biology Research Laboratory, College Station, Texas; 1953, Report on oyster experiments at Bay Sainte Elaine Oil Field. Research Conducted for the Texas A. & M. Research Foundation, Biology Research Laboratory, College Station, Texas.

Moffitt, James and Robert T. Orr, 1930, Recent disastrous effects of oil pollution on birds in the San Francisco Bay region—Calif. Fish and Game, Vol. 24, No. 3.

McKee, Jack Edward, 1956, Report on oily substances and their effects on the beneficial uses of water. State Water Pollution Control Board, Room 316, 1227 O Street, Sacramento 14, Calif. Excellent Bibliography.

Peterson, Roger Troy, 1942, Birds and floating oil. Audubon Magazine, Vol. XLIV, No. 4, p. 217. National Audubon Society, New York City.

Proceedings International Conference on Oil Pollution of the Sea, 1953, Coordinating Advisory Committee on Oil Pollution of the Sea, c/o Miss Phyllis Barclay-Smith, British Museum (Natural History), Cromwell Road, S.W.7, London—27 Oct.

Proceedings Merchant Marine Council—United States Coast Guard, 1958, Vol. 15, No. 2. p. 28, Feb., Vol. 15. No. 7, p. 128, July; 1959, Vol. 16, No. 5, p. 101, May, Vol. 16, No. 10, pp. 198-203, Oct., Vol. 16, No. 12, pp. 242-243, Dec.; 1960, Vol. 17, No. 2. pp. 28-31, Feb., Vol. 17, No. 4, pp. 64-65, Apr., Vol. 17, No. 6, pp. 94-97, Jun., Vol. 17. No. 8, pp. 140-141, Aug., Vol. 17, No. 11, pp. 194-195, Nov.

Prokop, J. F., 1950, Report on a study of the microbial decomposition of crude oil. Research Conducted for the Texas A. & M. Research Foundation, Biology Research Laboratory, College Station, Texas.

Ripley, Dillon, 1942, Oil on the sea. Audubon Magazine, Vol. XLIV, No. 2, p. 86 National Audubon Society, New York.

Tuck, Leslie M., 1959, Oil pollution in Newfoundland. Address before the International Conference on Oil Pollution of the Sea, Copenhagen, Denmark.

Tufts, R. W., 1942a, Preliminary report covering investigation of damage to seafowl by crude oil along the Nova Scotia Coast. Report to: Chief, Canadian Wildlife Service, Ottawa, Canada, Mar. 18; 1942b, Informal report on investigation of damage being done to waterfowl in coastal Nova Scotia as a result of floating crude oil. Report to: The Controller, National Parks Bureau, Dept. of Mines and Resources, Ottawa, Canada, May.

Wilson, John E., 1960, Oil contamination in relation to waterfowl kill records—1960—Lake Ontario—St. Lawrence River. Report for the New York State Department of Conservation and Natural Resources, N.Y.

Radiation and Nature

Commentary

Ever since the atomic bomb was dropped on Nagasaki and Hiroshima, violently ushering in the atomic age, the impact of nuclear radiation on life on earth has been of major concern. Although the threat of atomic weapons is always present, of more immediate concern is the effect of much lower levels of irradiation on life. Major questions revolve around the effects of nuclear power plants, which might well supply us with 50 percent of our power needs in the next twenty years. What will be the effect of these plants on humans and on ecosystems?

In this selection George Woodwell explores the effects of chronic radiation on ecosystems, specifically an oak pine forest. The forest is more sensitive to radiation than any other natural ecosystem, and radiation tends to revert it back to an earlier stage of succession. Woodwell and others find[1] five well-defined zones of modification of vegetation: a central devastated zone, a sedge zone, a shrub zone, an oak zone where pine had been eliminated, and a normal oak-pine forest. The strata were removed layer by layer, with all but the herbaceous layer gone close to the source. Upright forms were at a particular disadvantage, whereas plants with underground stems and buds survived the best. In effect, radiation changed the structure of ecosystem and altered species diversity. The changes were somewhat suggestive of the effects of fire[2] or other severe environmental damage. Such radiational effects one would expect after an atomic blast. The levels of radiation are many times greater than what one could expect from nuclear power stations. Yet the very fact that such plants do involve nuclear piles and fission reactions has created considerable uneasiness about nuclear power plants, because most of them are being located near populated areas.

There can be no denial of the fact that pressurized water reactors, commonly used in nuclear power plants, release low levels of radioactivity to the air and to condenser water. The nuclear release of radioisotopes to the environment around the plant site is about one-millionth of that produced during the fission reaction. As determined by the Federal Radiation Council, the permissible exposure levels for a general population in a five- to twenty-mile radius about the plant is 170 millirems (mrem) per year, and the maximum nonoccupational single dose exposure is 7500 mrem a year. The Atomic Energy Commission in turn establishes the FRC guidelines at the plant boundary. The maximum possible exposure five to ten miles from the plant is supposedly 2 to 5 percent of FRC limits.

Radioactive contamination of water from nuclear power plants comes from several sources. When water passes through the intense neutron flux of the reactor, trace elements in the water are activated, producing radioisotopes. Added to this are radioactive corrosive products from the surface of metal cooling tubes. Except for tritium, most of the radioisotopes are removed in a radioactive waste removal process. Those left have a short half-life and rapidly decay below detection levels.

Radioactive materials that enter the water become incorporated into bottom sediments and circulate between mud and water. Some become absorbed by organisms and concentrated at various trophic levels. In fact, a sort of equilibrium is established between retention in the biomass and in the bottom sediment, the water, daily input, and decay.[3]

When a strike shut down the Hanford water reactor on the Columbia River for forty days in 1966, a rapid and extensive decline took place in the concentration of radionucleides, particularly chromium-51, phosphorus-

[1] J. F. McCormick, "Effects of Ionizing Radiation on a Pine Forest," in D. J. Nelson and F. C. Evans (eds.), *Proc. Second Nat. Symp. on Radioecology*, CONF-670503, Clearinghouse for Fed. Sci. and Tech. Inf. Nat. Bur. Stand., Springfield, Va., 1969, pp. 78—87.

[2] G. M. Woodwell, "Effects of Pollution on the Structure and Physiology of Ecosystems," *Science* **168**, 1970, pp. 429—433.

[3] C. D. Jennings and C. Osterberg, "Sediment Radioactivity in the Columbia River Estuary," in D. J. Nelson and F. C. Evans (eds.), *Proc. Second Nat. Symp. on Radioecology*, CONF 670503, Clearinghouse for Fed. Sci. and Tech. Inf. Nat. Bur. Stand., Springfield, Va., 1969, pp. 300—306.

52, and zinc-75, in both fish and phytoplankton.[4,5] When the plant resumed operations, the old equilibrium was reestablished within two or three weeks. Although the levels of radioactivity in the biota were too low to cause any short-range biological damage, the biological effects of long-term exposure to low levels of radiation is totally unknown.

The tritium produced, however, is released with no reduction. Possessing a half-life of 12.5 years, tritium tends to concentrate in the ocean. It can substitute biochemically for stable isotopes of hydrogen in body tissues. Globally, an equilibrium level of about 100 million curies of tritium exists, a balance between decay and production by cosmic ray flux. Hydrogen bomb testing raised that level to 1.7 billion curies. Providing that no additional testing of hydrogen bombs takes place, the level of global tritium should drop to a normal equilibrium level of 100 million curies again. But if nuclear power supplies one-half of the world's needs of electricity, as is predicted, then the tritium levels in the world will increase exponentially until it reaches a concentration of that of the residual from hydrogen bomb tests.[6] After the year 2000, nuclear reactors could become the dominant source of tritium unless adequate treatment methods for its removal are developed. World population would be exposed to 0.002 mrem of tritium from all sources.

A second source of radiation pollution comes from gaseous effluents. The most important source of radioactive pollutants, however, comes not from the nuclear power station itself but from the fuel reprocessing plants. Although gaseous emissions are contained forty-five days in a holding system, two radioactive elements, the so-called noble gases krypton and xenon, are still released to the atmosphere. Of the two, krypton-85 is still the most important, and the total global content comes from nuclear reactors of all types. At present the level of exposure of man to krypton is less then 0.1 percent of the combination from background cosmic radiation and natural radioactivity. But if nuclear power production increases as predicted, then the exposure "due to krypton-85 could increase to 2 milliroentgen or 1000 times that of tritium and about one percent of the radiation protection guides recommended by national international standards groups."[6] Necessary efforts to reduce this amount of krypton emission should be undertaken now—before the turn of the century, when the problem will be upon us.

Radioactive wastes removed and concentrated at fuel reprocessing plants must be disposed of safely; therein lies another environmental threat. At present these highly radioactive wastes are stored in about 200 large underground steel and concrete tanks. These wastes, mostly from weapons production, may run as high as 1000 curies per gallon. This amount is so lethal that three gallons, if distributed equally around the world, would expose everyone to damaging radiation. One hundred million gallons of such wastes are now stored in tanks that require perpetual care. Not only must they be continually cooled, but tanks have to be replaced about every twenty years. One tank of 60,000 has already failed, releasing radioactive material to work its way through the soil.

Woodwell's paper is concerned with only one aspect of nuclear radiation, chronic radiation as it affects ecosystems and would affect ecosystems after an atomic detonation. His observations on the effects of radiation, however, should alert us to possible chromosomal changes induced by long-term, low-level radiation, even if below federal guidelines.

GLOSSARY OF TERMS

Roentgen (R) The original unit of radiation. It is the amount of X- or gamma-radiation that is produced in one cubic centimeter of standard dry air ionization equal to one electrostatic unit of charge. It is used to describe the radiation field to which one may be exposed.

Rad (radiation absorbed dose) The quantity of radiation that delivers 100 ergs of energy to 1 gram of substance (almost equivalent to a roentgen when referred to body tissue).

Rem (roentgen equivalent, man) A biological (rather than physical) unit of radiation damage, the quantity of radiation that is equivalent in biological damage to 1 rad of 250-kilovolt peak X-rays.

[4]S. C. Renfro and C. Osterberg, "Radiozinc Decline in Starry Flounders after Temporary Shutdown of Hanford Reactors," in D. J. Nelson and F. C. Evans (eds.), *Proc. Second Nat. Symp. on Radioecology*, CONF-670503. Clearinghouse for Fed. Sci. and Tech. Inf. Nat. Bur. Stand., Springfield, Va., 1969, pp. 372–379.
[5]D. G. Watson, C. E. Cushing, C. C. Coutant, W. V. Templeton, "Effects of Hanford Reactor Shutdown on Columbia River Biota," in D. J. Nelson and F. C. Evans (eds.), *Proc. Second Nat. Symp. on Radioecology*, CONF-670503. Clearinghouse for Fed. Sci. and Tech. Inf. Nat. Bur. Stand., Springfield, Va., 1969, pp. 291–299.
[6]J. H. Wright, "Electric Power Generation and the Environment," *Westinghouse Engineer* **30**, 1970, pp. 66–80.

Curie (Ci) A measure of radioactivity. One curie is the amount of any radioactive nuclide that undergoes 37 billion transformations per second.

Half-life The average time required for half the atoms of an unstable nuclide to transform.

Dose A measure of the energy actually absorbed in tissue by interactions with ionizing radiation.

Exposure A measure of X- or gamma-radiation at any point, used to describe the energy of the radiation field outside the body.

Selection 27

Radiation and the Patterns of Nature

by George M. Woodwell

The partial answers we have to the question of what radiation does *in* and *to* nature are revealing not only of the effects of radiation on living systems, but also of the architecture of the systems themselves. My object is to show the patterns of the effects of radiation on natural communities, and how the patterns parallel and help to explain the normal patterns of structure, function, and development of these communities. It is important in this discussion to remember that most life as we know it has evolved in environments in which total exposures to ionizing radiation have amounted to less than a few tenths of 1 roentgen per annum, and that ionizing radiation is generally thought to have played a very minor role among the selective processes of evolution. It is somewhat surprising therefore that the effects of radiation on natural communities follow predictable patterns apparently related to the evolution of life.

The significance of natural communities to biology and to man is not immediately apparent. For my purposes it is important to recognize that all organisms have evolved as functional units in communities of organisms, and that the structure and function of these communities have determined in some measure the structure and function of the organisms themselves. So we can think of Darwin's struggle for existence as operative in the evolution of not only species but also groups of species and whole communities. This is not a new concept; it was set down by Darwin in his *Origin of Species*, published in 1859.

The evolutionary implications of Darwin's struggle for existence at the community level are shown most clearly by a simple example, which is based rather freely on Darwin's own studies in the Galápagos Islands. Let us assume a small group of islands in the tropics, volcanic, and therefore young in a geologic sense, but supporting the limited flora and fauna that have arrived from the mainland some 1000 kilometers away. The climate is diversified, ranging from desert to moist forest. The islands have trees, grasses, and shrubs, but no mammals and few birds.

Over the years, probably hundreds of years, chance, possibly in the form of westering storms, brought small flocks of birds. From among these flocks at various times some finches survived and found a favorable habitat, rich in a diversity of foods and free of both mammalian and avian predators; reproducing rapidly, each new immigrant population became a plague, much as the Japanese beetle, the sparrow, the starling, the gypsy moth, and a host of other introductions have become plagues in our own experience. Food, although at first abundant, quickly became limiting, and the struggle for existence intensified. Competition for food was fierce and a premium attached to any ability to exploit new food

---

THIS SELECTION is reprinted with permission of the author and publisher from *Science*, Vol. 156, pp. 461–470, April 1967. Copyright 1967 by the American Association for the Advancement of Science.

supplies—foods different from those exploited by competitors. Small differences in behavior or in size or shape of beak resulted in small differences in survival and in ability to rear young. These differences, when hereditary and useful, were passed on and amplified in the population, and on each island there developed a population of finches peculiarly adapted to that environment and different from populations on other islands.

There was one additional complication. Exchanges of individuals or small groups of individuals occurred occasionally among the islands, continually testing the degree of genetic isolation achieved by the evolution of different races. Frequently these transported populations failed on the new island or were absorbed into the now-indigenous population; occasionally, however, a small one found itself partially isolated ecologically, by behavior, food supply, or local preference of habitat, from the indigenous population and survived as a distinct population, competition and evolution tending to accentuate the isolating mechanisms. Thus the islands gradually acquired a diverse bird fauna consisting largely of races of finches; ground finches, tree finches, a warbler finch, a woodpecker finch—each race using a set of resources used elsewhere in the world by a totally different species. Ecologists call the resources used by any one species a niche; where niches overlap and resources are shared, they say that competition occurs.

We see from this example, which is a grossly simplified version of *Darwin's Finches* (1), that the evolution of life proceeds toward reduction of competition, toward utilization of space and other resources, toward diversity in form and function, toward the filling of niches. We see, moreover, that the evolution of a race is affected not only by its physical environment, but also by the evolution of other races whose evolutions are in turn affected. Thus the chain of cause and effect here becomes entangled in bewildering ways. The product is a complex and, in some degree, mutable array of plants and animals which, itself, has clear and predictable patterns of structure, function, and development; these are "natural communities." Thus physical environments that are similar tend to support organisms that are similar in form and function, if not in species. So certain climates support forests the world over; others, grasslands; others, desert; and these words—

forest, grassland, desert, and tundra—have meaning for us in terms of climate and flora and fauna.

Thus, where environments are similar, we find organisms that may have little or no common genetic past performing parallel functions. In Australia the marsupials, for instance, fill the grazing niches filled by placental mammals elsewhere; and the genus *Eucalyptus* has filled the tree niches occupied elsewhere by a score of other genera. The communities in which these organisms participate are one answer, tested through millions of years of evolution, to the very fundamental question: How can the resources of environment be used to perpetuate life? This is, of course, a fundamental objective of man: the use of environment to best advantage.

The evolutionary answer is a magnificently durable one and, in terrestrial communities, usually a surprisingly stable one, free of plagues or rapid changes in sizes of population. By this I mean that controls of population size have evolved, building stability into these complex biological systems—putting the "balance" into nature.

Now let us consider for a moment certain other characteristics of natural communities. It is clear that the communities have developed over long periods and are very much a product of the evolution of life; and that they vary in a spatial sense with geography, climate, topography, and a host of other environmental factors. They also vary with time.

To show the variation with time, let us assume for a moment that after we harvest our corn crop in the eastern United States we simply abandon the land. The weeds of the garden take over; crabgrass, at first; later, grasses; then, pine forest; and finally, after 100 years or so, an oak forest. The general pattern is familiar; environmental circumstance may modify details. The change from herbaceous weed field to forest involves not only changes in the species forming the communities, but also changes in the total weight of living matter on a unit of land, in the total amount of essential nutrients available, in the total amount of water used, in the total number of niches available, and probably in the rates of biologic evolution itself. This process—succession—becomes one of the great central principles of biology.

We can examine one succession, from abandoned field to forest, most easily by considering stored energy in plants over time. By plotting such data (my own, and those produced by workers elsewhere in eastern North America) we obtain an S-shaped curve similar to the growth curve of a single organism. It rises slowly during the early herbaceous stages, rises much more rapidly during the pine-forest stage, and levels during the deciduous-forest stage as the degree of stability increases. Along this curve several very fundamental changes occur in community structure and function. There is, of course, a shift in species from herbaceous plants to trees. But there is also thought to be increase in diversity—total numbers of species present—from the few of the abandoned field to the many of the ultimate forest. There is change in degree of stability from the field, with its patches of ragweed and crabgrass which may be rapidly replaced by any of several species, to the forest with its spatial uniformity and slow replacement. There is increase in the total pool of minerals within the system: small amounts held within the herbaceous communities, large amounts in the forest. Total respiration and total photosynthesis increase, but at different rates, producing a regular change with time in the ratio of photosynthesis to respiration during the course of succession. We assume in addition that the total amount of water used increases along this succession (2).

If, in the course of such a succession, one or more factors essential to the system become exhausted or available only in short supply, the rate of succession is slowed and the climax is diverted, possibly by as much as from forest to grassland. Thus, in areas of low rainfall, succession ends in a stable grassland or woodland; where little mineral nutrient is available, whatever the reason, the succession is slowed and the S-shaped curve levels.

If, on the other hand, the environment is changed drastically by erosion or by sudden change in climate, or catastrophically by fire or windstorm or even by fallout from a bomb, then the changes that occur in these arrays tend to be just the reverse of those occurring during a normal succession: the communities are simplified, niches are opened, the nutrient inventory accumulated during succession is lost at least partially, the community becomes less stable, and a new succession begins, possibly marked by large fluctuations in populations that reproduce rapidly (such as insects)

and can exploit the open niches.

Succession, then, is such a fundamental part of biology that it forms the logical core for appraisal of the effects of any change in environment, most especially a change that has such far-reaching and basic implications for life as ionizing radiation.

At first glance the problems in appraisal of the effects of ionizing radiation on the communities along a successional gradient seem so complex as to be impossible. But we can borrow a trick from the mathematicians and examine the effects on the extremes: we can use a gradient of exposures from very high to very low and examine the early stages of succession, which, in eastern North America, are abandoned fields, and the later stages, which are forests. The question we ask is, in each of these stages: What are the effects of irradiation on the community? In the forest, for instance, we need to know what exposure to radiation changes the composition of the plant community. When the composition does change, how does it change? Do species behave individually, or are there groups of species having similar characteristics? After what exposures do we expect insect populations to change? Do we affect metabolism, use of water? How do we affect them? Are there any patterns of radiosensitivity that may be useful for prediction of effects of radiation or for interpretation of the structure and function of unirradiated communities? The overriding question is: What are the patterns of radiation effects on the structure, function, and development of natural communities? This was the question posed in 1961 when the work at Brookhaven, which I shall discuss, was started.

We had then considerable information on radiation effects on many species of plants (3). It was known that the amount of damage caused by any exposure was related to the size and number of chromosomes in the cell nucleus (4). Sparrow had observed that certain species of pine trees are killed by exposures in the same general range as those killing man. Other data had shown a very great range, more than 1000-fold, in the sensitivity of plants to damage by radiation (5). The sensitivity of pines had been confirmed (6), and it had been shown that forests are generally more sensitive than had been known (7). Field observations, however, were most limited, and there was good reason to explore that problem experimentally and in detail.

Our approach entailed the establishment of two experiments, in each of which we used a single large source of γ-radiation (equivalent to about 9500 curies of Cs[137]), arranged in such a way that it could be lowered into a shield (for safe approach) or suspended several meters above ground to provide radiation over a large area. The sources were large enough to administer several thousand roentgens per day within a few meters, the dose approaching background levels beyond 300 meters. The two experiments· were conducted in an irradiated old field in the now-well-known γ-radiation field established in 1949 (8), and in an irradiated forest—a completely new installation (9, 10); thus they gave us a sample from each end of the successional curve that I have discussed.

A section of the γ-radiation field was abandoned in the fall, after harvest, and the herbaceous communities common to abandoned gardens were allowed to develop. On Long Island about 40 herbaceous species participate in colonizing land prepared in this way; one of the most conspicuous is pigweed (*Chenopodium album*) because of its height (up to 1 meter) and abundance. During the 2nd year, horseweed (*Erigeron canadensis*) is the most conspicuous and one of the most abundant. In subsequent years, grasses such as broom sedge (*Andropogon* spp.) and asters (*Aster ericoides*) become dominants, to be followed by pine, and oak-hickory forest (11, 12).

Irradiation produced striking changes in the communities of the early stages of the succession. Although we have studied several of these communities over five summers at Brookhaven,

I shall discuss here only the 1st-year communities. The most conspicuous change was drastic simplification at high exposures. We can measure simplification as a reduction in numbers of species per unit area, or in "diversity." Figure 1 is a plot of diversity along the radiation gradient. Irradiation at 1000 roentgens per day reduced diversity to about 50 percent of that of the unirradiated community, another field 2 kilometers distant. This decrease was continuous along the radiation gradient and was not marked by any abrupt decline indicating exclusion of several species in a narrow range of rates of exposure. Certain species survived daily exposures that exceeded 2000 roentgens.

The pattern of distribution of standing crop, or total weight of plants, at the end of the growing season, was strikingly different (Fig. 2). Total standing crop along the radiation gradient ranged between about 400 grams per square meter in the control community and 800 grams at 1000 roentgens per day, with a consistent increase with increase in exposure between these extremes. While the significance of this increase is not entirely clear, it is plain that, at exposures exceeding 1000 roentgens per day, total standing crop dropped abruptly to a few grams per square meter and, although some species survived even higher exposures, production of plant mass was very low indeed. There is clear evidence that at intermediate exposures exclusion of one species freed resources for others, crabgrass being by far the most benefited; at exposures exceeding 200 roentgens per day it was the major contributor to the total standing crop. Thus these old-field communities appear to be plastic, maintaining

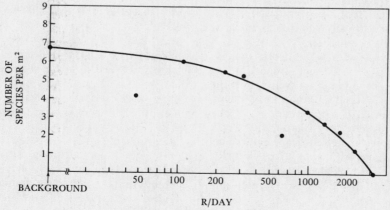

Figure 1. Diversity in the 1st-year-old field.

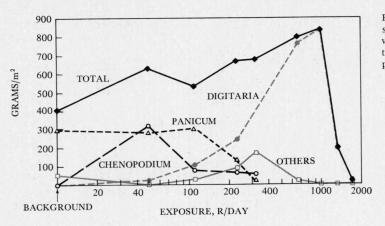

Figure 2. Total dry weight of plants, by species, in the irradiated old field. Dry weights were measured at the end of the season and do not represent total production.

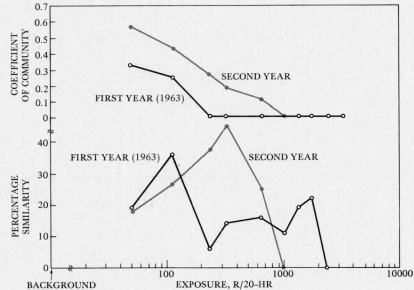

Figure 3. Coefficient of community and percentage similarity for irradiated communities, compared with the control community (2 kilometers distant). The linear relation between coefficient of community and the logarithm of exposure rate shows that species composition, alone, independent of density, is a useful criterion of the severity of disturbance by radiation.

and possibly even increasing the total amount of energy fixed, despite a reduction in diversity of up to 50 percent. It also appears that diversity of species is more sensitive to radiation effects than is organic production. This relation is borne out by a brief consideration of coefficient of community, and percentage similarity.

The coefficient of community is simply the total number of species common to two communities, expressed as a percentage of the total number of species in both communities; Fig. 3 shows an approximately linear relation between the coefficients of community along the radiation gradient, calculated for the control community, and the logarithm of radiation-exposure rate (11). There appears to be no threshold for effects on composition by species

at exposures as low as 50 roentgens per day. If we weight the coefficient of community with a measure of abundance of each species, we can calculate what is called percentage similarity, and Fig. 3 shows that there is no simple relation between these figures and radiation exposure, an observation that seems to confirm the earlier observation that the relative abundance of any species, however measured, is primarily controlled by competition with other species. Thus diversity and coefficient of community (and probably any other index of species diversity) emerge as relatively sensitive measures of radiation damage—and probably of any type of environmental change; abundance, density, and standing crop are insensitive.

Let us examine somewhat more closely the

310

characteristics of plants that survive high rates of exposure. Two characteristics seem particularly significant: first, at high exposures the incidence of species that normally grow close to the ground [prostrate, decumbent, or depressed (13)] is substantially higher than in unirradiated communities (Fig. 4); second, there appears to be sorting on the basis of chromosome size, plants with large chromosomes being excluded from the areas receiving high exposures. While it is difficult to venture a reason for apparent correlation between small size of chromosomes and a prostrate or decumbent growth habit among plants of old-field communities, these observations suggest that such a pattern may exist.

Thus the first year of succession is characterized by a loose array of herbaceous plants, most of them annuals or biennials, of varying life-forms and physiologies. Diversity in form and function allows rapid colonization of a wide variety of disturbed areas, and contributes toward making the community as a whole resilient in the face of disaster—such as a gardener's hoe or a gradient of ionizing radiation. The primary effect of stresses, including irradiation, is reduction of diversity. In the case of radiation, the reduction is continuous along the radiation gradient and not characterized by simultaneous exclusion of two or more closely associated species, an observation testifying to the looseness of the community organization. Although it is true that the plasticity of the community as a whole makes it resistant to radiation damage, it is certainly not true that all species in the community are equally resistant. Daily irradiation at 50 or more roentgens produced continuous sorting of species

according to life-form and according to the average volumes of their chromosomes.

Irradiation of the forest commenced in November 1961 after a detailed series of pre-irradiation studies. The approach was to make a case-history study of one relatively complex ecological system by examining as many aspects as possible of its structure and function, both normal and pathological (10). Six months after installation of the source the forest appeared as in Fig. 5; my data, with few exceptions, apply to the forest as it was in the summer of 1962, after approximately the same period of exposure as the old field.

Five zones were apparent along the radiation gradient: a central zone in which no higher plants survived; a sedge zone containing *Carex pensylvanica* and a few sprouts of the heath-shrub layer; a shrub zone where the two blueberries and huckleberry survived; an oak-forest zone at daily exposures less than about 40 roentgens; and the oak-pine forest in which radiation effects on growth were apparent, without change in species composition (14).

The zoning of vegetation reflected the decline in diversity along the gradient (Fig. 6). If the normal "plot" in this forest be accepted as having 5.5 species, then 50-percent diversity occurred at 160 roentgens per day, or less than one-fifth the exposure to reduce diversity by 50 percent in the herbaceous community. Shielding by the stems of large trees in the forest allowed survival by species at average exposures substantially greater than the normally lethal exposures. Therefore the differential is probably even greater, and the forest may have its diversity depressed by 50 percent at exposures as low as one-tenth of those re-

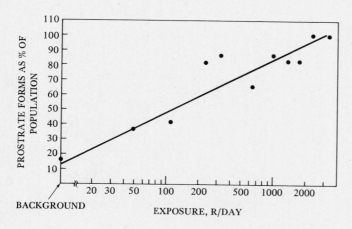

Figure 4. Life-forms in an irradiated field (1963, 1st year); "prostrate" forms include forms labeled normally prostrate, decumbent, or geniculate by Fernald (13).

Figure 5. Effects of 6-month exposure to gamma radiation ranging in intensity from several thousand roentgens per day near the center of the circle to about 60 roentgens at the perimeter of the defoliated area. The experiment is part of a study at Brookhaven National Laboratory of the effects of chronic exposure to ionizing radiation.

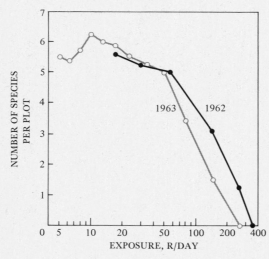

Figure 6. Species diversity along the radiation gradient in the irradiated forest in 1962 and 1963. Measurement of diversity in a forest requires differently sized samples for differently sized plants; thus the unit of diversity here is "species per plot" [from Woodwell and Rebuck (15)].

quired in the herb field (15).

Unlike the old field, standing crop in the forest declined at approximately the same rate as diversity (Fig. 7). This relation between diversity and abundance measured by standing crop is, of course, to be expected, since there is no possibility of a population of oak trees, 9 meters in height, expanding within a year to fill a niche vacated by pine. Nor was there invasion by any of the herbaceous species more resistant to radiation. There was, however, expansion of the population of *Carex*, a plant that normally occurs as a ubiquitous but very sparse herb, to cover as much as 20 percent of the total ground surface. This expansion was in response to the demise of the tree and shrub cover; it points to the potential importance of rare, or at least inconspicuous, species, capable of rapid regeneration, in maintaining certain aspects of function in disturbed communities.

Other examples of rapid response to the

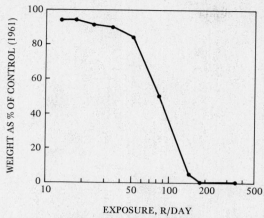

Figure 7. Total weight of above-ground shoots in irradiated forest in 1962.

changed resources in the damaged community abound, especially among insect populations. In general these populations have followed quite closely change in food supply (*16*). Populations that utilize dead organic matter and decay organisms increased in the central zone of high mortality to the vegetation; bark lice are a good example (Fig. 8). While this type of change seems quite straightforward and predictable, all changes in insect populations were not: during the 2nd year of the experiment, for instance, there was an unexpected and still-unexplained population explosion of aphids

on white oaks exposed to 5 to 10 roentgens per day (Fig. 9). Aphids share with certain fungi, such as wheat rust, ability to reproduce asexually very rapidly to exploit any available resource. Although mobile, they are not strong fliers and do not migrate far; it is unlikely that the high populations resulted from migration from neighboring forests. It seems much more probable that leaves of trees exposed to 5 to 10 roentgens per day differed qualitatively from leaves of unirradiated trees sufficiently to support large populations of aphids; the difference appears to be not in either total sugars or total proteins, but in some more subtle factor detectable by aphids but not yet by man (*17*).

The effects of irradiation on the forest are best summarized by the profile (Fig. 10) showing the five vegetation zones and their approximate distribution along the radiation gradient in 1962. The most striking observation is the relative sensitivity of all the higher plants. No higher plant indigenous to the forest survived the 1st year of exposures exceeding 350 roentgens per day; in the old field, certain species survived more than 3000 roentgens per day. The 50-percent diversity point occurred in the forest at less than 160 roentgens per day; in the field, at 1000 roentgens per day. It seems abundantly clear that the forest as a unit is substantially more sensitive than the herb field. A second important relation is that there is sorting by size along the radiation gradient, smaller forms of life being generally more

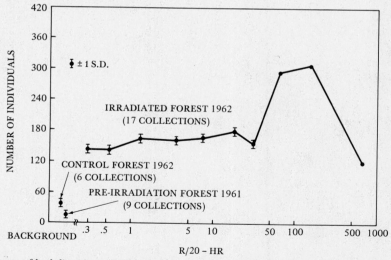

Figure 8. Abundance of bark lice (*Psocoptera*), which feed on decay organisms and dead organic matter, along the radiation gradient [from Brower (*16*)].

Figure 9. Abundance of aphids (*Myzocallis* sp.) on oak leaves in 1963 along the radiation gradient. At 9.5 roentgens per day, populations were more than 200 times normal.

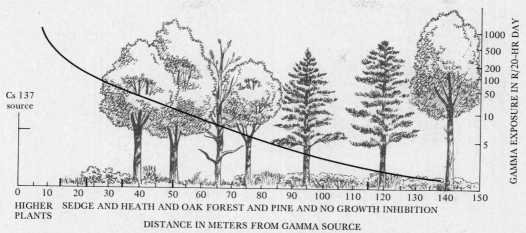

Figure 10. Pattern of radiation damage to oak-pine forest in 1962 after about 6 months of exposure.

resistant than trees; this relation also extends to mosses and lichens.

This sorting by size, which now seems to be a well-established characteristic of radiation damage, has interesting parallels elsewhere in nature. It occurs along gradients of increasing climatic severity, such as the transition from forest to tundra in the north, and on mountain slopes. At such transitions, forest is replaced by low-growing shrubs, frequently blueberries and other members of the heath-plant family. In more extreme environments the heath shrubs are replaced by a sedge mat formed by a species of *Carex*; in the most extreme, the *Carex* is restricted to protected spots, and mosses and lichens are the only vegetation. The parallel with the irradiated forest is quite remarkable, holding even to genera and species, in certain instances. The conclusion to be drawn from this relation is merely that characteristics that confer resistance to certain types of environmental extremes also, curiously enough, confer resistance to damage by radiation.

We can test the hypothesis a little more rigorously by examining in detail the shrub layer of the forest, which is itself a small community containing two species of blueberries, the huckleberry, and the sedge. Changes in this community after burning have been studied intensively (*18*); their general pattern appears in Fig. 11: with increased frequency of fire, the huckleberry populations decline, the blueberries increase, and the sedge increases. Under

irradiation the pattern is strikingly similar until the point at which radiation kills the blueberry. The parallelism between the effects of fire and of radiation should not be expected to be universal, for many factors are implicated. Nonetheless there seems to be a strong parallel

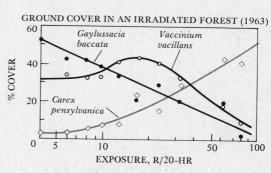

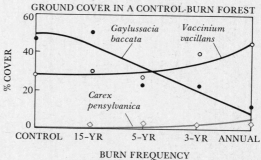

Figure 11. Comparison of effects of ionizing radiation and different frequencies of burning on the shrub and sedge community [from Brayton and Woodwell (*19*)].

315

between the effects of radiation and the effects of another extreme; and in both instances, as well as in the herb field, the correlation between durability and small stature applies (19).

While there is no completely satisfactory explanation of the parallels, one important contributory factor may be simply the size of the plant. Perennialism, height and complexity of structure all represent investments of energy in nonphotosynthesizing tissue, tissue that requires energy for maintenance. We might think of this tissue as a mortgage that must be paid off with income from photosynthesis. As the size of a plant increases, both mortgage and total income increase, but at different rates. In Fig. 12 are plotted the total weights of trees against $h \times d^2$, a measure of size (20). Since total weight of the tree is not a proper measure of total living tissue (there being considerable nonliving tissue in a tree), we have also plotted an estimate of the weight of tissue that may normally be considered living. It seems clear that in small trees leaves represent a substantially larger fraction of the total weight of live tissue than in large trees. An increase

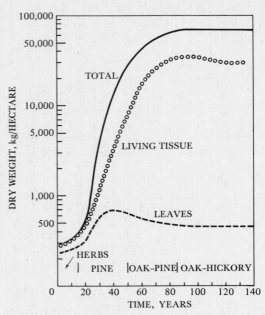

Figure 13. Approximate relations between total aboveground standing crop of plants, weight of living tissue, and weight of leaves in a normal field-forest succession of eastern North America.

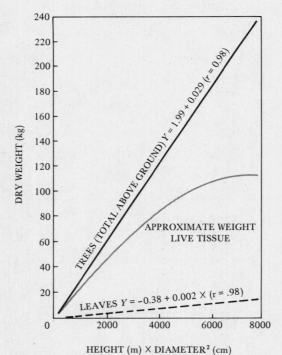

HEIGHT (m) × DIAMETER² (cm)

Figure 12. Relation between weights of leaves, weights of trees, and tree sizes for an oak-pine forest on Long Island.

in size thus puts greater demands on the photosynthetic mechanism simply for maintenance, leaving less for growth and repair.

A similar relation applies along the successional gradient that we have discussed (Fig. 13). In the early stages of succession most of the tissue produced is green, and the mortgage payments to support respiration are small. As succession progresses, the complexity of structure increases, but total living tissue increases more rapidly than the weight of leaves, which supply the energy for respiration; the mortgage increases, but income does not increase proportionally. It is true that the existence of the structure allows greater use of space, greater total photosynthesis up to a point, and greater diversity of species. But it is also true that the maintenance of the structure and diversity hinges on the annual interest paid from photosynthesis into the structural mortgage, and, if for any reason the interest is not paid, the structure begins to decay.

And here lies the crux of the matter: the mechanisms related to energy fixation—bud set, bud burst, lead production, photosynthesis —are at much greater hazard than mechanisms related to energy use. Almost any disturbance of a forest may reduce its capacity for fixing energy; it either increases respiration or reduces it relatively slightly. If the disturbance is chronic, the vegetation comes to a new equilibrium, supporting a less complex structure. For this reason we might expect a forest to be more sensitive to disturbance than is an herb field because the forest is less plastic in species composition and because its capacity for fixing energy must remain substantially intact or it will burn up more than it fixes and deteriorate. And that is exactly what happens, but it is far from the whole explanation.

We have shown for the herbaceous field that there was sorting along the radiation gradient, dependent on chromosome volume: plants with large average chromosome volumes are sensitive; those with small volumes, resistant. The pattern in the forest was similar. If we plot the average chromosome volumes (*8, 21*) against the daily exposure required to inhibit growth to 10 percent of growth of unirradiated plants (Fig. 14), it is abundantly clear that radiosensitivity correlates with size of the chromosomes, and that this correlation applies to populations in nature as well as to cultivated populations. Also, the larger plants tend to have larger chromosome volumes; the smaller

plants, smaller. Clearly, chromosome volume has played a role in the persistence of plants along the radiation gradient in the forest as well as in the field.

Now let me recapitulate briefly: the successional gradient we have used to explore effects of radiation on natural communities is characterized in the early stages by a loosely structured community or series of communities shifting in species composition, diversity, dominance, density, total mass of living matter, and probably in every other measurable parameter, within relatively broad limits, in response to disturbance. It is also true that the species of the early successional communities, including mosses and lichens, tend generally to be resistant to radiation. The forest does not share the plasticity of communities having simpler structure; in this respect the forest is more sensitive to any disturbance. In plants, large size alone, because of its effects on the ratio of photosynthesis to respiration, contributes to this type of sensitivity; but, more importantly, plants of the forest are inherently sensitive to radiation damage because they have large chromosomes and because woody species in general are more sensitive than herbaceous plants having the same-sized chromosomes (*22*).

Thus there seems to be a shift toward greater sensitivity to radiation as succession progresses. The shift is due to at least three factors: (i) what I term the relative plasticity of the communities; (ii) increase in the amount of structure in the communities, with its implications for the photosynthesis:respiration ratio; and (iii) changes in the intrinsic characteristics of the plants participating in these communities, including changes in size of chromosomes. All these factors work in the same direction, contributing toward greater sensitivity to radiation and probably to other types of disturbance later in succession.

What do the patterns of radiosensitivity mean? Could they be sheer coincidence on the one hand, a useful new clue to the mechanisms of evolution on the other?

It is difficult to discard them as mere coincidence: true, they are imperfect: there are radiation-resistant plants in the forest and radiosensitive plants in the field; furthermore, the pines, the most sensitive of all, are a minor part of the mature forest, and the pattern of increasing radiosensitivity along succession is

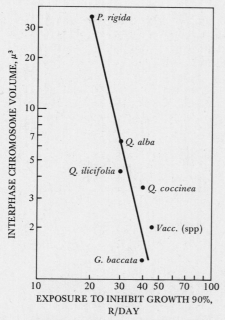

Figure 14. Relation between radiosensitivity, measured as inhibition of growth (90 percent), and interphase chromosome volume in irradiated forest (*21*).

imperfect in detail. Yet the difference in sensitivity between field and forest spans a factor of nearly 10; if we include lichen communities, which sometimes precede herbaceous communities in succession, there is a factor of 10 of additional resistance beyond that of the herbs (23). And the correlations between life-form and size and radiosensitivity, and the parallels between radiation effects and known effects of environmental gradients are too strong to be set aside lightly. There is no evidence at all that the enormous range of radiosensitivities among higher plants correlates in any way with the distribution of radioactivity in nature; nor is there reason to believe that radiation levels have changed appreciably during the quarter-billion years or so of existence of the higher plants. Rather, it seems that we must look further for other environmental factors or combinations of factors that have affected the evolution of that constellation of characteristics we measure when we measure radiosensitivity, including especially chromosome size.

It is an intriguing if somewhat oversimplified hypothesis that sensitivity to radiation damage is a measure of sensitivity to environmentally induced mutation (mutation is used in its broadest sense). It seems reasonable to accept the concept that rates of mutation tend toward some optimum, which is under hereditary control (24). If the rate were too high, there would be reduction in reproductive success; if too low, there would be insufficient variability to meet the evolutionary demands of constantly changing environments.

Certainly it is conceivable that environments vary in capacity to produce mutations. If, on the basis of current evidence about mutations, one were to seek a mutagenic natural environment (independent of radiation intensity), he would probably seek one characterized by extremes: extremes of temperature, moisture availability, and solar radiation. One thinks immediately of surfaces exposed to the sun: soil, rock, bark. The evidence that I report suggests strongly that plants that normally inhabit such surfaces—algae, lichens, mosses, and prostrate-growing vascular plants—are more resistant to ionizing radiation (and doubtless to many other stresses) than plants of more ameliorated environments such as forests.

Whether this suggestion will prove to be true when examined in a larger context than has yet been possible remains to be seen. Nonetheless, we now infer that ability to survive such rigorous environmental conditions also confers in some degree, at least, resistance to ionizing radiation. The factors that confer resistance involve growth form, length of life cycle, regenerative capacity, and cytological characteristics, especially average interphase chromosome volume. Experimental examination of this question is a current challenge to radiation research. Only by willingness to look at such really tough questions will we gain further insight into both radiation and the patterns of nature.

REFERENCES AND NOTES

1. D. Lack, *Darwin's Finches* (Cambridge Univ. Press, London, 1947).
2. This series of general statements is a synthesis of concepts current in ecology; for further discussion see R. Margalef, *Amer. Naturalist* **97**, 357 (1963); F. E. Clements, *Plant Succession and Indicators* (Wilson, New York, 1928).
3. Largely because of the efforts of A. H. Sparrow and colleagues at Brookhaven National Laboratory.
4. This work has been recently summarized: A. H. Sparrow, R. C. Sparrow, K. H. Thompson, L. A. Schairer, in *Proc. Use of Induced Mutations in Plant Breeding* (Pergamon, Oxford, 1965), pp. 101–32.
5. A. H. Sparrow and G. M. Woodwell, *Radiat. Bot.* **2**, 9 (1962).
6. By a 3-year study (Emory Univ., Atlanta; directed by R. B Platt) of the effects of radiation on vegetation surrounding an unshielded reactor in Georgia.
7. R. B. Platt, in *Ecological Effects of Nuclear War, BNL 917 (C–43)*, G. M. Woodwell, Ed. (Brookhaven National Laboratory, Upton, N.Y., 1965), pp. 39–60.
8. By A. H. Sparrow and colleagues, Brookhaven National Laboratory.
9. A. H. Sparrow, in *Large Radiation Sources in Industry* (Intern. Atomic Energy Agency, Vienna, 1960), vol. 3, pp. 195–219; ——— and W. R. Singleton, *Amer. Naturalist* **87**, 29 (1953).
10. G. M. Woodwell, *Radiat. Bot.* **3**, 125 (1963).
11. ——— and J. K. Oosting, *ibid.* **5**, 205 (1965).
12. G. E. Bard, *Ecol. Monographs* **22**, 195 (1952); H. J. Oosting, *Amer. Midland Naturalist* **28**, 1 (1942).
13. M. L. Fernald, *Gray's Manual of Botany* (American Book, New York, 1950).
14. G. M. Woodwell, *Science* **138**, 572 (1962).

15. ———— and A. L. Rebuck. *Ecol. Monographs,* **37**, 53 (1967).
16. J. H. Brower, dissertation, Univ. of Massachusetts, 1964.
17. G. M. Woodwell and J. H. Brower, *Ecology,* in press.
18. M. F. Buell and J. E. Cantlon, *ibid.* **34**, 520 (1953).
19. R. D. Brayton and G. M. Woodwell, *Amer. J. Bot.* **53**, 816 (1966).
20. G. M. Woodwell and P. Bourdeau, in *Proc. Symp. Methodol. Plant Ecophysiol.* (UNESCO, 1965), pp. 519—27.
21. G. M. Woodwell and A. H. Sparrow. *Radiat. Bot.* **3**, 231 (1963).
22. R. C. Sparrow and A. H. Sparrow, *Science* **147**, 1449 (1965).
23. G. M. Woodwell and T. P. Gannutz, Amer. *J. Bot.,* in press.
24. J. F. Crow, *Sci. Amer.* 201, 138 (1959); M. Kimura, *J. Genet.* **52**, 21 (1960).
25. R. H. Wagner (Brookhaven National Laboratory), unpublished data.
26. Research carried out at Brookhaven National Laboratory under the auspices of the AEC. Many have contributed for years to this work. I thank especially F. H. Bormann of Yale University, R. H. Whittaker of the University of California, Irvine, and A. H. Sparrow of Brookhaven National Laboratory for many long discussions.

Selection 28

The Land—Its Pollutants

Commentary

Whereas air and water pollution have become major concerns of the time, soil pollution is given little consideration. The manner in which land becomes polluted and the ecological implications of that pollution are considered by David Elrick in this selection.

The selection stimulates two comments. One concerns pollution from fertilizers, particularly as it relates to human health. Dr. Barry Commoner[1] argues that intensified application of nitrogenous fertilizers is stressing natural nitrogen cycles. In the United States the natural turnover of nitrogen in the soil is on the order of 7 or 8 million tons annually. Agriculture introduces into the system cycle nearly 10 million tons of nitrogen annually. Soil bacteria quickly convert fertilizer into nitrates. Because plants vary in their efficiency of uptake and utilization, and because soil and growing conditions differ widely, appreciable quantities of nitrates may be leached to the water and air (see Selection 23 and commentary). In addition to this, Dr. Commoner argues, nitrate fertilizer introduces a health hazard from excessive nitrites in food, particularly leafy vegetables, and in drinking water. Although not reported in the United States, some doctors in Europe have noted a rise in nitrite poisoning (methemoglobinemia) from spinach. While fresh spinach is high in nitrates, it contains insignificant amounts of nitrites. In the preparation of spinach, widely used in baby foods, the nitrates are converted to nitrites by bacteria. Increases in nitrate content and thus nitrites in prepared spinach are related to a heavier use of nitrogen fertilizer on the spinach crop. There is also evidence, in recent years, of increasing nitrate content in a number of vegetables, such as green beans, beets, and tomatoes.

On the other hand, an eminent agriculturist, Dr. T. C. Byerly,[2] states that a problem clearly exists and some control of the input of nitrogen from commercial fertilizers and other sources is needed. But he argues that we cannot reduce the level of nitrogen fertilization, for modern crops are genetically adapted to respond to intensive fertilization. Modern methods of intensive agriculture rely on heavy fertilization. However, because the rate of nitrogen utilization decreases as the rate of application increases, there is room for improvement on the timing of the application of fertilizer and a need for a nitrogen fertilizer that releases the nutrient more slowly. Because the best agricultural soils in the world are already under cultivation, increased food production can be achieved only by maximum use of that land, including heavy fertilization.

Another aspect of soil pollution is the effect of insecticides and herbicides on soil fauna. The effects are least severe when these materials reach only the surface soil. But what happens when these pesticides and herbicides are mixed with the soil by cultivation, bringing them in contact with large populations of soil animals?

Members of the soil fauna differ widely in their susceptibility to these substances.[3] A certain pesticide may eliminate one species and not affect another. A number of species of soil fauna are resistant to a wide range of pesticides, including most groups of springtails, symphylids, and enchytraeid worms. Susceptible groups include predatory mites, pauropods, springtails of the isotomid family, and the larvae of flies. There is a similar response to ionizing radiation.[4] In general, soil fauna are highly resistant to gamma radiation and can survive doses of several thousand rads. The lethal dose for humans is 400 rads. In spite of this high resistance, soil fauna are still more susceptible than the microflora. The least resistant to gamma radiation are those soil animals that are highly active, such as centipedes, wood lice, and parasitic mites. Least susceptible are relatively inactive species living deep in the soil.

---

[1]Barry Commoner, "Threats to the Integrity of the Nitrogen Cycle: Nitrogen Compounds in Soil, Water, Atmosphere and Precipitation," in Singer, S. F. (ed.), *Global Effects of Environmental Pollution*, New York, Springer-Verlag, 1970, pp. 70–95.
[2]T. C. Byerly, "Nitrogen Compounds Used in Crop Production," in S. F. Singer (ed.), *Global Effects of Environmental Pollution*, New York, Springer-Verlag, 1970, pp. 104–109.
[3]C. A. Edwards, "Effects of Pesticide Residues on Soil Invertebrates and Plants," in *Ecology and the Industrial Society*, Fifth Symp. British Ecol. Soc., 1965, pp. 239–261.
[4]C. A. Edwards, "Effects of Gamma Radiation on Populations of Soil Invertebrates," in D. F. Nelson and F. C. Evans (eds.), *Proc. Second Nat. Symp. on Radioecology*, CONF 670503, Clearinghouse for Fed. Sci. and Tech. Inf. Nat. Bur. Stand., Springfield, Va., 1969, pp. 68–77.

This fact has some ecological implications. The loss of the susceptible and usually predatory species permits the rapid multiplication of resistant forms. In some studies, populations of springtails important in the breakdown of organic matter increased by more than 400 percent after predatory mites were eliminated. Although such pollution reduces species diversity, eliminates many of the predators, and produces changes in food chains of soil communities, its ecological effects are not as far-reaching or important as they are in aquatic ecosystems. The major impact seems to occur above the soil, where the same pesticides and herbicides are transferred from soil to plants and animals in major terrestrial food chains.

Selection 28

The Land: Its Future-Endangering Pollutants

By David E. Elrick

One way of subdividing the subject of pollution is by slicing our environment into air, water and soil, a somewhat artificial but nevertheless convenient grouping. Of the three, air and water pollution are well-known evils to the general public. Pollution of the land is the least infamous of the trio, to a large extent due to the fact that both air and water are directly consumed by human beings, whereas soil is not (except for the 'peck of dirt' that accompanies infancy). In addition, soil pollution tends to stay hidden longer because of the soil's much greater density. The air around us can very easily become polluted and, fortunately, can often be depolluted just as easily, e.g. by filtering. Water has a much greater density and is more difficult to pollute; but once polluted, purification is more difficult than with air. The soil has a still greater density and consequently is even more difficult to purify once polluted.

In general, we tend to consider the soil as man's waste basket—but this practice cannot be carried too far. Because the soil is biologically alive, it does have the ability to degrade or break down organic compounds. This is a natural process in which leaves, dead grass and other sources of plant and animal matter are decomposed by the soil microflora, releasing nutrients to be used again in plant-life processes. However, there is a limit to the amount of material the soil can handle adequately and the soil is by no means a 'garbage can *par excellence*'.

WHAT IS THE SCOPE OF THE SOIL POLLUTION PROBLEM?

Is soil pollution an important problem in the world today? Is its priority high or low by comparison with air and water pollution, education, defence, and other problems? A direct answer is difficult to give because of insufficient statistical data on the extent of pollution of the world's land resources. We can say that the problem of soil pollutions, *per se*, is not yet an acute one, though the problem of pollution as a whole, including that of soil, air and water, is at the extreme end of the chronic stage, approaching the acute stage. Yet because of the great difficulty in decontaminating polluted soils, we must be much concerned with what will happen to the world's supply of soil if we perpetuate and expand our present practices.

It is only too easy to look into the future and see that soil pollution can become an overwhelming problem if proper planning is not undertaken immediately.

The major sources of contamination of soil are three: agriculture, industry and population agglomerations. In the technologically advanced countries, a revolution in agriculture—what we may call an industrialization of agriculture—has been taking place over the past two decades. This revolution has entailed, among other major revisions in

THIS SELECTION is from *Impact of Science on Society*, Vol. XIX, No. 2, 1969. Reprinted by permission of © Unesco.

agricultural practices, the widespread use of pesticides, commercial fertilizers and animal wastes. While these valuable materials are not pollutants in themselves, their misuse has often made them such.

The agricultural revolution is spreading to the developing countries of the world, virtually all of whom have agriculture as the base of their economy and their major source of national income. With its spread, vast additional areas of farmland will come under the application of pesticides, fertilizers and animal wastes. If these are not then used in a sound rational fashion, with some controls on their application, the resulting increased pollution of the world's land resources, cultivated and wild, will multiply the present problem severalfold.

Similarly, there is a great trend or ambition in developing countries toward industrialization. The inevitable establishment of new factories in developing regions will cause an enormous increase in the potentialities for pollution of land by industrial wastes, though factories pollute water and air far more than land. It is clear that the industrialization of presently backward economies will contribute to making the land pollution problem an acute one if proper measures are not taken at the present comparatively early stage.

In all countries of the world, there is a tide of movement from the land to the cities. In technologically advanced countries, this movement has reached a far advanced state, though it still continues. It has really only begun in the developing countries, but will approach springtide proportions before too long, especially as it correlates to increasing industrialization. Thus there will be many more and larger agglomerates of population, some attaining megalopolis dimensions, generating enormous quantities of wastes.

Increasing soil pollution in future years can intensify the present international aspect of this problem, even though the soil is much less mobile than air or water. International aspects of soil pollution can take place when soil contaminants pass across the border from one country to another, in ground water, surface water, air or food, fibres and animal products. The classic example is fall-out from nuclear-bomb testing where debris can be distributed anywhere in the hemisphere where the explosion occurred. Leaching and run-off of fertilizers or pesticides from agricultural land into international waters is another example.

A third example can be found in the insecticide, DDT. Today the chemical can be found in greater or lesser concentrations almost everywhere in the world environment. Bald eagles in the Arctic and penguins in the Antarctic have been found to have residues of DDT in their tissues. DDT residues have been found in the rain falling over the English country-side and in fishes of the Pacific coastal area from Alaska to Mexico. These levels of contamination, which are in general quite low, can vary from non-detectable, which with modern methods is down to one part per million million (1×10^{-12}), up to thousands of parts per million. In general, the contamination of fish and wild-life in areas where pesticides have not been directly applied is near the lowest level of detection.

Another very important aspect of pesticide pollution applies to international trade in food products. Tolerance levels in various food products are established by each country and products may be turned back at the border if they exceed the established tolerance levels. An interesting political aspect of this topic is that a country may reduce imports, not by adding duties or import restrictions but by lowering pesticide tolerance levels.

With this quick review of the soil pollution problem, I would like now to present a picture of the nature of the soil and of its interaction with some of the more important pollutants.

THE NATURE OF THE SOIL

A soil contains solid, liquid and gaseous phases consisting of various organic and inorganic compounds plus microflora and microfauna. The structure and arrangement of the solid phase determine the form of the porous soil matrix. The reactive surfaces of the soil grains are usually exposed to the aqueous phase and at these surfaces various reactions (both chemical and biological) can take place between the soil solids and dissolved or suspended material.

The gaseous phase is of importance with regard to the exchange of gases, such as oxygen and carbon dioxide, with the surface atmosphere. The biological component of the soil has to 'breathe' and it is the gaseous phase which regulates this activity.

The size of the 'garbage can' which the soil represents depends on the biological activity within the soil. It is the living component of the soil that is of the greatest importance for the break-down or degradation of organic materials, such as leaf litter, animal wastes and organochlorine insecticides. For example, it is the bacteria in the soil that are responsible for conversion of the nitrogen present in organic residues, such as dead plants or leaves, into simple inorganic compounds that can be utilized by living plants or into a gaseous form which returns to the atmosphere. Fungi and actinomycetes (an order of filamentous bacteria) help decompose soil herbicides, which otherwise might accumulate and make the soil unfit for many crops.

THE POTENTIAL SOIL POLLUTANT AND ITS TRANSPORT

Let us explain what might happen by tracing the possible pathways that a pollutant might follow in the soil. A potential pollutant usually falls (or is deposited) on the soil surface or is mixed (or injected) in the upper layer of the soil.

What happens from there depends on the chemical, physical and biological properties of the soil and the corresponding properties of the potential pollutant. Its solubility and volatility are extremely important. For example, a rather insoluble compound, such as the insecticide DDT, would probably be present at concentrations in the parts per billion[1] (ppb) range in the soil solution and even in much lower concentrations (non-detectable) in the soil gaseous phase. A much higher concentration of nitrate nitrogen, from both natural and artificial sources on fertilized land, would be present in the soil solution in about the parts per million range (ppm) and there would be no detectable nitrogen as nitrate present in the gaseous phase.

The potential pollutant can undergo various chemical and microbial reactions. Adsorption on soil solid surfaces, precipitation and transformation or degradation of the original substance are specific examples. Movement of potential pollutants in the soil can take place by diffusion (usually due to high concentrations near the soil surface) and by mass flow with the moving soil water or soil air (dispersion) (Fig. 1). This movement can possibly be toward

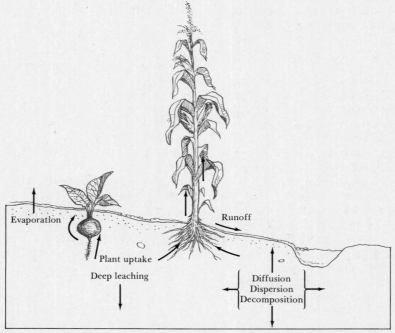

Figure 1. The movement of pollutants in the soil. Uptake of pollutants by food or fodder crops can lead to reduced yields, lowered quality, and toxic substances in food.

---

[1]'Billion' here has the North American definition, i.e., 1,000 million.—Ed.

plant roots or be downward leaching to ground-water supplies. There could also be upward flow to the soil surface when evaporation is taking place.

Some potential pollutants can be absorbed by crops. Studies have shown that there is some absorption of organochlorine residues from soils by root crops such as carrots and turnips but in general the residues did not exceed the tolerances that have been established for human consumption. Difficulties can some-times arise when food-stuffs fed to cattle contain only trace amounts of pesticides, particularly the organochlorine insecticides, dieldrin and DDT. These pesticides can be concentrated in some animal products, such as milk, resulting in a preferential magnification of the pesticide concentration. Some herbicides such as atra-zine, which is widely used for weed control in corn (maize), are quite persistent and can lower the yield of a subsequent susceptible crop, for example, oats or sugar beets, when present in the soil even in small amounts. This is usually a result of misuse, when recommendations are not followed. In many cases, it is appropriate to say that pesticide pollution equals pesticide misuse.

Subsequent water pollution can occur by leaching, by run-off, or by a combination of both. From a leaching standpoint, nitrate nitrogen and possibly some pesticides are the potential pollutants of most concern. From a run-off standpoint, the more insoluble com-pounds such as phosphates, the majority of the pesticides and animal wastes can be added. These problems will be discussed in detail in the following sections.

An ever increasing number and variety of chemicals are either applied directly to the soil or come in contact with the soil surface by wash-off from foliage, by leaf fall, and by other means. These chemicals are usually not considered as pollutants but are classified as insecticides, herbicides, fungicides, fertilizers, etc. However, the combination of high rates of application, widespread use of compounds that are toxic to wild-life and man, and the use of persistent chemicals that resist microbial attack and chemical break-down can produce a widespread problem.

The majority of crops and food products grown today in the technically advanced countries are either subjected to the use of some form of pesticide during the growth period or are grown on soil which has been chemically treated in the past. This is partic-ularly true in the United States and Canada.

The average citizen's awareness of the potential undesirable side effects of pesticides was stirred by Rachel Carson's *Silent Spring*.[2] Despite its emotional and partly inaccurate account of the consequences of pesticide use, this book has at least stimulated scientific interest in the over-all effects of pesticide usage on the environment.

The persistence of some pesticides in the soil and the possible incorporation of these com-pounds into some part of the food cycle of man and animals are some of the unforeseen prob-lems that have developed from pesticide usage. Most of these problems have developed with insecticides. Before 1945, many of the insecticides in general use were inorganic substances, such as arsenic and mercury com-pounds. In 1945 the first synthetic insecticide, DDT, became available for use. It was the be-ginning of a long list of synthetic insecticides that are highly effective, broad-spectrum poisons. Because these insecticides were effec-tive against a wide variety of foliar pests, they were used extensively. In retrospect, it is prob-ably correct to say that because of a lack of adequate information, these compounds were sometimes used at excessive rates or with methods of application that were detrimental and wasteful.

Although a considerable amount of time and effort was devoted to testing these materials for efficacy, little thought was given at first to possible side effects which might occur. Then, approximately five years after the introduction of organochlorine insecticides (DDT, aldrin, lindane, heptachlor), concern was voiced re-garding their persistence in soil. Since that time a number of studies have been carried out to determine the factors which affect the persist-ence or degradation of these materials in the soil.

It is difficult to formulate broad statements about pesticide behaviour in soils because of the large number and variety of chemical com-pounds coupled with the diversity of soil types (ranging from sands through clays to muck soils). However, it is known that the most

---

[2]Rachel Carson, *Silent Spring*, Greenwich, Connecticut, Crest Books, Fawcett, 1964.

important factors include the physical-chemical characteristics of the pesticide and its stability under microbial attack, climate, soil type (including physical and chemical properties), soil moisture, crop cover and frequency of cultivation.

Some materials, such as lindane, disappear relatively quickly. Others, such as dieldrin, persist in soils for many years. A major factor in the disappearance of residues from soils is the rate at which they evaporate. In some cases, relatively small amounts of the parent materials are converted into other compounds, apparently by soil micro-organisms. These conversion products may or may not be toxic, and may or may not be more persistent than the original parent material. Lindane, for example, is apparently degraded to a non-toxic material. On the other hand, small amounts of aldrin are converted to dieldrin and heptachlor to heptachlor epoxide within the soil. Both of these latter metabolites are toxic and considerably more persistent than the parent materials. DDT is also a very persistent insecticide, which is only slowly converted into two different metabolites.

If pesticide residues in soils were inert, perhaps there would be no problem. Unfortunately, this is not so. Pesticide residues in soil can possibly affect the microbiology of soil and ultimately influence the fertility levels (at present, this does not seem to be a problem). Some pesticides are absorbed by earth-worms. Although these materials may not be toxic to worms, some may be highly toxic to the birds that feed on these worms.

Pesticides may dissolve slightly in soil water, or may move with silt and ultimately end up in ponds, rivers and lakes. Fish may accumulate pesticides in the water and in turn may be eaten by birds and other fish. Thus one can speculate as to the manner in which pesticides move in the environment.

The development of resistance to insecticides and the absorption and translocation of organochlorine insecticide residues from soils into plants two unanticipated major problems that have resulted from pesticide use. A number of species of soil insects have become resistant to certain insecticides because of their extensive use and their persistence in the soil. In most cases, a mutant present in the population which carries the gene for resistance is responsible. It does not appear that the residues absorbed from the soil by vegetable and cereal crops exceed tolerances established for human consumption; however, when crops contaminated with even extremely small amounts of insecticides, particularly the organochlorines, are fed in bulk 'to animals over a relatively long period of time, the residues can build up in the animal tissues to much higher levels.

Absorption of residues from the soil also poses problems in the disposal of cannery wastes (such as pea vines), cull-grade vegetables (such as potatoes, turnips) and other vegetables which are usually fed to animals. Fortunately, there is now a trend away from these materials to other synthetic pesticides which do not appear to present such a formidable problem.

POLLUTION BY FERTILIZERS

As an agriculturist, it is difficult for this author to think of fertilizers as pollutants. However, when nutrient elements, such as phosphorus and nitrogen, are present in water supplies they can promote the growth of algae and aquatic plants. Also, in some cases, certain nitrogen compounds can act like poisons.

Although the presence of these nutrients in water supplies is normal because of leaching and run-off processes, sufficiently high concentrations of these nutrients in water supplies can lead to accelerated eutrophication.[3] How much of the fertilizer applied to agricultural land reaches surface water supplies? To answer this question, it is necessary to have an understanding of the reactions that fertilizers undergo in the soil and the more important transport mechanisms.

Phosphorus compounds in fertilizers react very quickly with iron, aluminium and calcium compounds in the soil to form new compounds which are only slightly soluble in water. On the other hand, the nitrogen compounds in fertilizers react quite differently. Under normal conditions, they are oxidized to the nitrate

---

[3]Eutrophication is the enrichment in water supplies (ponds, lakes, rivers) of nutrients that support the growth of plant and animal life. Eutrophication itself is a natural process, but accelerated eutrophication of water supplies by man's activities results in an excessive production of algae and other aquatic plant life. The decay of these can deplete the oxygen supply of the water, causing the death of fish and their disappearance from the affected pond, lake or river.

form; nitrates are soluble and mobile and free to move in association with the movement of soil water. Much of the fertilizer nitrogen is in the ammonium form which can be converted in the soil within several weeks by microbial action to the nitrate form. There are two important factors controlling the nitrate nitrogen level in soils: the rate and the time of application. Fortunately, pollution control and efficient farm management go hand-in-hand. Fertilizers must be purchased and it is to the farmer's advantage to get the maximum benefit from a minimum application. If rates higher than those recommended by the competent authorities are exceeded, it is possible that there may be some leaching of nitrogen into groundwater supplies.

Both nitrogen and phosphorus compounds may be directly transported to surface water supplies by soil erosion and surface run-off. It is also to the benefit of both the farmer and the conservationist to minimize this erosion process.

At present there is considerable controversy over the effects of nitrates in water supplies and food products on both animals and man. Drinking water tolerances have been set by most authorities at about 10 ppm of nitrogen in the nitrate form (a relatively low concentration).

As explained previously, nitrate nitrogen can build up to significant levels under certain conditions, particularly in ground-water supplies. In addition, the application of nitrogen fertilizers will usually increase the nitrogen content in the plants. Under certain exceptional circumstances a high nitrate intake can cause health problems. In infants and young animals, the nitrate ion can be reduced to nitrite by organisms in the stomach. (Apparently this does not occur in humans after about 6 months of age.) If the nitrite is absorbed into the bloodstream, it can cause a shortage of oxygen, a condition commonly referred to as 'blue baby' (methaemoglobinaemia). In extreme instances, death has resulted.

Care should certainly be taken with soils used to produce crops for baby foods.

MINERAL POLLUTION

The problem of mineral pollution in soil differs from that of many others in that minerals are normal constituents of soils whereas the majority of the other pollutants, such as pesticides, fertilizers, wastes, etc., are not. The question about minerals is whether or not they are present in soils in amounts capable of harming living things. For example, iron is common in soil and a fantastic amount of it would be necessary for it to be considered a pollutant. On the other hand, there is only a very small quantity of mercury in normal soils, less than 0.01 ppm, so that only a modest quantity of this element is capable of drastically changing the nature of the soil.

Lead lies between these two extremes. There are soils containing naturally occurring lead in harmful or near-harmful proportions.

A certain amount of lead added to a lead-free soil might be harmless, whereas the same amount added to soil containing lead could bring about deleterious effects. In the latter case it would be considered a pollutant.

Probably of more importance than the concentration or quantity of mineral in a soil, is the absorption capacity of the particular plants growing on the soil. Many soils are known to be naturally polluted with a high mineral content, but sometimes by experience and ingenuity they can be used safely. Farmers may graze their herds in different pastures during different times of the year. It is in this way that the farmers of North Wales (United Kingdom) avoid poisoning of their livestock grazing on heavily leaded land. Also there are fields where the soils have a high content of selenium or molybdenum and yet grazing for cattle or sheep is perfectly safe with some grasses. However, if some highly absorbent plant such as a legume were grown there, the pasture would be judged to be polluted.

Potentially harmful minerals have been added to soils in a number of ways. As mentioned previously, many of the older inorganic forms of pesticides contained elements such as arsenic, mercury and lead. Likewise, some of the phosphatic fertilizers contain lead and cadmium in relatively high proportions. In addition, industrial operations can release a number of mineral contaminants and, more recently, the particulate 'fall-out' from automobile exhausts is rapidly becoming an important source of lead pollution on the ground near highways, a consequence of the lead added to petrol to increase engine performance. It has been found that fodder and food crops growing close to well-travelled highways in parts of the United States have from four to twenty times the normal quantity of lead.

DISPOSAL OF WASTES

The soil is not only a medium for plant growth but it is also a ready-made treatment plant for the disposal of some wastes, particularly those of an organic nature. When properly carried out, animal and human wastes as well as municipal and some industrial wastes can be disposed of in the soil with no problems.

ANIMAL WASTES

Historically, animal manures have been spread on the soil and have been a necessary complement to crop production. This is a natural process which promotes a recycling of the nutrient elements and helps maintain a viable soil. However, the recent practice of confinement housing of poultry, swine and cattle in combination with small land holdings can create a severe problem in disposing of their wastes. For these situations, the concept of economic utilization of manures may perhaps have to be sacrificed for an approach that uses the land for disposal purposes at maximum rates without creating a pollution problem.

Research has indicated that frequent and heavy applications of manure have resulted in a build-up in the soil of phosphorus and potassium compounds with no reduction in crop yield or pollution of water supplies. As with synthetic fertilizers, it is the mobile element, nitrogen, which could create a problem. In Ontario, Canada, agricultural authorities have recommended that the amount of nitrogen applied to farm land in any one season, whether in manure or synthetic fertilizers, should be not more than double that recommended for the most efficient use. Higher rates could lead to a depression of crop yield and cause water contamination. Also, run-off of manure exposed on the soil surface during heavy storms or in areas where there is a snow melt must be minimized by proper management techniques.

MUNICIPAL WASTES[4]

For many years, society has accepted the statement that 'the solution to pollution is dilution'. Accordingly, cities have dumped wastes into rivers and lakes and hoped that the regenerative processes of moving water would degrade the wastes. The system in many cases is now beginning to backfire. Many streams and lakes are overloaded with wastes, there is not enough oxygen present in the water to decompose the material, and a polluted state results.

A strong argument can be offered for the disposal of municipal wastes on land. Nitrogen and phosphorus compounds are difficult to remove in sewage treatment plants. Consequently, most treatment plants simply discharge these nutrients dissolved in the effluent water. It is an established fact that these nutrients and the water can be of value for both crop production and recharge of ground-water when applied to the land, whereas when simply discharged into streams and lakes they promote algal growth and bring about accelerated eutrophication of the surface water supplies. It is somewhat paradoxical that the ancient 'night soil' is still the most efficient use of man's wastes.

The recycling of plant nutrients from the land, to food, to sewage waste water and back to crop and forest land again thus makes good sense. This technique is being used with good results in some European countries and the United States. For example, in an experimental programme at Pennsylvania State University, effluent from the sewage treatment plan was applied to field crops and forest areas. The average composition of water samples taken from various depths after three years of operation showed that the renovation capacity of the soil remained excellent. More than 99 percent of the phosphorus in the effluent was removed and the concentration of nitrates in the soil was lower than in a control area. At the same time, there was a substantial increase in the yield of hay and corn and the quantity of water which leached down into the ground water was equivalent to about 80 percent of that applied. Thus the sewage served both to increase crop production and to recharge the ground-water supply.

INDUSTRIAL AND SOLID WASTES

It is certainly possible to dispose of some industrial wastes, particularly those containing organic compounds, by application to the soil. Four general methods for disposal on land

---

[4]Some of the material in this section has been adapted from H. V. Warren, R. E. Delevault and C. H. Cross, 'Mineral Contamination in Soil and Vegetation,' in: A. De Vos *et al., The Pollution Reader*, Montreal, Harvest House, 1968.

are commonly used: (a) impounding lagoons, in which the liquid wastes are held until they break down; (b) absorption beds, (c) ridge and furrow irrigation and (d) sprinkler irrigation. In the latter three methods, pollutants are degraded during the process of filtration through the soil.

As an example of sprinkler irrigation waste disposal, I can mention a cannery in Ontario, Canada, which disposes of waste water from cleansing and cooking operations in the plant by sprinkling it on to grass plots. The waste water cannot be pumped directly to a nearby stream because of its content of degradable organic material, principally fruit skins and vegetable peelings.

If the soil is kept well aerated, perhaps by intermittent application of the waste, so that water does not remain ponded on the surface, and if the soil system is not overloaded, both stream and ground-water pollution as well as objectionable odours can be avoided.

Another problem arises with the disposal of solid wastes, i.e. the household and industrial garbage which commonly ends up in the dump. 'Sanitary landfills', dumping sites which are then given a protective cover of soil, are the least expensive disposal method. However, the site must be carefully selected to prevent surface water and ground-water contamination. High-temperature composting, as practised in some municipalities, offers an attractive means of disposal. The composted waste, although containing little plant nutritive value, may then be safely applied to the soil for ultimate disposal.

RADIO-ACTIVE CONTAMINATION

Radio-active substances, which are other possible contaminants of the soil, may be produced by several sources. Atmospheric fall-out from the testing of nuclear weapons has caused a great deal of public concern and is well known. However, radio-active pollution may also be produced by a number of other sources. One of these is the mining and refining of radio-active materials. For example, a constant check on the radio-activity level in waters near the uranium mining area of Eliot Lake is maintained by the Ontario Water Resources Commission, because of concern about leaching from the mine tailings.

There may also be accidental or unauthorized releases of radio-active isotopes from power generators or research laboratories. In addition, a very small amount of radio-active uranium or thorium may be present in some fertilizers because of their presence in some phosphate rocks which are the raw materials for the fertilizers.

Radio-active contaminants have caused some minor adverse effects on food production. Nuclear-bomb testing in the atmosphere produces a number of radio-active substances. If detonated in the atmosphere, these radio-active substances are widely dispersed in the stratosphere. Since the summer of 1962, when worldwide fall-out from nuclear-bomb testing reached its peak, the levels of the short-lived radio-active isotopes iodine-131, barium-140 and strontium-89 have significantly decreased. However, strontium-90 and cesium-137 are still present in significant quantities in milk, foodstuffs and soils.

Chemically, strontium is similar to calcium. It can enter into and behave in water, soil, plants, animal tissues, bones and milk much like calcium. Strontium-90 loses half of its radio-activity every 28 years. It is a potentially dangerous contaminant because of this long half-life and because of its ability to be part of the bone structure where it can give rise to bone cancer.

Cesium-137 is much like potassium. It has a long half-life of about 30 years and may collect in muscle tissue. Fortunately, cesium-137 is bound very tightly by the clay fraction of soils, thus lowering its probability of entering into the food chain.

Radio-active iodine may accumulate in the thyroid gland and induce cancer. Luckily, iodine-131 has only an 8-day half-life and thus disappears quite rapidly. During the spring of 1966, milk was confiscated on a dairy farm in Nevada because of a high level of iodine-131 in the area resulting from accidental venting during an underground weapons test.

On a much larger scale, dairymen in central Minnesota considered using stored feed instead of field pastures during the peak fall-out summer season of 1962.

Soils are also used for the dispersal of radio-active wastes. Parsons[5] found that different radio-active substances travel at different

[5]P. J. Parsons, 'Migration from a Disposal of Radioactive Liquid in Soils', Health Phys., Vol. 9, 1963, pp. 333—42.

rates in soils. Rutherium-106 migrated rapidly from the disposal area, travelling in the soil at about the same rate as the ground water. Strontium-90 moved much more slowly, taking about eight years to develop into a continuous tongue stretching 650 feet from the disposal site. Cesium-137 migrated even more slowly and remained in the unsaturated zone of sand beneath the disposal pit. At this particular site, it is estimated that when the strontium-90 front emerges in surface water in about 130 years, radio-active decay and dispersion will have reduced the concentration to within drinking-water tolerances.

Fortunately, the adverse effects of radio-active contaminants on the agricultural economy at the present time are quite small. However, any further atmospheric testing would considerably increase the present load of radio-active materials and their deleterious effects.

TO COMBAT POLLUTION

At present, the general problem of soil pollution on a world-wide basis cannot be considered as critical. However, the time is at hand for careful and wise planning. Modern technology has now brought us to the point where a careful appraisal must be made of the industrial, agricultural and urban practices that are potential polluters of the soil.

It is imperative that more technical information be obtained on land pollution. Data is needed on the present levels of potential pollutants in soils throughout the world (bench-mark studies). Further studies are also needed to establish the permissible levels of potential pollutants in soils, a determination which is complicated by the fact that the same pollutant will often react differently in different soils.

It is unfortunate that many of our present pollution problems are surfacing because 'dilution is not the solution' to pollution control. Population growth and increased use of water by municipalities, industries and agriculture have changed the perspective.

Most planning (or lack of planning) in the past has been on a unilateral basis. The farmer (the village, the factory, the town, the city, etc.) up-stream has tended to dump his wastes in the stream without worrying about what happens down-stream. It is unfortunate as well that many of our geographical divisions (cities, states, provinces, countries) do not have the locations or boundaries which are geographically best suited for pollution-control planning.

Pollutants have no respect for artificial geographical barriers, particularly those carried in air or in water. While soil is certainly not as mobile as water, it can be transported in water, giving rise to siltation problems as well as transporting any pollutant attached to the soil particles. The soil can thus act as a source for pollutants carried by water and air.

In the final analysis, there is no substitute for sound planning of land use, backed by effective legislation. To this end, it is imperative to realize that the different categories of land pollution, as under the headings used in this article, cannot be alloted to distinct pigeon-holes and studied in isolation. A broad systems-type approach is required which takes into account all the factors bearing on a particular problem. Computers can easily handle the numerical manipulations but there is a dire need for good reliable data to feed to the computers.

To be effective, land-use planning must aim to achieve sound location of industry, housing and means of transportation while assuring simultaneously the best use of the land for agriculture and recreation. At the same time, responsible political bodies or advisory bodies must take measures to ensure exploiting to the fullest the great potential of soil for decomposing organic materials, in order to have effective waste disposal and utilization.

To solve pollution problems, compromises will necessarily have to be made among the differing objectives of various groups: farmers, industries, conservationists, municipalities, the citizenry at large, and so on.

In most cases, the technology is available. However, reaching solutions of pollution problems depends upon an awakened population sufficiently motivated to insist that the necessary measures be taken.

Today, affluent societies are also unfortunately 'effluent' societies. Yet, with wise planning and public support, this need not be the case.

VI/The Prospect Before Us

Grant Heilman

Introduction

IN THE PREVIOUS parts we explored man's interaction with the planet earth. We examined how the earth functions as a complex of interacting systems involving the living elements and the nonliving, and how man fits into those systems. We noted man's early emergence and evolution, and his gradually evolving methods of channeling energy of natural ecosystems into artificial ecosystems to support his own populations and his animals. We observed how the exploitation of that energy was closely associated with the cultural development of man. This ability to channel energy for his own use changed man's attitudes toward the land, fostered the development of urban life, and encouraged technology through which man changed the face of the earth. The ability to increase the carrying capacity of the earth permitted an expansion of the human population which has reached a level at which it is placing too heavy a demand on the complex systems of the earth and is endangering man's habitat. The land is scarred and eroded, the waters of rivers, lakes, and oceans are so polluted with wastes that even the fish are unfit to eat. Air is being filled with both gaseous and particulate pollutants toxic to life. The environmental problems are the result of technology and population growth.

Yet man the world over strives for riches, for growth, for economic development. He has become enslaved to and obsessed by technology and the Gross National Product. This technology and population growth, as discussed in Part V, have despoiled the environment and are ruining the capacity of the earth to support life.

What, then, are the prospects before us? The technologist and the physical scientist are optimistic about the future. Technology will save us just as it has almost destroyed us and will support our burgeoning populations. Ecologists are pessimistic, talking of impending doom: the downfall of man destroyed by himself and the death of the earth.

Can man maintain himself as things are going now? Can increasing consumption and a soaring economy, increasing industrialization and an expanding population, be supported by the earth? Will man continue to give priority to technological advancement, such as nuclear power and supersonic transports, instead of to restoring and reclaiming the environment, slowing the population growth, and bringing back some of the vitality that life seems to have lost? As Part VI will suggest, the prospect before us is joyless, but *our very survival* depends upon a degree of guarded optimism, without which the world is lost. Some people say it is lost already, that earth will capitulate by the year 2000.

There will be a reason for optimism if man will place the maintenance of the earth ahead of technology and growth. To do so will mean a radically altered life style, but life can never remain static, and change is desirable so long as it is in harmony with the earth.

Modern man needs to reestablish that ancient respect and attachment to the earth, for he is as much a part of the earth as are the vegetation and the animals with which he shares it. He has to recognize the fact that he lives *in* the earth and not just *on* it, that for him it is the very source of life. As René Dubos says: "Man emerged on the earth, evolved under its influence, was shaped by it and biologically he is bound to it forever. He may dream of stars and engage in casual flirtation with other worlds, but he will remain wedded to the earth, his sole source of sustenance."[1]

---

[1]René Dubos, *So Human and Animal*, New York, Scribner, 1968, p. 262.

The World's Water Resources

Commentary

Three-fourths of the earth is covered with water, yet, paradoxically, water problems exist around the world. The problems of water are present in a number of forms: quantity, quality, source for new supplies, distribution, and allocation. Because of the global nature of the hydrological cycle, water problems are not local or national in scope, but international. The international aspect of water is reflected in the following selection by two Russian hydrologists who speculate on the methods of increasing water supply for human needs.

Examples of water problems as they exist today are the situations in the northeastern and southwestern United States. The arid region of the southwest is one of the most rapidly growing areas of the United States. Into this region the waters of the Colorado and Rio Grande Rivers have been diverted, but not without considerable interstate and international arguments and problems. Shortly, the water of the Feather River will be conveyed across a 2000-foot-high mountain to the same area. Most of the water of the Colorado, Rio Grande, and Feather Rivers go not to urban areas but to agriculture. Urban areas still depend largely on underground aquifers. In effect, ground water is being mined, while most of the surface and precipitation water which supports agriculture is lost through evaporation or is swiftly absorbed into the banks of irrigation ditches. Very little of the precipitation that does occur, about 1 percent, actually gets to replenish the underground water supplies.

Water for irrigation is supplied by large dams on the Colorado, from which it is diverted to irrigation canals. By the time the Colorado reaches the Gulf of California, little of its water is left. Desert agriculture is extremely hard on water, yet it is agricultural use of that water that provides the incentive for making water available and stimulates urban development. When water is made available for agriculture by damming rivers, the quantities at first are in excess of need. Then populations move toward the water supply. As populations build up, less water is allocated to agriculture and more is directed to urban growth. Because urban users pay rates that cover the cost of supplying water whereas agricultural users are largely subsidized by the public, urban growth is encouraged. As urban growth increases, heavier demands on water are made and additional steps are taken to increase and conserve the water supply.

To reduce losses from evaporation, phreatophytic vegetation (long-rooted plants that draw their water from the water table or the soil above it) is destroyed in an attempt to convert the watershed to bare ground or grass. The economic and ecological wisdom of such action is questioned, but it is being pursued actively in the name of water conservation. Not only does the destruction of phreatophytes expose the watershed to erosion, it also destroys wildlife habitat. The amount of water saved by the reduction in evaporation is minimal, and more water is better conserved by the use of impervious sides on irrigation canals and coverings over artificial reservoirs.

Ambitious plans have been suggested for the diversion of water from the Pacific northwest and Canada to the southwest and Mexico. Proposed is the North American Water and Power Alliance. It would collect water from the rivers of Alaska, British Columbia, and the Yukon; distribute 178-million-acre-feet of water annually to water-scarce parts of Canada, the United States, and Mexico; produce electricity through gravitational flow; and provide a canal from Alberta to South Dakota. Such a project would require a treaty among the United States, Canada, and Mexico, as well as cooperation among western states and Canadian provinces and between federal government and private utility companies. Such a project needs to be studied carefully for its economic feasibility and ecological damage, and for the possibility of viable alternatives. The probable minimal constructional cost of $150 billion and annual maintenance cost of $8.5 billion,[1] as well as opposition in some quarters, including Canada, make accomplishment of such a project quite unlikely. But it does indicate the extent to which man is ready to go to solve his water needs.

The northeastern part of the United States also experiences water problems but of a different sort. Blessed with 40 inches of rainfall annually and an abundance of rivers, it would seem that water would be no problem. But it is, as well illustrated by the drought and the urban water crisis of the early 1960s. The drought, which

---

[1]E. F. Murphy, *Governing Nature*, Chicago, Ill., Quadrangle Books, 1967, pp. 66–72, 127–128, 147–151, 264–267.

lasted three years, was experienced largely by urban areas and not by agriculture. In fact, if it had not been for the urban crisis, the drought might have escaped any real notice. The dry period became a problem because of urban demands for water and the methods of supplying it. The large urban areas go to the mountains for water. Large reservoirs are built miles from the cities and the water is transported through aqueducts. If the watershed experiences a drought, the natural flow of water into the reservoirs cannot balance the urban demands. In the early 1960s, reservoir levels dropped and water conservation measures had to be put into effect in northeastern cities. Meanwhile, rivers running past the cities went untapped because the waters were not considered potable. Water at the doorsteps of the cities is regarded only as a receptacle for waste.

The problems of the southwest and the northeast suggest the types of water problems that are and will be facing the world, and they inevitably face grand solutions such as that of the North American Water and Power Alliance. On a less grandiose scale is the proposal to desalt sea water, now in active pilot study. Use of desalted water has been considered a solution to the water problems, both of arid areas and of urban centers that border oceans. A number of desalination plants are already in operation, including one in Key West, Florida. Russia is building the world's largest desalination unit at Shevchenko, on the shores of the Caspian Sea, where no source of fresh water is available.

Desalination has problems. One is economic. Cost prohibits the wide-scale use of desalted water for agriculture for the near future at least, except for high value crops.[2] Another problem is ecological. A 150-million-gallon plant, for example, would produce 23,000 tons of salt every day.[3] The disposal problem would be enormous. The salt cannot be returned to the ocean, for local concentration of salt would kill marine life. Some industrial or commercial by-products may be developed, but the costs involved must be charged toward the cost of the water obtained.

A partial solution to the water problem is recycling. Major cities experience periods of inadequate water because of institutional and political failure to provide for sufficient supplies and to adequately utilize nearby sources of waters.[4] For many industrial nations the ultimate and most economical solution will not be the transport of water for great distances or desalinization, but rather the recycling of sewage and river water, all technically and economically possible. Strict pollution control could further improve the potability of nearby water sources.

Because water problems are not local but national and international, mutual regulatory use of water will be a challenge of the future, just as it is in the southwest today. There are precedents for regulation. Although both Anglo-American common law and English law recognize ownership of renewable resources on the owner's property, there are legal restrictions on the use of water. In Europe the owner of water-permeable underground layers and in America the owner of riparian rights can use the water on his own property for domestic, agricultural, and other needs so long as other users of the watershed are not injured by his actions. In Europe the use and withdrawal of water is limited and permits are required. Wells are so spaced by law that every owner is assured of at least one well on his property. Regulations control mining and underground storage of gas or other material that might pollute or upset underground water levels. When water shortages become acute, the permit holder is forced to set up priorities of use.

The world's water problems are reaching that stage at which it may be this resource rather than disarmament or some other political problem that will bring the world together in a common cause.

---

[2]G. Young, "Dry Lands and Desalted Water," *Science* **167**, 1970, pp. 339–343.
[3]Murphy, *op. cit.*
[4]*Ibid.*

The World's Water Resources, Present and Future

by G. P. Kalinin and V. D. Bykov

THE HYDROLOGIC CYCLE
AND THE WORLD WATER BALANCE

The world's water resources form a single entity. Nothing illustrates this more clearly than water in the atmosphere-hydrosphere-lithosphere cycle, basic mechanism of the relatively stable distribution of water as between land, sea and atmosphere. This cycle, the hydrologic cycle (Fig. 1), is influenced by solar activity and the latter's general effect on the circulation of air, by processes taking place in the sea and on land, reflecting the correlation of the heat budgets and water balances of land

and sea, and to some extent, by factors of cosmic origin.

The influence of the oceans, which occupy two-thirds of the earth's surface, on the natural hydrologic cycle must obviously be considerable but, although occupying a smaller area, the land mass is more varied, more complex and less stable in its properties and structure.

Considerable changes can be brought about in the natural conditions on land by human activity as well as by the forces of nature. The total balance of free water in historical times and even back into the prehistoric era may be regarded as constant. Aristotle was the first,

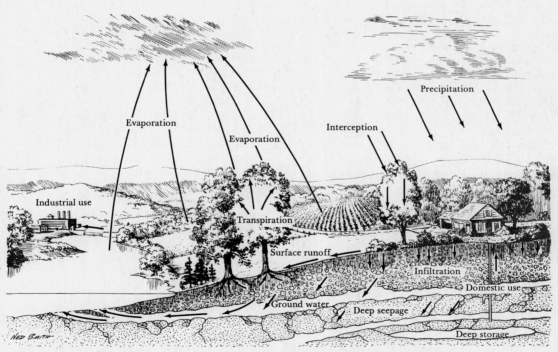

Figure 1. The water cycle. (From R. L. Smith, *Ecology and Field Biology*, Harper & Row, New York, 1966.)

THIS SELECTION is from *Impact of Science on Society*, Vol. XIX, No. 2, 1969. Reprinted by permission of © Unesco.

in his *Meteorology*, to express the view that the earth's water balance is constant. The same conclusion was reached, on the basis of calculations, by V. I. Vernadsky, P. Queney, Penck and others.

The water balances of the land and sea taken separately are a different matter. The distribution of water between the oceans and land can only remain stable when the "credit" and "debit" sides of the water account balance out for land and sea individually. Such stability can only occur if the natural hydrologic cycle is stable. But it is a dynamic process, governed by a number of variable factors which operate in unco-ordinated fashion. For this reason, at various geological epochs and during historical times, the balance between the waters on land and in the ocean has been upset, resulting in a change in the level of the oceans and consequently a change in the relative proportions between sea and land areas.

By analysing variations in surface waters and groundwater, variations of glaciation and changes in plant communities, A. V. Shnitnikov[1] has shown that these variations are governed by general laws and, more especially, that there is a 1,800–2,000 year cycle in terrestrial humidity. G. K. Tushinsky[2] arrived at much the same result by studying the rhythms of snow cover and glaciation.

According to Shnitnikov, we are at present passing through a period of transition from a humid phase to a dry one in which the continents are losing and the oceans are gaining water. Analysis of observations over the last sixty to eighty years has shown that the level of the ocean is rising by 0.05 inch (1.2 mm) a year, on the average. To put it another way, this means that about 105 cubic miles of water (430 cubic kilometres) are being lost yearly from the resources of the land. This yearly addition to the "credit" side of the ocean's balance is greater than the annual discharge of all rivers flowing into the Caspian Sea. If this situation continues, we can expect a further rise in the level of the seas and a corresponding decrease in the area of land and in its water resources.

It must also be recognized that over long periods of time—several thousands of years—there is a possibility of considerable changes in the world's water resources. The nature of these changes can be determined only by studying the hydrologic balance of the land and the oceans separately.

On the assumption that no changes occur in the earth's resources of moisture (as by loss into space) during the period under consideration, water gains and losses on land and sea balance out, as can be shown by a simple mathematical analysis. Hence, the total quantity of precipitation that falls on the earth is exactly equal to the quantity that evaporates from its surface. Table 1 (slightly adapted from M. I. Lvovich) shows the magnitudes of the component elements of the earth's water balance.

(In land areas where there is vegetation, a part of the return of moisture to the atmosphere results from the transpiration by plants of water which has been absorbed from the ground through their roots or which is a product of metabolism. 'Evapotranspiration' is the term generally applied to the combined return of moisture by both evaporation and transpiration. It shall be understood that in Table 1 and elsewhere in this article when evaporation from land areas is referred to this also includes transpiration.)

It would be well now to examine the world's water resources so we can see what proportion of it is disposable for man's use.

As Table 2 shows, over 90 per cent of the earth's water is found in the oceans. At present this water is not directly available for use, with insignificant exceptions. However, it is the evaporation of this water, which then falls as rain, which may be taken as the initiating step of the hydrologic cycle.

The rain-water is directly used, in the first instance, as it falls from the skies. Much of it, however, percolates through the surface and subsoil to replenish the ground-water supply, from which some of it is taken for use before it is eventually discharged, *via* rivers, into the oceans.

The ground water is that water which lies in the saturated region of the ground; the upper

[1] A. V. Shnitnikov, 'Cycles in Stream Flow and in Variations of the Level of Lakes in Northern Europe and Solar Activity', Proceedings of the All-Union Geographical Society, Vol. 93, No. 1, 1961. (In Russian.)

[2] G. K. Tushinsky, Outer Space and the Natural Rhythms of the Earth, Moscow, Prosvescenie Publishing House, 1966. (In Russian.)

Table 1. WORLD'S ANNUAL WATER BALANCE

AREA AND PROCESS	GAIN		LOSS	
	VOLUME (CU KM)	DEPTH[1] (MM)	VOLUME (CU KM)	DEPTH[1] (MM)
Peripheral areas of continents (117,504,000 sq km)				
Precipitation	101,000	860		
River discharge[2]			37,300	310
Evaporation			63,700	550
Landlocked areas of continents (31,124,000 sq km)				
Precipitation	7,400	240		
Evaporation			7,400	240
Continents as a whole (148,628,000 sq km)				
Precipitation	108,400	720		
River discharge[2]			37,300	250
Evaporation			71,100	470
The oceans (361,455,000 sq km)				
Precipitation	411,600	1,140		
Discharge from rivers[2]	37,300	100		
Evaporation			448,900	1,240
The earth as a whole (510,083,000 sq km)				
Precipitation	520,000	1,020		
Evaporation			520,000	1,020

[1]The depth of water if the volume involved in the process were distributed uniformly over the area in question.
[2]Including water originating from the melting of Arctic and Antarctic glaciers.

surface of this saturated region is the water table. As Table 2 shows, the total ground water (free gravitational waters) equals approximately 60 million cubic kilometres. However, most of this water lies so deeply down that for all practical purposes it does not participate in the hydrologic cycle and is not available for use. It is the 4 million cubic kilometres in the upper region of the crust which participates in active exchanges—into which rain-water percolates and which runs off into lakes, wells, irrigation networks, rivers and the ocean—which is of direct interest to us when we talk of directly usable water resources (though the deeper waters may be increasingly tapped

and brought into the hydrologic cycle in the future).

It is in the estimation of ground water that the greatest possibility of error occurs, though there are doubtless inaccuracies in the precipitation and evaporation figures. The average error in the figures shown in Table 2 is probably of the order of 10—15 per cent.

We might mention that the total volume of water in the earth's crust between subsoil and mantle is actually far larger than the figure shown. Most of this water, is, however, in various states physically or chemically bound to minerals. Taking into account water in these forms, Vernadsky[3] estimates that the total

[3]V. I. Vernadsky, History of Minerals in the Earth's Crust. Vol. 2: History of Natural Waters, Part I, Sections I—III, 1933, 1934, 1936. (In Russian.)

volume of water in the upper 20 to 25 kilometres of crust is of the order of 1,300 million cubic kilometres, approximately equalling the volume of the oceans.

Table 2 shows that the last two items, atmospheric moisture and river waters, represent the two most active agents of water exchange in the hydrologic cycle. River flow also helps to intensify the rate of ground-water exchange. (Two renewal periods have been shown for river waters. The twelve-day period is that for river systems having small catchment areas measuring only a few tens of thousands of square miles. Twenty days is the mean renewal period for major rivers which empty directly into the sea.)

Clearly, the exchange of water between atmosphere and earth's surface is of considerable practical interest. Let us look at some modern views on this point. It is recognized that a portion of the evaporated ocean moisture which falls as rain on land evaporates—the rest eventually making its way back to the ocean—and some of this re-evaporated moisture falls as rain onto the land again. The relative total quantity of rain which results from an initial precipitated quantity of ocean moisture before all this moisture gets back to the sea is expressed as the coefficient for the hydrologic cycle.

Holzman and Thornthwaite[4] using aerological observations, established that the coefficient

Table 2. WORLD'S WATER RESOURCES

RESOURCE	VOLUME (W) (IN THOUSANDS OF CU KM)	ANNUAL RATE OF REMOVAL (Q) (IN THOUSANDS OF CU KM) AND PROCESS		RENEWAL PERIOD $\left(T = \dfrac{W}{Q}\right)$
Total water on earth	1,460,000	520,	evaporation	2,800 years
Total water in the oceans	1,370,000	449,	evaporation	3,100 years
		37,	difference between precipitation and evaporation	37,000 years
Free gravitational waters in the earth's crust (to a depth of 5 km)	60,000	13,	underground run-off	4,600 years
(Of which), in the zone of active water exchange	4,000	13,	underground run-off	300 years
Lakes	750		—	
Glaciers and permanent snow	29,000	1.8,	run-off	16,000 years
Soil and subsoil moisture	65	85,	evaporation and underground run-off	280 days
Atmospheric moisture	14	520,	precipitation	9 days
River waters	1.2	36.3,[1]	run-off	12(20) days

[1] Not counting the melting of Antarctic and Arctic glaciers.

[4] B. Holzman and C. Thornthwaite, 'A New Interpretation of the Hydrologic Cycle', Trans. Amer. Geog. Union, Vol. 19, 1938, p. 11.

for the hydrologic cycle over the territory of the United States was 1.25. Similar calculations by K. I. Kashin and K. P. Pogosyan and later by M. I. Budyko and O. A. Drozdov[5] using different methods, showed coefficients for the territory of the European U.S.S.R. of 1.13 and 1.14 respectively.

Drozdov[6] points out that the coefficient increases somewhat more rapidly than the area of the territory covered, but comparison of coefficients with areas showed a fairly close connexion between them (Fig. 2). In Table 3 below is an approximate calculation of the coefficient of the hydrologic cycle for various continents, worked out from the graph of Fig. 2. Interesting results are obtained by applying Drozdov's observation on the coefficient/area relationship to measuring the influence of land-improvement schemes in which water normally lost as run-off is diverted to use. If by virtue of such schemes the evaporation from the southern part of the European U.S.S.R. were to be increased by 15 mm, precipitation would increase by 20 mm, mainly in the eastern

Table 3. CALCULATED HYDROLOGIC CYCLE COEFFICIENTS FOR THE CONTINENTS

TERRITORY	AREA (IN MILLIONS OF SQ KM)	COEFFICIENT FOR THE HYDROLOGIC CYCLE
Australia	7.96	1.15
Europe	9.67	1.20
South America	17.98	1.30
North America	20.44	1.35
Africa	29.81	1.45
Asia	42.28	1.55
Eurasia	51.95	1.65
Africa and Eurasia	81.76	1.90

part of the territory. However, the importance of local evaporation has been somewhat exaggerated in recent calculations. This is because an increase in precipitation leads to a substantial increase in the rate of run-off of that precipitation; the reduction in atmospheric moisture which results from this additional run-off was not taken into account in calculations. Likewise, the reciprocal links between humidity and precipitation were not fully taken into account in calculations: not only does the humidity of the air increase precipitation, but an increase in precipitation increases humidity.

There is no doubt, however, that large-scale land improvement schemes produce very favourable results in large areas with river systems that discharge into the ocean. In regions (continental interiors) without run-off and discharge to the oceans, all precipitation is given off again as evaporation. Roughly speaking, for a large territory of the scale of the Afro-Eurasian land mass the quantity of additional precipitation gained is nearly as great as the quantity of run-off which is diverted to use. About two-thirds of the diverted run-off falls again as precipitation, returning to the rivers where it can be re-used.

The present increase in precipitation for the Afro-Eurasian land mass due to the evaporation of diverted run-off cannot be very great,

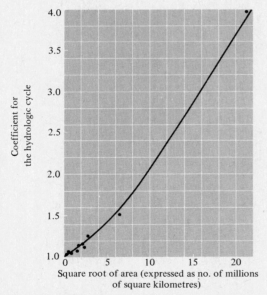

Figure 2. Relationship between land area and the coefficient for the hydrologic cycle.

[5]K. I. Kashin and K. P. Pogosyan, 'The Atmospheric Water Cycle. The Hydrometeorological Effect of Growing Trees as Wind Breaks'. Leningrad, Gidrometeoizdat, 1950. (In Russian.); M. I. Budyko and O. A. Drozdov, 'General Laws Governing the Atmospheric Water Cycle', Proceedings of the Academy of Sciences of the U.S.S.R., Geography Series, No. 4, 1953. (In Russian.)
[6]O. A. Drozdov, 'Data on the Water Cycle in the European Territory (of the U.S.S.R.) and Central Asia', Journal of the Main Geophysical Observatory, No. 45 (107), 1954. (In Russian.)

but as the demand for water is developing very rapidly and, according to calculations, is doubling every 10 to 15 years, it is to be expected that in 35 to 50 years the diversion of run-off, which subsequently evaporates, will reach 15—20 per cent. This will produce a noticeable increase in precipitation—of the order of 30 to 40 mm—over this territory, which in turn will lead to a return run-off of the order of 20 to 30 mm, so a significant portion of the diverted run-off will be regained.

We should not discount the possibility that in future man will learn to control the water cycle and will be able to accelerate changes in the humidity regimen of the continents, especially as it is theoretically possible to produce enormous increases in precipitation (hundreds of millimetres) by diverting run-off (including return run-off) and by increasing the evaporation of effluents.

SHORT-TERM VARIATIONS IN THE WATER CONTENT OF THE EARTH'S RIVERS

The spread of stream-flow gauging stations and modern methods of computing have permitted large-scale investigations into cyclic variations of stream flow. However, the observation periods being too short (at most 150 years), it is impossible to establish long-term cycles with sufficient reliability.

Processing of readings covering many years for sixty major rivers of the northern hemisphere by the spectral functions method have shown that cycles recur most frequently with periods of 2 to 3, 5 to 7, 11 to 13 and 22 to 28 years. The 11 to 13 year cycles are normally regarded as being governed by solar activity. The nature of the shorter cycles has not as yet been adequately explained. The 2 to 3 year cycle is observable not only in variations of stream flow but also in the level of the oceans. Similar cycles occur in a number of other geophysical phenomena.

Periods of greater and lesser humidity affect vast areas of the earth but never the earth as a whole. A period of increased humidity in one part of the world is simultaneously accompanied by reduced humidity elsewhere. Research has shown that, between 1881 and 1950, there was both a synchronous and an asynchronous variation in run-off in the drainage basins of the major rivers of the northern hemisphere. The zones affected by increased or reduced run-off (as compared with the mean) cover considerable areas, the boundaries of which are fairly constant, e.g. run-off was abundant in Europe and North America between 1926 and 1930, reduced in the rest of the northern hemisphere. For 1931–40, this relationship was reversed.

Synchronous and asynchronous variations of run-off are thus geographically localized, a fact of great importance for the calculation of water power and the water balance. There are important possibilities of economic gains by planning hydroelectrical installations not as individual units but as part of a broad, integrated geographical scheme taking into account the synchronous and compensating asynchronous variations in stream flow in different parts of the world, including the U.S.S.R.

One curious fact is that the peaks and lows of the cyclical variations of run-off (2 to 3 years, 5 to 7 years, etc.) occur at different times, in different well-defined, fairly large zones of the earth. This fact can be made use of for forecasting purposes.

Research has been done on this point by A. I. Davydova[7] under the supervision of G. P. Kalinin. By correlating time-graphs depicting run-off and various atmospheric factors, calculations were made of the future annual stream flow for a number of rivers in the northern hemisphere. These investigations proved that it is indeed possible to forecast the water content of rivers for a long time in advance (4 to 7 years, depending on the cycle).

Despite the possibilities for forecasting stream flow, considerable difficulties face us before water resources can be fully utilized. These arise from the way in which water is distributed in nature as compared to human needs for it. The latter are in direct ratio to solar energy received (because of the consequent potential evaporation), but the water resources annually renewed (surface and underground run-off) are equal to the difference between precipitation and evaporation, i.e. they are in inverse ratio to potential evaporation. (Exceptions to this general rule about

---

[7]G. P. Kalinin and A. I. Davydova, 'Cyclical Variations in the Stream Flow of Rivers in the Northern Hemisphere', in Problems of Stream Flow, Moscow, Moscow University Publishing House, 1968. (In Russian.)

water distribution *versus* need may be caused by local topographic or geographic conditions or peculiarities in the atmospheric circulation.) In the particular case of the U.S.S.R., 80 per cent of the 1,000 cubic kilometres of regular run-off are concentrated in its most sparsely inhabited parts, and only 20 per cent in those where the demand for water is highest.

Another problem in the utilization of water is its uneven seasonal distribution in time, particularly in the case of rivers of the plain. The stream flow of mountain rivers is greatest during the warm part of the year, which is good for agriculture in the southern regions, but even in this case considerable variations from one year to the next create economic difficulties.

FORECASTING WATER DEMAND

To evaluate future water requirements, we need to know about future economic and population growth. According to United Nations experts, the world population will reach 7,000 million by the year 2000, over 50 per cent living in towns. Apart from the quantity of drinking water this implies, all branches of the economy will require water in various quantities and qualities. The total is difficult to assess. A very approximate estimate (not counting water for power generation and transport, which do not actually consume water), is given in Table 4.

The figure for the dilution of industrial and domestic effluent wastes is an expert evalua-

tion assuming dilution with four times their volume of clean water after a preliminary treatment. This is undoubtedly a considerable under-estimate of the ratio of clean water to effluents.

It can be seen in Table 4 that, by the year 2000, half of all the earth's annually renewed waters—the 37,000 cubic kilometres of evaporated ocean water (Table 2) which precipitates on land rather than back into the ocean—will be in use by man. With so high a demand, and the uneven distribution in space and time, work will soon have to be undertaken on an unprecedented scale to regulate run-off and divert the waters of rivers into areas affected by drought. The problem is particularly acute, since demand is growing several times faster than the population. When the world population reaches 20,000 million in the twenty-first century, the demand will be several times greater than in the year 2000.

These water-demand forecasts are rough approximations only, because data on growth of population, irrigation, industry and consumption are also only approximate, and estimates of pollution are either too high or too low. Very likely, the future demand for clean, fresh water is exaggerated because: (a) as demand grows, means will be sought to reduce consumption per unit of industrial and agricultural production; (b) some branches of industry could use salt water or brackish water, as is already being done in some cases; (c) desalination of sea-water and brackish ground water will increase; and (d) the purifying of polluted water will be improved and accelerated.

Nevertheless, the figures must be regarded as approximately correct for the next thirty-five to fifty years, i.e. until A.D. 2000—15.

THE CONSERVATION OF CONTINENTAL WATERS

Until recently, the utilization of water was mainly regarded in local terms, e.g. a hydraulic scheme for a particular river, or reservoirs for a limited area. At best, the planning of the installations on a river or rivers might be co-ordinated with other objectives, such as obtaining the maximum hydroelectric yield, or ensuring free passage for shipping, and so on. The same limited approach was also true about fighting pollution, the factory effluents

Table 4. TOTAL ANNUAL WORLD WATER REQUIREMENTS BY YEAR 2000[1]

USAGE	WATER REQUIRED (CU KM)	
	TOTAL	IRRETRIEVABLE (LOST IN EVAPORATION)
Irrigation	7,000	4,800
Domestic	600	100
Industrial	1,700	170
Dilution of effluents and waste	9,000	
Other	400	400
Total	18,700	5,470

[1]From G. P. Kalinin, *Problems of Global Hydrology*, Leningrad. Gidrometeoizdat, 1968.

being to some extent purified upon the responsibility of the enterprise itself.

The inevitable consequence of this attitude is that as the demand for water has increased, so natural water resources are coming nearer and nearer to exhaustion, and with progressive deterioration in the quality of the water. In the areas most important to man, nature's own renewal of the quantity and quality of water has not compensated for the deterioration man has caused.

Clearly, the present approach to water utilization must be fundamentally changed, and science must provide the practical means for reversing this degrading of fresh-water resources. To do this: (a) man must put back at least as much water as he takes out; (b) the water he returns to nature must be of at least as high a quality as the water he takes out. It is only in this way that we can improve continental waters while still making active use of them.

To meet this objective, localized methods are obviously inadequate. Only large-scale integrated approaches will work.

Water use and conservation can be considered to be done at seven levels:

1. Local (watercourse and ground water).
2. A complete watercourse.
3. A hydrographic system.
4. An entire hydrographic basin (surface water and ground water).
5. Multiple-basin.
6. Intercontinental.
7. Global.

As industry develops, the scale of water use gradually moves from the local level upwards.

At the fourth level, the main methods of increasing quantity are: (a) carry-over storage: superfluous flood waters can be held over for periods of drought, and part of the run-off in plentiful years can be held over for low years; (b) transfer to regions of shortage within the same hydrographic system; (c) drainage of excessively wet land under agricultural and woodland improvement schemes; (d) agricultural engineering measures to reduce unproductive evaporation; (e) reduction of evaporation by deepening shallows and by charge of ground water by diverting surface water underground (afforestation, reservoirs, and so on).

Run-off control at the fifth level would also make it possible (a) to transfer water from high-rainfall areas to low-rainfall areas and (b) to increase evaporation of diverted run-off, thus increasing the coefficient for the hydrologic cycle.

Levels (6) and (7) involve modifying the hydrologic cycle in neighbouring continents or in all the continents by planned water management, and even possibly directly using the waters and ice of the world's oceans.

By 2000–15, the loss of water through evaporation may represent one-sixth of total run-off, and be highest in Afro-Eurasia (one-quarter to one-fifth of total run-off). Precipitation will increase (because of the higher moisture content of the atmosphere) by close to the quantity of normal run-off which is diverted to use, i.e. 40–50 mm. The increased precipitation which results will in turn cause a return run-off equivalent to about two-thirds of the original diverted run-off (25–35 mm). Thus, despite the high level of water consumption, total run-off is unlikely to be reduced by more than 5–8 per cent—probably even less, as some of the demand will by that time be met from new sources (primarily sea-water). This latter will introduce further moisture into the hydrologic cycle, thus increasing the moisture content of the atmosphere.

FULLY EXPLOITING THE EARTH'S HEAT

A number of major desalination plants are now in operation—in Kuwait, for instance. Here the development of atomic energy is very pertinent, as atomic energy and desalination at a single large plant make a very efficient combination.

Using new methods, it may prove possible, if only in the distant future, to carry out existing plans for transferring water from the Black Sea to the Caspian. The utilization of the Dead Sea, the Qattara Depression, and other enclosed basins in Africa and Eurasia could draw a considerable additional quantity of water from the ocean into the hydrologic cycle by increased evaporation, and this advantage could be further exploited by integrating several activities, e.g. production of fresh water, chemical industries, fisheries, recreation areas.

The earth has the enormous heat resources necessary to evaporate extra moisture, but in certain cases they might prove inadequate.

In fact, if we take the maximum possible evaporation (fully utilizing all the heat presently available, combined with unlimited irrigation of the continents) as being equivalent to 740 mm, and subtract from this the present evaporation from continents (470 mm, cf. Table 1), the remainder—the maximum additional evaporation we could get—is 270 mm. This is virtually equivalent to the present continental run-off figure (river discharge of 250 mm in Table 1).

Run-off redistributed to correspond to the distribution of the earth's heat resources would be the ideal solution, and would ensure maximum possible evaporation over the whole surface of the globe, but this is unattainable, even in the very distant future. This is why the argument advanced by many scientists, that by the end of the twenty-first century we will have been able to put all our water resources fully to use, has no adequate physical foundation.

To evaluate the actual potential for consumption of water by evaporation, the following factors must be taken into account: (a) water resources and the possibility of their redistribution; (b) heat resources and their distribution; (c) availability of land suitable for irrigation or the creation of reservoirs; (d) industrial consumption of water. In the long run, then, the diversion of run-off to use will be limited by the amounts of water, heat and land resources available. If the heat and land resources are limited, this will of course mean that by no means all the water resources can be used.

THE PLANET'S REFRIGERANT

So far we have not considered the changes in the earth's heat resources caused by power generation. Power is now generated and consumed by industry at such an accelerating rate that, even in the near future, this will seriously affect the earth's heat budget.

M. I. Budyko[8] has shown that the radiation balance at the earth's surface and the power generated by industry stand in the ratio of 49 : 0.02. (The radiation balance is the difference between the radiation arriving from the sun and that radiated back to space.) If power generated increases annually by 10 per cent, in 100 years it will be greater than the radiation

balance and will then have an effect comparable to that of solar radiation. There is thus clearly a real danger that the earth may become over-heated. Water resources accordingly become particularly important, since a large increase in water consumption (thus, evaporation) would lead to a corresponding cooling effect.

Here we see water resources in an entirely new light: as one of the main means of preventing the overheating of the earth. In the future world, power production and water consumption will have to be combined in such a way as to ensure optimum moisture and heat conditions.

In sum, it appears highly probable to us that, against the general background of cyclical and incidental variations of climate, there will be a general tendency towards greater humidity (greater quantity of precipitation) of the continents as a result of increased water consumption.

In the U.S.S.R. there are a number of projects for diverting northern Soviet rivers southwards to get greater water utilization. Some (e.g. the scheme for diverting the waters of northern rivers into the Volga-Kama chain of reservoirs and the Caspian) are relatively near to becoming operational. Others (e.g. the diversion of Siberian rivers into Central Asia) are unlikely in the next ten to fifteen years, not only because of the cost, but also because of the problem of the side effects of flooding. The difficulties will eventually be overcome, however, since the problem of water supply cannot be solved without using the run-off of the northern and Siberian rivers.

The measures indicated above for increasing the quantity of water and converting it in the final stage of consumption into evaporation must be taken together with the 'debit' items in the water management balance to attain the optimum utilization.

THE QUESTION OF POLLUTION

The quantitative and qualitative aspects of water utilization cannot be separated. This brings up the matter of pollution.

The main forms of pollution are: (a) basin

---

[8]M. I. Budyko, The Heat Balance of the Earth's Surface, Leningrad, Gidrometeoizdat, 1956. (In Russian.)

pollution caused by sediments produced by erosion, poisonous chemicals washed out of the soil by irrigation, etc.; (b) watercourse pollution—the dumping of organic and inorganic waste compounds by sewers and factories, pollutants produced by shipping, minerals leached out of the river bed, etc.; (c) heat pollution—the dumping of water at high temperature by thermal power stations and factories; this increasingly common form of contamination causes a drop in the oxygen content of water which harms fish life and encourages excessive growth of aquatic plants; (d) hydrobiological contamination from a variety of factors, such as run-off control producing shallows with abundant vegetation, the dumping of organic compounds whose residual decomposition products (nitrogen, phosphorus, carbon) encourage the growth of vegetation, etc.

As a result of the increasing use of chemicals in agriculture and of the development of irrigated farming, increasing quantities of chemicals which may be classified as pollutants (weed killers, pesticides, etc.) are bound to enter rivers. Also, large quantities of minerals in solution are washed into rivers during reclamation work on saline soils.

At the basin level, methods of controlling pollution include: (a) on-the-spot processing of sewage and industrial effluents; (b) dilution of effluents, making use of opportunities to control the flow; (c) improvement of the sanitary condition of natural water by purification, by eliminating shallows, and by measures to reduce the quantity of organic and inorganic compounds washed out of agricultural land and woodlands into rivers; (d) improvement of the quality of brackish natural water by diverting part of the purer surface run-off underground; (e) recycling of water used in industry to prevent its being dumped into rivers; (f) putting waste-carrying effluents to use in agriculture.

At the multiple-basin, intercontinental and global levels, another pollution-combating measure is to supply additional fresh water from diverted rivers (and perhaps from the sea) while increasing the return of water to the hydrologic cycle by diverting part of used river water for evaporation.

The methods of controlling the quantity and quality of natural waters can and must be harmoniously combined.

CONCLUSIONS

The following conclusions may be drawn.

The development of society inevitably involves increased consumption of water and increased return of used water into the hydrographic system. Since water consumption and the deterioration in the quality of available natural water will inevitably continue, it is imperative that, to allow society to develop normally, the replenishment and qualitative improvement of natural waters must proceed faster than their consumption and deterioration.

As all natural waters form a single entity, with which there is constant interchange, control and conservation must be organized at the level of river basins, continents, even groups of continents.

The time is coming when mankind will have to face up to the problem of reorganizing the hydrographic system in such a way as to divert water in the necessary quantities from areas where there is a surplus to areas where there is a shortage. The creation of irrigated zones in what are now deserts will undoubtedly become extremely urgent in the very near future.

Reorganization of the hydrographic system and control of the hydrologic cycle will become a matter of great importance in the next decades because of the enormously high level which water consumption will reach by the beginning of the twenty-first century. There is growing recognition of the importance of research on these subjects.

The particular feature of water resources which offers prospects for overcoming the water shortage is that not only do they constantly renew themselves but that the intensity with which they renew themselves is proportional to that with which they are used. However, water withdrawn from the hydrologic cycle in one place returns only in minute quantities to the same place. Renewal of resources takes place by: (a) increase in underground run-off; (b) increase in precipitation due to increased humidity of the atmosphere as a result of extraction of water. A study of the mechanisms involved in these processes provides important information for the scientific control of water resources.

Localized water management schemes touch off processes which affect all continents and the planet as a whole. Since the waters of the continents are in constant interaction with the physical and geographical environment, investigation and exploitation must be integrated. Water management is already on such a scale as to have a direct effect on physical, geographical and geological processes as a whole. Hence, hydrological factors are of the greatest importance in working out the theoretical foundations for forecasting changes in the totality of the environment.

We already dispose of considerable knowledge enabling us to predict the environmental effects of our various interventions in our water resources. We have: (a) the principles and methods for calculating the deformation of the beds of streams and reservoirs and forecasting the state of these beds for many years ahead; (b) a theory of interaction between surface water and ground water—this can be used to assess changes in the level of ground water and the exchanges of water between elements of the hydrographic system and the surrounding territory; (c) experimental data on and theories relating to the movement of masses of air over open water—these can be used to evaluate meteorological changes immediately above the water and its adjacent areas; (d) general laws showing how changes in the elements of the water balance bring about related changes in soil-forming processes; (e) principles and methods for calculating the transport of suspended sediments both in surface run-off and in streams; these enable the determination of changes in the processes of denudation of the earth's crust which are taking place or which will take place with the reorganization of the hydrographic system (these will be on such a large scale that they will have a considerable influence on the future face of the planet).

As far as man is concerned, rivers have two functions: (a) to supply fresh water; (b) to channel off the polluted waste created by domestic and industrial activities. There is such a sharp contradiction between these two functions that in the not too distant future their head-on collision will have grave consequences.

The organic world as we know it today is the end product of an evolutionary process whereby the waters of the continents and the rest of the geographical environment have reached a certain equilibrium. However, the quality of these waters is now being changed by human activity at such an ever-increasing rate that the organic world (and man himself) can hardly adapt itself undamaged to these changes. This situation cannot continue forever. The scale of human activities is becoming such that man cannot go on simply helping himself recklessly to what nature has provided. There is only one way out. Man cannot do without fresh water, therefore he must organize the environment at a higher level. As in the living organism, in addition to the arteries—in this case rivers—he must also have veins to carry away the industrial and domestic waste. This is an enormous challenge, but one which must sooner or later be met.

To create such a purification system, adequate to the needs, he will have to take advantage of all the possibilities. In addition to the methods previously mentioned, these possibilities include: (a) developing supplementary artificial surface and underground hydrographic systems into which industrial and domestic effluents can be dumped (using part of the existing system, suitably modified); (b) dumping waste directly into deep seas; (c) underground dumping of industrial waste, taking care not to contaminate usable ground water.

The question of dumping into the oceans must be handled with extreme care. The zone of active and direct interaction between rivers and seas is the relatively small continental shelf, with depths of up to 200 metres, which makes up about 8 per cent of the area of the oceans. It is the part of the ocean richest in vegetable and animal life; this falls off by factors of tens and even thousands as one goes away from the coasts and towards the deep ocean. The sea coasts have played and have an extremely important role to play in the evolution of life on earth—an intermediate zone enriching both seas and land.

Contamination of the ocean by industrial effluents, oil and petroleum products is greatest in coastal waters and in the surface layers of the deep ocean—precisely in those places where biological productivity is greatest. With increasing use of the oceans, care must be taken both to protect them and to assure them an inflow of needed mineral and organic substances. Thus, even when the hydrographic system is reorganized to keep clean and polluted water separate, the problem of purifying effluents will not lose its importance. We shall always have to dump waste into the ocean but it must be so purified and dumped at such a depth that it does not represent a threat to marine life; it must enter into natural processes without lessening the biological productivity of the seas.

Run-off causes both mechanical denudation of land surfaces and chemical denudation—that is, by taking ground minerals into solution. Most of the substances carried away in suspension as a result of mechanical denudation and part of those carried away in solution are deposited on the continental shelf at a rate of 130 metres of sediment in 100,000 years. This is undoubtedly a major reason for the continental shelf's biological productivity.

Therefore, when managing run-off we must be careful to take into account the possible consequences of altering the existing conditions of denudation of the earth's surface.

In view of all the above considerations, it is clear that our problem today is to secure an optimum level of control of the run-off and of the exchange of matter for each physical and geographical zone. To do this, we must simultaneously take into consideration water consumption requirements, changes induced in the physical and geographical environment by the retention of run-off, and changes induced in the hydrological cycle and in the circulation of materials in the earth's natural processes.

Selection 30

Mineral Resources

Commentary

The earth is finite, and in no area is that finiteness more revealing than in the supply of minerals. Unlike food and timber, minerals are not renewable. Once extracted and consumed, they are, under present-day technology, largely gone. At no time in man's tenure on earth has the mineral supply been exploited to the limit it is being exploited today. Judging by the current rate of consumption, more metals have been used in the past thirty-year period than have been consumed in all previous time.[1] With the possible exception of coal, most of the accessible and the best deposits of minerals in the United States, the United Kingdom, and other Western countries have been exhausted. Most of the industrialized world now depends upon raw materials from foreign nations, mostly the underdeveloped ones, making such nations extremely vulnerable economically, to say the least.

As sources of minerals become exhausted, billions of tons of metals and other exhaustable resources pollute the land as solid wastes. "The disposal of trash and other solid wastes," Dr. Hibbard writes in this selection, "is nearly as acute an environmental problem as the pollution of air and water." Solid wastes at once represent an enormous financial drain on the public, a wastage of valuable raw materials, and pollution of the land.

The removal of refuse costs the United States $4.5 billion a year. Seventy-five per cent of this cost is

Recycling of waste is part of the answer to the solid waste problem and the conservation of natural resources. Here baled waste paper is being removed from yard storage for pulping and use in manufacture of corrugated shipping containers. (Photo courtesy of Georgia-Pacific.)

---

[1]T. S. Lovering, "Mineral Resources from the Land," Nat. Acad. Sci., *Resources and Man*, San Francisco, Calif., Freeman, 1969.

borne by urban waste disposal; the cost is close behind schools and highways as the major item in municipal budgets. Much of this urban waste comes from increased and improved food packaging of nondegradable plastics, from glass bottles and cans, from old appliances, and from paper. A great deal of the trash is a result of planned obsolescence designed to keep industry going. Industry generates 15 million tons of scrap metal annually, and paper mills are responsible for 30 million tons of waste paper each year.[2] These wastes accumulate because both industry and the consumer are geared to the processing of raw materials rather than to the recycling of waste materials. Solid wastes are disposed on open dumps, and in sanitary land fills or reduced to ashes and molten material in incinerators. Very rarely some biodegradable materials may be decomposed. Waste materials buried in sanitary land fills or resting in unsightly open dumps represent rich stores of mineral matter. If the materials were utilized, environmental degradation would be controlled and losses of mineral wealth would be reduced to a point where the only new resources needed would be those required to replace natural losses from manufacture and to meet increased demand. Just as the ecosystem recycles its materials, so man must recycle his solid wastes, utilizing them as much as possible to increase the supply of usable materials and to create new products.

The problem involved in recycling is not so much one of technology as it is of economics and psychology. For example, glass and metal used in bottle and cans can be recycled economically. But we have no economical means of segregating the waste products initially from other forms of trash. Consumers lack the enthusiasm for returning bottles and cans, and efforts to encourage such returns, the returnable bottle notwithstanding, meet with resistance. During the 1940s and the recession years of the 1950s, before the advent of aluminum cans and nonreturnable bottles, even the affluent would faithfully return their bottles each week and claim their two- or five-cent deposit on each. What adults failed to return, children collected for candy money. Today the returnable bottle has become a bother. Supermarkets and the corner store are annoyed at both collecting and returning the deposit. Consumers don't like bottles accumulating around the house, nor will they tolerate the inconvenience of loading them in the car and taking them to the store. So glass bottles, capable of being both reused and recycled, clutter the roadsides and fill the dumps. There has yet to be developed a total and systematic approach for solid waste management.

Meanwhile the accelerating and often exponential worldwide demands for minerals and for fossil fuel for both power and metallurgical needs are creating major solid and associated environmental problems. Mining accounts for 31 percent of all solid wastes. Of the estimated 1.1 billion tons of solid wastes generated each year by the mineral industry in the United States, 80 percent comes from eight largely extractive industries: copper, iron and steel, bituminous coal, phosphate rock, lead, zinc, aluminum, and anthracite coal.[3] Before 1965 over 7000 square miles of the United States were buried under mountains of coal waste piles, slag heaps, smelter wastes, and strip mine overburdens. Since 1965 some 20,000 active surface and strip mining operations have destroyed 157,000 acres each year. Strip mining of coal, the price of which has nearly doubled in several years' time, is increasing at an enormous rate in spite of some restrictive legislation. In the coal regions of West Virginia, strip mining has increased 200 percent in two years. The growing demand for power by urban areas is destroying the central Appalachian area and the corn lands of Ohio and Illinois, and it threatens other coal-producing areas of the west. Except for those who have visited or live in coal-producing regions, few appreciate the environmental destruction caused by strip mining. The impact and magnitude of damage vary with the region. The most environmental destruction occurs in the Appalachians.

There are two types of strip mining in the mountains: contour and area. Contour strip mining is done on the slope. The operator bulldozes a haul road to the seam and proceeds to remove the overburden from the bed starting at the outcrop and working around the hillside, carving out a long, broad bench. Left on the inside is a high wall, often as high as 100 feet. On the outside is the overburden, shoved over the side of the hill to create a precipitous downslope. Some mountains contain one seam of coal. Others may contain up to four seams. The strip mine operator starts on the lowest seam first, and when that is mined he moves on to the next seam until he reaches the topmost. If the upper seam is close to the top, the operator will area strip. In this method, a trench or box cut is made through the overburden to expose a portion of the seam. When that part is removed, a parallel cut is made and the spoil is deposited in the cut previously excavated. The final cut leaves an open trench equal to the overburden and coal bed recovered. In mountain country this means the removal of the mountain top. Thus, where several seams of coal exist, an entire mountain can be converted into one huge pile of overburden.

The spoils are highly unstable. Water seeping into and percolating through the overburden wets the clays and the shales. The slipperiness of the clays, the weight of the overburden, and gravity combine to cause massive landslides that block mountain roads and dam mountain streams. Water rushing down the steep slopes carries with it tons of sediment that are washed far downstream.

[2]R. Eliassen, "Solid Waste Management," in H. D. Johnson (ed.), *No Deposit, No Return,* Reading, Mass., Addison-Wesley, 1970, pp. 55—56.
[3]*Ibid.*

Strip mining alters the ground water regime. Water tables, once deep in the underlying rock strata, are exposed and flow freely to the newly created surface. Water rushing down the precipitous slopes during storms collects in the pits and benches and rushes down the slopes. During periods of intense spring and summer storms, water flows from the strip mines with tremendous force, intensifying the height and damage from flash floods and washing out stream channels and narrow flood plains below.

To complicate the problem, the spoils are not easily vegetated. The spoil material, a mixture of rock fragments, sand, silt and clay high in iron, aluminum, magnesium, and sulfur, is too acidic and toxic to support life. Revegetation on many spoils is nearly impossible because of the acid and toxic soil of the overburden, the extremely unstable slope, and severe environmental conditions. For the exposed acid materials to leach out to a point that they might support life again may require 800 to 1000 years. Thus, for short-term gains extensive areas in eastern Kentucky and southwestern West Virginia mountain land are destroyed for hundreds if not thousands of years.

Of all the ecological changes brought about by coal mining, both deep and strip, none are more damaging or affect a wider area than mine acid water pollution. Lying above and below the seams of coal are layers of rock strata containing pyrite or iron sulfide. Before mining operations these sulfite-bearing rocks are not exposed to air, which causes oxidation. But mining allows the air and water to reach these rocks and even lowers the ground water table to the floor of the mine. Once exposed to air and water the pyritic materials react to produce sulfuric acid and iron sulfate. As the mine acid water flows through the materials, it dissolves and holds great quantities (relative to neutral water) of aluminum, calcium, magnesium, potassium, sodium, and iron sulfate. Once in the receiving stream, the iron sulfate hydrolyzes to sulfuric acid and ferric hydroxide, which precipitates out as a yellowish sediment that colors the water and coats the stream bottom.

Mine acid entering the stream destroys it. For the most part, aquatic life associated with clear-running streams is killed from the high concentrations of acid, the ions of iron sulfate, and the deposition of a smothering blanket of iron precipitates on the stream bottom. In addition, copper, zinc, and aluminum may be at lethal concentrations. Streams with a pH lower than 4.5 hold no fish, although in some places the bullhead may survive.

There are other effects. Sewage is also poured into water. Normal streams, if not subject to too heavy loads of sewage, purify themselves further downstream. This self-purification is dependent upon activities of bacteria and other microorganisms. The low pH of acid-polluted streams inhibits the activity of these purifying bacteria; in fact, the organic material in the water is actually pickled, and intestinal bacteria such as *Escherichia coli* are held to very low counts. Once this sewage-laden acid water reaches areas of higher pH, bacterial counts rise quickly and oxygen demands by decomposing bacteria increase rapidly, often depleting the oxygen supply in downstream waters. Acid water is also unfit for recreational swimming because it can burn the eyes. Industrial and domestic use necessitates additional treatment of polluted water and often early replacement of equipment. Acid water rusts out steel and iron structures such as bridges, locks, and boat pumps.

In such a manner do the mineral requirements represent a threat. Only careful planning by man on an international scale can meet the challenge of mineral depletion and environmental degradation in the future.

Selection 30

Mineral Resources: Challenge or Threat?

by Walter R. Hibbard, Jr.

For I dipt into the future,
   far as human eye could see,
Saw the Vision of the World.
   and all the wonders that would be
          TENNYSON, *Locksley Hall* (1842)

Soothsayers are popular when they foresee good things and predict fulfillment of widespread longings and expectations. Consequently, Edward Bellamy's utopian novel, *Looking Backward*, was a best seller when it appeared

THIS SELECTION is reprinted with permission of the author and publisher from *Science*, Vol. 160, pp. 143–148, April 1968. Copyright 1968 by the American Association for the Advancement of Science.

in 1881 (1). It foretold that in the year 2000 there would be a very good thing in Boston—an ideal society.

Those who foresee dangers and darkness are less likely to be listened to. Cassandra predicted that Troy would fall, and no one believed her. Malthus reasoned that population would outstrip food supply, and all kinds of refutations were marshaled against him. Lindbergh in 1938 warned that the air force which the Nazis possessed was the best in the world, and he was doubted.

It is the same today. We tend to ignore predictions of bad news. We respond to alarms only when the house is already on fire.

Bellamy, whose book is enjoying a modest revival now, believed that it would be "the limit of human felicity" if people could have "music in their homes, perfect in quality, unlimited in quantity, suited to every mood, and beginning and ceasing at will" (2). This describes the phonographs and stereo tape recorders now in many American and European homes.

Many of today's and tomorrow's problems also have long been predicted, but we are accustomed to undertake seriously and purposefully solutions to only those problems that present a clear and immediate danger. Too often solutions come too late, and it becomes necessary to apply remedies which are expensive and difficult; the answers would have been cheaper and easier had we started earlier.

Thus, in a society whose standard of living is the highest ever attained for so many people, the opinion that our economic growth may decelerate and our living standard decline would be highly unpopular.

LET SCIENCE FIX IT

We are called an affluent society, and we want to believe it; but is it really true? Secretary of the Interior Udall has called our vaunted superabundance a myth inherited from the 19th century. And this myth is rapidly being supplanted, he says, by a "myth of scientific supremacy . . . we tolerate great imbalance" in the use of our natural resources and "shrug off the newer forms of erosion with a let-science-fix-it-tomorrow attitude" (3).

Our ability to handle some of our greatest present threats—war, poverty, crime, urban crowding and ugliness, growing damage to our environment—is seldom thought of as resource-limited. Whatever material resources we need to solve these problems, most of us apparently assume are already here at hand—or if not, don't worry; the economics of the market place will soon provide them!

A requisite for affluence, now or in the future, is an adequate supply of minerals—fuels to energize our power and transportation; nonmetals, such as sulfur and phosphates to fertilize farms; and metals, steel, copper, lead, aluminum, and so forth, to build our machinery, cars, buildings, and bridges. These are the materials basic to our economy, the multipliers in our gross national product. But the needed materials which can be recovered by known methods at reasonable cost from the earth's crust are limited, whereas their rates of exploitation and use obviously are not. This situation cannot continue.

A warning to that effect was sounded early in the last decade by the President's Materials Policy Commission after a careful review and appraisal of our materials balance sheet (4). The report, Resources for Freedom, popularly known as the Paley Commission Report, was published before the full impact of the current population increase was widely recognized, and before the full extent of the postwar expansion of the U.S. economy was identified. Therefore many of its forecasts of mineral supply and demand turned out to be too conservative, too comforting. The commision has been widely criticized for not sounding the alarm. Its cautious conclusions have been questioned—and largely ignored or forgotten.

Although there were obvious inconsistencies between their forecasts and subsequent events, the philosophy that underlay the Paley Commission study was sound, and its general conclusions apply today as much as they did 15 years ago. In area after area the same pattern was discernible: soaring demands, shrinking resources, the consequent pressure of rising real costs, the risk of wartime shortages, the ultimate threat of an arrest or decline in the standard of living we cherish and hope to help others attain.

Last year, President Johnson, in a message to Congress on air pollution (5), summed it up in another way.

Sharply rising world demands threaten to

exhaust the best and most accessible deposits of minerals. Rapidly changing demands for materials are bringing changes in our mineral needs. We must understand the technological and economic changes taking place.

SEVERE STRAIN ON MINERAL SUPPLY

With only about 9 percent of the Free World population in 1965, the United States consumed between 30 and 40 percent of the Free World's mineral supply (6). Simple projection based on growth of the population and the gross national product suggest that by 1980 consumption of minerals by the United States will in general increase by 50 percent and in many cases double. Although by 1980 it is estimated that the United States will include 7.7 percent of the Free World's population, the number of people in the nation will increase by some 29 percent, and the Free World's population is projected to increase by 50 percent. This sheer weight of numbers is going to place a severe strain on the mineral supply of the Free World to maintain and improve the standard of living in most of the Free World.

With the rapid expansion of the economy during and since World War II, the United States has consumed a correspondingly large increase in mineral output. The result has been greater dependence of U.S. industry on foreign sources of raw materials. Today, imports supply over 75 percent of our needs for 20 different mineral commodities (6). Also world mineral development and depletion of the higher grade domestic reserves and development of mineral industries in other nations have led the U.S. mineral producer into widening world competition for key resources.

Recognizing our increasing reliance on foreign resources, the Paley Commission recommended: (i) government measures to encourage investment of risk capital in the mineral industries; (ii) a continuous appraisal of the nation's mineral and energy supply position; and (iii) accelerated research and development to expand the base of our mineral and fuel resources.

These recommendations are still valid. Indeed, events since the Paley Report make it more urgent than ever to expand the technical and economic base of our resources by every feasible means.

NEW PALEY COMMISSION STUDY URGENT

Industrial growth in many parts of the world, the population explosion, advances in transportation and in communications, changing marketing patterns, shifting needs and requirements stemming from wars (Vietnam and the Middle East), and the emergence of new nations—all these, and other trends barely discernible now, make it imperative that another study similar to the Paley Commission review be made as soon as possible so that we may anticipate and undertake as soon as possible the steps necessary to avert serious calamity. Although such a study may also fail in precision of forecasting, new and continuously revised estimates of each mineral requirement and each type of fuel or energy source would provide a sound basis for action by both government and private industry.

Raw materials are powerful economic multipliers. Cost changes in ores are reflected throughout the economic structure, from metal producer, to fabricator, and ultimately to the consumer. But we cannot depend upon the law of supply and demand in a free economy to spur the necessary investment. Mineral production cannot be turned on like a faucet. Substantial capital (hundreds of millions of dollars per venture) and substantial time (often 5 to 10 years) are required to complete a new mineral-producing facility.

THE TIME PROBLEM

Prain points out that the mining investor has to wait many years, perhaps a quarter of a century, before a mine can be built and can operate long enough to repay his investment and make a reasonable profit (7).

Winning from the earth the minerals needed for prosperity and well-being depends not only on the capital available for investment, but also on the technology that can be applied. As Boyd has pointed out, our resources are limited less by the amounts of raw materials than by the technology of treatment and extraction and by the capacity to produce at a reasonable cost (8). Spencer believes that one mineral industry, petroleum, will be "bumping against the ceiling, not of resources, but of technology, and therefore of capital. Unlike land, which becomes more valuable as population increases and good prospects are snapped up, technology can be improved, and the supply of capital can be stretched" (9).

Although technology may stretch capital by less-expensive production facilities, permitting utilization of lower grade ores, only long-range planning can remedy the time problem. It is already too late to initiate new production capability for 1970; facilities for that year must be well along in development now.

Technology, willingness to risk capital, and planning have made the United States a major producer of minerals. The U.S. Bureau of Mines shows complete world production data on 54 mineral commodities for 1966 (10); U.S. led in the production of 27. In the case of 11 additional commodities for which complete figures were not available, it is believed the United States led in the production of six.

However, as long as mineral deposits in other parts of the world can be profitably developed, the incentives for radical innovation in technology are slight and investment capital is attracted abroad. It is axiomatic that investors seek out ventures that are the most profitable. Hence, capital will flow to those countries with lower labor costs, greater government incentives (such as tax benefits and subsidies), and minimum costs for pollution control (relative to the United States) as well as high-grade reserves which can be readily exploited by well-established procedures and available equipment. Already, American investment in mining is going abroad at an increasing rate—to Australia, Canada, Spain, South Africa, and South America. If this trend continues, by 1985 we may be importing a major portion of our large-tonnage metals such as iron, copper, lead, and zinc, thus adding commodities for which the United States is already primarily dependent on overseas sources. Advanced technology at home, economically applied to domestic reserves, can reverse this trend.

TECHNOLOGY CAN EXPAND RESOURCE BASE

Most of our mineral industries are mature; they have been operating for a long time, and the cream has been skimmed from the richest and most easily recovered ores. Yet technological innovation is continually injecting new life into these mature industries. I believe that technolgoy can help increase our mineral resource base in following four ways:

1) Exploration and discovery. The minerals so far used by man have come from very near the surface. Most were discovered from outcrops. We must learn how to explore at depths, and we must develop methods to find and extract minerals in the deeper layers of the earth's crust and from under the sea.

2) Improved mining, benefication, and processing. More efficient methods for mining ores and for upgrading them before smelting and refining can make the use of leaner ores technically and economically feasible.

3) Recycling of scrap and waste. There is tremendous opportunity in "mining" our scrap heaps and junkyards. Already about 40 percent of this year's production of lead and 25 percent of this year's copper comes, not from primary ores, but from reclaimed scrap. Such salvage programs could be greatly extended through research and improved collection and processing techniques.

4) Substitution. Using abundant materials in place of those in short supply is the challenge of the physical metallurgist—and of the polymer chemist. Not only is there strong economic pressure to find substitutes (because they are usually cheaper), but there is technical pressure also. The materials engineer, redesigning from basic principles, often finds that the traditional materials are not the best technically.

Potentially one of the most rewarding opportunities for dramatic expansion of our mineral resource base—and one of the greatest challenges to our ingenuity—is the exploration and exploitation of the almost untapped three-quarters of the earth's crust beneath the oceans. The deepwater sections are beyond our reach at present, but very encouraging progress has been made on the continental shelves, defined as offshore sea bottom to a depth of 200 meters. These shelves are geologically similar to the adjacent dry land; and we can assume with some confidence that they contain ore bodies of similar types and distributions.

Let us imagine a map of the United States with a 200-meter depth line offshore, showing the approximate extent of our 2.3 million square kilometers of continental shelf. If we were to flip the shelf over onto dry land, using the coast line as a hinge, we would have a mirror image of the shelf. The value of the

352

minerals produced from this onshore mirror image is estimated at $160 billion (in 1966 dollars), exclusive of the value of the oil and gas produced.

It is entirely reasonable to expect several billion dollars worth of minerals in our continental shelf, but we must develop the technology to explore, identify, and sample them; and then the technology of delineating and mining these undersea deposits. About 60 percent of the shelf area has a thick cover of sediment; 20 percent is believed to have a thin cover; and another 20 percent to be essentially bare bedrock or outcrop.

INVISIBLE GOLD

The technology of improved exploration and processing is typified by recent developments in gold production. Gold has traditionally been discovered in visible deposits, where material can be crushed and physically separated by panning. Extracting the ores from a wide variety of geologic settings, at varying ocean depths in all kinds of weather, is a formidable challenge requiring new technology. Elemental gold can generally be picked out because it is heavier than other minerals in the mix. So-called invisible gold, identified only by sophisticated chemical analysis, has been discovered. One such discovery, at Carlin, Nevada, was largely responsible for the 1965 increase in U.S. gold production.

Chemical extraction of gold from ore is also being improved, supplanting methods that are 50 years old. With massive new techniques for bulk ore-handling, low-grade ore deposits known as dry placers may be surface mined.

Thus, discoveries (including anticipated development of offshore gold placers in the estuaries of once-productive gold-bearing stream and beaches), better mining, and progressive technology should ultimately make it possible to increase U.S. gold production three- or fourfold.

Recycling to further extend our resource base is certainly not a new concept; it is an established business of great social usefulness and should not be deprecated as junk. Most of its value is in metal scrap. Even in our disposable, no-deposit-no-return, throw-away mode of living, sales of nonferrous scrap alone amount to $1.5 billion annually. This figure represents only that portion of recycled non-ferrous metals that go through obsolescence, discard, and scrap dealers; it is only a fraction of the total, for home scrap produced in metal and fabricating plants is recycled without going through the scrap dealer and its value cannot be accurately computed.

Two reforms are urgently needed to extend the use and to expand the reuse of valuable materials, even though they may seem to run counter to the affluent status our society seems to be trying to maintain. (i) We should design our durable, mineral-containing products to last longer before they go out of style or wear out, and (ii) we should design such products to make it easier to collect and separate their mineral content for recycling after they are discarded.

An American automobile, for instance, lasts about 7 years, or 160,000 kilometers. From a technical standpoint, doubling those figures should not be difficult, and there would be a tremendous saving in metals and other materials.

Moreover, most automobiles seem to be designed on the assumption that no one, not even a mechanic, will ever want to take one apart. Workers at the Bureau of Mines have dismantled several dozen cars of different ages and makes in the course of current work on solid-waste disposal problems. The manufacturers were unable to tell them the composition and distribution of materials in their cars, since many components were supplied by vendors. The placement of these components and the overall design of the car are subject to many restrictions: conservation of space, esthetic appeal, ease of manufacture, safety, and others. The result is that not only the exterior design but also the materials which are used in automobiles change from year to year. Wiring becomes more complex in order to take care of additional electrical equipment. Increasing use is made of stainless, aluminized, and galvanized steel and of aluminum and zinc castings and other materials which make salvage difficult.

I propose that in designing automobiles— and refrigerators, ranges, and other metallic consumer products—manufacturers should provide greater durability, retard obsolescence, and anticipate the need for recycling. If engineering design were to include this concept, valuable materials could then be readily saved when the product is obsolete or worn out. This is a stiff requirement but a necessary one. The

353

annual addition to the scrap market of millions of tons of metal is such a valuable potential resource that we cannot afford to overlook any means of making it easier to salvage.

The continuing failure, on the one hand, to retard the flow of usable materials into the scrap piles, and, on the other hand, to utilize this above-ground bonanza more fully to satisfy our proliferating requirements is shortsighted, in fact, criminal.

There is no reason why, with skill in design and materials application, we cannot make products more durable while we salvage every bit we can from our unusable and discarded products, and thereby extend the mineral resource base of the nation.

The rising need for minerals creates the corollary problem of controlling the detrimental effects of mining on man's living space and on his environment. The same increases in population and living standards that require more minerals also require intensified and multiple use of land for homes and other buildings, for roads and airports, for parks and recreational areas.

MECHANICAL MONSTERS AT WORK

Our current mining operations, for reasons of economy, are, where feasible, conducted from the surface rather than underground. These open-pit, strip or surface mines (Fig. 1) already produce most of the tonnage of some materials such as copper, and in the foreseeable future will extract an even larger proportion of coal and ore in the United States. Big machines—

Figure 2. One of the world's largest excavating machines used in open-pit mining for coal in Ohio. This machine digs 400,000 pounds of earth in a single bite, swings 180 degrees, and deposits the load 325 feet away from the digging points at heights up to 120 feet. (Photo courtesy of Consolidation Coal.)

large electric shovels and draglines, some of which can handle up to 152 cubic meters at a single pass and cost as much as a jet plane—are making it profitable to mine deposits under a considerable overburden of earth and waste rock (Fig. 2).

But mounting public protests against alteration of the land surface (Fig. 3) and the past failure of numerous operators to restore mined lands to satisfactory condition may reverse the trend. Several states already have passed or strengthened their strip-mining laws and enforcement procedures. Other states—and possibly the federal government—may also take action along these lines. These measures will obviously add to the costs of surface-

Figure 1. An open pit or surface mine for coal. Note the removal of overburden which exposes the bed of coal. (Photo courtesy of U.S. Soil Conservation Service.)

Figure 3. Contour strip mining in Appalachia (Boone County, West Virginia) results in total destruction of the mountain environment. (Photo courtesy of Genevive Rasmussen.)

mining operations and can shrink the available resources. Marginal producers may be discouraged, but the necessities of the situation will stimulate more economical and efficient mining and transportation techniques.

In addition, there are finite limits to deposits minable by surface access. Consequently there is an urgent need to develop more efficient underground mining equipment, analogous to the gigantic, economic, high-speed surface machines concurrently with new systems of procedures and techniques for high-capacity underground operations. Some equipment has already been developed (such as the giant boring machines, see Fig. 4) to bore vertical holes as large as 2 meters in diameter in soft rock (Fig. 5); and horizontal holes up to about 13 meters in diameter. Such machines can chew their way along at satisfactory speeds, but the broken rock and ore pile up too fast to be removed by present conveyor systems. Other problems are proper ventilation at a rapidly moving cutting face, fast and efficient propping to keep the tunnel intact, means of handling water intrusion, and methods of geological reconnoitering to locate obstacles or hazards before the cutter reaches them. All of these challenges await technical solutions which I believe the future burgeoning demands for minerals will bring about.

RAPID EXCAVATION FOR URBAN DEVELOPMENT

Incidentally, development of rapid tunneling methods would benefit many aspects of modern life other than mining. Subway systems and vehicular tunnels would be easier

Figure 5. Vertical holes drilled by auger mining to remove coal. (Photo courtesy of Samuel Brock.)

and cheaper to build. Greater portions of our water, sewer, electric power, and communication systems could be installed underground. Buildings in metropolitan centers might grow downward as well as upward, thereby creating new living and working space.

Our increasing need for minerals has created the additional environmental problem of air pollution, largely the result of the burning of fossil fuels and the processing of minerals, which adds to our costs. If their emissions are not carefully controlled, coal-fueled electric power stations, steel mills, and other industrial plants pour sulfur oxides and fly ash into the air. Automobiles, trucks, and diesel-powered vehicles produce hydrocarbons and nitrogen oxides. All fuels produce carbon dioxide—in itself harmless and necessary for plant life, but potentially harmful if it should accumulate enough to change the world's atmospheric composition. Imperfectly burned fuel produces carbon monoxide, a deadly poison. Awareness of the hazards of these pollutants to people,

Figure 4. An auger mining machine at work on a coal seam. (Photo courtesy of Samuel Brock.)

animals, and crops is bringing about laws and regulations that upset normal patterns of fuel use. Consequently, the cost of air-pollution control increases the costs not only of power production, space heating, and manufacture, but also that of fuels treated or modified to meet new standards.

TECHNOLOGY OF AIR-POLLUTION CONTROL

In general, the technology of controlling air pollution is known. Many government agencies and industry are working on these problems, but, in every case I know of, the cost is still too high for voluntary adoption by the industries involved. People must be educated and their habits changed. The social force of public opinion, backed by legislation when necessary, is needed before much progress can be made, and research and development work must be continued and expanded.

Work on one aspect of air pollution at the U.S. Bureau of Mines points to the encouraging prospect of getting valuable products from the poisons taken from air. A process used by the Bureau to remove sulfur dioxide from the stack gases of coal-burning plants recovers part of the process cost from the sale of elemental sulfur. The prospect of using a crop-killing pollutant to make fertilizer is intriguing. Technology to control air pollution is also being applied to the fuels themselves, as in the removal of sulfur before burning. These developments as well as legislation, regulations, and social pressure will have a bearing on the kinds of fuels we use and on their costs. Will we have enough of the prescribed kind to meet our needs in the future?

Disposal of trash and other solid waste is nearly as acute an environmental problem as the pollution of air and water. We pay dearly for space in which to dump discarded material that may contain valuable metals. We bury in sanitary landfills tons of iron and other metals mixed together in residues from municipal incinerators. Even as we bury metal in one place we are looking elsewhere for ores that may well be leaner than our sanitary landfills.

BONANZA IN THE TRASH HEAPS

The 34 million metric tons of municipal refuse incinerated annually in this country contain more than 2.8 million metric tons of iron and some 180,000 metric tons of aluminum, zinc, copper, lead, and tin (*11*). Archeologist-miners of the future may well go prospecting in our city dumps, which for the present are lost resources.

The disposal, control, and reclamation of mineral waste products also pose technologic and social problems, and in addition are economic factors in the effective conservation and use of mineral resources. The problem must be attacked from the standpoint of conservation by minimizing the amount of waste produced. Specifically, methods must be sought to improve recovery systems in order to reduce mineral losses and to reduce the volume of products finally discarded. In addition, more efficient techniques must be devised for reclamation and reuse of mineral-based materials that currently are wastefully discarded—a practice we may no longer be able to afford.

We should develop the technology to mine waste of all types. Recovering metals and other minerals from mine tailings, industrial refuse, and incinerator ash are likely places to start.

Of course, these objectives in themselves do not provide adequate direct economic gains to industry. On the contrary, they would frequently add costs that would probably have to be passed on to consumers. Nevertheless, the problems arising from mineral supply cannot be treated apart from environmental degradation stemming from the mining, treatment, or use of any mineral substance.

In our political and economic system, it is the responsibility of private industry to develop and exploit resources to meet demands at the market place. It is the federal government's role, however, to assume a position of leadership in determining the projected needs, in supplying the long-range scientific and technologic support for the minerals industry, and in using techniques such as education, communication of information, and cooperation to encourage industry to attack the vital problems of minerals supply. Such assistance is especially necessary where the risks are too costly to be undertaken by a corporate entity, and where the rewards benefit the public rather than a particular industry. Research and engineering are under way to devise methods for processing marginal reserves, improving efficiency of extraction and recovery, recycling mineral materials, and making alternatives or substitutes for mineral materials in short supply.

All these efforts of the government are aimed at promoting the wise development and use of the nation's mineral resources to sustain the economy and to assure adequate, dependable supplies at the lowest economic and social cost. But these efforts, with those of cooperating state and local governments and the mineral industries, are not enough. A broad public understanding is needed to insure support for the concerted action by all sectors of our society to alleviate the coming threats to our mineral resources.

UNDERSTANDING BY SCIENTIFIC COMMUNITY

Understanding by our scientific community is especially needed, for, although I have stressed the technical and utilitarian aspects of the problems we will face, there is a tremendous need for scientific backup. The challenges herein are not just to engineers, industrialists, and statesmen: they are as well to scientists of many disciplines; for, unless we acquire the fundamental knowledge to apply, our progress may be too slow to avert the threats to our standards of living and future security.

These threats—or challenges—can be summed up. (i) Minerals are essentially and in the long run nonrenewable, and some of our mineral reserves, exploitable by today's technology, are becoming exhausted. (ii) The population explosion and rising living standards impose unprecedented demands that will hasten the depletion of our mineral resources. (iii) Pollutants from the extraction and use of minerals and the sheer bulk of inert wastes are degrading our environment and must be controlled, even at increased real costs for the minerals we need. Whether these predictions are optimistic or pessimistic depends upon one's temperament and point of view. I believe they are optimistic, that the tasks we face are demanding, but not impossible.

REFERENCES AND NOTES

1. E. Bellamy, *Looking Backward: 2000—1887* (Boston, 1888; New American Library, New York, 1960).
2. ———, *ibid.*, chap. 11.
3. S. L. Udall, "Conservation challenge of the sixties," Albright Lecture, University of California, Berkeley, 19 April 1963.
4. W. S. Paley *et al.*, in *Resources for Freedom*, President's Materials Policy Commission (Government Printing Office, Washington, D.C., 1952). Five volumes, also summary of vol. 1.
5. Lyndon Johnson, "Message to Congress" 30 January 1967, in *Presidential Documents*, 6 February 1967 (Government Printing Office, Washington, D.C.), vol. 3, No. 5, p. 139.
6. U.S. Department of the Interior, Bureau of Mines, *Minerals Yearbook 1966*, vols. 1 and 2 (Government Printing Office, Washington, D.C., 1967), chap. 1.
7. Sir Ronald Prain, "Investment climate for the developing countries," address to Institute of Mining Engineers of Peru, Lima, 8 November 1967.
8. J. Boyd, *Mining Eng.* **19**, (No. 3), 54 (1967).
9. W. I. Spencer, "Exploration, key to the future," address to American Association of Petroleum Landmen, New Orleans, La., 23 June 1967.
10. Mineral Industry Survey, U.S. Bureau of Mines, *World Mineral Production in 1966* (Government Printing Office, Washington, D.C., 1967).
11. C. B. Kenahan and P. M. Sullivan, *Amer. Public Works Assoc. Reporter*, March 1967, pp. 5–8.

Photosynthesis and Fish Production in the Sea

Commentary

The illimitable seas. To some they represent a vast untapped storehouse of food that can solve the protein problems of the world. The oceans will be farmed, they believe, and the world will be sustained by the sea. But the oceans are finite, and what they can produce in the way of food is determined by the very same conditions that limit productivity on land. There is a limit to the photosynthetic capacity of the ocean plankton and the dynamics of energy transfer through the food chain. The production of organic matter by the oceans and its conversion to higher forms of life usable by man are discussed in this selection. Ryther's estimated productivity of the ocean implies careful management and husbandry of the resource. If the past and the present are any indication of the future, then the oceans stand to be overexploited and productivity impaired if not destroyed.

The stories of the sardine on a national scale and of the whales on an international level illustrate how man has exploited the seas, and they suggest the future of the ocean's food resources. What is true of the sardine and the whale is also true of the northwest Pacific salmon, the Alanto-Scandian herring, and the Barent Sea cod; it foretells the future of such important species as the North Sea and British Columbia herring, the Newfoundland cod, menhaden, and haddock, yellow-finned tuna, and Bering Sea flatfish.

The Pacific coast sardine industry had its beginnings back in 1915 and reached its peak in 1936–1937, when the fishing netted 800,000 tons. It was first in the nation in the number of pounds of fish caught and ranked third in the commercial fishing industry, grossing $10 million annually. The fish went into canned sardines, fish bait, dog food, oil, and fertilizer. The prosperity of the industry was supported by overexploitation. The declines in the catch per boat and success per unit of fishing were compensated for by adding more boats to the fleet. In spite of the fact that older fish were removed early, and that the later catch consisted of young fish, indicating overexploitation and an impending collapse of the industry, the fishing industry rejected all forms of regulation. The British Columbia sardine fishery went under in 1945–1946, the first to fail. In 1947–1948 the Washington–Oregon fishery failed. Then, in 1951, the San Francisco fleet returned with only 80 tons. The fishery closed down and never has recovered.[1]

The story of the sardine has been repeated on an international scale with the whale.[2] Early whalers armed with hand lances and harpoons sought only those whales that could be overtaken and killed from small boats. As whales became scarce along the shore, whalers took to the high seas. In the sixteenth century, whalers hunted off Newfoundland and Iceland until the stock failed. The population of Spitsbergen and the Davis Strait were the next to go. The colorful New England whaling industry, which first exploited the stock of right whales, peaked in the first half of the nineteenth century, but as stocks of slow-moving, easily exploited species were depleted and as petroleum replaced whale oil as a fuel, the New England whaling industry died. Then two developments put international whaling into business. One was the invention of the explosive harpoon in 1865, and the other was the development of more powerful, faster boats that could overtake the swifter whales. The revitalized industry began to concentrate on the plankton-feeding blue whale and its relatives the fin and the sei whales. Again stocks were overexploited. Blue whale fishery in Norway ended in 1904, followed by a decline of the species off Iceland, the Faeroes, the Shetlands, the Hebrides, and Ireland. When these areas failed, whalers sailing free-ranging factory ships turned to the Antarctic and the Falklands. The catches rose and the stocks again collapsed. Antarctic whaling was over and most of the whaling nations were out of business. Japan and the U.S.S.R. developed a whaling industry and now hunted the sei and sperm and other whales wherever they could be found. Investments were made into large factory ships equipped with helicopters and accompanied by catcher boats that captured more whales but with less oil per effort and per ship.

---

[1] G. I. Murphy, "Population Biology of the Pacific Sardine (Sardinops caerulea), *Calif. Acad. Sci. Proc.* **34**(1), 1966, pp. 1–84.
[2] C. P. Idyll, "The Dodo, the Passenger Pigeon and the Whale," *Oceans* **3**(3), 1970, pp. 37–45.

The history of the several species are an example of exploitation.[3] After 1860 the blue whale became the most important commercial species. Catches peaked in 1931 with 150,000 animals and declined to 1000–2000 in 1963. For the past forty years the average age of the blue whale caught in the Antarctic has been six years, mostly immature females or females carrying their first calf. The species is near extinction. The industry turned next to the fin whale. In 1960–1961 catches of this whale amounted to 31,790; in 1966–1967 the catch dropped to 6342. If catch continues at the level of 5000 a year, this species will be extinct in ten years. Kills of the humpbacked whale peaked in 1912; in 1961–1962 only 452 were taken, and whaling for this species was suspended for at least two years. Estimates place a minimum of fifty years for the blue and the humpbacked whales to recover to an abundance that will permit maximum sustainable yield.

The situation of the sardine and the whale is being repeated throughout the world fisheries. The growth rate of fisheries in 1950 was 4 percent; in 1968 it rose to 7 percent. This growth rate is being supported by exploitation of new stocks of less marketable fish, by exploitation of new fishing grounds, especially the Humboldt Current of Peru and the Benguela Current of southwest Africa, by the use of new fleets of fishing vessels equipped to freeze, salt, dry, or can the catch, by electronic methods of fish finding, by aerial spotting, and by improved methods of netting fish.

The leading fishery nations are the same ones that are actively exploiting the dwindling whale populations, Japan and the U.S.S.R. Japan fishes in the Pacific, Indian, Atlantic Oceans and the Mediterranean Sea. Most of her fishing operates from land bases scattered in a number of countries, and she exports much of the fish. The Japanese catch amounts to 7 million metric tons. The Russians, on the other hand, possess large fishing fleets that carry a working city of 25,000 to 30,000 men each. All processing is done at sea, and the catch is carried back by transport vessels. The Soviet catch amounted to 5.6 million metric tons in 1968 and is expected to expand to at least 10 million tons in 1972. A new giant among the fishery nations is Peru, which is exploiting the Humboldt Current. Her annual take in 1967 amounted to 12 million metric tons, consisting largely of anchovies, a plankton-feeding fish. The stock is being overfished. Biologists estimate that the maximum sustained yield of the fishery is 7 million metric tons.

Of the catch of world fisheries, 45 percent is converted to fish meal, most of which is fed to livestock and poultry. One-third of the fish taken goes to developed countries of the world, and only 17 percent or 8 million metric tons goes to underdeveloped nations and their hungry people. One of the largest consumers of fish is the United States, which purchases 65 percent of the world's canned packs of tuna. The bulk of world fishery involves less marketable, low-quality fish, whereas the take of haddock and hake as measured by catch per unit effort is declining.

Instead of being managed for sustained yield, many species of ocean fish are being overexploited to a point where the catch is declining and the stock is showing the same danger signs that preceded the collapse of the sardine and whaling industries. And there is little indication that the exploitation will cease. Major fishery nations have so much money tied up in equipment that they need to continue heavy fishing to repay their original investment. In addition, in many countries the fishing industry is a source of local income and employment, and there is little incentive to reduce the take to an acceptable biological level. To the fishing nations, what is biologically necessary is economically unsatisfactory.

If the world fisheries are to provide a sustained source of protein for man, international regulation of fishing is needed. But the past history of such regulations is one of noncooperation. It has been impossible to get the nations of the world together to regulate whaling. The International Whaling Commission controlled by whalers is not interested in sustained yield management.[4] And Japan is insisting on continuing the killing of whales until the industry collapses. If it is impossible to get an agreement on whaling, how much more difficult will it be to get cooperation on international regulation of fishing?

Overfishing is one man-imposed limitation to the productivity of the seas; another is the destruction of estuaries, the nursery and spawning grounds for many food species, such as the flounder. Estuaries also support larval stages of many marine organisms and account for the high shellfish and fish productivity of coastal waters. Dredging, filling, and pollution are destroying estuaries at a rapid rate, thus reducing the productivity of the seas.

A third problem is contamination of the food resource of the sea, making it unsuitable as food. The accumulation of DDT in the coho salmon of Lake Michigan and the presence of mercury above tolerable levels in tuna and swordfish are warnings enough that pollution of the seas with pesticides and heavy metals that tend to concentrate in food chains can limit the usefulness of the oceans as a source of food for man.

---

[3]Noel Simon, "Of Whales and Whaling," *Science* **149**, 1965, pp. 943–946.
[4]*Ibid.*

The productivity of the sea depends not only on the photosynthetic capacity of the oceans; potential productivity will, to a considerable extent, be influenced by man. With continued overexploitation of fishery resources and accelerated pollution of the seas, even in the face of warning signs of danger, the future of the seas as a source of food looks rather grim.

Selection 31

Photosynthesis and Fish Production in the Sea

by John H. Ryther

Numerous attempts have been made to estimate the production in the sea of fish and other organisms of existing or potential food value to man (*1—4*). These exercises, for the most part, are based on estimates of primary (photosynthetic) organic production rates in the ocean (*5*) and various assumed trophic-dynamic relationships between the photosynthetic producers and the organisms of interest to man. Included in the latter are the number of steps or links in the food chains and the efficiency of conversion of organic matter from each trophic level or link in the food chain to the next. Different estimates result from different choices in the number of trophic levels and in the efficiencies, as illustrated in Table 1 (*2*).

Implicit in the above approach is the concept of the ocean as a single ecosystem in which the same food chains involving the same number of links and efficiencies apply throughout. However, the rate of primary production is known to be highly variable, differing by at least two full orders of magnitude from the richest to the most impoverished regions. This in itself would be expected to result in a highly irregular pattern of food production. In addition, the ecological conditions which determine the trophic dynamics of marine food chains also vary widely and in direct relationship to the absolute level of primary organic production. As is shown below, the two sets of variables—primary production and the asso-

Table 1. ESTIMATES OF POTENTIAL YIELDS (PER YEAR) AT VARIOUS TROPHIC LEVELS, IN METRIC TONS [AFTER SCHAEFFER (*2*)]

	ECOLOGICAL EFFICIENCY FACTOR					
	10 PERCENT		15 PERCENT		20 PERCENT	
TROPHIC LEVEL	CARBON (TONS)	TOTAL WEIGHT (TONS)	CARBON (TONS)	TOTAL WEIGHT (TONS)	CARBON (TONS)	TOTAL WEIGHT (TONS)
0. Phytoplankton (net particulate production)	1.9×10^{10}		1.9×10^{10}		1.9×10^{10}	
1. Herbivores	1.9×10^{9}	1.9×10^{10}	2.8×10^{9}	2.8×10^{10}	3.8×10^{9}	3.8×10^{10}
2. 1st stage carnivores	1.9×10^{8}	1.9×10^{9}	4.2×10^{8}	4.2×10^{9}	7.6×10^{8}	7.6×10^{9}
3. 2nd stage carnivores	1.9×10^{7}	1.9×10^{8}	6.4×10^{7}	6.4×10^{8}	15.2×10^{7}	15.2×10^{8}
4. 3rd stage carnivores	1.9×10^{6}	1.9×10^{7}	9.6×10^{6}	9.6×10^{7}	30.4×10^{6}	30.4×10^{7}

ciated food chain dynamics—may act additively to produce differences in fish production which are far more pronounced and dramatic than the observed variability of the individual causative factors.

PRIMARY PRODUCTIVITY

Our knowledge of the primary organic productivity of the ocean began with the development of the C^{14}-tracer technique for *in situ* measurement of photosynthesis by marine plankton algae (*6*) and the application of the method on the 1950–52 *Galathea* expedition around the world (*5*). Despite obvious deficiencies in the coverage of the ocean by *Galathea* (the expedition made 194 observations, or an average of about one every 2 million square kilometers, most of which were made in the tropics or semitropics), our concept of the total productivity of the world ocean has changed little in the intervening years.

While there have been no more expeditions comparable to the *Galathea*, there have been numerous local or regional studies of productivity in many parts of the world. Most of these have been brought together by a group of Soviet scientists to provide up-to-date world coverage consisting of over 7000 productivity observations (*7*). The result has been modification of the estimate of primary production in the world ocean from 1.2 to 1.5 × 10^{10} tons of carbon fixed per year (*5*) to a new figure, 1.5 to 1.8 × 10^{10} tons.

Attempts have also been made by Steemann Nielsen and Jensen (*5*), Ryther (*8*), and Koblentz-Mishke *et al.* (*7*) to assign specific levels or ranges of productivity to different parts of the ocean. Although the approach was somewhat different in each case, in general the agreement between the three was good and, with appropriate condensation and combination, permits the following conclusions.

1) Annual primary production in the open sea varies, for the most part, between 25 and 75 grams of carbon fixed per square meter and averages about 50 grams of carbon per square meter per year. This is true for roughly 90 percent of the ocean, an area of 326 × 10^6 square kilometers.

2) Higher levels of primary production occur in shallow coastal waters, defined here as the area within the 100-fathom (180-meter) depth contour. The mean value for this region may be considered to be 100 grams of carbon fixed per square meter per year, and the area, according to Menard and Smith (*9*), is 7.5 percent of the total world ocean. In addition, certain offshore waters are influenced by divergences, fronts, and other hydrographic features which bring nutrient-rich subsurface water into the euphotic zone. The equatorial divergences are examples of such regions. The productivity of these offshore areas is comparable to that of the coastal zone. Their total area is difficult to assess, but is considered here to be 2.5 percent of the total ocean. Thus, the coastal zone and the offshore regions of comparably high productivity together represent 10 percent of the total area of the oceans, or 36 × 10^4 square kilometers.

3) In a few restricted areas of the world, particularly along the west coasts of continents at subtropical latitudes where there are prevailing offshore winds and strong eastern boundary currents, surface waters are diverted offshore and are replaced by nutrient-rich deeper water. Such areas of coastal upwelling are biologically the richest parts of the ocean. They exist off Peru, California, northwest and southwest Africa, Somalia, and the Arabian coast, and in other more localized situations. Extensive coastal upwelling also is known to occur in various places around the continent of Antarctica, although its exact location and extent have not been well documented. During periods of active upwelling, primary production normally exceeds 1.0 and may exceed 10.0 grams of carbon per square meter per day. Some of the high values which have been reported from these locations are 3.9 grams for the southwest coast of Africa (*5*), 6.4 for the Arabian Sea (*10*), and 11.2 off Peru (*11*). However, the upwelling of subsurface water does not persist throughout the year in many of these places—for example, in the Arabian Sea, where the process is seasonal and related to the monsoon winds. In the Antarctic, high production is limited by solar radiation during half the year. For all these areas of coastal upwelling throughout the year, it is probably safe, if somewhat conservative, to assign an annual value of 300 grams of carbon per square meter. Their total area in the world is again difficult to assess. On the assumption that their total cumulative area is no greater than 10 times the well-documented upwelling area off Peru,

Table 2. DIVISION OF THE OCEAN INTO PROVINCES ACCORDING TO THEIR LEVEL OF PRIMARY ORGANIC PRODUCTION

PROVINCE	PERCENTAGE OF OCEAN	AREA (KM^2)	MEAN PRODUCTIVITY (GRAMS OF CARBON/M^2/ YR)	TOTAL PRODUCTIVITY (10^9 TONS OF CARBON/YR)
Open ocean	90	326 × 10^6	50	16.3
Coastal zone*	9.9	36 × 10^6	100	3.6
Upwelling areas	0.1	3.6 × 10^5	300	0.1
Total				20.0

*Includes offshore areas of high productivity.

this would amount to some 3.6×10^5 square kilometers, or 0.1 percent of the world ocean. These conclusions are summarized in Table 2.

FOOD CHAINS

Let us next examine the three provinces of the ocean which have been designated according to their differing levels of primary productivity from the standpoint of other possible major differences. These will include, in particular, differences which related to the food chains and to trophic efficiencies involved in the transfer of organic matter from the photosynthetic organisms to fish and invertebrate species large and abundant enough to be of importance to man.

The first factor to be considered in this context is the size of the photosynthetic or producer organisms. It is generally agreed that, as one moves from coastal to offshore oceanic waters, the character of these organisms changes from large "microplankton" (100 microns or more in diameter) to the much smaller "nanno-plankton" cells 5 to 25 microns in their largest dimensions (12, 13).

Since the size of an organism is an essential criterion of its potential usefulness to man, we have the following relationship: the larger the plant cells at the beginning of the food chain, the fewer the trophic levels that are required to convert the organic matter to a useful form. The oceanic nannoplankton cannot be effectively filtered from the water by most of the common zooplankton crustacea. For example, the euphausid *Euphausia pacifica,* which may function as a herbivore in the rich subarctic coastal waters of the Pacific, must turn to a carnivorous habit in the offshore

waters where the phytoplankton become too small to be captured (13).

Intermediate between the nannoplankton and the carnivorous zooplankton are a group of herbivores, the microzooplankton, whose ecological significance is a subject of considerable current interest (14, 15). Representatives of this group include protozoans such as Radiolaria, Foraminifera, and Tintinnidae, and larval nuplii of microcrustaceans. These organisms, which may occur in concentrations of tens of thousands per cubic meter, are the primary herbivores of the open sea.

Feeding upon these tiny animals is a great host of carnivorous zooplankton, many of which have long been thought of as herbivores. Only by careful study of the mouthparts and feeding habits were Anraku and Omori (16) able to show that many common copepods are facultative if not obligate carnivores. Some of these predatory copepods may be no more than a millimeter or two in length.

Again, it is in the offshore environment that these small carnivorous zooplankton predominate. Grice and Hart (17) showed that the percentage of carnivorous species in the zooplankton increased from 16 to 39 percent in a transect from the coastal waters of the northeastern United States to the Sargasso Sea. Of very considerable importance in this group are the Chaetognatha. In terms of biomass, this group of animals, predominantly carnivorous, represents, on the average, 30 percent of the weight of copepods in the open sea (17). With such a distribution, it is clear that virtually all the copepods, many of which are themselves carnivores, must be preyed upon by chaetognaths.

The oceanic food chain thus far described

involves three to four trophic levels from the photosynthetic nannoplankton to animals no more than 1 to 2 centimeters long. How many additional steps may be required to produce organisms of conceivable use to man is difficult to say, largely because there are so few known oceanic species large enough and (through schooling habits) abundant enough to fit this category. Familiar species such as the tunas, dolphins, and squid are all top carnivores which feed on fishes or invertebrates at least one, and probably two, trophic levels beyond such zooplankton as the chaetognaths. A food chain consisting of five trophic levels between photosynthetic organisms and man would therefore seem reasonable for the oceanic province.

As for the coastal zone, it has already been pointed out that the phytoplankton are quite commonly large enough to be filtered and consumed directly by the common crustacean zooplankton such as copepods and euphausids. However, the presence, in coastal waters, of protozoans and other microzooplankton in large numbers and of greater biomass than those found in offshore waters (15) attests to the fact that much of the primary production here, too, passes through several steps of a microscopic food chain before reaching the macrozooplankton.

The larger animals of the coastal province (that is, those directly useful to man) are certainly the most diverse with respect to feeding type. Some (mollusks and some fishes) are herbivores. Many others, including most of the pelagic clupeoid fishes, feed on zooplankton. Another large group, the demersal fishes, feed on bottom fauna which may be anywhere from one to several steps removed from the phytoplankton.

If the herbivorous clupeoid fishes are excluded (since these occur predominantly in the upwelling provinces and are therefore considered separately), it is probably safe to assume that the average food organism from coastal waters represents the end of at least a three-step food chain between photoplankton and man.

It is in the upwelling areas of the world that food chains are the shortest, or—to put it another way—that the organisms are large enough to be directly utilizable by man from trophic levels very near the primary producers. This, again, is due to the large size of the phytoplankton, but it is due also to the fact that many of these species are colonial in habit, forming large gelatinous masses or long filaments. The eight most abundant species of phytoplankton in the upwelling region off Peru, in the spring of 1966, were *Chaetoceros socialis, C. debilis, C. lorenzianus, Skeletonema costatum, Nitzschia seriata, N. delicatissima, Schroederella delicatula,* and *Asterionella japonica* (11, 18). The first in this list, *C. socialis,* forms large gelatinous masses. The others all form long filamentous chains. *Thalossiosira subtilis,* another gelatinous colonial form like *Chaetoceros socialis,* occurs commonly off southwest Africa (19) and close to shore off the Azores (20). Hart (21) makes special mention of the colonial habit of all the most abundant species of phytoplankton in the Antarctic—*Fragiloriopsis antarctica, Encampia balaustrium, Rhizosalenia alata, R. antarctica, R. chunii, Thallosiothrix antarctica,* and *Phaeocystis brucei.*

Many of the above-mentioned species of phytoplankton form colonies several millimeters and, in some cases, several centimeters in diameter. Such aggregates of plant material can be readily eaten by large fishes without special feeding adaptation. In addition, however, many of the clupeoid fishes (sardines, anchovies, pilchards, menhaden, and so on) that are found most abundantly in upwelling areas and that make up the largest single component of the world's commercial fish landings, do have specially modified gill rakers for removing the larger species of phytoplankton from the water.

There seems little doubt that many of the fishes indigenous to upwelling regions are direct herbivores for at least most of their lives. There is some evidence that juveniles of the Peruvian anchovy (*Engraulis ringens*) may feed on zooplankton, but the adult is predominantly if not exclusively a herbivore (22). Small gobies (*Gobius bibarbatus*) found at midwater in the coastal waters off southwest Africa had their stomachs filled with a large, chain-forming diatom of the genus *Fragilaria* (23). There is considerable interest at present in the possible commercial utilization of the large Antarctic krill, *Euphausia superba,* which feeds primarily on the colonial diatom *Fragilariopsis antarctica* (24).

In some of the upwelling regions of the world, such as the Arabian Sea, the species of fish are not well known, so it is not surprising

363

that knowledge of their feeding habits and food chains is fragmentary. From what is known, however, the evidence would appear to be overwhelming that a one- or two-step food chain between phytoplankton and man is the rule. As a working compromise, let us assign the upwelling province a 1½-step food chain.

EFFICIENCY

The growth (that is, the net organic production) of an organism is a function of the food assimilated less metabolic losses or respiration. This efficiency of growth or food utilization (the ratio of growth to assimilation) has been found, by a large number of investigators and with a great variety of organisms, to be about 30 percent in young, actively growing animals. The efficiency decreases as animals approach their full growth, and reaches zero in fully mature or senescent individuals (25). Thus a figure of 30 percent can be considered a biological potential which may be approached in nature, although the growth efficiency of a population of animals of mixed ages under steady-state conditions must be lower.

Since there must obviously be a "maintenance ration" which is just sufficient to accommodate an organism's basal metabolic requirement (26), it must also be true that growth efficiency is a function of the absolute rate of assimilation. The effects of this factor will be most pronounced at low feeding rates, near the "maintenance ration," and will tend to become negligible at high feeding rates. Food conversion (that is, growth efficiency) will therefore obviously be related to food availability, or to the concentration of prey organisms when the latter are sparsely distributed.

In addition, the more available the food and the greater the quantity consumed, the greater the amount of "internal work" the animal must perform to digest, assimilate, convert, and store the food. Conversely, the less available the food, the greater the amount of "external work" the animal must perform to hunt, locate, and capture its prey. These concepts are discussed in some detail by Ivlev (27) and reviewed by Ricker (28). The two metabolic costs thus work in opposite ways with respect to food availability, tending thereby toward a constant total effect. However, when food availability is low,

the added costs of basal metabolism and external work relative to assimilation may have a pronounced effect on growth efficiency.

When one turns from consideration of the individual and its physiological growth efficiency to the "ecological efficiency" of food conversion from one trophic level to the next (2, 29), there are additional losses to be taken into account. Any of the food consumed but not assimilated would be included here, though it is possible that undigested organic matter may be reassimilated by members of the same trophic level (2). Any other nonassimilatory losses, such as losses due to natural death, sedimentation, and emigration, will, if not otherwise accounted for, appear as a loss in trophic efficiency. In addition, when one considers a specific or selected part of a trophic level, such as a population of fish of use to man, the consumption of food by any other hidden members of the same trophic level will appear as a loss in efficiency. For example, the role of such animals as salps, medusae, and ctenophores in marine food chains is not well understood and is seldom even considered. Yet these animals may occur sporadically or periodically in swarms so dense that they dominate the plankton completely. Whether they represent a dead end or side branch in the normal food chain of the sea is not known, but the effect can hardly be negligible when they occur in abundance.

Finally, a further loss which may occur at any trophic level but is, again, of unknown or unpredictable magnitude is that of dissolved organic matter lost through excretion or other physiological processes by plants and animals. This has received particular attention at the level of primary production, some investigators concluding that 50 percent or more of the photoassimilated carbon may be released by phytoplankton into the water as dissolved compounds (30). There appears to be general agreement that the loss of dissolved organic matter is indirectly proportional to the absolute rate of organic production and is therefore most serious in the oligotrophic regions of the open sea (11, 13).

All of the various factors discussed above will affect the efficiency or apparent efficiency of the transfer of organic matter between trophic levels. Since they cannot, in most cases, be quantitatively estimated individually, their total effect cannot be assessed. It is known only that the maximum potential growth efficiency is about 30 percent and that at least some of the factors which reduce this further are more pronounced in oligotrophic, low-productivity waters than in highly productive situations. Slobodkin (29) concludes that an ecological efficiency of about 10 percent is possible, and Schaeffer feels that the figure may be as high as 20 percent. Here, therefore, I assign efficiencies of 10, 15, and 20 percent, respectively, to the oceanic, the coastal, and the upwelling provinces, though it is quite possible that the actual values are considerably lower.

CONCLUSIONS AND DISCUSSION

With values assigned to the three marine provinces for primary productivity (Table 2), number of trophic levels, and efficiencies, it is now possible to calculate fish production in the three regions. The results are summarized in Table 3.

These calculations reveal several interesting features. The open sea—90 percent of the ocean and nearly three-fourths of the earth's surface—is essentially a biological desert. It produces a negligible fraction of the world's fish catch at present and has little or no potential for yielding more in the future.

Upwelling regions, totaling no more than about one-tenth of 1 percent of the ocean surface (an area roughly the size of California) produce about half the world's fish supply. The other half is produced in coastal waters and the few offshore regions of comparably high fertility.

One of the major uncertainties and possible sources of error in the calculation is the estimation of the areas of high, intermediate, and low productivity. This is particularly true of the upwelling area off the continent of Antarctica,

an area which has never been well described or defined.

A figure of 360,000 square kilometers has been used for the total area of upwelling regions in the world (Table 2). If the upwelling regions off California, northwest and southwest Africa, and the Arabian Sea are of roughly the same area as that off the coast of Peru, these semitropical regions would total some 200,000 square kilometers. The remaining 160,000 square kilometers would represent about one-fourth the circumference of Antarctica seaward for a distance of 30 kilometers. This seems a not unreasonable inference. Certainly, the entire ocean south of the Antarctic Convergence is not highly productive, contrary to the estimates of El-Sayed (32). Extensive observations in this region by Saijo and Kawashima (33) yielded primary productivity values of 0.01 to 0.15 gram of carbon per square meter per day—a value no higher than the values used here for the open sea. Presumably, the discrepancy is the result of highly irregular, discontinuous, or "patchy" distribution of biological activity. In other words, the occurrence of extremely high productivity associated with upwelling conditions appears to be confined, in the Antarctic, as elsewhere, to restricted areas close to shore.

An area of 160,000 square kilometers of upwelling conditions with an annual productivity of 300 grams of carbon per square meter would result in the production of about 50×10^6 tons of "fish," if we follow the ground rules established above in making the estimate. Presumably these "fish" would consist for the most part of the Antarctic krill, which feeds directly upon phytoplankton, as noted above, and which is known to be extremely abundant in Antarctic waters. There have been numerous attempts to estimate the annual production of

Table 3. ESTIMATED FISH PRODUCTION IN THE THREE OCEAN PROVINCES DEFINED IN TABLE 2

PROVINCE	PRIMARY PRODUCTION [TONS (ORGANIC CARBON)]	TROPHIC LEVELS	EFFICIENCY (%)	FISH PRODUCTION [TONS (FRESH WT.)]
Oceanic	16.3×10^9	5	10	16×10^5
Coastal	3.6×10^9	3	15	12×10^7
Upwelling	0.1×10^9	$1\frac{1}{2}$	20	12×10^7
Total				24×10^7

krill in the Antarctic, from the known number of whales at their peak of abundance and from various assumptions concerning their daily ration of krill. The evidence upon which such estimates are based is so tenuous that they are hardly worth discussing. It is interesting to note, however, that the more conservative of these estimates are rather close to figures derived independently by the method discussed here. For example, Moiseev (34) calculated krill production for 1967 to be 60.5×10^6 tons, while Kasahara (3) considered a range of 24 to 36×10^6 tons to be a minimal figure. I consider the figure 50×10^6 tons to be on the high side, as the estimated area of upwelling is probably generous, the average productivity value of 300 grams of carbon per square meter per year is high for a region where photosynthesis can occur during only half the year, and much of the primary production is probably diverted into smaller crustacean herbivores (35). Clearly, the Antarctic must receive much more intensive study before its productive capacity can be assessed with any accuracy.

In all, I estimate that some 240 million tons (fresh weight) of fish are produced annually in the sea. As this figure is rough and subject to numerous sources of error, it should not be considered significantly different from Schaeffer's (2) figure of 200 million tons.

Production, however, is not equivalent to potential harvest. In the first place, man must share the production with other top-level carnivores. It has been estimated, for example, that guano birds alone eat some 4 million tons of anchovies annually off the coast of Peru, while tunas, squid, sea lions, and other predators probably consume an equivalent amount (22, 36). This is nearly equal to the amount taken by man from this one highly productive fishery. In addition, man must take care to leave a large enough fraction of the annual production of fish to permit utilization of the resource at something close to its maximum sustainable yield, both to protect the fishery and to provide a sound economic basis for the industry.

When these various factors are taken into consideration, it seems unlikely that the potential sustained yield of fish to man is appreciably greater than 100 million tons. The total world fish landings for 1967 were just over 60 million tons (37), and this figure has been increasing at an average rate of about 8 percent per year for the past 25 years. It is clear that, while the

yield can be still further increased, the resource is not vast. At the present rate, the industry can continue to expand for no more than a decade.

Most of the existing fisheries of the world are probably incapable of contributing significantly to this expansion. Many are already overexploited, and most of the rest are utilized at or near their maximum sustainable yield. Evidence of fishing pressure is usually determined directly from fishery statistics, but it is of some interest, in connection with the present discussion, to compare landings with fish production as estimated by the methods developed in this article. I will make this comparison for two quite dissimilar fisheries, that of the continental shelf of the northwest Atlantic and that of the Peruvian coastal region.

According to Edwards (38), the continental shelf between Hudson Canyon and the southern end of the Nova Scotian shelf includes an area of 110,000 square miles (2.9×10^{11} square meters). From the information in Tables 2 and 3, it may be calculated that approximately 1 million tons of fish are produced annually in this region. Commercial landings from the same area were slightly in excess of 1 million tons per year for the 3-year period 1963 to 1965 before going into a decline. The decline has become more serious each year, until it is now proposed to regulate the landings of at least the more valuable species such as cod and haddock, now clearly overexploited.

The coastal upwelling associated with the Peru Coastal Current gives rise to the world's most productive fishery, an annual harvest of some 10^7 metric tons of anchovies. The maximum sustainable yield is estimated at, or slightly below, this figure (39), and the fishery is carefully regulated. As mentioned above, mortality from other causes (such as predation from guano birds, bonito, squid, and so on) probably accounts for an additional 10^7 tons. This prodigious fishery is concentrated in an area no larger than about 800×30 miles (36), or 6×10^{10} square meters. By the methods developed in this article, it is estimated that such an upwelling area can be expected to produce 2×10^7 tons of fish, almost precisely the commercial yield as now regulated plus the amount attributed to natural mortality.

These are but two of the many recognized examples of well-developed commercial fisheries now being utilized at or above their levels of maximum sustainable yield. Any appreciable continued increase in the world's fish landings must clearly come from unexploited species and, for the most part, from undeveloped new fishing areas. Much of the potential expansion must consist of new products from remote regions, such as the Antarctic krill, for which no harvesting technology and no market yet exist.

REFERENCES AND NOTES

1. H. W. Graham and R. L. Edwards, in *Fish and Nutrition* (Fishing News, London, 1962), pp. 3—8; W. K. Schmitt, *Ann. N.Y. Acad. Sci.* **118**, 645 (1965).
2. M. B. Schaeffer, *Trans. Amer. Fish. Soc.* **94**, 123 (1965).
3. H. Kasahara, in *Proceedings, 7th International Congress of Nutrition, Hamburg* (Pergamon, New York, 1966). vol. 4, p. 958.
4. W. M. Chapman, "Potential Resources of the Ocean" (Serial Publication 89—21, 89th Congress, first session, 1965) (Government Printing Office, Washington, D.C., 1965), pp. 132—156.
5. E. Steemann Nielsen and E. A. Jensen, *Galathea Report*, F. Bruun *et al.*, Eds. (Allen & Unwin, London, 1957), vol. 1, p.49.
6. E. Steemann Nielsen, *J. Cons. Cons. Perma. Int. Explor. Mer* **18**, 117 (1952).
7. O. I. Koblentz-Mishke, V. V. Volkovinsky, J. G. Kobanova, in *Scientific Exploration of the South Pacific*, W. Wooster, Ed. (National Academy of Sciences, Washington, D.C., in press).
8. J. H. Ryther, in *The Sea*, M. N. Hill, Ed. (Interscience, London, 1963), pp. 347—380.
9. H. W. Menard and S. M. Smith, *J. Geophys. Res.* **71**, 4305 (1966).
10. J. H. Ryther and D. W. Menzel, *Deep-Sea Res.* **12**, 199 (1965).
11. ———, E. M. Hulburt, C. J. Lorenzen, N. Corwin, "The Production and Utilization of Organic Matter in the Peru Coastal Current" (Texas A & M Univ. Press, College Station, in press).
12. C. D. McAllister, T. R. Parsons, J. D. H. Strickland, *J. Cons. Cons. Perma. Int. Explor. Mer* **25**, 240 (1960); G. C. Anderson, *Limnol. Oceanogr.* **10**, 477 (1965).
13. T. R. Parsons and R. J. Le Brasseur, in "Symposium Marine Food Chains, Aarhus (1968)."
14. E. Steemann Nielsen, *J. Cons. Cons. Perma. Int. Explor. Mer* **23**, 178 (1958).
15. J. R. Beers and G. L. Stewart, *J. Fish. Res. Board Can.* **24**, 2053 (1967).
16. M. Anraku and M. Omori, *Limnol. Oceanogr.* **8**, 116 (1963).
17. G. D. Grice and H. D. Hart, *Ecol. Monogr.* **32**, 287 (1962).
18. M. R. Reeve, in "Symposium Marine Food Chains, Aarhus (1968)."
19. Personal observation; T. J. Hart and R. I. Currie, *Discovery Rep.* **31**, 123 (1960).
20. K. R. Gaarder, *Report on the Scientific Results of the "Michael Sars" North Atlantic Deep-Sea Expedition 1910* (Univ. of Bergen, Bergen, Norway).
21. T. J. Hart, *Discovery Rep.* **21**, 261 (1942).
22. R. J. E. Sanchez, in *Proceedings, 18th Annual Session, Gulf and Caribbean Fisheries Institute, University of Miami Institute of Marine Science, 1966*, J. B. Higman, Ed. (Univ. of Miami Press, Coral Gables, Fla., 1966), pp. 84—93.
23. R. T. Barber and R. L. Haedrich, *Deep-Sea Res.* **16**, 415 (1952).
24. J. W. S. Marr, *Discovery Rep.* **32**, 34 (1962).
25. S. D. Gerkings, *Physiol. Zool.* **25**, 358 (1952).
26. B. Dawes, *J. Mar. Biol. Ass. U.K.* **17**, 102 (1930—31); *ibid.*, p. 877.
27. V. S. Ivlev, *Zool. Zh.* **18**, 303 (1939).
28. W. E. Ricker, *Ecology* **16**, 373 (1946).
29. L. B. Slobodkin, *Growth and Regulation of Animal Populations* (Holt, Rinehart & Winston, New York, 1961), chap. 12.
30. G. E. Fogg, C. Nalewajko, W. D. Watt, *Proc. Roy. Soc. Ser B Biol. Sci.* **162**, 517 (1965).
31. G. E. Fogg and W. D. Watt, *Mem. Inst. Ital. Idrobiol. Dott. Marco de Marshi Pallanza Italy* **18**, suppl., 165 (1965).
32. S. Z. El-Sayed, in *Biology of the Antarctic Seas III*, G. Llano and W. Schmitt, Eds. (American Geophysical Union, Washington, D.C., 1968), pp. 15—47.
33. Y. Saijo and T. Kawashima, *J. Oceanogr. Soc. Japan* **19**, 190 (1964).
34. P. A. Moiseev, paper presented at the 2nd Symposium on Antarctic Ecology, Cambridge, England, 1968.
35. T. L. Hopkins, unpublished manuscript.
36. W. S. Wooster and J. L. Reid, Jr., in *The Sea*, M. N. Hill, Ed. (Interscience, London, 1963), vol. 2, p. 253.
37. *FAO Yearb. Fish. Statistics* **25** (1967).
38. R. L. Edwards, *Univ. Wash. Publ. Fish.* **4**, 52 (1968).
39. R. J. E. Sanchez, in *Proceedings, 18th Annual Session, Gulf and Caribbean Fisheries Institute, University of Miami Institute of Marine Science* (Univ. of Miami Press, Coral Cables, 1966), p. 84.
40. The work discussed here was supported by the Atomic Energy Commission, contract No. AT(30-1)-3862, Ref. No. NYO-3862-26. This article is contribution No. 2327 from the Woods Hole Oceanographic Institution.

Selection 32

Outlook for Conventional Agriculture

Commentary

The resources of the sea, if properly managed, will supply a fraction of the world's needs; our major source of food will be land-based agriculture. The ability of the world's conventional agriculture to meet the nutritional needs of the world's population is discussed by Lester Brown in this selection.

The ability of agriculture to meet the food demands of the future is tied closely to the size of the population drawing on it. At present the developed nations of the world possess adequate and even an abundance of food, yet, paradoxically, even in these countries, including the United States, hunger exists in the midst of plenty.

But two-thirds of the world's people, those of Asia, with the exception of Japan and Israel, all of Africa, with the exception of the southern tip, and most of Central and South America live on nutritionally inadequate diets. Their caloric intake is about three-fourths that of the people of the developed nations. To balance the caloric difference would require an additional 10 pounds of grain for each person. To provide this for the underdeveloped nations (excluding those of communist world, where the food situation is not well known) would require some 25 million metric tons of grain or 10 percent of current agricultural production. Two-thirds of this would be needed in India, Pakistan, Indonesia, and Egypt. Forty-five percent would be needed for India alone. Although the food production in these countries is increasing at the rate of $\frac{1}{3}$ of 1 percent per year, food consumption because of population growth is increasing at the rate of 1 percent per year.

The gap in food production is made up by imports. Before World War II the underdeveloped countries of the world imported 2.3 million metric tons of grain annually. In the past few years these same nations have imported 30 million tons, one-fourth of which went to India.

Agricultural production can be increased in several ways. One is to increase production per acre. A second is to bring more land under cultivation. Both sound relatively easy but they are not. The best agricultural lands in the world are already under cultivation. Production on many of these lands can be increased by improved varieties of crops, by increased fertilization, and by the use of pesticides. But there is a limit to the expansion of production by such means, and in some places it probably has already been reached.

Economics, too, enters the picture. As production costs increase or as prices go down, farmers have no incentive to increase crop production, however desperate the need for food may be (see Selection 9 and commentary). Even in the affluent United States the demand for milk is strong, yet production is declining because of the price structure. A \$.50/hr labor return above investment is hardly an incentive to increase milk production, regardless of demand. The production of "miracle" rice and wheat in Asia is depressing grain prices in some underdeveloped countries, which in turn reduces the incentives for production, even though people may be starving in the streets.

Opening up new land for agriculture is possible only if it is economically sound to do so. In some parts of the world, agriculture is encroaching on marginal land. This land usually is the most easily eroded and better suited to production of timber, water, and wildlife. As this land is brought under cultivation, fewer natural areas necessary for ecological balance and diversity remain.

Associated with the ability of agriculture to feed the world is the ability and willingness of the world's peoples to modify their food habits. Cultural taboos and tastes limit foods that will be accepted by many people. Cattle and other livestock kept more as a measure of wealth than as a source of food destroy natural productivity of land in such places as Africa and displace wildlife. Inefficient agricultural practices that cannot economically be changed will not be changed because of cultural traditions, and serve to reduce productivity per acre. Increased use of pesticides and inorganic fertilizers, especially nitrogen (see Selection 28 and commentary), may introduce certain amounts of toxicity into the food being raised, just as mercury and DDT have done to aquatic food sources, and thus reduce the utilization of food produced. Increased urbanization and the concentration of consumers in cities away from food-producing areas create massive distribution problems that are not easily solved in underdeveloped nations. All these place serious limitations on the ability of agriculture to feed a rapidly expanding population.

The World Outlook for Conventional Agriculture

by Lester R. Brown

The problem of obtaining enough food has plagued man since his beginnings. Despite the innumerable scientific advances of the 20th century, the problem becomes increasingly serious. Accelerating rates of population growth, on the one hand, and the continuing reduction in the area of new land that can be put under the plow, on the other, are postponing a satisfactory solution to this problem for at least another decade and perhaps much longer.

Conventional agriculture now provides an adequate and assured supply of food for one-third of the human race. But assuring an adequate supply of food for the remaining two-thirds, in parts of the world where population is increasing at the rate of 1 million weekly, poses one of the most nearly insoluble problems confronting man.

DIMENSIONS OF THE PROBLEM

Two major forces are responsible for expanding food needs: population growth and rising per capita incomes.

Populations in many developing countries are increasing at the rate of 3 percent or more per year. In some instances the rate of increase appears to be approaching the biological maximum. Populations growing by 3 percent per year double within a generation and multiply 18-fold in a century.

According to projections, world population, now just over 3 billion, will increase by another 3 billion over the remaining one-third of this century (Fig. 1). Even with the most optimistic assumptions concerning the effect of newly initiated family-planning programs in developing countries, we must still plan to feed an additional 1 billion people by 1980. The world has never before added 1 billion people in 15 years. More significantly, four-fifths of these

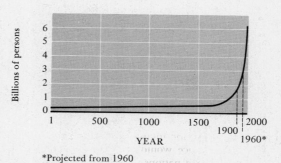

*Projected from 1960

Figure 1. Twenty centuries of world population growth. [U.S. Department of Agriculture]

will be added to the less-developed countries, where food is already in short supply.

Rising income levels throughout the world are generating additional demand on the world's food-producing resources. Virtually every country in the world today has plans for raising income levels among its people. In some of the more advanced countries the rise in incomes generates far more demand for food than the growth of population does.

Japan illustrates this well. There, population is increasing by only 1 percent per year but per capita incomes are rising by 7 percent per year. Most of the rapid increase in the demand for food now being experienced in Japan is due to rising incomes. The same may be true for several countries in western Europe, such as West Germany and Italy, where population growth is slow and economic growth is rapid.

Comparisons between population growth and increases in food production, seemingly in vogue today, often completely ignore the effect of rapidly rising incomes, in some instances an even more important demand-creating force than population growth.

THIS SELECTION is reprinted with permission of the author and publisher from *Science*, Vol. 158, pp. 604–611, November 1967. Copyright 1967 by the American Association for the Advancement of Science.

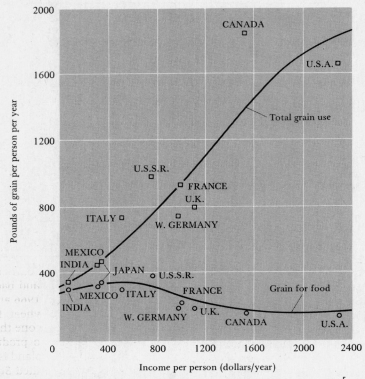

Figure 2. Income and per-capita grain consumption, total and for food (data for 1959–1961). [U.S. Department of Agriculture]

The relationships between increases in per capita income and the consumption of grain are illustrated in Fig. 2. The direct consumption of grain, as food, rises with income per person throughout the low-income brackets; at higher incomes it declines, eventually leveling off at about 150 pounds per year.

The more significant relationship, however, is that between total grain use and income. Historically, as incomes have risen, the use of grain, both that consumed directly and that consumed indirectly in the form of meat, milk, and eggs, has risen also. The upper curve in Fig. 2 indicates that every $2 gain in annual per capita income requires one pound of additional grain.

The rapid increases in both population and income are recent phenomena, in historical terms. Both have occurred since the war, and both are gaining momentum on a worldwide scale.

The effect of the resulting explosive increase in the demand for food is greater pressure on the world's food supplies. . . .

Meeting future food needs will require immense increases in output. The expected increase of 1 billion in world population over the next 15 years will require expansion of world grain production, now totaling about 1 billion tons, by about one-third, or 335 million tons. Additional demand generated by rising per capita incomes, even if only half as large as the population-generated component, could push the total needed increase toward 500 million tons.

What are the prospects of meeting these future increases in world food needs through conventional agriculture? There are two methods of increasing food production: expanding the cultivated area or raising the productivity (output per unit) of land already under cultivation. Throughout most of history, increases in food production have come largely from expanding the area under cultivation. Only quite recently, in historical terms, have some regions begun to rely on raising output per acre for most of the increases in their food supply (1).

Over the past 30 years, all of the increases in

agriculture production in North America and western Europe have come from raising the productivity of land. Food output has about doubled in both regions, while the area cultivated has actually declined somewhat. Available technology has made it more profitable to raise output per acre than to increase the area under cultivation.

EXPANDING THE CROPLAND AREA

The world's present cultivated land area totals some 3 billion acres (1.2 billion hectares). Estimates of the possibilities for expanding this area vary from a few hundred million acres to several billion. However, any such estimate of the area of new land likely to be brought under cultivation must, to be meaningful, specify at what cost this is to be accomplished.

Some land which was farmed a few decades ago has now been abandoned because it is no longer profitable. Much of the abandoned farmland in New England and Appalachia in the United States, or in other countries, such as portions of the Anatolian Plateau in Turkey, falls into this category.

In several countries of the world the area of cultivated land is actually declining. Japan, where the area of cultivated land reached a peak in 1920 and has declined substantially since, is a prominent example. Other countries in this category are Ireland, Sweden, and Switzerland.

Most of the world's larger countries are finding it difficult to further expand the area under cultivation. India plans to expand the cultivated-land area by less than 2 percent over its Fourth Plan period, from 1966 to 1971; yet the demand for food is expected to expand by some 20 percent over this 5-year span. Mainland China, which has been suffering from severe population pressure for several decades, has plowed nearly all of its readily cultivable land.

Most of the countries in the Middle East and North Africa, which depend on irrigation or on dry-land farming, cannot significantly expand the area under cultivation without developing new sources of water for irrigation. The Soviet Union is reportedly abandoning some of the land brought under cultivation during the expansion into the "virgin-lands" area in the late 1950s.

The only two major regions where there are prospects for further significant expansion of the cultivated area in the near future are sub-Saharan Africa and the Amazon Basin of Brazil. Any substantial expansion in these two areas awaits further improvements in our ability to manage tropical soils—to maintain their fertility once the lush natural vegetation is removed.

Aside from this possibility, no further opportunities are likely to arise until the cost of desalinization is reduced to the point where it is profitable to use seawater for large-scale irrigation. This will probably not occur before the late 1970s or early 1980s at best.

The only country in the world which in recent years has had a ready reserve of idled cropland has been the United States. As recently as 1966, some 50 million acres were idled, as compared with a harvested acreage of 300 million acres. The growing need for imported food and feed in western Europe, the Communist countries, Japan, and particularly India is bringing much of this land back into production. Decisions made in 1966 and early 1967 to expand the acreage of wheat, feed grains, and soybeans brought some one-third of the idled U.S. cropland back into production in 1967.

Even while idled cropland is being returned to production in the United States and efforts are being made to expand the area of cultivated land in other parts of the world, farmland is being lost because of expanding urban areas, the construction of highways, and other developments. On balance, it appears that increases in world food production over the next 15 years or so will, because of technical and economic factors, depend heavily on our ability to raise the productivity of land already under cultivation.

INCREASING LAND PRODUCTIVITY

Crop yield per acre in much of the world has changed little over the centuries. Rates of increase in output per acre have, in historical terms, been so low as to be scarcely perceptible within any given generation. Only quite recently—that is, during the 20th century—have certain countries succeeded in achieving rapid, continuing increases in output per acre—a yield "takeoff." Most of the economically advanced countries—particularly those in North America, western Europe, and Japan—have achieved this yield-per-acre takeoff (2).

The first yield-per-acre takeoff, at least the first documented by available data, occurred for

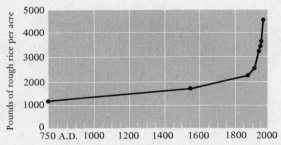

Figure 3. Rice yields in Japan from A.D. 750 to 1960. Historical estimates from Japanese ministry of agriculture. [U.S. Department of Agriculture]

rice in Japan during the early years of this century (see Fig. 3). Yield takeoffs occurred at about the same time, or shortly thereafter, in several countries in northwestern Europe, such as Denmark, the Netherlands, and Sweden. Several other countries, such as the United Kingdom and the United States, achieved yield-per-acre takeoffs in the late 1930s and early 1940s (Fig. 4).

Increasing food output per acre of land requires either a change in cultural practices or an increase in inputs, or both. Nearly all increases in inputs or improvements in cultural practices involve the use of more capitals (3). Many (mechanization itself is an exception) require more labor as well (4).

A review of the yield trends shown in Figs. 3 and 4, or of any of several others for the agriculturally advanced countries, raises the obvious question of how long upward trends may be expected to continue. Will there come a time when the rate of increase will slow down or cease altogether? Hopefully, technological considerations, resulting from new research breakthroughs, will continue to postpone that date.

Differing Sources of Productivity. One way of evaluating future prospects for continuing expansion in yields is to divide the known sources of increased productivity into two broad categories: "nonrecurring" and "recurring" sources of increased productivity (5). Nonrecurring inputs are essentially of a one-shot nature; once they are fully adopted, further increases in yields are limited. Recurring inputs, even when fully adopted, offer further annual increases in output through more intensive application.

Corn provides a good illustration. Yields have expanded sharply in the United States (see Fig. 4). Total production now exceeds 100 million tons of grain annually, or about half the total U.S. grain crop. Much of the increase in corn yields, however, was due to two nonrecurring sources of productivity: the replacement of open-pollinated or traditional varieties with hybrids and, to a lesser extent, the use of herbicides.

Hybrid corn has replaced open-pollinated varieties on more than 97 percent of the corn acreage in the United States (see Fig. 5). Further improvements in hybrid varieties are to

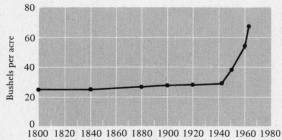

Figure 4. Corn yields in the United States. [U.S. Department of Agriculture]

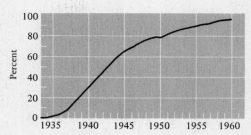

Figure 5. Share of U.S. corn acreage planted with hybrid seed. [U.S. Department of Agriculture]

be expected. (Hybrids in use today are superior to hybrids developed in the mid-1930s.) The big spurt in yields, however, is usually associated with the initial transition from open-pollinated or traditional varieties to hybrids. Consequently, the big thrust in corn yields in the United States resulting from the adoption of hybrids is probably a thing of the past. Likewise, once herbicides are widely used and virtually all weeds are controlled, there is little, if any, prospect of future gains in productivity from this source.

Some sources of increased yields are of a recurring nature. Among these, there is still ample opportunity for further yield increases as a result of the use of additional fertilizer. As plant populations increase, provided moisture is not a limiting factor, corn yields will rise further as more fertilizer is used.

Just how far the yield increase will go in the United States, however, is not clear. Paul Mangelsdorf of Harvard University, speaking recently at the National Academy of Sciences, asked this vital question (6):

> With more than 95 percent of the corn acreage already planted to hybrid corn, with the genetic potentials of the hybrids having reached a pla-

teau, with 87 percent of the acreage in the Corn Belt and Lake States already using fertilizer, and with many farmers already employing herbicides, from where will come the future improvements that will allow us to continue our present rate of improvement?

The same question may be asked of other crops in some of the other agriculturally advanced countries.

The S-Shaped Yield Curve. As the nonrecurring sources of productivity are exhausted, the sources of increased productivity are reduced until eventually the rate of increase in yield per acre begins to slow. This might be depicted by that familiar biologic function the S-shaped growth curve (Fig. 6). John R. Platt of the University of Chicago recently explained the curve this way (7):

> Many of our important indices of technical achievement have been shooting up exponentially for many years, very much like the numbers in the biologists' colonies of bacteria, that double in every generation as each cell divides into two again. But such a curve of growth obviously cannot continue indefinitely in any field. The growth

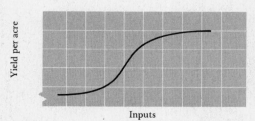

Inputs

Figure 6. S-shaped yield curve (schematic representation). [U.S. Department of Agriculture]

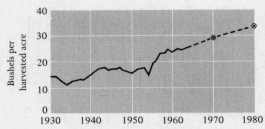

Figure 7. Wheat yields in the United States, with projections. Plotted as a 3-year sliding average. [U.S. Department of Agriculture]

of the bacterial colony slows up as it begins to exhaust its nutrient. The exponential curve bends over and flattens out into the more general "S-curve" or "logistic curve" of growth.

We do not know with any certainty when the rate of yield increase for the major food crops on which man depends for sustenance will begin to slow, but we do know that ultimately it will.

The key questions are: Is the slowdown near for some of the major food crops in some of the agriculturally advanced countries? Will the slowdown come gradually, or will it occur abruptly and with little warning? Finally, to what extent can the level at which the final turn of the S-shaped yield curve occurs be influenced? Can the level be raised by increasing the prices received by farmers, by adopting technological innovations, and by stepping up investment in crop research?

Most of those countries which have achieved takeoffs in yield per acre are continuing to raise yields at a rapid rate. But there are indications that the rate of gain may be slowing for some crops in some of the more agriculturally advanced countries.

Projected per-acre yield levels for the major grains in the United States show a substantial slowing of the rate of yield increase over the next 15 years as compared with the last 15. The rate of yield increase for wheat, averaging 3.5 percent yearly from 1950 to 1965, is projected to drop to less than 2 percent per year between 1965 and 1980 (Fig. 7). Sorghum yields, recently increasing at a rate of nearly 6 percent annually, are projected to increase at just over 2 percent per year between now and 1980 (Fig. 8). For corn, the projected slowdown is less dramatic, with yield increases dropping from about 4 percent to 3 percent. Per-acre yields of wheat and grain sorghum have apparently achieved their more rapid gains as the use of nonrecurring technologies becomes almost universal. In Platt's words (7), they may already be "past the middle of the S-curve."

The rate of increase could also be slowing down for certain crops elsewhere in the world.

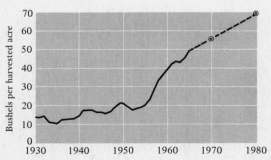

Figure 8. Grain sorghum yields in the United States, with projections. Plotted as a 3-year sliding average. [U.S. Department of Agriculture]

Rice yields in Japan may be a case in point. Yields were relatively static before 1900 but began to rise steadily shortly after the turn of the century. This rise continued until about 1959 (except for a brief period around World War II, and a period from 1949 to 1953, when production was disrupted by land reform). Since 1959, U.S. Department of Agriculture estimates (*8*) indicate, the rate of increase has slowed appreciably and, in fact, has recently nearly leveled off (Fig. 9). Whether or not this is a temporary plateau or a more permanent one remains to be seen. Interestingly, projections of per-acre rice yields made by the Japanese Institute of Agricultural Economic Research, using a 1958—1960 base period (*9*), did not anticipate the recent slowdown in the rate of increase in rice yields.

This recent leveling off of yields, however, may be caused by economic as well as technological factors. One key factor contributing to the very high yields obtained in Japan has been the intensive use of what was once low-cost labor. In recent years there has been a withdrawal of labor from rice production as rural workers have found more remunerative urban jobs. If economic development continues, it is unlikely that recent trends in labor costs will ever be reversed. Thus, it may well be that per-acre rice yields in Japan are approaching what is, in the immediately foreseeable future at least, a plateau.

A slowdown in the rate of yield increase seems also to be occurring for some of the grain crops in the Netherlands. This is not particularly surprising since yields there are already among the highest in the world. Further yield responses of some grains to the use of additional inputs, such as fertilizer, now seem limited by genetic constraints—the inherent ability of the plant to effectively use additional plant nutrients.

There are, on the other hand, some crops in the agriculturally developed countries which have not yet begun their upward advance on the growth curve. One of the major U.S. crops, the soybean, has thus far stubbornly resisted efforts to generate a yield-per-acre takeoff (*10*). The combination of near-static yields, on the one hand, and the very rapid growth in demand for soybeans, on the other, means that the necessary increases in the soybean supply are obtainable only through a rapid continuing expansion in the area planted to soybeans—an expansion which is steadily reducing the area available for other crops.

During the two decades since World War II, projections of increases in per-acre yields in the United States have invariably underestimated the increases actually achieved. This may be due in part to the yield-raising effect of idling large areas of marginal cropland during this period. There is now a risk that our faith in technology will cause us to overestimate future increases in yields if, in fact, the rate of yield increase ultimately slows as the sources of further gains in productivity diminish.

It is significant that the major sources of increased agricultural productivity—the use of chemical fertilizer; the use of improved varieties, including hybrids; the use of pesticides and irrigation—have all been known for decades, if not longer. The key question now is: Are there any sources of increased productivity in existence or in the process of development comparable to the traditional ones listed above?

The concept of the S-shaped curve is not new, but its implications for future agricultural

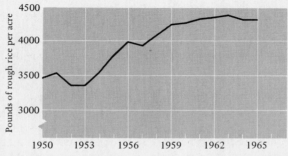

Figure 9. Rice yields in Japan, 1950—1965. Plotted as a 3-year sliding average. [U.S. Department of Agriculture]

375

production have not been fully explored. Although the S-shaped yield curve for crops is, at this point, still an untested hypothesis, it is, in Platt's words (7), "at least as plausible as the uncritical assumption that changes like those of the twentieth-century will go on forever."

Photosynthetic Efficiency and Research. The ultimate factor limiting crop output per acre is the crop's photosynthetic efficiency (*11*). Defined as the percentage of solar energy used relative to that which is available on a given area occupied by a particular crop, photosynthetic efficiency is always quite low, usually less than 3 percent. Density of plant population, actual position of the leaves on the plant, and temperature are key factors accounting for variations within this range.

In 1962, James Bonner of the California Institute of Technology stated (*11*):

> . . . the upper limit of crop yield, as determined by the factors that regulate photosynthetic efficiency, is already being approached today in those regions with the highest level of agricultural practice—in parts of Japan, of Western Europe, and of the United States.

Obviously, research into ways of increasing the upper limit of yield is needed. This increase could be achieved by developing plants which have greater photosynthetic efficiency or by improving present cultural practices so as to increase efficiency per acre, or by both means. The development of smaller and more efficient corn plants, along with reduction in the need for cultivation during the growing season, makes it possible to reduce the width between corn rows—a width that was initially determined by the width of a horse, in the age of the horse-drawn cultivator. The result is a dramatic gain in the number of corn plants per acre, and increased output.

More productive hybrid wheats have been developed, but they are still in the experimental stage and are not yet being grown commercially. Work on breeding new varieties with higher nutritive value—a potentially promising activity—is also under way. The adoption of a new technology takes time, even in an agriculturally advanced country. It took a quarter of a century for U.S. farmers to adopt hybrid corn (see Fig. 5). Hybrid grain sorghum, introduced

in the early 1950s, required about a decade to become widely disseminated.

Both corn and wheat have been the subject of many years of research in the United States and other developed nations. Much less work has been done in rice. To help rectify this situation, the Rockefeller and Ford foundations established the International Rice Institute in the Philippines several years ago. The Institute devotes its efforts not only to the development of new varieties but to the whole range of cultural practices as well.

The need for such research is further emphasized by a recent statement by Harvey Brooks, chairman of the Committee on Science and Public Policy of the National Academy of Sciences (*12*):

> Future food production, even for domestic purposes, will be strongly dependent on the quality and direction of both the basic and applied research undertaken within the next few years. Most of the potential of past basic research has already been realized, and new knowledge will be needed even to maintain present levels of productivity.

Clearly, much more research is essential if we are to (i) get the underdeveloped nations to the yield takeoff point, and (ii) maintain the upward thrust of yields in the developed countries by postponing the final turn on the S-shaped curve (*13*).

RESEARCH AND REALITY

Two groups of factors should be kept in mind in evaluating the real potential of research results for significantly increasing food output on a worldwide basis. The first group centers about the pronounced variations in natural resources and managerial abilities, which can lead to wide differences between record yields and average national yields obtained by individual farmers under localized conditions. The second group concerns the matter of costs and returns, which spells the difference between technical potential and economic reality.

Record Yields Versus Average Yields. It is often assumed that record yields attained on experimental plots can be easily and quickly translated into national average yields. Such is not, however, the case. Maximum yields obtained on experimental plots under closely controlled conditions usually far exceed those generally obtained in practice. Average yields of wheat in this country, for example, are far below those attained on experimental plots during the latter part of the last century. The same is true for many other crops.

Equally common and equally unwarranted is the assumption that all countries will eventually attain the average yield prevailing in the nation which now has the highest yield. Potential yield levels attainable by individual countries vary widely with variations in rainfall, temperature, soil types and topography, production costs, managerial abilities of farmers, and other factors.

Wheat yields in the United Kingdom now average about 60 bushels per acre (52 hecto-liters per hectare) as contrasted with only 18 bushels per acre in Australia. This does not mean that wheat-production technology is less advanced in Australia than in the United Kingdom. The yield differences do reflect the difference between growing conditions in Australia, where rainfall in the wheat-growing regions averages 12 to 15 inches (30 to 38 centimeters) annually, and those in the United Kingdom, where rainfall may average 40 to 50 inches. Although wheat yields in both the United Kingdom and Australia may continue to rise, there is no reason to assume that the differences in yields between the two countries will narrow appreciably in the foreseeable future.

The average national rice yield in Japan is nearly four times that in India. A large part of this difference is accounted for by a much greater volume of inputs, including labor as well as modern practices and management. Not to be overlooked, however, is the fact that virtually all of the rice crop produced in Japan is irrigated, whereas only part of India's rice crop is irrigated. A large share of India's rice fields are rainfed, thus the yield levels attained depend greatly on the vagaries of the monsoon.

There are also very wide variations in yield within individual countries. Variations in corn yields within various corn-producing states in the United States are almost as pronounced as variations in corn yields between the various corn-producing countries of the world. Average yields in principal U.S. corn-producing states in 1965, for instance, varied from more than 90 bushels per acre in some states in the Midwest

to less than 40 bushels in some states in the southern Mississippi Valley.

It is significant that the leveling off of rice yields in Japan has occurred at a time when average rice yields in the more productive and the less productive prefectures vary widely. Some individual villages in Japan obtain rice yields at least double the national average.

Per-acre yields obtained by individual farmers in the same area may vary even more than do those for various states or prefectures. It is often assumed that the performance of the best farmers can be emulated by all. There are and will continue to be some very basic differences in the innate capacities or motivations of farmers. There is no more reason for assuming that all farmers can or really want to attain a record yield of corn or wheat than to assume that all students can or want to become Harvard Phi Beta Kappas. The distribution of talent and motivation is probably at least as wide within the world's rural communities as in any other area.

Technical Potential Versus Economic Reality. The failure to distinguish between the technical potential for expanding food production and the economically profitable possibilities for doing so has resulted in confusing variations in estimates of future food production. The difference between estimates based on these two criteria is often very great. The earlier discussion of the experience in Japan—where rice yields seem to have leveled off in recent years—suggests the importance of economic relationships.

A recent reduction in milk production in the United States closely parallels the Japanese experience with rice yields. Through the early months of 1966, milk production in the United States was 3 to 5 percent below production in comparable months of the preceding year. At prevailing prices it was not profitable for dairy farmers to use some of the existing resources. During 1966, dairy farmers in New York State received scarcely 40 cents an hour for their labor (when allowance is made for interest on their investment), and farmers in Wisconsin received only 50 cents an hour. At a time when slaughter prices were high and there were many job opportunities to choose from—with a 5-day, 40-hour week in industry and a minimum wage of $1.25 per hour (*14*)—it comes as no surprise to learn that many dairy farmers liquidated their holdings and took other jobs. In order to help increase returns to farmers and expand milk production, the Department of Agriculture raised milk support prices twice during 1966, for a total increase of 23 percent.

Both prices received by farmers and costs of production must be taken into consideration in assessing potential increases in production. As farmers move up the per-acre yield curve, the point of diminishing returns is eventually reached. Additional costs begin to exceed additional returns. Thus it is unrealistic to expect farmers to produce up to the full technical potential.

Therefore, while many farmers can produce much more under a given technology, it is sometimes uneconomic, at existing prices and costs, for them to do so. If society is willing to pay higher prices—and it may have to some day—much greater production may be expected.

CONCLUSIONS

1) The worldwide demand for food will continue to be strong in the coming decades. Two forces—rapidly growing population and, in much of the world, rapidly rising incomes—are expected to result in increases in the demand for food even more rapid than those that have occurred during the past.

2) Conventional agriculture has assured an adequate food supply for the economically advanced one-third of the world. The challenge now is to assure an adequate food supply for the remaining two-thirds, where population is now increasing at the rate of 1 million people per week and where malnutrition is already widespread.

3) Economically feasible prospects for significantly expanding the world's area of cultivated land in the 1960s and 1970s are limited and largely confined to sub-Saharan Africa and the Amazon Basin. Even here, agronomic problems will limit the rate of expansion. When the cost of desalting seawater is substantially reduced—probably not before the late 1970s or early 1980s at best—it may become feasible to irrigate large areas of desert.

4) Given the limited possibilities for expanding the area of land under cultivation, most of the increases in world food needs must be met, for the foreseeable future, by raising the productivity of land already under cultivation. Food output per acre, rather static throughout most of history, has begun to increase rapidly in some of the more advanced countries in recent decades. All of the increases in food production over the past quarter century in North America, western Europe, and Japan have come from increasing the productivity of land already under cultivation. The area under cultivation has actually declined.

5) Achieving dramatic gains in land productivity requires a massive investment of capital and the widespread adoption of new technology. A similar effort must now be made in the less-developed nations if these nations are to feed their people. The most important single factor influencing this rate of investment is food prices, more particularly the relationship between the price farmers receive for their food products and the cost of modern inputs such as fertilizer.

6) In some of the more-developed countries where per-acre yields have been rising for a long time, there is now evidence that the rate of yield increase may be slowing. Nonrecurring inputs may have made their maximum contribution to output in the case of some crops, pushing yield levels past the middle of the S-shaped logistic curve. Although this cannot be determined with any certainty, the possibility that the middle of the curve has been passed in some instances should be taken into account in viewing the long-term future.

7) If the rate of increase in yield per acre does in fact begin to slow in some of the agriculturally advanced countries, additional pressure will be put on the less-developed countries—which have much of the world's unrealized food-production potential—to meet the continuing future increases in world food needs.

8) Man has not yet been able to bypass the process of photosynthesis in the production of food. This dependence on photosynthesis plays a significant role in determining the upper levels of the S-shaped yield curve. Additional research is urgently needed to increase the photosynthetic efficiency of crops and to raise the upper levels of economically feasible yields.

REFERENCES AND NOTES

1. I have previously examined these matters in some detail in "Man, Land and Food," *U.S. Dept. Agr. Foreign Agr. Econ. Rep. No. 11* (1963).

2. I have discussed this concept at length in "Increasing World Food Output," *U.S. Dept. Agr. Foreign Agr. Econ. Rep. No. 25* (1965).

3. For further discussion of this point, and the role that may be played by private industry, see L. R. Brown, *Columbia J. World Business* **2**, No. 1, 15 (1967).

4. As one leading agricultural economist recently stated, there is considerable evidence that in most low-income countries "technological advance requires a complementary input of labor" [J. Mellor. *The Economics of Agricultural Development* (Cornell Univ. Press, Ithaca, N.Y., 1966), p. 157].

5. The "nonrecurring" concept was introduced by Paul C. Mangelsdorf (see 6).

6. P. C. Mangelsdorf. *Proc. Nat. Acad. Sci. U.S.* **56**, 370 (1966).

7. J. R. Platt, *The Road to Man* (Wiley, New York, 1966) [originally published in *Science* **149**, 607 (1965)].

8. Estimates published by the Food and Agriculture Organization show a continued increase in rice yields up until 1963—64, followed by successive declines in each of the three following seasons; see annual issues of *Production Yearbook* (Rome) and *Monthly Bull. Agr. Economics Statistics* **15**, No. 12, 26 (1966).

9 *Japanese Import Requirement: Projections of Agricultural Supply and Demand for 1965, 1970 and 1975* (Institute of Agricultural Economic Research, University of Tokyo, 1964), p. 84.

10. Soybeans cannot be commercially hybridized and show only limited response to nitrogen: see *The World Food Problem* (Government Printing Office, Washington, D.C., 1967), vol. 2, p. 197.

11. J. Bonner, Science **137**, 11 (1962).

12. *The Plant Sciences Now and in the Coming Decade* (National Academy of Sciences, Washington, D.C., 1966), p. iv.

13. A detailed discussion of the technical problems and issues faced in intensifying plant production in the developing nations is presented in *The World Food Problem* (Superintendent of Documents, Government Printing Office, Washington, D.C., 1967), pp. 215—233.

14. The minimum wage was recently raised to $1.40 per hour.

15. I am indebted to Dana G. Dalrymple of the U.S. Department of Agriculture for his suggestions and assistance.

Selection 33

Tragedy of the Commons

Commentary

The world, Garrett Hardin points out in this selection, is rapidly facing the problem of the commons. At one time in the development of agriculture, each community had its commons, grazing land open to all. As one could predict, each herdsman ran as many cattle or sheep on the grazing land as possible, because each additional unit accrued more wealth for him. Each pursued his own short-range interest, regardless of its effect on himself or his fellow herdmen. Eventually the number of animals utilizing the commons was much greater than the resource of the commons could support. The economy of the herdsman collapsed and the commons as a functioning, productive ecosystem was impaired, if not destroyed. The commons ended with enclosure; grazing was restricted to a few.

The tragedy of the commons came about for many reasons. Inherent was the concept pointed out several decades ago by Aldo Leopold,[1] that land is a commodity. The herdsman of old and his modern-day counterparts—the agriculturalist, the industrialist, the real estate speculator, and society in general—view land and resources much the same way: no one has any interest in ensuring the future productivity of the resource. More important is short-term economics. How many head of cattle a herdsman might be able to put on the commons a decade hence was of no immediate importance. Is the tragedy of the commons also about to become the tragedy of the earth?

The problem cannot be solved by technology in which so many of us have an almost blinding and religious faith.[2] The solution is dependent upon an extension of a morality which involves "mutual coercion, mutually agreed upon by the majority of people affected," coupled with an administrative system possessing a sound basis for judgment and the power to force the coercion.

But in a companion selection, "The Tragedy of the Commons Revisited," Beryl Crowe argues that mutual coercion is not the solution, for the solution would simply be reduced to the establishment of administrative agencies, and who is to keep the administrative custodian honest? In the end the staffing of such regulatory agencies comes from the ranks of the regulated. This is already the situation in local, state, and national governments, not only in the United States but in other countries as well.

The whaling and fishing industry, discussed in the commentary to Selection 31, is an excellent example of the exploitation of the commons and proposed regulation in action. The high seas beyond all territorial limits are common fishing grounds. No one owns the resource; therefore it is available to all. No attempt is made to manage it on the basis of sound ecology. If the catch declines and the revenues fall, the solution is that of the herdsman—add another unit of production. More boats and newer technology are applied. There is no concern for the future, and exploitation continues until the productivity of the commons collapses. The tragedy of the commons is a real one on the high seas.

There are efforts at mutual coercion. An International Whaling Commission exists which attempts to impose quotas on the number of animals killed. In spite of the recognition by the major whaling nations that the resource is in danger and that the kill must be regulated, the countries can come to no agreement. The limitations finally imposed are much higher than the resource can sustain. The commons is still to be overgrazed.

Created in 1946, the International Whaling Commission supposedly was empowered to regulate the whale catch and ensure the conservation of the stock of the world's whales. But the Commission has no legal powers of enforcement. Although there may be hints of mutual coercion, there is no administrative organization strong enough to enforce it. And, except for the United States, the Commission has drawn its members from the ranks of the regulated, the whaling nations.

Similarly, there was established in Geneva in 1958 a Convention on Fishing and Conservation of the Living Resources of the High Seas, which is to provide a framework within which the world's fisheries might be managed. It spells out in detail the methods by which conservation regulations on the high seas are to be established and the means for handling disputes. But the Convention has not yet begun to function.

The success of the Whaling Commission and the Convention on Fishing, in spite of all regulatory devices

---

[1] Aldo Leopold, "The Conservation Ethic," *J. Forestry* **31**, 1933, pp. 634–643.
[2] Lewis Mumford, *The Myth of the Machine. The Pentagon of Power*, New York, Harcourt Brace Jovanovich, 1970.

and mutual coercion, will depend upon ethics, "the fundamental extension of morality." This is obviously not being achieved, and Beryl Crowe writes that he is "very suspicious of success of either demands or pleas for fundamental extensions in morality." Yet this appears to be the only ultimate solution.

The ethical consideration was suggested by Aldo Leopold as an ecological ethic that places a "limitation on the freedom of action in the struggle for existence." He wrote, "All ethics, so far evolved rest on the single premise that the individual is a member of a community of interdependent parts." Within the context of the spaceship earth these interdependent parts make up the global ecosystem.

Writing at the time only of man's relation to the land, Leopold noted that industrial landowners, stockmen, and lumbermen did not and would not develop voluntary practices of conservation on the land. They failed to develop a land ethic that reflected an "existence of an ecological conscience." Yet the ethical obligations on the part of landowners are the only visible remedy to the situation. The same idea can be expressed on a national and international level and can be applied not just to land but to ecosystems. Nations must develop an ethical obligation toward ecosystems, the commons.

Such ethical obligations will come about only when people of all nations develop some ethical relationship toward the environment. Leopold continues, "Perhaps the most serious obstacle impeding the evolution of a land ethic is the fact that our educational and economic system is headed away from rather than toward an intense consciousness of the land." We have "no vital relation to it." The word *ecosystem* can be substituted for *land*. Today the urban masses are so far removed from natural ecosystems upon which they depend that they have no real relationship to it.

Developing such an ecological conscience is difficult, although the groundwork for such an achievement can be found in the current concern for the environment. It is hard to develop an ecological consciousness in poor people or nations. Their concerns are on the present, not the future. Future benefits requiring current expenditures are inconceivable. As Kenneth Boulding writes:

> It is always hard to find a convincing answer to the man who says, "What has posterity ever done for me?" and the conservationist has always had to fall back on rather vague ethical principles postulating the identity of the individual with some human community or society which extends not only back into the past but forward into the future. Unless the individual identifies with some community of this kind, conservation is obviously "irrational."[3]

In spite of the current environmental concerns that seem to make the development of such a conscience possible, there are two anti-ecology movements, the business establishment on the right[4] and the radicals on the left.[5] Although businesses appear to be showing strong interest in ecology, they are for the most part doing so only because they are forced to. First comes their economic well-being, which still involves technological expansion regardless of the environment. On the other hand, the activists interpret the current interest in the environment as a "cop-out" to meet other social problems. They look upon conservation as "a diabolical master plot to preserve the status quo and the Corporate Capitalist Economy, which has duped the academicians, captured regulatory agencies and manipulated the grassroots."[6] Both fail to grasp the very concepts of ecology. They are so fixed on the human situation that they fail to understand the close relationship that exists between man and ecology. They fail to recognize that the continued prosperity of the establishment and the solution to social ills are ecological. The solution begins with the development of an ecological ethic. Once accepting such an ethic man might, as René Dubos puts it, "try to insert himself into the environment in such a manner that his technology and way of life relate him more intimately to nature. He might thereby become once more a part of nature instead of its uneasy overlord."[7]

[3] K. Boulding, "The Economics of the Coming Spaceship Earth," in H. Jarrett (ed.), *Environment Quality in a Growing Economy*, Baltimore, Md., Resources for the Future and Johns Hopkins Press, 1966, pp. 3—14.
[4] "The Environment—a National Mission for the Seventies," *Fortune Magazine*, February, 1970.
[5] Editors of *Ramparts* magazine, *Eco-Catastrophe*, San Fransisco, Calif., Canfield Press (a department of Harper & Row), 1970.
[6] P. Shepard, "Establishment and Radicals on the Environmental Crisis," *Ecology* **51**, 1970, pp. 941—942.
[7] René Dubos, "Uneasy Overlords Must Learn to Collaborate with Nature," *Catalyst*, Spring 1970, pp. 5—8.

The Tragedy of the Commons

by Garrett Hardin

At the end of a thoughtful article on the future of nuclear war, Wiesner and York (1) concluded that: "Both sides in the arms race are ... confronted by the dilemma of steadily increasing military power and steadily decreasing national security. *It is our considered professional judgment that this dilemma has no technical solution.* If the great powers continue to look for solutions in the area of science and technology only, the result will be to worsen the situation."

I would like to focus your attention not on the subject of the article (national security in a nuclear world) but on the kind of conclusion they reached, namely that there is no technical solution to the problem. An implicit and almost universal assumption of discussions published in professional and semipopular scientific journals is that the problem under discussion has a technical solution. A technical solution may be defined as one that requires a change only in the techniques of the natural sciences, demanding little or nothing in the way of change in human values or ideas of morality.

In our day (though not in earlier times) technical solutions are always welcome. Because of previous failures in prophecy, it takes courage to assert that a desired technical solution is not possible. Wiesner and York exhibited this courage; publishing in a science journal, they insisted that the solution to the problem was not to be found in the natural sciences. They cautiously qualified their statement with the phrase, "It is our considered professional judgment...." Whether they were right or not is not the concern of the present article. Rather, the concern here is with the important concept of a class of human problems which can be called "no technical solution problems," and, more specifically, with the identification and discussion of one of these.

It is easy to show that the class is not a null class. Recall the game of tick-tack-toe. Consider the problem, "How can I win the game of tick-tack-toe?" It is well known that I cannot, if I assume (in keeping with the conventions of game theory) that my opponent understands the game perfectly. Put another way, there is no "technical solution" to the problem. I can win only by giving a radical meaning to the word "win." I can hit my opponent over the head; or I can drug him; or I can falsify the records. Every way in which I "win" involves, in some sense, an abandonment of the game, as we intuitively understand it. (I can also, of course, openly abandon the game—refuse to play it. This is what most adults do.)

The class of "No technical solution problems" has members. My thesis is that the "population problem," as conventionally conceived, is a member of this class. How it is conventionally conceived needs some comment. It is fair to say that most people who anguish over the population problem are trying to find a way to avoid the evils of overpopulation without relinquishing any of the privileges they now enjoy. They think that farming the seas or developing new strains of wheat will solve the problem—technologically. I try to show here that the solution they seek cannot be found. The population problem cannot be solved in a technical way, any more than can the problem of winning the game of tick-tack-toe.

Population, as Malthus said, naturally tends to grow "geometrically," or, as we would now say, exponentially. In a finite world this means that the per capita share of the world's goods must steadily decrease. Is ours a finite world?

A fair defense can be put forward for the view that the world is infinite; or that we do not know that it is not. But, in terms of the practical problems that we must face in the next few generations with the foreseeable technology, it is clear that we will greatly increase human misery if we do not, during the immediate future, assume that the world available to the terrestrial human population is finite. "Space" is no escape (*2*).

A finite world can support only a finite population; therefore, population growth must eventually equal zero. (The case of perpetual wide fluctuations above and below zero is a trivial variant that need not be discussed.) When this condition is met, what will be the situation of mankind? Specifically, can Bentham's goal of "the greatest good for the greatest number" be realized?

No—for two reasons, each sufficient by itself. The first is a theoretical one. It is not mathematically possible to maximize for two (or more) variables at the same time. This was clearly stated by von Neumann and Morgenstern (*3*), but the principle is implicit in the theory of partial differential equations, dating back at least to D'Alembert (1717–1783).

The second reason springs directly from biological facts. To live, any organism must have a source of energy (for example, food). This energy is utilized for two purposes; mere maintenance and work. For man, maintenance of life requires about 1600 kilocalories a day ("maintenance calories"). Anything that he does over and above merely staying alive will be defined as work, and is supported by "work calories" which he takes in. Work calories are used not only for what we call work in common speech; they are also required for all forms of enjoyment, from swimming and automobile racing to playing music and writing poetry. If our goal is to maximize population it is obvious what we must do: We must make the work calories per person approach as close to zero as possible. No gourmet meals, no vacations, no sports, no music, no literature, no art. . . . I think that everyone will grant, without argument or proof, that maximizing population does not maximize goods. Bentham's goal is impossible.

In reaching this conclusion I have made the usual assumption that it is the acquisition of energy that is the problem. The appearance of atomic energy has led some to question this assumption. However, given an infinite source of energy, population growth still produces an inescapable problem. The problem of the acquisition of energy is replaced by the problem of

its dissipation, as J. H. Fremlin has so wittily shown (*4*). The arithmetic signs in the analysis are, as it were, reversed; but Bentham's goal is still unobtainable.

The optimum population is, then, less than the maximum. The difficulty of defining the optimum is enormous; so far as I know, no one has seriously tackled this problem. Reaching an acceptable and stable solution will surely require more than one generation of hard analytical work—and much persuasion.

We want the maximum good per person; but what is good? To one person it is wilderness, to another it is ski lodges for thousands. To one it is estuaries to nourish ducks for hunters to shoot; to another it is factory land. Comparing one good with another is, we usually say, impossible because goods are incommensurable. Incommensurables cannot be compared.

Theoretically this may be true; but in real life incommensurables *are* commensurable. Only a criterion of judgment and a system of weighting are needed. In nature the criterion is survival. Is it better for a species to be small band hideable, or large and powerful? Natural selection commensurates the incommensurables. The compromise achieved depends on a natural weighting of the values of the variables.

Man must imitate this process. There is no doubt that in fact he already does, but unconsciously. It is when the hidden decisions are made explicit that the arguments begin. The problem for the years ahead is to work out an acceptable theory of weighting. Synergistic effects, nonlinear variation, and difficulties in discounting the future make the intellectual problem difficult, but not (in principle) insoluble.

Has any cultural group solved this practical problem at the present time, even on an intuitive level? One simple fact proves that none has: there is no prosperous population in the world today that has, and has had for some time, a growth rate of zero. Any people that has intuitively identified its optimum point will soon reach it, after which its growth rate becomes and remains zero.

Of course, a positive growth rate might be taken as evidence that a population is below its optimum. However, by any reasonable standards, the most rapidly growing populations on earth today are (in general) the most miserable. This association (which need not be invariable) casts doubt on the optimistic assumption that the positive growth rate of a population is evidence that it has yet to reach its optimum.

We can make little progress in working toward optimum population size until we explicitly exercise the spirit of Adam Smith in the field of practical demography. In economic affairs, *The Wealth of Nations* (1776) popularized the "invisible hand," the idea that an individual who "intends only his own gain," is, as it were, "led by an invisible hand to promote . . . the public interest" (5). Adam Smith did not assert that this was invariably true, and perhaps neither did any of his followers. But he contributed to a dominant tendency of thought that has ever since interfered with positive action based on rational analysis, namely, the tendency to assume that decisions reached individually will, in fact, be the best decisions for an entire society. If this assumption is correct it justifies the continuance of our present policy of laissez-faire in reproduction. If it is correct we can assume that men will control their individual fecundity so as to produce the optimum population. If the assumption is not correct, we need to reexamine our individual freedoms to see which ones are defensible.

TRAGEDY OF FREEDOM IN A COMMONS

The rebuttal to the invisible hand in population control is to be found in a scenario first sketched in a little-known pamphlet (6) in 1833 by a mathematical amateur named William Forster Lloyd (1794—1852). We may well call it "the tragedy of the commons," using the word "tragedy" as the philosopher Whitehead used it (7): "The essence of dramatic tragedy is not unhappiness. It resides in the solemnity of the remorseless working of things." He then goes on to say, "This inevitableness of destiny can only be illustrated in terms of human life by incidents which in fact involve unhappiness. For it is only by them that the futility of escape can be made evident in the drama."

The tragedy of the commons develops in this way. Picture a pasture open to all. It is to be expected that each herdsman will try to keep as many cattle as possible on the commons. Such an arrangement may work reasonably satisfactorily for centuries because tribal wars, poaching, and disease keep the numbers of both man and beast well below the carrying capacity of the land. Finally, however, comes the day of reckoning, that is, the day when the long-desired goal of social stability becomes a reality. At this point, the inherent logic of the commons remorselessly generates tragedy.

As a rational being, each herdsman seeks to maximize his gain. Explicitly or implicitly, more or less consciously, he asks, "What is the utility *to me* of adding one more animal to my herd?" This utility has one negative and one positive component.

1) The positive component is a function of the increment of one animal. Since the herdsman receives all the proceeds from the sale of the additional animal, the positive utility is nearly +1.

2) The negative component is a function of the additional overgrazing created by one more animal. Since, however, the effects of overgrazing are shared by all the herdsmen, the negative utility for any particular decision-making herdsman is only a fraction of −1.

Adding together the component partial utilities, the rational herdsman concludes that the only sensible course for him to pursue is to add another animal to his herd. And another; and another. . . . But this is the conclusion reached by each and every rational herdsman sharing a commons. Therein is the tragedy. Each man is locked into a system that compels him to increase his herd without limit—in a world that is limited. Ruin is the destination toward which all men rush, each pursuing his own interest in a society that believes in the freedom of the commons. Freedom in a commons brings ruin to all.

Some would say that this is a platitude. Would that it were! In a sense, it was learned thousands of years ago, but natural selection favors the forces of psychological denial (8). The individual benefits as an individual from his ability to deny the truth even though society as a whole, of which he is a part, suffers. Education can counteract the natural tendency to do the wrong thing, but the inexorable succession of generations requires that the basis for this knowledge be constantly refreshed.

A simple incident that occurred a few years ago in Leominster, Massachusetts, shows how perishable the knowledge is. During the Christmas shopping season the parking meters downtown were covered with plastic bags that bore tags reading: "Do not open until after Christmas. Free parking courtesy of the mayor and city council." In other words, facing the prospect of an increased demand for already scarce space, the city fathers reinstituted the system of the commons. (Cynically, we suspect that they gained more votes than they lost by this retrogressive act.)

In an approximate way, the logic of the commons has been understood for a long time, perhaps since the discovery of agriculture or the invention of private property in real estate. But it is understood mostly only in special cases which are not sufficiently generalized. Even at this late date, cattlemen leasing national land on the western ranges demonstrate no more than an ambivalent understanding, in constantly pressuring federal authorities to increase the head count to the point where overgrazing produces erosion and weed-dominance. Likewise, the oceans of the world continue to suffer from the survival of the philosophy of the commons. Maritime nations still respond automatically to the shibboleth of the "freedom of the seas." Professing to believe in the "inexhaustible resources of the oceans," they bring species after species of fish and whales closer to extinction (9).

The National Parks present another instance of the working out of the tragedy of the commons. At present, they are open to all, without limit. The parks themselves are limited in extent—there is only one Yosemite Valley—whereas population seems to grow without limit. The values that visitors seek in the parks are steadily eroded. Plainly, we must soon cease to treat the parks as commons or they will be of no value to anyone.

What shall we do? We have several options. We might sell them off as private property. We might keep them as public property, but allocate the right to enter them. The allocation might be on the basis of wealth, by the use of an auction system. It might be on the basis of merit, as defined by some agreed-upon standards. It might be by lottery. Or it might be on a first-come, first-served basis, administered to long queues. These, I think, are all the reasonable possibilities. They are all objectionable. But we must choose—or acquiesce in the destruction of the commons that we call our National Parks.

POLLUTION

In a reverse way, the tragedy of the commons reappears in problems of pollution. Here it is not a question of taking something out of the commons, but of putting something in—sewage, or chemical, radioactive, and heat wastes into water; noxious and dangerous fumes into the air; and distracting and unpleasant advertising signs into the line of sight. The calculations of utility are much the same as before. The rational man finds that his share of the cost of the wastes he discharges into the commons is less than the cost of purifying his wastes before releasing them. Since this is true for everyone, we are locked into a system of "fouling our own nest," so long as we behave only as independent, rational, free-enterprisers.

The tragedy of the commons as a food basket is averted by private property, or something formally like it. But the air and waters surrounding us cannot readily be fenced, and so the tragedy of the commons as a cesspool must be prevented by different means, by coercive laws or taxing devices that make it cheaper for the polluter to treat his pollutants than to discharge them untreated. We have no progressed as far with the solution of this problem as we have with the first. Indeed, our particular concept of private property, which deters us from exhausting the positive resources of the earth, favors pollution. The owner of a factory on the bank of a stream—whose property extends to the middle of the stream—often has difficulty seeing why it is not his natural right to muddy the waters flowing past his door. The law, always behind the times, requires elaborate stitching and fitting to adapt it to this newly perceived aspect of the commons.

The pollution problem is a consequence of population. It did not much matter how a lonely American frontiersman disposed of his waste. "Flowing water purifies every 10 miles," my grandfather used to say, and the myth was near enough to the truth when he was a boy, for there were not too many people. But as population became denser, the natural chemical and biological recycling processes became overloaded, calling for a redefinition of property rights.

HOW TO LEGISLATE TEMPERANCE?

Analysis of the pollution problem as a function of population density uncovers a not generally recognized principle of morality, namely: *the morality of an act is a function of the state of the system at the time it is performed* (10). Using the commons as a cesspool does not harm the general public under frontier conditions, because there is no public; the same behavior in a metropolis is unbearable. A hundred and fifty years ago a plainsman could kill an American bison, cut out only the tongue for his dinner, and discard the rest of the animal. He was not in any important sense being wasteful. Today, with only a few thousand bison left, we would be appalled at such behavior.

In passing, it is worth noting that the morality of an act cannot be determined from a photograph. One does not know whether a man killing an elephant or setting fire to the grassland is harming others until one knows the total system in which his act appears. "One picture is worth a thousand words," said an ancient Chinese; but it may take 10,000 words to validate it. It is as tempting to ecologists as it is to reformers in general to try to persuade others by way of the photographic shortcut. But the essense of an argument cannot be photographed: it must be presented rationally—in words.

That morality is system-sensitive escaped the attention of most codifiers of ethics in the past. "Thou shalt not . . ." is the form of traditional ethical directives which make no allowance for particular circumstances. The laws of our society follow the pattern of ancient ethics, and therefore are poorly suited to governing a complex, crowded, changeable world. Our epicyclic solution is to augment statutory law with administrative law. Since it is practically impossible to spell out all the conditions under which it is safe to burn trash in the back yard or to run an automobile without smog-control, by law we delegate the details to bureaus. The result is administrative law, which is rightly feared for an ancient reason—*Quis custodiet ipsos custodes?*—"Who shall watch the watchers themselves?" John Adams said that we must have "a government of laws and not men." Bureau administrators, trying to evaluate the morality of acts in the total system, are singularly liable to corruption, producing a government by men, not laws.

Prohibition is easy to legislate (though not necessarily to enforce); but how do we legislate temperance? Experience indicates that it can be accomplished best through the mediation of administrative law. We limit possibilities unnecessarily if we suppose that the sentiment of *Quis custodiet* denies us the use of administrative law. We should rather retain the phrase as a perpetual reminder of fearful dangers we cannot avoid. The great challenge facing us now is to invent the corrective feedbacks that are needed to keep custodians honest. We must find ways to legitimate the needed authority of both the custodians and the corrective feedbacks.

FREEDOM TO BREED IS INTOLERABLE

The tragedy of the commons is involved in population problems in another way. In a world governed solely by the principle of "dog eat dog"—if indeed there ever was such a world—how many children a family had would not be a matter of public concern. Parents who bred too exuberantly would leave fewer descendants, not more, because they would be unable to care adequately for their children. David Lack and others have found that such a negative feedback demonstrably controls the fecundity of birds (*11*). But men are not birds, and have not acted like them for millenniums, at least.

If each human family were dependent only on its own resources; *if* the children of improvident parents starved to death; *if*, thus, overbreeding brought its own "punishment" to the germ line—*then* there would be no public interest in controlling the breeding of families. But our society is deeply committed to the welfare state (*12*), and hence is confronted with another aspect of the tragedy of the commons.

In a welfare state, how shall we deal with the family, the religion, the race, or the class (or indeed any distinguishable and cohesive group) that adopts overbreeding as a policy to secure its own aggrandizement (*13*)? To couple the concept of freedom to breed with the belief that everyone born has an equal right to the commons is to lock the world into a tragic course of action.

Unfortunately this is just the course of action that is being pursued by the United Nations. In late 1967, some 30 nations agreed to the following (*14*):

> The Universal Declaration of Human Rights describes the family as the natural and fundamental unit of society. It follows that any choice and decision with regard to the size of the family must irrevocably rest with the family itself, and cannot be made by anyone else.

It is painful to have to deny categorically the validity of this right; denying it, one feels as uncomfortable as a resident of Salem, Massachusetts, who denied the reality of witches in the 17th century. At the present time, in liberal quarters, something like a taboo acts to inhibit criticism of the United Nations. There is a feeling that the United Nations is "our last and best hope," that we shouldn't find fault with it; we shouldn't play into the hands of the arch-conservatives. However, let us not forget what Robert Louis Stevenson said: "The truth that is suppressed by friends is the readiest weapon of the enemy." If we love the truth we must openly deny the validity of the Universal Declaration of Human Rights, even though it is promoted by the United Nations. We should also join with Kingsley Davis (15) in attempting to get Planned Parenthood-World Population to see the error of its ways in embracing the same tragic ideal.

CONSCIENCE IS SELF-ELIMINATING

It is a mistake to think that we can control the breeding of mankind in the long run by an appeal to conscience. Charles Galton Darwin made this point when he spoke on the centennial of the publication of his grandfather's great book. The argument is straightforward and Darwinian.

People vary. Confronted with appeals to limit breeding, some people will undoubtedly respond to the plea more than others. Those who have more children will produce a larger fraction of the next generation than those with more susceptible consciences. The difference will be accentuated, generation by generation.

In C. G. Darwin's words: "It may well be that it would take hundreds of generations for the progenitive instinct to develop in this way, but if it should do so, nature would have taken her revenge, and the variety *Homo contracipiens* would become extinct and would be replaced by the variety *Homo progenitivus*" (16).

The argument assumes that conscience or the desire for children (no matter which) is hereditary—but hereditary only in the most general formal sense. The result will be the same whether the attitude is transmitted through germ cells, or exosomatically, to use A. J. Lotka's term. (If one denies the latter possibility as well as the former, then what's the point of education?) The argument has here

been stated in the context of the population problem, but it applies equally well to any instance in which society appeals to an individual exploiting a commons to restrain himself for the general good—by means of his conscience. To make such an appeal is to set up a selective system that works toward the elimination of conscience from the race.

PATHOGENIC EFFECTS OF CONSCIENCE

The long-term disadvantage of an appeal to conscience should be enough to condemn it; but it has serious short-term disadvantages as well. If we ask a man who is exploiting a commons to desist "in the name of conscience, what are we saying to him? What does he hear?—not only at the moment but also in the wee small hours of the night when, half asleep, he remembers not merely the words we used but also the nonverbal communication cues we gave him unawares? Sooner or later, consciously or subconsciously, he senses that he has received two communications, and that they are contradictory: (i) (intended communication) "If you don't do as we ask, we will openly condemn you for not acting like a responsible citizen"; (ii) (the unintended communication) "If you *do* behave as we ask, we will secretly condemn you for a simpleton who can be shamed into standing aside while the rest of us exploit the commons."

Everyman then is caught in what Bateson has called a "double bind." Bateson and his co-workers have made a plausible case for viewing the double bind as an important causative factor in the genesis of schizophrenia (17). The double bind may not always be so damaging, but it always endangers the mental health of anyone to whom it is applied. "A bad conscience," said Nietzsche, "is a kind of illness."

To conjure up a conscience in others is tempting to anyone who wishes to extend his control beyond the legal limits. Leaders at the highest level succumb to this temptation. Has any President during the past generation failed to call on labor unions to moderate voluntarily their demands for higher wages, or to steel companies to honor voluntary guidelines on prices? I can recall none. The rhetoric used on such occasions is designed to produce feelings of guilt in noncooperators.

For centuries it was assumed without proof that guilt was a valuable, perhaps even an indispensable, ingredient of the civilized life. Now, in this post-Freudian world, we doubt it.

Paul Goodman speaks from the modern point of view when he says: "No good has ever come from feeling guilty, neither intelligence, policy, nor compassion. The guilty do not pay attention to the object but only to themselves, and not even to their own interests, which might make sense, but to their anxieties" (18).

One does not have to be a professional psychiatrist to see the consequences of anxiety. We in the Western world are just emerging from a dreadful two-centuries-long Dark Ages of Eros that was sustained partly by prohibition laws, but perhaps more effectively by the anxiety-generating mechanisms of education. Alex Comfort has told the story well in *The Anxiety Makers* (19); it is not a pretty one.

Since proof is difficult, we may even concede that the results of anxiety may sometimes, from certain points of view, be desirable. The larger question we should ask is whether, as a matter of policy, we should ever encourage the use of a technique the tendency (if not the intention) of which is psychologically pathogenic. We hear much talk these days of responsible parenthood; the coupled words are incorporated into the titles of some organizations devoted to birth control. Some people have proposed massive propaganda campaigns to instill responsibility into the nation's (or the world's) breeders. But what is the meaning of the word responsibility in this context? Is it not merely a synonym for the word conscience? When we use the word responsibility in the absence of substantial sanctions are we not trying to browbeat a free man in a commons into acting against his own interest? Responsibility is a verbal counterfeit for a substantial *quid pro quo*. It is an attempt to get something for nothing.

If the word responsibility is to be used at all, I suggest that it be in the sense Charles Frankel uses it (20). "Responsibility," says this philosopher, "is the product of definite social arrangements." Notice that Frankel calls for social arrangements—not propaganda.

MUTUAL COERCION
MUTUALLY AGREED UPON

The social arrangements that produce responsibility are arrangements that create coercion, of some sort. Consider bank-robbing. The man who takes money from a bank acts as if the bank were a commons. How do we prevent such action? Certainly not by trying to control his behavior solely by a verbal appeal to his sense of responsibility. Rather than rely on propaganda we follow Frankel's lead and insist that a bank is not a commons; we seek the definite social arrangements that will keep it from becoming a commons. That we thereby infringe on the freedom of would-be robbers we neither deny nor regret.

The morality of bank-robbing is particularly easy to understand because we accept complete prohibition of this activity. We are willing to say "Thou shalt not rob banks," without providing for exceptions. But temperance also can be created by coercion. Taxing is a good coercive device. To keep downtown shoppers temperate in their use of parking space we introduce parking meters for short periods, and traffic fines for longer ones. We need not actually forbid a citizen to park as long as he wants to; we need merely make it increasingly expensive for him to do so. Not prohibition, but carefully biased options are what we offer him. A Madison Avenue man might call this persuasion; I prefer the greater candor of the word coercion.

Coercion is a dirty word to most liberals now, but it need not forever be so. As with the four-letter words, its dirtiness can be cleansed away by exposure to the light, by saying it over and over without apology or embarrassment. To many, the word coercion implies arbitrary decisions of distant and irresponsible bureaucrats; but this is not a necessary part of its meaning. The only kind of coercion I recommend is mutual coercion, mutually agreed upon by the majority of the people affected.

To say that we mutually agree to coercion is not to say that we are required to enjoy it, or even to pretend we enjoy it. Who enjoys taxes? We all grumble about them. But we accept compulsory taxes because we recognize that voluntary taxes would favor the conscienceless. We institute and (grumblingly) support taxes and other coercive devices to escape the horror of the commons.

An alternative to the commons need not be perfect just to be preferable. With real estate and other material goods, the alternative we have chosen is the institution of private property coupled with legal inheritance. Is this system perfectly just? As a genetically trained biologist I deny that it is. It seems to me that, if there are to be differences in individual inheritance, legal possession should be perfectly correlated with biological inheritance—that those who are biologically more fit to be the custodians of property and power should legally inherit more. But genetic recombination continually makes a mockery of the doctrine of "like father, like son" implicit in our laws of legal inheritance. An idiot can inherit millions, and a trust fund can keep his estate intact. We must admit that our legal system of private property plus inheritance is unjust—but we put up with it because we are not convinced, at the moment, that anyone has invented a better system. The alternative of the commons is too horrifying to contemplate. Injustice is preferable to total ruin.

It is one of the peculiarities of the warfare between reform and the status quo that it is thoughtlessly governed by a double standard. Whenever a reform measure is proposed it is often defeated when its opponents triumphantly discover a flaw in it. As Kingsley Davis has pointed out (*21*), worshippers of the status quo sometimes imply that no reform is possible without unanimous agreement, an implication contrary to historical fact. As nearly as I can make out, automatic rejection of proposed reforms is based on one of two unconscious assumptions: (*i*) that the status quo is perfect; or (*ii*) that the choice we face is between reform and no action; if the proposed reform is imperfect, we presumably should take no action at all, while we wait for a perfect proposal.

But we can never do nothing. That which we have done for thousands of years is also action. It also produces evils. Once we are aware that the status quo is action, we can then compare its discoverable advantages and disadvantages with the predicted advantages and disadvantages of the proposed reform, discounting as best we can for our lack of experience. On the basis of such a comparison, we can make a rational decision which will not involve the unworkable assumption that only perfect systems are tolerable.

RECOGNITION OF NECESSITY

Perhaps the simplest summary of this analysis of man's population problems is this: the com-

mons, if justifiable at all, is justifiable only under conditions of low-population density. As the human population has increased, the commons has had to be abandoned in one apsect after another.

First we abandoned the commons in food gathering, enclosing farm land and restricting pastures and hunting and fishing areas. These restrictions are still not complete throughout the world.

Somewhat later we saw that the commons as a place for waste disposal would also have to be abandoned. Restrictions on the disposal of domestic sewage are widely accepted in the Western world; we are still struggling to close the commons to pollution by automobiles, factories, insecticide sprayers, fertilizing operations, and atomic energy installations.

In a still more embryonic state is our recognition of the evils of the commons in matters of pleasure. There is almost no restriction on the propagation of sound waves in the public medium. The shopping public is assaulted with mindless music, without its consent. Our government is paying out billions of dollars to create supersonic transport which will disturb 50,000 people for every one person who is whisked from coast to coast 3 hours faster. Advertisers muddy the airwaves of radio and television and pollute the view of travelers. We are a long way from outlawing the commons in matters of pleasure. Is this because our Puritan inheritance makes us view pleasure as something of a sin, and pain (that is, the pollution of advertising) as the sign of virtue?

Every new enclosure of the commons involves the infringement of somebody's personal liberty. Infringements made in the distant past are accepted because no contemporary complains of a loss. It is the newly proposed infringements that we vigorously oppose; cries of "rights" and "freedom" fill the air. But what does "freedom" mean? When men mutually agreed to pass laws against robbing, mankind became more free, not less so. Individuals locked into the logic of the commons are free only to bring on universal ruin; once they see the necessity of mutual coercion, they become free to pursue other goals. I believe it was Hegel who said, "Freedom is the recognition of necessity."

The most important aspect of necessity that we must now recognize, is the necessity of abandoning the commons in breeding. No technical solution can rescue us from the misery of overpopulation. Freedom to breed will bring ruin to all. At the moment, to avoid hard decisions many of us are tempted to propagandize for conscience and responsible parenthood. The temptation must be resisted, because an appeal to independently acting consciences selects for the disappearance of all conscience in the long run, and an increase in anxiety in the short.

The only way we can preserve and nurture other and more precious freedoms is by relinquishing the freedom to breed, and that very soon. "Freedom is the recognition of necessity" —and it is the role of education to reveal to all the necessity of abandoning the freedom to breed. Only so, can we put an end to this aspect of the tragedy of the commons.

REFERENCES

1. J. B. Wiesner and H. F. York, *Sci. Amer.* **211** (No. 4), 27 (1964).
2. G. Hardin, *J. Hered.* **50**, 68 (1959); S. von Hoernor, *Science* **137**, 18 (1962).
3. J. von Neumann and O. Morgenstern, *Theory of Games and Economic Behavior* (Princeton Univ. Press, Princeton, N.J., 1947), p. 11.
4. J. H. Fremlin, *New Sci.*, No. 415 (1964), p. 285.
5. A. Smith, *The Wealth of Nations* (Modern Library, New York, 1937), p. 423.
6. W. F. Lloyd, *Two Lectures on the Checks to Population* (Oxford Univ. Press, Oxford, England, 1833), reprinted (in part) in *Population, Evolution, and Birth Control*, G. Hardin, Ed. (Freeman, San Francisco, 1964), p. 37.
7. A. N. Whitehead, *Science and the Modern World* (Mentor, New York, 1948), p. 17.
8. G. Hardin, Ed. *Population, Evolution, and Birth Control* (Freeman, San Francisco, 1964), p. 56.
9. S. McVay, *Sci. Amer.* **216** (No. 8), 13 (1966).
10. J. Fletcher, *Situation Ethics* (Westminster, Philadelphia, 1966).
11. D. Lack, *The Natural Regulation of Animal Numbers* (Clarendon Press, Oxford, 1954).
12. H. Girvetz, *From Wealth to Welfare* (Stanford Univ. Press, Stanford, Calif., 1950).
13. G. Hardin, *Perspec. Biol. Med.* **6**, 366 (1963).
14. U. Thant, *Int. Planned Parenthood News*, No. 168 (February 1968), p. 3.
15. K. Davis, *Science* **158**, 730 (1967).
16. S. Tax, Ed., *Evolution after Darwin* (Univ. of Chicago Press, Chicago, 1960), vol. 2, p. 469.
17. G. Bateson, D. D. Jackson, J. Haley, J. Weakland, *Behav. Sci.* **1**, 251 (1956).
18. P. Goodman, *New York Rev. Books* **10**(8), 22 (23 May 1968).
19. A. Comfort, *The Anxiety Makers* (Nelson, London, 1967).
20. C. Frankel, *The Case for Modern Man* (Harper, New York, 1955), p. 203.
21. J. D. Roslansky, *Genetics and the Future of Man* (Appleton-Century-Crofts, New York, 1966). p. 177.

The Tragedy of the Commons Revisited

by Beryl L. Crowe

There has developed in the contemporary natural sciences a recognition that there is a subset of problems, such as population, atomic war, and environmental corruption, for which there are no technical solutions (*1, 2*). There is also an increasing recognition among contemporary social scientists that there is a subset of problems, such as population, atomic war, environmental corruption, and the recovery of a livable urban environment, for which there are no current political solutions (*3*). The thesis of this article is that the common area shared by these two subsets contains most of the critical problems that threaten the very existence of contemporary man.

The importance of this area has not been raised previously because of the very structure of modern society. This society, with its emphasis on differentiation and specialization, has led to the development of two insular scientific communities—the natural and the social—between which there is very little communication and a great deal of envy, suspicion, disdain, and competition for scarce resources. Indeed, these two communities more closely resemble tribes living in close geographic proximity on university campuses than they resemble the "scientific culture" that C. P. Snow placed in contrast to and opposition to the "humanistic culture" (*4*).

Perhaps the major problems of modern society have, in large part, been allowed to develop and intensify through this structure of insularity and specialization because it serves both psychological and professional functions for both scientific communities. Under such conditions, the natural sciences can recognize that some problems are not technically soluble and relegate them to the nether land of politics, while the social sciences recognized that some problems have no current political solutions and then postpone a search for solutions while they wait for new technologies with which to attack the problem. Both sciences can thus avoid responsibility and protect their respective myths of competence and relevance, while they avoid having to face the awesome and awful possibility that each has independently isolated the same subset of problems and given them different names. Thus, both never have to face the consequences of their respective findings. Meanwhile, due to the specialization and insularity of modern society, man's most critical problems lie in limbo, while the specialists in problem-solving go on to less critical problems for which they can find technical or political solutions.

In this circumstance, one psychologically brave, but professionally foolhardy soul, Garrett Hardin, has dared to cross the tribal boundaries in his article "The tragedy of the commons" (*1*). In it, he gives vivid proof of the insularity of the two scientific tribes in at least two respects: first, his "rediscovery" of the tragedy was in part wasted effort, for the knowledge of this tragedy is so common in the social sciences that it has generated some fairly sophisticated mathematical models (*5*); second, the recognition of the existence of a subset of problems for which science neither offers nor aspires to offer technical solutions is not likely, under the contemporary conditions of insularity, to gain wide currency in the social sciences. Like Hardin, I will attempt to avoid the psychological and professional benefits of this insularity by tracing some of the political and social implications of his proposed solution to the tragedy of the commons.

The commons is a fundamental social institution that has a history going back through our own colonial experience to a body of English common law which antidates the Roman

THIS SELECTION is reprinted with permission of the author and publisher from *Science*, Vol. 166, pp. 1103–1107, November 1969. Copyright 1969 by the American Association for the Advancement of Science.

conquest. That law recognized that in societies there are some environmental objects which have never been, and should never be, exclusively appropriated to any individual or group of individuals. In England the classic example of the commons is the pasturage set aside for public use, and the "tragedy of the commons" to which Hardin refers was a tragedy of overgrazing and lack of care and fertilization which resulted in erosion and underproduction so destructive that there developed in the late 19th century an enclosure movement. Hardin applies this social institution to other environmental objects such as water, atmosphere, and living space.

The cause of this tragedy is exposed by a very simple mathematical model, utilizing the concept of utility drawn from economics. Allowing the utilities to range between a positive value of 1 and a negative value of 1, we may ask, as did the individual English herdsman, what is the utility to me of adding one more animal to my herd that grazes on the commons? His answer is that the positive utility is near 1 and the negative utility is only a fraction of minus 1. Adding together the component partial utilities, the herdsman concludes that it is rational for him to add another animal to his herd; then another, and so on. The tragedy to which Hardin refers develops because the same rational conclusion is reached by each and every herdsman sharing the commons.

ASSUMPTIONS NECESSARY TO AVOID THE TRAGEDY

In passing the technically insoluble problems over to the political and social realm for solution, Hardin has made three critical assumptions: (i) that there exists, or can be developed, a "criterion of judgment and a system of weighting..." that will "render the incommensurables...commensurable..." in real life; (ii) that, possessing this criterion of judgment, "coercion can be mutually agreed upon," and that the application of coercion to effect a solution to problems will be effective in modern society; and (iii) that the administrative system, supported by the criterion of judgment and access to coercion, can and will protect the commons from further desecration.

If all three of these assumptions were correct, the tragedy which Hardin has re-

cognized would dissolve into a rather facile melodrama of setting up administrative agencies. I believe these three assumptions are so questionable in contemporary society that a tragedy remains in the full sense in which Hardin used the term. Under contemporary conditions, the subset of technically insoluble problems is also politically insoluble, and thus we witness a full-blown tragedy wherein "the essence of dramatic tragedy is not unhappiness. It resides in the remorseless working of things."

The remorseless working of things in modern society is the erosion of three social myths which form the basis for Hardin's assumptions, and this erosion is proceeding at such a swift rate that perhaps the myths can neither revitalize nor reformulate in time to prevent the "population bomb" from going off, or before an accelerating "pollution immersion," or perhaps even an "atomic fallout."

ERODING MYTH OF THE COMMON VALUE SYSTEM

Hardin is theoretically correct, from the point of view of the behavioral sciences, in his argument that "in real life incommensurables *are* commensurable." He is, moreover, on firm ground in his assertion that to fulfill this condition in real life one needs only "a criterion of judgment and a system of weighting." In real life, however, values are the criteria of judgment, and the system of weighting is dependent upon the ranging of a number of conflicting values in a hierarchy. That such a system of values exists beyond the confines of the nation-state is hardly tenable. At this point in time one is more likely to find such a system of values within the boundaries of the nation-state. Moreover, the nation-state is the only political unit of sufficient dimension to find and enforce political solutions to Hardin's subset of "technically insoluble problems." It is on this political unit that we will fix our attention.

In America there existed, until very recently, a set of conditions which perhaps made the solution to Hardin's problem subset possible: we lived with the myth that we were "one people, indivisible...." This myth postulated that we were the great "melting pot" of the world wherein the diverse cultural ores of

Europe were poured into the crucible of the frontier experience to produce a new alloy—an American civilization. This new civilization was presumably united by a common value system that was democratic, equalitarian, and existing under universally enforceable rules contained in the Constitution and the Bill of Rights.

In the United States today, however, there is emerging a new set of behavior patterns which suggest that the myth is either dead or dying. Instead of believing and behaving in accordance with the myth, large sectors of the population are developing life-styles and value hierarchies that give contemporary Americans an appearance more closely analogous to the particularistic, primitive forms of "tribal" organizations living in geographic proximity than to that shining new alloy, the American civilization.

With respect to American politics, for example, it is increasingly evident that the 1960 election was the last election in the United States to be played out according to the rules of pluralistic politics in a two-party system. Certainly 1964 was, even in terms of voting behavior, a contest between the larger tribe that was still committed to the pluralistic model of compromise and accommodation within a winning coalition, and an emerging tribe that is best seen as a millennial revitalization movement directed against mass society—a movement so committed to the revitalization of old values that it would rather lose the election than compromise its values. Under such circumstances former real-life commensurables within the Republican Party suddenly became incommensurable.

In 1968 it was the Democratic Party's turn to suffer the degeneration of commensurables into incommensurables as both the Wallace tribe and the McCarthy tribe refused to play by the old rules of compromise, accommodation, and exchange of interests. Indeed, as one looks back on the 1968 election, there seems to be a common theme in both these camps—a theme of return to more simple and direct participation in decision-making that is only possible in the tribal setting. Yet, despite this similarity, both the Wallaceites and the McCarthyites responded with a value perspective that ruled out compromise and they both demanded a drastic change in the dimension in which politics is

played. So firm were the value commitments in both of these tribes that neither (as was the case with the Goldwater forces in 1964) was willing to settle for a modicum of power that could accrue through the processes of compromise with the national party leadership.

Still another dimension of this radical change in behavior is to be seen in the black community where the main trend of the argument seems to be, not in the direction of accommodation, compromise, and integration, but rather in the direction of fragmentation from the larger community, intransigence in the areas where black values and black culture are concerned, and the structuring of a new community of like-minded and like-colored people. But to all appearances even the concept of color is not enough to sustain commensurables in their emerging community as it fragments into religious nationalism, secular nationalism, integrationists, separatists, and so forth. Thus those problems which were commensurable, both interracial and intraracial, in the era of integration become incommensurable in the era of Black Nationalism.

Nor can the growth of commensurable views be seen in the contemporary youth movements. On most of the American campuses today there are at least ten tribes involved in "tribal wars" among themselves and against the "imperialistic" powers of those "over 30." Just to tick them off, without any attempt to be comprehensive, there are: the up-tight protectors of the status quo who are looking for middle-class union cards, the revitalization movements of the Young Americans for Freedom, the reformists of pluralism represented by the Young Democrats and the Young Republicans, those committed to New Politics, the Students for a Democratic Society, the Yippies, the Flower Children, the Black Students Union, and the Third World Liberation Front. The critical change in this instance is not the rise of new groups; this is expected within the pluralistic model of politics. What is new are value positions assumed by these groups which lead them to make demands, not as points for bargaining and compromise with the opposition, but rather as points which are "not negotiable." Hence, they consciously set the stage for either confrontation or surrender, but not for rendering incommensurables commensurable.

Moving out of formalized politics and off

the campus, we see the remnants of the "hippie" movement which show clear-cut tribal overtones in their commune movements. This movement has, moreover, already fragmented into an urban tribe which can talk of guerrilla warfare against the city fathers, while another tribe finds accommodation to urban life untenable without sacrificing its values and therefore moves out to the "Hog Farm," "Morning Star," or "Big Sur." Both hippie tribes have reduced the commensurables with the dominant WASP tribe to the point at which one of the cities on the Monterey Peninsula felt sufficiently threatened to pass a city ordinance against sleeping in trees, and the city of San Francisco passed a law against sitting on sidewalks.

Even among those who still adhere to the pluralistic middle-class American image, we can observe an increasing demand for a change in the dimension of life and politics that has disrupted the elementary social processes: the demand for neighborhood (tribal?) schools, control over redevelopment projects, and autonomy in the setting and payment of rents to slumlords. All of these trends are more suggestive of tribalism than of the growth of the range of commensurables with respect to the commons.

We are, moreover, rediscovering other kinds of tribes in some very odd ways. For example, in the educational process, we have found that one of our first and best empirical measures in terms both of validity and reproducibility—the I. Q. test—is a much better measure of the existence of different linguistic tribes than it is a measure of "native intellect" (6). In the elementary school, the different languages and different values of these diverse tribal children have even rendered the commensurables that obtained in the educational system suddenly incommensurable.

Nor are the empirical contradictions of the common value myth as new as one might suspect. For example, with respect to the urban environment, at least 7 years ago Scott Greer was arguing that the core city was sick and would remain sick until a basic sociological movement took place in our urban environment that would move all the middle classes to the suburbs and surrender the core city to the "... segregated, the insulted, and the injured" (7). This argument by Greer came at a time when most of us were still talking about

compromise and accommodation of interests, and was based upon a perception that the life styles, values, and needs of these two groups were so disparate that a healthy, creative restructuring of life in the core city could not take place until pluralism had been replaced by what amounted to geographic or territorial tribalism; only when this occurred would urban incommensurables become commensurable.

Looking at a more recent analysis of the sickness of the core city, Wallace F. Smith has argued that the productive model of the city is no longer viable for the purposes of economic analysis (8). Instead, he develops a model of the city as a site for leisure consumption, and then seems to suggest that the nature of this model is such that the city cannot regain its health because it cannot make decisions, and that it cannot make decisions because the leisure demands are value-based and, hence, do not admit of compromise and accommodation; consequently there is no way of deciding among these various value-oriented demands that are being made on the core city.

In looking for the cause of the erosion of the myth of a common value system, it seems to me that so long as our perceptions and knowledge of other groups were formed largely through the written media of communication, the American myth that we were a giant melting pot of equalitarians could be sustained. In such a perceptual field it is tenable, if not obvious, that men are motivated by interests. Interests can always be compromised and accommodated without undermining our very being by sacrificing values. Under the impact of the electronic media, however, this psychological distance has broken down and we now discover that these people with whom we could formerly compromise on interests are not, after all, really motivated by interests but by values. Their behavior in our very living room betrays a set of values, moreover, that are incompatible with our own, and consequently the compromises that we make are not those of contract but of culture. While the former are acceptable, any form of compromise on the latter is not a form of rational behavior but is rather a clear case of either apostasy or heresy. Thus, we have arrived not at an age of accommodation but one of confrontation. In such an age "incommensurables" remain "incommensurable" in real life.

EROSION OF THE MYTH
OF THE MONOPOLY
OF COERCIVE FORCE

In the past, those who no longer subscribed to the values of the dominant culture were held in check by the myth that the state possessed a monopoly on coercive force. This myth has undergone continual erosion since the end of World War II owing to the success of the strategy of guerrilla warfare, as first revealed to the French in Indochina, and later conclusively demonstrated in Algeria. Suffering as we do from what Senator Fulbright has called "the arrogance of power," we have been extremely slow to learn the lesson in Vietnam, although we now realize that war is political and cannot be won by military means. It is apparent that the myth of the monopoly of coercive force as it was first qualified in the civil rights conflict in the South, then in our urban ghettos, next on the streets of Chicago, and now on our college campuses has lost its hold over the minds of Americans. The technology of guerrilla warfare has made it evident that, while the state can win battles, it cannot win wars of values. Coercive force which is centered in the modern state cannot be sustained in the face of the active resistance of some 10 percent of its population unless the state is willing to embark on a deliberate policy of genocide directed against the value dissident groups. The factor that sustained the myth of coercive force in the past was the acceptance of a common value system. Whether the latter exists is questionable in the modern nation-state. But, even if most members of the nation-state remain united around a common value system which makes incommensurables for the majority commensurable, that majority is incapable of enforcing its decisions upon the minority in the face of the diminished coercive power of the governing body of the nation-state.

EROSION OF THE MYTH
OF ADMINISTRATORS
OF THE COMMONS

Hardin's thesis that the administrative arm of the state is capable of legislating temperance accords with current administrative theory in political science and touches on one of the concerns of that body of theory when he suggests that the ". . . great challenge facing us now is to invent the corrective feedbacks that are needed to keep the custodians honest."

Our best empirical answers to the question—*Quis custodiet ipsos custodes?*—"Who shall watch the watchers themselves?"—have shown fairly conclusively (9) that the decisions, orders, hearings, and press releases of the custodians of the commons, such as the Federal Communications Commission, the Interstate Commerce Commission, the Federal Trade Commission, and even the Bureau of Internal Revenue, give the large but unorganized groups in American society symbolic satisfaction and assurances. Yet, the actual day-to-day decisions and operations of these administrative agencies contribute, foster, aid, and indeed legitimate the special claims of small but highly organized groups to differential access to tangible resources which are extracted from the commons. This has been so well documented in the social sciences that the best answer to the question of who watches over the custodians of the commons is the regulated interests that make incursions on the commons.

Indeed, the process has been so widely commented upon that one writer has postulated a common life cycle for all of the attempts to develop regulatory policies (10). This life cycle is launched by an outcry so widespread and demanding that it generates enough political force to bring about the establishment of a regulatory agency to insure the equitable, just, and rational distribution of the advantages among all holders of interest in the commons. This phase is followed by the symbolic reassurance of the offended as the agency goes into operation, developing a period of political quiescence among the great majority of those who hold a general but unorganized interest in the commons. Once this political quiescence has developed, the highly organized and specifically interested groups who wish to make incursions into the commons bring sufficient pressure to bear through other political processes to convert the agency to the protection and furthering of their interests. In the last phase even staffing of the regulating agency is accomplished by drawing the agency administrators from the ranks of the regulated.

Thus, it would seem that, even with the existence of a common value system accompanied by a viable myth of the monopoly of coercive force, the prospects are very dim for

395

saving the commons from differential exploitation or spoilation by the administrative devices in which Hardin places his hope. This being the case, the natural sciences may absolve themselves of responsibility for meeting the environmental challenges of the contemporary world by relegating those problems for which there are no technical solutions to the political or social realm. This action will, however, make little contribution to the solution of the problem.

ARE THE CRITICAL PROBLEMS OF MODERN SOCIETY INSOLUBLE?

Earlier in this article I agreed that perhaps until very recently, there existed a set of conditions which made the solution of Hardin's problem subset possible; now I suggest that the concession is questionable. There is evidence of structural as well as value problems which make comprehensive solutions impossible and these conditions have been present for some time.

For example, Aaron Wildavsky, in a comprehensive study of the budgetary process, has found that in the absence of a calculus for resolving "intrapersonal comparison of utilities," the governmental budgetary process proceeds by a calculus that is sequential and incremental rather than comprehensive. This being the case ". . . if one looks at politics as a process by which the government mobilizes resources to meet pressing problems" (11) the budget is the focus of these problem responses and the responses to problems in contemporary America are not the sort of comprehensive responses required to bring order to a disordered environment. Another example of the operation of this type of rationality is the American involvement in Vietnam; for, what is the policy of escalation but the policy of sequential incrementalism given a new Madison Avenue euphemism? The question facing us all is the question of whether incremental rationality is sufficient to deal with 20th-century problems.

The operational requirements of modern institutions makes incremental rationality the only viable form of decision-making, but this only raises the prior question of whether there are solutions to any of the major problems raised in modern society. It may well be that the emerging forms of tribal behavior noted in this article are the last hope of reducing political and social institutions to a level where incommensurables become commensurable in terms of values *and* in terms of comprehensive responses to problems. After all, in the history of man on earth we might well assume that the departure from the tribal experience is a short-run deviant experiment that failed. As we stand "on the eve of destruction," it may well be that the return to the face-to-face life in the small community unmediated by the electronic media is a very functional response in terms of the perpetuation of the species.

There is, I believe, a significant sense in which the human environment is directly in conflict with the source of man's ascendancy among the other species of the earth. Man's evolutionary position hinges, not on specialization, but rather on generalized adaptability. Modern social and political institutions, however, hinge on specialized, sequential, incremental decision-making and not on generalized adaptability. This being the case, life in the nation-state will continue to require a singleness of purpose for success but in a very critical sense this singleness of purpose becomes a straightjacket that makes generalized adaptation impossible. Nowhere is this conflict more evident than in our urban centers where there has been a decline in the livability of the total environment that is almost directly proportionate to the rise of special purpose districts. Nowhere is this conflict between institutional singleness of purpose and the human dimension of the modern environment more evident than in the recent warning of S. Goran Lofroth, chairman of a committee studying pesticides for the Swedish National Research Council, that many breast-fed children ingest from their mother's milk "more than the recommended daily intake of DDT" (12) and should perhaps be switched to cow's milk because cows secrete only 2 to 10 percent of the DDT they ingest.

HOW CAN SCIENCE CONTRIBUTE TO THE SAVING OF THE COMMONS?

It would seem that, despite the nearly remorseless working of things, science has some interim contributions to make to the alleviation of those problems of the commons which Hardin has pointed out.

These contributions can come at two levels:

1) Science can concentrate more of its attention on the development of technological responses which at once alleviate those problems and reward those people who no longer desecrate the commons. This approach would seem more likely to be successful than the "... fundamental extension in morality ..." by administrative law; the engagement of interest seems to be a more reliable and consistent motivator of advantage-seeking groups than does administrative wrist-slapping or constituency pressure from the general public.

2) Science can perhaps, by using the widely proposed environmental monitoring systems, use them in such a way as to sustain a high level of "symbolic disassurance" among the holders of generalized interests in the commons—thus sustaining their political interest to a point where they would provide a constituency for the administrator other than those bent on denuding the commons. This latter approach would seem to be a first step toward the "... invention of the corrective feedbacks that are needed to keep custodians honest." This would require a major change in the behavior of science, however, for it could no longer rest content with development of the technology of monitoring and with turning the technology over to some new agency. Past administrative experience suggests that the use of technology to sustain a high level of "dis-assurance" among the general population would also require science to take up the role and the responsibility for maintaining, controlling, and disseminating the information.

Neither of these contributions to maintaining a habitable environment will be made by science unless there is a significant break in the insularity of the two scientific tribes. For, if science must, in its own insularity, embark on the independent discovery of "the tragedy of the commons," along with the parameters that produce the tragedy, it may be too slow a process to save us from the total destruction of the planet. Just as important, however, science will, by pursuing such a course, divert its attention from the production of technical tools, information, and solutions which will contribute to the political and social solutions for the problems of the commons.

Because I remain very suspicious of the success of either demands or pleas for fundamental extensions in morality, I would suggest that such a conscious turning by both the social and the natural sciences is, at this time, in their immediate self-interest. As Michael Polanyi has pointed out, "... encircled today between the crude utilitarianism of the philistine and the ideological utilitarianism of the modern revolutionary movement, the love of pure science may falter and die" (*13*). The sciences, both social and natural, can function only in a very special intellectual environment that is neither universal nor unchanging, and that environment is in jeopardy. The questions of humanistic relevance raised by the students at M.I.T., Stanford Research Institute, Berkeley, and wherever the headlines may carry us tomorrow, pose serious threats to the maintenance of that intellectual environment. However ill-founded *some* of the questions raised by the new generation may be, it behooves us to be ready with at least some collective, tentative answers—if only to maintain an environment in which both sciences will be allowed and fostered. This will not be accomplished so long as the social sciences continue to defer the most critical problems that face mankind to future technical advances, while the natural sciences continue to defer those same problems which are about to overwhelm all mankind to false expectations in the political realm.

REFERENCES AND NOTES

1. G. Hardin, *Science* **162**, 1243 (1968).
2. J. B. Wiesner and H. F. York, *Sci. Amer.* **211** (No. 4), 27 (1964).
3. C. Woodbury, *Amer. J. Public Health* **45**, 1 (1955); S. Marquis, *Amer. Behav. Sci.* **11**, 11 (1968); W. H. Ferry, *Center Mag.* **2**, 2 (1969).
4. C. P. Snow, *The Two Cultures and the Scientific Revolution* (Cambridge Univ. Press, New York, 1959).
5. M. Olson, Jr., *The Logic of Collective Action* (Harvard Univ. Press, Cambridge, Mass., 1965).
6. G. A. Harrison *et al.*, *Human Biology* (Oxford Univ. Press, New York, 1964), p. 292; W. W. Charters, Jr. in *School Children in the Urban Slum* (Free Press, New York, 1967).
7. S. Greer, *Governing the Metropolis* (Wiley, New York, 1962), p. 148.
8. W. F. Smith, "The Class Struggle and the Disquieted City," a paper presented at the 1969 annual meeting of the Western Economic Association, Oregon State University, Corvallis.

9. M. Bernstein, *Regulating Business by Independent Commissions* (Princeton Univ. Press, Princeton, N.J., 1955); E. P. Herring, *Public Administration and the Public Interest* (McGraw-Hill, New York, 1936); E. M. Redford, *Administration of National Economic Control* (Macmillan, New York, 1952).

10. M. Edelman, *The Symbolic Uses of Politics* (Univ. of Illinois Press, Urbana, 1964).

11. A. Wildavsky, *The Politics of the Budgetary Process* (Little Brown, Boston, Mass., 1964).

12. Corvallis *Gazette-Times*, 6 May 1969, p. 6.

13. M. Polanyi, *Personal Knowledge* (Harper & Row, New York, 1964), p. 182.

Selection 35

Growth and the Quality of Life

Commentary

During his tenure on the planet earth, man has related to his environment as a herdsman related to the commons. The resources of the world in one manner or another were free for exploitation, their use unrestricted. For a while the approach worked well enough. The commons were rich, capable of sustaining man once he acquired the knowledge and developed the technology to exploit them. If one area became depleted, man could move on to another waiting to be exploited. Now there are few places left to go.

As the commons rapidly deteriorate, there is an awakening realization that resources are limited. As clean air and water, space, and quiet places become scarcer and have to be shared by an ever-growing population, many begin to sense a decline in the quality of life. The evidence is everywhere, it has become painfully obvious during the past thirty years. The population of the United States in that time has increased by 50 percent. The automobile has increased several times faster than that until now there is nearly one car for every two persons. Energy production has expanded many times faster than that of the population. The ever-increasing economic growth rate has brought on environmental degradation, crowding, and social problems. Thousands of acres of countryside have been buried beneath concrete to make roads for cars, which in turn pollute the air. Valleys are drowned for power production and mountains are destroyed to recover coal. Housing developments and urban expansion eat up agricultural land, garbage fills up estuaries, the wilderness retreats and familiar animals grow fewer and head toward extinction.

A great deal in the decline of the quality of life is the result of the interaction between population growth, which added more units to the commons; technology, which improved means of extracting more from the commons; and politics, which provides the expediency for exploitation and environmental degradation. Rich resources encourage technology; the technology that makes riches available spurs population growth and economic development. This in turn encourages more technology and more exploitation, resulting in more material riches. The rich who at one time were the only ones privileged to enjoy the good life became richer, but so did the poor. The gap between the two never really narrowed, but the emancipated poor were able to enjoy many of the privileges of the rich—better food, cars, vacations away from home, ability to buy material goods. It was all accomplished, as Kenneth Boulding puts it, by "economic output," and increasing the output "inevitably increases the strain on the environment."[1]

This strain on the environment is demonstrated in the model presented by J. A. Wagar in this selection. The standard of living, states one of the models, is the sum of the production divided by the population. The standard of living is increased by increasing production or by reducing population. Since our population has not been reduced, the standard of living has been raised by increasing production. Increase of production is measured by the Gross National Product, and the objective of every nation is to ensure that its GNP is always increasing. To have it otherwise is to admit economic failure. To keep the GNP growing, environmental degradation is tolerated, and population expansion is encouraged as necessary for economic growth.

But is growing GNP or an expanding population desirable? We have already lost much of the value. We possess cars, but pleasure rides on crowded highways are no longer pleasurable. Campgrounds and beaches are overcrowded, people are trampling our national parks, and the hearts of our cities rot away with unemployment, ghettoes, racial strife, and economic deterioration. Life isn't what it used to be.

An answer to the problem is, as Raymond Dasmann puts it, is to plan against progress.[2] But to plan for a lower growth rate and stabilize the GNP is obviously economic heresy. To bring an ethic of stability to economic activity is the antithesis of American or any other business philosophy.

Stability could not be achieved without far-reaching effects and upheavals in society. It would require a slowdown in population growth which would in itself decrease the demand on the environment. It would mean recycling materials already drawn from the earth rather than disposing of the material as garbage. It would demand that the costs of containing pollution and environmental restoration be added to the

[1]K. E. Boulding, "No Second Chance for Man," in editors of *Progressive, The Crisis of Survival*, New York, Morrow, 1970, pp. 160–171.
[2]R. F. Dasmann, *A Different Kind of Country*, New York, Macmillan, 1968.

costs of production. The transition from a growing to a stabilized economy would mean fewer jobs and diminish demands for primary products and raw materials. This in turn would slow down or inhibit the further development of underdeveloped countries, who must rely on the export of raw materials to finance their own economic development. This could be frustrating to such nations, who recognize their poverty and yearn for a level of affluence comparable to that of the United States.

All nations are committed to increasing their Gross National Product by some minimal rate each year. A rise in GNP means further inroads on the commons. Attempts to control growth by reducing the GNP and controlling population growth appear to the poor as if the rich want to continue an unequal distribution of wealth and to limit the numbers of people simply so they can remain rich. To the underdeveloped nations and to the poor within the country, conservation movements which are at the heart of maintaining some quality to life are irrelevant. What is a bit of landscape, a wild river, or a country's wildlife when its destruction may mean the betterment of their life, even if only for a short period of time? The poor do not look far into the future, for the present has already seemingly unsolvable problems. As William R. Burch, Jr., has stated, "Persons of the underclass cannot be expected to hold a faith that a limited consumption world is any more certain a way toward a community of equal and free men than is a world of relative plenty."[3]

Yet if an impending future catastrophe is to be avoided, America and all nations must reach some level of ecological stability in which non-renewable resources are recycled, waste is minimized, and energy sources are stabilized, in which qualitative pursuits replace quantative ones and social planning replaces planning for profit. Such stability can be brought about only by a considerable and traumatic restructuring of society as we know it.

As Burch writes:

> We are being asked to limit consumption of children and goods, to substitute for expectation of plenty, expectation of decreasing subsistence, and to so confine our actions that very often we must opt for death or at least emptiness rather than life. To save a world order we know and love we must consciously rearrange it beyond recognition, while we are given a sea of information but no knowledge as to who is to allocate options within this delimited set of margins. Can we place faith in the industrialist or the state bureaucrat? The technician seems more guilty than clean, and democracy is not likely to willingly provide the means for its extinction. Can we count on our leadership class to prepare for a transformation as great as the market society and the frontier forced upon the feudal lords? Are those in command of our social system likely to push the levers which if not sending them to the underclass, at least deprive them of their customary range of power and action?[4]

Such questions as these lie behind the concern of growth and the quality of life.

---

[3]W. R. Burch, "Fishes and Loaves: Some Sociological Observations on the Environmental Crisis," in *Man and His Environment. The Ecological Limits of Optimism*, New Haven, Conn., Yale University School of Forestry Bull. No. 76, 1970, pp. 30—53.
[4]*Ibid.*

Selection 35

Growth Versus the Quality of Life

by J. Alan Wagar

In economics, as in most other matters, past experience provides a major basis for current decisions, even though changing circumstances may have diminished the appropriateness of such experience. Such use of "conventional wisdom" may explain our continuing emphasis on economic and other types of growth despite the many problems created by such growth.

When the United States was sparsely populated, emphasis on growth made good sense.

THIS SELECTION is reprinted with permission of the author and publisher from *Science*, Vol. 168, pp. 1179—1184, June 1970. Copyright 1970 by the American Association for the Advancement of Science.

Growth of many kinds permitted exploitation of the rich environment at an accelerating rate and provided a phenomenal increase in wealth.

Growth still increases material wealth but has a growing number of unfortunate side effects, as each of us tries to increase his own benefits within an increasingly crowded environment. These spillover effects, which were of minor importance when settlement was sparse and neighbors farther apart, are now of major consequence. For example a firm may make the most money from a downtown tract of land by erecting a tall office building there. Construction of the building will add to the gross national product, and the builders will be hailed for their contribution to "progress." However, the building will add to traffic congestion, exhaust fumes, competition for parking, the need for new freeways, and social disorder. These problems, which must be handled by someone else, become part of the "environmental mess" or "urban crisis."

Too few people have recognized the connection between uncontrolled growth and our environmental ills. Growth has become so widely accepted that, in *The Costs of Economic Growth*, Mishan (1) found it necessary to emphasize at some length that his criticism of economic growth was to be taken seriously. Yet, because rising levels of congestion, pollution, and social and biological disorder accompany our growing material wealth, an increasing portion of what passes for progress is illusory. We face the choice either of using more of each gain to offset the problems of growth or of accepting such threats to the quality of life as smog, rising crime rates, dead fish, and vanishing species. Rather than getting full measure for our resources and toil, we seem to be on a treadmill that makes us run faster and faster just to inch forward.

Growth is not an unmixed blessing, and the purpose of this article is to argue that growth is no longer the factor we should be trying to increase.

Unfortunately, growth is as deeply entrenched in our economic thinking as rain dancing has been for some other societies. In each case there is faith that results will come indirectly if a capricious and little-understood power is propitiated. Thus, instead of concentrating directly on the goods and values we want, we emphasize growth, exploit the environment faster, and assume that good things will follow by some indirect mechanism.

From time to time, the correlation between rainfall and rain dancing must have been good enough to perpetuate the tradition. Similarly, the correlations between exploitation of the environment, growth, and progress were usually excellent in our recent past. So great have been the successes of our economic habits that they have become almost sacrosanct and are not to be challenged.

However, here in the United States as in most of the world, the relationships between people and environment have changed drastically, and past experience is no longer a reliable guide. While we rush headlong through the present with frontier-day attitudes, our runaway growth generates noxious physical and sociological by-products that threaten the very quality of our lives. Although we still seem confident that technology will solve all problems as they arise, the problems are already far ahead of us, and many are growing faster than their solutions (2).

We cannot return to some golden and fictionally perfect era of the past, and we certainly should extend the knowledge on which not only our comfort but our very existence depends. However, to cope with the future, we may need a fundamental reanalysis of the economic strategy that directs our application of knowledge. Instead of producing more and more to be cast sooner and sooner on our growing piles of junk, we need to concentrate on improving our total quality of life.

If environmental resources were infinite, as our behavior seems to assume, then the rate at which we created wealth would depend mainly on our rate of exploitation, which is certainly accelerated by growth. However, the idea of an unlimited environment is increasingly untenable, in spite of our growing technological capacity to develop new resources.

Boulding has beautifully contrasted the open or "cowboy" economy, where resources are considered infinite, with the closed "spaceman" economy of the future (3). He has pointed out that, as the earth becomes recognized as a closed space capsule with finite quantities of resources, the problem becomes one of maintaining adequate capital stocks with the least possible production and consumption (or "throughput"). However, this idea of keeping the economic plumbing full, with the least possible pressure and flow, is still almost unthinkable. Experience to the contrary is still too fresh.

CULT OF GROWTH

The economic boom of World War II, in contrast with the stagnation of the Great Depression, seemed to verify the Keynesian theory that abundance will follow if we keep the economy moving. As a result, continuing growth has been embraced as a cornerstone of our economy and the answer to many of our economic problems. At least for the short run, growth seems to be the answer to distribution of wealth, debt, the population explosion, unemployment, and international competition. Let us start with the distribution of wealth.

Probably no other factor has contributed as much to human strife as has discontentment or competition concerning wealth. Among individuals and nations, differences in wealth separate the "haves" from the "have-nots." The "have-nots" plot to redress the imbalance, and the "haves" fight to protect their interests and usually have the power to win. However, the precariousness of their position, if recognized, demands a more just balance. But, rather than decrease their own wealth, they find it much more comfortable to enrich the poor, both within a nation and among the nations. Only growth offers the possibility of bringing the poor up without bringing the rich down.

In our market society, the distribution of wealth has come to depend on jobholding, consumption, and, to an increasing extent, on creating dissatisfaction with last year's models. Unless this year's line of larger models can be sold, receipts will not be sufficient to pay the jobholders and assure further consumption. Inadequate demand would mean recession. We have therefore been urged: Throw something away. Stir up the economy. Buy now. And if there are two of us buying where there had been only one, wonderful! Rapid consumption and a growing economy help to distribute income and goods and have been accepted as part of "progress."

Problems of debt also seem to be answered by growth. To keep up with production, consumption may need to be on credit, or personal debt. But debt is uncomfortable. However, if we are assured that our income will grow, then we can pay off today's debt from tomorrow's

expanded income. Growth (perhaps with just a little inflation) is accepted as an answer.

The same reasoning applies to corporate debt, the national debt, and the expansion of government services. As long as debt is not increasing in proportion to income, why worry? Debt is something we expect to outgrow, especially if we can keep the interest paid.

The population explosion is growth that is finally causing widespread concern. Yet many businessmen can think of nothing worse than the day our population stops growing. New citizens are the customers on which our economic growth depends. Conversely, economic growth can meet the needs of added people—if we are careful not to look beyond our borders.

Growth might also handle unemployment problems, and Myrdal (4) has indicated that only an expanding economy and massive retraining can incorporate our increasingly structural "underclass" into the mainstream of American life.

Finally, there is the problem of international competition. In an era when our sphere of influence and overseas sources of economic health are threatened, strength is imperative. Yet our main adversary has grown from a backward nation to a substantial industrial and military power. To counter the threat, we expect to outgrow the competition.

The evidence suggests that growth is good and that we have always grown. Isn't it reasonable to believe that we always will? This question takes us from the short run to the middle and long run.

DYNAMICS OF GROWTH

Viewed in the most general terms, growth will continue as long as there is something capable of growing and the conditions are suitable for its growth. The typical growth pattern starts slowly because growth cannot be rapid without an adequate base, be it capital, number of cells or organisms, or surfaces for crystallization. However, if other conditions are suitable, growth can proceed at a compound rate, accelerating as the base increases. But growth is eventually slowed or stopped by "limiting factors." These factors can include exhaustion of the materials needed for growth. They can also include lack of further space; the predation, disease, or parasitism encouraged by crowding; social or psychological disorganization; and concentrations of wastes or other products of growth. For example, the concentration of alcohol eventually limits the growth of yeast in wine.

Perhaps it is worth examining the U.S. economy within this frame of reference. Although its vigor has been attributed solely to free enterprise, or to democracy, or to divine grace, it fits the general growth model of a few well-adapted entities with growth potential (settlers) landing on an extremely rich and little exploited growth medium (North America).

Our settlers had, or soon acquired, the technological skills of Europe. They also had the good fortune to inherit and elaborate a political philosophy of equality, diffused power, and the right to benefit from one's own efforts. So armed, they face a rich and nearly untouched continent. The growth we are still witnessing today is probably nothing more than the inevitable.

But the end of growth is also inevitable. In a finite environment no pattern of growth can continue forever. Sooner or later both our population growth and our economic growth must stop. The crucial questions are When? and How will it come about?

Malthus once saw food shortages as the factor that would limit population growth. At least half of the world lives with Malthusian realities, but the technological nations have so far escaped his predictions. To what extent can technology continue to remove the limiting factors? Will we use foresight and intelligence? Or will we wait until congestion, disease, social and psychological disorganization, and perhaps even hunger finally limit our growth?

Perhaps there is little time to spare (5). Many factors already in operation could stop or greatly curtail the economic growth of the United States within the next 10 to 30 years. Furthermore, the multiplier effect of many economic factors could transform an apparently low-risk decline into an accelerating downward spiral. If devastating results are to be avoided, the adjustment from a rapidly growing to a much slowed economy will take time, and we should examine the problems and possibilities far enough in advance to be prepared.

THE CASE FOR PESSIMISM

Some of the very problems we hope to outgrow result in part from growth. Certainly the rapid changes brought by a growing economy contribute strongly to unemployment, migration to the cities, and the uneven distribution of wealth. A great deal of our debt can also be attributed to growth, as people try to keep up with what is new. Even the population explosion may result in part from confidence that the future offers increasing abundance. By trying to inundate the problems with more growth, we may actually be intensifying the causes.

If there were no other powers in the world, technology might be sufficient to sustain our growth, replace our shortages, and keep us ahead of the problems. Boulding (6) has suggested that we may have a chance, and probably only one, to convert our environmental capital into enough knowledge so that we can henceforth live without a rich natural environment.

But we are not alone. The Communists have vowed to bury us, one way or another, and can be expected to do whatever they can to upset our applecart. We can expect competition in many places in a struggle for spheres of influence and the roots of power. The nation or bloc that can extend its influence can gain raw materials and markets and can deny them to its competitors.

It is doubtful that we can retain the hegemony enjoyed in the late 1940s, and technology cannot fully fill the breach. Our competitors have access to the same technology that we do, and, if they gain control of rich resources and markets while ours are declining, they can increase their power relative to ours.

Closely related to competion for spheres of influence are the rising nationalism and aspirations of the underdeveloped countries. Extractive economies have seldom made them wealthy, and they aspire increasingly toward industrialization. As elements in the global struggle for power, they can demand technological assistance by threatening to go elsewhere for it if refused. From their point of view, it would be rational to put their resources on the world market, to try to get enough for them to support aspirations toward technology, and to let us bid without privileged status.

The problem is compounded by rapid communication and increasing awareness by the aspiring nations that wealth and consumption are disproportionate. The United States, for example, has about 6 percent of the world's population and consumes about 40 percent of the world's annual production. Until such differences in wealth are substantially reduced, they will create constant tension and antagonism. While enduring the many frustrations and setbacks of incipient economic growth, the aspiring nations may be happy to do whatever they can to reduce our wealth. The possible effect is suggested by England's economic woes since she lost her empire and her control over vast resources and markets.

If the aspiring nations and the Communists are not enough to slow us down, perhaps our friends will add the finishing touch. Western Europe is becoming increasingly powerful as an economic bloc and will compete for many of the resources and markets we would like to have. From another quarter, we can expect increasing competition from the Japanese.

In addition to these external forces, there are processes within our own nation that could slow our rate of growth. One of them is the increasing recognition that the products of runaway growth can damage the quality of living, especially for adults who remember a different past. When our rivers are choked with sewage, our cities are choked with automobiles and smog, and our countryside is choked with suburbs, some people begin to wonder if "the good life" will be achieved through more growth and goods. When goods are so abundant and the environment so threatened, will people continue to want even more goods at the expense of environmental quality?

Even the growth promised by automation may be self-limiting. The machines used by "management" to replace "labor" are not going to engage in collective bargaining. However, labor outnumbers management at the ballot box and may well counter such threats by demanding government control of automation and the protection of jobs, even at the cost of slowing our economic growth.

We already have a rising number of permanently unemployed and unemployable people who probably threaten our domestic tranquillity far more than "have-not" nations threaten international stability. Our traditions of self-reliance seem increasingly inadequate now that jobholding depends largely on technological skills that are so much easier to acquire in some settings than in others.

In addition to such technological unemployment, Heilbroner (7) has listed three other factors that may slow our growth. The first is the extent to which we now depend on defense expenditures to maintain growth and the likelihood that these outlays will eventually stabilize. His second point is that capitalism is inherently unstable, even though the factors that caused the Great Depression are now better understood and largely under control. His third point concerns the size of government expenditures that might be needed for antirecession policy in the future. If investments in plant, equipment, and construction are all low in 1980, he has estimated that government expenditures of $50 to $75 billion per year may be required to maintain growth and that Congress may well balk at such appropriations.

Another factor that could slow growth was suggested by Brown (8). Growth can be slowed by the increasing amount of energy and organization required for subsequent units of output from resources of decreasing richness. So far, as we have used up the richest mineral resources, improved technology, imports, newly located deposits, and the redefinition of resources have kept us ahead of the problem. But, if the difficulty of extracting essential materials from the environment should ever happen to increase more rapidly than our technological efficiency, our economy could become static and then decline.

Perhaps of greater importance, Brown predicted that the level of organization needed for a very populous society would become so interdependent that failure at one point could trigger failures elsewhere until a chain reaction led to total collapse. In relation to his prediction, the chain reaction aspects of power failures in the Northeast, the Southwest, and elsewhere are sobering. Also sobering is the growing power of strikes to disrupt our economy.

As stated earlier, growth must inevitably stop, and the major uncertainties are When? and How? Despite these uncertainties, the factors examined above could limit our growth within the next few decades, and they merit careful thought. Because growth has become such an integral part of our economy, any sudden setback is greatly feared and could be disastrous. Nevertheless, transition from accelerating growth to some other economic pattern must eventually be made, and it is desirable that we make a smooth transition to something other than total collapse.

Perhaps there is an acceptable alternative to growth or collapse.

A SIMPLIFIED CALCULUS FOR "THE GOOD LIFE"

If we look only at the production side of economics, it is easy to visualize the average standard of living (SL) as the sum of material goods that have been produced divided by the total population (9):

$$SL = \frac{\Sigma \text{ production}}{\text{population}}$$

It follows that the average standard of living can be raised only by increasing production faster than we increase population. Quite conceivably, we could have a static or even declining population and a rising standard of living. For example, the Black Death, which decimated the population of Europe in the 14th century, has been credited with providing the surplus that kicked off the Renaissance. However, other factors are involved.

Goods often have a limited useful life and are depleted by a variety of losses. Thus, for a better computation of the average standard of living, we can subtract the total of everything that has been lost from the total of everything that has been produced and divide this difference by the population:

$$SL = \frac{\Sigma \text{ production} - \Sigma \text{ losses}}{\text{population}}$$

The per capita share of wealth now includes antiques, the serviceable old, and the new. From this relationship it appears that we can increase the average standard of living by reducing losses as well as by increasing production. However, in our economy, production is closely related to consumption, and we face the seemingly illogical fact that we can increase the standard of living by increasing waste! Such losses as normal wear and tear, designed obsolescence, and accidents can increase consumption enough to stimulate production.

Even if we grant that technology can create and exploit new resources as needed, we must deal with the quality of living (QL) as well as the purely material standard of living. In addition to material goods, the quantity and quality of both services and experiences available to each person will be included. The model must therefore be expanded to

$$QL = \frac{\Sigma \text{ production} - \text{losses}}{\text{population}}$$
$$+ \frac{\text{services/time}}{\text{population}} + \frac{\text{experiences/time}}{\text{population}}$$

As material comforts increase, it is likely that "the good life" will be defined to a greater degree by services. And, as services become more abundant, the emphasis may shift toward experiences. Services may well increase in abundance and excellence with continued growth. The quantity of experiences may also increase. However, the quality of many experiences is likely to decline, especially if the environment deteriorates seriously.

Our values will undoubtedly shift toward what is available, but this shift will lag enough to leave many desires for things that are remembered and cherished but no longer available. This "memory gap" between what is remembered and wanted and what is available will mean a decrease in the quality of living unless it is at least offset by new advantages. Right now, for example, how many families no longer have a "view" from their picture window because of growth? What will be the impact of added growth on activities that let the imagination run free without an overdose of organization, regulation, and spectatorship? As growth continues, how many of us will long for such things as a picnic by an unpolluted lake, fishing in a clear stream, room for a family dog, or even places to walk, ride, boat, or fly with a minimum of regulation and traffic?

In mastering the details of production and distribution we seem to forget the environmental base on which our productive forces and many enjoyable experiences depend. Even in our outdoor recreation, we still tend to emphasize access to new areas rather than management of existing areas for continued enjoyment. One wonders if the rise in our standard of living can be sustained or whether it is the result of a rising rate of exploitation of a limited and exhaustible environment. To what extent are we drawing on the capital as well as the interest of our global savings account? Can technology replace environmental capital? Can it do so in time?

We may grow into a "Brave New World" where pleasures come from happiness pills and electrodes in the brain. Conversely, we may grow into a "1984," where repressive measures

405

are necessary to keep society from falling apart. As a third alternative, we may exhaust the resources or disrupt the organization needed for a dynamic technology and then collapse to a thin population of subsistence farmers. To find a better alternative, we may have to rethink our entire economic strategy. How can we do it?

SOME CRITERIA
FOR A FUTURE ECONOMY

As the product of a long and often stormy evolution, our economic system is not something that can be overhauled by a few armchair critics. Yet one need not be an expert to identify some difficulties with our present system and to suggest what it ought to be doing for us. Too often we seem to view the economy as a mysterious creature operating by its own inscrutable laws and to which we humans must be subservient. Instead, we should see it as a human institution which must serve human needs as directly as possible.

Now that we are so capable of fouling our own nest, dare we assume that an "invisible hand" will somehow guide us automatically along the correct course to survival? Although modern technology can work many wonders, it can also permit enormous mistakes to be made before we have learned the consequences of our actions. Now that we are on the threshold of such things as weather modification and massive transfers of water between regions, one wonders how sure we can be of avoiding unexpected and undesirable side effects. Yet shortages induced by rapid growth may force us to act before we understand the full implications of our actions. As examples, DDT killed many fish and threatened many species of birds before we knew that it would, and some Eskimos ingested dangerous amounts of cesium-137 from what were considered harmless tests of nuclear devices. Smog alerts, epidemics of hepatitis, unemployment, riots, and other problems already demonstrate that personal greed does not necessarily aggregate to public good in a populous and highly interrelated society.

A few criteria for an ideal economy are obvious. It must provide a decent quality of living for every citizen. For the foreseeable future, it must also maintain enough national strength to prevent another nation from overwhelming us. Beyond these criteria, perhaps our major concern with any future economic system is that it not repress individual freedom any more than is inevitable because of population density and technological complexity.

Two factors seem of particular importance in maintaining individual freedom. The first is representative government. Although many voters are apathetic and poorly informed, it would be an awful and probably irreversible step to lose the power to turn an unsatisfactory government out of office by peaceful processes. Yet, as we speculate on the future, it is not difficult to imagine political instability and chaos as the electorate votes "no confidence" in the economic policies of successive governments that deal unsuccessfully with resource and environment problems. Problems resulting from population growth, worldwide as well as domestic, seem especially likely to create a serious challenge to representative government everywhere in the years ahead.

A second factor of importance to individual freedom is diffused decision-making. There is safety in a redundant system in which many suppliers estimate needs and many purchasers select among competing goods and services. Such redundancy guards against a crisis in one sector mushrooming into total collapse throughout a highly interdependent technological society. As society becomes more complex, it is unlikely that centralized decision-makers, even with the best computers, can foresee all our needs and all the effects of each decision. In addition, the centralization of decision-making is likely to decrease individual freedom.

Self-interest is also important as a strong motive force that needs to be retained in any future economy. However, in a complex society where one person's actions affect many other people, self-interest must operate within the constraints needed to guard the interests of the total society.

The market system is probably still the most effective means of maintaining the abundance, individual freedom, redundant decision-making, and self-interest we desire. However, it is less effective than it could be in achieving high levels of human benefit. For example, as we chase the rainbow of economic growth, our marketplace decisions are usually based only on the costs incurred by the individual or firm and ignore the costs borne by society in general. Thus industries have been allowed to save money by dumping their wastes, often untreated, into the atmosphere, lakes and streams, or onto the land. But the costs are borne by the public in terms of respiratory disease, dead fish, and lost amenity and recreation opportunities.

Perhaps rather subtle controls on the economy would enhance the quality of our living by forcing a consideration of *all* costs of economic activity. Included would be such social costs as air and water pollution, building suburbs on prime agricultural land, and spoiling scenic or recreation areas.

One means of bringing hidden costs into the market system would be to tax or charge the responsible party for the full costs of repairing, replacing, or cleaning up whatever was damaged by his economic activity (*10*). Water users might be required either to return water of equal quality or to pay a pollution charge. Road builders might be required to provide lands of quality and acreage equal to park lands taken for highways. Such costs would simply enter into the total allocation process. If protection of the environment were accepted as a legitimate cost of production, many abuses would simply become too expensive to perpetuate and some activities that are now profitable would become uneconomic.

A second difficulty results because marketplace decisions are usually short-run decisions that de-emphasize the future. Currently we usually discount every future benefit by assuming that it can be equated to whatever present investment would give the same value at a selected rate of interest. For example, at an interest rate of 6 percent, each dollar in benefits 50 years from now would discount to a present worth of approximately 5 cents.

Such discounting may be perfectly appropriate for decisions that can be readily reversed. However, irreversible decisions should not be based on discounting. For example, the depletion of soils, water tables, minerals, interesting species, and space and amenity values must be curbed if future generations are to have a rich life.

I am not saying that we must go "back to nature," which is clearly impossible. A technological society can live only by greatly modifying nature on much of its land. But at some point we must admit that future people are just as important as present people and that we cannot justly discount the value of their environment. Unless we use the environment responsibly, we will greatly reduce the range of opportunities and alternatives available to our descendants.

Again, some fairly subtle controls on the economy might be effective. Tax laws are already being used to encourage or discourage specific practices, and some changes in direction might become essential. For example, to accelerate the discovery and exploitation of mineral resources, we now give generous depletion allowances. However, to encourage more efficient use of such resources, we may need to institute resource depletion taxes. We might also need a space depletion tax to encourage effective use of land and to discourage our urban sprawl.

There may be some merit in a replacement tax for durable goods. By taxing people on the frequency with which they replace things, we might encourage them to make things last as long as possible and might reestablish a belief that durability means quality. This belief might in turn improve the quality of living by greatly weakening the link we have developed between waste, production, and distribution in our economic system. For example, if each automobile lasted twice as long, we could have just as many automobiles per family by producing only half as many cars. The effect could be less industrial smoke, fewer junkyards, and fewer new scars on the landscape due to mining. It could also mean that more resources, energy, and leisure would be available for purposes other than building automobiles.

Yet, true to the assumption that man is subservient to the economic system, we hear waste defended as necessary for our prosperity. Surely we can organize our economy efficiently enough to avoid having to throw things away to have more! Are we inescapably on such a treadmill?

As we approach the "spaceman" economy suggested by Boulding, we must come into better equilibrium with the environment instead of trying to sustain the continual disequilibrium implied by our treadmill pattern of growth. We have tried to keep our economic plumbing full by increasing the pressure and flow rather than by fixing the leaks. Improved knowledge, efficiency, and durability can repair the leaks in the economic vessel that contains society's wealth, and their achievement will probably always be a desirable kind of progress. But we face enormous problems if we continue to insist that everything must grow.

First we must stop the population growth that is the major stimulus to many other kinds of growth. Thus far we have been unwilling and unable to take this step, and it seems tragic that we may reproduce ourselves back into scarcity just as we are within reach of affluence for all. Unless population growth is slowed on a world-wide basis, the "have" nations may soon face the ethical dilemma of reducing their own per capita wealth by sharing with the "have-not" nations or reverting to increasing "defense" operations to control desperate people who are trying to better their own lot.

In addition to stabilizing population levels, we need to recycle our environmental resources. For some structural purposes, we might develop reusable polymers that can be assembled, used, separated into constituents, and reassembled with minimum losses. Such materials seem well within reach of foreseeable technology and might be preferable to the problems of unscrambling and reusing alloyed metals. Human wastes should go back to agricultural lands rather than into our water supplies. Because fossil fuels will not last long if the rest of the world begins to consume them at anywhere near our own rates of consumption, much of our energy may have to come from the sun. At current levels of technology, nuclear fission and fusion may both be too dirty for widespread use. Petroleum may need to be conserved primarily for lubrication, with re-

processing after use, or perhaps for aircraft use where other energy sources might be too heavy.

My comments may amount to a redefinition of "progress." Too often, progress has been equated with mere growth, change, or exploitation rather than with a real improvement in the per capita quality of life. Thus a new smokestack has usually passed as progress, and the odors generated by new factories have been said to "smell like money." But getting rid of the stacks already in town may now be a more rational view of progress. Developing a smokeless process, a product that lasts longer, or a process that requires less expenditure of human energy, or something that makes life more meaningful—all these may better qualify as progress.

In its time the treadmill pattern of growth was progress enough and served us well. But as the relationships change between human numbers and the total environment, we must abandon unregulated growth before it strangles us.

The essential tasks ahead are to stabilize human population levels and to learn to recycle as much of our material abundance as possible. Ideally, the change to new ways would be by incremental, evolutionary, and perhaps experimental steps, although some writers believe an incremental approach may not work (11). But if steps of some kind are not started soon, they may well be outrun by the pace of events. Unless we can slow the treadmill on which we have been running faster and faster, we may stumble—and find ourselves flung irretrievably into disaster.

REFERENCES AND NOTES

1. E. J. Misham, *The Costs of Economic Growth* (Praeger, New York, 1967).
2. Although we have generally assumed our wellbeing to be a linear function of total size (X), it has turned out to be the curvilinear function $Y = a + bX - cX^n$, where n is greater than 1. Thus at some point we can expect added growth to decrease our wellbeing rather than add to it.
3. K. E. Boulding, in *Environmental Quality in a Growing Economy*, H. Jarrett, Ed. (Resources for the Future, Washington, D.C., 1966). pp. 9–10.
4. G. Myrdal, *Challenge to Affluence* (Pantheon, New York, 1963).
5. For a summary of threats to our survival, see J. Platt. *Science* **166**, 1115 (1969).
6. K. E. Boulding, in *Future Environments of North America*, F. F. Darling and J. P. Milton, Eds. (Natural History, Garden City, N.Y., 1966), p. 234.
7. R. L. Heilbroner, *The Future as History* (Grove Press, New York, 1959), pp. 136–140.
8. H. Brown, *The Challenge of Man's Future* (Viking, New York, 1954), pp. 222–225.
9. To be precise, we should exclude production used to replace capital goods. However, the general logic of this analysis does not depend on such refinement.
10. M. M. Gaffney, *Bull. At. Sci.* **21** (6) 20 (1965); A. V. Kneese, *Pap. Proc. Reg. Sci. Ass.* **11**, 231 (1963).
11. B. L. Crowe, *Science* **166**, 1103 (1969).

Selection 36

Ecosystem and Public Land Policy

Commentary

If the quality of life is declining and the degradation of the environment is increasing, it is because man for too long a time has considered himself apart from nature rather than a part of nature. Nature is governed by one set of rules, he thinks, and he by another, largely of his own making. And therein lies the reason for the ecological crisis. Man has looked upon the earth as an infinite source of materials. But there is a growing, even if not universal, awareness that perhaps man does fit somewhere within the larger framework of natural processes and has managed to upset or impair them to his own disadvantage.

Man has approached the planet earth as an open ecosystem. There is a constant flow of imputs of energy and raw materials and outputs of products and waste that ultimately are lost to the system. But all the while man has been treating the earth as an open system, he has in fact been operating within a closed system which he has been constantly short-circuiting. Except for the energy of the sun, all of the materials available to him, air, water, space, and collective resources, are those that already exist or within limits can be biologically renewed. The earth that has been regarded as infinite is now being discovered as finite. And if man is to exist in a finite world, then he has to work with nature's rules, under which he evolved. Man has to operate within a complex of dynamic interrelated systems of which he is an integral part and the existence of which modern man is just beginning to comprehend. Man needs to develop an ecosystem approach to the management of his world.[1]

In his relation to ecosystems man, unlike other members of the total complex, operates at two levels, the physical level, which relates to the alteration of environments, and the decision-making level, which relates to man's behavior toward the environment.[2] Thus, the impact of man on natural ecosystems is mediated through human society. Since this is the case, society itself must be a part of ecosystems.

To work within the context of ecosystems involves a number of implications. For one, all of man's activities must be in harmony with the functioning of ecosystems. This does not mean that man must work only within natural ecosystems. For thousands of years man has been dependent upon artificial ecosystems of his own creation (see Selections 6 to 9). But it does mean that artificial and natural ecosystems modified under management must benefit to the fullest from the functional processes common to natural ecosystems. To accomplish this, man must develop an understanding and respect for the potentialities of natural ecosystems. An ecosystem approach also involves a change from a consumptive economy to an economy oriented toward the maintenance of capital stock and the recycling of materials. The concept of the ecosystem must be viewed more broadly than that held by ecology. Man's ecosystem also includes social, political, and economic systems superimposed on the environment.

It is within such a conceptual view of the ecosystem that Lynton Caldwell, a political economist, explores the application of the ecosystem theory to public land management. Although the selection relates primarily to public lands, Caldwell describes how man's ecosystem transcends a purely ecological one and demonstrates the decisive role of social, political, and economic systems in fate and the functioning of naturally operating ecosystems. What Caldwell writes of public lands applies to other resources as well.

---

[1]G. VanDyne (ed.), *The Ecosystem Concept in Natural Resource Management*, New York, Academic Press, 1969.
[2]A. M. Schultz, "Ecosystems and Environment," San Francisco, Calif., Canfield Press (a department of Harper & Row), 1971.

Selection 36

The Ecosystem as a Criterion
for Public Land Policy

by Lynton K. Caldwell

A public lands policy restricted to lands in governmental ownership has been politically expedient but ecologically unrealistic. The natural processes of physical and biological systems that comprise the land do not necessarily accommodate themselves to the artificial boundaries and restrictions that law and political economy impose upon them. The stress of human demands upon the land tends to displace natural processes throughout its ecosystems and to impair the capacity of the natural environment for self-renewal. American public land policy is based upon a set of historically derived assumptions—legal, economic, and political—that provide no means for taking the fundamental ecological context of land use into account. It is, of course, necessary to cope with land problems within the conventional context of public attitudes, laws, and economic arrangements, inadequate though they may be to encompass all of the land related needs of contemporary society. But it is also important to know that there is a larger context for policy with which laws and governments must ultimately reckon: it is the condition of the land as the physical base for human welfare and survival. If human demands upon the natural environment continue to mount, it will become necessary as a matter of welfare and survival to abandon present land policy assumptions for a policy of public management of human environment on ecologically valid principles. The proposed National Land Use Policy Act of 1970 (S. 3354, Jackson) specifical-

ly indicates ecological factors as criteria for sound land use planning and establishes a national-state-local system for obtaining comprehensive land use planning and management in which ecologically sound principles are favored.

How would a public land policy based upon ecosystems concepts differ from policies based upon other considerations? Public land policies here and abroad have traditionally been based on juridic, economic, or demographic concepts.[1] Land planning based on sectoral analysis (essentially on economic and social uses) has been the predominant source of policy in those countries in which the rational allocation of natural resources in land has become an accepted public responsibility. Spatial planning, "which considers man and his natural environment in their geographical and historical associations," is an alternative complementary approach to land policy, but does not necessarily take ecological considerations fully into account.[2] Ecological considerations, although not always by that name, have sometimes influenced land policies. But an ecosystems approach to public land policy has seldom been attempted on national or regional scales. The reason does not lie wholly in the complexity and ambiguity of ecosystems, although these are deterring factors. Failure to apply ecological criteria to land use policies is primarily the consequence of two related causes. The first is the inability of society, because of inadequate knowledge, insufficient

THIS SELECTION is reprinted with the author's permission and with permission from *Natural Resources Journal*, Vol. 10, pp. 203—220, 1970, published by the University of New Mexico School of Law. This paper is an elaboration and extension of an earlier version, *An Ecosystem Approach to Public Land Policy*, presented at the Tenth Annual Western Resources Conference, Colorado State University, July 1—3, 1968.

[1]C. Haar, Land-Use Planning (1959), Law and Land: Anglo-American Planning Practice (1964). *See also*, C. Berger, Land Ownership and Use (1968).

[2]E. Ackerman, *A View of Terrestrial Space* (a review of L'Organization de l'espace: Élémentes de géographie volontaire by Jean Labasse, Paris; Hermann, 1966, 157 Science 1031. Labasse's book is a major contribution to the literature of land policy and planning.)

wealth, or incompatible institutions, to build ecologically based land policies into a general system of environmental management. The second, and more obvious, is incompatible interests among conflicting land users.

An ecosystems approach to land policy encounters resistance to the degree that it is inconsistent with the values, assumptions, institutions, and practices that shape the prevailing social arrangement which affect the custody and care of the land. Ecological considerations may, in themselves, be compatible with specific aspects of traditional land use arrangements. For example, specific legal restrictions in Denmark, the Netherlands, and the United Kingdom are designed to protect and perpetuate certain traditional uses of the land for ecological reasons as well as for sentimental and esthetic purposes. Incompatibility among uses derives as often from the structuring of land use arrangements—from the way in which the various institutions influencing the use of land are related—as it does from contradictions among the uses themselves. Thus the factors involved in banking, taxation, insurance, and property law, when woven into a non-ecological matrix of public land policy, afford a very resistant, inadvertent barrier to an ecosystems approach. To establish rapidly a land policy in which ecological principles predominated would require that the conventional matrix be unravelled and rewoven in a new pattern. In a colony on the moon there would be an overwhelming presumption in favor of a predominately ecological approach. The arguments for survival would outweigh all others. On earth, ecological criteria will increasingly modify or replace other indices of value as the constraints of the closed-system environment of Spaceship Earth become increasingly apparent.

The context of land policy changes when the ecosystems concept is introduced. The discourse can no longer be confined realistically to lands in governmental ownership, but must take into account whatever lands are included in particular ecosystems, regardless of who holds title to them. This broadening of the policy context may be opposed by persons committed to the inviolate right of private landownership, or who hold specific interests in land use that they believe might be threatened by public action. Ecological principles are more often and more easily applied to government lands than to private holdings. Pressure for rapid economic return, and the financial or technological inability of the private owner to apply ecological concepts, are the more common explanations. But if the management of whole ecosystems becomes a matter of public policy, then the formulation of public land policy must proceed upon the basis of the proposition that all land is in some degree public.

To conceive an ecosystems approach to public land policy, one must have first arrived at an ecological viewpoint toward the world of man and nature. But this is not the viewpoint from which pioneers, land speculators, farmers, miners, stockmen, lawyers, bankers, or local government officials have commonly seen the land. To institute an ecosystems approach to public land policy, a great many other things besides land must be considered. An ecosystems approach is essentially a total systems approach. It therefore includes in its purview many things omitted in less comprehensive systems. It would impose constraints upon single purpose approaches to the environment and would arouse hostility among individuals whose single purpose pursuits would thereby be constrained.

I. IMPLICATIONS OF AN ECOSYSTEMS LAND POLICY

Before examining more closely the ecosystem concept and the opposition to its implied modification of rights of landownership, the implications of the term "public land policy" must be identified, as they are basic to the questions: What approach to land policy is most consistent with the public interest? All things considered, what policy is best? The term "best" arouses a multitude of subsidiary questions. It is certain to arouse objections among persons unwilling or unable to consider normative concepts. It may fail to interest persons who believe that the only practical focus of public policy is upon the condition of things as they are. Nevertheless, goals and values are implicit in the concept of "policy." The student concerned with the public interest must examine the relevance of public policies to changes in the condition of society and to future stability and welfare. Not all criteria for the formulation and application of a policy afford equally effective means to its specified ends. Moreover, not

411

all goals or objectives serve equally well the general or long-term interests of society. For example, policies that permitted massive and continuing loss of top soil or encouraged price-escalating land speculation would not be a good *public* land policy under any criteria, however beneficial they might appear to be to the immediate interests of particular land users or owners.

In the United States, and particularly in the West, ambiguity can easily occur in the use of the expression "public land policy." Does the expression connote a public policy for land generally—all land? Or does it refer only to policies regarding lands in public ownership? Conventional American assumptions and word usage take the latter definition as the more practical and appropriate. Yet eminent domain, land use zoning, and sale of land for tax delinquency, make it clear that public jurisdiction over land is general and not confined to public ownership. An ecosystems approach to public land policy assumes a scope that embraces all land regardless of its ownership or custody under law. The metes and bounds of ecosystems are determined by physical, biological, and cultural forces. Men may impose their own arrangements on natural systems, but engineers, surveyors, and lawyers neither amend nor repeal the so-called laws of nature. Ecosystems form a complex unity embracing the entire earth. And although men have never been able to deal with the ultimate unity of the ecosphere, they have been learning more and more about its interrelated workings. As more has been learned, the practicality of introducing ecological concepts into land use policy is enhanced. But the word "practicality" may be given two different interpretations. There is a conventional short-run practicality of socially sanctioned arrangements. There is also a long-run practicality that takes account of ecological trends, assesses the consequences of their continuation into the future, and estimates the effects of modifying forces that may impinge upon them.

Implicit in the ecosystems concept is recognition that maintenance of the ecosystem depends upon the consistency of man-made standards, laws, and boundaries with those that have evolved through natural processes. For example, man's structural works or artificial boundaries when forced into or across a natural system may alter, impair, or destroy it.

The Southern Pacific Railroad causeway altered the ecology of the Great Salt Lake, and land fills on the Eastern Seaboard estuaries are impairing numerous and valuable marine and salt-marsh ecosystems. Persistent mining of ground water has changed the ecology of soils and land surfaces in many parts of the United States, notably in central Arizona. It is obvious that man-made ecosystems will inevitably affect those of natural origin where civilized society exists. It is not obvious, however, that human changes must always be destructive to natural systems or that, with thoughtful planning, man-made and natural ecosystems could not more often coexist in harmony.

But why this concern with an ecological basis for land policy? By what reasoning is an ecosystems approach to land use more useful or more valid than any other? Are ecological criteria merely the tools or overt expressions of a naturalistic ideology—an ecological mystique—which some nature lovers and a few apprehensive scientists would substitute for the economic common sense of people who know that the practical business of life continues to be the procuring of food, clothing, and shelter? Does an ecosystems concept impute some teleological design to nature? Is man required to seek out nature's purposes and adapt his laws and practices to nature's ends regardless of his own needs and purposes? The ancient Christian, substituting God's purposes for nature's, could have affirmed this proposition. Adherents to natural law concepts might still do so. But in the dominant societies of this technoeconomic age, mastery or manipulation of nature has become a goal that sometimes approaches a secular religion. Nature, if she has purposes, does not reveal them in language that contemporary man has been able to understand. Technological man, however, has defined and developed his own purposes in relation to nature. These purposes basically require the obtaining of food, clothing, and shelter from nature, and to this end man has organized his relationships with his environment on the basis of the uses he makes of particular components of the natural world. These components are the familiar "natural resources."

As long as man's numbers were few, his technology simple, and his demands upon the natural world limited, it was feasible to deal with the land and its products as if they were no more than discrete resources. Man was unable simultaneously to make both rapid and far-reaching changes in natural ecosystems. Major ecological changes, such as deforestation or the spread of cultivation over the grasslands, required time, measured in Europe and Asia by centuries. Some of these changes, as in the brittle, sub-arid ecosystem of the Middle East, were cumulatively destructive. Other changes, as in the clearing of forests for agriculture in Western Europe, largely substituted one ecological system for another of comparable stability and productivity. But modern science and technology have permitted man to upset longstanding ecological balances. His numbers have multiplied without restraint. His technology has become powerful and complex with unpredictable side-effects, and his demands upon his environment have grown inordinate. Competition for resources has rapidly increased and conflicts among resource users have become a major phenomenon of politics.

If the categorizing of the products of nature into "natural resources" had been based upon a comprehending, selective utilization of the ecosystem, the implications of this "development process" for the integrity and survival of the ecosystem would have been available as a source for principles by which conflicts over resource uses might have been mediated. But ecosystems integrity as a criterion for policy choices has followed, not preceded, the natural resources concept of man-environment relationships. As a consequence, public land policy has shared in the contentiousness associated with the politics of natural resources, and the ecosystem concept has had as yet little mediating effect upon land-use conflicts. Neither in politics nor in administration has there been a generally accepted body of knowledge or doctrine by which conflicts over resource uses could be readily resolved. In the absence of an "ordering" or organizing concept, efforts to coordinate natural resources policies have been largely ineffectual or have been used as covers to impose or prevent one use over others. Prior to the recent intensification of the water pollution issue, the major impetus toward coordinative efforts in water policy may be seen as efforts to restrain the autonomous and arbitrary exercise of power by the Corps of Engineers, or it may be seen as efforts to reconcile differences between the Corps and competing

agencies, most frequently the Bureau of Reclamation.

Public policy for land use, as for resources use generally, has been decided chiefly through trial by political combat. "Conservation" as a concept has been helpful principally as an intermediary proposition, midway between unrestricted competition among resource users and an ecologically based view of public responsibility for the self-renewing capabilities of ecosystem. Aphorisms such as "conservation means wise use" are of little help in the absence of objective criteria for wisdom. An ecosystems approach to public land policy implies the possibility of public decisions based upon empirical principles of public interest in environmental quality and in the self-renewing capabilities of natural systems.

Availability of an objectively rational basis for land policy decisions (if such a basis is actually possible) does not imply, as a matter of course, that this basis will be accepted or acted upon. Human beings may be expected to act more often on a subjective level of rationality than upon more objective and enduring principles. But, until the ecosystems concept has been articulated and its amenability to practical application demonstrated, it is unavailable as a basis for policy. Yet, although the ecosystems approach to land policy remains largely on the theoretical level, it is nevertheless available for practical application at such time as it is perceived as a means of coping with the ecological predicament into which man has blundered.

To understand the ecological predicament of modern man is to begin to understand why an ecosystems approach may ultimately become necessary to human well-being and even to survival. Unfortunately, an understanding of the circumstances, now often described as the "ecological crisis," carries no automatic insight in how to correct or prevent conditions that are almost universally conceded to be harmful. If, as we shall presently contend, application of the ecosystems concept implies a wholly new way of organizing man's relations with the natural world, an ecosystems approach to public land policy implies fundamental changes in the rights and responsibilities of individuals and corporations in the possession and use of land.

It may not be too much to say that ecologically based public policies imply a thorough-

413

going transformation of some major sectors of the nation's political economy. The nature and scope of a public land policy based on ecological principles would be comprehensive and coordinative. The individual land-owner would lose certain rights and gain certain protections. Controversies over land use would be more often settled by administrative than by judicial means, and the criteria for settlement more often ecological fact than statutory law. Substantial changes could be expected to take place in the practical economics of land use. Application of ecological concepts would find a major obstacle in the treatment of land as a commodity. Private possession of land under ecological ground-rules could be made consistent with an ecosystems approach to land policy. But the freedom to buy, sell, or transfer land without regard to the ecological consequences of the intended or resulting action would not be consistent with an ecosystems approach. *Laissez faire* land economics, although deeply rooted in American folkways, is becoming increasingly inconsistent with the interests of the vast majority of citizens—a majority of citizens who live in great cities, own no land, and for whom the needs and amenities of life are becoming increasingly costly and difficult of access. All the same, the transition to an ecological approach will be painful, for as John Ise once remarked, ". . . Americans are land value animals. For three hundred years they have been moving westward seeking titles to land they hoped would rise in value; for three hundred years they have been following the lure of unearned increment, the beacon light of 'something for nothing'. . . ."[3]

II. THE SUBSTANCE OF AN ECOSYSTEMS APPROACH

The ecosystems approach has been advanced as a new way of defining public land policy. It would clearly be different from policies now dominant in the United States and to a large extent in other countries also. But the specific ways in which ecosystems relationships could be used as criteria for public policy for land must be defined before their operational feasibility can be assessed. The following summary of the salient properties of ecosystems criteria suggests some of the practical advantages to be gained from their application to land policies.

The first and essential characteristic of the ecosystems approach is its wholistic emphasis. In a pluralistic political-economy that has generally eschewed wholistic thinking, this comprehensive outlook and analysis is a salutary corrective to the tendencies of society to attack problems on a linear or single purpose basis. The novelty of wholistic analysis is now greatly reduced by the growth of systems thinking in government and industry. Indeed, ecosystems criteria may be taken as an application of systems thinking to relationships among natural and artificial environments. Ecosystems criteria, for example, are absolutely essential to the construction of life-support systems for the exploration of the moon and outer space.

Secondly, ecosystems criteria are based on scientific knowledge, although science does not yet have adequate answers to all ecological problems. Public land policies are not notably based on scientific considerations. To enlist science in determining the *goals* of domestic policy is a departure from tradition, although science has often been invoked on behalf of policies adopted by other than scientific reasoning. For example, the Bureau of Land Management applies many scientific concepts in its administration of federal public lands, but there is much less science in the laws under which the total public land system operates. Obviously, science does not contain the answers to all policy questions, but in the present state of confusion and contradiction that characterizes land law, at least in the United States, scientific criteria might afford an objective basis for mediating otherwise irreconcilable disputes.[4]

Thirdly, an ecosystems approach uses administrative means in preference to adjudication.

---

[3] Ise, *Too Much and Too Poor*, in The American Way 103 (1955) (published by members of the Faculty Department of Economics, School of Business, University of Kansas). John Ise was for many years a stimulating and productive professor of economics at the University of Kansas and wrote extensively in the field of public policy for natural resources.

[4] The need for more adequate criteria for policy to remedy the present confusion and contradiction in the laws governing public (government) land has been outlined by Irving Senzel, Assistant Director, Bureau of Land Management, U.S. Department of the Interior in a paper, *Public Land Laws and Effective Management*, in Proceedings of the 10th Annual Western Resources Conference, Fort Collins, Colorado, July 1—3, 1968.

This becomes possible to the extent that laws, policies, and actions are based on scientifically ascertainable facts rather than on political or technological fiat. Questions of fact become more important than questions of law (at least in a technical sense). Numerous issues, once litigated in the courts, cease to be issues when certain rights, practices, or beliefs associated with land ownership are confirmed, modified, or extinguished by demonstrable evidence.

The substance of an ecosystems approach appears simple, although ecosystems are themselves infinitely complex. The approach begins with an assumption derived from scientific inquiry. The natural world is a composite of interrelating life-systems subsisting in a highly improbable terrestrial environment. This environment—the ecosphere—is finite. Some of the components are naturally renewable, others are not. Of its renewable components (or resources) some are capable of restoration within a time dimension meaningful to man. But others, fossil fuels, for example, are incapable of renewal, although for some resources substitutes may be found.

The ultimate necessity of an ecosystems approach to environmental policy, including land, follows from the finite amount of land, water, air, and other substances upon which the human economy depends, and the infinite character of human demands upon the environment. The heavier the stress of human demands upon the environment, the greater the degree to which those demands must be coordinated and policed in order that the economy continue to function. In an economy of scarce essentials and pressing demands either the strong preempt resources and deprive the weak, or, where democratic collectivism prevails, socialization, rationing, licensing, and summary police action are instituted to insure fair shares. Political *laissez faire* in relation to the environment is feasible only when the demands that man makes upon it are relatively light and when natural ecological processes are permitted to operate, continually renewing the ecosystem so that what man uses today is replaced for his use tomorrow. The argument for ecological sophistication in public policies for land and the environment is no longer primarily the threat of shortages of food, energy, or raw materials for industry that troubled the "classic conservationists." The more fundamental danger is to the quality of life and to human freedom—

especially personal freedom—that will follow from a course of action that presses society to extremities in the maximum utilization of resources and space. Total resource utilization may well require total social control and the loss of choice and variety in life as the price of continuing subsistence.

Throughout nearly all human history man appears to have enjoyed a generally favorable ecological equilibrium. There were, of course, exceptional circumstances in which natural disasters or human errors disrupted a particular localized part of the ecosystem. Earthquakes, floods, droughts, epidemics, and famines have disturbed the equilibrium, but the ecosphere as a whole has maintained its stability over thousands of years even though suffering and death have resulted from its localized oscillations. Technology and science have enabled man to cope more effectively with natural disasters, and in some measure to prevent them. But the very success of the human enterprises has created its greatest danger. Technoscience has now given man free rein to increase his numbers and his demands. The result has been a runaway increase in human populations and unremitting pressure on all resources, including land.

This rapid inflation of people and their demands has already impaired the quality of the human environment over large areas of the earth and threatens more serious damage in the years ahead. But at the present stage of human affairs, contemplation of the almost certain consequences of ecological folly is less painful than undergoing the changes that would be required to bring man-environment relationships into ecological balance. There may yet be time to preserve a margin of personal freedom, of environmental variety, and of unforeclosed opportunities that would be comparable to what man has experienced in the past. But the prospect of these conditions surviving into the next century is lessened every day. Science fiction, which often assumes a role of prophecy, presents the bleakest of prospects for human freedom and variety. The triumphs of science and technology do not seem to include the timely mastery by man of the cybernetics of his ecosystems. To accomplish this, he would first have to bring his impulses under control and to exercise a collective self-restraint that has not yet become one of man's strong characteristics.

The idea of instituting lesser controls *now* to protect basic values and to avoid more drastic measures later has little contemporary appeal. It is the American way, and indeed the human way, to react to crises rather than to forestall them. For who can be sure that the threatened crisis will actually materialize? There is no end to conventional wisdom on behalf of procrastination. What candidate for elective public office would advocate action in the face of dangers that were neither clear nor present in the perception of his constituents? How many politicians would commit themselves to the prevention of dangers that, if real, could only be prevented by an inconvenient rearranging of present institutions and relationships, and would cost prospective voters the happy prospect of something-for-nothing gains?

Contrary to allegations sometimes made by persons who see it threatening their particular interests, ecosystems policy is not anti-people. Human welfare, now and in the future, is its objective. But the welfare of the individual is ultimately dependent upon the viability of the life-supporting ecosystem. Impoverishment of an ecosystem means impoverishment of all society dependent upon it. For example, to preserve wetlands and estuaries from being drained or filled for dry land uses is not to prefer ducks and muskrats to people. It is rather to prefer the interests of the whole of society in a viable ecosystem to those self-centered interests that would jeopardize the ecosystem for immediate and personal monetary gain.

The substance of an ecosystems approach to land policy is to identify, to protect, and, in the interest of human welfare, to manage the natural ecosystems upon whose continuing viability human welfare depends.[5] So far as feasible, an ecosystems approach allows natural processes to carry on the work of self-renewal unassisted by human effort. To the extent that man can rely upon nature to renew the ecosystem, human effort that might otherwise be required for the management of nature is freed for other purposes. The pressure of human needs has forced man under certain conditions into the substitution of artificial for natural ecosystems. Elabo-

rate systems of irrigation, drainage, and flood control are examples of artificial environments that are safe and productive only at the price of unremitting attention to maintenance of their systems. The great city is, of course, the most artificial and vulnerable environment of all and exacts from its inhabitants a heavy toll for systems maintenance.

To describe these systems as artificial is not to condemn them or to suggest that they are intrinsically inferior to natural systems. Civilization requires the construction of artificial ecosystems. The ecosystems approach to their management is not to return them to nature, but rather to benefit to the fullest extent from the operation of natural processes. The ecosystems approach implies an understanding of and respect for the potentialities of natural systems. To substitute wherever possible the economy of nature for human effort is the essence of economic as well as ecological good sense. Obviously, it is often necessary to channelize and direct natural forces in order to benefit from them. The extent to which human intervention in natural systems is economically or ecologically justifiable cannot be determined in the absence of demonstrable evidence. A particular high level dam, for example, may or may not be justifiable under an ecosystems approach and in comparison with optional ways of achieving its objectives. It is, however, safe to surmise that a blanket injunction to put *all* rivers under engineering management, or to ignore them altogether, would be very dubious ecological or economic wisdom.

When society works itself into an ecological straight-jacket, the ecosystem itself may be destroyed in efforts to break out of self-induced but unintended deprivations and constraints. Ecologically overstressed societies are impelled to further intensification of pressure on their environments in an effort to survive. Political leaders of overpopulated, ecologically impoverished nations are seldom apt pupils in the school of resources conservation.[6] Survival for them often means getting from the environ-

---

[5] For specific examples of ecosystems criteria for policy and management see a recently published Masters thesis by B. McClelland, *The Ecosystem—A Unifying Concept for the Management of Natural Areas in the Natural Park System*, Colorado State University, 1968, and George M. Van Dyne, ed., *The Ecosystem Concept in Natural Resource Management*, New York, Academic Press, 1969.

[6] Impressive documented evidence to this effect has been assembled by the Conference on the Ecological Aspects of International Development, Warrenton, Virginia, December 8–11, 1968. A published volume containing the papers and proceedings of this conference is being edited by John P. Milton of the Conservation Foundation and M. Faghi Farvar of the Center for the Biology of Natural Systems, Washington University.

ment whatever can be gotten today, regardless of the consequences for tomorrow. An ecosystems approach to land policy thus also implies a policy of population control. Unless population pressure is manageable, no other aspect of the ecosystem can be freely managed indefinitely. Ultimately the pressure of sheer numbers and the attendant demands upon the ecosystem would force all environmental policies into serving the one overpowering objective of maintaining a minimal existence for the human masses.

There are alternatives to such a course of constrained futility. Among these might be one classed under the heading of unthinkable thoughts. This course would be for a tough-minded and ecologically sophisticated elite to impose ecological order on their less perceptive or self-disciplined brethren. How this might be done, however, is not clear. Unfortunately, political astuteness and charisma seem more often to be found among the ecologically illiterate members of society. Compulsory population control through biomedical science if possible, or Malthusian control if all other means fail, could very well be the outcome of the present unwillingness of human societies to assess their ecological predicament realistically. Land is a substantially inelastic resource and this means that as human population multiplies, land policy is increasingly determined by population policy. The inseparable connections between land use, population, and the public interest have been identified with exceptional clarity by Garrett Hardin in his essay, *The Tragedy of the Commons*.[7]

Among the conflicts in our future-oriented technoscientific society is its fragmented and contradictory treatment of time. The relativity of time has become commonplace, and for certain purposes as in space flight, atomic technology, and medicine, very refined concepts of time are employed. With respect to the dynamics of the ecosystem, however, the time perceptions of modern man are perhaps less developed than those that characterized his agrarian ancestors. Modern man has not learned to perceive the world as a complex of dynamic interrelated systems. His behavior suggests that he believes the world to be an infinitely open system. Within this open system, time and change have a different meaning than they have when the system is closed. When closed, there is no escape from mistakes, and the consequences of a chain-reaction once started in time cannot be avoided by inter-planetary flight. Space exploration has reinforced the illusion that the infinity of the cosmos offers a way out for earthbound man. The reality for society in the ascertainable future is that the earth must be considered a closed system, even though it is in continual interaction with the galaxy.[8]

Within this essentially closed system, change is continuous. Man's future is inextricably involved with changes in the air, water, and land which are the gross elements of the ecosphere. He has himself become a principal change agent. His numbers and technologies have the effect of accelerating changes in time, of wearing down land forms, of increasing the salinity of the sea, and of altering the chemistry of the atmosphere. Only the most comprehensive surveillance of the side effects of technology, and the most carefully evaluated application of science and technology to the ecosystem, can prevent unadvertent damage to its self-regenerating capabilities. To be effective, management of the ecosystem must conform to the appropriate time table of nature, not merely to the·convenience of man. To illustrate, a dollar crisis or a Far Eastern war may offer politically defensible but ecologically invalid arguments for delaying efforts to save the Great Lakes from death by pollution. Today there may be higher political priorities, but, ecologically, tomorrow may be too late.

III. IN DEFENSE OF AN ECOSYSTEMS LAND POLICY

The intention in this article is not to describe the content of an actual ecosystems land policy. To attempt this without reference to specific

---

[7] 162 Science 1243. The population versus land issue has also been forcefully stated by P. Sears, *The Inexorable Problem of Space*, 127 Science 9, and by G. Macinko, *Saturation: A Problem Evaded in Planning Land Use*, 149 Science 516.

[8] The impact of the closed system on politics and economics was most clearly enunciated by K. Boulding, *The Economics of the Coming Spaceship Earth*, in Environmental Quality in a Growing Economy (H. Jarrett ed. 1966). The implications of the closed system for resources policy and human society have been explained by M. Kelso in a paper, *Man, Natural Resources and the Quality of Life*, prepared for a seminar at Montana State University, December, 1967.

plates, times, and circumstances would be to contradict the very thesis that has been developed. It is the ecosystems *approach* to policy that has been introduced. It was conceded at the outset that no such comprehensive approach to land policy exists in the United States. If such a policy based on ecological concepts were to be adopted, some major changes in the laws, expectations, and governmental arrangements in American society would also have to occur. These changes are not of the kinds that have been of primary concern to the Public Land Law Review Commission nor have they been the responsibility of the Division of Lands and Natural Resources of the United States Department of Justice. But if they are not the practical problems of the present, they may well be the compelling problems of the future. If the implications of this article are correct, American society and indeed mankind generally will eventually be forced into something like an ecosystems policy for land.

In essence this article asserts that man's predicament is that of passengers on a spaceship whose destination is unknown, whose numbers and appetites are increasing, and who have been long accustomed to quarrelsome and improvident conduct. The passengers assume that the builders of the spaceship endowed it with self-renewing mechanisms so that they need take little thought of its maintenance. Moreover, because the ship is very large, they act as though it were infinite, although they are quite capable of calculating its carrying capacity for given levels of safety and convenience. They know that there may come a day when its resources will be taxed beyond capacity. But they are also possessed by the optimistic thought that before the day of disaster arrives, they will land on some habitable planet. And so there is doubt among them as to the practical necessity for restraint.

This is the paradigm of Spaceship Earth whose passengers are only now beginning to realize where they are. Only the ecologically informed among them are aware of the growing precariousness of their condition. Unfortunately, the practical men who are the leaders and managers of the enterprise, although well-informed in many important ways, are generally uninformed or misinformed in this important respect. Their attention is on the lesser mechanics of the enterprise and on the mediation of quarrels among the passengers that might destroy the ship prematurely. Is it then to be conceded that the outcome of the voyage is hopeless, that the passengers cannot be taught, and that the officers and crew are unwilling to learn? No incontrovertible evidence compels this conclusion. It is equally plausible to assume, because human civilization is in itself a highly improbable phenomenon, that the limits of its improbability have not yet been reached. Unlikely as it may be, it is possible that American society, if not mankind generally, may reassess its circumstances with sufficient realism and insight to avoid ecological foreclosure. It is conceivable that people may voluntarily adopt ways of organizing their economy and of behaving in relation to the natural environment so as to bring the economy and the ecosystem into a dynamic, self-sustaining equilibrium.

It is hardly to be expected that the ecosystems policy can be made attractive to persons who would suffer real economic or psychological loss through its implementation. These persons, however, constitute a relatively small, although disproportionately influential, force in society. A greater number of Americans appear to have been wedded to certain fundamental concepts and institutions that do not serve them well. This incongruity between real needs and postulated values has been especially strong in matters of land use regulation and environmental management. Urban apartment dwellers appear in large numbers to subscribe environmental policies appropriate only to the life and times of Daniel Boone. A more adequate understanding of the values, attitudes, and understandings of urban Americans in relation to natural systems is greatly needed.

If present demographic projections are valid, the America of the 21st Century, and even before, will be politically dominated by the residents of great cities. Their beliefs and wishes could reshape public policies toward land. Few of the millions of urban residents will be owners of land; few will have a personal stake in returns from its rental, sale, or exploitation. But all would be in some measure dependent on it for the realization of other values. The great mass of urban dwellers are therefore not likely to be hostile to ecosystems concepts. They are likely to be totally unfamiliar with it, and to be unable to appraise its significance or its meaning for their lives. Defense of the concept among landless urbanites is thus largely a matter of including an understanding of ecology, and its implications for human welfare and public policy. Under present circumstances this would be a difficult task but it is even now being undertaken. For example, the Wave Hill Environmental Science Center in New York City works in close cooperation with the New York City public schools to bring a better understanding of the relationship between man and his environment to the children of the city. A similar effort is under way at High Rock Park Conservation Center on Staten Island.

A practical objection to the plausibility of an ecologically oriented public policy is the complexity of the ecosystems themselves. Taking as their target for criticism an exaggerated interpretation of ecology, critics say that because ecologists insist that everything relating to an ecosystem must be taken into account, nothing can be taken into account. This, they say, is because ecology provides no method for assessing priorities among the properties of ecosystems in relation to human values. The conclusion follows that the findings of ecological science are largely inapplicable (although not necessarily irrelevant) to the economics and politics of land policy. This criticism would have validity if an ecosystems approach to public land policy did in fact imply an extension of ecological concepts to everything having to do with land tenure and management, or required every aspect of an ecosystem to be examined in relation to every land use decision. But this totalitarian interpretation is neither necessary nor feasible. The fact is that ecologists *are* sometimes able to present alternative sets of policies for public consideration, together with their probable consequences. These may be reviewed by the public or by its representatives who may then establish priorities in public law policy.

It is doubtful that a public land policy designed to preserve and protect ecosystems would necessarily be more complex than the mass of laws, policies, and regulations affecting the ownership and use of land today. The effectiveness of an ecosystems land policy does not depend upon its mirroring the complexities of ecosystems. On the contrary, an ecosystems approach might simplify and clarify public land policy. A policy for the protection and ecologically

intelligent management of ecosystems could, by the establishment of standards and guidelines, reduce the confusion, conflict, and uncertainty that characterizes land use policy throughout the United States. It may be unrealistic to believe that the American people will adopt an ecosystems approach to land policy on its merits, but an ecological approach would almost certainly be more realistic in its treatment of the real problems of land than are some of the present policies. For the truth is that a great part of public policy for land is only tangentially concerned with the land as a major element in the human life support system. Land policies are not necessarily framed with reference to the land itself, but are often consequent to decisions made in banks, bars, and bedrooms. In any case, land use policy has been and will continue to be instrumental to broader social objectives. The nature of these objectives and their relevance to the continuing maintenance of the land as an element in the ecosphere must therefore be taken into account in any serious effort to understand or to modify land use policy and practices.

Public land policy does not begin with the land, but with man's dependencies upon it. Measured by ultimate human welfare, the most important of these dependencies is the basic function of land in the ecosystems through which life on earth is sustained. But these ecological functions are not the ones accorded the higher priorities in our society. Matters of land economics, of law, of land use technologies, and of public relations are in the forefront of our attention. Our concepts of public law and private property split our thought and action so that we tend to think of public land policy *only* as policy for publicly owned lands. The idea of a public land policy for all lands regardless of formal title would be consistent with ecological realities. From a legal viewpoint, however, a public land policy for "private" lands might appear to be a contradiction in terms. The immediate and practical problems of land policy under the prevailing laws and assumptions require attention, and most students of public land policy will examine them in this context.[9] Yet the larger view is also needed. Our

---

[9] Nevertheless the National Forest Products Association, representative of large interests in land use under both public and private ownership, has urged (at its 1968 annual meeting on September 5, in Washington, D.C.) that the need for a national policy for land use generally should be examined.

preoccupation with immediate and practical problems should not prevent our questioning whether we are indeed addressing ourselves to the right questions, at the right time, and in the right way. Public land policy is amenable to treatment at several levels of discourse. This article has sought a broad and theoretical level of treatment on the premise that unless the context of public land policy is consistent with ecological realities, specific land policies will ultimately prove to be ineffectual or harmful.

The argument of this article has been that the socio-political context of land use policy in America has been ecologically unwise, unrealistic, and uneconomic. The conclusion follows that a fundamental change of public attitude will be required if the broad range of needs and interests of the American people are to be served from the limited amount of land whose future use has not already been determined by law or events.

Epilogue

Epilogue

AS THE WORLD watched by television the earth recede into the distance as the astronauts neared the moon and watched the world grow larger as the astronauts returned to earth, and as the world listened to the successful efforts to bring a stricken spacecraft back home, only those with little imagination could fail to see the earth for what it really is, a spaceship traveling alone in empty space. The earth, once so large and so incomprehensible, could be seen as a single object, a sphere of blues and greens and browns and swirls of white bathed in sunlight. Nations vanished; the strange lines drawn on maps weren't there at all. The colors demarked tropical forests, mountains, plains, and seas. People of the earth were no longer nationals of many countries but all occupants of a spacecraft on an endless journey through space.

Like all spaceships the earth is self-contained. Its support systems are essentially closed, the only real input coming from the energy of the sun. This input supplies through photosynthesis the energy needed to provide nourishment for life aboard; it circulates the air masses, mixes the oxygen and carbon dioxide, recycles and circulates the water, and drives the cycling of nutrients and materials. Like power-packed batteries, fossil fuels supply additional energy those aboard require, because the spaceship needs more energy than man's existing technology can capture from the sun. Man has imposed upon the built-in automatic systems his own systems of human organization and technology. The very existence of the spacecraft depends upon the manner in which the crew, governments, and administration handle and care for the support systems, which are many and complex.

The spaceship earth consists of many special interrelated compartments of nations and regions. But the occupants of each do not seem to understand that the manner in which they manage their own compartment affects not only the welfare of other compartments but of their own as well. Because the materials stored for the journey are abundant, they are used wastefully; because some compartments contain richer stores, there is avarice as the occupants of one compartment connive to utilize not only their own supplies but the supplies of other compartments as well. Added to the mismanagement of the spaceship is another serious problem, the distribution and number of occupants in each compartment. At the outset of the journey, when man took over the controls the occupants were few, but as the journey lengthened and time passed, passengers and crews increased, slower in one compartment, faster in another, until many became overcrowded. Thus, some compartments live more comfortably than the occupants of others. The supplies are not equally and fairly distributed. There is dissension aboard the craft, and those in some compartments are armed to protect themselves from or subdue the occupants of other compartments.

Because of the dissension and greed among the crew and passengers, the present becomes most important, There is no concern for the future or interest in keeping the spacecraft operating efficiently. The spacecraft is cared for poorly, poisons spread through the system—into the air supply, the water supply, the food supply. No action is ever taken by the crew and passengers until a crisis is at hand. There is little effort to understand how the spacecraft operates, and what manuals do exist are ignored. If all else fails, read the directions; by then it is usually too late. There is no real understanding of the recycling processes involved in the support system. No effort is made to ensure that the activities of the occupants fit into the recycling processes that keep the ship in operating condition. Breakdown in the system occurs more frequently and seems irreparable, and the storehouses of supplies are squandered. Nor do the occupants seem to understand that each compartment is capable of supporting satisfactorily only a certain number of occupants, that overloading each compartment destroys the stability of the spaceship.

The spaceship earth is becoming overcrowded, the quality of life aboard is deteriorating, and the support systems are functioning less efficiently and in many places are damaged. There are warning lights flashing all over the boards, yet most of the occupants seem totally unconcerned. They are still more interested in what they can steal from the supplies.

Meanwhile the spaceship, partially crippled, sweeps on through space, still powered by the sun's energy but with major malfunctions. Unless the spacemen aboard awaken to the rapidly developing and increasing problems, the spaceship earth will become a lifeless craft, a ghostly spaceship, continuing on an endless journey around the sun.

Contributors

Gerald C. Anderson
Professor of Animal Science
West Virginia University

Joel Bitman
Leader of Hormone Physiology Laboratory
U.S. Department of Agriculture

Lester R. Brown
Senior Fellow, Overseas Development Council

V. D. Bykov
Professor of Surface Hydrology
Moscow University

Leslie A. Chambers
Professor and Chairman of Department of
    Environmental Health
University of Texas, Houston

Frank Fraser Darling
Director of Research
Conservation Foundation

Wayne H. Davis
Associate Professor of Zoology
University of Kentucky

Constantinos A. Doxiadis
President of Doxiadis Associates
Athens, Greece

H. Epstein
Professor of Animal Breeding
Faculty of Agriculture
Hebrew University
Rehovat, Israel

David R. Harris
Lecturer in Department of Geography
University College, London

Walter R. Hibbard, Jr.
Vice President of Research and Development
Owens-Corning Fiberglas Corporation

Nathan Keyfitz
Professor of Sociology
Department of Demography
University of California, Berkeley

George J. Armelagos
Associate Professor of Anthropology
University of Massachusetts

C. Loring Brace
Professor of Anthropology
University of California, Santa Barbara

W. E. Bullard
Environmental and Land Use Specialist
U.S. Soil Conservation Service

Lynton K. Caldwell
Professor of Political Science
Indiana University

Beryl L. Crowe
Assistant Professor of Political Science
Oregon State University

Raymond F. Dasmann
Senior Ecologist
International Union for the Conservation of Nature
Morges, Switzerland

John R. Dewey
Professor of Biology
Chico State College

David E. Elrick
Professor of Soil Physics
Ontario Agricultural College
University of Guelph

Garrett Hardin
Professor of Biology
University of California, Santa Barbara

Alfred L. Hawkes
Executive Director
The Audubon Society of Rhode Island

G. P. Kalinin
Professor and Head of Faculty of Surface Hydrology
Moscow University

Richard B. Lee
Professor of Anthropology
Rutgers University

423

Aldo Leopold (deceased, 1948)
formerly Professor of Wildlife Management
University of Wisconsin

Eugene P. Odum
Professor of Zoology; also
Director of Institute of Ecology
University of Georgia

John H. Ryther
Marine Biologist
Woods Hole Oceanographic Institute

D. H. Stott
Lecturer in Psychology
Glasgow University

Yi-Fu Tuan
Professor of Geography
University of Minnesota

Clifton R. Wharton, Jr.
Vice President of Agricultural Development
  Council

Lewis Mumford
Author and critic
Amenia, New York

Wayne D. Rasmussen
Chief of Agricultural History Branch
Economic Research Service
U.S. Department of Agriculture

Paul B. Sears
Professor Emeritus of Conservation
Yale University

N. Tinbergen
Lecturer in Animal Behavior
Oxford University

J. Alan Wagar
Outdoor Recreation Specialist
Pacific Northwest Forest and Range Experiment
  Station
U.S. Forest Service

George M. Woodwell
Senior Ecologist
Brookhaven National Laboratory

Selected References

The following references are for those readers who may wish to pursue certain topics or ideas in more depth. The books and papers listed are only a sampling of what is available. Perhaps the most important sources of reference are the footnotes and bibliographies throughout the book. Except for a few important titles, books and papers cited in the body of the book are not repeated here.

GENERAL

Damas, David (ed.). 1969. Contributions to Anthropology: Ecological Essays. Bull. No. 230. National Museum of Canada. Ottawa.

Darling, F. Fraser, and John P. Milton (eds.). 1966. *Future Environments of North America.* Natural History Press. Garden City, N. Y.

Dasmann, Raymond F. 1968. *Environmental Conservation.* 2nd ed. Wiley. New York.

Dubos, René. 1965. *Man Adapting.* Yale University Press. New Haven, Conn.

————. 1968. *So Human an Animal.* Scribner. New York.

Ehrlich, Paul R., and Anne H. Ehrlich. 1970. *Population, Resources, Environment. Issues in Human Ecology.* Freeman. San Francisco.

Leopold, Aldo. 1966. *A Sand County Almanac.* Enlarged edition. Oxford University Press. New York.

Mergen, Francois. 1970. *Man and His Environment: The Ecological Limits of Optimism.* Yale University School of Forestry Bull. No. 76. New Haven, Conn.

Murdock, William (ed.). 1971. *Environment: Sourcebook on Resources, Pollution, Society.* Sinauer Associates. Stamford, Conn.

Shepard, Paul, and Daniel McKinley (eds.). 1969. *The Subversive Science.* Houghton Mifflin. Boston.

Thomas, William L., Jr. (ed.). 1956. *Man's Role in Changing the Face of the Earth.* University of Chicago Press. Chicago, Ill.

Udall, Stewart. 1963. *The Quiet Crisis.* Holt, Rinehart and Winston. New York.

U.S. Department of Agriculture. 1967. Yearbook of Agriculture. *Outdoors, U.S.A.* Washington, D.C.

Vayda, Andrew P. (ed.). 1969. *Environment and Cultural Behavior.* Ecological Studies in Cultural Anthropology. Natural History Press. Garden City, N.Y.

I/ECOSYSTEMS AND MAN

Billings, W. D. 1970. *Plants, Man and the Ecosystem.* 2nd ed. Wadsworth. Belmont, Calif.

Cole, LaMont C. 1966. Man's ecosystem. BioScience 16(4): 243–248.

424

Daubenmire, Rexford. 1968. *Plant Communities*. Harper & Row. New York.

Goldman, C. R. (ed.). 1969. *Primary Productivity in Aquatic Environments* (Symposium). University of California Press. Berkeley and Los Angeles, Calif.

Kormondy, E. J. 1969. *Concepts of Ecology*. Prentice-Hall. Englewood Cliffs, N.J.

Odum, E. P. 1963. *Ecology* (Modern Biology Series). Holt, Rinehart and Winston. New York.

————. 1959. *Fundamentals of Ecology*. Saunders. Philadelphia, Pa.

Oosting, H. J. 1956. *The Study of Plant Communities*. Freeman. San Francisco, Calif.

Rodin, L. E., and N. E. Bazilevich. 1968. *Production and Mineral Cycling in Terrestrial Vegetation*. Transl. by G. E. Fogg. Oliver & Boyd. Edinborough.

Smith, Robert Leo. 1966. *Ecology and Field Biology*. Harper & Row. New York.

Van Dyne, George (ed.). 1969. *The Ecosystem Concept in Resource Management*. Academic Press. New York.

Whittaker, R. H. 1970. *Communities and Ecosystems*. Macmillan. New York.

II/MAN AND THE FOOD CHAIN

Allee, David. 1967. American agriculture—its resource issues for the coming years. Daedalus 96(4): 1071–1081.

Anderson, Edgar. 1967. *Plants, Life and Man*. University of California Press. Berkeley, Calif.

Axelrod, D. I. 1967. Quaternary extinctions of large mammals. Univ. Calif. Publ. Geol. Sci. 75: 1–42.

Brown, Lester R. 1970. *Seeds of Change: The Green Revolution and Development in the 1970's*. Praeger. New York.

Carneiro, R. L. 1961. Slash-and-burn cultivation among the Kuikuru and its implications for cultural development in the Amazon basin. Antropologica Supp. No. 2.

Childe, V. Gordon. 1951. *Man Makes Himself*. New American Library. New York.

Curwen, E. C., and G. Hatt. 1953. *Plough and Pasture*. Schuman. New York.

Cutler, H. C. 1954. Food sources in the New World. Agricultural History 28(1): 43–49.

Harris, Marvin. 1966. The cultural ecology of India's sacred cattle. Current Anthropology 7: 51–66.

Hopcraft, Arthur. 1968. *Born to Hunger*. Houghton Mifflin. Boston.

Isaac, Erich. 1959. The influence of religion on the spread of citrus. Science 129: 179–186.

Kark, R. M. (ed.). 1966. *World Review of Nutrition*. Vol. 6. *Food and Hunger in a World of Turmoil*. Hafner. New York.

Lee, Richard B., and Irvin Devore (eds.). 1968. *Man, the Hunter*. Aldine. Chicago.

Leeds, Anthony (ed.). 1965. *Man, Culture and Animals: The Role of Animals in Human Ecological Adjustment*. Amer. Assoc. Advance. Sci. Washington, D.C.

Lord, Russell. 1962. *Care of the Earth. A History of Husbandry*. Nelson. New York.

Matley, I. M. 1968. Transhumance in Bosnia and Herzegovina. Geographical Review 58: 231–261.

Paddock, William, and Paul Paddock. 1967. *Famine 1975!* Little, Brown. Boston.

Prentice, E. P. 1939. *The Influence of Hunger on Human History*. Harper & Row. New York.

Reed, Charles A. 1959. Animal domestication in the prehistoric Near East. Science 130: 1629–1639.

————. 1970. Extinction of mammalian megafauna in the Old World Late Quaternary. BioScience 20(5): 284–288.

Sauer, Carl. 1969. *Agricultural Origins and Dispersals*. 2nd ed. M.I.T. Press. Cambridge, Mass.

Service, E. R. 1966. *The Hunters*. Prentice-Hall. Englewood Cliffs, N.J.

U.S. Department of Agriculture. 1964. Yearbook of Agriculture. *Farmer's World*. Washington, D.C.

————. 1966. Yearbook of Agriculture. *Protecting Our Food*. Washington, D.C.

————. 1969. Yearbook of Agriculture. *Food for All of Us*. Washington, D.C.

III/MAN AND HIS HABITAT

Adams, Robert. 1966. *The Evolution of Urban Society*. Aldine. Chicago, Ill.

Beyer, Glenn (ed.). 1967. *The Urban Explosion in Latin America*. Cornell University Press. Ithaca, N.Y.

Breese, Gerald (ed.). 1969. *The City in Newly Developing Countries*. Prentice-Hall. Englewood Cliffs, N.J.

Chard, Chester S. 1969. *Man in Prehistory*. McGraw-Hill. New York.

Hauser, Philip M., and Leo F. Schnore (eds.). 1965. *The Study of Urbanization*. Wiley. New York.

Homans, G. C. 1941. *English Villagers of the Thirteenth Century*. Harvard University Press. Cambridge, Mass.

Howell, F. Clark. 1965. *Early Man.* (Life Nature Library). Time, Inc. Chicago.

Howell, F. Clark, and Francois Bourliere. 1963. *African Ecology and Human Evolution.* Aldine. Chicago, Ill.

U.S. Department of Agriculture. 1958. Yearbook of Agriculture. *Land.* Washington, D.C.

————. 1963. Yearbook of Agriculture. *A Place to Live.* Washington, D.C.

Wolf, Eric R. 1966. *Peasants.* Prentice-Hall. Englewood Cliffs, N.J.

IV/POPULATIONS

Blake, Judith. 1969. Population policy for Americans: is the government being misled? Science 164: 522–529.

Borgstrom, Georg. 1969. *Too Many: A Story of Earth's Biological Limitations.* Macmillan. New York.

Calhoun, J. B. 1966. The role of space in animal sociology. J. Soc. Issues 22(4): 46–58.

Cook, Robert C. 1965. World Population Projections 1965–2000. Pop. Bull. 21: 73–93.

Davis, Kingsley. 1967. Population policy: will current programs succeed? Science 158: 730–739; 1968. Comments 159: 481–482, 827–829.

DeJong, Gordon F. 1968. *Appalachian Fertility Decline: A Demographic and Social Analysis.* University of Kentucky Press. Lexington, Ky.

Dorn, H. F. 1962. World population growth: an international dilemma. Science 135: 283–290.

Ehrlich, Paul R. 1968. *The Population Bomb.* Ballantine. New York.

Fredericksen, H. 1969. Feedbacks in economic and demographic transition. Science 166: 837–847.

Hardin, Garrett. 1964. *Population, Evolution and Birth Control.* Freeman. San Francisco, Calif.

Keyfitz, Nathan, and Wilhelm Fleiger. 1968. *World Population: An Analysis of Vital Data.* University of Chicago Press. Chicago, Ill.

Langer, William L. 1964. The black death. Scientific American 210(2): 114–118, 121.

Malthus, Thomas, Julian Huxley, and Fredrick Osborn. 1960. *Three Essays on Population.* New American Library. New York.

Morris, Desmond. 1967. *The Naked Ape.* McGraw-Hill. New York.

Mudd, Stuart (ed.). 1964. *The Population Crisis and the Use of World Resources.* Indiana University Press. Bloomington, Ind.

Myint, H, 1964. *The Economics of the Developing Countries.* Hutchinson & Co. Ltd. London.

National Academy of Sciences. 1963. *The Growth of World Population.* Nat. Research Council Publ. 1091. National Academy of Sciences. Washington, D.C.

Osborn, Fairfield (ed.). 1962. *Our Crowded Planet: Essays on the Pressures of Population.* Doubleday. Garden City, N.Y.

United Nations Demographic Yearbook. United Nations. New York. Published annually since 1949.

Washburn, S. L. (ed.). 1961. *Social Life of Early Man.* Aldine. Chicago, Ill.

Young, Louise B. (ed.). 1968. *Population in Perspective.* Oxford University Press. New York.

Zinsser, Hans. 1963. *Rats, Lice and History.* Little, Brown. Boston.

V/ENDANGERED ENVIRONMENT

American Association for the Advancement of Science. 1965. *Air Conservation.* Washington, D.C.

Arnold, D. E. 1971. Lake Erie, alive but changing. Conservationist 25(3): 23–30, 36.

Bernarde, Melvin A. 1970. *Our Precarious Habitat.* Norton. New York.

Brady, N. C. 1967. *Agriculture and the Quality of Our Environment.* American Association for the Advancement of Science. Washington, D.C.

Carson, Rachel. 1962. *Silent Spring.* Houghton Mifflin. Boston.

Commoner, Barry. 1966. *Science and Survival.* Viking. New York.

Degler, S. E. (ed.). 1969. *Oil Pollution: Problems and Policies.* Environmental Management Service. Bureau of National Affairs, Washington, D.C.

Egler, F. E. 1964. Pesticides in our ecosystem. Amer. Sci. 52: 110–136.

Elton, Charles S. 1958. *The Ecology of Invasions by Animals and Plants.* Methuen. London.

Esposito, Jolin. 1970. *Vanishing Air.* Ralph Nader's Study Group Report on Air Pollution. Grossman. New York.

Gabrielson, I. R. 1970. Oil pollution. National Parks Magazine 44(270): 4–9.

Goldman, Marshall I. (ed.). 1967. *Controlling Pollution.* Prentice-Hall. Englewood Cliffs, N.J.

Helfrich, H. W. (ed.). 1970. *The Environmental Crisis.* Yale University Press. New Haven, Conn.

Hoult, D. P. (ed.). 1969. *Oil on the Sea*. Plenum Press. New York.

Landsberg, H. E. 1970. Man-made climatic changes. Science 170: 1265—1274.

Lauff, G. H. (ed.). 1967. *Estuaries*. American Association for the Advancement of Science. Washington, D.C.

Lauwerys, J. A. 1970. *Man's Impact on Nature*. Natural History Press. Garden City, N.Y.

Laycock, George. 1969. The beginning of the end for DDT. Audubon 71(4): 37c—43.

Love, L. B., and E. P. Seskin. 1970. Air pollution and human health. Science 169: 723—732.

Marine, Gene. 1969. *America, the Raped*. Simon and Schuster. New York.

Marx, Wesley. 1971. *Man and His Environment: Waste*. Harper & Row. New York.

Matthiessen, Peter. 1959. *Wildlife in America*. Viking. New York.

Moore, N. W. (ed.). 1966. Pesticides in the environment and their effects on wildlife. J. Appl. Eco. Supp. 3: 311.

Olson, T. A., and F. J. Burgess (eds.). 1967. *Pollution and Marine Ecology*. Wiley (Interscience). New York.

Osborn, Fairfield. 1968. *Our Plundered Planet*. Pyramid. New York.

Pruitt, William O., Jr. 1963. Lichen, caribou, and high radiation in Eskimos. Audubon 65: 284—287.

Reinow, Robert, and Leona T. Reinow. 1967. *Moment in the Sun*. Dial. New York.

Rudd, Robert L. 1964. *Pesticides and the Living Landscape*. University of Wisconsin Press. Madison, Wis.

Stern, Arthur (ed.). 1968. *Air Pollution*. 2nd ed. 3 vols. Academic Press. New York.

Stewart, Ronald, and S. P. Malhur. 1971. Handling hot water with a payoff. Conservationist 25(3): 16—20.

Whiteside, Thomas. 1970. *Defoliation*. Ballantine (Friends of the Earth). New York.

VI/THE PROSPECT BEFORE US

American Assembly. 1969. *Overcoming World Hunger*. Prentice-Hall, Englewood Cliffs, N.J.

Anderson, Walt. 1970. *Politics and Environment*. Goodyear. Pacific Palisades, Calif.

Borgstrom, Georg. 1965. *The Hungry Planet*. Macmillan. New York.

Brown, Harrison (ed.). 1967. *The Next Ninety Years*. California Institute of Technology. Pasadena, Calif.

Brown, Harrison, James Bonner, and John Wier. 1957. *The Next One Hundred Years*. Viking. New York.

Caldwell, L. K. 1970. *Environment—A Challenge to Modern Society*. Natural History Press. Garden City, N.Y.

Ciriacy-Wantrup, S. V., and James J. Parsons (eds.). 1967. *Natural Resources Quality and Quantity*. University of California Press. Berkeley, Calif.

Clawson, Marion. 1964. *Man and the Land in the United States*. University of Nebraska Press. Lincoln, Nebr.

Clawson, Marion, and Jack L. Knetsch. 1966. *Economics of Outdoor Recreation*. Johns Hopkins. Baltimore, Md.

Cloud, Preston (ed.). 1969. *Resources and Man*. Freeman. San Francisco, Calif.

Cooley, Richard A., and G. Wandesforde-Smith (eds.). 1970. *Congress and the Environment*. University of Washington Press. Pullman, Wash.

Darling, F. Fraser, and Noel Eichorn. 1969. *Man and Nature in the National Parks*. 2nd ed. Conservation Foundation. Washington, D.C.

Dasmann, Raymond F. 1968. *A Different Kind of Country*. Macmillan. New York.

Ewald, William R., Jr. 1968. *Environment and Policy: The Next 50 Years*. Indiana University Press, Bloomington, Ind.

Freeman, O. L. 1968. *World Without Hunger*. Praeger. New York.

Goldman, Marshall I. (ed.). 1967. *Controlling Pollution*. Prentice-Hall, Englewood Cliffs, N.J.

Helfrich, H. W. (ed.). 1970. *Agenda for Survival*. Yale University Press, New Haven, Conn.

Hutchison, J. Blair. 1969. Bringing resource conservation into the main stream of American thought. Nat. Resources J. 9(4): 518—536.

Jarrett, Henry (ed.). 1966. *Environmental Quality in a Growing Economy*. Johns Hopkins (Resources for the Future). Baltimore, Md.

Krutilla, J. V. 1967. Some environmental effects of economic development. Daedalus 96: 1058—1070.

Landsberg, H. H. 1967. The U.S. resource outlook: quantity and quality. Daedalus 96: 1034—1057.

McHarg, Ian. 1969. *Design with Nature.* Natural History Press. Garden City, N.Y.

Moss, Frank E. 1967. *The Water Crisis.* Praeger. New York.

Mudd, Stuart (ed.). 1964. *The Population Crisis and the Use of World Resources.* Indiana University Press. Bloomington, Ind.

Murphy, Earl F. 1967. *Governing Nature.* Quadrangle. Chicago, Ill.

————. 1971. *Man and His Environment: Law.* Harper & Row. New York.

Osborn, Fairfield (ed.). 1962. *Our Crowded Planet: Essays on the Pressures of Population.* Doubleday. New York.

Park, Charles, F., Jr. 1968. *Affluence in Jeopardy.* Freeman, Cooper. San Francisco, Calif.

Pincus, John A. (ed.). 1968. *Reshaping the World Economy: Rich and Poor Countries.* Prentice-Hall. Englewood Cliffs, N.J.

Popkin, Roy. 1968. *Desalination: Water for the World's Future.* Praeger. New York.

Russell-Hunter, W. D. 1970. *Aquatic Productivity.* Macmillan. New York.

U.S. Department of Agriculture, 1970. Yearbook of Agriculture. *Contours of Change.* Washington, D.C.

Watt, K. E. F. 1968. *Ecology and Resource Management.* McGraw-Hill. New York.

Wollman, Nathaniel. 1967. The new economics of resources. Daedalus 96: 1099—1114.

Wolman, Abel. 1969. *Water, Health, and Society.* University of Indiana Press. Bloomington, Ind.

Index

Aborigines, 213
Achondroplasia, 94
Adreno-pituitary exhaustion, 204, 208, 215
Age pyramids, 175–176
Age structure, 175–176
Aggression, 132–134, 216, 224–229, 240–241
        See also War
Agricultural ecosystems, 23, 32–33
Agriculture, attitudes toward, 103
    characteristics of, 102
    detritus, 35
    development of, 72, 102–111, 190
    economics of, 103, 110, 117–118, 119
    nutrient cycles in, 23, 24, 25, 26, 102
    productivity of, 48–49, 104, 195, 371–376
    and spread of disease, 224
    and urban development, 103, 132
Air pollution, and atmospheric physics,
        292–293
    concepts of, 289–294
    control of, 355–356
    ecological effects of, 281–284
    future problems of, 294
    and public health, 285–287
Amaranth, 83, 86
Anchovies, 363, 366
Anencephaly, 214–215
Animal domestication, 91–101
    and disease, 224
    reasons for, 91–101
Animal wastes, disposal of, 327
Animals, domestication effects upon, 91
Aphids, 207, 313
Arsenic, 263, 324
Artificial breeding, 111
Atmosphere, physics of, 279–281
        See also Air pollution
ATP, 4
Australopithecus, 180, 183
Automobile, impact of, on environment, 149,
        157, 194, 287–289, 291, 353, 399, 407

Baboon, 62
Bananas, 81, 121
Bark lice, 313
Barley, 21, 74, 76, 79, 81
Beans, 71, 74, 83, 85, 102, 105, 121
Bear, 88
Beef cattle, 23, 94, 97–98

Behavior, development of, 237–240
    of fish in heated water, 273–274
Biomass, 8–9, 19, 30
Birds, effect of DDT on, 246, 247–248, 249–252
    effect of oil pollution on, 300–301
Birth control, 201, 212–213, 386–387
Birth rate, 174–175
    and diet, 131
Bison, 88, 132, 385
Black Death, 185, 221, 405
Bog, 257
Bos taurus, 89

Calcium, 205, 251–253
Calcium chloride, as pollutant, 266
Calcium cycle, 13, 24–26
Camel, 132
Carbohydrates, 121
Carbon dioxide, 4, 256, 282–283, 289
Carnivore, 7
Carrying capacity, 177–179
Cassava, 121
Cattle, 77, 89, 90, 92, 93, 94
        See also Beef cattle; Dairy cattle
Centuriation, 168
Chlorinated hydrocarbons, 264, 324–325
        See also DDD; DDE; DDT
City, characteristics of, 156–157
    development of, 103, 132, 140–142, 143–146,
        191, 192
    and disease, 156–157, 224–225
    as ecological system, 43
    food supply of, 141, 191–192
    future size of, 162
    man's adaptation to, 153, 189, 193
    and pollution, 256–266
    problems of, 154, 156–158, 394
    relation of, to land, 104, 139, 145, 146, 191
    and transportation, 149–150, 153, 161–162
    in undeveloped vs. developed countries,
        196–197
Coal, 147
    and air pollution, 285–286, 287, 350
    strip mining of, 348–349, 354–355
Commons, administration of, 359, 381, 395
        396–397
    concept of, 380, 383–385
    exploitation of, 380
Community stability, 130

Competition, 17, 18, 41, 179, 205, 285, 402, 403
Conservation, 169, 170–171, 400, 413
Corn, 71, 111, 112, 113, 114, 372, 373, 377
Cotton, 74, 84, 109–110
Cowboy economy, 401
Cro-Magnon man, 180
Crop rotation, 105, 106
Crops, origin of, 71, 73–87
    production of, 371–378
Cultural eutrophication, 255–257
Culture, and disease, 221–226
    evolution of, 52–53, 72, 82–90, 102–109,
        181–182, 236–237
    hunting-gathering, 52–53, 190
    political organization of, 53
    village, 72, 89, 190, 191
Cycles, 204, 205, 208, 257

Dairy cattle, 92–93, 98–99, 100, 103, 110
Dams, 33, 136
DDD, 246
DDE, 246, 252, 253
DDT, 15, 45, 146, 201, 246–264, 322, 324, 406
    characteristics of, 248
    and eggshell thickness, 245, 250–252
    and human milk, 396
    and mammalian uterus, 248–249
    and population growth, 187
    in soil, 323, 324
Death rates, 174–175, 187
Deer, 88
Demographic transition, 186
Density, 176–177
    effect of, on freedom, 194–195
    man's response to, 44–45, 194
    relation of, to wealth, 195
    types of, 177–178, 179, 198–199, 206
        See also Carrying capacity
Desalinization, 342
Desert, development of, 134–135
    semi-urban, 150
Detritus, 7, 31
Detritus agriculture, 35
Disease, control of, 221–222, 226
    and cultural practices, 222, 224–225, 226
    ecological types of, 221
    evolutionary response to, 225–226
    and population, 185, 221
Diseases, kinds of, 221, 223, 224, 225
Dispersal, 205
Diversity, 20, 27
    as measure of stability, 19–20
    and succession, 31
Dogs, 67, 89, 94–95, 97
Dominance, 31, 205, 255
Draft animals, 102, 103
        See also Horses
Dust as air pollutant, 282–283

Earth, as ecosystem, 407, 417
    limitations of, 382–383
    as spaceship, 418
Ecological conscience, 381
Ecological efficiency, 364–365
Ecological equivalents, 307
Ecological pyramids, 8–9
Ecological stability, 133, 137, 381, 416
Ecology, defined, 3–4
Economic competition, 402, 403
Economic growth, dynamics of, 402–404
    and environment, 401, 402, 403–404
Economics, of agriculture, 110, 118–119, 368
    of a city, 155, 157
    and food consumption, 370
    Keynesian concept of, 200
Economy, ecosystem approach to, 409
    of marketplace, 143
    Neolithic, 141–143
    stabilization of, 399–400
    subsistence, 54–55
Ecosystem, agricultural, 32
    and air pollution, 279, 281–282
    concept of, 1–24
    as criterion for land use policy, 410–420
    defined, 3–4
    development of, 33
    homeostasis in, 16–17, 33
    man's place in, 2, 39, 43, 46, 129–130
    planning of, 34, 46
    structure of, 15
    thermal pollution of, 274–275
Ecumenopolis, 153–162, 189
Ekistics, 161
Emigration, 17, 18, 187, 205, 209
Energy flow, in ecosystem, 4, 8, 19, 29–30,
        31, 316–317
    and populations, 10
    and succession, 28
Environment, changes produced by man,
        132–136, 139, 147–148, 149
    and economic growth, 401, 405
    technical solutions to problems of, 382–383
Epidemic, 225
Erosion, 132–133, 134, 135, 142, 260–261, 262
Eskimo, 190, 225
Estuaries, 34
Ethics, land, 137, 381, 386
Ethology, 230–233
Eutrophic state, 30, 255
Eutrophication, 30, 36, 255–257
Evaporation, 333, 340–341
Evolution, of aggression, 229
    of crops, 71
    cultural, 236–237
    and disease, 225–226
    of economic systems, 55, 63
    of man, 184

Fallowing, 104–105
Famine, 121, 185
Farm machinery, development of, 106–108
Farms, decline in, 49
   size and food production of, 48
Fats, 121
Fear, 234
Feng-shui, 168–169
Fertile Crescent, 102, 128, 145
Fertility, effects of crowding on, 210
Fertilizers, and Green Revolution, 115
   and pollution, 108, 122, 265, 320
Fire, 34, 132, 143
Fish, and pollution, 256, 261, 298–299
   temperature tolerances of, 273–274
Fisheries, overexploitation of, 358–359
   world outlook on, 359–360
Floods, 135–136
Food, amount of, consumed by Americans, 48
   distribution systems of, 50, 52
   of !Kung Bushman, 60–61, 65–67
   and population density, 207, 213
   world demands for, 368, 369–370, 378
Food chain, 5–7, 30
   and man, 21, 246–247
   marine, 360–361, 362–364
   and pesticides, 246, 247
Food preservation, 107, 111
Food production, 71–72, 103–104, 374–376
Food storage, 117
Forest, effect of nuclear radiation on, 304
   man's impact on, 133, 142, 145, 169, 170
   and mineral cycling, 20
   and water cycle, 134
Forest fires, 169, 315

"Garden-city" principle, 151
Geomancy, 168–169
Geronticide, 53
Goats, 77, 79, 89–100, 132
Grassland, 89, 132, 134–135
Grassland farming, 102
Green Revolution, defined, 112, 114
   ecological effects of, 113–114
   economics of, 118–119
   political implications of, 120
   problems of, 115–117
Gross National Product, 2, 27, 332, 339, 400
Gross production, 19
Gourd, 83, 85, 86
Guano, 83, 108, 366

Habitat, elimination of natural, 88, 129–130
Heat as resource, 342–343
Herbicides, 264–265
   as soil pollutant, 324
Herbivores, 5–7, 88, 363
Herd instinct in man, 139–140

Highways, 139, 194, 259, 261, 262
Homeostasis of ecosystem, 16–17, 33
Homo erectus, 180, 223
Homo sapiens, 180, 182, 183, 184
Horses, 93, 95–97, 108
Horticulture, 72–73, 102
Hunting, as sport, 90
   as subsistence, 52–53, 60, 88
Hyena, 241

Immigration, 187
"Indian equivalents," 199, 200
Industrial revolution, 185–186
   and air pollution, 281–286
Industrial wastes, disposal of, 327
   soil pollution by, 322
Industry, effects on environment, 147–148
      See also Air pollution; Water pollution
Infanticide, 53, 58, 212
Ionizing radiation, effect of, on chromosomes, 308, 311, 317
   effect of, on forest, 309, 312, 313
   species sensitivity to, 308, 309
   and succession, 308, 309, 312, 313, 318
Irrigation, 102, 108, 132–133

Krill, 365–366, 367
!Kung Bushman, caloric requirements of, 67
   ecological energetics of, 62–66
   food habits of, 60, 66, 68
   population dynamics of, 56–58
   sex ratios of, 58
   subsistence efforts of, 58, 62–64
   and water, 58

Lake Erie, pollution of, 256
Lakes, 16, 338
Land, agricultural, 149
   pollution of, 321–329
   public jurisdiction over, 412
   rehabilitation of, 262
   Roman impact on, 168
Land use, and ecology, 165, 413
   ecosystem approach to, 414–417
   ethics of, 163, 381
   and population size, 133, 413
   principles of, 163–165
   and soil disturbance, 259–263
   and water resources, 258–269
Land use planning, 329
   and population policy, 417
   to protect ecosystems, 36, 417–420
   and resistance to ecosystem approach, 411
Lead, 326
Legumes, 105

Magnesium, 23

Maize, 83, 85, 146
  See also Corn
Malaria, 222–223, 224, 225, 226
Malformations, 212, 214
Malnutrition, 122–125
Mammoth, 88, 132
Man, behavior of, 139, 229, 235–236
  competition in, 192–193
  cultural revolution of, 69, 181, 184, 223
  and disease, 223–224
  and ecosystem, 25–28, 409
  evolution of, 180, 181, 183, 207
  as hunter-gatherer, 52–53, 88, 179, 183, 217
  impact of, on environment, 128, 129, 130, 132–136
  niche of, 42–44, 189, 190, 192
  nutritional requirements of, 121, 185
  territoriality in, 228–229
Market system, 50–51, 118, 406–407
Marsh, 34
Megalopolis, 145, 156, 159, 192
Mercury, 2, 263, 324
Mesolithic man, 224
Metallurgy, 142
Millet, 80, 81, 86
Mineral cycling, 14–15, 24
Minerals, 129
  recycling of, 353–354
  resources of, 136, 349–357
Mining, and pollution, 262, 267
  and technology, 351–352
    See also Strip mining
Mongongo nut, 60, 65–66, 67
Moose, 203
Morrill Land Grant College Act, 108, 112
Mortality, 175, 216
    See also Death rates
Mosquitoes, 222–223
Mountain lion, 203
Municipal wastes, 325
Muskrat, 209
Mussels, 275
Mutton, 97

National Land Use Policy Act, 410
National Parks, 88, 385
Natural communities, 307, 309, 311
Natural selection, 207, 209, 235
Nature, 163, 165–167
  attitudes toward, 163, 165–167, 168
  elements of, in city, 154
  urban displacement of, 144
Neanderthal man, 180, 183, 184
Neolithic agriculture, 71–72, 75–76, 78, 90, 141–142
Neolithic revolution, 71–72
Neolithic village, 140, 141–142
Net reproductive rate, 174

New Towns Act of 1947 (Great Britian), 151
Niche, 39, 40–44, 53, 95, 129–130, 189
Night soil, 141, 145, 327
Nitrate poisoning, 320, 326
Nitrates, 267
Nitrogen, 11–12, 23–25, 103, 141, 290, 320, 326
Nitrogen cycle, 11–12
Nitrogen-fixing legumes, 25, 105
Noise, 244–245
Nomadism, 89, 98
Nuclear fallout, 322
Nuclear power, 305
Nuclear radiation, 304–319
Nutrient cycles, 11–15, 32
  and agriculture, 23, 103
  and thermal pollution, 275
Nutrients, removal from ecosystem, 23, 32
  required by man, 121
Nutrition and population, 124, 125, 216–217

Oats, 74
Oceans, as commons, 385
  pollution of, 345
    See also Oil, pollution by
Oil, 136, 288
  pollution by, 292–303
Oligotrophic state, 30
Oligotrophy, 255, 257
Omnivore, 7
Oxygen, 4, 283
Oysters, 35, 247, 274, 299
Ozone, 283, 284, 291

Paleolithic man, 185
Paper, 143
Paranthropus, 180, 183
Parasites, 223, 403
Parasitism, 403
Pastoralism, 79, 89, 132
Peanut, 83
Peas, 76, 80, 105, 121
Peasantry, 103, 120, 142, 191, 195, 213
Pepper, 83, 84, 85
Pesticides, 2, 201, 246–254, 263–265, 324, 325
    See also Birds; DDT; Fish
Phosphorus, 23, 103, 141, 205, 257–258, 267, 325–327
Photosynthesis, 4, 283, 360–361, 376
Phreatophytes, 333
Pig, 77, 89, 111
Pine, 283–284
Pithecanthropus, 183
Plant domestication, 71–87
Pleistocene, 132, 183, 184
Pleistocene overkill, 80, 167
Pollution, from agriculture, 263–265, 320
  control of, 329, 344, 385, 407
  industrial, 147–148

Pollution *(Continued)*
    from mining, 267–268, 349
    and population growth, 245, 385
    from urban areas, 268, 349
        See also Air pollution; Oil, pollution by;
        Soil pollution; Thermal pollution;
        Water pollution
Population, control of, 201, 203, 209–210,
    212–218, 386–388, 395, 408, 415–416
    density of, 120, 174, 177–179, 185, 189, 190–197,
    203, 213
    in ecosystem, 10, 16–18
Population growth, 174–177
Population optimum, 198, 383
Population projections, 188
Potassium, 23–25, 204, 242
Potato, 71, 74, 82, 84, 112, 121, 146
Predation, 88, 203–204, 207–208
Production, economic, 405–406
    gross, 5
    net, 5, 9, 361–362
    and succession, 29–36
Productivity of ecosystems, 5, 365–366, 371–379
Protein, 121
Public health and air pollution, 293–294
Public land policy, ecosystem approach to,
    410–420
Pumpkin, 83, 220

Quality of life, 189, 198–199, 399–407

Radioactive contamination, 304–319
Rate of population increase, 175
Rats, 209–210, 248–249
Refrigeration, 108–109
Reindeer, 88, 99
Resources, conservation of, 81, 131
    food, in sea, 365–367
    mineral, 349–357
    as population limitation, 401
    water, 335–343
Rice, 34, 78, 79, 112–113, 114, 117, 375, 377
Riparian rights, 334
River and Harbor Act of 1899, 301
Rivers, 337, 338, 345
Roads, 143–144, 145, 168
Ruffed grouse, 88, 209
Run-off, 265–266, 268, 342, 346
Rye, 71, 74

Sardines, 358–359
Schistosomiasis, 113
Sedimentation, 259–263
Sewage, 327, 349
Sheep, 77, 89, 93, 98, 99–101, 106, 107, 132
Shock disease, 208, 210–211
Sickle cell anemia, 224, 226
Smog, 45, 286

Snowshoe hare, 204, 208, 215
Social behavior, 205, 209, 235–236
Soil, nature of, 322
Soil erosion, 133, 134, 259–263, 346
Soil pollution, 320–329
Solid waste, 2, 223–224, 328, 347–349
    353–354, 356–357, 408
Sorghum, 80, 81, 374
Spaceman economy, 401, 407
Species diversity, 310–311
Spinach, 320
Squash, 71, 83, 84, 85, 102
Stable age distribution, 175
Standing crop, 5, 309, 316
Steam electric stations, 270
Stickleback, 233–234, 239
Stratification, of forest, 15
    of grassland, 16
    of lakes and ponds, 16
Streamflow, 260, 261, 340
Stress, 17–18, 209, 210, 214, 215, 218, 315
Strip mining, 348–349, 354–355
Suburbia, 148–149
Suburbs, 139, 148–149
Succession, 18–19, 28–30, 31, 33, 39, 307–308, 318
Sugar beets, 107
Sulphur dioxide, 45, 283, 290, 291
Supermarkets, 51
Supersonic plane, 245
Swidden agriculture, 72–73, 102
System, defined, 3

Tax policy, as regulatory device, 407
Temperature inversions, 279–281
Territoriality, 36, 171, 205, 206, 234, 236
Territory, 17, 211, 228–229, 235–236
Thermal pollution, 270–278
Thermal shock, 273
Thermodynamics, laws of, 9, 130
Timber harvesting, 259, 261
Tomatoes, 71, 83
TPN, 4–5
Transhumance, 89
Transportation, 161, 162
Tribalism, 393–394
Trophic-dynamic concept, 9–10, 20, 360–361
Trophic levels, 9

Urbanization, effects of, on environment,
    147–148, 139–140, 142–144, 150–152
    stages of, 145–146
    in underdeveloped countries, 139–140, 195

Vetch, 76
Village, 72, 89, 140, 143, 190, 191, 193,
    196, 223–224
Vitamins, 121, 157, 211

War, 22, 228–229, 237
Waste, agricultural, 265–266
  disposal of, 327–328
  recycling of, 327
Water, for cooling, 273
  demand for, 135, 271–272, 341
  development plans for, 333
  quality of, 135
  recycling of, 334
  types of, 336–340
  world supply of, 338
Water conservation, 341–342, 345
Water cycle, 15, 24, 124, 255, 258, 337–340,
    344–345
  control of, 344–345
Water pollution, 255–269, 304–305, 349
Water power, 146–147
Water table, 132
Watershed, 258–259
Weeds, 75, 80, 132
Whales, 235, 358, 365–366
Whaling industry, 380
Wheat, 71, 109, 114, 374
Wolf, behavior of, 203, 205, 235
Wool, 99–101, 109

Yams, 80, 81, 82
Yield, 5
  of crops, 373–375, 376
  of ocean, 360–367

Zero population growth, 188
Zinjanthropus, 183
Zoning, 36, 133
Zooplankton, 363–364

73 74 7 6 5 4